The Interactional Nature of Depression

ADVANCES IN INTERPERSONAL APPROACHES

The Interactional Nature of Depression

Edited by

Thomas Joiner
James C. Coyne

American Psychological Association
Washington, DC

Published by
American Psychological Association
750 First Street, NE
Washington, DC 20002

Copies may be ordered from
APA Order Department
P.O. Box 92984
Washington, DC 20090-2984

In the U.K., Europe, Africa, and the Middle East, copies may be ordered from
American Psychological Association
3 Henrietta Street
Covent Garden, London
WC2E 8LU England

Typeset in Goudy by EPS Group Inc., Easton MD

Printer: Data Reproductions Corporation, Auburn Hills, MI
Cover Designer: Minker Design, Bethesda, MD
Technical/Production Editor: Catherine R. W. Hudson

Library of Congress Cataloging-in-Publication Data
The interactional nature of depression : advances in interpersonal approaches /
    edited by Thomas Joiner and James C. Coyne.—1st ed.
        p.   cm.
    Includes bibliographical references and index.
    ISBN 1-55798-534-0
    1. Depression, Mental—Social aspects.   2. Interpersonal
psychotherapy.   I. Joiner, Thomas   II. Coyne, James C., 1947–
RC537.I565   1999
616.85'27—dc21   98-31115
                                                                                              CIP

British Library Cataloguing-in-Publication Data
A CIP record is available from the British Library.

Printed in the United States of America
First Edition

To my son and wife, Malachi and Graciela (TJ)

In memory of Mr. C., role model and teacher of patience
and tolerance (JCC)

To N. B.: "*Si non, l'on n'y peut rien.*" (JCC)

CONTENTS

List of Contributors xi

Preface xiii

I. The Study of Interpersonal Variables in Depression 1

    Chapter 1.   On the Interpersonal Nature of Depression:
                      Overview and Synthesis 3
                      Thomas Joiner, James C. Coyne, and
                      Janice Blalock

    Chapter 2.   The Emergence of an Interpersonal Approach
                      to Depression 21
                      Constance Hammen

II. The Interpersonal and the Personal in Depression 37

    Chapter 3.   Social Context and Depression: An Integrative
                      Stress and Coping Framework 39
                      Charles J. Holahan, Rudolf H. Moos, and
                      Liza A. Bonin

    Chapter 4.   Interpersonal and Cognitive Pathways Into
                      the Origins of Attributional Style:
                      A Developmental Perspective 65
                      Beth A. Haines, Gerald I. Metalsky,
                      Aimee L. Cardamone, and Thomas Joiner

Chapter 5.   Loneliness, Shyness, and Depression:
             The Etiology and Interrelationships of
             Everyday Problems in Living 93
             Jody C. Dill and Craig A. Anderson

Chapter 6.   Schematic and Interpersonal Conceptualizations
             of Depression: An Integration 127
             *Norman B. Schmidt, Kristen L. Schmidt, and
             Jeffery E. Young*

Chapter 7.   Vulnerable Self-Esteem and Social Processes in
             Depression: Toward an Interpersonal Model of
             Self-Esteem Regulation 149
             John E. Roberts and Scott M. Monroe

Chapter 8.   Striving for Confirmation: The Role of
             Self-Verification in Depression 189
             R. Brian Giesler and William B. Swann, Jr.

III. Emerging Interpersonal Models of Depression 219

Chapter 9.   Silencing the Self: Inner Dialogues and Outer
             Realities 221
             Dana Crowley Jack

Chapter 10. Sociophysiology and Depression 247
             Russell Gardner, Jr. and John S. Price

IV. Depression and the Response of Significant Others 269

Chapter 11. Marital Discord and Depression: The Potential
             of Attachment Theory to Guide Integrative
             Clinical Intervention 271
             *Page Anderson, Steven R. H. Beach, and
             Nadine J. Kaslow*

Chapter 12. Depressed Parents and Family Functioning:
             Interpersonal Effects and Children's Functioning
             and Development 299
             E. Mark Cummings and Patrick T. Davies

Chapter 13. A Social–Cognitive Model of Interpersonal
Processes in Depression 329
William P. Sacco

V. Postscript 363

Chapter 14. Thinking Interactionally About Depression:
A Radical Restatement 365
James C. Coyne

Author Index 393

Subject Index 411

About the Editors 423

CONTRIBUTORS

Craig A. Anderson, PhD, Department of Psychology, University of Missouri—Columbia

Page Anderson, MS, Department of Psychology, University of Georgia

Steven R. H. Beach, PhD, Department of Psychology, University of Georgia

Janice Blalock, PhD, Department of Psychiatry and Behavioral Sciences, University of Texas Medical Branch at Galveston

Liza A. Bonin, MA, Department of Psychology, University of Texas at Austin

Aimee L. Cardamone, BA, Department of Psychology, Lawrence University

James C. Coyne, PhD, Department of Family Medicine and Department of Psychiatry, University of Michigan Medical Center

E. Mark Cummings, PhD, Department of Psychology, University of Notre Dame

Patrick T. Davies, PhD, Department of Psychology, West Virginia University

Jody C. Dill, PhD, Department of Psychology, Lenoir-Rhyne College

Russell Gardner, Jr., MD, Department of Psychiatry and Behavioral Sciences, University of Texas Medical Branch at Galveston

R. Brian Giesler, PhD, Indiana University School of Nursing and Medicine

Beth A. Haines, PhD, Department of Psychology, Lawrence University

Constance Hammen, PhD, Department of Psychology, University of California, Los Angeles

Charles J. Holahan, PhD, Department of Psychology, University of Texas at Austin

Dana Crowley Jack, EdD, Fairhaven College, Western Washington University

Thomas Joiner, PhD, Department of Psychology, Florida State University

Nadine J. Kaslow, PhD, Department of Psychology, Emory University

Gerald I. Metalsky, PhD, Department of Psychology, Lawrence University

Scott M. Monroe, PhD, Department of Psychology, University of Oregon

Rudolf H. Moos, PhD, Department of Veterans Affairs Medical Center, Palo Alto and Stanford University

John S. Price, DM, Plumpton near Lewes, East Sussex, United Kingdom

John E. Roberts, PhD, Department of Psychology, State University of New York at Buffalo

William P. Sacco, PhD, Department of Psychology, University of South Florida

Kristen L. Schmidt, PhD, Prevention Research Center, Department of Mental Hygiene, Johns Hopkins School of Hygiene and Public Health

Norman B. Schmidt, PhD, Department of Psychology, Ohio State University

William B. Swann, Jr., PhD, Department of Psychology, University of Texas at Austin

Jeffery E. Young, PhD, Department of Psychology, Columbia University

PREFACE

Even if theorists and scientists sometimes forget, depressed people will tell you that their involvement in interpersonal relationships matters. They will tell you that good relationships buffer them from depression; they will tell you that their involvement in bad relationships causes and maintains their depression; they will tell you that they are in a catch-22 dilemma of needing the very people their symptoms seem to disaffect; and they will tell you that treatment needs to be focused on improving their relationships. On all counts they are right. It is this insight—that depressed people are right—that is a lasting and profound contribution of the interpersonal approach. Since 1976, James Coyne has argued consistently and passionately for this perspective, criticizing models of depression that neglected one of its most salient features. This line of thought and argument has become one of the most influential in depression research; it has produced several lines of empirical work as well as therapeutic innovations. One goal of this volume is to claim the place of this tradition of thought and science in the collection of basic views on depression.

Thomas Joiner, inspired by Coyne, has attempted to understand the particulars of the interpersonal process in depression and the response of others. In so doing, concepts such as excessive reassurance seeking and negative feedback seeking have been invoked. It is notable that these behaviors, although quite interpersonal in emphasis, contain elements of social–cognitive approaches to depression (e.g., negative feedback seeking is thought to be undergirded by low self-esteem, as Giesler and Swann eloquently argue in chapter 8). Many authors of chapters of the current volume have also been influenced by social–cognitive science and have attempted comprehensive treatments of depression that, while highlighting the interpersonal, incorporate the cognitive.

There are promises and potential pitfalls in this approach and thus in this compilation. In terms of promise, a true and balanced integration of genuinely interpersonal thought with cognitive models of depression has the potential to fulfill the currently unrealized goal of a full psychological account of the causes, features, and consequences of depression. In terms of potential pitfalls, it has been strongly argued by Coyne (and is provocatively stated in the volume's concluding chapter) that there is the potential to obscure the substantive with the epiphenomenal by neglecting the interpersonal at the price of the intrapsychic. This volume confronts this two-edged sword, as the field must.

Efforts such as these are by definition communal, and so the list of people to whom we are grateful is long. Thomas Joiner wishes to thank those who schooled him, either directly or from afar, in various aspects of the science of clinical psychology, including a host of brave psychotherapy patients, as well as Jerry Metalsky, Bill Swann, Josh Holahan, Richard Campbell, Jim Coyne, Lyn Abramson, David Rudd, Sam Catanzaro, Lauren Alloy, and Karen Wagner. Donna Eberhardt, JoAnn Hale, and Becky Jones in Galveston were diligent in editorial and general assistance. Margaret Schlegel and Ted Baroody of the American Psychological Association have been patient and, when needed, directive. The volume's authors deserve congratulations and gratitude for scholarship, creativity, and, sometimes as important, timeliness and cooperation. I add this from a personal standpoint: As I put the finishing touches on this book, my wife and son are downstairs playing in the tub, laughing and shouting for me to come down. How lucky to have such work and to love such people. How sad that my dad, now deceased, cannot see this scene—he would have been proud of it.

James Coyne first wishes to acknowledge the good fortune of having had a number of mentors who valued independent thinking and who tolerated sometimes outrageous displays of such independence: Alex Buchwald, Richard Young, Richard Price, Fernando Melendez, Bruce Denner, Paul Watzlawick, and especially John Weakland. I also wish to acknowledge some younger colleagues who have stimulated my continued development: Anita DeLongis, Niall Bolger, Geraldine Downey, Thomas Joiner, Michael Klinkman, and Nili Benazon.

Thomas Joiner
James C. Coyne

I

THE STUDY
OF INTERPERSONAL
VARIABLES IN DEPRESSION

1

ON THE INTERPERSONAL NATURE OF DEPRESSION: OVERVIEW AND SYNTHESIS

THOMAS JOINER, JAMES C. COYNE, AND JANICE BLALOCK

The main theme of this volume is that depression needs to be understood in its interpersonal context. Regardless of what other factors may be involved, the interpersonal context affects greatly whether a person becomes depressed, the person's subjective experience while depressed, and the behavioral manifestations and resolution of the disorder. Consideration of the interpersonal context of depression is simply a necessity for an adequate account of the disorder. A failure to take into account the intricacies of depressed persons' involvement with other people causes one to attribute to depressed persons characteristics they do not possess and to leave significant aspects of their experience unexplained.

Clinicians have long been impressed by the impact of depressed patients on others. Consider the following passages from clinicians:

> Sigmund Freud (1917/1951): Their complaints are really "plaints" in the legal sense of the word ... everything derogatory that they say of themselves at bottom relates to someone else.... They give a great deal of trouble, perpetually taking offense and behaving as if they had been treated with great injustice. (p. 247)

Edward Bibring (1955): By demonstrating their sufferings they try to obtain the "narcissistic supplies" which they need, or they may exploit the depression for the justification of the various aggressive impulses toward external objects. (p. 46)

Lewinsohn, Weinstein, and Shaw (1969): Since most people in the depressed person's environment (and eventually even his family) find his behavior aversive, they will avoid him as much as possible. (p. 232)

Nacht and Racamier (1961): We wish to insist on the important and little realized fact that the depressed person ... is always truly aggressive toward others through the very medium of the manifestations of his depression. His suffering is an accusation. His sense of incurableness is a reproach. His demands are perhaps humbling, but devastating. His depression is tyrannical. He wallows in suffering, whilst trying to enmesh his object in it as well. (p. 486)

In each instance, the aversiveness of others' experience with depressed persons is explained solely in terms of what depressed persons do to others, with a corresponding neglect of what is being done to the depressed persons. Any sense on the part of depressed persons that they are being mistreated or caught up in some processes beyond their control is invalidated. There is the recurring hint that depressed persons may actively seek to have such a negative effect on others. The Nacht and Racamier quotation is most blatant in castigating depressed persons for their ill intentions and, in doing so, releasing clinicians and everyone else from responsibility for the interpersonal process in which such impressions arise. Such a depiction of depressed persons goes far to justify the negative response of others to them. Contrast this view with what is implicit in the following passage from Herman Melville's (1856/1984) quietly disturbing short story "Bartleby." Melville's protagonist is describing his reactions to the melancholic and mysterious scrivener, Bartleby:

> My first emotions had been those of pure melancholy and sincerest pity; but just in proportion as the forlornness of Bartleby grew and grew in my imagination, did that same melancholy merge into fear, that pity into repulsion. So true it is, and so terrible too, that up to a certain point the thought or sight of misery enlists our best affections; but, in certain special cases, beyond that point it does not. They err who would assert that invariably this is owing to the inherent selfishness of the human heart. It rather proceeds from a certain hopelessness of remedying excessive and organic ill. To a sensitive being, pity is not seldom pain. And when at last it is perceived that such pity cannot lead to eventual succor, common sense bids the soul be rid of it. (p. 112)

Melville's insightful protagonist acknowledges his own contribution to his reaction to Bartleby, rather than portraying himself as a hapless victim. The protagonist despairs of being able to remedy Bartleby's distress and wants to rid himself of his sight. It is in such an awareness, in such a direct implication of others in depression, that we move from what is simply an interpersonal perspective to an interactional perspective on depression. An interactional perspective not only addresses the interpersonal impact of depressed persons but also calls for an exploration of the mutually causative, reciprocal processes occurring between depressed persons and others. An article from the mid-1970s by one of the present chapter authors, James C. Coyne (1976; see also chap. 14 of this book), provided a rudimentary outline for how one might begin to construct such an interactional perspective.

In that article, Coyne (1976) was intentionally noncommittal about how depressed behavior might initially come about, leaving open the possibility that depression has multiple causes and that it is not necessary to understand the full range of these causes to track the contribution of depressed persons' exchanges with their environment. What is crucial, however, is the notion that depressed individuals seemingly seek reassurance from others to alleviate their doubts concerning their own worth and whether others truly care about them. Although others often provide reassurance, it is to little avail, because the depressed person doubts its genuineness, attributing it instead to others' sense of pity or obligation. The depressed person now faces a dilemma: He or she both needs and doubts others' reassurance. The need is emotionally compelling and thus predominates, leading the depressed individual again to request others' feedback. Once received, the reassurance is again doubted, and the pattern is repeated. Because the pattern is repetitive and resistant to attempts to change it, the depressed person's significant others become frustrated and irritated, and thus they are increasingly likely to reject the depressed individual and also increasingly likely to become distressed themselves. Rejection furthers the shrinkage and disruption of the depressed person's interpersonal environment, which, in turn, maintains or exacerbates the depressed person's symptoms and predicament. The theory describes a process that evolves over time within the crucible of close relationships.

The formulation offered in that article was in important respects vague and underdeveloped, but it filled a theoretical vacuum of sorts, even if it was not without precedent. The influence of Harry Stack Sullivan should be clear. However, Sullivan (1956) himself confessed that in working with a few severely depressed patients, "I did not get to first base in being able to deduce anything from that experience that was any good to me in terms of making a theoretical contribution" (p. 284). Thomas Szasz (1961) and Ernest Becker (1964; reprinted in Coyne, 1986) had each previously developed provocative interpersonal formulations of depression. Unfortunately, each had chosen to present these ideas in the context of a strident attack on the very foundations of psychiatry, and their ideas about depression were largely ignored in the ensuing controversy. At the time of Coyne's (1976) article, Weissman and Paykel (1974) had already published their landmark study of the social and personal lives of depressed women. However, this work was woefully short on theory. Even as the empirically validated interpersonal psychotherapy (IPT) emerged from the work of Myrna Weissman and colleagues, including Gerald Klerman (Klerman, Weissman, Rounsaville, & Chevron, 1984), their theory remained largely limited to the broad notion that understanding and renegotiating interpersonal relationships are crucial to the treatment of depression, regardless of how the disorder comes about.

In the same time period, Brown and Harris (1978) were developing their precise model of the role of social factors in depression. They showed that severe life events, often involving loss and disappointments in close relationships, had a key role in precipitating depression. Furthermore, interpersonal factors were crucial in the creation of vulnerability to such life stress, and the most potent of these vulnerability factors was the lack of an intimate, confiding relationship. However, explaining just how the interpersonal environment is implicated in what happens after the onset of depression was left by Brown and Harris as an agenda for future work. "Future research will need to focus on the role of the immediate social context, on individuals and their households, how they get caught up in a crisis or difficulty, try to cope with it, and the resources they have for this" (p. 293). In setting this agenda, Brown and Harris (1978) cautioned about the need to preserve the right level of analysis: "It is too easy for the broader approach to ignore the complexities of the individual's immediate social milieu and for the more detailed approach to get lost in the intricacies of the individual personality" (p. 293).

Interpersonal and interactional theories of depression have remained underdeveloped over the past two decades, even though this has been a period of rich and intense empirical work concerning the marriages, parenting, children, and family life of depressed persons, as well as work demonstrating depressed persons' fleeting contacts with strangers in the laboratory and the social psychological processes that can be uniquely observed in that context. This book presents the efforts of some of the key contributors to this accumulation of literature, including their predictions of future developments.

Besides summarizing and integrating empirical work, the authors of the chapters that follow make a determined effort to advance theory and to highlight the clinical implications of this work. There is no consensus as to how this is to be done. Some of the authors push theoretical development in ways that heighten the contrast with conventional views of depression. It should be noted that one of the explicit purposes of Coyne's (1976) article was to pose a challenge to cognitive theorists' assumption that the complaints of depressed persons are to be understood as the products of biased and distorted thinking. The alternative view is that depressed persons engage the environment in ways that lose support and elicit depressing feedback. In numerous subsequent publications (Coyne, 1982, 1989b; Coyne & Gotlib, 1983; Coyne & Whiffen, 1995), Coyne tried to show how invoking concepts like *schema* or *attributional style*, or the more recently fashionable *attachment style*, carries the risk of distracting researchers from otherwise readily observable interpersonal processes. Most of the authors of the chapters that follow take a distinctly different route, actively seeking a rapprochement and integration of just such concepts into interpersonal formulations of depression. However, Coyne resists being drawn into the mainstream and, in a somewhat discordant postscript to the volume, takes a defiant stand against casually integrating interactional and cognitive perspectives on depression. He argues that efforts at integration tend to end up "head first," with causal priority given to presumed cognitive structures without any attention to how contemporary involvement in relationships shapes people's thinking and sense of self. Such a causal priority is presumed by theorists without being critically examined or empirically tested, and it serves to constrain rather than enrich the understanding of the interactional context of depression.

It remains to be seen over the next decade whether the interactional perspective develops further as a distinctive alternative to intrapersonal and intrapsychic formulations of depression or whether it has its greatest impact in an integration into a more comprehensive model of depression. It is inevitable that efforts at theoretical integration will occur. One does not have to deny that depressed persons think about their experiences to assert that these experiences cannot be understood outside the interpersonal context in which they arise. However, it is unclear whether efforts to develop an integrative perspective will degenerate into *Cognition Über Alles* (Coyne, 1989b, 1990), the subordination of any consideration of depressed persons' involvement with their environment to cognitive theorists' construction of their cognitive processes. The task of integrating interactional and cognitive perspectives is more difficult than it first looks, unless one is prepared to settle for a Rube Goldberg construction in which concepts are joined together without regard for their necessity or redundancy. However the next decade unfolds, the directions that are taken are likely to be presaged in the chapters that follow, and many of the authors will undoubtedly prove to be important influences regarding these developments. In the following sections, we abstract several themes that are well articulated and elaborated in the chapters.

DEPRESSION IS ESSENTIALLY INTERPERSONAL

The strongest implication of the interpersonal approach is that depression not only has interpersonal features and consequences but also is fundamentally interpersonal in nature. From different perspectives, both Russell Gardner, Jr., and John S. Price (chap. 10) and Dana Crowley Jack (chap. 9) take this position, as each describes an emerging interpersonal model of depression. Adopting a sociophysiological perspective, Gardner and Price argue that depression-related states and behaviors represent evolved forms of a primordial "involuntary subordinate strategy," which arose as a means to cope with social competition and, particularly, losses in this competition. The functions of the involuntary subordinate strategy—and thus of depression—are to inhibit aggressive (and potentially costly) behaviors toward rivals and superiors (but not toward inferiors); to create a subjective self-view of incapacity (which encourages the inhibition of aggressive behaviors); to communicate to rivals and superiors a "no threat" signal (which discourages aggression from others); to communicate to allies an "out of action—can't help you" signal (which encourages them to fend for themselves); and to promote self-acceptance of a subordinate rank. Although most accounts of depression highlight the functional incapacity it engenders, the sociophysiological account of Gardner and Price emphasizes the survival value, during the course of human evolution, of a functional behavioral system for experiencing incapacity and of signaling it to others. This perspective claims empirical support from animal studies in which defeated animals display behavioral and neurochemical similarities to depressed people (e.g., Mehlman et al., 1995; cf. Seligman, 1974, 1975, regarding learned helplessness). Leading empirical support to the sociophysiological account, Joiner (1997) showed that college students high in shyness (cf. the "involuntary subordinate strategy") and low in social support (cf. lack of allies) tend to become lonely and thus depressed.

From a quite different, feminist perspective, Jack (chap. 9) reaches what can be viewed as similar conclusions. In her theory of self-silencing and women's depression, Jack argues that women's sense of self is organized around interpersonal themes of connectedness, intimacy, and mutuality. These are natural and healthy needs, which, in themselves, are not pathogenic. However, for women in many cultures, satisfaction of these needs requires a price that is pathogenic—self-silencing. Jack takes the well-established notion that depression is often the result of loss and expands it to encompass the idea that women often find that they must lose themselves to preserve harmony in their close relationships. According to this position, many women learn that self-sacrifice and self-denial are the keys to being "good" and are required to maintain closeness to others. The dilemma is that self-sacrifice and self-denial lead to lowered self-value as well as anger, and the "reward," closeness to others, engenders loneliness and hopelessness because it is not true closeness. For the self-silencing woman, legitimate needs for intimacy are framed as incompatible with needs for self-care and self-assertion; the result of this intractable dilemma is the appearance of depressive symptoms.

For Jack, as for Gardner and Price, depression cannot be understood without attention to its interpersonal function and grounding. In both accounts, depression results from a suppression of usual and healthy functioning, which, in turn, is a direct response to the interpersonal environment.

THE CAUSES OF DEPRESSION ARE INTERPERSONAL

Other chapters suggest that interpersonal factors may be causally related to depression. For example, William P. Sacco (chap. 13) advances the hypothesis that others' views of oneself may represent an enduring vulnerability factor for depression. The argument is that depression may instill in others a view of the sufferer, which, like the sufferer's self-view, is negative. This negative view of the depressed person appears to persist even after depressive symptoms remit (whereas the formerly depressed person may experience an enhanced self-view on symptom remission). This persistent negative view on the part of those who are close to recovered depressed persons may render the person vulnerable to relapse or recurrence of symptoms, perhaps through the expression of criticism or the lack of social support from the other to the formerly depressed person. Support for this proposition comes from the intriguing finding that a strong predictor of depression relapse is perceived criticism (Hooley & Teasdale, 1989). More generally, what has been termed *expressed emotion* in the family members of people with mental disorders increases relapse rates for the target person (Hooley, 1985; Leff & Vaughn, 1981).

The implication that negative evaluation by significant others may represent an enduring vulnerability factor is troubling, especially when applied to depressed children and negative evaluations of them by family members, including parents (cf. chaps. 11, 12, & 4, by P. Anderson, S. R. H. Beach, & N. J. Kaslow; E. M. Cummings & P. T. Davies; B. A. Haines, G. I. Metalsky, A. L. Cardamone, & T. E. Joiner, respectively). On a more optimistic note, an understanding of this process points to specific therapeutic interventions (e.g., changes in the attitude of significant others) to buffer the recovering depressed person from relapse or recurrence.

Norman B. Schmidt, Kristen L. Schmidt, and Jeffery E. Young (chap. 6) also focus on interpersonal factors as antecedents of depressive symptoms. Drawing on Young's theory of early maladaptive schemas, these authors argue that interpersonally relevant schemas (such as lack of connection to others, overconnection, and self-sacrifice) are developed through interactions with caregivers and persist to guide adult interpersonal behaviors in dysfunctional ways. For example, an individual who has developed a strong overconnection schema will attend to and select relationship partners who allow and foster excessive dependence. This is problematic; for example, Joiner, Metalsky, and colleagues (Joiner, Alfano, & Metalsky, 1992, 1993; Joiner & Metalsky, 1997; Pottholf, Holahan, & Joiner, 1995) showed that a dependent, excessively reassurance-seeking interpersonal style represents a vulnerability factor for future depression. The relevant theoretical and empirical work supports the idea that excessive reassurance seeking alienates others, which, in turn, increases or exacerbates depressive symptoms. It is interesting to note that this focus on schemas is quite compatible with the account of Jack and that of Gardner and Price, who emphasize self-silencing (cf. self-sacrifice schema) and submission–inadequacy (cf. involuntary subordination strategy), respectively.

The views of Schmidt et al. also are quite consistent with the work of Constance Hammen and colleagues, as summarized in Hammen's introductory chapter (chap. 2). Hammen and colleagues have articulated a stress generation model of depression, in which depressed people contribute to the occurrence of their own stress, which, in turn, maintains or exacerbates vulnerability to depression. Hammen's group has provided an impressive series of empirical studies to support this view. The stress generation perspective is similar to the views of several other authors in this volume in emphasizing the interpersonal while incorporating the intrapsychic; that is, interpersonal behaviors and relationships represent the key constructs of the model, yet the cognitive (intrapsychic) construct of attachment-related schemas is included in the model as well.

Also relevant to the interpersonal causes of depressive symptoms is R. Brian Giesler and W. B. Swann's provocative chapter (chap. 8), which expands on the notion that people need self-confirming feedback from others. In the case of people with negative self-concepts, this need for self-verification becomes a motivation to actively obtain negative responses from others. Swann and colleagues have provided impressive empirical evidence that such a need exists and operates with pernicious consequences in close relationships. Giesler and Swann argue that, among people with negative self-concepts, depressed people may be the most likely to engage in negative feedback seeking. With regard to the causes of depression, these authors suggest that initially nondepressed people with low self-esteem, in response to negative affect (occasioned, perhaps, by a negative life event), have heightened access to negatively valenced constructs in memory (e.g., specific negative self-views) as well as experience increased levels of self-awareness. Taken together, these two processes may, in turn, guide the solicitation of negative feedback. Over time, the person may increasingly receive and become receptive to unfavorable feedback. As Joiner (1995) showed, people who both solicit unfavorable feedback and receive it are vulnerable to increased depression.

In a comprehensive review of the connections among shyness, loneliness, and depression, Jody C. Dill and Craig A. Anderson (chap. 5) take a position similar to Schmidt et al. in that they frame shyness as a schematic, guiding perception, motivation, and interpersonal behaviors in depressotypic ways. Specifically, these authors assert that shy people have difficulty in establishing and maintaining close interpersonal ties, because social fear and anxiety interfere with attempts to initiate and sustain close relationships. Failures and embarrassments created by these unsuccessful (or untried) attempts create a negative self-view, as well as the motivation to avoid social encounters. Loneliness thus ensues. As Dill and Anderson state, "the lack of positive social reinforcers and dissatisfaction with one's interpersonal life produce the cognitive, affective, and behavioral states characteristic of depression." In a recent study, Joiner (1997) provided empirical support for this account: Shy undergraduates who were low in social support were likely to become lonely and, as a function thereof, were likely to experience increases in depression. Shyness has also been emphasized in other accounts of vulnerability to depression and related problems. For example, shyness may be linked to the "affective style" variable (i.e., relative left frontal hypoactivation on electroencephalography) studied by Davidson and colleagues (e.g., Davidson & Fox, 1982), and it is certainly associated with behavioral inhibition and its negative sequelae, as studied by Kagan and colleagues (e.g., Kagan, Resnick, & Snidman, 1987).

Rather than emphasizing interpersonal deficits (such as excessive reassurance seeking, self-silencing, overconnection schema, or shyness), Charles J. Holahan, Rudolph H. Moos, and Liza A. Bonin (chap. 3) focus on adaptive interpersonal functioning and its role in protecting individuals from depression and other health problems. In an impressive series of studies on community and clinical samples, Holahan et al. show that coping strategies involving approach as opposed to avoidance, such as direct problem solving and seeking information from others, can buffer people against the depressogenic effects of negative life events. By contrast, avoidant coping strategies, such as denial of problems and withdrawal from others (cf. Dill & Anderson on shyness, chap. 5), are associated with a variety of maladaptive behavioral outcomes, including depression. Furthermore, there is evidence that avoidant coping strategies not only increase the likelihood of psychological dysfunction but also may bring on negative life events, which, in turn, may lead to psychological problems. It is interesting—and also relevant to causation but at a more distal level—that Holahan, Moos, and Bonin have found that close support in families leads to more approach coping in the members of such families.

Anderson et al. (chap. 11) frame marital distress as a key risk factor for depression and, like Holahan et al. (chap. 3), construe harmonious marriage as a "secure base" from which healthy attachments and functioning may flow. In their account of the relation of marital processes to depression, Anderson et al. emphasize attachment processes, particularly the internal working models of self and other that guide selection of relationships, as well as social cognition within relationships—an approach that complements well the positions of Schmidt et al. (chap. 6) on schemas, Dill and Anderson (chap. 5) on shyness, and Giesler and Swann (chap. 8) on self-verification processes. Whether their work is viewed from the perspective of attachment theory, cognitive theory, or personality theory, these authors converge in their belief that early interpersonal experience lays down psychological models that influence, sometimes in pernicious ways, later adaptation. This is not to say that childhood experiences have a direct, inevitable effect on adult relationships and risk for depression (Coyne, Pepper, & Cohen, in press). As Caspi and Elder (1988) noted in another context, "it is not so much a personality trait or a psychoanalytic-like residual of early childhood experience that is maintained across time, but an interactional style that evokes reciprocal maintaining responses from others" (p. 231).

Cummings and Davies (chap. 12) also emphasize the influence of family environment on child development and, particularly, risk for depression. They go beyond the reviews of the past decade (Cummings & Davies, 1994; Downey & Coyne, 1990; Kaslow, Deering, & Racusin, 1994) in giving a fresh sense of the rapidly accumulating research concerning the family context of depression. They argue that marital conflict of the parents, as well as dysfunctional parent–child relationships, lead to a disrupted sense of emotional security and thus to a variety of negative outcomes, including depression. Reminiscent of the schema-related conceptualizations of Schmidt et al. (chap. 6) and Dill and Anderson (chap. 5), these authors define *emotional security* as children's "interpretation of the meaning of family relations, for their own well-being and for the well-being of the family," and they argue, supported by several lines of empirical evidence, that emotional security plays a key role in children's regulation of emotion and in their ability to face life stress adaptively (cf. Holahan et al., chap. 3). Furthermore, Cummings and Davies theorize that children's views of parental, intrafamilial, and personal relations, imbued by disrupted emotional security, accumulate to form a schema that has important implications for long-term adjustment.

Haines et al. (chap. 4) also provide a developmental model, and they also emphasize a schema-related construct—attributional style for negative interpersonal events. At a general level, these authors argue that negative early interpersonal experience, such as negative feedback from parents, peers, and teachers, may lead children to adopt a pessimistic worldview. It is interesting that younger children may be prone to develop pessimistic explanatory styles, despite relative lack of cognitive sophistication, because their less complex reasoning and limited experience may combine to form a broadly negative view of self and world. Again, the argument is that interpersonal experience affects outcome through its effect on interpersonally relevant intrapsychic structures, such as negative attributional style.

It is interesting to compare the approach of Haines et al. (chap. 4) with that of Jack (chap. 9). As Haines et al. show, on the basis of the work of Dweck and colleagues (Dweck, Davidson, Nelson, & Enna, 1978), young girls receive less praise than boys do for the intellectual quality of their work, and girls' shortcomings are more likely to be attributed by teachers to lack of ability than to lack of effort or motivation. This pattern of feedback is likely to lead to negative attributions about school-related ability and may be one early source of the tendency, emphasized by Jack, for women to doubt their ability and their right to assert themselves.

In summary, the book's contributors make a strong case that interpersonal factors should be considered in explaining vulnerability to depression. Many of the chapters converge around the following theme: Interpersonal experience, especially that involving significant others (e.g., parents), affects mood outcomes by laying down a negative and stable view of the interpersonal world. An exciting research agenda would involve delineation of interrelations of the proposed factors to one another as well as to other putative risk factors, such as various neurobiological indexes (e.g., serotonin system dysfunction). Once the various interpersonal and other risk factors are well defined and categorized, treatment and prevention efforts will be better informed.

DEPRESSION IS INTERPERSONALLY MEDIATED

Several authors argue that, whatever the cause of depression, interpersonal factors are involved in the pathway from vulnerability to manifestation of symptoms. As mentioned earlier, Dill and Anderson (chap. 5) frame loneliness as an important interpersonal mediator between causal factors and depressive outcomes. Many of the interpersonal risk factors, such as self-silencing, involuntary subordination, shyness, and the lack-of-connection schema, could contribute to loneliness, which, in turn, heightens depression vulnerability (i.e., loneliness may mediate the relations between all of these risk factors and depressive symptoms).

Although their chapter is also clearly relevant to the issue of vulnerability, John E. Roberts and Scott M. Monroe (chap. 7) frame vicissitudes of self-esteem regulation as a key mediator between causes (such as interpersonal loss and threat) and eventual symptoms. These authors observe that previous work has not firmly established that level of self-esteem is an antecedent of depression, and they suggest that other aspects of self-esteem, such as its stability and reactivity, may be more relevant in the development of depressive symptoms. In their view, people who can maintain their self-esteem, using such strategies as favorable social comparisons or emphasis of nonthreatened aspects of self-esteem, are able to fend off the depressogenic effects of negative life events. It is important to note that the availability and quality of close attachment relationships contribute to the ability to regulate and maintain self-esteem. This view is similar to the sociometer theory of self-esteem (Leary, Tambor, Terdal, & Downs, 1995), in that both level and stasis of self-esteem are intertwined with the interpersonal environment.

Roberts and Monroe's (chap. 7) emphasis on self-esteem regulation shares similarities to Holahan et al.'s (chap. 3) view of coping; like self-esteem regulation, coping processes may be viewed as both a risk factor and a mediator. With regard to the mediational role of coping, Holahan et al. report that, for high-stress individuals, personal and social resources (e.g., self-confidence, social support) relate to future psychological adjustment through coping. That is, those with good resources displayed better coping strategies and thus experienced better psychological functioning. This finding also appeared among women facing breast biopsy and possibly cancer: Dispositional optimism predicted adaptive coping and, therefore, better psychological adjustment.

The schema-based perspectives of both Schmidt et al. (chap. 6) and Dill and Anderson (chap. 5) lend themselves naturally to a mediational interpretation. Both accounts frame interpersonally relevant schemas (e.g., lack of connection) as distal diatheses that guide subsequent interpersonal behaviors and cognitions in ways that eventuate in depression. The interpersonal behaviors and cognitions, guided by schemas, play the role of mediators in these accounts. One such interpersonal behavior mentioned by Schmidt et al.—reassurance seeking—may indeed stem from interpersonally relevant schemas (such as shyness or lack of connection), and it seems to play an important role in bringing on negative outcomes in depression, such as interpersonal rejection and heightened symptoms (e.g., Joiner & Metalsky, 1995).

The focus of the chapter by Giesler and Swann (chap. 8) is self-confirming interpersonal behavior, especially when negative. When viewed in broader scope, however, an implication of the self-verification position is that self-confirming behavior is a mediator between negative self-concept (presumably obtained developmentally) and negative psychological and interpersonal outcomes. This model can be viewed as a self-esteem theory of depression with an interpersonal mediator.

In summary, the authors of these chapters, like the authors of the chapters emphasizing vulnerability, argue that various interpersonal behaviors, attitudes, and processes precede depression. However, these chapters focus more on the mechanism by which risk factors eventuate in depression. Of course, an understanding of both risk factors and mechanisms is crucial to the development and refinement of interventions for depression.

DEPRESSION IS INTERPERSONALLY REMEDIABLE

Many chapters provide rich clinical implications. For therapists interested in interpersonal psychotherapy (IPT), many of the book's clinical implications can be incorporated as refinements of IPT. IPT includes four areas of interpersonal focus: grief, role disputes, role transitions, and social skills. With regard to vicissitudes in roles, the chapter by Giesler and Swann (chap. 8) has potentially important implications. These authors make the case that both identity and roles are interpersonally negotiated between people and that a driving force in the negotiation process is confirmation and validation of self-concept, whether positive or negative. It is interesting that the change from a negative identity or role to a more positive one may be resisted, because role change brings with it a sense of uncertainty and unfamiliarity. The work of Swann and colleagues suggests that such changes will be resisted unless the preexisting self-view is acknowledged first. In working with a depressed person on self-esteem change, therefore, the person's negative self-views must be acknowledged—and, to a degree, accepted—in order to position the person to change those views.

With regard to the area of social skills, the chapters in this volume identify a number of attitudes and behaviors that either represent or lead to unskilled interpersonal behavior. For example, Giesler and Swann highlight the deleterious effects of negative feedback seeking; Schmidt et al., on the basis of the work of Coyne, Joiner, and colleagues, note the potential negative impact of excessive reassurance seeking; Haines et al. emphasize the role of negative attributional style for interpersonal events; Holahan et al., of avoidant coping strategies; and Dill and Anderson, of inhibited and avoidant interpersonal behaviors. Each of these behaviors or attitudes represents potential leverage points for successful intervention.

Another interesting clinical note comes from the chapter by Holahan et al. (chap. 3), who found that general family support is the crucible from which adaptive coping springs. In the family therapy of depressed people, particularly depressed children and adolescents, communication and provision of support among family members should be considered as exercises for each family session.

Anderson et al. (chap. 11) include clear implications for the work of marital therapy when one partner is depressed. In a vignette of an interaction between a couple and their therapist, the therapist draws out the attachment-related concerns of each partner. For the wife, feeling dismissed and out-of-touch was central; for the husband, feeling controlled was problematic. The therapist, working from an attachment perspective, assumes that each partner desires the marriage to be a "secure base." Specifically identifying the features of this secure base for each partner, as well as current obstacles, the therapist generates an agenda for the couple's therapy and for the interpersonal resolution of the partners' depressive symptoms.

Jack provides case examples in which women struggle with competing and conflicting needs for self-assertion and intimacy. This struggle can be paralyzing if one need circumvents the other, as can be the case for women caught in the "self-silencing" trap described by Jack. As a solution, Jack advises that therapists help depressed people to explicitly voice the standards that guide their behavior and then encourage a sense of personal choice and control regarding which standard to embrace. In addition, monitoring of self-silencing thoughts and behaviors is suggested as a way to identify underlying fears that keep one's authentic voice from gaining free expression. Once these fears are identified (perhaps, in part, by Jack's Silencing the Self Scale), they can be mastered.

In his postscript, Coyne argues that an interactional perspective can be used to take the treatment of depression in some radically new directions. He points out that IPT retains many of the psychodynamic and Sullivanian inhibitions about therapists making direct suggestions to clients as to how they might take action to resolve the negativity in their relationships with others. Of course, couples therapists work directly with the relationships of depressed persons, but Coyne argues that conventional couples therapy is too limiting in requiring that depressed persons be able to enlist their partners in a conjoint therapeutic process or assuming that they even want their partners to accompany them to therapeutic sessions. Drawing on his work with the Palo Alto Mental Research Institute Group (Coyne, 1989a; Watzlawick & Coyne, 1980), Coyne calls for alternative formats and therapeutic strategies for intervening directly in the relationships of depressed persons, enlisting whoever is willing to become involved.

CONCLUSION AND FUTURE RESEARCH DIRECTIONS

A notable feature of many of the book's chapters is the emphasis on theory development. Virtually all chapters abound with theoretical insights and attendant testable hypotheses. For example, the developmental accounts of Haines et al. (chap. 4) and Cummings and Davies (chap. 12) chart areas of research in developmental psychopathology that have received little empirical attention.

In addition, as mentioned earlier, an array of interpersonal risk factors have been proposed by the book's authors. As a first line of investigation, these factors must be tested to determine whether they predict future depressive symptoms and episodes. Many of the chapter authors suggest broadly conceived frameworks of depression and its interpersonal roots and consequences. The empirical examination of these frameworks, across time and lives, as well as the integration of these frameworks into a more comprehensive interpersonal theory of depression, represents an exciting and substantial agenda for future science.

REFERENCES

Becker, E. S. (1964). *The revolution in psychiatry*. New York: Free Press.

Bibring, E. (1955). The mechanism of depression. In P. Greenacre (Ed.), *Affective disorders* (pp. 13–48). London: International Universities Press.

Brown, G. W., & Harris, T. (1978). *Social origins of depression: A study of psychiatric disorder in women*. New York: Free Press.

Caspi, A., & Elder, G. (1988). Childhood precursors of the life course: Early personality and life disorganization. In E. M. Hetherington, R. Lerner, & M. Perlmutter (Eds.), *Child development in life-span perspective* (pp. 115–142). Hillsdale, NJ: Erlbaum.

Coyne, J. C. (1976). Toward an interactional description of depression. *Psychiatry, 39*, 28–40.

Coyne, J. C. (1982). A critique of cognitions as causal entities with particular reference to depression. *Cognitive Therapy and Research, 6*, 3–13.

Coyne, J. C. (Ed.). (1986). *Essential papers on depression*. New York: New York University Press.

Coyne, J. C. (1989a). Employing therapeutic paradoxes in the treatment of depression. In M. L. Ascher (Ed.), *Paradoxical procedures in psychotherapy* (pp. 163–183). New York: Guilford Press.

Coyne, J. C. (1989b). Thinking post-cognitively about depression. In A. Freeman, K. Simon, L. Beutler, & H. Arkowitz (Eds.), *Comprehensive handbook of cognitive therapy* (pp. 227–244). New York: Plenum Press.

Coyne, J. C. (1990). Concepts for understanding marriage and developing techniques of marital therapy: Cognition Uber Alles? *Journal of Family Psychology, 4*, 185–194.

Coyne, J. C., & Gotlib, I. (1983). The role of cognition in depression: A critical appraisal. *Psychological Bulletin, 94*, 472–505.

Coyne, J. C., Pepper, C. M., & Cohen, N. (in press). Marital distress, ways of coping with conflict, and the backgrounds of depressed patients and husbands. *Journal of Personal and Social Relationships*.

Coyne, J. C., & Whiffen, V. E. (1995). Issues in personality as diathesis for depression: The case of sociotropy/dependency and autonomy/self-criticism. *Psychological Bulletin, 118*, 358–378.

Cummings, E. M., & Davies, P. T. (1994). Maternal depression and child development. *Journal of Child Psychology and Psychiatry, 35*, 73–112.

Davidson, R. J., & Fox, N. A. (1982). Asymmetrical brain activity discriminates between positive versus negative affective stimuli in human infants. *Science, 218*, 1235–1237.

Downey, G., & Coyne, J. C. (1990). Children of depressed parents: An integrative review. *Psychological Bulletin, 108,* 50–76.

Dweck, C. S., Davidson, W., Nelson, S., & Enna, B. (1978). Sex differences in learned helplessness: II. The contingencies of evaluative feedback in the classroom and III. An experimental analysis. *Developmental Psychology, 14,* 268–276.

Fenichel, O. (1945). *The psychoanalytic theory of neurosis.* New York: Norton.

Freud, S. (1951). Mourning and melancholia. In J. Strachey (Ed. and Trans.), *The standard edition of the complete psychological works of Sigmund Freud* (Vol. 14). London: Hogarth Press. (Original work published 1917)

Hooley, J. (1985). Expressed emotion: A review of the critical literature. *Clinical Psychology Review, 5,* 119–139.

Hooley, J., & Teasdale, J. (1989). Predictors of relapse in unipolar depression: Expressed emotion, marital distress, and perceived criticism. *Journal of Abnormal Psychology, 98,* 229–235.

Joiner, T. E., Jr. (1995). The price of soliciting and receiving negative feedback: Self-verification theory as a vulnerability to depression theory. *Journal of Abnormal Psychology, 104,* 354–372.

Joiner, T. E., Jr. (1997). Shyness and low social support as interactive diatheses, and loneliness as mediator: Testing an interpersonal-personality view of vulnerability to depression. *Journal of Abnormal Psychology, 106,* 386–394.

Joiner, T. E., Jr., Alfano, M. S., & Metalsky, G. I. (1992). When depression breeds contempt: Reassurance-seeking, self-esteem, and rejection of depressed college students by their roommates. *Journal of Abnormal Psychology, 101,* 165–173.

Joiner, T. E., Jr., Alfano, M. S., & Metalsky, G. I. (1993). Caught in the crossfire: Depression, self-consistency, self-enhancement, and the response of others. *Journal of Social and Clinical Psychology, 12,* 113–134.

Joiner, T. E., Jr., & Metalsky, G. I. (1995). A prospective test of an integrative interpersonal theory of depression: A naturalistic study of college students. *Journal of Personality and Social Psychology, 69,* 778–788.

Joiner, T. E., Jr., & Metalsky, G. I. (1997). *Reassurance-seeking and depression.* Manuscript submitted for publication.

Kagan, J., Resnick, J. S., & Snidman, N. (1987). The physiology and psychology of behavioral inhibition in children. *Child Development, 58,* 1459–1473.

Kaslow, N. J., Deering, C. G., & Racusin, G. R. (1994). Depressed children and their families. *Clinical Psychology Review, 14,* 39–59.

Klerman, G. L., Weissman, M. M., Rounsaville, B. J., & Chevron, E. S. (1984). *Interpersonal therapy for depression.* New York: Basic Books.

Leary, M. R., Tambor, E. S., Terdal, S. K., & Downs, D. L. (1995). Self-esteem as an interpersonal monitor: The sociometer hypothesis. *Journal of Personality and Social Psychology, 68,* 518–530.

Leff, J. P., & Vaugh, C. E. (1981). The role of maintenance therapy and relatives' expressed emotion in relapse of schizophrenia: A two-year follow up. *British Journal of Psychology, 139,* 102–104.

Lewinsohn, P. M., Weinstein, M. S., & Shaw, D. A. (1969). Depression: A clinical research approach. In R. D. Rubin & C. M. Franks (Eds.), *Advances in behavior therapy* (pp. 229–248). New York: Academic Press.

Mehlman, P. T., Higley, J. D., Faucher, I., Lilly, A. A., Taub, D. M., Vickers, J., Suomi, S. J., & Linnoila, M. (1995). Correlation of CSF5-HIAA concentration with sociality and the timing of emigration in free-ranging primates. *American Journal of Psychiatry, 152,* 907–913.

Melville, H. (1984). Bartleby. In *Billy Budd, sailor, and other stories* (pp. 95–130). New York: Bantam Books. (Original work published 1856)

Nacht, S., & Racamier, P. C. (1961). The depressive states. *Psyche, 14,* 417–574.

Potthoff, J. G., Holahan, C. J., & Joiner, T. E., Jr. (1995). Reassurance-seeking, stress generation, and depressive symptoms: An integrative model. *Journal of Personality and Social Psychology, 68,* 664–670.

Seligman, M. E. P. (1974). Depression and learned helplessness. In R. J. Friedman & M. M. Katz. (Eds.), *The psychology of depression: Contemporary theory and research* (pp. 3–28). Washington, DC: Winston-Wiley.

Seligman, M. E. P. (1975). *Helplessness: On depression, development, and death.* San Francisco: Freeman.

Sullivan, H. S. (1956). *Clinical studies in psychiatry.* New York: Norton.

Szasz, T. S. (1961). *The myth of mental illness.* News York: Hoeber-Harper.

Watzlawick, P. W., & Coyne, J. C. (1980). Depression following stroke: Brief problem-focused family treatment. *Family Process, 19,* 13–18.

Weissman, M. M., & Paykel, E. S. (1974). *The depressed woman.* Chicago: University of Chicago Press.

2

THE EMERGENCE OF AN INTERPERSONAL APPROACH TO DEPRESSION

CONSTANCE HAMMEN

An interpersonal approach to depression represents both an attitude or philosophy about the research focus and substantive content about the social nature, origins, and consequences of the disorder. It is an "approach," or "focus," rather than a model or theory, because it is not well enough articulated or tested to attain the status of the latter. Indeed, behavioral science in general offers a relatively modest and limited understanding of human interpersonal functioning. Furthermore, an interpersonal approach is not only incomplete but also emergent and changing, as evidenced by the wide array of topics represented in this volume and the works in progress that are described.

The sections that follow describe first the philosophy and content of an interpersonal perspective as they have emerged in my work of the past 25 years; subsequently, they describe in general terms some of my group's current work that reflects these themes and interests. Finally, some gaps and future directions for further research are noted.

THE EMERGENCE OF AN INTERPERSONAL PERSPECTIVE: THE INTERPERSONAL "ATTITUDE"

Interpersonal emphases in depression research are defined in part by an attitude or philosophy that requires a focus on context and the understanding of the individual as embedded in an environment that influences, and is influenced by, the person. In contrast to an intraindividual perspective, which focuses on processes within the person, the interpersonal perspective includes the factors that have an impact on those intrapersonal activities. From this point of view, the social context of relationships between and among persons is the primary focus, although the context may additionally include numerous other important variables. By definition, the interpersonal perspective is about transactions, or reciprocal influences, among individuals, and these transactions create a dynamic process of change and flow. It contrasts with research strategies that may be viewed as unidirectional, linear, and perhaps static.

Although additional characteristics of the interpersonal perspective might be claimed, all writers would not agree on what they are. For instance, I argue that an interpersonal-based model of depression would likely be complex, requiring multiple interacting or mutually influencing factors, and would include both cognitive and behavioral variables representing both learned and cognitively represented social beliefs and behaviors as well as current behaviors and reactions. A particular research priority, however, need not require the elaboration of multiple factors, and the scope of an interpersonal research agenda depends on the nature of the question being asked.

The interpersonal approach, of course, also concerns the content of social and interpersonal experiences that characterize the nature, causes, and consequences of depressive experiences. There have been a number of exciting empirical developments in the study of mood disorders over the past 25 years or so that have increasingly convinced many that depression is fundamentally rooted in social experiences and that social consequences of depression are crucial to understanding and treating the disorder. This volume traces many such developments.

A HISTORICAL PERSPECTIVE ON THE ORIGINS OF INTERPERSONAL APPROACHES

Why or how did an interpersonal perspective arise? I venture the following list of critical contributions; I am certain that these will not be universally agreed on but submit them as the ones most influential in my own emerging interpersonal perspective.

A Reaction to the Excesses of a Cognitive Model of Depression

Aaron Beck's (1967) cognitive model of depression was one of the most fortunate developments for clinical psychology of recent times. In many ways, it was the intellectual heir and synthesis of the three "forces" of psychology in the twentieth century: psychodynamic, behavioral, and humanistic. Each of the forces made important contributions but was notably lacking in important elements, especially when applied to the complex and difficult-to-treat phenomenon of depression. Beck's model returned human internal experiences and conscious processes to the fore, while integrating behavioral and empirical principles that promoted a tidal wave of often elegant research on depressive processes and treatment. However, just as the success of any paradigm leads not only to celebrations of its achievements but also to discovery of its shortcomings, weaknesses of the cognitive model emerged (e.g., Coyne & Gotlib, 1983; Haaga, Ernst, & Dyck, 1991; Hammen, 1992).

In my view, the weaknesses were relative rather than absolute; they were emphases that weakened the empirical predictability of depression because of the exclusive focus on intrapersonal—cognitive—factors to the relative neglect of real-life situations. In reaction, the nearly exclusive emphasis on cognition promoted greater attention both to the philosophical features of the interpersonal perspective (contextual, interpersonal, transactional) and to the focus on additional content featuring social processes as they pertained to the etiology and treatment of depressive disorders. Some of my earlier chapters and talks reflected critiques of the "overly" cognitive focus that downplayed or ignored situational and contextual factors that influence individuals' cognitions and mood (e.g., Hammen, 1992; Hammen & Mayol, 1982).

Sex Differences in Depression

The reality of women's excess rates of depression was not readily explained by the cognitive (or any) model, which led many of us who were intrigued by this issue to consider the ways in which women's experiences differ from those of men in depressogenic ways. Considerable research was conducted in the 1970s on contributors to women's depressive experiences, including focus on women's roles and barriers—that is, the contexts of their lives. Myrna Weissman's work on sex differences and women's experiences (Weissman & Klerman, 1977; Weissman & Paykel, 1974) contributed to an interest in the lives of depressed women. These authors noted that depressed women often reported continuing impairment in relationship roles, even during remission.

Some of my earliest work addressed issues concerning gender differences, among them the question of whether depressed men and women elicited different reactions. Borrowing from Coyne's (1976) methods and ideas, my colleagues and I tested the hypothesis that depressed people elicit negative reactions from others and that men fare worse—with the implication that men may learn not to express depressive symptoms (Hammen & Peters, 1977, 1978). By definition, much of the research on gender differences focused on the interpersonal context of women's lives—their marriages and families and their social networks—as sources of stress and potentially of inadequate or diminished support.

Coyne's Interactional Perspective

Coyne's (1976) emphasis on the depressed person's elicitation of negative reactions from others was an important contributor to an interpersonal perspective. This work not only stimulated some of my group's sex differences research, noted previously, but also encouraged an emphasis on potentially problematic (and, hence, stressful) relationships of depressed people. Subsequent research on depression in marriages and in families has confirmed the notion when one member of the family is depressed, others are likely to be depressed as well (e.g., Downey & Coyne, 1990).

Brown and Harris's (1978) *Social Origins of Depression*

I consider the volume *Social Origins of Depression* (Brown & Harris, 1978) another significant contributor to the interpersonal focus in depression. In this book about women's depression and the experiences associated with the onset of depression, Brown and Harris described their contextual threat method, which represented an elegant approach to quantifying the context of women's lives. Life stress research played an important role in the explication of the etiology of depressive experiences, but it proceeded in relative isolation from the dominant cognitive model of depression. However, Brown and Harris (1978) formulated a theory of depression in which the situational (largely interpersonal) context of a stressor was the critical ingredient determining its meaning. Thus, "meaning," a cognitive construct, was created by the circumstances of a person's life surrounding the occurrence of a stressful life event. These investigators also factored in the chronic, or ongoing, circumstances of a woman's life, including difficult role enactments such as having multiple young children and not working outside the home, as well as lack of a confiding relationship. In short, depression was viewed not as a result of idiosyncratic or distorted interpretations of a negative or even minor event but as a predictable outcome following a severe event occurring in the context of relatively limited resources for dealing with it, with understandable meaning in terms of its importance in an individual's life.

The book *Social Origins of Depression* (Brown & Harris, 1978) played an important role in my work. It stimulated an abiding interest in understanding and assessing the stress context of depressive reactions. Although stress was dutifully given lip service in cognitive diathesis–stress models of depression, little or no attention was devoted to real-life tests of stressors in evaluating Beck's or attributional models. In the late 1970s and early 1980s, my group attempted to measure stressors and bring them into the tests of hypotheses (e.g., Gong-Guy & Hammen, 1980; Hammen, 1978; Hammen, Krantz, & Cochran, 1981; Hammen, Marks, Mayol, & deMayo, 1985). As we began to use our own version of a contextual threat assessment of stressors modeled after Brown's Life Events and Difficulties Schedule, we not only performed the empirical function of testing diathesis–stress hypotheses but also experienced an enormously rich glimpse into the lives of depressed individuals. This glimpse convinced us more than ever of the significance of interpersonal relationships in the depression process, about which more is discussed later.

Bowlby's Attachment Theory and Developmental Psychopathology

Bowlby's (1969, 1980) work is important to an interpersonal perspective on depression because it hypothesizes a fundamental, universal, and indeed psychobiologically based need for relatedness. Bowlby wrote that the quality of the earliest caretaker–infant relationship is a major factor in personality and vulnerability to depressive disorders, which reminded us that loss of an important relationship is a universally understood trigger for depression. Although the jury is still out on many features of Bowlby's model, there is impressive evidence that security of attachment is an important determinant of young children's socioemotional development (e.g., Sroufe, 1983) and that it may set the stage for the competencies and attitudes that affect lifelong functioning. Developmental psychopathology is an emerging field that has been influenced by Bowlby's theories and that emphasizes the study of the origins of vulnerabilities for psychopathology as they are rooted in early childhood experiences. An important part of the context of a person's life is the historical context, with the development and unfolding of competencies or deficiencies as the individual interacts with the world over time. Developmental psychopathology also is a perspective about healthy and unhealthy development that is compatible with an interpersonal model as described earlier—it is transactional, dynamic, and complex.

In my group's research, both the spirit of Bowlby (1969, 1980) and the field of developmental psychopathology have played a significant role in an emerging interpersonal focus. Together, they contributed to a strong interest in the childhood origins of vulnerability to depression, an interest that led directly to a project involving the study of children of depressed mothers. We believed that this high-risk sample would provide a good laboratory for testing a variety of psychosocial hypotheses about vulnerability, and indeed the work revealed a great deal about interpersonal processes in the families of depressed women and their children (e.g., Hammen, 1991a). Moreover, attachment theory provided a content and substance to the vague notions of cognitive models of depression, in which dysfunctional schemas are assumed to be acquired in early experiences. Childhood experiences seemed far too important to be left to psychoanalytic theorizing and nonempirical pronouncements. Because in many ways attachment theory is about acquisitions of cognitions about the self and the world, it seemed desirable to include such notions in models of depression. Specifically, my group made use of measures of attachment cognitions for adults, which are fundamentally about interpersonal functioning—one's desires and abilities to be close and connected with others and one's beliefs about others' reliability, availability, and warmth (e.g., Hammen et al., 1995).

This brief overview of five contributions to an emerging interest in interpersonal aspects of depression is not meant to be all-inclusive nor to minimize the importance of other influential models or findings that have helped stimulate this focus. Indeed, many such works are included or reviewed in this volume.

EMPIRICAL UNDERPINNINGS OF AN INTERPERSONAL APPROACH TO DEPRESSION

My research team has come to view social relationships as critical features of vulnerability to depression, with a particular focus on interpersonal contributions to recurrent depression in the individual and to intergenerational transmission of depression in families. The following sections provide a brief overview of these ideas and their origins in our work.

Stressful Life Events and the Interpersonal Context

Specific Vulnerability to Stressors

Long after Freud emphasized object loss as a trigger of depression (mourning and melancholia), researchers continue to discover that a key trigger to depression is loss of interpersonal connectedness with significant others. Both as a diathesis and as a stressor, interpersonal experiences are commonly—although of course not invariably—implicated in the onset of depressive reactions.

In my group's earliest work, we tested cognitive formulations of depression, but as noted previously, we included measures of stressful life events and cognitions about events. An early indication of the relative importance of social relationships as triggers of depressive reactions arose from the testing of hypotheses of "specific vulnerability." Both cognitive and psychodynamic formulations posited different pathways to depression (Arieti & Bemporad, 1980; Beck, 1983), suggesting that individuals might be susceptible to depression in particular domains of personal relevance. That is, depression likely follows the occurrence not of any stressful event but, more particularly, of an event that occurs within the domain of experiences to which the individual attaches particular significance with respect to self-worth and competence. Several of my group's earlier studies demonstrated that a match between event content and either interpersonal or achievement domains of personal importance resulted in depression to a greater extent than did stressors occurring in the nonrelevant content domain. Various methods were used in different studies to characterize the relative salience and personal significance of achievement and relationships with others, and participants were followed longitudinally to observe occurrence of stressors and depression.

A particularly noteworthy feature of these findings was the relative importance of the interpersonal domain to most individuals. In several studies involving different populations, such as college students (Hammen et al., 1985), adult outpatients with unipolar or bipolar mood disorder (Hammen, Ellicott, & Gitlin, 1992; Hammen, Ellicott, Gitlin, & Jamison, 1989), and children of depressed women (Hammen & Goodman-Brown, 1990), my colleagues and I demonstrated that the match between interpersonal negative life events and attribution of personal importance to relationships with others was especially predictive of depressive reactions. Whereas "matches" between achievement- or autonomy-oriented individuals and failures or disappointments in the achievement domain also produced depressive reactions, such matches were neither as frequent nor as reliable a predictor of depression as matches in the interpersonal domain. It seemed that negative life events in the interpersonal domain were simply more likely to elicit depressive reactions than were equally negative but noninterpersonal events.

Attachment Cognitions and Vulnerability to Interpersonal Stressors

In an attempt both to broaden the content of potentially dysfunctional depressive cognitions and to integrate a developmental psychopathology approach to the origin of such maladaptive beliefs, my group included "attachment cognitions" in a test of the cognitive diathesis–stress model of depression; the work was based on Bowlby's model of the acquisition of secure or insecure "working models" of the self and others as internal cognitive representations derived from the nature of the caretaker–infant bond (Bowlby, 1969, 1980). Negative working models confer vulnerability to depression when negative interpersonal events occur that are viewed as confirming the beliefs that others will abandon one or fail to provide reliable and responsive close connections. Hammen et al. (1995) found that the interaction of negative interpersonal events and insecure attachment cognitions (measured on the Revised Adult Attachment Scale; Collins & Read, 1990) predicted level of depressive symptoms as well as other psychopathology over a longitudinal course.

Studies such as these persuaded my group that depressive symptoms and episodes often represent responses to negative interpersonal events but that vulnerability is especially predictable among those whose interpersonal attitudes and beliefs either strongly emphasize the importance of relations with others or who have "insecure" beliefs and expectations of others. The origin of such maladaptive beliefs and their specificity to depression are topics of ongoing interest and research.

Intergenerational Transmission of Depression: Children of Depressed Women

An interest in the development of depressive vulnerability stimulated the undertaking of a high-risk study comparing school-age children of women with recurrent unipolar disorder with children of normal parents, with the additional comparison groups of bipolar women and chronically medically ill women to control for the nonspecific effects of stress and illness (Hammen, 1991a). In contrast to other high-risk depression studies of the time (which significantly languished behind the elegant high-risk schizophrenia studies in design), this study was longitudinal and included various child outcomes besides psychopathology, as well as psychosocial predictor variables, instead of implicitly assuming genetic mechanisms of risk.

The findings confirmed what has subsequently become a consistent theme regarding children's risk for depression: Maternal depression is probably the strongest predictor of depression in children and adolescents as well as of other psychopathology (Downey & Coyne, 1990; Hammen, Burge, Burney, & Adrian, 1990). However, my colleagues and I argued that it is not necessarily depression per se that conveys the risk, inasmuch as depression occurs in a context of impaired maternal functioning and chronically stressful family conditions as well as the mothers' dysphoric mood. Therefore, various clinical and psychosocial outcomes in children may be affected as much by stress, for example, as by depression history alone (Hammen et al., 1987). Moreover, the current quality of the mother–child relationship was a strong predictor of children's outcomes, with unipolar depressed women (who were studied during remission) typically displaying more negative and critical interactions with their youngsters than women in the other groups (Gordon et al., 1989). A mother's negativity was affected by her stress level; because of the transactional nature of the process, it was also significantly affected by the negative behavior of the child, which may have elicited some of her critical or avoidant style of interaction (Burge & Hammen, 1991; Conrad & Hammen, 1989; Hammen, Burge, & Stansbury, 1990). The mutual influence of depressed mothers and their ill children is further illustrated by the finding that over the course of observation, there was a significant temporal association in the timing of mothers' and children's episodes of disorder (Hammen, Burge, & Adrian, 1991).

My group also determined that many of the depressed women were themselves the offspring of depressed mothers and fathers who had other psychopathology (Hammen, 1991a), suggesting a long-term process in which dysfunctional parenting begets dysfunctional parenting. It is also not surprising that the marriages of these women were highly likely to have resulted in divorce or ongoing conflict and that the biological fathers of the children had elevated rates of disorders themselves. In short, children inherited not only any transmittable genetic liability for depression and other psychopathology but also an environment that included a distressed and stressed mother whose own childhood experiences portended maladaptive family life and marital disruption. So marked are the parenting (and perhaps more generally, interpersonal) difficulties of depressed women that Karlen Lyons-Ruth (1995) posed the intriguing question of whether risk to offspring is due to the maternal depression itself or to what she terms "relational pathology."

Critical lessons were learned in this high-risk project, not the least of which was about context and the role of dysfunctional environments in contributing to a recurrent pattern of depression. Both the children and their mothers were seemingly locked into lives and circumstances that challenged them beyond their capacities to cope, and their behaviors toward each other contributed to further disorder (Hammen, 1997). Another of the great lessons of this project was the observation of the phenomenon that we called "stress generation," discussed in the following section.

Stress Generation: Blurring the Diathesis–Stress Distinction

My group's research on stressful life events had an additional and unexpected payoff that went beyond the testing of diathesis–stress models of depression. In-depth interviews about the lives and circumstances of depressed patients and families during the assessment of stressors and ongoing (chronic) stress in various studies not only confirmed the importance of studying the individual in context but also clearly demonstrated the transactions between the person and the environment.

Specifically, my colleagues and I observed during the high-risk study in particular that many individuals contribute to the occurrence of stressful events through their behaviors, characteristics, attitudes, and levels of competencies. On testing this hypothesis formally over a portion of the longitudinal follow-up of this project, we found that the unipolar depressed women were significantly more likely than women in the other groups to have elevated rates of "dependent" events (as opposed to events that are independent of the person, or "fateful" events). Interpersonal events, the largest category of dependent events, were especially elevated for unipolar depressed women, who also had significantly more conflict events— disagreements, fights, and disruptions in relationships with others including partners, family members, friends, and coworkers (Hammen, 1991b). We found a similar stress generation pattern in the children of depressed women (Adrian & Hammen, 1993), and we subsequently replicated the finding among depressed young women in the community (Daley et al., 1997).

My associates and I learned several additional things about stress generation patterns. They do not occur only during depression; most of the events occurred outside periods of significant depression. As we expected, these stressors precipitate further depression, confirming our theory of a self-perpetuating process (e.g., Daley et al., 1997; Davila, Hammen, Burge, Paley, & Daley, 1995). Other psychopathology besides depression may be implicated; women with comorbid depression and other disorders were especially likely to have high rates of interpersonal negative events as well as elevated personality disorder pathology (Daley, Hammen, Davila, & Burge, 1998; Daley et al., 1997). Women who had the tendency to contribute to interpersonal negative events appeared to have poorer social problem-solving skills (Davila et al., 1995); more generally, such individuals have high rates of parent pathology and early onset of their own disorders (Daley et al., 1997; Hammen, Davila, Brown, Ellicott, & Gitlin, 1992).

There is much more to be learned about characteristics that contribute to interpersonal negative events, including conflict. One can speculate that both maladaptive cognitions about others and dysfunctional interpersonal skills contribute to the occurrence of and failure to resolve social difficulties. Given the triggering effect of interpersonal loss and conflict experiences on depression, it is likely that a recurrent course of depression can be predicted from maladaptive interpersonal beliefs and behaviors.

Perhaps no other stress generation issue is more salient than mate selection, and a tendency of depressed women to marry men with diagnoses was observed in both the high-risk study and a more recent study of depressed children in a clinical sample (Hammen, Rudolph, Weisz, Rao, & Burge, in press). My associates and I hope to learn more about the assortative mating process in our current study of young women in the transition from high school to adulthood.

ISSUES FOR FURTHER RESEARCH IN INTERPERSONAL ASPECTS OF DEPRESSION

As this volume attests, there is a limitless terrain to explore to understand the effects of depression on interpersonal behavior and the effects of interpersonal behavior on depression. From internal representations of relationships to complex transactional, eliciting patterns of interaction, there is considerable uncharted territory. Therefore, I conclude with a modest statement of some of the bigger gaps in my work that I hope to address—or hope that others will address.

Specificity to Depression

Many of the interpersonal processes and content that appear to be related to or predictive of depressive reactions may also be relevant to other forms of psychopathology. For instance, borderline personality pathology can be defined partly in terms of disrupted and disrupting relationships with close others (Daley et al., 1998). To what extent, therefore, are some features specific to depression or shared with other disorders? Indeed, additional work on "interpersonal pathology" describing the behaviors and consequences of social interaction styles would help to broaden the intraindividual focus of most psychopathology and psychiatric research. Moreover, characterizing the differences between depressive disorders and other forms of maladjustment would also help to flesh out more general models of interpersonal behavior than currently exist.

Attachment Processes

There is a great deal to be learned about attachment theory predictions and the psychopathology of depression. To what extent is Bowlby's (1969, 1980) model valid for depression (compared, e.g., with anxiety disorders)? Can depression vulnerability be predicted from caretaker–child interaction in infancy, and to what extent are such processes modified or consistent through childhood and adolescence? Is dysfunctional attachment a necessary or sufficient vulnerability factor?

Assortative Mating and Dysfunctional Mate Selection

As noted earlier, the choice of a mate is a strong determinant of stress level and overall family adjustment, and these choices appear to be dysfunctional for women at risk for depression. What determines women's mate choices? Many mechanisms come to mind, all requiring empirical evaluation: women's perceived limited choices that are due to poor self-concept, similarity and familiarity leading to bonding with "damaged" partners, "reenactment" of dysfunctional family patterns, complementarity in which depressed women seek "exciting" or "risk-taking" men, and others.

Nature and Acquisition of Interpersonal Skills and Schemas in Childhood

A particular focus on the developmental psychopathology of depression through emphasis on interpersonal relatedness would help to flesh out mechanisms of children's risk for depression or adult risk through childhood experience. Little is known about the acquisition and stability of maladaptive schemas or working models and about interpersonal problem-solving skills.

Questions of Depression Heterogeneity and Causal Unity

Clearly, not all depressions are the same, and no models should assume that chronic depressions have the same correlates and predictors as acute depressive reactions or that there is only one etiological pathway to depression. It would be useful to determine whether there are uniquely "interpersonal" forms or etiologies that are distinct from depressions that are not defined by interpersonal features or predictors.

CONCLUSION

This chapter has briefly defined the meaning of an interpersonal perspective and has provided a personal inventory of the contributions that fostered the emegence of this focus in my own work. My colleagues and I have increasingly learned about depression from studying the interpersonal lives of depressed people. This volume reminds the reader that there is a great deal left to discover about depression despite the enormous accomplishments of the past 20 years. I hope it will be the first of many specifically devoted to the interpersonal arena and that pursuit of these themes will not only broaden the understanding and treatment of depressive disorders but also enrich the theoretical and empirical base of social processes in psychopathology.

REFERENCES

Adrian, C., & Hammen, C. (1993). Stress exposure and stress generation in children of depressed mothers. *Journal of Consulting and Clinical Psychology, 61*, 354–359.

Arieti, S., & Bemporad, J. (1980). The psychological organization of depression. *American Journal of Psychiatry, 137,* 1360–1365.

Beck, A. T. (1967). *Depression: Clinical, experimental, and theoretical aspects.* New York: Harper & Row.

Beck, A. T. (1983). Cognitive therapy of depression: New perspectives. In P. J. Clayton & J. E. Barrett (Eds.), *Treatment of depression: Old controversies and new approaches.* New York: Raven Press.

Bowlby, J. (1969). *Attachment and loss: Vol. 1. Attachment.* New York: Basic Books.

Bowlby, J. (1980). *Loss: Sadness and depression.* New York: Basic Books.

Brown, G. W., & Harris, T. (1978). *Social origins of depression: A study of psychiatric disorders in women.* New York: Free Press.

Burge, D., & Hammen, C. (1991). Maternal communication: Predictors of outcome at follow-up in a sample of children at high and low risk for depression. *Journal of Abnormal Psychology, 100,* 174–180.

Collins, N., & Read, S. (1990). Adult attachment, working models, and relationship quality in dating couples. *Journal of Personality and Social Psychology, 58,* 644–663.

Conrad, M., & Hammen, C. (1989). Role of maternal depression in perceptions of child maladjustment. *Journal of Consulting and Clinical Psychology, 57,* 663–667.

Coyne, J. C. (1976). Depression and the response of others. *Journal of Abnormal Psychology, 85,* 186–193.

Coyne, J. C., & Gotlib, I. (1983). The role of cognition in depression: A critical appraisal. *Psychological Bulletin, 94,* 472–505.

Daley, S., Hammen, C., Burge, D., Davila, J., Paley, B., Lindberg, N., & Herzberg, D. (1997). Predictors of the generation of episodic stress: A longitudinal study of late adolescent women. *Journal of Abnormal Psychology, 106,* 251–259.

Daley, S. E., Hammen, C., Davila, J., & Burge, D. (1998). Axis II symptomatology, depression, and life stress during the transition from adolescence to adulthood. *Journal of Consulting and Clinical Psychology, 66,* 595–603.

Davila, J., Hammen, C., Burge, D., Paley, B., & Daley, S. (1995). Poor interpersonal problem-solving as a mechanism of stress generation in depression among adolescent women. *Journal of Abnormal Psychology, 104,* 592–600.

Downey, G., & Coyne, J. C. (1990). Children of depressed parents: An integrative review. *Psychological Bulletin, 108,* 50–76.

Gong-Guy, E., & Hammen, C. (1980). Causal perceptions of stressful life events in depressed and nondepressed outpatients. *Journal of Abnormal Psychology, 89,* 662–669.

Gordon, D., Burge, D., Hammen, C., Adrian, C., Jaenicke, C., & Hiroto, D. (1989). Observations of interactions of depressed women with their children. *American Journal of Psychiatry, 146,* 50–55.

Haaga, D. A., Ernst, D., & Dyck, M. J. (1991). Empirical status of cognitive theory of depression. *Psychological Bulletin, 110,* 215–236.

Hammen, C. L. (1978). Depression, distortion, and life stress in college students. *Cognitive Therapy and Research, 2,* 189–192.

Hammen, C. (1985). Predicting depression: A cognitive-behavioral perspective. In P. Kendall (Ed.), *Advances in cognitive-behavioral research and therapy* (Vol. 4, pp. 29–71). San Diego, CA: Academic Press.

Hammen, C. (1991a). *Depression runs in families: The social context of risk and resilience in children of depressed mothers.* New York: Springer-Verlag.

Hammen, C. (1991b). The generation of stress in the course of unipolar depression. *Journal of Abnormal Psychology, 100,* 555–561.

Hammen, C. (1992). Cognition and depression: Some thoughts about new directions. *Psychological Inquiry, 3,* 247–250.

Hammen, C. (1997). Depressed parents. In S. Wolchik & I. Sandler (Eds.), *Handbook of children's coping with common stressors: Linking theory, research, and interventions* (pp. 131–157). New York: Plenum Press.

Hammen, C., Adrian, C., Gordon, D., Burge, D., Jaenicke, C., & Hiroto, D. (1987). Children of depressed mothers: Maternal strain and symptom predictors of dysfunction. *Journal of Abnormal Psychology, 96,* 190–198.

Hammen, C., Burge, D., & Adrian, C. (1991). Timing of mother and child depression in a longitudinal study of children at risk. *Journal of Consulting and Clinical Psychology, 59,* 341–345.

Hammen, C., Burge, D., Burney, E., & Adrian, C. (1990). Longitudinal study of diagnoses in children of women with unipolar and bipolar affective disorder. *Archives of General Psychiatry, 47,* 1112–1117.

Hammen, C., Burge, D., Daley, S., Davila, J., Paley, B., & Rudolph, K. (1995). Interpersonal attachment cognitions and prediction of symptomatic responses to interpersonal stress. *Journal of Abnormal Psychology, 104,* 436–443.

Hammen, C., Burge, D., & Stansbury, K. (1990). Relationship of mother and child variables to child outcomes in a high risk sample: A causal modeling analysis. *Developmental Psychology, 26,* 24–30.

Hammen, C., Davila, J., Brown, G., Ellicott, A., & Gitlin, M. (1992). Psychiatric history and stress: Predictors of severity of unipolar depression. *Journal of Abnormal Psychology, 101,* 45–52.

Hammen, C., Ellicott, A., & Gitlin, M. (1992). Stressors and Sociotropy/ Autonomy: A longitudinal study of their relationship to the course of bipolar disorder. *Cognitive Therapy and Research, 16,* 409–418.

Hammen, C., Ellicott, A., Gitlin, M., & Jamison, K. (1989). Sociotropy/Autonomy and vulnerability to specific life events in patients with unipolar depression and bipolar disorders. *Journal of Abnormal Psychology, 98,* 154–160.

Hammen, C., & Goodman-Brown, T. (1990). Self-schemas and vulnerability to specific life stress in children at risk for depression. *Cognitive Therapy and Research, 14,* 215–227.

Hammen, C. L., Krantz, S., & Cochran, S. (1981). Relationships between depression and causal attributions about stressful life events. *Cognitive Therapy and Research, 5,* 351–358.

Hammen, C., Marks, T., Mayol, A., & deMayo, R. (1985). Depressive self-schemas, life stress, and vulnerability to depression. *Journal of Abnormal Psychology, 94*, 308–319.

Hammen, C., & Mayol, A. (1982). Depression and cognitive characteristics of stressful life event types. *Journal of Abnormal Psychology, 91*, 165–174.

Hammen, C. L., & Peters, S. D. (1977). Differential responses to male and female depressive reactions. *Journal of Consulting and Clinical Psychology, 45*, 994–1001.

Hammen, C. L., & Peters, S. D. (1978). Interpersonal consequences of depression: Responses to men and women enacting a depressed role. *Journal of Abnormal Psychology, 87*, 322–332.

Hammen, C., Rudolph, K., Weisz, J., Rao, U., & Burge, D. (in press). The context of depression in clinic-referred children: Neglected areas in treatment. *Journal of the American Academy of Child and Adolescent Psychiatry.*

Lyons-Ruth, K. (1995). Broadening our conceptual frameworks: Can we reintro-duce relational strategies and implicit representational systems to the study of psychopathology? *Developmental Psychology, 31*, 432–436.

Sroufe, L. A. (1983). Infant–caregiver attachment and patterns of adaptation in preschool: The roots of maladaption and competence. In M. Perlmutter (Ed.), *Minnesota Symposium in Child Psychology* (Vol. 16, pp. 41–81). Hillsdale, NJ: Erlbaum.

Weissman, M. M., & Klerman, G. (1977). Sex differences in the epidemiology of depression. *Archives of General Psychiatry, 34*, 98–111.

Weissman, M. M., & Paykel, E. S. (1974). *The depressed woman: A study of social relationships.* Chicago: University of Chicago Press.

II

THE INTERPERSONAL
AND THE PERSONAL
IN DEPRESSION

3

SOCIAL CONTEXT AND DEPRESSION: AN INTEGRATIVE STRESS AND COPING FRAMEWORK

CHARLES J. HOLAHAN, RUDOLF H. MOOS, AND LIZA A. BONIN

The last two decades have witnessed a growing societal concern with stress and its psychological toll (see Goldberger & Breznitz, 1993). Avison and Gotlib (1994) recently concluded that "a fundamental task of mental health researchers has been to understand the nature of the association between stress and mental health" (p. vii). In fact, psychological theories of depression increasingly are recognizing the central role of life stressors in the etiology and course of depression (see Coyne & Whiffen, 1995; Monroe & Simons, 1991). In this chapter, we review our program of research on stress and coping, highlighting its relevance to understanding and treating depression.

Our approach to studying stress and coping has been shaped by a social–ecological perspective. In general, three social–ecological principles

Parts of this manuscript were adapted from chapters by Holahan and Moos (1994), Holahan, Moos, and Bonin (1997), and Moos (1991). The research summarized in this chapter was supported in part by National Heart, Lung, and Blood Institute Grant 1-RO3-HL48063; National Institute on Alcohol Abuse and Alcoholism Grant AA06699; and Department of Veterans Affairs Health Services Research and Development Service funds.

have provided the foundation for our research program. First, we focus primarily on positive *adaptation*, that is, healthy and effective functioning. In addition, we emphasize the power of *social context* in shaping individual personality and behavior. Finally, we are sensitive to *interdependence*, or dynamic interrelationships among variables rather than static one-to-one influences.

We begin by describing a general conceptual framework relevant to predicting depressive reactions and show how it flowed from and guided our work. We then consider how our findings can be applied to understanding depressive reactions in the contexts of individual treatment, preventive interventions with children and families, and rehabilitation with medical patients. We conclude by reflecting on the implications of our findings for a more general appreciation of health, resilience, and adaptive competence.

DEVELOPING A CONCEPTUAL FRAMEWORK

Researchers have identified a wide range of stressors that operate as vulnerability factors for depressive reactions (see Avison & Gotlib, 1994; Goldberger & Breznitz, 1993). In general, severe life events and, less strongly, severe chronic difficulties are linked to major depression; minor life events and minor daily hassles are linked to depressive symptoms (Coyne & Whiffen, 1995; Monroe & Simons, 1991). Moreover, among both severe events (Kendler, Kessler, Neale, Heath, & Eaves, 1993) and minor stressors (Bolger, DeLongis, Kessler, & Schilling, 1989), interpersonal problems and losses are most closely associated with depressive reactions.

At the same time, individuals show highly variable reactions to stressors, and researchers have focused increasingly on identifying resilience factors in the stress process (Coyne & Downey, 1991). For example, a variety of dispositional factors that relate broadly to personal control provide personal resources during stressful periods (Cohen & Edwards, 1989). Similarly, social support offers a contextual resource that can bolster healthy functioning when stressors occur (Cohen, 1992; Russell & Cutrona, 1991; Thoits, 1992).

An Integrative Framework

We use the general conceptual framework shown in Figure 1 to help clarify how personal and social resources aid people in confronting acute and chronic life crises (Moos & Schaefer, 1993). The framework helps to unify research on predicting adjustment and coping responses.

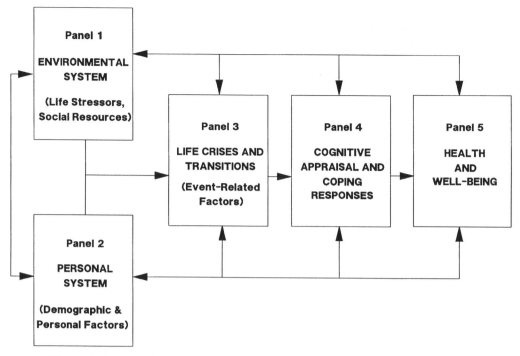

Figure 1. A general conceptual framework of the stress and coping process.

The environmental system (Panel 1) is composed of ongoing life stressors, such as chronic physical illness, as well as social coping resources, such as support from family members. The personal system (Panel 2) includes an individual's sociodemographic characteristics and personal coping resources, such as self-confidence. These relatively stable environmental and personal factors influence the life crises and transitions that an individual faces (Panel 3), which reflect significant changes in life circumstances. In turn, these combined influences shape health and well-being (Panel 5) both directly and indirectly through cognitive appraisal and coping responses (Panel 4). The bidirectional paths in the framework indicate that reciprocal feedback can occur at each stage.

This conceptualization is consistent with diathesis–stress theories of depression (see Coyne & Whiffen, 1995; Monroe & Simons, 1991) in that it postulates that characteristics of the person and of the social context interact in shaping vulnerability to life stressors. However, the framework goes beyond diathesis–stress models by highlighting the central role of coping strategies in the stress process. Because the framework emphasizes that the individual's capacity for effective coping is dependent on underlying personal and social resources, we have described our conceptualization as a *resources model* of coping (Holahan, Moos, & Bonin, 1997; Holahan, Moos, Holahan, & Brennan, 1995).

Personal and Social Resources

Several investigators have speculated that personality strengths and social support may be linked to staying healthy under adaptive challenge in significant part because they encourage more adaptive coping strategies. Lazarus and Folkman (1984) defined personal and social resources as what an individual "draws on in order to cope" (p. 158). Similarly, Thoits (1995) conceptualized social support as a source of coping assistance, as "a social 'fund' from which people may draw when handling stressors" (p. 64). Likewise, Bolger (1990) proposed that "coping is personality in action under stress" (p. 525).

In a series of longitudinal studies of two community samples, we examined personal and social stress-resistance resources (Holahan & Moos, 1981, 1986, 1987b). We began with a representative sample of more than 500 adults, and we then used a second representative sample of more than 400 adults to cross-validate and extend our findings.

Making use of the conceptual framework shown in Figure 1, we found that family support (Panel 1), personality strengths such as self-confidence (Panel 2), and less reliance on avoidance coping (Panel 4) predicted lower levels of depression (Panel 5) over a 1-year period, even when prior depression was controlled (Holahan & Moos, 1986, 1987b). We then progressed to asking a new question: How does coping function as a link between adaptive resources and psychological adjustment when an individual faces a high level of stressors?

Determinants of Coping

Coping is a stabilizing factor that can help individuals maintain psychosocial adaptation during stressful periods; it encompasses cognitive and behavioral efforts to reduce or eliminate stressful conditions and associated emotional distress (Lazarus & Folkman, 1984). Although coping responses may be classified in many ways, most approaches distinguish between strategies oriented toward confronting the problem and strategies oriented toward reducing tension by avoiding dealing with the problem directly (Holahan, Moos, & Schaefer, 1996; Moos & Schaefer, 1993).

Approach coping strategies, such as problem solving and seeking information, can moderate the potential adverse influence of both negative life change and enduring role stressors on psychological functioning (Sherbourne, Hays, & Wells, 1995). In contrast, avoidance coping, such as denial and withdrawal, generally is associated with psychological distress and maladaptive behavioral outcome, particularly when adjustment is assessed beyond the initial crisis period (Rohde, Lewinsohn, Tilson, & Seeley, 1990).

When we examined the predictors of coping, we found that individuals in supportive families engage in more active, problem-focused coping and less avoidance coping than do individuals in less supportive families (Cronkite & Moos, 1984; Holahan & Moos, 1987a). For example, both adults (Moos, Brennan, Fondacaro, & Moos, 1990) and youths (Ebata & Moos, 1994) who enjoyed more social resources from their family and friends relied more on approach coping, such as positive reappraisal and seeking guidance and support, and less on avoidance coping, especially emotional discharge. Similarly, increases in family support over a 1-year interval were related to increases in problem-solving coping among women and to declines in emotional discharge among men (Fondacaro & Moos, 1987).

Coping as a Mediator

Next, we examined the role of coping as a mediator between personal and social resources and depression (Holahan & Moos, 1990, 1994). In the model, personal and social resources relate to subsequent functioning both directly and indirectly through coping strategies. Because coping is a stabilizing factor that helps maintain psychological adjustment during stressful periods (Lazarus & Folkman, 1984), the advantage of coping efforts should be greatest when an individual is faced with many stressors.

We tested our model with a sample of more than 400 respondents in a two-group structural equation analysis (Holahan & Moos, 1991). A high stressor group experienced multiple (two or more) negative life events during the year prior to the follow-up assessment; a low stressor group experienced no negative life events during the year. Family support, the personality strength of self-confidence, and an easygoing disposition operated prospectively over 4 years, either directly or indirectly through coping responses, to protect individuals from depressive reactions. The results are presented graphically in Figure 2, which shows standardized estimates of parameters in the structural model. To simplify the presentation, the measurement model is not depicted. Parameter estimates for all hypothesized paths in the structural model are significant at the .05 level.

As hypothesized, the pattern of predictive associations differed according to level of stressors. With high stressors, resources were related to future psychological adjustment indirectly, through their link to increased approach coping strategies. Under adaptive challenge, personality characteristics and family support operated prospectively as coping resources; in turn, coping mediated between initial resources and later depressive symptoms. With low stressors, more resources were directly related to better psychological adjustment.

Investigators who have examined the personal coping resource of dispositional optimism have obtained further support for the mediational role

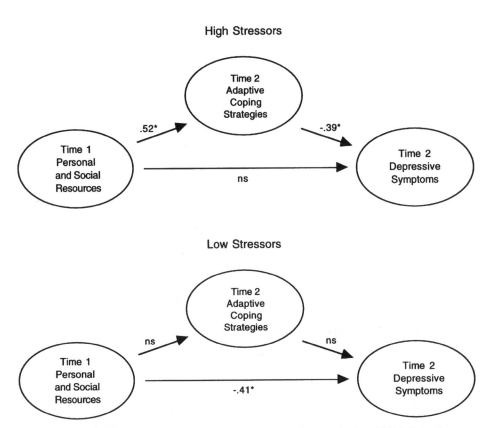

High Stressors

Low Stressors

Figure 2. Results of a two-group structural equation analysis with high and low stressor groups. *$p < .05$; *ns* indicates a nonsignificant parameter. Adapted from "Life Stressors, Personal and Social Resources, and Depression: A Four-Year Structural Model," by C. J. Holahan and R. H. Moos, 1991, *Journal of Abnormal Psychology, 100,* 31–38. Copyright 1991 by the American Psychological Association.

of coping in the stress and coping process. Among women coping with breast cancer and breast biopsy, more active coping efforts served as mediating routes through which optimism relates to better psychological adjustment (Carver et al., 1993; Stanton & Snider, 1993). Similarly, among first-year students adjusting to college, active coping strategies mediated the relation between optimism and subsequent adjustment (Aspinwall & Taylor, 1992). Moreover, researchers studying the cognitive coping strategy of rumination (Nolen-Hoeksema, Parker, & Larson, 1994) demonstrated that maladaptive coping responses mediate between poor social support and increased depression.

Some theorists have suggested that the adaptive significance of approach coping strategies may depend also on the controllability of the stressors that are confronted (Cutrona & Russell, 1990; Folkman, 1984). We examined the moderating effect of appraisals of controllability (Panel

4 in the conceptual framework shown in Figure 1) on the coping process in a 2-year prospective study with 175 college students (Valentiner, Holahan, & Moos, 1994). When individuals confronted a controllable event, family support was related to psychological adjustment indirectly through the fostering of more approach coping efforts. When events were uncontrollable, however, family support was not associated with coping but instead was related to psychological adjustment directly.

IMPLICATIONS FOR TREATMENT AND PREVENTION

At an applied level, our conceptual framework encourages innovations in mental health care that are appropriate to a variety of populations. The framework has implications for intervention at both the environmental and the individual levels. For example, each path in the model identifies a process that is potentially alterable. The framework emphasizes that treatment and preventive programs, which are one aspect of the environmental system, are part of an open system in which the program is only one of multiple factors that influence psychiatric disorders and other aspects of adaptation.

Individual Treatment and Outcome

Treatment for psychiatric and behavioral disorders has short-term beneficial effects, but many patients relapse over time (Brownell, Marlatt, Lichtenstein, & Wilson, 1986). Recognizing that stressful or relapse-inducing life situations inevitably occur, clinicians can identify coping skills and associated coping resources that clients can use to help them deal with these situations more effectively (see Moos, 1991). An especially important point is that a focus on coping processes encourages a competence-enhancing view of the client's adaptive strengths and of his or her potential for resilience and personal growth.

A Broadened Therapeutic Framework

Applying our conceptual framework to treatment can broaden the conventional psychotherapeutic framework by focusing attention on the interactive relationships among the individual, the family, and the related social settings. In studying clinical populations, we have found that the same factors that protect normally adjusted persons from depressive symptoms under stress also are related to remission among clinically depressed individuals after treatment (also see Sherbourne et al., 1995). Accordingly, we extended our program of research to examine the role of these factors in the process of remission and relapse among more than 400 patients who entered psychiatric treatment for unipolar depression (Moos, 1991).

Compared with demographically matched case controls, depressed patients at intake reported more stressful life circumstances and less family and work support. Depressed persons also were more likely to use avoidance coping and less likely to use problem-solving coping responses. Moreover, patients who experienced more life stressors and fewer social resources tended to be more severely depressed and to have more physical symptoms and less self-confidence. Avoidance coping also was linked to more severe depression, whereas patients who used more problem-solving coping reported higher self-confidence and less severe depression (Billings & Moos, 1984; Moos, 1991).

In terms of remission, posttreatment life stressors and social resources were predictably related to patients' posttreatment functioning, even when intake functioning and social background were controlled. Patients who experienced more life stressors (both life events and chronic strains) after treatment reported more severe depression and more physical symptoms at a 1-year follow-up. Life stressors predicted almost 13% additional variance in depression and 10% additional variance in physical symptoms beyond that accounted for by intake functioning and social background. The links among chronic stressors in the areas of health, housing, family, and work and the outcome criteria were somewhat stronger and more consistent than those for negative life events.

Conversely, patients who enjoyed more family and work support and those who had a better relationship with a confidant experienced less depression at a 1-year follow-up. Social resources added almost 18% incremental variance in predicting depression and 5% incremental variance in predicting physical symptoms after accounting for intake functioning and social background (Billings & Moos, 1985). In general, the quality of support was somewhat more strongly related to outcome than was the number of network members or social interactions.

Relationship quality with a confidant also was associated with depression at a 4-year follow-up. More broadly, postintake life stressors and social resources still predicted 4-year treatment outcome after the severity of depression at intake and the preintake levels of these life context factors were considered. Changes in life stressors and social resources during the treatment−posttreatment interval seem to have an independent influence on remission and relapse. Moreover, it is important to consider both chronic stressors and negative life events (see Kessler, Kendler, Heath, Neale, & Eaves, 1992). The associations between ongoing stressors and treatment outcome were as strong and consistent as those between negative events and outcome (Swindle, Cronkite, & Moos, 1989).

Interplay of Personal and Contextual Factors

To understand the probable influence of intervention programs that focus on one aspect of an individual's life context, one needs to take a social–ecological perspective and to consider the interconnections with other aspects of the individual's life context. For example, the conceptualization of stressors needs to be broadened to reflect the interplay between acute and enduring demands (Pearlin, 1989; Pillow, Zautra, & Sandler, 1996). Also needed is a fuller understanding of how different types of life stressors and social resources influence each other (Kaniasty & Norris, 1993).

Our group examined these issues in a sample of 500 older adults who were problem drinkers (Brennan & Moos, 1990). In terms of mutual influences between stressors and resources, results indicated that stressors and lack of support typically are closely connected in domains in which a single person or a few individuals are sources of both stressors and support. For example, ongoing difficulties involving spouse and children were associated with fewer resources in these domains. In contrast, in life domains in which many individuals were sources of problems and assistance, such as friends, stressors and social resources were more independent.

Interplay of Events and Ongoing Stressors and Resources

In a longitudinal assessment with a functionally diverse sample of 80 adults (Moos, Fenn, & Billings, 1988), data from an initial assessment were used to predict changes in stressors and resources over an 18-month interval. Respondents who experienced more stressful events during this interval initially reported more ongoing stressors and fewer ongoing resources. New stressful events foreshadowed increases in ongoing stressors in the financial, work, spouse, child, and extended family domains. They also led to a decline in spouse or partner resources. Therefore, ongoing stressors and a lack of social resources can predict new stressful events; in turn, such events can contribute to a rise in chronic stressors and to an erosion of social resources.

Reciprocal Influence of Functioning and Social Context

In a dynamic way, an individual's functioning shapes his or her social environment (Bolger, Foster, Vinokur, & Ng, 1996). For example, Hammen (1991) showed that depressed individuals generate additional life stressors, particularly interpersonal stressors. In a similar vein, Coyne (Coyne & Downey, 1991; Coyne et al., 1987) found that depressed individuals' repeated demands for more frequent and extreme reassurance resulted in aggravation of and consequent rejection by their significant others (also see Joiner, Alfano, & Metalsky, 1992). In this way, depression can be "contagious" (Coyne & Downey, 1991; Joiner, 1994); Joiner (1994) suggested couples or family therapies to help "inoculate" depressed individuals' significant others against becoming depressed themselves.

We used a longitudinal design with a sample of college students (Potthoff, Holahan, & Joiner, 1995) to investigate how Hammen's (1991) stress generation model might be integrated with Coyne's (Coyne & Downey, 1991; Coyne et al., 1987) interpersonal theory of depression. We showed that an excessive reassurance-seeking style operates indirectly in predicting more subsequent depressive symptoms through engendering minor social stressors. Being depressed gives rise to a social milieu fraught with frustration and disappointment. In turn, this stressful social context provides ongoing negative feedback that can feed both resentment and self-blame.

Life Context Profiles

In light of these issues, we developed the Life Stressors and Social Resources Inventory (LISRES; Moos & Moos, 1994) to provide a comprehensive picture of the various interrelated stressors and social resources in a person's life. The inventory includes nine indexes of life stressors (e.g., work stressors, spouse or partner stressors). It also includes seven indexes of social resources (e.g., work resources, spouse or partner resources).

Such information can be used in clinical case descriptions to help clinicians understand how their clients manage specific stressful circumstances, identify stressors and resources associated with symptom remission and relapse, and plan intervention programs that target clients' life contexts. An integrated picture of the overall balance of stressors and resources in a person's life also can provide a prognostic index of longer term outcome.

For example, Figure 3 shows an illustrative LISRES profile for a 60-year-old married woman (scores are standardized; $M = 50$, $SD = 10$). Because the woman was not employed, she had no ongoing stressors or resources in the work area. She reported several negative life events in the past year, including her own hospitalization and her husband's increased alcohol abuse and involvement in an automobile accident. In addition, she experienced above-average chronic stressors in most life domains. For example, she had serious ongoing health problems, including cancer, high blood pressure, and severe back pain. Moreover, her spouse, children, and extended family were a source of arguments and excessive demands.

Although this woman had moderate support from friends and slightly above-average spouse support and financial resources, she had few resources from her children and other relatives. Overall, these data show that this woman had an unfavorable balance of high stressors and only low-to-moderate resources; the profile was consistent with her low self-confidence and many symptoms of depression 1 year later (Moos & Moos, 1994).

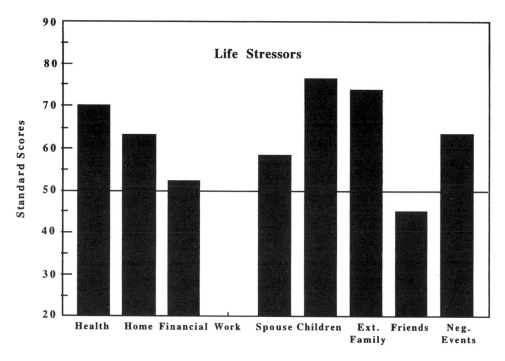

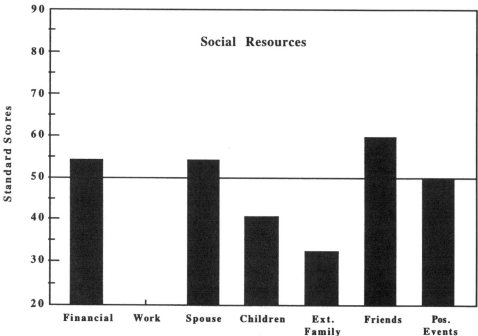

Figure 3. Life Stressors and Social Resources profile for a depressed woman. Reprinted from *Life Stressors and Social Resources Inventory: Adult Form Manual* (p. 25), by R. H. Moos and B. S. Moos, 1994, Odessa, FL: Psychological Assessment Resources. Reprinted with permission. Copyright 1994 by PAR, Inc. Further reproduction is prohibited without permission of PAR, Inc.

Prevention With Families and Children

In studying families and children, we discovered that factors that predict the health of one family member operate indirectly to affect the health of his or her spouse and children. For example, chronic depression tends to impair an individual's functioning as spouse and parent, which can promote family conflict and erode family cohesion. In this vein, Coyne and Smith (1991) found that 6 months after husbands suffered a heart attack, wives' distress was significantly related to their husbands' distress and was at least as pronounced. These findings demonstrate the potential health-promoting value of preventive interventions directed toward coping skills training for spouses.

Interdependencies Between Spouses

A key facet of the stress process in married couples is the interplay among the partners' functioning, personal resources, and coping responses. For example, we found that high work stressors (in outside jobs) in married women were associated with husbands' reports of less family cohesion and more physical symptoms (Billings & Moos, 1982). Not only are one spouse's symptoms stressful for the other, but the personal resources and coping strategies of each partner affect the other partner's reaction to and selection of coping responses.

In longitudinal analyses (controlling for prior functioning) with a community sample, we found that being married to a woman who was distressed was more closely associated with a husband's own subsequent depressed mood when he relied more heavily on avoidance coping. This adverse effect strengthened as his wife's reliance on avoidance coping increased. In contrast, a wife's self-esteem had a stronger influence in reducing her subsequent depression when her husband also experienced high self-esteem (Cronkite & Moos, 1984).

Similarly, in cross-sectional analyses with our sample of depressed patients, we found that negative events and chronic stressors experienced by a spouse were positively related to the severity of the partner's depression. High family support was associated with less depression. In addition, spouses in stressful conditions were less prone to depression when they used more problem-focused coping. Further analyses, controlling for a married individual's own negative events and strains, suggested that the link between a partner's stressors and his or her own depression may be mediated by a reduction in family support (Mitchell, Cronkite, & Moos, 1983).

The risk factors of stressful life conditions and avoidance coping also were linked to poorer current functioning among spouses of alcoholic patients, whereas the resistance factor of family support was related to better functioning among the spouses. Follow-up analyses over a 2-year period demonstrated that spouses of relapsed alcoholics experienced more negative events and less family support than spouses of either alcoholics in remission or community controls. Moreover, in a longer term assessment, initial spouse drinking and depression were related predictively to patients' alcohol consumption and depression, respectively, 8 years later (Finney & Moos, 1991; Moos, Finney, & Cronkite, 1990).

Furthermore, transactions intended to be supportive, such as the ministrations of an overprotective spouse, may engender threats to self-esteem and reduced feelings of self-efficacy. For example, excessive support in the context of chronic illness may be perceived as suggesting that the recipient is incompetent to manage for him- or herself (Quittner, Glueckauf, & Jackson, 1990). Coyne, Ellard, and Smith (1990) observed that deciding whether to give both emotional and practical help to a spouse recovering from a heart attack versus providing only emotional support can be difficult. Offering practical assistance may feel rewarding to the provider, but in some circumstances it can leave the recipient with a sense of helplessness.

Parent–Child Relationships

In work with a second community sample, our group found that risk and resistance factors in parents' lives predicted emotional and physical health problems in their children. In examining children's distress, we broadened our concept of risk to include parental functioning. The strongest findings emerged for family support and for maternal risk factors such as depression, physical symptoms, and avoidance coping, each of which was predictably associated with children's concurrent psychological health. Family support and mothers' physical symptoms also were tied to children's concurrent physical health.

Family support and parental risk together accounted for between 20% and 30% of the variance in children's concurrent psychological and physical health problems. Family support also was linked to children's subsequent psychological and physical health 1 year after the initial assessment, but these relationships did not hold when children's initial distress was controlled. Compared with adults, children may be more resilient to past adversity, although they are also less protected by past environmental support (Holahan & Moos, 1987b).

When we compared the children of parents in our sample of depressed patients with children of nondepressed parents in our initial community sample, we identified specific risk and resistance factors associated with the likelihood of a family having a child with multiple problems. Two groups of risk factors were identified: the presence and acuteness of parental depression and high family stressors. We also examined the resistance value of a supportive family climate.

In cross-sectional analyses, less than 3% of the families with no risk factors had a multiproblem child. Among families with a depressed parent, the prevalence of multiproblem children rose to 26%. This rate increased to 38% in the presence of high levels of stressors, but it dropped to 22% among families with a depressed parent with few stressors and to less than 11% among those with few stressors and high support (Billings & Moos, 1983). Family support was as strongly associated with children's functioning at a 1-year follow-up as was the severity of the parents' depressive symptoms (Billings & Moos, 1986).

Similarly, emotional disturbance among children in alcoholic families was associated with their parents' health, as well as with parents' use of avoidance coping, high conflict and lack of cohesion in the family, and negative life change (Moos, Finney, & Cronkite, 1990).

Adolescents' Adjustment

Life stressors and social resources play an important role in adolescent adjustment. We used the Youth Form of the LISRES to focus on how life context factors differentiated between depressed and other groups of youths. Seven of the life stressor and five of the social resource indexes discriminated between the depressed and other groups of youths (Daniels & Moos, 1990).

Compared with healthy youths, depressed youths reported more stressors involving chronic physical health problems, home and money, parents, extended family, and school, as well as more acute negative life events. Looking at resources, we found that, compared with healthy youths, depressed youths experienced fewer social resources with parents and extended family, at school, and with friends. These group differences identify specific domains of stressors and resources that can become foci for prevention programs for adolescents.

We also examined how parental support is related to psychological adjustment during the transition from adolescence to young adulthood in a college sample. The transition to young adulthood, which entails the developmental task of leaving the parental home and forming new social networks outside the family of origin, presents significant adaptive challenges for many individuals (Maughan & Champion, 1990; Zirkel & Cantor, 1990). We studied almost 200 new college freshmen who had relocated geographically on beginning college. An initial inventory was administered at the beginning of the students' freshman year, and a comparable inventory was completed 2 years later.

Social support from both mother and father and a nonconflictual relationship between parents played an important adaptive role during the transition to young adulthood. Also, consistent with recent conceptualizations of the significance of fathers in adolescent psychopathology (Phares

& Compas, 1992), paternal support played a strong predictive role in students' adjustment. In addition, congruent with research on parental marital conflict and children's and adolescents' maladjustment (Grych & Finchman, 1990), parents' marital conflict was as strongly linked to students' maladjustment as was maternal and paternal support.

Rehabilitation of Medical Patients

Understanding protective psychosocial factors and mechanisms in the context of physical illness can inform secondary prevention efforts with medical patients (see Blumenthal & Matthews, 1993). Depression can be a central obstacle in recovery from physical illness (Jenkins, Jono, Stanton, & Stroup-Benham, 1990; Kaplan, 1990). Moreover, new medical treatments that enhance survival increase the need to understand psychosocial functioning among persons living with long-term chronic illness (Allen, Fitzgerald, Swank, & Becker, 1990).

Fear and uncertainty are common among medical patients, with a significant subset of patients vulnerable to serious depression (Banks & Kerns, 1996). For example, depressive symptoms are common among cardiac patients (Forrester et al., 1992) and are a central aspect of diminished quality of life in cardiac illness (Jenkins et al., 1990). Psychological disability also is prevalent following the diagnosis and treatment of cancer (Anderson, 1992) and among patients coping with arthritis (Young, 1992). Moreover, physical illness is a major factor in depression among older persons; more than 80% of people older than 65 have at least one chronic illness (McGrath, Keita, Strickland, & Russo, 1990).

Depression Among Cardiac Patients

Our group conducted a program of research examining psychosocial adjustment in a late-middle-aged sample of patients with chronic cardiac illness. Moderate-to-severe depression has been reported for a significant number of individuals approximately 1 year postinfarction (Follick et al., 1988) and after cardiac surgery (Langeluddecke, Fulcher, Baird, Hughes, & Tennant, 1989). Moreover, among men recovering from myocardial infarction, one third showed substantial depressed mood 3 years later (Waltz, Badura, Pfaff, & Schott, 1988), and one fifth failed to achieve emotional adjustment 5 years later (Havik & Maelands, 1990).

We tested predictive models of depressive symptoms among almost 400 patients with chronic cardiac illness at a baseline assessment and at 1-year and 4-year follow-ups (see Holahan et al., 1995, 1996, 1997a, 1997b). The cardiac illness group was three-fourths men, and the average age was approximately 62 years at baseline. A healthy control group consisted of almost 400 individuals who reported no diagnosed illnesses of any type.

Individuals with chronic cardiac illness reported significantly more depressive symptoms than did persons free of illness at all three assessments. On average, cardiac patients scored almost one-half standard deviation higher than did healthy persons on measures of depressed mood and ideation and on behavioral manifestations of depression. It is especially important from a stress resistance perspective that the level of depressive symptoms in the cardiac group varied markedly at all three assessments. Some individuals with cardiac illness reported no depressive symptoms, whereas others reported high levels. Therefore, we examined the determinants of depressive symptoms in the cardiac group.

Cardiac Patients' Social Liabilities and Social Assets

We found that more social support at baseline was significantly related to fewer depressive symptoms at all three assessments (Holahan et al., 1995, 1996, 1997a). Previous research on psychosocial adjustment to cardiac illness has focused mostly on spousal support. However, our findings showed that all three components of social support we tapped—family, work, and broader social network—were related comparably to adjustment.

Furthermore, we broadened our predictive framework to include social liabilities as well as social assets. Social support researchers traditionally have focused almost entirely on the health-promoting aspects of social support (Schuster, Kessler, & Aseltine, 1990). Coyne and DeLongis (1986) argued that investigators have assumed a linear relation between close involvement and psychological well-being, ignoring the troublesome aspects of social ties. In fact, support and conflict occur together in most relationships (Abbey, Andrews, & Halman, 1995; Pagel, Erdly, & Becker, 1987; Pierce, Sarason, & Sarason, 1991; Schuster et al., 1990).

Therefore, we broadened our resources model of coping to encompass negative as well as positive aspects of social relationships, and we applied this expanded predictive framework in a 4-year prospective model with 183 cardiac patients (Holahan et al., 1997b). We found that negative aspects of relationships, such as conflict with and criticism from family and friends, were as damaging to adjustment as positive aspects of support were beneficial. This result is consistent with the idea that the benefits of social resources in cardiac rehabilitation derive from reduced interpersonal stressors as well as emotional support (Helgeson, 1993). For example, the psychosocial benefits of a healthy marital relationship for recovering cardiac patients derive from a low level of interpersonal stressors as well as a positive emotional quality (Waltz, 1986).

A conceptually important aspect of these findings is that they broaden a resources model of coping (Holahan & Moos, 1994) to include negative as well as positive aspects of social relationships. Just as coping is a key adaptive mechanism through which social support operates, so too coping provides a mechanism through which ongoing social stressors operate. Whereas ongoing social support enhances coping efforts, ongoing social stressors erode coping efforts (see Ebata & Moos, 1994; Fondacaro & Moos, 1989). This may be especially true of social stressors, which Bolger et al. (1989) observed are "by far the most upsetting of all daily stressors" (p. 814).

We found that negative components of social ties were reported much less frequently by cardiac patients than were positive features of relationships; this was consistent with findings of other investigators (see Helgeson, 1993). The fact that negative interactions relate strongly to maladjustment, even though they occur infrequently, underscores the importance of such interactions. As Helgeson (1993) observed, "the relative infrequency with which most negative social interactions occur, and their unexpectedness after the onset of chronic illness, may make the experience more vivid and more consequential" (p. 838).

Cardiovascular Rehabilitation

The conceptual framework and measurement tools used in our program of research may be applied to psychosocial intervention and assessment efforts related to cardiovascular rehabilitation. Ewart (1990) argued that the traditional emphasis in cardiovascular rehabilitation on individual behavior change, which ignores social context and coping factors, is an overly simplistic way to view the enduring lifestyle changes required for cardiac recovery.

Our results show that social support and social stressors in patients' lives are central to understanding long-term depressive reactions among cardiac patients. In a review of the literature on psychosocial adjustment to cardiac illness, Fielding (1991) concluded that depression is a central obstacle to full recovery. Moreover, because psychosocial debilitation may predict increased risk for reinfarction and cardiac death after myocardial infarction (Anda et al., 1993), efforts to enhance psychosocial adjustment may facilitate cardiac recovery.

Psychosocial goals for an individual recovering from cardiac illness, as well as assessment of progress toward such goals, can be indexed with the measures used in our program of research (see Figure 3). In addition, our finding that coping strategies operate as a mechanism through which social resources are linked to subsequent functioning suggests a point of intervention for enhancing cardiac patients' coping efforts. For example, a patient's social support, social stressors, coping efforts, and psychological well-being might be assessed along with more traditional medical and functional criteria in evaluating quality of life after cardiac surgery (see Blumenthal & Emery, 1988).

CONCLUSION

Overall, our findings highlight the need to develop broad and conceptually integrated views of life context factors in mental and physical health care. Depressed patients' life contexts play a key role in their post-treatment course. Life context factors shape the course of depression almost as much as do demographic factors and symptom severity at intake to treatment. However, clinicians tend not to focus on these factors, which generally are thought to be extraneous to treatment. Yet life context factors continue long after treatment ends, are pervasive and intense, and have a strong impact on outcome.

Most traditional assessment procedures focus on obtaining an accurate diagnosis. In contrast, clinicians should emphasize the "treatment utility of assessment" — that is, the extent to which assessment contributes to better treatment outcome, most often by enhancing treatment planning (Hayes, Nelson, & Jarrett, 1987). An assessment of ongoing life stressors can help to identify patients who have a high risk for relapse and who might profit from a special aftercare group to integrate them into the community. An assessment of long-term family stressors can help a family therapist decide whether to focus on communication skills training (whether there is lack of communication) or clarification of family roles (whether there is a lack of organization).

Most broadly, our work on stress and coping offers an optimistic portrait of individuals' adaptive strengths and of their capacity for resilience and constructive action in the face of challenge (Holahan et al., 1996). The findings that the conditions of life play an essential role in the course of remission from relatively severe depressive disorders are a hopeful sign. They suggest that depression need not become a chronic disorder and that patients who are in relatively benign circumstances are likely to experience a remission. Thus, a central challenge for clinicians is to guide recovering patients along a healthful trajectory of interpersonal relatedness (see Carnelley, Pietromonaco, & Jaffe, 1994).

In this optimistic spirit, clinicians also can recognize in life crises an opportunity for individuals to mature and grow emotionally stronger. We found that adaptively confronting life stressors can provide an opportunity for personal growth (Holahan & Moos, 1990). Of course, beneficial outcomes to life crises may emerge only after a process of assimilation that follows an initial period of emotional upheaval (Stewart, Sokol, Healy, & Chester, 1986). However, as Schaefer and Moos (1992) observed, "resilience develops from confronting stressful experiences and coping with them effectively. . . . Crisis situations . . . promote new coping skills and lead to new personal and social resources" (p. 150).

REFERENCES

Abbey, A., Andrews, F. M., & Halman, J. (1995). Provision and receipt of social support and disregard: What is their impact on the marital life quality of infertile and fertile couples? *Journal of Personality and Social Psychology, 68*, 455–469.

Allen, J. K., Fitzgerald, S. T., Swank, R. T., & Becker, D. M. (1990). Functional status after coronary artery bypass grafting and percutaneous transluminal coronary angioplasty. *American Journal of Cardiology, 65*, 921–925.

Anda, R., Williamson, D., Jones, D., Macera, C., Eaker, E., Glassman, A., & Marks, J. (1993). Depressed affect, hopelessness, and the risk of ischemic heart disease in a cohort of U.S. adults. *Epidemiology, 4*, 285–294.

Anderson, B. L. (1992). Psychological interventions for cancer patients to enhance the quality of life. *Journal of Consulting and Clinical Psychology, 60*, 552–568.

Aspinwall, L. G., & Taylor, S. E. (1992). Modeling cognitive adaptation: A longitudinal investigation of the impact of individual differences and coping on college adjustment and performance. *Journal of Personality and Social Psychology, 63*, 989–1003.

Avison, W. R., & Gotlib, I. H. (1994). *Stress and mental health: Contemporary issues and prospects for the future.* New York: Plenum.

Banks, S. M., & Kerns, R. D. (1996). Explaining high rates of depression in chronic pain: A diathesis-stress framework. *Psychological Bulletin, 119*, 95–110.

Billings, A. G., & Moos, R. H. (1982). Work stress and the stress-buffering roles of work and family resources. *Journal of Occupational Behaviour, 3*, 215–232.

Billings, A. G., & Moos, R. H. (1983). Comparisons of children of depressed and nondepressed parents: A socio-emotional perspective. *Journal of Abnormal Child Psychology, 11*, 463–485.

Billings, A. G., & Moos, R. H. (1984). Coping, stress, and social resources among adults with unipolar depression. *Journal of Personality and Social Psychology, 46*, 877–891.

Billings, A., & Moos, R. (1985). Life stressors and social resources affect posttreatment outcomes among depressed patients. *Journal of Abnormal Psychology, 94*, 140–153.

Billings, A. G., & Moos, R. H. (1986). Children of parents with unipolar depression: A controlled one-year follow-up. *Journal of Abnormal Child Psychology, 14*, 149–166.

Blumenthal, J. A., & Emery, C. F. (1988). Rehabilitation of patients following myocardial infarction. *Journal of Consulting and Clinical Psychology, 56*, 374–381.

Blumenthal, S. J., & Matthews, K. A. (1993). Psychosocial aspects of cardiovascular disease in women: Introduction and overview. *Annals of Behavioral Medicine, 15*, 109–111.

Bolger, N. (1990). Coping as a personality process: A prospective study. *Journal of Personality and Social Psychology, 59*, 525–537.

Bolger, N., DeLongis, A., Kessler, R. C., & Schilling, E. A. (1989). Effects of daily stress on negative mood. *Journal of Personality and Social Psychology, 57*, 808–818.

Bolger, N., Foster, M., Vinokur, A. D., & Ng, R. (1996). Close relationships and adjustment to a life crisis: The case of breast cancer. *Journal of Personality and Social Psychology, 70*, 283–294.

Brennan, P. L., & Moos, R. H. (1990). Life stressors, social resources, and late-life problem drinking. *Psychology and Aging, 5*, 491–501.

Brownell, K. D., Marlatt, G. A., Lichtenstein, E., & Wilson, G. T. (1986). Understanding and preventing relapse. *American Psychologist, 41*, 765–782.

Carnelley, K. B., Pietromonaco, P. R., & Jaffe, K. (1994). Depression, working models of others, and relationship functioning. *Journal of Personality and Social Psychology, 66*, 127–140.

Carver, C. S., Pozo, C., Haris, S. D., Noriega, V., Scheier, M. F., Robinson, D. S., Ketcham, A. S., Moffat, F. L., Jr., & Clark, K. C. (1993). How coping mediates the effect of optimism on distress: A study of women with early stage breast cancer. *Journal of Personality and Social Psychology, 65*, 375–390.

Cohen, S. (1992). Stress, social support, and disorder. In H. O. F. Veiel & U. Baumann (Eds.), *The meaning and measurement of social support* (pp. 109–124). New York: Hemisphere.

Cohen, S., & Edwards, J. R. (1989). Personality characteristics as moderators of the relationship between stress and disorder. In R. W. J. Neufeld (Ed.), *Advances in the investigation of psychological stress* (pp. 235–283). New York: Wiley.

Coyne, J. C., & DeLongis, A. (1986). Going beyond social support: The role of social relationships in adaptation. *Journal of Consulting and Clinical Psychology, 54*, 454–460.

Coyne, J. C., & Downey, G. (1991). Social factors and psychopathology: Stress, social support, and coping processes. *Annual Review of Psychology, 42*, 401–425.

Coyne, J. C., Ellard, J. H., & Smith, D. A. F. (1990). Social support, interdependence, and the dilemmas of helping. In B. R. Sarason, I. G. Sarason, & G. R. Pierce (Eds.), *Social support: An interactional view* (pp. 129–149). New York: Wiley.

Coyne, J. C., Kessler, R. C., Tal, M., Turnbull, J., Wortman, C. B., & Greden, J. F. (1987). Living with a depressed person. *Journal of Consulting and Clinical Psychology, 55*, 347–352.

Coyne, J. C., & Smith, D. A. F. (1991). Couples coping with a myocardial infarction: A contextual perspective on wives' distress. *Journal of Personality and Social Psychology, 61,* 404–412.

Coyne, J. C., & Whiffen, V. E. (1995). Issues in personality as diathesis for depression: The case of sociotropy–dependency and autonomy–self-criticism. *Psychological Bulletin, 118,* 358–378.

Cronkite, R. C., & Moos, R. H. (1984). The role of predisposing and moderating factors in the stress–illness relationship. *Journal of Health and Social Behavior, 25,* 372–393.

Cutrona, C. E., & Russell, D. W. (1990). Type of social support and specific stress: Toward a theory of optimal matching. In B. R. Sarason, I. G. Sarason, & G. R. Pierce (Eds.), *Social support: An interactional view* (pp. 319–366). New York: Wiley.

Daniels, D., & Moos, R. H. (1990). Assessing life stressors and social resources among adolescents: Applications to depressed youth. *Journal of Adolescent Research, 5,* 268–289.

Ebata, A. T., & Moos, R. H. (1994). Personal, situational, and contextual determinants of coping in adolescents. *Journal of Research on Adolescence, 4,* 99–125.

Ewart, C. K. (1990). A social problem-solving approach to behavior change in coronary heart disease. In S. Schumaker, E. Schron, & J. Ockene (Eds.), *Handbook of health behavior change* (pp. 153–190). New York: Springer.

Fielding, R. (1991). Depression and acute myocardial infarction: A review and reinterpretation. *Social Science and Medicine, 32,* 1017–1027.

Finney, J. W., & Moos, R. H. (1991). The long-term course of treated alcoholism: II. Predictors and correlates of 10-year functioning and mortality. *Journal of Studies on Alcohol, 53,* 1–12.

Folkman, S. (1984). Personal control and stress and coping processes: A theoretical analysis. *Journal of Personality and Social Psychology, 46,* 839–852.

Follick, M. J., Gorkin, L., Smith, T. W., Capone, R. J., Visco, J., & Stablein, D. (1988). Quality of life post-myocardial infarction: Effects of a transtelephonic coronary intervention system. *Health Psychology, 7,* 169–182.

Fondacaro, M., & Moos, R. H. (1987). Social support and coping: A longitudinal analysis. *American Journal of Community Psychology, 15,* 653–673.

Fondacaro, M., & Moos, R. H. (1989). Life stressors and coping: A longitudinal analysis among depressed and nondepressed adults. *Journal of Community Psychology, 17,* 330–340.

Forrester, A. W., Lipsey, J. R., Teitelbaum, M. L., DePaulo, J. R., Andrzejewski, P. L., & Robinson, R. G. (1992). Depression following myocardial infarction. *International Journal of Psychiatry in Medicine, 22,* 33–46.

Goldberger, L., & Breznitz, S. (Eds.). (1993). *Handbook of stress: Theoretical and clinical aspects* (2nd ed.). New York: Free Press.

Grych, J. H., & Finchman, F. D. (1990). Marital conflict and children's adjustment: A cognitive-contextual framework. *Psychological Bulletin, 108,* 267–290.

Hammen, C. (1991). Generation of stress in the course of unipolar depression. *Journal of Abnormal Psychology, 100,* 555–561.

Havik, O. E., & Maelands, J. G. (1990). Patterns of emotional reactions after a myocardial infarction. *Journal of Psychosomatic Research, 34,* 271–285.

Hayes, S. C., Nelson, R. O., & Jarrett, R. B. (1987). The treatment utility of assessment: A functional approach to evaluating assessment quality. *American Psychologist, 42,* 963–974.

Helgeson, V. S. (1993). Two important distinctions in social support: Kind of support and perceived versus received. *Journal of Applied Social Psychology, 23,* 825–845.

Holahan, C. J., & Moos, R. H. (1981). Social support and psychological distress: A longitudinal analysis. *Journal of Abnormal Psychology, 90,* 365–370.

Holahan, C. J., & Moos, R. H. (1986). Personality, coping, and family resources in stress resistance: A longitudinal analysis. *Journal of Personality and Social Psychology, 51,* 389–395.

Holahan, C. J., & Moos, R. H. (1987a). Personal and contextual determinants of coping strategies. *Journal of Personality and Social Psychology, 52,* 946–955.

Holahan, C. J., & Moos, R. H. (1987b). Risk, resistance, and psychological distress: A longitudinal analysis with adults and children. *Journal of Abnormal Psychology, 96,* 3–13.

Holahan, C. J., & Moos, R. H. (1990). Life stressors, resistance factors, and psychological health: An extension of the stress–resistance paradigm. *Journal of Personality and Social Psychology, 58,* 909–917.

Holahan, C. J., & Moos, R. H. (1991). Life stressors, personal and social resources, and depression: A four-year structural model. *Journal of Abnormal Psychology, 100,* 31–38.

Holahan, C. J., & Moos, R. H. (1994). Life stressors and mental health: Advances in conceptualizing stress resistance. In W. R. Avison & I. H. Gotlib (Eds.), *Stress and mental health: Contemporary issues and prospects for the future* (pp. 213–238). New York: Plenum.

Holahan, C. J., Moos, R. H., & Bonin, L. A. (1997). Social support, coping, and psychological adjustment: A resources model. In G. Pierce, B. Lakey, I. Sarason, & B. Sarason (Eds.), *Sourcebook of theory and research on social support and personality.* New York: Plenum Press.

Holahan, C. J., Moos, R. H., Holahan, C. K., & Brennan, P. (1995). Social support, coping, and depressive symptoms in a late-middle-aged sample of patients reporting cardiac illness. *Health Psychology, 14,* 152–163.

Holahan, C. J., Moos, R. H., Holahan, C. K., & Brennan, P. (1996). Social support, coping strategies, and psychological adjustment to cardiac illness: An integrative model. *Journal of Prevention and Intervention in the Community, 13,* 33–52.

Holahan, C. J., Moos, R. H., Holahan, C. K., & Brennan, P. (1997a). Psychological adjustment in patients reporting cardiac illness. *Psychology and Health, 12,* 345–357.

Holahan, C. J., Moos, R. H., Holahan, C. K., & Brennan, P. (1997b). Social context, coping strategies, and depressive symptoms: An expanded model with cardiac patients. *Journal of Personality and Social Psychology, 72*, 918–928.

Holahan, C. J., Moos, R. H., & Schaefer, J. (1996). Coping, resilience, and growth: Conceptualizing adaptive functioning. In M. Zeidner & N. Endler (Eds.), *Handbook of coping: Research, theory, and application* (pp. 24–43) New York: Wiley.

Jenkins, C. D., Jono, R. T., Stanton, B. A., & Stroup-Benham, C. A. (1990). The measurement of health-related quality of life: Major dimensions identified by factor analysis. *Social Science and Medicine, 31*, 925–931.

Joiner, T. E. (1994). Contagious depression: Existence, specificity to depressive symptoms, and the role of reassurance seeking. *Journal of Personality and Social Psychology, 67*, 287–296.

Joiner, T. E., Alfano, M. S., & Metalsky, G. I. (1992). When depression breeds contempt: Reassurance-seeking, self-esteem, and rejection of depressed college students by their roommates. *Journal of Abnormal Psychology, 101*, 165–173.

Kaniasty, K., & Norris, F. H. (1993). A test of the social support deterioration model in the context of natural disaster. *Journal of Personality and Social Psychology, 64*, 395–408.

Kaplan, R. M. (1990). Behavior as the central outcome in health care. *American Psychologist, 45*, 1211–1220.

Kendler, K. S., Kessler, R. C., Neale, M. C., Heath, A. C., & Eaves, L. J. (1993). The prediction of major depression in women: Toward an integrated etiological model. *American Journal of Psychiatry, 150*, 1139–1148.

Langeluddecke, P., Fulcher, G., Baird, D., Hughes, C., & Tennant, C. (1989). A prospective evaluation of the psychosocial effects of coronary artery bypass surgery. *Journal of Psychosomatic Research, 33*, 37–45.

Lazarus, R. S., & Folkman, S. (1984). *Stress, appraisal, and coping.* New York: Springer.

Maughan, B., & Champion, L. (1990). Risk and protective factors in the transition to young adulthood. In P. B. Baltes & M. M. Baltes (Eds.), *Successful aging: Perspectives from the behavioral sciences* (pp. 296–331). Cambridge, MA: Cambridge University Press.

McGrath, E., Keita, G. P., Stickland, B. R., & Russo, N. F. (Eds.). (1990). *Women and depression: Risk factors and treatment issues.* Washington, DC: American Psychological Association.

Mitchell, R. E., Cronkite, R. C., & Moos, R. H. (1983). Stress, coping, and depression among married couples. *Journal of Abnormal Psychology, 92*, 433–448.

Monroe, S. M., & Simons, A. D. (1991). Diathesis-stress theories in the context of life stress research: Implications for the depressive disorders. *Psychological Bulletin, 110*, 406–425.

Moos, R. H. (1991). Life stressors, social resources, and the treatment of depression. In J. Becker & A. Kleinman (Eds.), *Psychosocial aspects of depression* (pp. 187–214). Hillsdale, NJ: Erlbaum.

Moos, R. H., Brennan, P. L., Fondacaro, M., & Moos, B. S. (1990). Approach and avoidance coping responses among older problem and nonproblem drinkers. *Psychology and Aging, 5,* 31–40.

Moos, R. H., Fenn, C., & Billings, A. (1988). Life stressors and social resources: An integrated assessment approach. *Social Science and Medicine, 27,* 999–1002.

Moos, R. H., Finney, J. W., & Cronkite, R. C. (1990). *Alcoholism treatment: Process and outcome.* New York: Oxford University Press.

Moos, R. H., & Moos, B. S. (1994). *Life Stressors and Social Resources Inventory: Adult Form manual.* Odessa, FL: Psychological Assessment Resources.

Moos, R. H., & Schaefer, J. A. (1993). Coping resources and processes: Current concepts and measures. In L. Goldberger & S. Breznitz (Eds.), *Handbook of stress: Theoretical and clinical aspects* (2nd ed., pp. 234–257). New York: Free Press.

Nolen-Hoeksema, S., Parker, L. E., & Larson, J. (1994). Ruminative coping with depressed mood following loss. *Journal of Personality and Social Psychology, 67,* 92–104.

Pagel, M. D., Erdly, W. W., & Becker, J. (1987). Social networks: We get by with (and in spite of) a little help from our friends. *Journal of Personality and Social Psychology, 53,* 793–804.

Pearlin, L. I. (1989). The sociological study of stress. *Journal of Health and Social Behavior, 30,* 241–256.

Phares, V., & Compas, B. E. (1992). The role of fathers in child and adolescent psychopathology: Make room for daddy. *Psychological Bulletin, 11,* 387–412.

Pierce, G. R., Sarason, I. G., & Sarason, B. R. (1991). General and relationship-based perceptions of social support: Are two constructs better than one? *Journal of Personality and Social Psychology, 61,* 1028–1039.

Pillow, D. R., Zautra, A. J., & Sandler, I. (1996). Major life events and minor stressors: Identifying mediational links in the stress process. *Journal of Personality and Social Psychology, 70,* 381–394.

Potthoff, J. G., Holahan, C. J., & Joiner, T. E. (1995). Reassurance seeking, stress generation, and depressive symptoms: An integrative model. *Journal of Personality and Social Psychology, 68,* 664–670.

Quittner, A. L., Glueckauf, R. L., & Jackson, D. N. (1990). Chronic parenting stress: Moderating versus mediating effects of social support. *Journal of Personality and Social Psychology, 59,* 1266–1279.

Rohde, P., Lewinsohn, P. M., Tilson, M., & Seeley, J. R. (1990). Dimensionality of coping and its relation to depression. *Journal of Personality and Social Psychology, 58,* 499–511.

Russell, D. W., & Cutrona, C. E. (1991). Social support, stress, and depressive symptoms among the elderly: Test of a process model. *Psychology and Aging, 6,* 190–201.

Schaefer, J. A., & Moos, R. H. (1992). Life crises and personal growth. In B. N. Carpenter (Ed.), *Personal coping: Theory, research, and application* (pp. 149–170). New York: Praeger.

Schuster, T. L., Kessler, R. C., & Aseltine, R. H. (1990). Supportive interactions, negative interactions, and depressed mood. *American Journal of Community Psychology, 18,* 423–438.

Sherbourne, C. D., Hays, R. D., & Wells, K. B. (1995). Personal and psychosocial risk factors for physical and mental health outcomes and course of depression among depressed patients. *Journal of Consulting and Clinical Psychology, 63,* 345–355.

Stanton, A. L., & Snider, P. R. (1993). Coping with breast cancer diagnosis: A prospective study. *Health Psychology, 12,* 16–23.

Stewart, A. J., Sokol, M., Healy, J. M., & Chester, N. L. (1986). Longitudinal studies of psychological consequences of life changes in children and adults. *Journal of Personality and Social Psychology, 50,* 143–157.

Swindle, R. W., Cronkite, R. C., & Moos, R. H. (1989). Life stressors, social resources, coping, and the four-year course of unipolar depression. *Journal of Abnormal Psychology, 98,* 468–477.

Thoits, P. A. (1992). Social support functions and network structures: A supplemental view. In H. O. F. Veiel & U. Baumann (Eds.), *The meaning and measurement of social support* (pp. 57–62). New York: Hemisphere.

Thoits, P. A. (1995). Stress, coping, and social support processes: Where are we? What next? *Journal of Health and Social Behavior, 36,* 53–79.

Valentiner, D. P., Holahan, C. J., & Moos, R. H. (1994). Social support, appraisals of event controllability, and coping: An integrative model. *Journal of Personality and Social Psychology, 66,* 1094–1102.

Waltz, M. (1986). Marital context and post-infarction quality of life: Is it social support or something more? *Social Science and Medicine, 22,* 791–805.

Waltz, M., Badura, B., Pfaff, H., & Schott, T. (1988). Marriage and the psychological consequences of a heart attack: A longitudinal study of adaptation to chronic illness after 3 years. *Social Science and Medicine, 27,* 149–158.

Wheaton, B. (1994). Sampling the stress universe. In W. R. Avison & I. H. Gotlib (Eds.), Stress and mental health: Contemporary issues and prospects for the future (pp. 77–114). New York: Plenum.

Young, L. D. (1992). Psychological factors in rheumatoid arthritis. *Journal of Consulting and Clinical Psychology, 60,* 619–627.

Zirkel, S., & Cantor, N. (1990). Personal construal of life tasks: Those who struggle for independence. *Journal of Personality and Social Psychology, 58,* 172–185.

4

INTERPERSONAL AND COGNITIVE PATHWAYS INTO THE ORIGINS OF ATTRIBUTIONAL STYLE: A DEVELOPMENTAL PERSPECTIVE

BETH A. HAINES, GERALD I. METALSKY, AIMEE L. CARDAMONE
AND THOMAS JOINER

The hopelessness theory of depression (Abramson, Metalsky, & Alloy, 1989) posits that a stable, global attributional style for negative events is a cognitive diathesis that, in conjunction with negative life stressors, contributes to the development of a specific subtype of depression—hopelessness depression. Research based on the hopelessness theory and its predecessor, the reformulated learned helplessness model of depression (Abramson, Seligman, & Teasdale, 1978), has established a link between attributional style and childhood depression (e.g., Dixon & Ahrens, 1992; Hilsman & Garber, 1995; Kaslow, Rehm, & Siegel, 1984; Nolen-

Preparation of this chapter was supported by grants from Lawrence University to Beth A. Haines and Gerald I. Metalsky, by a grant from the Hogg Foundation for Mental Health to Gerald I. Metalsky, by a Young Investigator Award to Thomas Joiner, from the National Alliance for Research on Schizophrenia and Depression, and by a research grant to Thomas Joiner, from the John Sealy Memorial Endowment Fund and Pearl and Aaron Forman Research Foundation at the University of Texas Medical Branch at Galveston.

Hoeksema, Girgus, & Seligman, 1986). Nevertheless, a critical omission in the developmental research on the helplessness and hopelessness theories of depression concerns the developmental origins of attributional style. Although the hopelessness theory explicitly calls for a search for distal causes of attributional style, such a search was beyond the scope of the 1989 statement of the theory. The main purpose of the present chapter, therefore, is to extend the hopelessness theory by proposing a developmental model of the origins of attributional style. Because much of the research conducted to date has involved the generalized tendency to attribute negative events to internal, stable, and global causes, for simplicity we refer to this tendency as a *negative attributional style*.

Our intent is to provide a heuristic for examining the origins of the negative attributional style rather than to propose an exclusive model that specifies an exact combination of factors that will produce this attributional style. In doing so, we examine a variety of interpersonal and cognitive pathways into the origins of attributional style, including analysis of how attributional style may interface with cognitive development and early life experiences from a developmental perspective.

In our view, it is important to understand the origins of attributional style to allow investigators to intervene in the early years with the goal of primary prevention. Research with adults (Metalsky, Halberstadt, & Abramson, 1987; Metalsky, Joiner, Hardin, & Abramson, 1993) and with children (Hilsman & Garber, 1995) has suggested that depressive symptoms develop rapidly, soon after exposure to a negative life event. Therefore, primary prevention efforts ideally should focus on identifying at-risk individuals, *before* they develop a negative attributional style.

Before presenting our model, we consider the developmental evidence concerning the relationship between attributional style and depression. We begin by briefly reviewing this research and subsequently present our developmental model of the origins of attributional style.

NEGATIVE ATTRIBUTIONAL STYLE AND DEPRESSION IN CHILDREN

The Research

Many studies have documented a relationship between negative attributional style and depressive symptoms in children and adolescents (e.g., Hilsman & Garber, 1995; Kaslow et al., 1984; McCauley, Mitchell, Burke, & Moss, 1988; Seligman et al., 1984; Tems, Stewart, Skinner, Hughes, & Emslie, 1993). This relationship has been found to hold for a range of ages, from children in the first grade to adolescents (16 and 17 years of age). Only two of these studies made developmental comparisons of attributional style. One found that depressogenic attributional style became more negative with age (McCauley et al., 1988), and the other (Kaslow et al., 1984) found no developmental differences in the relationship between attributional style and depression in first, fourth, and eighth graders, but this study had small samples of depressed children (ns = 5–11).

A smaller group of studies were performed to test the diathesis–stress component of hopelessness theory (e.g., Cole & Turner, 1993; Turner & Cole, 1994), and an even smaller subset of studies have been reported to do so longitudinally (Dixon & Ahrens, 1992; Hammen, Adrian, & Hiroto, 1988; Hilsman & Garber, 1995; Nolen-Hoeksema et al., 1986; Nolen-Hoeksema, Girgus, & Seligman, 1992). Cole and Turner (1993) used structural equation modeling to examine the mediating and moderating roles of stressful events, cognitive errors, and negative attributional style in childhood depression. In line with Baron and Kenny (1986), we use the term *moderator* to refer to a variable that qualifies the effect of an independent variable (IV) on a dependent variable (DV). Therefore, *moderators* interact with an IV in the latter's effect on a DV. In contrast, a variable *mediates* the relationship between an IV and a DV if the IV has an effect on the DV indirectly through the operation of the mediator variable. Cole and Turner found that the relationship between adverse *interpersonal* events (peer's competency evaluations) and self-reported depression was almost completely mediated, but not moderated, by negative attributional style and cognitive errors. For positive and negative *environmental* events (as measured by the Children's Activity Inventory; Shelton & Garber, 1987), attributional style and cognitive variables only partially mediated the relationship with self-reported depressive symptoms. Cole and Turner found a strong relationship between negative attributional style and depressive symptoms, but they did not find developmental differences between fourth, sixth, and eighth graders in scores on the Children's Attributional Style Questionnaire (Kaslow, Tanenbaum, & Seligman, 1978) scores. Consequently, they collapsed data from 9- to 15-year-olds in testing their models.

From a developmental perspective, it is important to emphasize that grouping broad age ranges of children is common in the childhood depression literature, presumably because of small sample sizes, but it is counterproductive to the study of developmental processes. There is certainly ample evidence of sufficient knowledge base and processing differences between elementary school children and adolescents (e.g., Siegler, 1991) to justify increased attention to the role of developmental level in the origins of attributional style.

Turner and Cole (1994) suggested that negative cognitions are a consequence rather than a moderator of the effect of negative life events on depression for younger children (fourth and sixth graders). For older children (their eighth-grade sample), their data supported the hopelessness model in that attributional style interacted with negative life events in predicting depression. Turner and Cole hypothesized, on the basis of earlier research (Rholes, Blackwell, Jordan, & Walters, 1980) and theory (Fincham & Cain, 1986), that young children may not have stable attributional or cognitive styles and, consequently, that attributions may not play a significant role in the development of depression in younger children. Turner and Cole (1994) also reported interesting domain-specific effects in the relationship between negative events and attributional style in predicting depression. Stronger Attributional Style × Events interactions were found in domains that were personally relevant to the children, underscoring the need for developmental attention to this factor in future research.

The short-term longitudinal studies have produced mixed support for the hopelessness theory. Nolen-Hoeksema et al. (1986), in a study of third, fourth, and fifth graders, showed that negative attributional style predicted later depression and that the interaction of stress with attributional style predicted change in depressive symptoms in two of the four 3-month testing intervals (although only marginally in one period). Furthermore, maladaptive attributional style was a significant predictor of depression after the effects of depression at times n and $n - 1$ were controlled. A significant relationship between current depression and future attributional style suggests that an episode of depression may contribute to the development of a negative attributional style.

Dixon and Ahrens (1992) also found that attributional style in interaction with stress predicted later depression. Similar to work by Nolen-Hoeksema et al. (1986), a strength of the study was an appropriate age grouping of participants (9–12 years). Seligman et al. (1984) used a slightly broader age range of children (8–13 years) but found that negative attributional style predicted depressive symptoms over a 6-month interval.

One other short-term longitudinal study (Hammen et al., 1988) did not find support for the hopelessness theory. Previous depression and life stress predicted later depression over a 6-month interval. The sample included a broad age range (8–16 years), however, and the data were not analyzed developmentally. Therefore, these results should be interpreted cautiously, especially in view of the developmental findings of Nolen-Hoeksema et al. (1992), discussed later.

Hilsman and Garber (1995) suggested that the inconsistent findings in the short-term longitudinal studies may be due, in part, to differences across studies with regard to the time period between the occurrence of stress and the assessment of symptoms of depression. Replicating the findings of Metalsky et al. (1987), Hilsman and Garber reported that, irrespective of attributional styles, fifth- and sixth-grade children showed a depressive reaction on the morning after receipt of unacceptable grades on a report card. Attributional style did not interact with unacceptable grades at this time period. In contrast, 5 days after receipt of unacceptable grades, children who had a negative attributional style remained depressed, whereas children who had a positive attributional style recovered from their initial depressive reaction (cf. Metalsky et al., 1987, 1993). In view of the convergence of these findings in children and adults, we urge childhood depression researchers to pay particular attention to the time lag between the occurrence of negative life events and the assessment of symptoms of depression.

On the basis of the only long-term multiwave longitudinal study of the attributional style–depression link, Nolen-Hoeksema et al. (1992) reported several important findings. First and foremost, attributional style was found to predict depression when children were older (approximately 10–12 years old). With younger children (approximately 8–10 years), negative life events predicted later depressive symptoms, as did earlier depression. Support for the hopelessness theory was found in the final two 6-month periods: Life events in interaction with attributional style predicted depressive symptoms. The authors suggested that attributional style is still developing during the 8- to 10-year age range and that, consequently, negative life events may play a more significant role than cognitions in the development of depressive symptoms during this period. The authors also implied that a stable, negative attributional style does not develop until after age 10 years.

In the study by Nolen-Hoeksema et al. (1992), attributional style for both positive and negative events was quite stable over time, and attributional style and depressive symptoms were correlated at all time periods. Depressed children were also found to remain negative in their attributional style after their depression levels declined. This study also provided support for the "scar" hypothesis, which states that an episode of depression can lead to the development of a fixed and negative attributional style, leading to increased risk of further depressive episodes.

Discussion

The studies reviewed suggest that negative attributional style plays a significant role in the development of depressive symptoms in children, particularly older children. However, the origins of attributional style have not been established, although a variety of hypotheses about origins have been generated. First, a frequent assertion, articulated by Seligman et al. (1984), is that negative interpersonal experiences (e.g., poor peer relationships, negative feedback from teachers) lead to the development of a negative attributional style. Several authors also have asserted that attributional style must be well established and stable to cause depressive symptoms (e.g., Turner & Cole, 1994). However, the type of experience (i.e., quality, amount, intensity) and level of cognitive development necessary for the development of a stable attributional style are not clear. In the only long-term longitudinal study, attributional style was found to be relatively stable over a 5-year period (third and fourth grade to eighth and ninth grade), yet the impact of attributional style on depression appeared to change with development. In the only study in which very young children (first graders) participated, the data revealed an association between attributional style and depression even at this early age (Kaslow et al., 1984). Clearly, future research is needed to address how and when children acquire attributional style and also to examine when it starts to affect emotion and self-concept. This research suggests one possible origin of negative attributional style: the experience of an episode of depression in childhood. Depression may lead to negatively biased information processing, resulting in greater access to negative cognitions (Nolen-Hoeksema et al., 1992).

Overall, although some investigators have not found an association between attributional style and childhood depression, taken as a whole, the research in this area suggests that attributional style may indeed serve as a risk factor for depression, particularly in older children. We therefore turn to the question of origins.

MODEL OF THE ORIGINS OF ATTRIBUTIONAL STYLE

The research on childhood depression implicates interpersonal experiences as important antecedents to a negative attributional style. We propose a heuristic model of origins (see Figure 1) that identifies three interpersonal realms that are expected to play important and interrelated roles in the development of attributional style: (a) family experiences and parent–child relationships, (b) peer relationships, and (c) teacher–child relationships. A fourth process, based on the research reviewed earlier, highlights the significance of experiencing an episode of depression in early childhood to the development of a negative attributional style. We also speculate regarding possible genetic contributors to attributional style and suggest that genetic predispositions contribute indirectly to the development of attributional style. The developmental–interpersonal–cognitive nature of the model is evident in the sequencing of interpersonal relationships (early parent–child relationships precede peer and teacher relationships) and in the discussion of how cognitive development influences the origin of attributional style. Furthermore, we emphasize the importance of consistency, chronicity, and intensity in determining the impact of interpersonal experiences on attributional style. That is, consistent negative experiences across interpersonal domains (e.g., poor parental relationships, peer rejection, and negative feedback from teachers) are expected to increase the child's likelihood of developing a negative attributional style. Similarly, the chronicity and intensity of negative experiences in any particular domain are expected to increase the child's risk of negative inter-

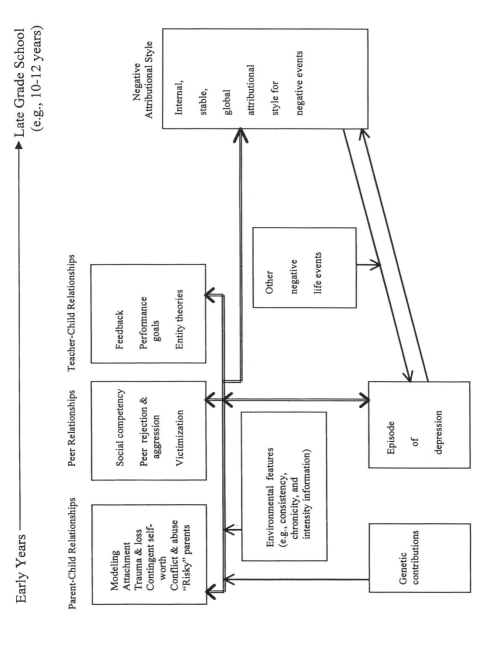

Early Years ──────▶ Late Grade School
(e.g., 10-12 years)

Figure 1. Developmental origins of attributional style: A heuristic model. Double lines refer to bidirectional relationships, and single lines refer to unidirectional relationships.

personal experiences in other domains (e.g., poor parent–child relationships may spill over into the academic domain and affect teacher relationships) and also increase the likelihood of establishing a negative attributional style.

On the basis of Crick and Dodge's (1994) social information-processing model, we suggest three probable sources of cognitive developmental influences on the origins of children's attributional styles: (a) increases in database and cognitive skills, (b) increases in speed or efficiency of processing, and (c) increased rigidity of processing patterns. Increases in children's database, in the form of greater experience with and knowledge of personal outcomes, goals, social events, and so on, presumably increase the likelihood that children will form a cohesive, internal, stable, global attributional style. Therefore, older children would be more likely than younger children to have an internal, stable, global attributional style in several domains (e.g., achievement, interpersonal). Nevertheless, younger children may display a stable attributional style in specific domains in which they have sufficient experience or that are personally relevant to them, such as interpersonal domains that they perceive as being relevant to their self-worth.

Also, the ability to attend to all the relevant features of stimuli improves with development. Older children, therefore, would be expected to show more complex processing of stimuli and greater accuracy in identifying subtle features of stimuli. For example, older children may be able to correctly identify a displaced cause of parental anger, whereas younger children may only consider a proximal cause—themselves—in their attributions. Consequently, older children's attributional style may be less affected by inconsistent negative experiences because they are able to consider other relevant factors and generate attributions drawing on previous feedback and self-assessments based on this feedback.

Developmental evidence suggests that increased efficiency in executing cognitive strategies facilitates rapid and more sophisticated processing in social situations. Therefore, children may simply be more likely to engage in more sophisticated causal attributional processing with age because of increased cognitive efficiency. Younger children's processing efforts may be more easily overwhelmed by affect and personal threat, and consequently, causal analysis may not consistently occur (see Grych & Fincham, 1990).

A final cognitive–developmental issue relevant to the origins of attributional style is the prediction of increased rigidity in processing patterns. Crick and Dodge (1994) discussed the role of early experiences in creating children's working models of the world. Experiences in the first few years of life (e.g., attachment quality) are hypothesized to create processing patterns that become more efficient and complex with age but also more rigid and resistant to change. These processing patterns begin to take on the qualities of personality characteristics in that they are stable and predictable across a wide range of situations. An important implication of this developmental tendency is that a negative worldview and maladaptive processing patterns acquired early in life can become ingrained and create a lens that children use for interpreting their social world (Bartlett, 1932; Binet & Henri, 1894; see Metalsky & Abramson, 1981, for a review of work in this area).

With this important work in mind, we turn to a discussion of each interpersonal realm of the model. Empirical evidence linking particular interpersonal relationships with the origins of attributional style is quite limited in some cases, but we hope the discussion will invite direct tests and future elaborations of the model.

Family Experiences and Parental Relationships

Modeling and Direct Tuition

There are several ways in which family experiences may influence children's attributional style (although family variables may coincide with potential genetic contributors). Peterson and Seligman (1984) offered three hypotheses about the origins of attributional style. First, they suggested that children may acquire attributional style from their mothers, learned either through observation or from the causal explanations for children's behavior that parents share with their children. In support of this hypothesis, these authors reported correlations between mother's attributional style and children's attributional style. The same pattern did not hold for fathers and children, but the authors suggested that mothers' more frequent role as primary caretaker may account for this difference. Fincham and Cain (1986) also hypothesized that children acquire attributional style through modeling. Consequently, the developmental state as well as the emotional state of caregivers is expected to affect children's attributional style. For example, Fincham and Cain suggested that elderly caretakers might create a risk factor for the development of negative attributional style because old age is associated with perceptions of decreased control.

Fincham and Cain (1986) also suggested that children may learn attributional styles on the basis of the attributions that significant others make for their behavior. In an interesting study, Fincham and Cain (1985) found that parents who attributed their child's failure to their own lack of effort (a mastery-oriented attribution on the parents' part) had children who displayed a learned helplessness pattern. This curious finding suggested that the children also attributed their failure to their parents' lack of effort (an external attribution that may also be perceived as stable and global). This is a potentially alarming result in that it implies that a mastery-oriented attribution by the parent (internal, unstable, specific) could contribute to an external, stable, global attribution by the child. In the same study, when fathers attributed children's failures to children's ability, children's performance deteriorated, providing further support for the conclusion that children directly adopt parental attributions for their behavior. Hokoda and Fincham (1995) also provided evidence that children adopt parental attributions for their behavior and asserted that parent–child interactions play a central role in the origins of helpless or mastery-oriented achievement patterns.

Parent–Child Attachment

Eisner (1995) suggested that trust in close relationships promotes a positive attributional style, whereas mistrust leads to the development of a negative attributional style. Eisner conceptualized trust as a personality trait and, like Erikson (1950), argued that early trust provides the foundation for positive personality development. Attachment theory portrays a similar picture of the attachment relationship; that is, attachment relationships provide children with internal working models of social relationships and expectations of how others will respond. Ford and Thompson (1985) asserted that attachment relationships contribute to infants' concept of personal agency—that is, to their perceptions of control (resulting from responsive, contingent environments) and their perceptions of self-competence (evolving from personal success in achieving desired outcomes). Secure attachments, presumably fostered by warm, responsive caregiving (Ainsworth, 1979), create a tendency in children to view the world as responsive and supportive and to see themselves as worthy of love (Bretherton, 1987; Sroufe, 1979). In contrast, insecure attachments have been associated with a variety of negative outcomes, such as lower social competence in boys (Cohn, 1990), lower personal and peer competence, and higher dependency (Sroufe, 1979). Moreover, infant maltreatment and maternal depression have both been related to a higher incidence of insecure attachment (e.g., Lyons-Ruth, Connell, Grunebaum, & Botein, 1990). Eisner (1995) reported that in college students, lower trust scores (based on trust in maternal, paternal, intimate, and closest friend relationships) predicted negative attributional style. Clearly, the link between early attachment relationships and the origins of attributional style is in need of further research.

Traumatic Early Experiences

Peterson and Seligman (1984) hypothesized that children's first traumatic experience may set their attributional style for life. Intense, stable, and global traumas, such as the loss of a parent, may create a propensity to make stable, global, and internal attributions about negative events, because the child has no control over the loss or ability to relieve the suffering. Peterson and Seligman emphasized the child's first loss, but this hypothesis could be extended to include prolonged or intense exposure to other negative events early in life (e.g., abuse; see the discussion below). Lefkowitz and Tesiny (1984) provided some support for the hypothesis that trauma in the early parent–child relationship, in the form of parental rejection, leads to childhood depression. Clearly, in exploring this hypothesis, one will need to further define the characteristics of a single traumatic event or other negative life events that increase the likelihood of developing a negative attributional style.

Contingent Self-Worth

Because of the evidence that young children do not view ability as a fixed personal trait, it generally has been concluded that young children are not vulnerable to helplessness (e.g., Dweck & Elliot, 1983). Consequently, until recently, little attention was given to young children's attributions. In recent work, Dweck and colleagues (Burhans & Dweck, 1995; Heyman, Dweck, & Cain, 1992; Smiley & Dweck, 1994) expanded their motivational model, arguing that young children are indeed susceptible to helplessness and that this vulnerability is based on the young child's conception of self as "good" or "bad." In particular, they argued that "a concept of self as an object of contingent worth is a sufficient condition for helplessness to occur" (Burhans & Dweck, 1995, p. 1722) and that this global sense of self can be acquired early in childhood (preschool years). In three studies (see Burhans & Dweck, 1995), 36%–51% of 4- to 7-year-old children showed the learned helplessness pattern—that is, lack of persistence following failure accompanied by attributions of low ability, lowered future expectations, and negative affect. Furthermore, Burhans and Dweck argued that the critical difference between helpless responses in older versus younger children centers around how the children conceptualize ability. Older children view ability as related to intelligence in a traitlike way. In contrast, Heyman et al. (1992) found that some young children associate ability simply with whether they know how to do a particular task, whereas others view poor task performance as indicating that they are "bad" or "unworthy"; the latter children tended to internalize negative feedback in a global way. Therefore, Burhans and Dweck presented an expanded model of motivation in which a general conception of self as an object of contingent self-worth is a sufficient condition for helpless responses to occur. Specifically, children who believe that their self-worth is contingent on others' judgments are vulnerable to helplessness (see Olinger, Kuiper, & Shaw, 1987, for a contingent self-worth model of depression). Burhans and Dweck have not yet articulated what leads children to view their self-worth as contingent on others' judgments; however, they have implied that feedback from significant adults (e.g., parents) conveying that children's value is contingent on good and successful behavior may lead children to adopt "self-valuation" goals.

In summary, even very young children appear to make attributions, but the content and type of attribution vary with age and task. In early childhood, attributions about global "badness" may have a strong impact on the development of a negative attributional style. Thus, it is plausible that a negative attributional style in a specific domain (e.g., parent–child relationships), acquired early in development, could put children at risk for acquiring a negative attributional style across several domains. Later in development, consistency of negative relationships across domains may further increase the risk of developing a negative attributional style across domains.

Family Conflict and Child Abuse

The field of research in which links between family conflict and children's attributional styles are examined directly is fairly limited. There is strong evidence that exposure to family conflict sensitizes children to conflict and that conflict that is frequent, physical, or intense is particularly disruptive to children (e.g., Cummings & Davies, 1994; Grych & Fincham, 1990). Also, conflict that involves children is more distressing for them than conflict over other matters (Grych & Fincham, 1993). How might exposure to high levels of family conflict affect children's attributional style?

Grych and Fincham (1993) examined the effects of intensity differences in interparental conflict. Children reported significantly higher levels of worry, shame, and helplessness in response to high-intensity conflicts than to low-intensity conflicts. Although the authors did not measure attributional style directly, the presence of shame and helplessness is suggestive of negative attributions. That is, when children express shame, they express the feeling that the situation occurred through some stable, global fault of their own. On the basis of our clinical work with children and adults, we have concluded that shame is an exceptionally good marker for a negative attributional style.

Barahal, Waterman, and Martin (1981) examined the cognitive-processing patterns of 6- to 8-year-old children who experienced physical maltreatment. They found that maltreated children were more likely to display a generalized external locus of control; therefore, they had little confidence in their ability to control the outcome of either positive or negative events. Kaufman (1991) directly tested the relationship between maltreatment and attributional style and also included precise measures of the severity and type of maltreatment, including emotional maltreatment (e.g., being called unworthy, being degraded, or being rejected). Maltreatment (emotional or physical abuse or both) was associated with negative attributional style and depression, and the more severe the maltreatment, the stronger the relationship. Maltreated children who tended to attribute the causes of negative events to internal, stable, and global factors, but attributed positive events to external, unstable, and specific factors, were more likely to be depressed. Maltreated depressed children reported fewer social supports and believed that their parents cared less for them than did maltreated nondepressed children. Cerezo and Frias (1994) also found that abused children were more likely to have a negative attributional style than their nonabused peers. They argued that abused children's depressogenic attributions evolve from exposure to aversive, noncontingent environments rather than from a bias in their thinking.

Allen and Tarnowski (1989) examined the effects of physical abuse on children's social cognitions. Abused children had significantly lower self-esteem than nonabused children and were more likely to display an external locus of control. In addition, abused children reported higher ratings of hopelessness, had more negative outcome expectancies, and tended to blame themselves for negative outcomes, suggesting the presence of internal, global, stable attributions. Dean, Malik, Richards, and Stringer (1986) also reported that maltreated children, more often than nonmaltreated children, believed that parents were justified in being unkind to children in response to children's misbehavior.

The tendency of children to accept blame for parental anger has been established for other groups as well. Covell and Abramovitch (1988) found that 5- and 6-year-olds tended to blame themselves exclusively for maternal anger, overlooking other possible contributors to the anger. Haines, Triesch, and Jome (1995) studied children's perceptions of displaced parental anger, that is, anger caused by some other source but directed at them. Young children (5–8 years) were more likely than older children (9–12 years) to blame themselves for parental anger (an internal attribution). Also, young children from high-conflict families reported greater sadness in response to parental anger than did children from low-conflict families. Older children were more successful at identifying the displaced cause of parental anger but still frequently (in more than 40% of their responses) asserted that they were responsible, at least partially, for the parent's anger. Grych and Fincham (1993) also reported that children frequently blame themselves for interparental conflict.

In summary, children may have a tendency to make internal attributions for parental anger. High levels of family conflict or abuse may serve to augment this tendency, ingraining self-blame and shame and leading to the development of a negative attributional style.

"Risky" Parents

Parental depression (see Downey & Coyne, 1990, for a review) and substance abuse (Perez-Bouchard, Johnson, & Ahrens, 1993) both have been associated with depressive symptoms in children, and recent work has suggested that attributional style may moderate this relationship. Perez-Bouchard et al. (1993) found that 8- to 14-year-old children of substance abusers had more negative attributional styles than did children of non-substance abusers. These researchers also included a measure of children's attributions about home events relevant to substance-abusing families. Children of substance abusers viewed negative events in their home environments as being more enduring than did children of non-substance abusers. This work suggests that repeated experience with negative home-life events may lead to the development of a negative attributional style.

Seligman (1990) also discussed work tying attributional style to chronic family stress. Children from lower socioeconomic families who experienced the economic crisis of the Depression, but did not experience financial recovery afterward, fared worse than children from middle socioeconomic families who also experienced the financial crisis but whose families recovered. People exposed to chronic economic stress acquired stable, global attributional styles and came to believe that negative events were inescapable and likely in the future.

Maternal depression has also been associated with negative attributional styles and poorer self-concepts in children (Jaenicke et al., 1987; Seligman & Peterson, 1986). Nolen-Hoeksema, Wolfson, Mumme, and Guskin (1995) examined the relationship between maternal depression and very young children's (5–7 years) helpless behaviors on a puzzle task. Depressed mothers were more negative in tone during the task, but group comparisons showed them to be comparable to nondepressed mothers in most ways. Parents with more negative tones and more hostile behavior (which was more common among severely depressed mothers) had children who exhibited more helpless behaviors (less enthusiasm, less persistence, lower competence). The variability in parenting competence of depressed mothers may be due to a variety of moderating factors (e.g., poverty, family support). In view of the studies reviewed previously, we suggest that the variability in child outcomes may also be moderated by attributional style. In our view, the relationship between parental depression and child functioning is a reciprocal one; this view is consistent with Hammen, Burge, and Stansbury's (1990) analysis (see also Coyne, Kahn, & Gotlib, 1987).

Peer Relationships

Although peer relationships enter children's interpersonal sphere in early childhood, most work on attributional style and peer relationships has focused on older (school-age) children. Of particular interest to the question of origins is the impact of peer rejection on attributional style. Various subgroups of rejected children have been identified including (a) aggressive–rejected children (actively disliked by peers and high in aggression), (b) aggressive–controversial children (disliked by some and liked by others), and (c) victimized peers (targets of aggression who are frequently rejected by their peers). It is not surprising that investigators have reported a relationship between peer rejection and depression (Cole, 1990; Lefkowitz & Tesiny, 1984). Of greater interest is recent work showing that depressed children display a hostile attributional bias—the tendency to attribute hostile intent to peers even in ambiguous provocation situations—which is also characteristic of aggressive children (Quiggle, Garber, Panak, & Dodge, 1992). The fact that aggressive children displayed the hostile attributional bias but did not show a more negative (depressogenic) attributional style is interesting in that it suggests that attributional biases in a specific domain do not necessarily generalize to other domains. Aggressive and depressed children processed information differently from and less competently than other children, but each group also showed unique information-processing patterns that corresponded to its presenting problems. The challenge for researchers is to map out how particular types of peer experiences interact with information processing in producing attributional style.

Panak and Garber's (1992) work sheds light on the relationship between rejection and attributional style. They found that increases in aggression were associated with increases in depression and that this relationship was partially mediated through increases in peer rejection. Strong support for hopelessness theory was provided by the finding that increases in peer rejection interacted with negative attributional style in predicting depression 1 year later. Critical to an understanding of origins was the finding that perceived rejection mediated the relationship between peer-reported rejection and self-reported depressive symptoms. Thus, aggression and peer rejection may put children at risk for developing depressive symptoms only if they perceive the rejection and attribute it to some flaw in themselves.

Crick and Ladd (1993) have partially addressed this hypothesis by examining the relationships between children's perceptions of their social problems, peer-reported rejection, and attributional style. Children with three peer statuses involving rejection—controversial, aggressive–rejected, and neglected (children ignored by their peers)—were compared to popular and average-status children. On the basis of group comparisons, only aggressive–rejected children expressed higher social distress than other groups; neither controversial nor neglected children showed high social distress or loneliness. However, there was variability within each group in reported social distress, and it was related to attributional style. The popular, average, and controversial children who experienced high levels of social distress despite their social status showed a *non*-self-serving bias in their attributional style. They attributed failures to themselves and did not take credit for social successes; being well-liked by peers was not sufficient to protect children from a maladaptive attributional style. Why children discounted their peer experiences was not established. Even popular children exhibited a maladaptive attributional style if they were high in social distress. In contrast, aggressive–rejected children displayed a self-serving attributional style. They externalized negative outcomes by blaming peers for their social problems and took credit for their successes.

Crick and Ladd's (1993) research suggests that how children perceive their peer status and the attributions they make about why they are accepted or rejected play a critical role in the impact of peer relationships on children's adjustment. Presumably, children's previous interpersonal experiences, perhaps based on parent–child relationships, lead some children to interpret positive peer relationships in a negative light, further ingraining a negative attributional style.

Victimized peers provide another interesting perspective on how peer relationships affect the development of attributional style. As Perry, Kusel, and Perry (1988) pointed out, whether peer rejection leads to internalizing problems (e.g., depression) or externalizing problems (e.g., aggression) may depend on whether a child is victimized by peers, is aggressive toward peers, or a combination of the two. We suggest that the child's attributions surrounding rejection will moderate this relationship: When rejection is perceived by a child, external, stable, global attributions (e.g., other children are mean) should lead to both aggression and depression, whereas internal, stable, global attributions (e.g., "I'm a 'geek'") should lead to depression.

Victimized children are frequent targets of peer aggression from bullies and even from typically nonaggressive peers (Perry, Williard, & Perry, 1990). Victimized preschoolers are anxious and vulnerable and often have a history of anxious–resistant attachments to their parents (Troy & Sroufe, 1987). Adolescent male victims show lowered self-esteem and social isolation (Olweus, 1984). Victimized peers reward their attackers by displaying great distress and providing tangible rewards. The reasons for children's lack of empathy to the distress of victimized children are of great concern; however, the critical issue in the present context is the kinds of attributions victimized children make about their peer relationships. Although direct measures of attributional style are not available for victimized children, some patterns are suggested. The fact that victims do not typically retaliate and the fact that victimization may be fairly stable over time (Perry et al., 1990) and across situations (e.g., "Most children treat me as a 'geek'") suggest that victims feel helpless and make internal, stable, global attributions about being victimized. Crick and Dodge (1994) suggested that children rely on cognitive heuristics to help them in interpreting situational or internal cues but that their heuristics may be biased. Heuristics originate from memory and working models of past experiences, and they affect future behavior indirectly through their influence on on-line processing. Thus, heuristics may play a role in the development of negative attributional style by reflecting children's worldviews and leading them to attend to certain cues to the exclusion of others (see also Metalsky & Abramson, 1981).

This hypothesis is similar to Ingram's (1984, 1990) analysis of how cognitive processing connects with depressive affect and results in priming the individual to attend to depressogenic information over other types of information. Beck's (1967) theory also implies that depressed people have negatively biased schemas that result in selective attention to certain cues more than others. Victimized children's life experiences may lead to heuristic processing characterized by stable negative attributions that affect their processing of future experiences. However, this heuristic processing may also be true to experience; that is, peers' cognitions about victimized children have been found to be fairly resistant to change, even when victims modify their behavior (Hymel, Wagner, & Butler, 1990). Victimized peers also seem to experience low self-esteem, a correlate of negative attributional style. Important questions remain, however: (a) Do victims make internal attributions, blaming themselves for aggressors' attacks? and (b) Do victims see their peer problems as indicative of a stable, global weakness in their character? If the answers to these questions are yes, victimization may be a strong predictor of negative attributional style.

Of course, information processing can be highly automated rather than conscious and reflective. Rabiner, Lenhart, and Lochman (1990) found, in their research on peer relations, that maladjusted children show deficits in automatic processing conditions but not in reflective processing situations. It will be important to determine whether the automatic and reflective processing of depressed children is similar to that of nondepressed children. For example, if some rejected children engage in more reflective processing and are also exposed to more negative peer interactions, it is possible that these children will show a processing pattern analogous to the "sadder but wiser" effect found with adults (Alloy & Abramson, 1979). This processing pattern could lead to an "evidence-based" negative attributional style (Metalsky & Abramson, 1981).

Teacher Relationships

As mentioned previously, negative correlations between academic competence and depressive symptoms in children are found throughout the childhood depression literature. Cole (1990) argued that academic competence defined by feedback for performance is linked most directly to depression and reported a strong relationship between academic competence and depressive symptoms. Most of the research on achievement-based helplessness has been done with school-age children (third grade and older) because young children's conceptions of ability, effort, and failure have been viewed as protecting them from helplessness. First, young children (less than 5 years) typically do not admit to failure (see Fincham & Cain, 1986, for a review). Consequently, vulnerability to negative attributional style on the basis of perceptions of failure appears unlikely in children under 5 years of age. Very young children (preschoolers) have been found to focus on specific knowledge or skills rather than on effort in explaining achievement. Effort attributions increase over the preschool years, becoming much more common by 6 years of age. Subsequently, children attribute outcomes to effort, and only in the later elementary years do they treat effort and ability as interdependent.

Peterson and Seligman (1984) hypothesized that children may learn attributional style from the type of feedback they receive from teachers. This hypothesis is based in part on Dweck's research on achievement-based helplessness (e.g., Dweck & Leggett, 1988; Licht & Dweck, 1984). Dweck, Davidson, Nelson, and Enna (1978) found that girls received less praise than boys for the intellectual quality of their work (girls' praise often focused on nonacademic aspects of their work, such as neatness) and more specific criticism about the intellectual quality of their performance. In contrast, although boys were criticized more frequently than girls, the criticism was directed at nonintellectual aspects of the boys' work or at their conduct. Also, teachers were more likely to attribute boys' failure to a lack of effort or motivation than they were girls' failures. On the basis of these results and those of a second study in which feedback style was experimentally manipulated, Dweck and colleagues concluded that the pattern of feedback girls received was more likely to lead to negative attributions about ability, associated with the helplessness orientation.

Dweck and Leggett (1988) presented a model of motivation that organizes the literature on achievement-based helplessness; they suggested that children's achievement attributions arise from the goals they set for themselves and their personal theory of intelligence. Mastery-oriented children are more likely to hold learning goals in which they seek to increase their competence. They view effort and ability as directly related; that is, they attribute failures to insufficient effort, and they increase their self-monitoring and persistence when faced with a challenge. In contrast, helplessness-oriented children often set performance goals and seek to obtain positive assessments of their ability and avoid negative assessments. They view effort and ability as inversely related; that is, high effort implies low ability. If they try hard and fail, they may conclude that they lack the ability to succeed. Thus, Dweck and Leggett argued that children's goals (i.e., learning vs. performance) affect how they process experiences and feedback and also how they judge their own contributions. A performance goal would lead a child who has expended a high amount of effort on a task and failed to attribute the failure to low ability. Thus, when children with performance goals experience failure, they have difficulty sustaining confidence in their ability, which may create a threat to their self-esteem and may increase depressed affect.

Dweck and Leggett's (1988) model further asserts that children's goal frameworks are based on their personal theories of their own intelligence. Children who are "entity theorists" view intelligence as fixed (and set performance goals), whereas children who are "incremental theorists" view intelligence as malleable (and set learning goals). Although entity theorists hold performance goals (which are implicitly less adaptive), if they have high confidence in their ability, they are predicted to display a mastery-oriented style. However, Henderson and Dweck (1990) found that high-confidence entity theorists did not achieve as well as expected in the seventh grade on the basis of their sixth-grade grade point average. This finding supports the contention that performance goals make it difficult to sustain confidence and also suggests that not all children view ability as a stable and global trait. Rather, some children seem to hold a developmental theory according to which ability is viewed as sufficient for tasks of a particular developmental level but not for tasks beyond that level. That is, they may view intelligence as fixed but base their judgments regarding their ability on the external assessments of others (i.e., grades reflect ability, so poor grades mean insufficient ability and an identified ceiling in ability). However, even low-confidence incremental theorists performed well after the middle-school transition, supporting the theory's assertion that learning goals lead to a positive response to challenge.

Dweck and Leggett (1988) argued that children's personal theory of intelligence is established by late grade school but can be experimentally manipulated by the type of feedback given. The cycle that emerges from Dweck and colleagues' work is that adult feedback leads children to view intelligence as either fixed or malleable, which in turn leads them to set goals and make attributions in the achievement domain in accordance with that view.

Early Episode of Depression

As mentioned earlier, the work of Turner and Cole (1994) and Nolen-Hoeksema et al. (1992) has suggested an additional pathway to the development of negative attributional style. Experience of a sustained clinical episode of depression may be one life experience that is sufficient to result in the acquisition of a negative attributional style that will persist even after the depression subsides. Other evidence (Tems et al., 1993) has suggested that successful treatment of depression can lead to more normalized cognitions in children and adolescents. Consequently, how a depressive episode affects cognition needs further study (cf. Gotlib, Lewinsohn, Seeley, Rohde, & Redner, 1993), with careful attention to developmental level. Perhaps an episode of depression has a stronger impact on attributional style when children are younger and their attributional style is still forming. In later years, previous attributional style may be the more critical determinant of the impact of a depressive episode on subsequent attributional style.

Support for this hypothesis comes from consideration of preemptive processing (rapid, automatic, script-based processing). Crick and Dodge (1994) asserted that preemptive processing is most likely to occur in highly emotional situations and in matters of great personal relevance. With results that are consistent with this assertion, Shaughnessy and Teglasi (1989) reported that children made more global attributions in important negative situations and that they rated these situations as more upsetting and as having a greater likelihood of future occurrence than less important situations. The children also explained that they classified the importance of situations on the basis of their emotional reactions. Preemptive processing may be particularly relevant in young children because it may interfere with adaptive causal attributional processing in favor of negative self-focused attributions. In a similar vein, Grych and Fincham (1990) asserted that the emotional arousal involved in the primary processing (i.e., assessing threat and self-relevance) of negative experiences can interfere with more sophisticated causal analysis (secondary processing). They also argued that primary processing may be more common among younger children because of their more limited cognitive skills. Therefore, preemptive processing may help to explain the finding that exposure to negative life events leads directly to depression for younger children.

Genetic Contributors

It is interesting to note that Schulman, Keith, and Seligman (1993) reported higher concordance in attributional style among monozygotic (MZ) than dizygotic (DZ) twins. In fact, the intraclass correlations for DZ twins on the composite attributional style subscale were zero. Although one interpretation of their data is that attributional style has a genetic component, these authors argued, on the basis of the extremely low correlation for DZ twins, that attributional style is indirectly heritable. Because their DZ twin sample was small, replication is needed as well as further exploration of familial correlates of attributional style. In the proposed model, we speculate that genetics is indirectly linked to attributional style through the impact on parent–child relationships (e.g., abuse), peer relationships, or teacher relationships, or through a genetic propensity toward depression, or both.

CONCLUSION

We have identified three interpersonal domains that we believe are likely to have a significant impact on the development of attributional style: (a) parent–child relationships, (b) peer relationships, and (c) teacher–child relationships. Furthermore, we have suggested possible risk factors within each of these domains that might lead to cognitive vulnerability to negative attributional style. As we indicated earlier, our intent has been to provide a heuristic for examining the origins of attributional style rather than an exclusive model that specifies an exact combination of factors necessary to producing a negative attributional style.

Certain interesting patterns emerge from the literature reviewed. First, it seems that very young children may be vulnerable to acquiring a negative attributional style despite their less sophisticated cognitive skills. That is, an insecure attachment relationship or an abusive environment may lead children to adopt a pessimistic worldview. Limited experience coupled with a tendency to blame themselves for negative parent–child experiences may lead very young children to view negative events as caused by enduring and global factors that reflect their own personal shortcomings. In this sense, young children's less complex reasoning and much more limited database may lead to a broader (less domain-specific) negative attributional style and self-view. Ford and Thompson (1985) similarly argued that children's perceptions of control and competency are initially global and undifferentiated and that they are applied broadly in both social and object domains. Later, with increased cognitive development and more breadth of experience, self-attributions become more complex and domain specific.

This consideration of young children also creates a methodological challenge. Most of the existing studies of attributional style have focused on older children, and when different age groups have been included, data have frequently been combined across age groups. Strikingly absent in most of the studies reviewed earlier are children younger than 8 years. On the basis of recent research on achievement helplessness (e.g., Burhans & Dweck, 1995; Heyman et al., 1992), we suggest that children may display a negative attributional style as early as age 5 (cf. Nolen-Hoeksema et al., 1992). Furthermore, measures of attributional style need to be developed that reflect relationships and interactions most relevant to young children. Whereas Dweck and colleagues looked at young children's helpless reactions in achievement domains, the domains to be explored in future work need to be expanded to include interpersonal domains that are most central to very young children's lives, namely, parent–child interactions.

Dweck and colleagues, who studied these issues in young children, suggested another important contributor to the development of a negative attributional style: contingent self-worth. Burhans and Dweck (1995) reported that some young children acquire a belief that their worth is contingent on the feedback of significant others. These authors argued that this sense of contingent self-worth leads children to seek positive evaluations from others and is associated with helpless responses when the children are faced with negative feedback. This pattern may be similar to the reassurance seeking seen in depressed individuals (Coyne, 1976; Joiner, Alfano, & Metalsky, 1992; Joiner & Metalsky, 1995). It also may explain why some children are particularly sensitive to negative feedback from teachers, which is associated with maladaptive attributional style in the achievement domain.

The issue of domain specificity in the development of attributional style is also of considerable interest (Abramson et al., 1989; Metalsky et al., 1987). We have argued that early in development, a sense of contingent self-worth or chronic exposure to a negative home environment may create a negative attributional style in the parent–child domain. However, we also speculate that because of the centrality of this domain to children, their pessimistic worldview and poor interpersonal self-concept may easily spill over into other domains, putting children at risk to develop negative attributional styles in other domains. In contrast, older children's more complex self-image (Linville, 1987) may provide a buffer against negative feedback in a particular domain if they have competent self-concepts in other domains. However, the bidirectional arrows in Figure 1 indicate that negative domain-specific experiences can affect other interpersonal domains. With findings that are consistent with this argument, Cole (1990) reported that children with multiple incompetencies (social and academic) showed stronger depressive symptoms.

Finally, the specific cognitive and affective mechanisms connecting interpersonal experiences to attributional style need further delineation. The research on peer rejection highlights this need for articulation of cognitive mechanisms. For example, as Quiggle et al. (1992) showed, both depressed and aggressive children displayed a hostile attributional bias, but each also had a distinctive processing style specific to their presenting symptoms. Also, the research reviewed earlier suggests that children's responses to peer rejection (e.g., aggression, maladaptive internalizing problems) depends in part on how they interpret the rejection (e.g., Crick & Ladd, 1993; Panak & Garber, 1992). Research on attributional styles of victimized peers may help to illuminate the processes involved. Perhaps feedback from significant others (parents, peers, teachers) helps children to define their self-concept, worldview, and way of explaining events in their world. Negative feedback or experience will lead to the development of a negative attributional style to the extent that such experiences are consistent over time and nondistinctive across domains (Kelley, 1967; Metalsky & Abramson, 1981), thereby creating a heuristic that children use in interpreting their life experiences.

REFERENCES

Abramson, L. Y., Metalsky, G. I., & Alloy, L. B. (1989). Hopelessness depression: A theory-based subtype of depression. *Psychological Review, 96,* 358–372.

Abramson, L. Y., Seligman, M. E. P., & Teasdale, J. (1978). Learned helplessness in humans: Critique and reformulation. *Journal of Abnormal Psychology, 87,* 49–74.

Ainsworth, M. D. S. (1979). Attachment related to mother–infant interaction. In L. S. Rosenblatt, R. A. Hinde, C. Beer, & M. Busnel (Eds.), *Advances in the study of behavior* (Vol. 9, pp. 1–51). New York: Academic Press.

Allen, D. M., & Tarnowski, K. J. (1989). Depressive characteristics of physically abused children. *Journal of Abnormal Child Psychology, 17,* 1–11.

Alloy, L. B., & Abramson, L. Y. (1979). Judgment of contingency in depressed and non-depressed students: Sadder but wiser? *Journal of Experimental Psychology: General, 108,* 441–485.

Barahal, R. M., Waterman, J., & Martin, H. P. (1981). The social-cognitive development of abused children. *Journal of Consulting and Clinical Psychology, 49,* 508–516.

Baron, R. M., & Kenny, D. A. (1986). The moderator–mediator variable distinction in social psychological research: Conceptual, strategic, and statistical considerations. *Journal of Personality and Social Psychology, 51,* 1173–1182.

Bartlett, F. (1932). *Remembering.* London: Cambridge University Press.

Beck, A. T. (1967). *Depression: Clinical, experimental, and theoretical aspects.* New York: Harper & Row.

Binet, A., & Henri, V. (1894). La mémoire des phrases (mémoire des idées) [Memory of sentences (memory of ideas)]. *Année Psychologique, 1,* 24–59.

Bretherton, I. (1987). New perspectives on attachment relations: Security, communication, and internal working models. In J. Osofsky (Ed.), *Handbook of infant development* (pp. 1061–1100). New York: Wiley.

Burhans, K. K., & Dweck, C. S. (1995). Helplessness in early childhood: The role of contingent worth. *Child Development, 66,* 1719–1738.

Cerezo, M. A., & Frias, D. (1994). Emotional and cognitive adjustment in abused children. *Child Abuse and Neglect, 18,* 923–932.

Cohn, D. A. (1990). Child–mother attachment of six-year-olds and social competence at school. *Child Development, 61,* 152–162.

Cole, D. A. (1990). Relation of social and academic competence to depressive symptoms in childhood. *Journal of Abnormal Psychology, 99,* 422–429.

Cole, D. A., & Turner, J. E., Jr. (1993). Models of cognitive mediation and moderation in child depression. *Journal of Abnormal Psychology, 102,* 271–281.

Covell, K., & Abramovitch, R. (1988). Children's understanding of maternal anger: Age and source of anger differences. *Merrill-Palmer Quarterly, 34,* 353–368.

Coyne, J. C. (1976). Toward an interactional description of depression. *Psychiatry, 39*, 28–40.

Coyne, J., Kahn, J., & Gotlib, I. (1987). Depression. In T. Jacob (Ed.), *Family interaction and psychopathology: Theories, methods, and findings* (pp. 509–533). New York: Plenum Press.

Crick, N. R., & Dodge, K. A. (1994). A review and reformulation of social information-processing mechanisms in children's social adjustment. *Psychological Bulletin, 115*, 74–101.

Crick, N. R., & Ladd, G. W. (1993). Children's perceptions of their peer experiences: Attributions, loneliness, social anxiety, and social avoidance. *Developmental Psychology, 29*, 244–254.

Cummings, E. M., & Davies, P. (1994). *Children and marital conflict: The impact of family dispute and resolution.* New York: Guilford Press.

Dean, A. L., Malik, M. M., Richards, W., & Stringer, S. A. (1986). Effects of parental maltreatment on children's conceptions of interpersonal relationships. *Developmental Psychology, 22*, 617–626.

Dixon, J. F., & Ahrens, A. H. (1992). Stress and attributional style as predictors of self-reported depression in children. *Cognitive Therapy and Research, 16*, 623–634.

Downey, G., & Coyne, J. C. (1990). Children of depressed parents: An integrative review. *Psychological Bulletin, 108*, 50–76.

Dweck, C. S., Davidson, W., Nelson, S., & Enna, B. (1978). Sex differences in learned helplessness: II. The contingencies of evaluative feedback in the classroom and III. An experimental analysis. *Developmental Psychology, 14*, 268–276.

Dweck, C. S., & Elliot, E. S. (1983). Achievement motivation. In P. H. Mussen (Series Ed.) & E. M. Hetherington (Vol. Ed.), *Handbook of child psychology: Vol. 4. Socialization, personality, and social development* (4th ed., pp. 643–691). New York: Wiley.

Dweck, C. S., & Leggett, E. L. (1988). A social-cognitive approach to motivation. *Psychological Review, 95*, 256–273.

Eisner, J. P. (1995). The origins of explanatory style: Trust as a determinant of optimism and pessimism. In G. M. Buchanan & M. E. P. Seligman (Eds.), *Explanatory style* (pp. 49–55). Hillsdale, NJ: Erlbaum.

Erikson, E. (1950). *Childhood and society.* New York: Norton.

Fincham, F. D., & Cain, K. M. (1985, April). *The role of attributions in learned helplessness.* Paper presented at the biennial meeting of the Society for Research in Child Development, Toronto, Ontario, Canada.

Fincham, F. D., & Cain, K. M. (1986). Learned helplessness in humans: A developmental analysis. *Developmental Review, 6*, 301–333.

Ford, M. E., & Thompson, R. A. (1985). Perceptions of personal agency and infant attachment: Toward a life-span perspective on competence development. *International Journal of Behavioral Development, 8*, 377–406.

Gotlib, I. H., Lewinsohn, P. M., Seeley, J. R., Rohde, P., & Redner, J. E. (1993).

Negative cognitions and attributional style in depressed adolescents: An examination of stability and specificity. *Journal of Abnormal Psychology, 102,* 607–615.

Grych, L. H., & Fincham, F. D. (1990). Marital conflict and children's adjustment: A cognitive-contextual framework. *Psychological Bulletin, 108,* 267–290.

Grych, L. H., & Fincham, F. D. (1993). Children's appraisals of marital conflict: Initial investigations of the cognitive contextual framework. *Child Development, 64,* 215–230.

Haines, B. A., Triesch, S. K., & Jome, M. A. (1995, March). *Perceptions of displaced parental anger in children from low- and high-conflict families.* Paper presented at the biennial meeting of the Society for Research in Child Development, Indianapolis, IN.

Hammen, C., Adrian, C., & Hiroto, D. (1988). A longitudinal test of the attributional vulnerability model in children at risk for depression. *British Journal of Clinical Psychology, 27,* 37–46.

Hammen, C., Burge, D., & Stansbury, K. (1990). Relationship of mother and child variables to child outcomes in a high-risk sample: A causal modeling analysis. *Developmental Psychology, 26,* 24–30.

Henderson, V. L., & Dweck, C. S. (1990). Motivation and achievement. In S. Feldman & G. Elliot (Eds.), *At the threshold: The developing adolescent* (pp. 308–329). Cambridge, MA: Harvard University Press.

Heyman, G. D., Dweck, C. S., & Cain, K. M. (1992). Young children's vulnerability to self-blame and helplessness: Relationship to beliefs about goodness. *Child Development, 63,* 401–415.

Hilsman, R., & Garber, J. (1995). A test of the cognitive diathesis–stress model of depression in children: Academic stressors, attributional style, perceived competence, and control. *Journal of Personality and Social Psychology, 69,* 370–380.

Hokoda, A., & Fincham, F. D. (1995). Origins of children's helpless and mastery oriented achievement patterns in the family. *Journal of Educational Psychology, 87,* 375–385.

Hymel, S., Wagner, E., & Butler, L. J. (1990). Reputational bias: View from the peer group. In S. R. Asher & J. D. Coie (Eds.), *Peer rejection in childhood* (pp. 156–186). New York: Cambridge University Press.

Ingram, R. E. (1984). Toward an information processing analysis of depression. *Cognitive Therapy and Research, 8,* 443–478.

Ingram, R. E. (1990). Self-focused attention in clinical disorders: Review and a conceptual model. *Psychological Bulletin, 107,* 156–176.

Jaenicke, C., Hammen, C., Zupan, B., Hiroto, D., Gordon, D., Adrian, C., & Burge, D. (1987). Cognitive vulnerability in children at risk for depression. *Journal of Abnormal Child Psychology, 15,* 559–572.

Joiner, T. E., Jr., Alfano, M. S., & Metalsky, G. I. (1992). When depression breeds contempt: Reassurance seeking, self-esteem, and rejection of depressed college students by their roommates. *Journal of Abnormal Psychology, 101,* 165–173.

Joiner, T. E., Jr., & Metalsky, G. I. (1995). A prospective test of an integrative theory of depression: A naturalistic study of college roommates. *Journal of Personality and Social Psychology, 69*, 778–788.

Kaslow, N. J., Rehm, L. P., & Siegel, A. W. (1984). Social-cognitive and cognitive correlates of depression in children. *Journal of Abnormal Child Psychology, 12*, 605–620.

Kaslow, N. J., Tanenbaum, R. L., & Seligman, M. E. P. (1978). *The KASTAN: A Children's Attributional Style Questionnaire.* Unpublished manuscript, University of Pennsylvania, Philadelphia.

Kaufman, J. (1991). Depressive disorders in maltreated children. *Journal of the American Academy of Child and Adolescent Psychiatry, 30*, 257–265.

Kelley, H. H. (1967). Attribution theory in social psychology. In D. Levine (Ed.), *Nebraska Symposium on Motivation* (Vol. 15, pp. 192–238). Lincoln: University of Nebraska Press.

Lefkowitz, M. M., & Tesiny, E. P. (1984). Rejection and depression: Prospective and contemporaneous analyses. *Developmental Psychology, 20*, 776–785.

Licht, B. G., & Dweck, C. S. (1984). Determinants of academic achievement: The interaction of children's achievement orientations with skill area. *Developmental Psychology, 20*, 628–636.

Linville, P. W. (1987). Self-complexity as a buffer against stress-related illness and depression. *Journal of Personality and Social Psychology, 52*, 663–676.

Lyons-Ruth, K., Connell, D. B., Grunebaum, H. U., & Botein, S. (1990). Infants at social risk: Maternal depression and family support services as mediators of infant development and security of attachment. *Child Development, 61*, 85–98.

McCauley, E., Mitchell, J. R., Burke, P., & Moss, S. (1988). Cognitive attributes of depression in children and adolescents. *Journal of Consulting and Clinical Psychology, 56*, 903–908.

Metalsky, G. I., & Abramson, L. Y. (1981). Attributional styles: Toward a framework for conceptualization and assessment. In P. C. Kendallt & S. P. Hollon (Eds.), *Cognitive-behavioral interventions: Assessment methods* (pp. 13–58). New York: Academic Press.

Metalsky, G. I., Halberstadt, L. J., & Abramson, L. Y. (1987). Vulnerability to depressive mood reactions: Toward a more powerful test of the diathesis-stress and causal mediation components of the reformulated theory of depression. *Journal of Personality and Social Psychology, 52*, 386–393.

Metalsky, G. I., Joiner, T. E., Jr., Hardin, T. S., & Abramson, L. Y. (1993). Depressive reactions to failure in a naturalistic setting: A test of the hopelessness and self-esteem theories of depression. *Journal of Abnormal Psychology, 102*, 101–109.

Nolen-Hoeksema, S., Girgus, J. S., & Seligman, M. E. P. (1986). Learned helplessness in children: A longitudinal study of depression, achievement, and explanatory style. *Journal of Personality and Social Psychology, 51*, 435–442.

Nolen-Hoeksema, S., Girgus, J. S., & Seligman, M. E. P. (1992). Predictors and consequences of childhood depressive symptoms: A 5-year longitudinal study. *Journal of Abnormal Psychology, 101*, 405–422.

Nolen-Hoeksema, S., Wolfson, A., Mumme, D., & Guskin, K. (1995). Helplessness in children of depressed and nondepressed mothers. *Developmental Psychology, 31*, 377–387.

Olinger, L. J., Kuiper, N. A., & Shaw, B. F. (1987). Dysfunctional attitudes and stressful life events: An interactive model of depression. *Cognitive Therapy and Research, 11*, 25–40.

Olweus, D. (1984). Aggressors and their victims: Bullying at school. In N. Frude & H. Gault (Eds.), *Disruptive behaviors in schools* (pp. 57–76). New York: Wiley.

Panak, W. F., & Garber, J. (1992). Role of aggression, rejection, and attributions in the prediction of depression in children. *Development and Psychopathology, 4*, 145–165.

Perez-Bouchard, L., Johnson, J. L., & Ahrens, A. H. (1993). Attributional style in children of substance abusers. *American Journal of Drug and Alcohol Abuse, 19*, 475–489.

Perry, D. G., Kusel, S. J., & Perry, L. C. (1988). Victims of peer aggression. *Developmental Psychology, 24*, 807–814.

Perry, D. G., Williard, L. C., & Perry, L. C. (1990). Peers' perceptions of the consequences that victimized children provide aggressors. *Child Development, 61*, 1310–1325.

Peterson, C., & Seligman, M. E. P. (1984). Causal explanations as a risk factor for depression: Theory and evidence. *Psychological Review, 91*, 347–374.

Quiggle, N. L., Garber, J., Panak, W. F., & Dodge, K. A. (1992). Social information processing in aggressive and depressed children. *Child Development, 63*, 1305–1320.

Rabiner, D. L., Lenhart, L., & Lochman, L. E. (1990). Automatic versus reflective social problem solving in relation to children's sociometric status. *Developmental Psychology, 26*, 1010–1016.

Rholes, W. S., Blackwell, J., Jordon, C., & Walters, C. (1980). *Developmental Psychology, 16*, 616–624.

Schulman, P., Keith, D., & Seligman, M. E. P. (1993). Is optimism heritable? A study of twins. *Behavioral Research and Therapy, 31*, 569–574.

Seligman, M. E. P. (1990). *Learned optimism.* New York: Pocket Books.

Seligman, M. E. P., Peterson, C., Kaslow, N. J., Tanenbaum, R. L., Alloy, L. B., & Abramson, L. Y. (1984). Attributional style and depressive symptoms among children. *Journal of Abnormal Psychology, 93*, 235–238.

Shaughnessy, M. S., & Teglasi, H. (1989). Situational importance, affect, and causal attribution. *Psychological Reports, 64*, 839–850.

Shelton, M. R., & Garber, J. (1987, August). *Development and validation of children's pleasant and unpleasant events schedule.* Paper presented at the 95th Annual Convention of the American Psychological Association, New York.

Siegler, R. S. (1991). *Children's thinking* (2nd ed.). Englewood Cliffs, NJ: Prentice Hall.

Smiley, P., & Dweck, C. S. (1994). Individual differences in achievement goals among young children. *Child Development, 65,* 1723–1743.

Sroufe, L. A. (1979). The coherence of individual development. *American Psychologist, 34,* 837–841.

Tems, C. L., Stewart, S. M., Skinner, J. R., Jr., Hughes, C. W., & Emslie, G. (1993). Cognitive distortions in depressed children and adolescents: Are they state dependent or traitlike? *Journal of Clinical Child Psychology, 22,* 316–326.

Troy, M., & Sroufe, A. (1987). Victimization among preschoolers: Role of attachment relationship history. *Journal of the American Academy of Child and Adolescent Psychiatry, 26,* 166–172.

Turner, J. E., Jr., & Cole, D. A. (1994). Developmental differences in cognitive diatheses for child depression. *Journal of Abnormal Child Psychology, 22,* 15–32.

5

LONELINESS, SHYNESS, AND DEPRESSION: THE ETIOLOGY AND INTERRELATIONSHIPS OF EVERYDAY PROBLEMS IN LIVING

JODY C. DILL AND CRAIG A. ANDERSON

And indeed there will be time
To wonder, "Do I dare?" and, "Do I dare?"
Time to turn back and descend the stair,
With a bald spot in the middle of my hair ...
Do I dare
Disturb the universe?
(From *The Love Song of J. Alfred Prufrock,* 1917, by T. S. Eliot
[1888–1965], Anglo-American poet.)

Shyness, loneliness, and depression—these are the bane of modern U.S. society. Like the four horsemen of the Apocalypse, this troika of "everyday problems in living" (Anderson & Arnoult, 1985a) rides down the unsuspecting and undeserving with no regard for age or income, education or status, race or gender. Recent statistics show that 8% to 10% of the U.S. population will experience a major depressive episode during their lifetime and that at any given time, roughly 15% of the population show some significant depressive signs (B. Brown, 1974; Secunda, 1973). Loneliness characterizes about 26% of the population at any given point in time (Bradburn, 1969). Zimbardo, Pilkonis, and Norwood (1974) reported that 40% of the population indicate that they have serious problems that are due to shyness.

93

EVER-WIDENING IMPACT

In addition to the emotional trauma and psychological suffering inflicted on the victims, these problems exact a heavy monetary toll on society. Like a pebble tossed into a pond, these problems have their most obvious effects at the point of entry, but the impact radiates outward in an ever-widening circle. Perhaps this simile is too optimistic: It implies that one can observe and predict relatively low-level effects as the modest-sized waves dissipate at increasing distances from the initial point of impact. A coastal earthquake may provide a better analogy. The most obvious victims are those at the epicenter—the shy, the lonely, and the depressed. However, such traumatic events can lead to unexpected problems at quite some distance, just as the tsunami created by the earthquake can appear suddenly and unexpectedly thousands of miles away. For example, it is not simply the immediate family who suffer with the shy, lonely, and depressed; coworkers, friends, and acquaintances of the family may also be adversely affected. The health care costs, lost days at work, increased accident rates, and decreased productivity of the immediate victims and these "ripple effect" victims are all consequences of shyness, loneliness, and depression.

Other hidden costs also accrue. For instance, there are theoretical and empirical reasons to suspect that these problems in living increase the likelihood of a variety of violent behaviors, ranging from child abuse to murder. For instance, Lee, Zimbardo, and Bertholf (1977) showed that convicted murderers who had no prior history of violence were unusually shy. Shyness, loneliness, and depression may all increase a variety of aggressive behaviors through at least three separate mechanisms (e.g., Anderson, Anderson, & Deuser, 1996; see also Berkowitz, 1993; Geen, 1990). First, the lack of satisfying interpersonal ties may contribute to a lower or less effective set of inhibitions against aggression. Second, the high level of negative affect characteristic of these problems in living may increase unwarranted aggression. Finally, these problems may prime aggressive thoughts, thus producing increases in aggression.

THE ROLE OF MODERN SOCIETY

Numerous characteristics of modern society contribute to shyness, loneliness, and depression. The high mobility in U.S. society makes it difficult to develop and maintain close interpersonal relationships, even within families. Similarly, the loss of intergenerational ties and the rise of single-parent families contribute to the social isolation that underlies many of the problems in living. These characteristics of modern U.S. society, and of most industrial societies, in conjunction with traditional values of individualism, have contributed to the development of an unhealthy focus on the self, the individual, and the "me" perspective.

One of the authors (Craig A. Anderson) has described this pattern of values as the "myth of materialism" in annual addresses to new Psi Chi (the Psychology honor society) members. It is fascinating to watch the facial expressions of this select group of students as they hear, perhaps for the first time, a challenge to the belief that happiness is best obtained by making and spending large sums of money. Some clearly do not believe the challenge; others display a surprised look, revealing that they had never seriously considered the possibility that there are values that are more important than "materialism." Of most interest, however, are the subsequent discussions. Many students have been taught at some intellectual level to value their interpersonal relationships. Many even seem to believe that "helping others" is a valuable goal; however, they also report tremendous peer pressure to have "nice things." They feel that others judge them by the quality of their car, clothes, and stereo. Furthermore, they realize that "society" often judges the success of a person by his or her salary or investment portfolio. Is it any wonder that in such a society people feel threatened, unworthy, and isolated? Even those who are successful by these materialistic standards are likely to feel nagging self-doubts as their interpersonal world continues to wither because of lack of attention.

These societal effects are beyond the scope of this chapter, but they are important to bear in mind when attempting to understand various everyday problems in living. As we articulate in greater detail in later sections, the societal effects provide a background on which we paint our portraits of three problems in living.

EVERYDAY PROBLEMS IN LIVING

Definitions

The main focus of this chapter is on the interrelationships among three everyday problems in living: shyness, loneliness, and depression. The latter has received by far the most theoretical and empirical attention by psychologists, and for good reason. It is an extremely common condition with major negative outcomes.

Depression is itself a broad category that has been subdivided in numerous ways. In this chapter we focus on the type of depression that has been termed *unipolar* and *reactive*. Many of the studies we cite do not explicitly include "clinically depressed" populations, mainly because the investigators used standardized self-report measures of depression (such as the Beck Depression Inventory) on normal populations.

Some scholars prefer to label the distressed people in these studies *dysphoric* rather than *depressed*, in part because of a belief that the clinically depressed are (or might be) very different from the moderately depressed. We eschew this distinction for two reasons. First, as noted in the opening paragraph, a substantial portion of the general population is clinically depressed at any given time. Therefore, the studies of general populations (e.g., university students) are likely to include truly depressed individuals. Second, our theoretical orientation suggests that differences in the most common forms of unipolar depression are largely a matter of degree, not of kind. However, it is important to note that some independent variables of interest (e.g., attributional effort) may not be linearly (or monotonically) related to self-reported depression. For instance, Weary and her colleagues (Weary, Marsh, Gleicher, & Edwards, 1993) suggested a curvilinear relation between depression and attributional effort. Specifically, these authors have shown that moderately depressed college students engage in more attributional work than either the nondepressed or the severely depressed.

Shyness and loneliness have also occasionally been split into various subcategories. However, there is less empirical work on these constructs than on depression. Furthermore, there is no evidence that the various subtypes of shyness and loneliness require substantially different theoretical treatment. Therefore, we focus on the general categories of shyness and loneliness, rather than on subtypes of each.

Interrelationships

We view shyness, loneliness, and depression as a highly interrelated set of problems. The three are interrelated at two different levels of analysis. At one level, they share many common etiological, preventive, and treatment features. For example, stressful environments and maladaptive attributional styles contribute to each problem. These common features, as well as distinctive ones, are discussed in greater detail in subsequent sections of the chapter.

At a second level of analysis, these problems are causally related to each other. For example, being shy has important implications for the development of loneliness and depression. Shy people avoid social interactions, mainly because they feel anxious in them. They typically display poor social skills when they are in social situations. As a result, they may have few solid social relationships and may become lonely individuals. Finally, the lack of social support and positive social interactions may well lead to depression.

In a similar way, depression can contribute to loneliness. Some depressed people repeatedly seek reassurance from their friends and family. After a while, such constant reassurance seeking may become so annoying that it harms the positive relationships that initially existed. In other words, depressed people sometimes drive away those who had been their best friends. This loss of social support can exacerbate the depression and create intense feelings of loneliness as well.

There has been relatively little empirical or theoretical work on the causal connections among shyness, loneliness, and depression. What work has been done is consistent with the model we present in Figure 1. This model displays what we believe to be the modal set of relations among these three problems in living. Note that we also believe that each of the three problems can, under some circumstances, have a causal impact on the other two, as the depression → loneliness example described earlier illustrates.

Shyness

In this model, shyness is seen as playing a causal role in the development of loneliness. Shy people have a hard time establishing and maintaining strong interpersonal relationships. The fear and anxiety that characterize shyness interfere with attempts to interact with others. The embarrassments and failures created by these poor attempts eventually lead shy people to avoid social encounters. If this pattern leads the shy person to have fewer social contacts than he or she desires, loneliness results.

Shyness can also have a causal effect on depression, both directly and indirectly through loneliness. We believe that the indirect effect is the more common one: Shyness interferes with the healthy development of satisfying interpersonal relationships, which in turn may lead to depression. The direct effect is probably weaker. The social failures and concomitant anxiety all produce negative affect and, hence, an increase in depression.

Loneliness

Loneliness itself can come about for a variety of reasons, some of which may have to do with the lonely person's interpersonal failures. The shyness route to loneliness is one such example. Social anxiety combined with poor social skills results in a meager social life that the person finds unacceptable. There are other routes to loneliness as well. Poor social skills, even in the absence of social anxiety, may yield loneliness rather than interpersonal satisfaction. Alternatively, the social environment may be such that there are few social options available—too few to prevent loneliness. For example, the new kid in school may be lonely because she lost all her friends when her family moved to a new city. It can be particularly hard to develop a new set of friends in the teen years because the social structure of classmates may already be firmly established. Other problematic situations arise for adults moving to new jobs and for people moving into retirement communities or nursing homes. Divorce and death are additional external sources of loneliness. Being clearly different from other people in one's environment may also hamper the formation of close inter-

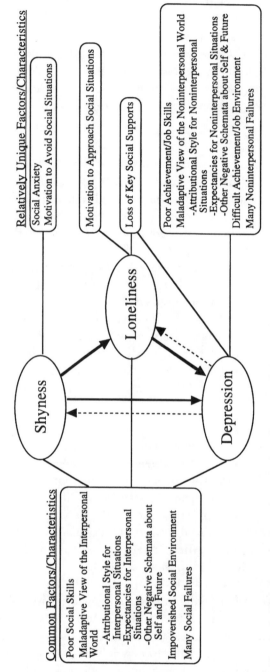

Figure 1. Relations among shyness, loneliness, and depression.

personal ties. Membership in a racial minority group and having some physical stigma are examples of conditions that can get in the way of the formation of new interpersonal relationships.

In many of these externally caused cases of loneliness, the problem may be temporary. If the person has good social skills, and if the environment has appropriate social opportunities, new interpersonal relationships may eventually develop. However, as we note in a later section, some of the motivational and affective consequences of loneliness may lead to a pattern of self-defeating behaviors that prevent resolution of the problem.

Regardless of the initial reason for the onset of loneliness, one possible consequence is depression. Indeed, one could create a category of depression that is specifically composed of those who are depressed primarily because of persistent loneliness. The lack of positive social reinforcers and dissatisfaction with one's interpersonal life produce the cognitive, affective, and behavioral states characteristic of depression.

Depression

The model includes interpersonal causes of depression (e.g., loneliness) as well as noninterpersonal causes of depression. Career setbacks and similar achievement-related failures can certainly cause a depressive episode to begin. Regardless of the initial source, however, the consequences of depression can serve to maintain and even expand the depression. As noted earlier, reassurance-seeking behavior patterns of depressed people can produce additional interpersonal problems (such as loneliness and shyness), even when the initial precipitating cause of depression had nothing to do with interpersonal relationships.

Treatments

We also focus on treatment implications of the shyness, loneliness, and depression models. In each problem, treatments vary as a function of the specific difficulties underlying the problem. For example, loneliness caused by poor social skills may be treated by assigning social skill acquisition tasks. Depression caused by the same type of loneliness may be treated in a similar manner, although complicating factors may require additional treatment elements.

Prevention

A thorough understanding of shyness, loneliness, and depression gives rise to implications for prevention. Use of proper parenting styles can lead to the acquisition of more adaptive attachment styles, which in turn encourage the development of strong social skills and relationships. Values training (e.g., Rokeach, 1973), at home, church, or school, can result in the development of a more adaptive set of values than the distorted "me first" perspective modeled in the mass media. (We are reminded of the challenge issued by John F. Kennedy in his inaugural address [January 20, 1961, Washington, DC] to "ask not what your country can do for you— ask what you can do for your country.") Other important suggestions for preventive interventions designed to improve the social functioning of those most at risk include modified classroom settings (e.g., jigsaw classroom; Aronson & Osherow, 1980; Aronson, Stephan, Sikes, Blaney, & Snapp, 1978), changes in housing design (e.g., Festinger, Schachter, & Back, 1950), and poverty reduction and employment programs.

In short, improving the social behaviors of people of all ages through training or education, through modifying the structure of social situations or of the physical environments in which social interactions occur, or by reducing of the stresses of poverty and parenthood can reduce the problems of shyness, loneliness, and depression. We turn now to a more detailed discussion of each of these problems in living.

A NOTE ON ATTRIBUTIONAL STYLE

In subsequent sections of this chapter, we outline characteristic features, major antecedents, typical consequences, and potential treatments for shyness, loneliness, and depression. One major antecedent factor and potential treatment target for each of these problems in living is a maladaptive attributional style. Because other authors represented in this volume discuss attributional style in some detail, we do not provide extensive coverage in this chapter. However, a brief word seems appropriate to aid readers in obtaining an overall view of shyness, loneliness, and depression.

For all three problems in living, the most common maladaptive attributional style is one in which the person attributes his or her failures to causes that are simultaneously uncontrollable, stable, and internal, such as poor social skills or personal worthlessness. Similarly, a shy, lonely, and depressed person tends to attribute his or her successes to causes that are simultaneously uncontrollable, unstable, and external, such as getting a lucky break.

One major difference between the characteristic maladaptive attributional styles of persons with these problems concerns the range of situations to which they apply. Shy and lonely people tend to have maladaptive attributional styles primarily for interpersonal situations, whereas depressed people display the same maladaptive attributional styles for interpersonal and noninterpersonal (e.g., achievement) situations (e.g., Anderson & Arnoult, 1985a, 1985b; Anderson, Miller, Riger, Dill, & Sedikides, 1994; Johnson, Petzel, & Johnson, 1991; Renshaw & Brown, 1993; Teglasi & Hoffman, 1982).

A final point to keep in mind while exploring these problems in living is that temporarily modifying people's attributional styles causes corresponding changes in their behavior. That is, inducing shy, lonely, or depressed people to make adaptive attributions for a particular event leads to behaviors that are indistinguishable from those of their nonshy, nonlonely, nondepressed counterparts, whereas inducing normal people to make the maladaptive attributions typical of shy, lonely, or depressed people makes them behave as if they were suffering from these problems in living (e.g., Anderson, Jennings, & Arnoult, 1988; Brodt & Zimbardo, 1981).

SHYNESS

Shy and proud men . . . are more liable than any others to fall into the hands of parasites and creatures of low character. For in the intimacies which are formed by shy men, they do not choose, but are chosen.
(From *The Statesman*, 1836, p. 76, Sir Henry Taylor [1800–1886], English author.)

As they have for many psychological constructs, researchers have struggled to gain a consensual definition of shyness. The conceptions that exist focus on different characteristics of shyness that different researchers believe to be most important. Buss (1980) referred to shyness as a form of social anxiety, or discomfort in the presence of others, akin to what most people feel when in the presence of an audience. Tomkins (1963), on the other hand, defined shyness as an aspect of the underlying fundamental emotion of shame. Cheek, Melchior, and Carpentieri (1986) proposed that shyness is "the tendency to feel tense, worried, or awkward during social interactions, especially with unfamiliar people" (p. 115). This account emphasizes the importance of anxiety in response to face-to-face social interactions; it emphasizes the feeling of shyness. Leary (1986) defined shyness as "an affective-behavioral syndrome characterized by social anxiety and interpersonal inhibition that results from the prospect or presence of interpersonal evaluation" (p. 30). Here, the importance of felt anxiety is joined by a behavioral dimension—one of inhibition and withdrawal. An additional hypothesized component to shyness is found within a description provided by van der Molen (1990). In his conception, shyness is distinguished by three important components:

1. Fear (a component similar to anxiety or arousal)
2. Social skills deficit (behavioral inhibition)

3. Irrational thoughts. The third component consists of unrealistically maladaptive attributions of past interpersonal failures and negative anticipations of future interpersonal performance.

All these definitions have in common one major motivational implication. The dominant motive in all cases is social avoidance. In other words, shy people are strongly motivated to avoid social interactions because of the anxiety and negative arousal experienced in such situations.

Each of the three hypothesized components of shyness has received some empirical support. Regarding the anxiety component, Cheek and Melchior (1990) reported that 40%–60% of shy high school and college students have trouble with multiple symptoms of anxiety. In addition, in a study in which shy women were asked to describe freely why they considered themselves shy, 38% listed at least one somatic anxiety symptom (Cheek & Watson, 1989).

The associated behavioral inhibition is an extremely common symptom of shyness. Pilkonis (1977a) described shy participants as speaking less frequently, allowing more silences to occur in the conversation, and breaking silences less often than nonshy participants. Awkward bodily movements, gaze aversion, and general social unresponsiveness are typical behavior patterns of shy individuals (Buss, 1984).

The percentage of shy people estimated to have cognitive symptoms ranges from 44% (Cheek & Watson, 1989) to 77% (Fatis, 1983). Whatever the frequency of the cognitive component embedded in the experience of shyness, the nature of these symptoms is fairly clear. Shy individuals, compared with nonshy individuals, exhibit a self-defeating attributional style in which positive self-relevant events are considered due to luck and other unstable characteristics, and negative self-relevant events are considered due to ability and other stable characteristics (Anderson & Arnoult, 1985a, 1985b; Arkin, Appelman, & Burger, 1980; Leary, Atherton, Hill, & Hur, 1986; Teglasi & Hoffman, 1982).

The fact that shyness can manifest itself acutely through any of the aforementioned three criteria has led to the proposition that there are different types of shyness. For instance, Pilkonis (1977b) defined the publicly shy as those for whom the behavioral component is most salient. In contrast, the privately shy are those who are most sensitive to the internal characteristics of shyness such as arousal and cognitive distortions. Although researchers have debated which of these three components predominates in the concept of shyness, it is generally agreed that all are necessary to circumscribe completely the boundaries of the concept. In general, these three components act together to form a modal interpersonal tendency toward anxiety, negative thinking, and behavioral awkwardness, which serves as a great motivator to avoid the presence of others.

Antecedents of Shyness

The causes of shyness are difficult to isolate, primarily because of the inherently correlational nature of relevant data. Cross-lagged panel designs and causal modeling have improved the understanding of correlational data but do not wholly solve the correlation–causation problem. The following section explores some potential antecedents of shyness and cites evidence, when available, of variables that may play a role in the etiology of shyness. At the least, the following variables seem to be concurrent predictors of shyness and have a role in its maintenance. They may also play causal roles in the development of shyness.

High Arousal and Anxiety (Especially Social)

As one of the three most accepted characteristics of shyness, anxiety may play some role in its etiology. Consider the likely developmental consequences of a constitutionally anxious child. At low levels of arousal, he or she is quite comfortable. However, the presence of others is a particularly arousing condition (Zajonc, 1965), especially if negative outcomes are expected (Geen, 1979) or a task to be accomplished in the presence of the audience is perceived as difficult (Smith, Baldwin, & Christenson, 1990). The child may perceive most interpersonal situations as overarousing or anxiety producing, and the behavioral result may be withdrawal from social situations.

Of course, if children repeatedly cope with overarousal by withdrawal, their interpersonal experiences will frequently be failures, and their interpersonal skills will have little opportunity to develop. Awareness of such failures only adds to the arousal until it blossoms into full-blown anxiety. After many such instances, the arousal, anxiety, cognitive distortions, and behavioral withdrawal patterns become what we call *shyness*. In brief, the low arousal threshold of those who are by temperament highly anxious can lead to the development of the full syndrome of shyness.

Recent evidence supports this basic line of reasoning. Eisenberg, Fabes, and Murphy (1995) showed shyness to be associated with high emotionality and empathic overarousal (or personal distress) and inversely related to attentional shifting. The authors interpreted these findings in the following manner: The empathic overarousal created by social situations is turned inward because the individual is poor at shifting his or her attention to the other. Repeated exposure to anxious self-preoccupation in social situations leads to the perception that such situations are generally aversive and are to be avoided. Stated in this manner, overarousal spirals into anxiety, which, over time, evolves into shyness.

In the shyness literature, it is common to find relationships between shyness and anxiety, specifically social anxiety (Eisenberg et al., 1995;

Lahey & Carlson, 1991; Lawton, Powell, Kleban, & Dean, 1993; Neto, 1992). Indeed, Anderson and Harvey (1988) showed that the most popular self-report measures of shyness and social anxiety are indistinguishable. One insight into the relationship between shyness and anxiety comes, somewhat unexpectedly, from research on sleep. Hartmann (1973) found that "long sleepers," individuals who consistently require more sleep than average, tended to be shy and showed considerable anxiety in an experimental interview. Hartmann added that "several consciously placed great value on sleep and even saw it as an escape from a somewhat painful waking life" (pp. 98–99). Some participants in Hartmann's study noted that they "value the isolation of sleep" or "sleep a lot to get away from things" (p. 99). Perhaps the drive for isolation or to "get away from things" is in the service of avoiding the anxiety that, for shy individuals, is a fundamental part of social existence.

Shy individuals do, indeed, tend to be prone to physiological arousal, especially when anticipating social interaction. Granger, Weiss, and Kauneckis (1994) found that neuroendocrine activity (i.e., cortisol increase) was associated with social withdrawal and social anxiety (referred to as *internalizing behavior problems*). Whether the neuroendocrine activity leads to social withdrawal and anxiety or the internalizing behavior problems lead to a reduced threshold for mildly stressful environmental events, arousal seems to play a role in the etiology and maintenance of shyness. Furthermore, Kagan and Snidman (1991) reported that physiological changes indicative of increased autonomic activity are characteristic of children who are prone to extreme withdrawal from unfamiliar social situations. The authors also reported that 15% of Caucasian children exhibit this pattern that is so stereotypical of shyness.

Because arousal plays such a major role in shyness, understanding factors that predispose to overarousal becomes important. Because arousal regulation is believed to have a biological basis (Kagan, Snidman, & Arcus, 1993; Larsen & Deiner, 1987; Plomin & Stocker, 1989; Rothbart & Derryberry, 1981), one would expect shyness to have a genetic component.

Genetic Component

Shyness has been considered one of the most heritable dimensions of temperament throughout the life span (Plomin & Daniels, 1986). Most of the research on the heritability of shyness has focused on its behavioral component. Behavioral inhibition has repeatedly been found to have a genetic or biological foundation for children, adolescents, and adults (Bell, Jasnoski, Kagan, & King, 1990; Kagan, Resnick, & Snidman, 1988; Kagan & Snidman, 1991; Matheny & Dolan, 1975; Plomin & Daniels, 1986; Plomin & Rowe, 1979). The 15% of Caucasian children mentioned earlier who exhibit behavioral withdrawal (Kagan & Snidman, 1991) appear to be stable in that characteristic over the first 7 years of life; they can even be identified at 24 months by their high levels of motor activity and crying to unfamiliar stimuli.

Bell et al. (1990) found that parents who suffer from panic disorder and depression have an unusually high incidence of shy children and that these children have a heightened sensitivity to allergies, especially hay fever. The latter finding is interpreted as a genetic correlate of shyness, indicating that the stable temperamental characteristic of shyness is found in those who also have a genetic susceptibility to nasal allergies. It is interesting to note that the shy participants of the Bell et al. study reported more anxiety than did the extroverted participants.

Much of the research on the genetic basis for shyness involves the study of monozygotic and dizygotic twins (Kagan et al., 1988; Matheny & Dolan, 1975; Plomin & Daniels, 1986; Plomin & Rowe, 1979). These investigators have found, in general, that genetically identical (monozygotic) twins are more similar to one another with regard to shyness than are genetically nonidentical (dizygotic) twins.

Poor Social Skills

In addition to arousal–anxiety as an antecedent to shyness, possessing poor social skills may also be important. The causal relationship between arousal and social skills is still unresolved; one possibility is that heightened arousal and anxiety coupled with internalizing behaviors (e.g., social withdrawal and social anxiety) merely reduce one's ability to learn social skills adequately. Alternatively, lacking adequate social skills (or even believing that one lacks social skills) may lead to heightened arousal when a social situation is encountered. Investigations into the role of arousal and anxiety in shyness often involve the participant's anticipation of a social interaction. Expectations of failure and perceptions of difficulty frequently lead to anxiety and arousal. Therefore, poor social skills (real or imagined) can exacerbate the arousal problems by increasing the perceived difficulty and risk of failure. In other words, poor social skills can be a cause and a consequence of maladaptive levels of arousal in social situations.

It is also possible that poor social skills alone lead to shyness. The behavioral inhibition component of shyness can, itself, be seen as a poor social skill. McCullough et al. (1994) reported that individuals who were overly submissive in social situations showed inhibited, introverted behaviors. To tease apart lack of social skills from behavioral inhibition and to show that the relative absence of social skills can lead to shyness, it would be important to locate previously nonshy individuals who, for some reason, have lost their ability to maintain adequate social skills and have, therefore, fallen into the state of shyness. Knutson and Lansing (1990) showed that lost social skills can lead to shyness in a study involving individuals who acquired profound hearing loss. They proposed that the typical relationship between hearing loss and psychological disturbance (Thomas, 1984) is mediated by personal or environmental variables or both:

> Among the personal attributes that could mediate the effect of acquired hearing loss on psychological functioning are the communication behaviors adopted by persons with a hearing loss and the degree to which those communication strategies meet their unique personal, occupational, and familial demands for communication. (p. 656)

Their results showed that the decline in communication skills following hearing loss led to social introversion, social anxiety, and even loneliness and depression.

Consequences of Shyness

The consequences of shyness are numerous. Some are relatively minor, such as feeling a bit awkward in novel social situations. Other consequences are so severe that they can cause major disruptions in all areas of one's life. A full description of these is beyond the scope of this chapter. Interested readers may refer to useful discussions by Leitenberg (1990), Pilkonis (1977a, 1977b), and Zimbardo (1977).

Shyness also has a major consequence that is particularly relevant to this chapter, namely, loneliness (Cheek & Busch, 1981; Ekkehard, Fäth, & Lamm, 1988; Kalliopuska & Laitinen, 1991; Moore & Schultz, 1983). In the following sections, we turn our focus from shyness to loneliness, which we discuss not only as a consequence of shyness but also as a diverse, potentially multidimensional problem with its own unique antecedents and consequences. We then turn our focus to depression, which is a major potential consequence of both shyness and loneliness.

LONELINESS

> The whole conviction of my life now rests upon the belief that loneliness, far from being a rare and curious phenomenon, peculiar to myself and to a few other solitary men, is the central and inevitable fact of human existence.
> (From *The Anatomy of Loneliness*, 1941 by Thomas Wolfe [1900–1938], American novelist.)

Like shyness, loneliness does not have a universally accepted definition (Horowitz, French, & Anderson, 1982; Ryan & Patterson, 1987). Andersson (1992) noted that there is disagreement on whether loneliness should be considered a unidimensional construct (e.g., a simple discrepancy between an individual's desired and obtained social contacts) or a multidimensional construct (e.g., dividing loneliness on distinct and separate dimensions). The unidimensional approach is exemplified in the work of Peplau and Perlman (1982), who described loneliness as the unpleasant experience that occurs when an individual's social network is deficient either qualitatively or quantitatively. The multidimensional view is espoused by Hsu, Hailey, and Range (1987), who described emotional loneliness (resulting from the absence of close personal attachments) as distinct from social loneliness (resulting from the absence of a social network). Blai (1989) suggested a similar distinction. On the basis of available research, it appears that loneliness is a multidimensional construct that can be reliably measured with a unidimensional scale, presumably because there is so much overlap in the various dimensions. The following definition provided by Rook (1984) is consistent with both sides of the dimensional issue: "Loneliness is defined as an enduring condition of emotional distress that arises when a person feels estranged from, misunderstood, or rejected by others and/or lacks appropriate social partners for desired activities, particularly activities that provide a sense of social integration and opportunities for emotional intimacy" (p. 1391).

All these definitions imply the same motivational state. Lonely people believe that they feel so bad because of insufficient interpersonal relationships. The insufficiency may be quantitative (e.g., too few friends), qualitative (e.g., no deeply intimate relationships), or both. In all cases, the dominant social motive is one of approach. Lonely people want more contacts, whereas shy people want to avoid social situations.

Approximately 26% of the population are lonely (Bradburn, 1969). In a more recent sample of undergraduate college students, Revenson (1981) reported that 51% sometimes felt lonely and 11% felt lonely often or most of the time. When they did feel lonely, 37% reported the intensity of their loneliness as severe. At any given time, one fourth of Americans feel painfully lonely (Ryan & Patterson, 1987). Adolescents are by far the loneliest subgroup of the population (Brage, Meredith, & Woodward, 1993; Ryan & Patterson, 1987). Loneliness has been considered to be distinct from aloneness, solitude, and grief (Ryan & Patterson, 1987). Like shyness, loneliness has a cognitive component (thinking one is separate and isolated from others), an affective component (negative feelings of sadness, anger, and depression), and a behavioral component (actions such as avoiding social contacts; Blai, 1989). It is interesting that the major features of a lonely person are a subset of the characteristic features of a depressed person (Horowitz et al., 1982).

Antecedents of Loneliness

Shyness

Shyness may lead to loneliness and therefore can be seen as a causal antecedent. Many researchers have reported a positive correlation between shyness and loneliness (e.g., Anderson & Harvey, 1988; Kalliopuska & Laitinen, 1991; Stephan, Fäth, & Lamm, 1988; Zimbardo, 1977). As one may expect because of its close relationship with shyness, social anxiety has also been found to be related to loneliness (Anderson & Harvey, 1988; Bruch, Kaflowitz, & Pearl, 1988; Neto, 1992). Jones, Rose, and Russell (1990) reported correlations between shyness and loneliness ranging from .40 to .51.

Cheek and Busch (1981) provided evidence that shyness causes loneliness. In their study, undergraduates completed a trait measure of shyness and a state measure of loneliness at both the beginning and the end of a spring semester course in introductory psychology. Although loneliness scores declined for both shy and nonshy individuals from the beginning to the end of the semester (presumably owing to habituation to the newness of the semester), shy participants were significantly lonelier than nonshy ones at both time periods. The findings were taken to indicate that both social situations, particularly novel ones, and personality characteristics, particularly shyness, contribute to the amount of loneliness an individual may experience.

The strong relationship between shyness and loneliness suggests that the two also share some causal antecedents. A review of the literature reveals that they do, indeed, share features that may contribute to their etiology—namely, anxiety, poor social skills, maladaptive attributional styles, and lack of social networks (e.g., loss of intimates).

High Anxiety (Especially Social)

A strong relationship has been found between loneliness and anxiety (Jones et al., 1990; Moore & Schultz, 1983; Ryan & Patterson, 1987), particularly social anxiety (Moore and Schultz, 1983; Neto, 1992). Moore and Schultz (1983) reported significant correlations between loneliness and both state and trait anxiety. As is usually the case in correlational studies, the direction of causality between loneliness and social anxiety is unclear. However, the results of Moore and Schultz (1983) indicated that high social anxiety is one factor that interferes with the ability to initiate and maintain contacts with others, resulting in loneliness.

Poor Social Skills

A great deal of attention has been devoted to the relationship between loneliness and social skills. As one would expect, lonely people are less socially skilled (Horowitz et al., 1982; Inderbitzen-Pisuruk, Clark, & Solano, 1992; Kalliopuska & Laitinen, 1991; Moore & Schultz, 1983; Stephan et al., 1988), display more withdrawn and inhibited social behaviors (Renshaw & Brown, 1993; Rubin, LeMare, & Lollis, 1990), are less willing to take social risks (Moore & Schultz, 1983), and are less willing to assert their rights to others (Bruch et al., 1988).

Some researchers have explored the direction of causation between loneliness and poor social skills, with fairly consistent results. For instance, Renshaw and Brown (1993) conducted a 1-year longitudinal study of children and found that withdrawn social behavior was a significant predictor of concurrent and future loneliness. Their interpretation was that possession of poor social skills lessens the ability to create needed friendship networks, a condition conducive to loneliness. Rubin et al. (1990) reported similar results. Moore and Schultz (1983) replicated these findings with an adolescent sample. They found that the low social risk-taking characteristic of lonely adolescents impedes initiation of social contacts. Peplau and Perlman (1979) made the following clear statement on the matter: "Individual characteristics that make it difficult for a person to establish or maintain satisfactory relationships may increase the likelihood of loneliness" (p. 103).

Lack of Social Networks–Loss of Intimates

Blai (1989) reported two additional and interrelated conditions that can lead to loneliness. One factor is the feeling of not belonging to a community; the other is the absence of an attachment figure. He also cited specific social situations that can lead to loneliness such as the ending of a marriage, friendship breakups, unemployment, retirement, imprisonment, and hospitalization. Both of the identified factors have empirical support. Loneliness has been linked to many facets of community involvement and acceptance, such as deficits in quality and quantity of social networks (Levin & Stokes, 1986), dissatisfaction with social contacts and with a steady partner (Ekkehard et al., 1988), and low peer acceptance with few or no friendships in adolescence (Renshaw & Brown, 1993). In fact, Levin and Stokes (1986) reported that lack of social networks partially mediated the relationship between introversion and loneliness.

Kivett (1979) found that inadequate transportation and unavailability of organized social activity were among the best predictors of loneliness in older adults. Inadequate transportation was also found by Berg, Mellstrom, and Persons (1981, cited in Ryan & Patterson, 1987) to be a correlate of loneliness, presumably because it has implications for the ability to maintain social contacts. Patients with chronic obstructive pulmonary disease and their caregivers have reported heightened feelings of loneliness as a result of the social separation that the disease causes for both (Keele-Card, Foxall, & Barron, 1993).

Townshend (1955) found that loneliness in old age is related more strongly to desolation, defined as recent separation from a loved one, than to isolation. Such a loss, whether due to death or divorce, can be devastating to one's psychological well-being. Both Townshend (1955) and Kivett (1979) listed widowhood among the conditions most related to loneliness in older adults.

Consequences of Loneliness

The consequences of loneliness, like those of shyness, are numerous, ranging from relatively minor to severely debilitating, and a discussion is beyond the scope of this chapter. Interested readers may consult useful discussions by Blai (1989), Peplau and Goldston (1984), and Peplau and Perlman (1982).

Loneliness also may serve as a factor in depression (e.g., G. W. Brown & Harris, 1978; Joiner, in press; Krietman, 1977). In the following section, we focus on depression, discussing its antecedents (including shyness and loneliness) and consequences.

DEPRESSION

If there is hell upon earth, it is to be found in a melancholy man's heart.
(From *The Anatomy of Melancholy*, 1621 by Robert Burton [1577–1640], English clergyman.)

Of the psychological problems discussed in this chapter, depression is the most severe and the most debilitating. Approximately 15% of the U.S. population show significant depressive symptoms at any given time (Secunda, 1973). Depression is a dysphoric mood state accompanied by a loss of enthusiasm, a general slowing of mental and physical activity, and a set of negative cognitive distortions (e.g., Beck, 1976). Other features include anger (Quiggle, Garber, Panak, & Dodge, 1992), anxiety, and unassertiveness (Nezu, Nezu, & Nezu, 1986). Although depression is related to loneliness and shyness (rs = .42 and .30, respectively; Anderson & Harvey, 1988), the three conditions are considered to be separate entities with somewhat different characteristics (Anderson & Harvey, 1988; Seligson, 1983; Weeks, Michela, Peplau, & Bragg, 1980; Weiss, 1973). For instance, loneliness is characterized by the emotion of longing, shyness by anxiety and embarrassment, and depression by sadness and anger. The lonely individual attempts to alleviate loneliness by forming relationships, whereas the depressed individual surrenders to the distress (Weiss, 1973). The shy individual is motivated to avoid social situations. All three constructs are stable across time (e.g., Plomin & Daniels, 1986; Weeks et al., 1980).

A review of the voluminous depression literature reveals several primary antecedents. Among these are shyness and loneliness, lack of social support, self-focusing, maladaptive attributional style, and, perhaps most important, cognitive distortions. Following is a discussion of the various etiological pathways to depression.

Antecedents of Depression

Shyness and Loneliness

Certainly, shyness, loneliness, and depression have much in common. All are associated with higher than normal levels of anxiety. As we noted previously concerning shyness and loneliness, all are associated with poor social networks and a disproportionately high attendance to negative information. These similarities are more than simple coincidence; there are causal links among the conditions.

Many researchers have found a link between depression and shyness (Alfano, Joiner, Perry, & Metalsky, 1994; Anderson & Arnoult, 1985a, 1985b; Anderson & Harvey, 1988; Traub, 1983) as well as between depression and loneliness (Andersson, 1985; Jackson & Cochran, 1991; Mullins & Dugan, 1990; Yang & Clum, 1994). Although some consider neither loneliness nor depression to be a direct cause of the other (Weeks et al., 1980), others have found that lonely and isolated people tend to be vulnerable to depression (Brown & Harris, 1978; Krietman, 1977; Rich & Bonner, 1987), that loneliness at the beginning of a semester predicted depression later in the semester (Rich & Scovel, 1987), and that experiencing feelings of loneliness at one point in time is significantly related to depression 3 years later (Green et al., 1992).

Cognitive Complexity, Attention to Negative Information, and Self-Focusing

Several additional cognitive phenomena are associated strongly enough with depression to deserve special mention. Depressed individuals, especially those who are moderately depressed, are highly motivated to process attributional information (Flett, Pliner, & Blankenstein, 1989; Kammer, 1983, 1984; Quiggle et al., 1992), particularly negative information (Weiner, 1985). This pattern holds for both hypothetical (McCaul, 1983) and real failures (Kammer, 1984) and for failures in achievement (Kammer, 1983) and interpersonal arenas (Rich & Bonner, 1987). According to Mullins, Seigel, and Hodges (1985), although a group of depressed children generated as many relevant solutions to hypothetical interpersonal problems as did nondepressed children, the depressed group generated more irrelevant solutions as well. Weary et al. (1993) found this effect, even when the attribution task involved attributions other than self-attributions. These findings are consistent with the reasoning of Pittman and Pittman (1980), who suggested that lack of control motivates attributional thinking. It stands to reason (and has been demonstrated empirically by Kaslow, Rehm, Pollack, & Siegel, 1988) that depressed individuals have chronic feelings of uncontrollability.

Another cognitive phenomenon associated with depression is that depressed individuals disproportionately attend to negative information in general (Quiggle et al., 1992). Hammen and Zupan (1984) found that depressed children, compared with nondepressed children, endorsed and recalled more negative and fewer positive self-referent words. Depressed individuals also were found to espouse a hostile attributional bias, perceiving a hostile intent in the actions of others (Quiggle et al., 1992).

Depressed people also engage in more self-focused thought in the face of negative events than nondepressed people. Ingram, Cruet, Johnson, and Wisnicki (1988) reported a positive relationship between the amount of self-focus and negative affect. There is even evidence that depressed individuals avoid self-focus in the face of success (Pyszczynski & Greenberg, 1986), unfortunately suggesting that depressed individuals are made deeply and personally uncomfortable by the idea that they have done a good thing. Pyszczynski and Greenberg (1986) stated that this self-focusing plays an important role in the development and maintenance of depression and that self-focusing can explain, at least in part, the motivational and performance deficits associated with depression.

Given the tendency for depressed individuals to engage in more attributional processing, and for that processing to be not only negative in general but also negatively self-focused, it is easy to see how these factors work together in maintaining a pernicious depressogenic attributional style that could be both the cause of the depression and a maintaining factor. Quiggle et al. (1992) summed up their findings, as well as the findings of several other researchers, in the following manner:

> Taken together, these findings depict a depressive cognitive pattern of attending to negative cues in the environment, interpreting the negative events as being due to global and stable factors, either of the world or of the self, generating irrelevant means of solving problems, expecting to be ineffective in changing the situation to a more desirable one, and ultimately interacting less with others. (p. 222)

Social Support

As in the research on loneliness, much attention has been given to the role of social support in the maintenance and etiology of depression. Depressed individuals report having fewer social contacts and a less self-affirming social environment, are likely to be less sociable and more interpersonally submissive (McCullough et al., 1994), and report a lack of confiding relationships (Eisemann, 1985). In fact, lack of close, confiding relationships is a well-established vulnerability factor for depression (Bebbington, Sturt, Tennant, & Hurry, 1984; G. W. Brown & Harris, 1978).

Depressive symptoms are also associated with loneliness, social isolation, retirement, and loss of close partners or relatives (Müller-Spahn & Hock, 1994), all conditions in which an individual's social networks are compromised. In line with other research that has shown an increased risk of depression in caregivers of patients with Alzheimer's disease (Crook & Miller, 1985; Eisdorfer, Kennedy, Wisnieski, & Cohen, 1983), George and Gwyther (1984, cited in Kiecolt-Glaser et al., 1987) found that the caregivers of patients with Alzheimer's disease reported decreased well-being when their caregiving interfered with their ability to maintain an active social life. Conversely, Rich and Bonner (1987) showed that social support, especially family support, served as a buffer on the effects of life stress on depression. The reality that humans are social animals is reflected in the debilitating effects of the removal of social support and in the buffering effects of its presence.

An objective social deficit is not the only aspect of social support that has implications for vulnerability to depression. An individual may experience dejection if his or her expectations for social support are greater than the level that is realized. Even an ample supply of social support can be seen as a deficit if one's expectations are too high. Indeed, vulnerability to depression is associated with abnormally high expectations for support (Beck, Rush, Shaw, & Emery, 1979) and an unexpected lack of support in times of crisis (Neeleman & Power, 1994).

Regarding the role of social support in the etiology of depression, Eisemann (1985) found that, prior to a depressive episode, depressed patients reported fewer activities involving other people than did individuals who did not become depressed. Bonner and Rich (1987; Rich & Bonner, 1987) have provided evidence that social support moderates the relationship between life stress and depression, and Barnett and Gotlib (1988) showed that, even when the effects of concurrent symptoms are controlled, low social integration may be involved in the etiology of depression. Leary (1990) also concluded that, although not all depression is caused by social exclusion, social exclusion generally causes depression.

Consequences of Depression

The consequences of depression in everyday life are too numerous to mention. They range from impaired job performance to suicide to aggression. Interested readers are referred to any current textbook on abnormal psychology (e.g., Barlow & Durand, 1995). However, one potential consequence of particular relevance to the current chapter is that depression may lead to loneliness and even shyness. Although depression is more likely to be caused by loneliness than the reverse, it is possible that a depressive reaction to a noninterpersonal stressor (e.g., job loss, financial problems) will put a strain on interpersonal relationships and lead to loneliness. In fact, Essex, Klein, Lohr, and Benjamin (1985) and Young (1982) have suggested that the cognitive negativity associated with depression may make the negative aspects of an individual's interpersonal relationships more salient, leading the individual to feel lonely. Persistent loneliness may cause one to develop a strained interpersonal style, which may ultimately lead to shyness.

TREATMENT OF SHYNESS, LONELINESS, AND DEPRESSION

Shyness

The treatment of shyness, loneliness, and depression should attack the underlying causes of each condition. Therefore, according to the material presented in this chapter, shyness may be especially amenable to treatments that lower feelings of anxiety and increase social skills. The treatment literature on shyness is consistent with these suggestions. For instance, Girodo, Dotzenroth, and Stein (1981) suggested that social skills training may be effective for overcoming shyness. Their contention is not that shy individuals lack social skills but rather that they need to be shown that successful social outcomes are contingent on their ability. Of course, social skills training would add to one's repertoire of social abilities; however, as Girodo et al. suggested, awareness that the application of these abilities can produce successful interpersonal exchanges can increase one's self-confidence and self-esteem while lowering social anxiety. Another suggestion for the treatment of shyness includes a combination of social skills training with cognitive restructuring and systematic desensitization (Cheek & Melchior, 1990).

Kelly and Keaten (1992) addressed the effectiveness of a behavioral modification program developed at Pennsylvania State University (PSU) known as the PSU Reticence Program. The program was designed as a treatment of reticence; individuals who are reticent avoid social situations because they feel unable to perform competently. The program does not directly attempt to reduce feelings of anxiety or apprehension in interpersonal situations. Rather, it focuses on changing reticent behavior through goal setting. Under the specific instruction that individuals adapt to the listener and take his or her perspective (an act usually omitted by shy, lonely, and depressed individuals), participants set goals, make specific plans for goal completion, and evaluate their performance. Kelly and Keaten (1992) showed the PSU Reticence Program to be more effective in reducing self-reported shyness and communication apprehension than either no treatment at all (a control group) or a performance-based public speaking course.

Loneliness

The literature on the treatment of loneliness indicates the effectiveness of training in social skills and cognitive restructuring and of providing situations that encourage the formation of friendship bonds (Blai, 1989; Brage et al., 1993; Seligson, 1983; Weeks, 1994). Because lonely individuals tend to have poor social skills (Chelune, Sultan, & Williams, 1980; Horowitz et al., 1982), teaching them to be more assertive (Blai, 1989), encouraging them to take social risks (a behavior that lonely individuals avoid; Moore & Schultz, 1983), and increasing their repertoire of appropriate interpersonal skills may prove useful in reducing their loneliness (Seligson, 1983; Weeks, 1994).

As mentioned earlier in this chapter, lonely individuals evince a negative pattern of thinking, both about themselves and about the intentions of others. For this reason, cognitive therapy may relieve the condition of loneliness. Beck et al. (1979) suggested that modification of dysfunctional beliefs and self-defeating thought patterns is an effective treatment for loneliness. Other researchers have concurred with this strategy (Blai, 1989; Brage et al., 1993; Rich & Bonner, 1987). However, cognitive therapy should target the alleviation of loneliness and not simply make one cognitively adept at coping with the problem. Therapy should not assist in the endurance of an unwanted problem but rather in the mitigation of it (e.g., Rook, 1984).

One of the most cited methods of reducing loneliness is establishing an environment that encourages the development of social contacts. Specifically, interventions should foster social support (Brage et al., 1993), provide enhanced opportunities for social contacts (Blai, 1989), and be directed at improving the lonely individual's links with others by providing settings where friendships may be easily formed (Weeks, 1994). Loneliness in older adults, therefore, could be somewhat relieved by placement in a residential setting where the individual's social network is facilitated by the proximity of neighbors and the establishment of apartment-sponsored activities (Mullins & Dugan, 1990). Seligson (1983) added that these activities should be noncompetitive in nature, such as volunteer work in hospitals and schools or perhaps group therapy, which provides multiple contacts with peers.

In addition to treatments that focus on loneliness per se, the implementation of a shyness clinic has been a suggestion for combating loneliness (Weeks, 1994). Because shyness serves as an antecedent to loneliness, an effective shyness clinic could also prevent loneliness. Of course, not everyone who is lonely became so because of preexisting shyness. However, the strong relationship between shyness and loneliness suggests that any treatment that is effective in reducing shyness should be examined for possible value as a treatment for loneliness.

Finally, research from several domains has shown that the physical structure of living environments (e.g., dormitories) has a significant impact on the frequency and quality of social interactions (Baum & Davis, 1980; Evans, Lepore, & Schroeder, 1996).

Depression

Because depression is considered the worst problem of the three discussed in this chapter, it follows that greater attention has been devoted to its treatment. Like the proposed treatments for shyness and loneliness, the proposed treatments for depression are consistent with the causes described in this chapter. Cognitive therapies, social skills training, and additional social support are most often cited for the alleviation of depression. Drug therapies are also a viable option, although, as we show, they are in some instances inferior to therapies that correct the distorted cognitions so prevalent in depressed patients.

Although they are not widely supported with empirical data, social support (Rich & Bonner, 1987) and social skills training (Bellack, Hersen, & Himmelhoch, 1980) have been proposed as treatments to depression. Rich and Bonner (1987) put forth the reasonable assertion that for those whose depression is at least partially caused by the lack of a social support network or the lack of social skills, group therapy may be especially useful. In the surroundings of a group, a social network is supplied, as is the opportunity both to learn and to apply newly acquired interpersonal skills.

By far the most common problem area that is targeted in treating depressed patients is their pronounced tendency toward distorted cognitions. Many researchers have advocated the use of therapies that revise the maladaptive nature of depressed individuals' attributions (Abramson, Seligman, & Teasdale, 1978; Anderson & Arnoult, 1985a; Beck et al., 1979; Foersterling, 1985; Helm, 1984; Miller & Norman, 1981). Especially important to such cognitive therapies is the dimension of control (Abramson et al., 1978; Anderson & Arnoult, 1985a; Anderson et al., 1994; Bandura, 1977; Beck et al., 1979). Firth-Cozens and Brewin (1988) found that both interpersonal therapy and cognitive–behavioral therapy had a significant impact on attributions in general but that the greatest impact was on the controllability dimension.

The usefulness of therapies that implement changes in the depressed individual's attributional style is clear. For instance, the effectiveness of psychotherapy does not differ from the effectiveness of psychotherapy combined with medication (Seligman, 1995). In addition, cognitive therapy rivaled antidepressant medication (i.e., imipramine) in the alleviation of depressive symptoms and resulted in a significantly lower dropout rate (Rush, Beck, Kovacs, & Hollon, 1977).

Rich and Bonner (1989) also suggested that because depression is a multidimensional problem, it should be treated with a multimodal strategy. The assessment of depression should be broad and able to individualize the root cause of an individual's depression. Therapy should then be tailored to the particular deficiency, whether it be the cultivating of interpersonal skills or the provision of an environment conducive to social bonds.

CONCLUSION

We have attempted to integrate the vast literatures on shyness, loneliness, and depression at several different levels. The overlap in causal factors as well as in treatments reflects the overlap between these three everyday problems in living. Additional research is needed on numerous aspects of our model of shyness, loneliness, and depression. For instance, additional work on the causal mechanisms involved in the link between loneliness and depression is needed. It also is important to examine these relationships for different subpopulations, such as adults, adolescents, and children. Great strides have been made in the last 20 years in understanding and treating depression, loneliness, and shyness, but a complete understanding is still some distance away. We hope that our synthesis aids others in the journey toward better understanding.

REFERENCES

Abramson, L. Y., Seligman, M. E. P., & Teasdale, J. D. (1978). Learned helplessness in humans: Critique and reformulation. *Journal of Abnormal Psychology, 87*, 49–74.

Alfano, M. S., Joiner, T. E., Perry, M., & Metalsky, G. I. (1994). Attributional style: A mediator of the shyness-depression relationship? *Journal of Research in Personality, 28*, 287–300.

Anderson, C. A., Anderson, K. B., & Deuser, W. E. (1996). Examining an affective aggression framework: Weapon and temperature effects on aggressive thoughts, affect, and attitudes. *Personality and Social Psychology Bulletin, 22*, 366–376.

Anderson, C. A., & Arnoult, L. H. (1985a). Attributional models of depression, loneliness, and shyness. In J. Harvey & G. Weary (Eds.), *Attribution: Basic issues and applications* (pp. 235–279). New York: Academic Press.

Anderson, C. A., & Arnoult, L. H. (1985b). Attributional style and everyday problems in living: Depression, loneliness, and shyness [Special issue: Depression]. *Social Cognition, 3*, 16–35.

Anderson, C. A., & Harvey, R. J. (1988). Discriminating between problems in living: An examination of measures of depression, loneliness, shyness, and social anxiety. *Journal of Social and Clinical Psychology, 6*, 482–491.

Anderson, C. A., Jennings, D. L., & Arnoult, L. H. (1988). Validity and utility of the attributional style construct at a moderate level of specificity. *Journal of Personality and Social Psychology, 55*, 979–990.

Anderson, C. A., Miller, R. S., Riger, A. L., Dill, J. C., & Sedikides, C. (1994). Behavioral and characterological attributional styles as predictors of depression and loneliness: Review, refinement, and test. *Journal of Personality and Social Psychology, 66*, 549–558.

Andersson, L. (1985). Loneliness, birth order and social loss among a group of elderly women. *Journal of Psychosomatic Research, 29*, 33–42.

Andersson, L. (1992). Loneliness and perceived responsibility and control in elderly community residents. *Journal of Social Behavior and Personality, 7*, 431–443.

Arkin, R. M., Appelman, A. J., & Burger, J. M. (1980). Social anxiety, self-presentation, and the self-serving bias in causal attribution. *Journal of Personality and Social Psychology, 38*, 23–35.

Aronson, E., & Osherow, N. (1980). Cooperation, prosocial behavior, and academic performance: Experiments in the desegregated classroom. In L. Bickman (Ed.), *Applied social psychology annual* (Vol. 1, pp. 163–196). Beverly Hills, CA: Sage.

Aronson, E., Stephan, C., Sikes, J., Blaney, N., & Snapp, M. (1978). *The jigsaw classroom*. Beverly Hills, CA: Sage.

Bandura, A. (1977). Self-efficacy: Toward a unifying theory of behavioral change. *Psychological Review, 84*, 191–215.

Barlow, D. H., & Durand, V. M. (1995). *Abnormal psychology: An integrative approach*. Pacific Grove, CA: Brooks/Cole.

Barnett, P. A., & Gotlib, I. H. (1988). Psychosocial functioning and depression: Distinguishing among antecedents, concomitants, and consequences. *Psychological Bulletin, 104*, 97–126.

Baum, A., & Davis, G. E. (1980). Reducing the stress of high-density living: An architectural intervention. *Journal of Personality and Social Psychology, 38*, 471–481.

Bebbington, P., Sturt, E., Tennant, C., & Hurry, J. (1984). Misfortune and resilience: A community study of women. *Psychological Medicine, 14*, 347–363.

Beck, A. T. (1976). *Cognitive therapy and the emotional disorders*. New York: International Universities Press.

Beck, A. T., Rush, A. J., Shaw, B., & Emery, G. (1979). *Cognitive therapy of depression*. New York: Guilford Press.

Bell, I. R., Jasnoski, M. L., Kagan, J., & King, D. S. (1990). Is allergic rhinitis more frequent in young adults with extreme shyness? A preliminary survey. *Psychosomatic Medicine, 52*, 517–525.

Bellack, A. S., Hersen, M., & Himmelhoch, J. (1980). Social skills training for depression: A treatment manual. *Catalog of Selected Documents in Psychology, 10*, 92.

Berkowitz, L. (1993). *Aggression: Its causes, consequences, and control*. New York: McGraw-Hill.

Blai, B. (1989). Health consequences of loneliness: A review of the literature. *Journal of American College Health, 37,* 162–167.

Bonner, R. L., & Rich, A. R. (1987). Toward a predictive model of suicidal ideation and behavior: Some preliminary data in college students. *Suicide and Life Threatening Behavior, 17,* 50–63.

Bradburn, N. (1969). *The structure of psychological well-being*. Chicago: Aldine.

Brage, D., Meredith, W., & Woodward, J. (1993). Correlates of loneliness among Midwestern adolescents. *Adolescence, 28,* 685–693.

Brodt, S. E., & Zimbardo, P. G. (1981). Modifying shyness-related social behavior through symptom misattribution. *Journal of Personality and Social Psychology, 41,* 437–449.

Brown, B. (1974, April 29). Depression roundup. *Behavior Today, 5,* 117.

Brown, G. W., & Harris, T. (1978). *Social origins of depression: A study of psychological disorder in women*. New York: Free Press.

Bruch, M. A., Kaflowitz, N. G., & Pearl, L. (1988). Mediated and nonmediated relationships of personality components to loneliness. *Journal of Social and Clinical Psychology, 6,* 346–355.

Buss, A. (1980). *Self-consciousness and social anxiety*. New York: Freeman.

Buss, A. (1984). A conception of shyness. In J. A. Daly & J. C. McCroskey (Eds.), *Avoiding communication: Shyness, reticence, and communication apprehension* (pp. 39–49). Beverly Hills, CA: Sage.

Cheek, J. M., & Busch, C. M. (1981). The influence of shyness on loneliness in a new situation. *Personality and Social Psychology Bulletin, 7,* 572–577.

Cheek, J. M., & Melchior, L. A. (1990). Shyness, self-esteem, and self-consciousness. In H. Leitenberg (Ed.), *Handbook of social evaluation anxiety* (pp. 47–82). New York: Plenum Press.

Cheek, J. M., Melchior, L. A., & Carpentieri, A. M. (1986). Shyness and self-concept. In L. M. Hartman & K. R. Blankstein (Eds.), *Perception of self in emotional disorder and psychotherapy* (pp. 113–131). New York: Plenum Press.

Cheek, J. M., & Watson, A. K. (1989). The definition of shyness: Psychological imperialism or construct validity? *Journal of Social Behavior and Personality, 4,* 85–95.

Chelune, G., Sultan, F., & Williams, C. (1980). Loneliness, self-disclosure and interpersonal effectiveness. *Journal of Counseling Psychology, 27,* 462–468.

Crook, T. H., & Miller, N. E. (1985). The challenge of Alzheimer's disease. *American Psychologist, 40,* 1245–1250.

Eisdorfer, C., Kennedy, G., Wisnieski, W., & Cohen, D. (1983). Depression and attributional style in families coping with the stress of caring for a relative with Alzheimer's disease. *Gerontologist, 23,* 115–116.

Eisemann, M. (1985). Depressed patients and non-psychiatric controls: Discriminant analysis on social environment variables. *Acta Psychiatrica Scandinavica*, *71*, 495–498.

Eisenberg, N., Fabes, R. A., & Murphy, B. C. (1995). Relations of shyness and low sociability to regulation and emotionality. *Journal of Personality and Social Psychology*, *68*, 505–517.

Ekkehard, S., Fäth, M., & Lamm, H. (1988). Loneliness as related to various personality and environmental measures: Research with the German adaptation of the UCLA Loneliness Scale. *Social Behavior and Personality*, *16*, 169–174.

Essex, M. J., Klein, M. H., Lohr, M. J., & Benjamin, L. S. (1985). Intimacy and depression in older women. *Psychiatry*, *48*, 159–178.

Evans, G. W., Lepore, S. J., & Schroeder, A. (1996). The role of interior design elements in human responses to crowding. *Journal of Personality and Social Psychology*, *70*, 41–46.

Fatis, M. (1983). Degree of shyness and self-reported physiological, behavioral, and cognitive reactions. *Psychological Reports*, *52*, 351–354.

Festinger, L., Schachter, S., & Back, K. (1950). *Social pressures in informal groups: A study of human factors in housing*. Stanford, CA: Stanford University Press.

Firth-Cozens, J., & Brewin, C. R. (1988). Attributional change during psychotherapy. *British Journal of Clinical Psychology*, *27*, 47–54.

Flett, G. L., Pliner, P., & Blankenstein, K. R. (1989). Depression and components of attributional complexity. *Journal of Personality and Social Psychology*, *56*, 757–764.

Foersterling, F. (1985). Attributional retraining: A review. *Psychological Bulletin*, *98*, 495–512.

Geen, R. G. (1979). Effects of being observed on learning following success and failure experiences. *Motivation and Emotion*, *3*, 355–371.

Geen, R. G. (1990). *Human aggression*. Pacific Grove, CA: Brooks/Cole.

Girodo, M., Dotzenroth, S. E., & Stein, S. J. (1981). Causal attribution bias in shy males: Implications for self-esteem and self-confidence. *Cognitive Therapy and Research*, *5*, 325–338.

Granger, D. A., Weiss, J. R., & Kauneckis, D. (1994). Neuroendocrine reactivity, internalizing behavior problems, and control-related cognitions in clinic-referred children and adolescents. *Journal of Abnormal Psychology*, *103*, 259–266.

Green, B. H., Copeland, J. R. M., Dewey, M. E., Sharma, V., Saunders, P. A., Davidson, I. A., Sullivan, C., & McWilliam, C. (1992). Risk factors for depression in elderly people: A prospective study. *Acta Psychiatrica Scandinavica*, *86*, 213–217.

Hammen, C., & Zupan, B. A. (1984). Self-schemas, depression, and social problem solving and social competence in preadolescents: Is inconsistency the hobgoblin of little minds? *Cognitive Therapy and Research*, *9*, 685–702.

Hartmann, E. (1973). Sleep requirement: Long sleepers, short sleepers, variable sleepers, and insomniacs. *Psychosomatics*, *14*, 95–103.

Helm, S. B. (1984). Nursing care of the depressed patient: A cognitive approach. *Perspectives in Psychiatric Care, 22,* 100–107.

Horowitz, L. M., French, R., & Anderson, C. A. (1982). The prototype of a lonely person. In L. Peplau & D. Perlman (Eds.), *Loneliness: A sourcebook of current theory, research, and therapy* (pp. 183–205). New York: Wiley.

Hsu, L. R., Hailey, B. J., & Range, L. M. (1987). Cultural and emotional components of loneliness and depression. *Journal of Psychology, 121,* 61–70.

Inderbitzen-Pisuruk, H., Clark, M. L., & Solano, C. H. (1992). Correlates of loneliness in midadolescence. *Journal of Youth and Adolescence, 21,* 151–167.

Ingram, R. E., Cruet, D., Johnson, B. R., & Wisnicki, K. S. (1988). Self-focused attention and depression: Self-evaluation, affect, and life stress. *Motivation and Emotion, 9,* 381–389.

Jackson, J., & Cochran, S. D. (1991). Loneliness and psychological distress. *Journal of Psychology, 125,* 257–262.

Johnson, J. M., Petzel, T. P., & Johnson, J. E. (1991). Attributions of shy persons in affiliation and achievement situations. *Journal of Psychology, 125,* 51–58.

Joiner, T. E. (in press). Shyness as diathesis, low social support as stress, and loneliness as mediator: Testing an interpersonal-personality view of vulnerability to depression. *Journal of Abnormal Psychology.*

Jones, W. H., Rose, J., & Russell, D. (1990). Loneliness and social anxiety. In H. Leitenberg (Ed.), *Handbook of social evaluation anxiety* (pp. 247–266). New York: Plenum Press.

Kagan, J., Resnick, J. S., & Snidman, N. (1988, April). Biological bases of childhood shyness. *Science, 240,* 167–171.

Kagan, J., & Snidman, N. (1991). Temperamental factors in human development. *American Psychologist, 46,* 856–862.

Kagan, J., Snidman, N., & Arcus, D. (1993). On the temperamental categories of inhibited and uninhibited children. In K. H. Rubin & J. B. Asendorpf (Eds.), *Social withdrawal, inhibition, and shyness* (pp. 19–28). Hillsdale, NJ: Erlbaum.

Kalliopuska, M., & Laitinen, M. (1991). Loneliness related to self-concept. *Psychological Reports, 69,* 27–34.

Kammer, D. (1983). Depression, attributional style, and failure generalization. *Cognitive Therapy and Research, 7,* 413–423.

Kammer, D. (1984). Attributional processing style differences in depressed and nondepressed individuals. *Motivation and Emotion, 8,* 211–220.

Kaslow, N. J., Rehm, L. P., Pollack, S. L., & Siegel, A. W. (1988). Attributional style and self-control behavior in depressed and nondepressed children and their parents. *Journal of Abnormal Child Psychology, 16,* 163–175.

Keele-Card, G., Foxall, M. J., & Barron, C. R. (1993). Loneliness, depression, and social support of patients with COPD and their spouses. *Public Health Nursing, 10,* 245–251.

Kelly, L., & Keaten, J. (1992). A test of the effectiveness of the reticence program at the Pennsylvania State University. *Communication Education, 41,* 361–374.

Kiecolt-Glaser, J. K., Glaser, R., Shuttleworth, E. C., Dyer, C. S., Ogrocki, P., & Speicher, C. E. (1987). Chronic stress and immunity in family caregivers of Alzheimer's disease victims. *Psychosomatic Medicine, 49,* 523–535.

Kivett, V. R. (1979). Discriminators of loneliness among the rural elderly: Implications for intervention. *Gerontologist, 19,* 108–115.

Knutson, J. F., & Lansing, C. R. (1990). The relationship between communication problems and psychological difficulties in persons with profound acquired hearing loss. *Journal of Speech and Hearing Disorders, 55,* 656–664.

Krietman, N. (Ed.). (1977). *Parasuicide.* London: Wiley.

Lahey, B. B., & Carlson, C. L. (1991). Validity of the diagnostic category of attention deficit disorder without hyperactivity: A review of the literature. *Journal of Learning Disabilities, 24,* 110–120.

Larsen, R. J., & Deiner, E. (1987). Affect intensity as an individual difference characteristic: A review. *Journal of Research in Personality, 21,* 1–39.

Lawton, M. P., Powell, M., Kleban, M. H., & Dean, J. (1993). Affect and age: Cross-sectional comparisons of structure and prevalence. *Psychology and Aging, 8,* 165–175.

Leary, M. (1986). Affective and behavioral components of shyness. In W. H. Jones, J. M. Cheek, & S. R. Briggs (Eds.), *Shyness: Perspectives on research and treatment* (pp. 27–38). New York: Plenum Press.

Leary, M. (1990). Responses to social exclusion: Social anxiety, jealousy, loneliness, depression, and low self-esteem. *Journal of Social and Clinical Psychology, 9,* 221–229.

Leary, M., Atherton, S. C., Hill, S., & Hur, C. (1986). Attributional mediators of social inhibition and avoidance. *Journal of Personality, 54,* 704–716.

Lee, M., Zimbardo, P. G., & Bertholf, M. (1977, November). Shy murderers. *Psychology Today, 11,* 69.

Leitenberg, H. (1990). *Handbook of social and evaluation anxiety.* New York: Plenum Press.

Levin, I., & Stokes, J. P. (1986). An examination of the relation of individual difference variables to loneliness. *Journal of Personality, 54,* 717–733.

Matheny, A. P., Jr., & Dolan, A. B. (1975). Persons, situations, and time: A genetic view of behavioral change in children. *Journal of Personality and Social Psychology, 32,* 1106–1110.

McCaul, K. D. (1983). Observer attributions of depressed students. *Personality and Social Psychology Bulletin, 9,* 74–82.

McCullough, J. P., McCune, K. J., Kaye, A. L., Braith, J. A., Friend, R., Roberts, W. C., Belyea-Caldwell, S., Norris, S. L. W., & Hampton, C. (1994). Comparison of a community dysthymia sample at screening with a matched group of nondepressed community controls. *Journal of Nervous and Mental Disease, 182,* 402–407.

Miller, I. W., & Norman, W. H. (1981). Effects of attributions for success on the alleviation of learned helplessness and depression. *Journal of Abnormal Psychology, 90,* 113–124.

Moore, D., & Schultz, N. R. (1983). Loneliness at adolescence: Correlates, attributions, and coping. *Journal of Youth and Adolescence, 12*, 95–100.

Müller-Spahn, F., & Hock, C. (1994). Clinical presentation of depression in the elderly. *Gerontologist, 40*, 10–14.

Mullins, L. C., & Dugan, E. (1990). The influence of depression, and family and friendship relations, on residents' loneliness in congregate housing. *Gerontologist, 30*, 377–384.

Mullins, L. L., Seigel, L. J., & Hodges, K. (1985). Cognitive problem-solving and life event correlates of depressive symptoms in children. *Journal of Abnormal Child Psychology, 13*, 305–314.

Neeleman, J., & Power, M. J. (1994). Social support and depression in three groups of psychiatric patients and a group of medical controls. *Social Psychiatry and Psychiatric Epidemiology, 29*, 46–51.

Neto, F. (1992). Loneliness among Portuguese adolescents. *Social Behavior and Personality, 20*, 15–21.

Nezu, A. M., Nezu, C. M., & Nezu, V. A. (1986). Depression, general distress, and causal attributions among university students. *Journal of Abnormal Psychology, 95*, 184–186.

Peplau, L. A., & Goldston, S. E. (1984). *Preventing the harmful consequences of severe and persistent loneliness.* Washington, DC: U.S. Government Printing Office.

Peplau, L. A., & Perlman, D. (1979). Blueprint for a social psychological theory of loneliness. In M. Cook & G. Wilson (Eds.), *Love and attraction* (pp. 101–110). New York: Pergamon Press.

Peplau, L. A., & Perlman, D. (1982). Perspectives on loneliness. In L. A. Peplau & D. Perlman (Eds.), *Loneliness: A sourcebook of current theory, research, and therapy* (pp. 1–18). New York: Wiley.

Pilkonis, P. A. (1977a). The behavioral consequences of shyness. *Journal of Personality, 45*, 596–611.

Pilkonis, P. A. (1977b). Shyness, public and private, and its relationship to other measures of social behavior. *Journal of Personality, 45*, 585–595.

Pittman, T. S., & Pittman, N. L. (1980). Deprivation of control and the attribution process. *Journal of Personality and Social Psychology, 39*, 377–389.

Plomin, R., & Daniels, D. (1986). Genetics and shyness. In W. H. Jones, J. M. Cheek, & S. R. Briggs (Eds.), *Shyness: Perspectives on research and treatment* (pp. 63–80). New York: Plenum Press.

Plomin, R., & Rowe, D. C. (1979). Genetic and environmental etiology of social behavior in infancy. *Developmental Psychology, 15*, 62–72.

Plomin, R., & Stocker, C. (1989). Behavioral genetics and emotionality. In J. S. Reznick (Ed.), *Perspectives on behavioral inhibition* (pp. 219–240). Chicago: University of Chicago Press.

Pyszczynski, T., & Greenberg, J. (1986). Evidence for a depressive self-focusing style. *Journal of Research in Personality, 20*, 95–106.

Quiggle, N. L., Garber, J., Panak, W. F., & Dodge, K. A. (1992). Social information processing in aggressive and depressed children. *Child Development, 63,* 1305–1320.

Renshaw, P. D., & Brown, P. J. (1993). Loneliness in middle childhood: Concurrent and longitudinal predictors. *Child Development, 64,* 1271–1284.

Revenson, T. A. (1981). Coping with loneliness: The impact of causal attributions. *Personality and Social Psychology Bulletin, 7,* 565–571.

Rich, A. R., & Bonner, R. L. (1987). Interpersonal moderators of depression among college students. *Journal of College Student Personnel, 28,* 337–342.

Rich, A. R., & Bonner, R. L. (1989). Support for a pluralistic approach to the treatment of depression. *Journal of College Student Development, 30,* 426–431.

Rich, A. R., & Scovel, M. (1987). Causes of depression in college students: A cross-lagged panel correlation analysis. *Psychological Reports, 60,* 27–30.

Rokeach, M. (1973). *The nature of human values.* New York: Free Press.

Rook, K. (1984). Promoting social bonding: Strategies for helping the lonely and socially isolated. *American Psychologist, 39,* 1389–1407.

Rothbart, M. K., & Derryberry, D. (1981). Development of individual differences in temperament. In M. E. Lamb & A. L. Brown (Eds.), *Advances in developmental psychology* (Vol. 1, pp. 37–86). Hillsdale, NJ: Erlbaum.

Rubin, K. H., LeMare, L. J., & Lollis, S. (1990). Social withdrawal in children: Developmental pathways to peer rejection. In S. R. Asher & J. D. Coie (Eds.), *Peer rejection in childhood* (pp. 217–252). Cambridge, England: Cambridge University Press.

Rush, A. J., Beck, A. T., Kovacs, M., & Hollon, S. (1977). Comparative efficacy of cognitive therapy and pharmacotherapy in the treatment of depressed outpatients. *Cognitive Therapy and Research, 1,* 17–37.

Ryan, M. C., & Patterson, J. (1987). Loneliness in the elderly. *Journal of Gerontological Nursing, 13,* 6–12.

Secunda, S. K. (1973). *Special report, 1973: The depressive disorders.* Washington, DC: National Institute of Mental Health.

Seligman, M. E. P. (1995). The effectiveness of psychotherapy: The Consumer Reports study. *American Psychologist, 50,* 965–974.

Seligson, A. G. (1983). The presentation of loneliness as a separate diagnostic category and its disentanglement from depression. *Psychotherapy in Private Practice, 1,* 33–37.

Smith, T. W., Baldwin, M., & Christenson, A. J. (1990). Interpersonal influence as active coping: Effects of task difficulty on cardiovascular reactivity. *Psychophysiology, 27,* 429–437.

Stephan, E., Fäth, M., & Lamm, H. (1988). Loneliness as related to various personality and environmental measures: Research with the German adaptation of the UCLA Loneliness Scale. *Social Behavior and Personality, 16,* 169–174.

Taylor, H. (1836). *The Statesman.* Westport, CT: Praeger.

Teglasi, H., & Hoffman, M. A. (1982). Causal attributions of shy subjects. *Journal of Research in Personality, 16*, 376–385.

Thomas, A. J. (1984). *Acquired hearing loss: Psychological and psychosocial implications.* San Diego, CA: Academic Press.

Tomkins, S. S. (1963). *Affect, imagery, consciousness.* New York: Sage.

Townshend, P. (1955). *The family life of old people.* Baltimore: Penguin Books.

Traub, G. S. (1983). Correlations of shyness with depression, anxiety, and academic performance. *Psychological Reports, 52*, 849–850.

van der Molen, H. T. (1990). A definition of shyness and its implications for clinical practice. In W. R. Crozier (Ed.), *Shyness and embarrassment: Perspectives from social psychology* (pp. 255–285). New York: Cambridge University Press.

Weary, G., Marsh, K. L., Gleicher, F., & Edwards, J. A. (1993). Depression, control motivation, and the processing of information about others. In G. Weary, F. Gleicher, & K. L. Marsh, (Eds.), *Control motivation and social cognition* (pp. 255–287). New York: Springer-Verlag.

Weeks, D. J. (1994). A review of loneliness concepts, with particular reference to old age. *International Journal of Geriatric Psychiatry, 9*, 345–355.

Weeks, D. J., Michela, J. L., Peplau, L. A., & Bragg, M. E. (1980). Relation between loneliness and depression: A structural equation analysis. *Journal of Personality and Social Psychology, 39*, 1238–1244.

Weiner, B. (1985). Spontaneous causal thinking. *Psychological Bulletin, 97*, 74–84.

Weiss, R. S. (1973). Issues in the study of loneliness. In L. A. Peplau & D. Perlman (Eds.), *Loneliness: A sourcebook of current theory, research, and therapy* (pp. 71–80). New York: Wiley.

Yang, B., & Clum, G. A. (1994). Life stress, social support, and problem-solving skills predictive of depressive symptoms, hopelessness, and suicide ideation in an Asian student population: A test of a model. *Suicide and Life Threatening Behavior, 24*, 127–139.

Young, J. E. (1982). Loneliness, depression, and cognitive therapy: Theory and application. In L. A. Peplau & D. Perlman (Eds.), *Loneliness: A sourcebook of current theory, research, and therapy* (pp. 379–405). New York: Wiley.

Zajonc, R. B. (1965). Social facilitation. *Science, 149*, (Whole No. 3681), 269–274.

Zimbardo, P. G. (1977). *Shyness: What it is and what to do about it.* Reading, MA: Addison-Wesley.

Zimbardo, P. G., Pilkonis, P. A., & Norwood, R. M. (1974). *The silent prison of shyness.* (ONR Tech. Rep. No. Z-17). Stanford, CA: Stanford University Press.

6

SCHEMATIC AND INTERPERSONAL CONCEPTUALIZATIONS OF DEPRESSION: AN INTEGRATION

NORMAN B. SCHMIDT, KRISTEN L. SCHMIDT, AND
JEFFERY E. YOUNG

Although the schema construct plays a central role in some formulations of depression (Beck, Rush, Shaw, & Emery, 1979), its discussion within interpersonal models of depression (Coyne, 1976b) is notably absent. The principal aim of this chapter is to highlight the usefulness of self-schemas for interpersonal conceptualizations of depression. We believe that many of the salient facets of social psychological conceptualizations of depression can be meaningfully augmented by schematic formulations, and we offer an integrationist account of interpersonal and schematic models of depression.

SCHEMATIC–COGNITIVE AND INTERPERSONAL MODELS OF DEPRESSION

Schematic–Cognitive Models of Depression

Schematic theories are premised on the existence of enduring cognitive structures referred to as *schemas*. These mental templates, which are

This research was supported by Uniformed Services University of the Health Sciences Grant CO72BO awarded to Norman B. Schmidt.

built up from historical experiences, serve to create cognitive generalizations about the self as well as about social experience (Markus, 1977; Segal, 1988; Turk & Speers, 1983). All cognitive theories of depression assume the existence of these schemas, although the descriptions and use of schemas vary considerably across different theories. Generally, cognitive theories of depression posit that depressed individuals maintain a negativistic style of thinking, which characterizes their interpretation of past and present life experiences as well as their expectations for the future (e.g., Abramson, Metalsky, & Alloy, 1989; Abramson, Seligman, & Teasdale, 1978; Beck, 1967). We begin this chapter by reviewing some of the prominent cognitive theories of depression that incorporate schematic conceptualizations.

According to the original learned helplessness theory of depression (Seligman, 1975), individuals show motivational, cognitive, and affective symptoms of depression when they come to believe that their actions are not related to and cannot appreciably influence the outcome of events in their lives. On the basis of investigations of Seligman's model, Abramson et al. (1978) reformulated the learned helplessness theory of depression. According to the reformulated theory, an individual develops depression (helplessness) if he or she believes either (a) that highly desired outcomes (e.g., having a romantic relationship) are very unlikely to happen or (b) that highly aversive outcomes (e.g., losing one's job) are very likely to happen—and that he or she is helpless to affect these outcomes. According to the theory, the degree to which an individual makes global, stable, and internalized attributions for events affects the generality and chronicity of depressive symptoms and whether the individual's self-esteem is lowered as a result. From this reformulation, Abramson et al. concluded that a relatively stable maladaptive cognitive style for making attributions about the causes and consequences of events plays an important role in the development of depression.

Another revision of learned helplessness theory, Abramson et al.'s (1989) hopelessness theory of depression, posits a hopelessness subtype of depression. Abramson et al. proposed a model of distal and proximal contributory causes that culminate in the development of a "hopelessness depression." As in the revised learned helplessness theory, in hopelessness theory the depressed person's negative attributional style for explaining life events is emphasized, but here it is considered a diathesis that interacts with negative life events (stressors) to produce hopelessness. Hopelessness requires both a negative outcome expectancy (or the belief that desired outcomes will not occur) and helplessness (the belief that one cannot affect one's outcome).

In the adult depression literature, an association between depressive symptoms and depressive attributional style has been supported (Peterson & Seligman, 1984; Sweeney, Anderson, & Bailey, 1986). Empirical support for the hopelessness theory of depression has also been reported (Metalsky & Joiner, 1992; Metalsky, Joiner, Hardin, & Abramson, 1993). Similarly, there is support for a depressive attributional style in children (Seligman et al., 1984), and a number of other studies have documented the relationship between depressive symptoms and hopelessness in children (Asarnow, Carlson, & Guthrie, 1987; Benfield, Palmer, Pfefferbaum, & Stowe, 1988; Kazdin, French, Unis, Esveldt-Dawson, & Sherick, 1983; Kazdin, Rodgers, & Colbus, 1986).

Beck's (1967) cognitive model of depression integrates relatively stable cognitive patterns (schemas); negative views about oneself, the world, and the future (the cognitive triad); and faulty information processing (cognitive distortions) to account for the psychological basis of depression. Schemas are the basic structural components of cognitive organization through which humans come to identify, interpret, categorize, and evaluate their experiences. The schemas of depressed people are characterized by negative views: views of the self as defective, inadequate, and undesirable; the world as demanding and defeating; and the future as hopeless and futile (Beck et al., 1979). Beck hypothesized that negative schemas are triggered by the occurrence (or perceived occurrence) of negative life events and are maintained by the person's tendency to distort incoming information systematically in a maladaptive or self-defeating manner.

According to Beck (Beck et al., 1979), an individual's affect and behavior are largely determined by the way in which he or she structures or thinks about the world. Beck suggested that early life experiences influence the nature of one's cognitive organization because they serve as the basis from which negative concepts about the self, the world, and the future are formed. Individuals who develop negative views about the self, world, and future and who maintain these views through cognitive distortions are predisposed to develop depression when the schemas are activated by negative life experiences analogous to those that contributed originally to the development of the negative schemas.

Beck's theory has generally been supported by empirical work with adults with depression (Olinger, Kuiper, & Shaw, 1987; Wise & Barnes, 1986; but see also Persons & Rao, 1985) and with depressed children. Kendall, Stark, and Adam (1990) and Haley, Fine, Marriage, Moretti, and Freeman (1985) found evidence of cognitive distortion (i.e., distorted self-evaluations) in depressed children. Leitenberg, Yost, and Carroll-Wilson (1986) demonstrated negatively biased information processing in young children. Kaslow, Stark, Printz, Livingston, and Tsai (1992) found that depressed children, and depressed–anxious children, maintained significantly more negative views of themselves, the world, and the future than did anxious and normal children, providing evidence for the negative cognitive triad in children. Other investigators have documented the presence of negative self-schemas in depressed children (Hammen & Zupan, 1984;

Zupan, Hammen, & Jaenicke, 1987) as well as negative expectations for the future (Benfield et al., 1988; Kazdin et al., 1986).

Young (1990) expanded schematic conceptualizations by enumerating a variety of specific maladaptive self-schemas. Although the focus of Young's work has been the association between schemas and Axis II personality disorders, there is compelling theoretical and empirical support for an association between several specific maladaptive self-schemas and depression. Young (1990) proposed that schemas, which he termed *early maladaptive schemas* (EMS), develop during childhood vis-à-vis relationships with significant caretakers. Once in place, the EMSs selectively filter for corroborating experience, and the schemas are extended and elaborated throughout the individual's lifetime. During childhood, an EMS is a means for the child to comprehend and manage the environment. In adulthood, the EMS outlives its limited usefulness and creates distress when it is activated by situations relevant to the particular schema.

Despite their maladaptive nature, EMSs are self-perpetuating and highly resistant to change. Because the EMS rests at the core of the individual's self-concept, it is familiar, comfortable, and unconditional (cf. Swann, 1983). The unconditional nature of an EMS prevents realistic processing of schema-inconsistent information. At the cognitive level, the schema is maintained by magnification of information that confirms the schema and negation or minimization of information that is inconsistent with the schema.

Young's (1990) schematic theory is largely consistent with other schema-based theories. Like Beck, Young has described schemas as stable and enduring structures that form the core of the individual's self-concept. Schemas distort information regarding the self and the environment, which gives rise to negative automatic thoughts and subjective distress. However, one important difference between the theories of Young and Beck is that EMSs are unconditional (e.g., "I am unlovable"), whereas Beck's underlying assumptions are conditional (e.g., "If I can please others all the time, I will be loved"). This difference suggests that EMSs are more frequently hypervalent than are underlying beliefs, which require that certain stressors or conditions be present.

Theoretical differences between diathesis–stress models of Axis I disorders and Young's (1990) hypervalent schematic conceptualization make for differential predictions regarding the consequences of negative life events in the context of schemas. The cognitive diathesis–stress models predict distress only when a negative life event is added to the cognitive diathesis (e.g., Beck's model of depression, Beck et al., 1979; hopelessness theory of depression, Abramson et al., 1989). According to Young's schematic model, however, the presence of negative life events should have less influence on individuals with hypervalent maladaptive schemas because these individuals chronically experience high levels of distress as a result of persistent triggering of the maladaptive schemas.

Young's (1990) hierarchical model of EMSs has received support from a factor analytic study of the Schema Questionnaire, a measure of the proposed maladaptive schemas (Schmidt, Joiner, Young, & Telch, 1995). Schmidt et al. found that the majority of proposed EMSs were clearly delineated in both nonclinical and clinical samples. A hierarchical factor analysis conducted with the nonclinical sample yielded three higher order factors: Disconnection, Overconnection, and Exaggerated Standards. The higher order factor Disconnection appears to reflect pathology that results from a sense of disconnection and defectiveness. This cluster of schemas describes disconnected individuals who feel defective and alienated from others. These individuals may be emotionally inhibited with considerable fear of losing control of their emotions and behavior. It is of particular interest that validity analyses indicated that individuals with this cluster of EMSs, in particular the Defectiveness EMS, may be vulnerable to depression, because scores on the Defectiveness index significantly predicted depressive symptoms over time.

The Overconnection cluster of EMSs appears to represent pathology that results from enmeshment. This cluster of schemas appears to describe individuals who feel incompetent, vulnerable, and excessively dependent. Validity analyses indicated that individuals who scored high on schemas measuring feelings of incompetence, inferiority, and vulnerability were particularly at risk for the development of anxiety symptoms (Schmidt et al., 1995). On the other hand, individuals scoring high on the Dependency EMS were at greater risk for the development of depressive symptoms. Of all the EMSs assessed, the Dependency index was the single best predictor of depression.

These findings suggest that a depressive reaction can emerge from maladaptive schemas that reflect either extreme on an interpersonal continuum ranging from disconnection from others (i.e., Defectiveness) to overconnection (i.e., Dependency). When changes in Beck Depression Inventory (BDI) scores over a 4-week period were predicted, the Dependency EMS accounted for 27% of the variance, and the Defectiveness EMS added 6% more variance to the model, suggesting that these two schemas are not only potent predictors of depressive symptoms but also unique contributors to depression. Because each may uniquely lead to the development of depression, individuals who feel both dependent and defective would be at increased risk for depression.

The third higher order factor, Exaggerated Standards, describes EMSs that pertain to exaggerated standards of behavior. This cluster of schemas refers to individuals who are excessively focused on achievement or self-sacrifice. Schemas related to the Exaggerated Standards higher order factor were predictive of overall distress and impairment, but they were not specifically predictive of mood or anxiety symptoms. These findings suggest that some EMSs are uniquely predictive of anxiety pathology, whereas others are predictive of depressive pathology. Overall, it appears that individual EMSs yield conceptually meaningful and discriminant predictions with respect to depressive psychopathology.

Schmidt and Joiner (1996) evaluated the relationship between maladaptive self-schemas, negative life events, and psychological distress. Young's (1970) model predicts that individuals with maladaptive schemas are chronically distressed because the schemas are chronically activated. Therefore, the experience of negative life events is unlikely to potentiate the level of distress experienced by those having maladaptive schemas. A nonclinical sample (N = 93) was assessed using the Schema Questionnaire (SQ), a measure of negative life events, and several measures of psychological distress. Consistent with prediction, results indicated a Schema × Negative Life Events interaction in which the distress level of participants who scored high on the SQ was less affected by negative life events than that of low SQ participants. However, schema-related negative life events were much more likely than schema-unrelated negative life events to increase distress among high SQ participants.

Overall, there is considerable empirical support for various aspects of schematic models of depression in both children and adults. Although this perspective does not account for the entire phenomenon of depressed mood, we believe the evidence suggests clear descriptive and predictive usefulness for schematic conceptualizations.

Interpersonal Models of Depression

Beck's (1967) theory, as well as the other cognitive theories of depression, has been challenged by those who argue for an interactive, interpersonal approach that includes aspects of an individual's social functioning and environment (Brown & Harris, 1978; Coyne, 1976b; Coyne & Gotlib, 1983). Detailed descriptions of interpersonal models of depression can be found elsewhere in the current volume; here, key aspects of this model are summarized. The interpersonal models of depression deemphasize the significance of cognitive factors and highlight the role of social environment, which is believed to be critical to the etiology of depressive symptoms. An understanding of the depressed person's social context (e.g., the quality of interpersonal interactions) is considered essential to the understanding of depression.

Lewinsohn (1974) proposed a behavioral and interpersonal model of depression. According to Lewinsohn, depressed individuals obtain insufficient positive reinforcement from significant others because they lack the social skills that are necessary for eliciting positive interpersonal responses. Furthermore, depressed people are seen as less capable of reinforcing others, thereby decreasing their chances for social reciprocity. The theory also contends that the maintenance of depression, as well as its severity, is influenced by the depressed individuals' tendency to engage in few social activities and relative inability to experience activities as pleasurable.

Lewinsohn's (1974) theory has received support in both the child and adult literatures (Gotlib & Robinson, 1982; Lewinsohn, Mischel, Chaplin, & Barton, 1980). Wierzbicki and McCabe (1988) found that children's social skill deficits were significantly related to their current levels of depression and were predictive of future levels of depression, thus suggesting that depressed children lack the skills necessary for engaging in positive social interactions. On an interpersonal level, depressed children have shown social deficits when interacting with parents, siblings, and peers (Altman & Gotlib, 1988; John, Gammon, Prusoff, & Warner, 1987; Kazdin, Esveldt-Dawson, Sherick, & Colbus, 1985; Puig-Antich et al., 1985; Sacco & Graves, 1984), and they have reported being less satisfied with their performance and perceiving themselves as less socially competent than others (Altman & Gotlib, 1988; Fauber, Forehand, Long, Burke, & Faust, 1987; Faust, Baum, & Forehand, 1985; Sacco & Graves, 1984).

Coyne (1976b) conceptualized depression as the result of a disruption in the provision of support and validation from the interpersonal environment. He described depression as an interpersonal process in which the depressed person seeks reassurance about the nature of his or her relationship to individuals with whom he or she interacts, along with the efforts to validate or deny the depressed person's needs for reassurance (Coyne, 1976b). Coyne pointed out that this process is complicated by the ability of humans to communicate conflicting information simultaneously in different modes. Communication includes contextual or relational factors that may contradict verbal statements. For example, vocal and linguistic patterns may be mismatched when informative body movements (i.e., "body language") contradict the salient verbal message.

According to Coyne (1976b), a person who is prone to depression seeks validation and reassurance from significant others when a loss or change in social structure occurs. He or she then faces an "interpersonal dilemma" about whether or not the elicited feedback is genuine. A cycle of reassurance seeking begins, and the individual's depressive symptoms worsen. Eventually, significant others become annoyed and frustrated with the depressed person and begin to give mixed signals to him or her—that is, positive verbal support but negative nonverbal information (e.g., avoidance). According to Coyne, this pattern increases the person's uncertainty and depressive symptoms, and it eventually leads the depressed person to the conclusion that he or she is unloved. The end result of this cycle of reassurance seeking and doubt can be a full-blown depressive episode. Studies testing Coyne's interpersonal theory of depression have provided generally supportive data regarding various aspects of his theory in samples of both adults (Coyne, 1976a; Gotlib & Robinson, 1982; Stephens, Hokanson, & Welker, 1987) and children (Kennedy, Spence, & Hensley, 1989; Mullins, Peterson, Wonderlich, & Reaven, 1986).

AN INTEGRATED MODEL OF DEPRESSION: THE PERCEPTION OF STRESSORS, REASSURANCE SEEKING, AND SOCIAL REINFORCEMENT

Our review of the interpersonal and cognitive models of depression, as well as supporting empirical evidence for each, suggests that each model offers a valid description of the development of depression. On the basis of the documented scientific merits, in this section we offer an incorporation of each model to highlight the potential usefulness of a combined schematic–interpersonal conceptualization. The key elements of interpersonal models of depression are summarized in Figure 1. As illustrated, the presence of a stressor (S), (in particular, the perceived loss of a social reinforcer) can lead to reassurance-seeking behavior in the potential depressed person (D), which results in some level of reciprocal reinforcement from the social environment (E). According to interpersonal theory, each

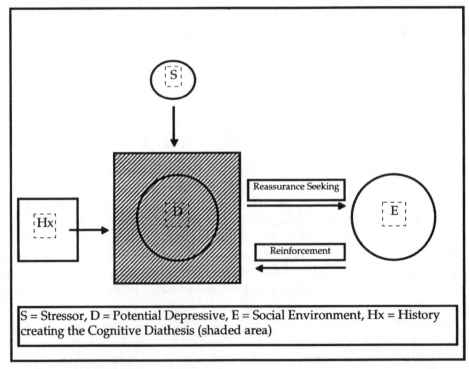

S = Stressor, D = Potential Depressive, E = Social Environment, Hx = History creating the Cognitive Diathesis (shaded area)

Figure 1. Potential influence of cognitive schemas on the essential parameters of interpersonal models of depression.

of these interrelated pathways constitutes a necessary conduit for the development of depressed mood. In what follows, we illustrate how each pathway can become disrupted or affected by schematic information-processing biases.

First, it may be useful to consider the integration of a schematic model of depression into the processes described in Figure 1. Cognitive models of depression focus on the relationship between the stressor (S) and the cognitive diathesis inherent in the potential depressed peerson (D). The contribution that is unique to the schematic model is straightforward—the cognitive diathesis. Yet this element can substantially add to the richness, complexity, and, we hope, usefulness of the interpersonal model. The cognitive diathesis adds history or context to the dynamic relationships that are described in Figure 1. As noted previously, schematic theories posit that the developmental history of the individual is critical in influencing responses to stressors. History is responsible for molding the cognitive diathesis that processes information relevant to all the pathways described.

Perception of Stressors

One of the central premises of cognitive models of depression is that schemas should exert a general influence on perception. It follows that schemas should influence the perception of each of the three processes described as necessary in the interpersonal model. The shaded area in Figure 1 represents the potential influence of the schematic template. It is consistent with the diathesis–stress cognitive models described that a proximal stressor poses the greatest risk for depression in individuals with a specific cognitive vulnerability for a negative interpretation of the stressor. In addition, individuals with depressogenic schemas should show attentional biases toward environmental stimuli that are relevant to the schema. Thus, individuals with a cognitive diathesis for depression are more apt to *detect* the proximal stressor as well as to *interpret* that stressor in a negative manner consistent with the schema.

Several predictions arise from the preceding. First, stressors that affect social reinforcement will be more likely to be perceived by those with relevant schemas. Given the same stressor, those with a cognitive diathesis are more likely than others to detect the stressor. For example, an individual with a dependency schema should report a greater frequency of potentially threatening and dependency-relevant environmental stressors such as changes in a loved one's social arena (e.g., a new project at work, new interests and hobbies).

Second, individuals with a cognitive diathesis will interpret the stressor in an exaggerated and negative manner relative to those without the cognitive bias. For example, those with dependency schemas will be more apt to interpret changes in the loved one's social environment as indicative of social loss (e.g., my spouse has lost interest in me; this will lead inevitably to divorce, abandonment, and isolation).

Because schemas affect the perception of stressors, they should also influence reassurance-seeking behaviors. The presence of a stressor, along with the potential depressive's increased capacity to detect and negatively interpret it, will lead to increased triggering of the schema. Negative affect resulting from schematic triggering should potentiate a greater frequency of reassurance seeking. In particular, Joiner, Katz, and Lew (1996) found that negative life events caused decreased self-esteem and increased anxiety, which appeared to completely mediate the initial reassurance-seeking behaviors. This finding leads to the following predictions: (a) Socially relevant stressors should lead to higher levels of reassurance seeking and (b) individuals with a cognitive diathesis, relative to those without, should show greater reassurance seeking in the context of schema-relevant triggering events. In other words, the onset of reassurance seeking in the context of stressors should be modified by the presence of stressor-specific schemas.

For example, in the context of perceived social rejection, most individuals should show increased reassurance seeking, but individuals with the defectiveness schema should show differentially greater reassurance seeking for evidence that they are not "defective" (e.g., "I'm not a bad person am I?" "Why don't people like me?"), whereas those with a dependency schema may show differentially greater reassurance seeking for evidence that they are not "being abandoned" (e.g., "Do you still love me?" "You aren't falling in love with someone else, are you?"). Whereas reassurance seeking has been well documented among depressed individuals (Joiner, Alfano, & Metalsky, 1992; Joiner & Metalsky, 1995), this schema-based conceptualization represents an elaboration of reassurance-seeking behaviors and should allow for differential predictions of specific reassurance-seeking behaviors on the basis of schematic content.

Taking these predictions one step further, we predict that the frequency of reassurance seeking is related to the degree of association between a schema and the stressor. Certain types of events may lead to reassurance seeking for those who can be primarily characterized as having a defectiveness schema but not for those with a dependency schema, and vice versa. For example, perceived social rejection may elicit greater reassurance seeking among those with dependency issues, whereas perceived negative evaluation may lead to greater reassurance seeking among those with defectiveness issues. Thus, reassurance-seeking behaviors may be induced by substantially different means among those possessing an underlying vulnerability to depressive reactions. It would follow that knowledge of specific maladaptive schemas may allow for more accurate differential predictions of reassurance seeking.

Perception of Reassurance-Seeking Behaviors

The individual's perception of his or her reassurance-seeking activity is yet another mechanism for the schema to exert its influence. Do reassurance-seeking people understand their stimulus value (i.e., the impact of their activity on others), or are they unaware of others' negative signals because they so desperately need to engage in the process itself? Some may view their excessive reassurance-seeking behaviors as effective means for maintaining closeness and intimacy with their confidants or for bringing about a resolution to their problems. The individual with a dependency schema may believe that friends and loved ones relish the excessive attention given them. In fact, the negative consequences of reassurance-seeking behaviors are likely to be overlooked as the person seeks relief from his or her distress and, in particular, when the individual perceives excessive reassurance seeking as a necessary behavior to provide relief. Consequently, some individuals do not easily learn which of their behaviors are aversive to others, thus maintaining, or creating greater, social skills deficits.

The prediction from this aspect of the model is that one's schema-driven perception of the reassurance-seeking process may predict the overall efficacy of the reassurance-seeking behaviors. Those who can more accurately understand the reassurance-seeking process and how best to monitor their social behaviors are more likely to engage in productive reassurance seeking. Similarly, there will be individual differences in the capacity to produce an aversive reaction in others, depending on one's accuracy in perceiving the reassurance-seeking process. It can be predicted that individuals who more accurately perceive their reassurance-seeking behaviors will be better received by social reinforcers, leading to a greater likelihood of positive feedback. Accurate perception of one's reassurance-seeking behaviors should lead to better implementation of the behaviors, including lower levels of aversive behavior and higher levels of positive responding, all of which translate into more effective reassurance seeking.

Perception of Social Reinforcement

The final link in the interpersonal pathway toward depression is the interpretation of feedback or reinforcement provided by the social environment. Perception of the feedback process is another area open to interpretation by the potential depressed individual. The ability of potential depressed individuals to be adequately reinforced or reassured depends on their ability to accept feedback that is inconsistent with their interpretation of the proximal stressor and, of course, inconsistent with their interpretation of themselves relevant to the self-schema.

The interpretation of feedback is perhaps the most likely candidate for information-processing biases. Assessment of multiple sources of feedback is central to Coyne's (1976b) model. Although Coyne focused on the depressed individuals' elicitation of negative responses from others, interpersonal feedback of any sort is open to interpretation. There appear to be two related questions: Are certain individuals prone to an ambiguous (i.e., simultaneously positive and negative) interpretation of feedback, and how do individuals interpret negative feedback?

Regardless of the true ambiguity of interpersonal feedback, those with maladaptive schemas are likely to perceive ambiguity. In any interpersonal scenario, the reassurance seeker is confronted with multiple sources of information, and any one of these data sources is potentially ambiguous. Depending on one's interpretive bias, a smile can be friendly or threatening, eye contact can reflect curiosity or disapproval, and voice inflections can indicate a sense of caring or malice. Information-processing biases should yield ambiguous interpretations of data; that is, positive or neutral feedback is more likely to be perceived as potentially negative among those with maladaptive schemas. Therefore, the level of schematic pathology should be predictive of perceived ambiguity in interpersonal feedback.

It also seems important to consider the information processing of negative feedback because of Coyne's emphasis on the elicitation of negative reactions from the social environment in response to excessive reassurance seeking. Along with positive and neutral feedback, the potential depressed individuals experience negative feedback during the reassurance-seeking process. As we noted earlier, maladaptive schemas should lead to a greater likelihood of detecting, and a more negative interpretation of, cues that are schema related. For example, individuals with a dependency schema should be more apt to detect feedback cues that are suggestive of rejection. The same issues raised in terms of detection and interpretation of stressors apply to this pathway of the model: Those with maladaptive schemas should be more likely to detect schema-consistent negative feedback. Of course, feedback that is more ambiguous and generally more negative for those with maladaptive schemas should elicit higher levels of reassurance seeking in the individuals' attempt to obtain nonambiguous, positive feedback.

Do the potential depressed individuals want to be reassured, or are they evaluating feedback in such a way as to verify their maladaptive views of themselves? Research on self-verification theory suggests that individuals selectively attend to information that is consistent with self-schemas (Swann, Wenzlaff, Krull, & Pelham, 1992; Swann, Wenzlaff, & Tafarodi, 1992). Accordingly, individuals with maladaptive views of themselves minimize reassuring information that is inconsistent with self-schemas, magnify nonreassuring information, and distort ambiguous information to be consistent with self-schemas. The level of maladaptive pathology should be related to the level of distortion of both reassuring, nonreassuring, and ambiguous information. Among those with considerable schematic pathology, any reassuring feedback is likely to be interpreted to confirm maladaptive self-schemas. Paradoxically, this affirmation should elicit continued reassurance-seeking behaviors, further social feedback, and so forth. In summary, self-verification theory suggests that for those with maladaptive self-schemas, almost any social feedback is likely to "reinforce" selectively the maladaptive views of the self.

We also note that two elements of the schema per se are related to each aspect of this model. There is a structural and a process element inherent to schemas (Segal, 1988). The degree of structural pathology reflects the absolute level of bias that a maladaptive template can produce. Individuals with a defectiveness schema may believe either that they are absolutely, unconditionally defective in every sense or that they are defective in some particular manner or in specific circumstances. The structural dimension should reflect the degree of bias contained within an individual schema, which should affect the interpretation of the stressor, the perception of reassurance-seeking behaviors, and the amount of reassurance necessary to change their interpretation. It would be expected that those evidencing higher levels of schematic bias, relative to those with less bias, will react with more negative interpretations of stressors, less adept reassurance-seeking behaviors, and greater reassurance seeking.

The process element of the schema refers to its level of activation. The level of activation of a particular schema, or valence, refers to the degree to which the schema is currently operating. Another way to conceptualize this activation would be the degree of belief the individual has in the biases captured by a given schematic template—the degree to which an individual "believes" a given bias will vary from day to day and situation to situation. Someone may generally believe that he or she is defective but may particularly believe this on days following a salient trigger (e.g., rejection) or when engaged in certain activities throughout the day (e.g., when alone vs. when involved in social interchange). Similar to the level of structural pathology, the level of activation of a schema should be related to perception of stressors, reassurance-seeking behaviors, and the overall amount of reassurance that is undertaken to ameliorate the negative valence.

It is evident that information-processing biases may influence each of the pathways described by interpersonal models of depression. The sheer number of potential effects for information processing suggests that these biases may dramatically affect the reassurance-seeking process. These potential schematic influences are summarized as follows:

1. Maladaptive schemas lead to a higher frequency of detection of stressors relevant to social reinforcement.
2. Maladaptive schemas produce more negative interpretations of stressors.

3. Schema-relevant stressors, compared with nonrelevant stressors, produce higher levels of reassurance seeking.
4. Maladaptive schemas produce less effective reassurance-seeking behaviors.
5. Maladaptive schemas produce more negative, and more ambiguous, perceptions of interpersonal feedback.

EMPIRICAL WORK INCORPORATING COGNITIVE AND INTERPERSONAL THEORIES

We next turn to an emerging line of empirical work on depression that combines aspects of both interpersonal and cognitive theory to explore the explanatory significance of interactions between social–familial factors and cognitive factors for the development of depression in both adults and children. Few studies in the adult literature explicitly incorporate both models, but those that are available suggest that the foregoing integration of schematic and interpersonal theories provides a viable springboard for future work. Hammen, Marks, Mayol, and DeMayo (1985) demonstrated that negative stressors relevant to individuals' particular schemas were more likely to produce depression than were schema-irrelevant negative events and that negative interpersonal events were much more closely associated with the development of depression than were negative achievement-related events. Dykman, Horowitz, Abramson, and Usher (1991) found that, relative to nondepressed people, depressed people's negative schemas and social skills deficits combined to bias negatively their interpretations of feedback. Results of a series of studies by Swann and colleagues (Swann, Wenzlaff, Krull, et al., 1992; Swann, Wenzlaff, & Tafarodi, 1992) have supported the assertion that, relative to nondepressed participants, depressed individuals seek interpersonal experiences and relationships that confirm their negative self-schemas.

Several investigators have examined the interaction between interpersonal experiences and cognitive vulnerability in children. Consistent with the activation of self-schemas in socially relevant stressors is the finding by Stark, Linn, Maguire, and Kaslow (in press) that depressed children, compared with normal controls, experienced a significant elicitation of negative automatic thoughts in the context of social situations. Several researchers have reported a relationship between negative verbal input, especially maternal criticism, and children's tendency to be self-critical or to make self-blaming attributions for negative events (Jaenicke et al., 1987; Radke-Yarrow, Belmont, Nottelmann, & Bottomly, 1990). Schmidt (1996), in a study of children with attention deficit hyperactivity disorder, reported that participants' views of self, world, and future; their attributional style; and their perceptions of paternal messages of self, world, and future were associated with the development of comorbid depressive disorders. Burge and Hammen (1991) found a relationship between children's depressive symptoms and critical maternal verbal behavior during a discussion–interaction task. Furthermore, Stark, Schmidt, and Joiner (1996) demonstrated that parental messages to children (categorized as messages about the child, the world, or the future) were predictive of children's depression and of the children's views of self, world, and future. In addition, the relationship between perceived parental messages and child depression was completely mediated by the children's views of self, world, and future.

Although these investigators have explored only some of the interactive pathways that interpersonal and schematic factors may contribute to depression, their findings indicate the potential usefulness of an integrated model in the prediction of childhood and adult depression.

GENERAL DISCUSSION

What do schematic conceptualizations add to interpersonal models of depression? This has been the question of principal interest in this chapter. We have suggested that there is a sound theoretical basis for the schema construct as well as considerable empirical support for the existence and development of self-schemas and their role in childhood and adult depression. We have focused our attention on the specific and necessary pathways for the generation of depression according to interpersonal models to highlight the diverse potential effects of schematic pathology. An incorporated conceptual model has begun to receive empirical attention, although much additional work is necessary. Despite the preliminary status of this work, we answer the question posed at the start of this section by tentatively concluding that the self-schema construct can substantially enrich interpersonal formulations of depression. We believe that an integrated model has additional explanatory potential with regard to the etiology, assessment, course, and treatment of depression.

Our discussions of schematic conceptualizations have necessarily focused on the psychopathogenicity of mood. Although we have emphasized the pathogenicity of maladaptive information processing, it is equally important to consider schema-based resiliency. In the same way that mild stressors can lead to pathological responses in some, severe stressors can have little effect on others. Schema-based resiliency should affect all aspects of the integrated model we have considered. For example, schema-based resiliency should lead to a differential interpretation of negative stressors. Similarly, some individuals are less affected by negative feedback than others, suggesting that negative feedback can be positively distorted or minimized. Just as negative information-processing biases increase the likelihood of depressive reactions, positive information-processing biases should minimize the impact of negative events. A fully incorporated model of depression should also consider protective information-processing biases.

An emphasis on schematic influences in the interpersonal processes does not negate the importance of a number of noncognitive factors. The proximal stressor should differentially affect the potential depressive in terms of its severity, generality, and chronicity. The facility or level of social skill or, conversely, any specific social skills deficit, will positively or negatively affect reassurance-seeking behavior. Finally, the number and quality of resources available in the social environment, including the communication skills of the potential reinforcers and their capacity to provide positive reinforcement despite being exposed to the aversively "needy" depressed individual, are elements of the social environment that will differentially affect the individual who is potentially depressed. These aspects of the necessary parameters of the interpersonal model all have the capacity to affect the vulnerability of the potential depressive to a depressive episode. Our assumption is, however, that the individual's interpretation of each of these factors, which represents an important index for vulnerability or resiliency, accounts for a substantial and unique share of the variance in predicting mood pathology.

What does this integrated theoretical model have to offer in terms of practical clinical implications? Despite considerable research evaluating theoretical aspects of Coyne's (1976b) interpersonal model of depression, on the one hand, a derivative treatment model has not been clearly delineated. On the other hand, schematic theory has been closely related to treatment interventions. An integrated model highlights two principal mechanisms—faulty information processing and faulty reassurance-seeking behaviors—that may be responsible for depressed mood. It is conceivable that cognitive therapy is more appropriate for schematic pathology, but a behaviorally oriented therapy may be better suited for interpersonally mediated mood pathology. A two-pronged treatment that addresses both types of deficits through cognitive and behavioral interventions should yield the greatest overall efficacy. It is likely, however, because the processes are interrelated, that either treatment mode (i.e., cognitive or behavioral) will have positive effects on the other domain. For example, in several outcome studies comparing behavioral and cognitive treatments for panic disorder, investigators found that the two treatment methods produced similar levels of improvement in both behavioral and cognitive domains (Telch et al., 1993; Telch, Schmidt, Kamphuis, Jaimez, & Frank, 1993). We are not aware of similar studies comparing behavioral and cognitive therapies for depression in which differential responding in information-processing and interpersonal deficits were evaluated, but we believe that this would be an interesting line for future research.

We conclude by offering final thoughts on a general conceptual framework for incorporating cognitive and interpersonal models. Given the empirical support for both cognitive and interpersonal mechanisms for depression, it is conceivable that these sets of mechanisms can act in combination, as we suggested earlier, or independently of one another. One way to consider these relations is to describe a 2 × 2 matrix that captures each of the dimensions. The first dimension, or mechanism, is the faulty information processing that is responsible for depressogenic misinterpretations. Some individuals will display substantial information-processing vulnerabilities that will be absent in others. The second dimension, or mechanism, would capture faulty reassurance seeking. Some individuals will display the depressogenic reassurance-seeking spiral described by Coyne, whereas others will remain relatively free from these tendencies. Each of these mechanisms should be sufficient to produce depression or may describe a particular type of depressed person. There may be some depressed people who show only maladaptive schemas with no reassurance-seeking deficits, whereas others may show the reverse. The absence of both mechanisms should describe individuals who are relatively resilient, or generally normothymic in the absence of endogenous or other exogenous factors. Of course, the combination of both factors is likely to indicate a substantial risk for depression. Individuals evidencing both mechanisms should generally show more severe mood pathology.

In conclusion, if one assumes that there is some validity to this typology, a variety of interesting questions arise. Do individuals remain stable within a given depressogenic mechanism, or do some manifest different mechanisms during separate depressive episodes? For example, some depressive episodes could be brought on primarily by reassurance seeking at one point but by maladaptive information processing at a different point. Do these separate mechanisms result in the same phenomenological expression of the depression? Perhaps the clinical manifestations of depression differ according to its etiology. It would also be of interest to understand whether the combination of factors results in a potentiated mood pathology. These two factors could interact in a variety of ways, perhaps resulting in mood pathology that is no greater than any singular mechanism, or perhaps resulting in additive or potentiated pathology. In summary, we hope these questions, and others related to an integrated model of depression, will begin to receive greater scientific attention.

REFERENCES

Abramson, L. Y., Metalsky, G. I., & Alloy, L. B. (1989). Hopelessness depression: A theory-based subtype of depression. *Psychological Review, 96,* 358–372.

Abramson, L. Y., Seligman, M. E. P., & Teasdale, J. (1978). Learned helplessness in humans: Critique and reformulation. *Journal of Abnormal Psychology, 87,* 49–74.

Altman, E. O., & Gotlib, I. H. (1988). The social behavior of depressed children: An observational study. *Journal of Abnormal Child Psychology, 16,* 29–44.

Asarnow, J. R., Carlson, G. A., & Guthrie, D. (1987). Coping strategies, self-perceptions, hopelessness, and perceived family environments in depressed and suicidal children. *Journal of Consulting and Clinical Psychology, 55,* 361–366.

Beck, A. T. (1967). *Depression: Causes and treatment.* Philadelphia: University of Pennsylvania Press.

Beck, A. T., Rush, A. J., Shaw, B. F., & Emery, G. (1979). *Cognitive therapy of depression.* New York: Guilford Press.

Benfield, C. Y., Palmer, D. J., Pfefferbaum, B., & Stowe, M. L. (1988). A comparison of depressed and nondepressed disturbed children on measures of attributional style, hopelessness, life stress, and temperament. *Journal of Abnormal Child Psychology, 16,* 397–410.

Brown, G. W., & Harris, T. (1978). *Social origins of depression: A study of psychiatric disorder in women.* New York: Free Press.

Burge, D., & Hammen, C. (1991). Maternal communication: Predictors of outcome at follow-up in a sample of children at high and low risk for depression. *Journal of Abnormal Psychology, 100,* 174–180.

Coyne, J. C. (1976a). Depression and the response of others. *Journal of Abnormal Psychology, 85,* 186–193.

Coyne, J. C. (1976b). Toward an interactional description of depression. *Psychiatry, 39,* 28–40.

Coyne, J. C., & Gotlib, I. H. (1983). The role of cognition in depression: A critical appraisal. *Psychological Bulletin, 94,* 472–505.

Dykman, B. M., Horowitz, L. M., Abramson, L. Y., & Usher, M. (1991). Schematic and situational determinants of depressed and nondepressed students' interpretation of feedback. *Journal of Abnormal Psychology, 100,* 45–55.

Fauber, R., Forehand, R., Long, N., Burke, M., & Faust, J. (1987). The relationship of young adolescent Children's Depression Inventory (CDI) scores to their social and cognitive functioning. *Journal of Psychopathology and Behavioral Assessment, 9,* 161–172.

Faust, J., Baum, C. G., & Forehand, R. (1985). An examination of the association between social relationships and depression in early adolescence. *Journal of Applied Developmental Psychology, 6,* 291–297.

Gotlib, I. H., & Robinson, L. A. (1982). Responses to depressed individuals: Discrepancies between self-report and observer-rated behavior. *Journal of Abnormal Psychology, 91,* 231–240.

Haley, B. M. T., Fine, S. L., Marriage, K., Moretti, M. M., & Freeman, R. J. (1985). Cognitive bias and depression in psychiatrically disturbed children and adolescents. *Journal of Consulting and Clinical Psychology, 53,* 535–537.

Hammen, C., Marks, T., Mayol, A., & DeMayo, R. (1985). Depressive self-schemas, life stress, and vulnerability to depression. *Journal of Abnormal Psychology, 94,* 308–319.

Hammen, C., & Zupan, B. A. (1984). Self-schemas, depression, and the processing of personal information in children. *Journal of Experimental Child Psychology, 37,* 598–608.

Jaenicke, C., Hammen, C., Zupan, B., Hiroto, D., Gordon, D., Adrian, C., & Burge, D. (1987). Cognitive vulnerability in children at risk for depression. *Journal of Abnormal Child Psychology, 15,* 559–572.

John, K., Gammon, G. D., Prusoff, B. A., & Warner, V. (1987). The social adjustment inventory for children and adolescents (SAICA): Test of a new semistructured interview. *Journal of the American Academy of Child and Adolescent Psychiatry, 26,* 898–911.

Joiner, T. E., Alfano, M. S., & Metalsky, G. I. (1992). When depression breeds contempt: Reassurance-seeking, self-esteem and rejection of depressed college students by their roommates. *Journal of Abnormal Psychology, 101,* 165–173.

Joiner, T. E., Katz, J., & Lew, A. (1996). *Harbingers of depressotypic reassurance seeking: Negative events, anxiety, and self-esteem.* Manuscript submitted for publication.

Joiner, T. E., & Metalsky, G. I. (1995). A prospective test of an integrative interpersonal theory of depression: A naturalistic study of college roommates. *Journal of Personality and Social Psychology, 69,* 778–788.

Kaslow, N. J., Stark, K. D., Printz, B., Livingston, R., & Tsai, S. L. (1992). Cognitive triad inventory for children: Development and relation to depression and anxiety. *Journal of Clinical Child Psychology, 21,* 339–347.

Kazdin, A. E., Esveldt-Dawson, K., Sherick, R. B., & Colbus, D. (1985). Assessment of overt behavior and childhood depression among psychiatrically disturbed children. *Journal of Consulting and Clinical Psychology, 53,* 201–210.

Kazdin, A. E., French, N. H., Unis, A. S., Esveldt-Dawson, K., & Sherick, R. B. (1983). Hopelessness, depression, and suicidal intent among psychiatrically disturbed inpatient children. *Journal of Consulting and Clinical Psychology, 51,* 504–510.

Kazdin, A. E., Rodgers, A., & Colbus, D. (1986). The hopelessness scale for children: Psychometric characteristics and concurrent validity. *Journal of Consulting and Clinical Psychology, 54,* 241–245.

Kendall, P. C., Stark, K. D., & Adam, T. (1990). Cognitive deficit or cognitive distortion in childhood depression. *Journal of Abnormal Child Psychology, 18,* 255–270.

Kennedy, E., Spence, S. H., & Hensley, R. (1989). An examination of the relationship between childhood depression and social competence amongst primary school children. *Journal of Child Psychology and Psychiatry, 30,* 561–573.

Leitenberg, H., Yost, L. W., & Carroll-Wilson, M. (1986). Negative cognitive errors in children: Questionnaire development, normative data, and comparisons between children with and without self-reported symptoms of depression, low self-esteem, and evaluation anxiety. *Journal of Consulting and Clinical Psychology, 54*, 528–536.

Lewinsohn, P. M. (1974). A behavioral approach to depression. In R. M. Friedman, & M. M. Katz (Eds.), *The psychology of depression: Contemporary theory and research* (pp. 132–149). New York: Wiley.

Lewinsohn, P. M., Mischel, W., Chaplin, W., & Barton, R. (1980). Social competence and depression: The role of illusory self-perceptions. *Journal of Abnormal Psychology, 89*, 203–212.

Markus, H. (1977). Self-schemata and processing information about the self. *Journal of Personality and Social Psychology, 35*, 63–78.

Metalsky, G. I., & Joiner, T. E., Jr. (1992). Vulnerability to depressive symptomatology: A prospective test of the diathesis–stress and causal mediation components of the hopelessness theory of depression. *Journal of Personality and Social Psychology, 63*, 667–675.

Metalsky, G. I., Joiner, T. E., Jr., Hardin, T. S., & Abramson, L. Y. (1993). Depressive reactions to failure in a naturalistic setting: A test of the hopelessness and self-esteem theories of depression. *Journal of Abnormal Psychology, 102*, 101–109.

Mullins, L. L., Peterson, L., Wonderlich, S. A., & Reaven, N. M. (1986). The influence of depressive symptomatology in children on the social responses and perception of adults. *Journal of Clinical Child Psychology, 15*, 233–240.

Olinger, L. J., Kuiper, N. A., & Shaw, B. F. (1987). Dysfunctional attitudes and stressful life events: An interactive model of depression. *Cognitive Therapy and Research, 11*, 25–40.

Persons, J. B., & Rao, P. A. (1985). Longitudinal study of cognitions, life events, and depression in psychiatric inpatients. *Journal of Abnormal Psychology, 94*, 51–63.

Peterson, C., & Seligman, M. E. P. (1984). Causal explanations as a risk factor for depression: Theory and evidence. *Psychological Review, 91*, 347–374.

Puig-Antich, J., Lukens, E., Davies, M., Goetz, D., Brennon-Quattrock, J., & Todak, G. (1985). Psychosocial functioning in prepubertal major depressive disorders. *Archives of General Psychiatry, 42*, 511–517.

Radke-Yarrow, M., Belmont, B., Nottelmann, E., & Bottomly, L. (1990). Young children's self-conceptions: Origins in the natural discourse of depressed and normal mothers and their children. In D. Cicchetti & M. Beeghly (Eds.), *The self in transition: Infancy to childhood* (pp. 345–361). Chicago: University of Chicago Press.

Sacco, W. P., & Graves, D. J. (1984). Childhood depression, interpersonal problem-solving, and self-ratings of performance. *Journal of Clinical Child Psychology, 13*, 10–15.

Schmidt, K. (1996). *Cognitive, behavioral, and family factors which differentiate between attention-deficit/hyperactivity disordered children with and without a comorbid mood disorder.* Unpublished doctoral dissertation University of Texas at Austin.

Schmidt, N. B., & Joiner, T. E., Jr. (1996). *The relationship between maladaptive schemas, negative life events and psychological distress.* Manuscipt submitted for publication.

Schmidt, N. B., Joiner, T. E., Jr., Young, J., & Telch, M. J. (1995). The Schema Questionnaire: Investigation of psychometric properties and the hierarchical structure of a measure of early maladaptive schemas. *Cognitive Therapy and Research, 19,* 295–321.

Segal, Z. (1988). Appraisal of the self-schema construct in cognitive models of depression. *Psychological Bulletin, 103,* 147–162.

Segal, Z. V., & Vella, D. D. (1990). Self-schema in major depression: Replication and extension of a priming methodology. *Cognitive Therapy and Research, 14,* 161–176.

Seligman, M. E. P. (1975). *Helplessness: On depression, development, and death.* New York: Freeman.

Seligman, M. E. P., Peterson, C., Kaslow, N. J., Tanenbaum, R. L., Alloy, L. B., & Abramson, L. Y. (1984). Attributional style and depressive symptoms among children. *Journal of Abnormal Psychology, 93,* 235–238.

Stark, K. D., Linn, J. D., Maguire, M., & Kaslow, N. J. (in press). The interpersonal functioning of depressed and anxious children: Social skills, social knowledge, automatic thoughts, and physical arousal. *Journal of Clinical Child Psychology.*

Stark, K. D., Schmidt, K. L., & Joiner, T. E., Jr. (1996). The depressive cognitive triad: Symptom specificity and relationship to children's depressive symptoms, parents' cognitive triad, and perceived parental messages. *Journal of Abnormal Child Psychology, 24,* 615–632.

Stephens, R. S., Hokanson, J. E., & Welker, R. (1987). Responses to depressed interpersonal behavior: Mixed reactions in a helping role. *Journal of Personality and Social Psychology, 52,* 1274–1282.

Swann, W. B., Jr. (1983). Self-verification: Bringing social reality into harmony with the self. In J. Suls & A. G. Greenwald (Eds.), *Social psychological perspectives on the self* (Vol. 2, pp. 33–66). Hillsdale, NJ: Erlbaum.

Swann, W. B., Jr., Wenzlaff, R. M., Krull, D. S., & Pelham, B. W. (1992). Allure of negative feedback: Self-verification strivings among depressed persons. *Journal of Abnormal Psychology, 101,* 293–306.

Swann, W. B., Jr., Wenzlaff, R. M., & Tafarodi, R. W. (1992). Depression and the search for negative evaluations: More evidence of the role of self-verification strivings. *Journal of Abnormal Psychology, 101,* 314–317.

Sweeney, P. D., Anderson, K., & Bailey, S. (1986). Attributional style in depression: A meta-analytic review. *Journal of Personality and Social Psychology, 50,* 974–991.

Telch, M. J., Lucas, J. A., Schmidt, N. B., Hanna, H. H., Jaimez, T. L., & Lucas, R. (1993). Group cognitive-behavioral treatment of panic disorder. *Behaviour Research and Therapy, 31,* 279–287.

Telch, M. J., Schmidt, N. B., Kamphuis, J., Jaimez, L., & Frank, J. (1993, September). *Singular and combined efficacy of in vivo exposure and CBT in the treatment of panic disorder with agoraphobia: Interim results.* Paper presented at the 23rd European Congress of Behaviour and Cognitive Therapies, London.

Turk, D. C., & Speers, M. A. (1983). Cognitive schemata and cognitive processes in cognitive-behavioral interventions: Going beyond the information given. In P. C. Kendall (Ed.), *Advances in cognitive-behavioral research and therapy* (Vol. 2, pp. 1–31). San Diego, CA: Academic Press.

Wierzbicki, M., & McCabe, M. (1988). Social skills and subsequent depressive symptomatology in children. *Journal of Clinical Child Psychology, 17,* 203–208.

Wise, E. H., & Barnes, D. R. (1986). The relationship among life events, dysfunctional attitudes, and depression. *Cognitive Therapy and Research, 10,* 257–266.

Young, J. (1990). *Cognitive therapy for personality disorders: A schema-focused approach.* Sarasota, FL: Professional Resource Exchange.

Zupan, B. A., Hammen, C., & Jaenicke, C. (1987). The effects of current mood and prior depressive history on self-schematic processing in children. *Journal of Experimental Child Psychology, 43,* 149–158.

7

VULNERABLE SELF-ESTEEM AND SOCIAL PROCESSES IN DEPRESSION: TOWARD AN INTERPERSONAL MODEL OF SELF-ESTEEM REGULATION

JOHN E. ROBERTS AND SCOTT M. MONROE

Numerous investigators have found that individuals with higher levels of subclinical depressive symptoms or with episodes of clinical depression report lower levels of self-esteem than their nondepressed counterparts (see Bernet, Ingram, & Johnson, 1993, for a review). Likewise, depressive disorders and symptoms have been repeatedly correlated with interpersonal difficulties, such as inadequate perceived social support (Barnett & Gotlib, 1988; Cohen & Wills, 1985), marital conflict and divorce (Beach, Sandeen, & O'Leary, 1990; Gotlib & Beach, 1995), interpersonal skill deficits (Dykman, Horowitz, Abramson, & Usher, 1991; Gotlib, 1982), and perceptions of inadequate care during childhood (Hickie, Parker, Wilhelm, & Tennant, 1991; Lizardi et al., 1995; MacKinnon, Henderson, & Andrews, 1993). Despite these robust cross-sectional associations between depression and both self-esteem and interpersonal difficulties, controversy remains concerning the nature of the underlying relationships. Although it is possible that many of these deficits are nothing more than correlates, consequences, or artifacts of depression (Coyne & Gotlib, 1983, 1986; Monroe & Steiner, 1986), there is evidence suggesting that certain aspects of self-esteem and the interpersonal environment play a more central role in depression, specifically, in the etiology and maintenance of depressive disorders and symptoms. Nonetheless, it is currently unclear how these factors operate in the development and maintenance of depression. The psychological pathways and mechanisms leading from social functioning and self-esteem to depression have not been adequately delineated.

In response to this void, investigators recently have begun to formulate models to integrate intra- and interpersonal aspects of depression in terms of understanding the etiology and maintenance of depressive disorders and symptoms (Carnelley, Pietromonaco, & Jaffe, 1994; Gotlib & Hammen, 1992; Joiner, Alfano, & Metalsky, 1993). One interesting possibility is that important attachment relationships contribute to the development and maintenance of positive self-esteem, which in turn buffers against depression. Conversely, adverse experiences in these relationships would lead to attachment insecurity, deficits in self-esteem, and vulnerability to depression. In the current chapter, we outline an approach to understanding depression that emphasizes the role of interpersonal processes in regulating and maintaining stable levels of self-esteem.

We begin the present chapter by discussing some of the complexities within the self-esteem construct, including distinctions between level of self-esteem and other dimensions of self-esteem, such as stability, reactivity, and regulatory processes. We want the reader to understand that "there's more to self-esteem than whether it is high or low" (Kernis, Cornell, Sun, Berry, & Harlow, 1993, p. 1190). The chapter continues with a review of associations between depression and four major aspects of self-esteem, namely, level of self-esteem, processes associated with self-esteem regulation, self-esteem reactivity, and self-esteem stability. On the basis of this review of the research literature, we suggest that difficulties in the latter three aspects of self-esteem might prove to be more indicative of risk for depressive symptoms, and perhaps episodes, than are chronic low levels of self-esteem. Rather than low self-esteem, it may be that depression-prone people are characterized by deficits in (a) the strategies or processes they use in evaluating and maintaining their self-worth; (b) the resilience of their self-esteem to the effects of various challenges, such as life stressors and dysphoric moods; and (c) the stability of their self-esteem over time. Finally, and of most relevance to the current volume, we further posit that depression-prone people evidence problems with close interpersonal relationships and attachment security, which in turn play an important role in regulating and maintaining self-esteem.

As we show, a broad characterization of thought and research on self-esteem and depression is clearly consistent with the idea that facets of self-esteem may at least in part contribute to the onset and maintenance of depression. However, there are many conceptual and operational matters that must be clarified to ensure that existing associations are not merely artifacts, correlates, or consequences of depression (Coyne & Gotlib, 1983, 1986; Monroe & Steiner, 1986). These issues range from the fact that low self-esteem is considered a defining symptom of depression (Bernet et al., 1993) to the related fact that self-report measures of self-esteem and depressive symptoms frequently share item content (Coyne & Gotlib, 1983). As we discuss later, use of prospective and remission designs, as well as eliminating self-esteem items from depression measures, can be helpful in dealing with such issues. Furthermore, studies investigating aspects of self-esteem other than simply level (i.e., high vs. low self-esteem), such as temporal stability of self-esteem, are somewhat less vulnerable to these potential confounds.

Another important issue when considering this research concerns the operationalization of depression. In this chapter, we review studies using samples of individuals suffering from clinical depression diagnosed through structured interviews as well as samples of individuals (typically college students) who report varying levels of depressive symptoms on self-report inventories. Although we are interested in processes associated with vulnerability to clinical depression, studies based on nonclinical samples can be useful in providing initial tests of hypotheses that can be further investigated in more severely ill populations. Frequently, novel and innovative ideas in the field are first tested in nonclinical samples (e.g., Joiner & Metalsky, 1995; Linville, 1987) and only later are examined among individuals with more severe depression. At this time, many of the studies testing hypotheses relevant to the current chapter are based on nonclinical samples. It is important to keep in mind that it is unclear to what extent the findings are generalizable to clinical populations.

SELF-ESTEEM AND DEPRESSION

Historically, the concept of self-esteem has played a crucial role in a number of theories of depression. Freud (1917/1986) introduced the notion that self-esteem is a critical factor in depression and believed that loss of self-worth was an important distinguishing feature between mourning and melancholia. Other psychoanalytic theorists expanded on this idea and suggested that loss of self-esteem plays a major causal role in the onset and maintenance of the disorder (Bibring, 1953; Fenichel, 1945; Jacobson, 1975; Rado, 1928, 1951). Many of these theorists posited that the disposition toward poor self-esteem regulation is laid down in early childhood as a result of inadequate parenting experiences (e.g., Fenichel, 1945; Jacobson, 1975; Kohut, 1987). As such, early interpersonal relationships are thought to set the stage for the development of vulnerable self-esteem, and depression. Some theorists have suggested that vulnerability to depression is represented by an overinvestment of self-esteem in external, difficult-to-maintain "supplies" and in excessive interpersonal dependency (e.g., Barnett & Gotlib, 1988; Blatt & Zuroff, 1992; Rado, 1928); this is consistent with the idea that interpersonal relationships are critical in establishing and maintaining self-esteem.

There has been a resurgence of interest in self-esteem in relation to depression. Cognitive theorists, such as Beck (1967; Pretzer & Beck, 1996) and Teasdale (1988), have suggested that negative cognitions about the self are critically involved in the maintenance of depression. It is thought that these cognitions are one of a number of interlocking elements that help perpetuate depression. From a sociological perspective, Brown and Harris (1978) suggested that social vulnerability factors, such as unemployment and inadequate social support, generate psychological vulnerability through their corrosive effects on self-esteem. Others have suggested that stressful life events lead to depression by thwarting important goals and aspirations related to an individual's sense of self-worth (Hyland, 1987; Oatley & Bolton, 1985; Pyszczynski & Greenberg, 1987). Of most relevance to the current volume is the suggestion of interpersonal theorists that several of the negative interactional cycles typical of depressed people's social relationships arise because they seek excessive reassurance about their personal worth (Coyne, 1976; Potthoff, Holahan, & Joiner, 1995), negative feedback to verify negative self-conceptions (Giesler, Josephs, & Swann, 1996; Joiner, 1995; Swann, Wenzlaff, Krull, & Pelham, 1992), or a combination of both excessive reassurance and negative feedback (Joiner et al., 1993; Joiner & Metalsky, 1995). It is quite possible, therefore, that a number of negative interpersonal processes documented in depression are driven, at least in part, by aspects of vulnerable self-esteem.

Nature of Self-Esteem

Before we proceed further, we want to define and develop conceptually the construct of self-esteem, particularly as it relates to vulnerability to depression. As noted by Robson (1988) and Mruk (1995), constructs that differ considerably are frequently camped under the tent of self-esteem, which has led to confusion and superficial understanding. According to William James (1890), self-esteem is one's evaluation of the degree to which important aspirations, ideals, and values are being met. Likewise, self-esteem can be seen as one's overall evaluation of self (Rosenberg, 1979). In Becker's (1979) words, self-esteem is "a cognitive-affective product of self-evaluation processes" (p. 319). Within these perspectives, the *process* of self-evaluation is as important as the end *product* or *outcome* of self-evaluation. We refer to this end product of self-evaluation as the *level of self-esteem*, which is a dimension of how positive or negative a person's feelings of self-worth are. Although many aspects of the process of self-evaluation might be nonconscious (Brewin, 1989; Power & Brewin, 1991), we consider the outcome of self-evaluation to be a person's consciously experienced feelings of worth.

Although level of experienced self-worth clearly is an important aspect of self-esteem and has received considerable attention within clinical, social, and personality psychology over the past 25 years, the self-esteem construct is likely to be considerably more complex than a simple determination of whether a person's self-worth is relatively high or low. For example, it is apparent that people differ in terms of the stability of their self-esteem over time (Kernis et al., 1993; Kernis, Grannemann, & Barclay, 1989), the resilience of their self-evaluations to the effects of stressors and dysphoric moods (Brown & Mankowski, 1993; Roberts & Kassel, 1996), the sources from which they derive feelings of global self-worth (Marsh, 1986; Pelham & Swann, 1989), as well as the strategies and processes by which they regulate self-esteem (Baumeister, Tice, & Hutton, 1989; Josephs, Larrick, Steele, & Nisbett, 1992; Rhodewalt, Morf, Hazlett, & Fairfield, 1991; Wayment & Taylor, 1995). Furthermore, it is unclear whether the end product of the process of self-evaluation (i.e., level of self-esteem) is a monolithic structure or, rather, should be conceptualized as composed of many semiautonomous domains or facets (Markus & Nurius, 1986; Marsh, 1986, 1993). For example, people may evaluate themselves favorably in some domains (e.g., worker, religious person), but not in others (e.g., parent). In terms of vulnerability to depression, an individual might become devastated by negative evaluations within an area of particular idiosyncratic importance and meaning, even though this person typically is able to maintain normal levels of global self-esteem because of positive evaluations across other domains. Furthermore, the degree to which these positive and negative self-representations are interconnected also might have important emotional consequences (see Linville, 1987; Showers, 1992; Stein & Markus, 1994).

Although multiple facets of self-esteem, such as stability, resilience, sources, and regulatory processes, are implicated in vulnerability to depression at a theoretical level (Kuiper & Olinger, 1986; Roberts & Monroe, 1994; Swallow & Kuiper, 1988), in the preponderance of empirical studies only global level of trait self-esteem (high vs. low self-esteem) has been examined. Unfortunately, there is reason to believe that such a perspective is less than ideal and that self-reported low self-esteem might not be a particularly good indicator of vulnerability to depression (Barnett & Gotlib, 1988; Butler, Hokanson, & Flynn, 1994; Roberts & Monroe, 1994). After reviewing studies addressing level of self-esteem as a potential causal factor, we discuss other facets of self-esteem that are hypothetically related to vulnerability, including processes associated with self-esteem regulation, self-esteem reactivity, and temporal stability of self-esteem, as well as initial research testing these ideas.

Empirical Investigations of Self-Esteem and Depression

Traditionally, the idea that self-esteem plays a causal role in depression has been supported by rich clinical descriptions of self-devaluation in depression (e.g., Beck, 1967; Kohut, 1987) as well as by cross-sectional studies that showed that currently depressed individuals suffer diminished self-worth compared with nondepressed individuals (e.g., Axford & Jerrom, 1986; Feather & Barber, 1983; Gara et al., 1993; Hewstone, Hooper, & Miller, 1981; Laxer, 1964; Lewinsohn, Steinmetz, Larson, & Franklin, 1981; Tarlow & Haaga, 1996). Although clearly demonstrating that depression is associated with self-esteem deficits, these clinical descriptions and cross-sectional designs preclude inferences about the precise nature of the relationship: Low self-esteem might be no more than a correlate, a consequence, or an artifact of depression (Bernet et al., 1993; Coyne & Gotlib, 1983, 1986). For example, Coyne and Gotlib (1983) noted that such associations could be tautological and could result from item overlap between self-report measures of self-esteem and depression, whereas Bernet et al. (1993) pointed out that low self-esteem is a defining symptom of depression.

More recently, researchers have used remission designs, which compare previously depressed individuals with never-depressed persons, and prospective designs, which attempt to determine whether a presumed risk factor, such as vulnerable self-esteem, exists prior to depression. If vulnerable self-esteem is a traitlike risk factor that causally contributes to depression, it should be apparent in depression-prone people before, during, and after episodes of the disorder. If vulnerable self-esteem is merely a correlate, symptom, or artifact of depression, however, it would be manifest only during episodes of depression (see Barnett & Gotlib, 1988). These types of designs have their limitations as well. They fail to rule out the possibility that vulnerable self-esteem is a prodromal symptom (in the case of prospective studies) or a consequence of depression (in the case of remission studies). Thus, investigators are advised to use ancillary procedures so that they can better substantiate the nature of associations found. For example, frequent measurement of constructs and symptoms may be useful to disaggregate them over time. Furthermore, some researchers have recommended removing self-esteem-related items from self-report measures of depression to guard against tautologies due to item overlap (e.g., Roberts & Monroe, 1992; Whisman & Kwon, 1993). Overall, the complexities and technicalities pertaining to this core concern with discriminant validity must be appreciated throughout any review of the literature.

Level of Self-Esteem

In two early studies, it was found that previously depressed individuals were characterized by a number of personality features, including low self-esteem, when compared with never-depressed individuals (Altman & Wittenborn, 1980; Cofer & Wittenborn, 1980). However, these findings are difficult to interpret because previously depressed and never-depressed participants were not matched on current levels of depressive symptoms. Subclinical depressive symptoms are known to remain elevated following remission (Depue & Monroe, 1986) and are strongly correlated with lower self-esteem. In this regard, in a recent study researchers found that previously depressed adolescents reported lower self-esteem than never-depressed adolescents (Lewinsohn et al., 1994). However, this difference became nonsignificant when initial depressive symptoms were statistically controlled. Similarly, Butler et al. (1994) and Lewinsohn et al. (1981) were unable to find differences in level of self-esteem between previously depressed and never-depressed individuals in college and community samples, respectively. Other investigators have also found that dysfunctional contingencies of self-worth (i.e., rigid beliefs concerning what is required for self-esteem; see Kuiper & Olinger, 1986) return to normal levels following remission of depression (e.g., Hamilton & Abramson, 1983; Silverman, Silverman, & Eardley, 1984). Overall, there is little evidence that previously depressed people are characterized by low self-esteem (but see Hartlage, Ardvino, & Alloy, 1998, for conflicting results).

Over the past decade, there have been a number of prospective studies conducted to determine whether low self-esteem predisposes to future depression. In a classic study, Lewinsohn et al. (1981) measured a wide variety of cognitive variables, including self-esteem, in a community sample of 998 individuals. Participants were followed for up to 9 months. Although concurrent depression was clearly associated with diminished self-esteem at baseline, cognitive measures (including self-esteem) failed to predict subsequent onsets of clinical depression. Unfortunately, all cognitive measures were analyzed simultaneously in a multivariate analysis of variance, raising the possibility that differences in self-esteem may have been "washed out," particularly if they were small. Consistent with this possibility, in a reanalysis of these data, Lewinsohn, Hoberman, and Rosenbaum (1988) found that a measure of baseline dissatisfaction with one's self discriminated participants who developed an episode of depression from those who remained well (Table 2, p. 257). However, these authors failed to control statistically for initial depressive symptoms in this analysis, leaving it unclear as to whether or not self-esteem made an independent contribution to the prediction of future depressive episodes. In terms of the onset of subclinical depressive symptoms, Lewinsohn et al. (1988) found that low self-esteem predicted higher levels of depressive symptoms over the 9-month prospective interval, even after initial depression was statistically controlled.

Ingham, Kreitman, Miller, Sashidharan, and Surtees (1987) found that low self-esteem predicted the onset of clinical depression in a large community sample. The relation between self-esteem and future onset of depressive episodes was small, however, and appeared to be due to overlap between low self-esteem and subclinical symptoms. Hokanson, Rubert, Welker, Hollander, and Hedeen (1989) also reported that low self-esteem predicted the onset of depressive episodes over a 9-month prospective interval in college students, but unfortunately these authors failed to control for initial subclinical depressive symptoms. Finally, Lewinsohn et al. (1994) found that low self-esteem predicted future onset of clinical depression over a 1-year prospective interval in a large sample of adolescents ($N = 1,508$) in the community. Unfortunately, these investigators also failed to control for initial depressive symptoms (which were elevated in those who eventually developed major depression), rendering conclusions ambiguous concerning whether low self-esteem predicted future onset of depression independently of initial subclinical symptoms.

In addition to examining the main effects of self-esteem, investigators have tested diathesis—stress hypotheses, which posit that deficiencies in self-esteem increase the negative impact of stressful life events (Alloy, Hartlage, & Abramson, 1988; Monroe & Simons, 1991). These models suggest that self-esteem buffers against the depressogenic impact of stressful life events. Specifically, the buffering hypothesis predicts that low self-esteem will be associated with the onset of depression more strongly in people who have undergone stressful life events than in those with relatively stress-free lives. This hypothesis is tested by examining the statistical interaction between self-esteem and life stressors: Individuals with low self-esteem should become more depressed following stressful life events than those with higher self-esteem.

Brown and his colleagues tested this hypothesis in a 2-year longitudinal study of 404 women who were initially nondepressed but who were considered at risk for clinical depression because of social factors (such as low socioeconomic status and having young children living at home). Negative life events were assessed through a well-validated interview-based approach (Brown & Harris, 1978; see also Monroe & Roberts, 1990). Likewise, self-esteem was measured through an interview designed to elicit thoughts and evaluations concerning the self (Brown, Andrews, Bifulco, & Veiel, 1990). Consistent with Brown, Andrews, et al.'s theory, negative evaluation of the self was associated with the onset of depressive episodes, but only in the face of a major life event. It is important that self-esteem interacting with life stress predicted future onsets of depression independently of its association with subclinical disorders (Brown, Bifulco, & Andrews, 1990a; Brown, Bifulco, Harris, & Bridge, 1986). Likewise, in a reanalysis of data from their community sample discussed earlier (Ingham et al., 1987), Miller, Kreitman, Ingham, and Sashidharan (1989) found that low self-esteem was associated with an increased risk of developing an episode of depression following major life stressors. However, this relation held only for people with a previous history of depression, and it is unclear whether the interaction was independent of subclinical symptomatology. Finally, Metalsky, Joiner, Hardin, and Abramson (1993) found that the pernicious combination of negative attributional style and academic disappointment was most apparent in participants with low self-esteem. That is, individuals with low self-esteem who tended to attribute negative events to global and stable causes were at increased risk of developing depressive symptoms following poor performance on an academic examination. High self-esteem buffered against the onset of depressive symptoms following failure, even among people with a negative attributional style (see also Robinson, Garber, & Hilsman, 1995, for similar findings with a sample of children).

In contrast, other researchers have been unable to replicate these diathesis–stress findings. Low self-esteem failed to predict changes in depressive symptoms in interaction with life stressors in five studies in which the participants were college students (Butler et al., 1994; Lakey, 1988; Roberts & Gotlib, 1997a; Roberts & Kassel, 1997; Roberts & Monroe, 1992). Likewise, the interaction between life stress and self-esteem failed to predict future onsets of depressive symptoms or episodes in a large community sample (Lewinsohn et al., 1988). Furthermore, although Whisman and Kwon (1993) found that self-esteem interacted with life events in predicting changes in depressive symptoms in a sample of college students, the form of this interaction was opposite to that of predictions: Low self-esteem predicted increases in depressive symptoms in people who were relatively low in life stress rather than in those who experienced relatively high levels of stress. Several additional prospective studies in which investigators attempted to test the buffering hypothesis (Hobfoll & Leiberman, 1987; Hobfoll & London, 1986) unfortunately have provided ambiguous results because self-esteem was measured only concurrently with follow-up depressive symptoms.

Overall, there has been weak and inconsistent support for the hypothesis that low levels of self-esteem precede the onset of, or remain subsequent to, depressive episodes and symptoms. Furthermore, the role of self-esteem in predicting depression was not much stronger in studies in which the combined effects of low self-esteem and stressful life events were tested. These findings argue against the hypothesis that low self-esteem plays a major causal role in depression. However, conceptual and methodological limitations might have precluded finding greater support for this hypothesis. According to Brown, Andrews, Harris, Adler, and Bridge (1986), it might be difficult to demonstrate self-esteem effects in prospective designs because the *drop* in self-esteem from an initially moderate-to-high baseline (in contrast to chronically low self-esteem) might be crucial in many onsets of depression. Consequently, loss of self-esteem might precede the onset of depression by only a brief interval. In fact, depression and the loss of self-esteem might co-occur in a downward spiral (Teasdale, 1988), making it methodologically difficult to demonstrate the temporal precedence of low self-esteem. Of particular relevance to the current volume is the possibility that self-esteem might plummet when vulnerable individuals are confronted with disappointments and negative revelations about their closest relationships (Brown et al., 1986), relationships that, as we later show, are likely to be critical in maintaining positive feelings of self-worth.

Strategies and Processes to Regulate Self-Esteem

Epstein (1980) posited that people are motivated to maintain stable self-concepts and positive feelings of self-esteem. Consistent with this view, a number of theorists (e.g., Crocker & Major, 1989; Steele, 1988; Tesser, 1988) have suggested that people use various strategies, processes, and mechanisms to maintain, protect, and enhance their self-esteem. In contrast, it is possible that depressed and depression-prone people experience deficits in these self-esteem regulation processes. In the current chapter, we focus on aspects of self-esteem regulation that might be related to vulnerability to depression, including social comparison processes, self-enhancement strategies, and self-affirmation.

Self-esteem regulation is in part based on the manner in which individuals evaluate or judge their talents, abilities, and performances in personally salient domains (Becker, 1979; James, 1890). One important way people self-evaluate is by comparing themselves with other individuals on various dimensions (Festinger, 1954). Indeed, an extensive social psychological literature has evolved investigating social comparison processes in nondepressed people (Suls & Wills, 1991; Wood, 1989). Social comparisons appear to be a critical aspect of self-evaluation that contributes to overall feelings of self-esteem. According to Gilbert, Price, and Allan (1995), self-esteem essentially represents a person's internal judgments of social rank and position (see also Leary, Tambor, Terdal, & Downs, 1995). Social comparisons are crucial in establishing these judgments of rank; consequently, they are critical in determining a person's feelings of self-esteem. Gilbert (1992) argued that comparisons in which the self is judged to be inferior and low in social rank have a devastating impact on the individual. These types of evaluations result in a biopsychosocial state representing defeat, helplessness, and depression (Gilbert, 1992; Price, Sloman, Gardner, Gilbert, & Rohde, 1994).

In the social comparison literature, a great deal of attention has been paid to the choice of comparison to others. Who serves as the reference by which people judge themselves? Downward social comparisons (i.e., comparing oneself to someone who is worse off) can be used in the service of maintaining positive illusions about the self (Taylor & Brown, 1988; Wayment & Taylor, 1995), particularly when individuals are experiencing stress or ego-threat (Aspinwall & Taylor, 1993; Wills, 1981). Therefore, one might expect that when stressed, healthy nondepressed individuals use downward comparisons to help protect, maintain, and even enhance their self-esteem. In contrast, upward comparisons (i.e., comparing oneself to someone who is better off) are likely to result in depletions in self-esteem, unless these comparisons are discounted for various reasons (Swallow & Kuiper, 1988). One would expect, therefore, that the tendency to use these types of upward comparisons, as well as an inability to make downward comparisons, would contribute to depression. These maladaptive strategies and processes in self-esteem regulation would increase the risk for developing depressive symptoms and, perhaps, episodes.

After failure experiences, nondepressed individuals were found either to inhibit the social comparison process altogether or to make downward comparisons, a finding that is consistent with the preceding formulation (Swallow & Kuiper, 1993). Inhibition of social comparison and downward comparisons after failures and disappointments would protect the self-esteem of these nondepressed individuals. However, subclinically depressed individuals were found to engage in frequent social comparisons regardless of their performance and the feedback they received (Swallow & Kuiper, 1992, 1993). Consequently, following failures and disappointments, these mildly depressed people would be exposed to a high degree of negative feedback, which is likely to corrode their self-esteem further (Swallow & Kuiper, 1988). Apparently, mildly depressed people fail to protect their self-esteem from these potentially damaging social comparisons. Wayment and Taylor (1995) found that people with low self-esteem reported engaging in more frequent upward comparisons than did those with high self-esteem. Although this study was cross-sectional, these findings are consistent with the possibility that upward social comparisons, particularly after failures and disappointments, contribute to depletions in self-esteem. Unfortunately, we are unaware of any researchers who have investigated these processes in previously depressed people or who have used prospective designs to determine whether these types of comparisons are associated with the onset of depressive symptoms or episodes. Research also needs to be conducted with clinically significant depression.

The social comparison literature suggests that members of one's social network play an important role in self-evaluation and the regulation of self-esteem because they serve as sources of comparative information. In addition, the nature and the quality of relationships with individuals within one's social sphere can have a more direct bearing on evaluations of self-worth. Positive, mutually rewarding relationships give individuals the message that they are worthy of care and affection, whereas rejection and hostility within close relationships give the message that they are unworthy. Indeed, self-esteem might serve as a gauge indicating an individual's degree of social connectedness, or what Leary et al. (1995) referred to as a *sociometer*. It is interesting that depressed and depression-prone individuals are thought to experience a wide range of difficulties in terms of their interpersonal relationships (see Barnett & Gotlib, 1988; Coyne, Burchill, & Stiles, 1991; Segrin & Abramson, 1994, for reviews). In fact, Coyne's (1976) interpersonal model of depression posits that to a great degree, the interpersonal rejection experienced by depressed people is due to the fact that these individuals are in some way aversive to other people.

With findings that are consistent with Coyne's hypothesis, researchers have documented that interpersonal rejection is associated with a combination of behaviors and characteristics, including mild depression, low self-esteem, excessive reassurance seeking that others "truly care," and negative feedback seeking (Joiner et al., 1992, Joiner, Alfano, & Metalsky, 1993; Joiner & Metalsky, 1995). Furthermore, depressed individuals and people prone to depression are more willing to engage in social comparison on topics that are normatively inappropriate (Kuiper & McCabe, 1985). These types of interactions are thought to lead to embarrassment and withdrawal on the part of their interaction partners (Gurtman, 1987) and to negative self-evaluations on the part of the depressed individuals. Although the evidence is somewhat mixed, symptomatically and clinically depressed individuals appear to induce negative emotional reactions in others who interact with them, particularly if the individuals are in longer term relationships with the depressed persons, such as roommates and marital partners (Coyne et al., 1987; Joiner, 1994). These findings suggest that depressed, and perhaps depression-prone, individuals are likely to create interpersonal milieus in which it is difficult to maintain positive self-evaluations; they are likely to be exposed to high levels of rejection, criticism, and conflict, which may impair self-esteem regulation.

In addition to social comparison processes and interpersonal feedback, there are a number of other possible contributors to self-esteem maintenance and regulation. For example, people engage in different strategies in the process of self-evaluation that have varying effects on self-esteem regulation. Some individuals evaluate themselves to obtain accurate self-views. However, self-consistency theorists suggest that people attempt to self-verify what they already know or believe about themselves (Swann, 1983). Finally, other theorists suggest that people use self-evaluation as an opportunity to self-enhance (Taylor & Brown, 1988). That is, they seek positive information about themselves, regardless of the validity of that information. In an impressive series of studies, Sedikides (1993) demonstrated that individuals (not selected in terms of depression) largely tend to self-evaluate on the basis of self-enhancement strategies and, to a lesser extent, self-verification strategies. Accurate self-assessment was rarely used by participants in her studies. This research suggests that many people use self-evaluation strategies that are likely to lead to positive self-esteem. Future investigations might profitably examine whether depression-prone individuals differ from less vulnerable individuals in terms of these strategies in self-evaluation. Findings indicating that depression is associated with "evenhanded" self-evaluations and cognitive processing (e.g., Alloy & Abramson, 1988; Alloy & Clements, 1992; Gilboa, Roberts, & Gotlib, 1997) suggest that depression-prone individuals would be less likely to self-enhance, which would have important implications concerning self-esteem regulation. Consistent with this view are findings that individuals with low self-esteem tend to make decisions that minimize potential future regret (Josephs et al., 1992) and tend to downplay their own accomplishments (John & Robins, 1994). These more "conservative" strategies are less likely to provide self-esteem boosts.

What happens when one's valued positive self-conceptions are threatened by failures and letdowns? How do people protect their self-esteem? According to Steele (1988), people often attempt to maintain self-esteem in the face of various threats by affirming another valued aspect of the self. For example, if a young woman does poorly on an examination, she might protect her self-esteem by thinking about how good a tennis player she is. In terms of vulnerability to depression, we hypothesize that, in addition to failing to self-enhance within a particular domain, depression-prone individuals would have difficulties in protecting self-esteem through affirmation of other self domains. Depression-prone individuals are thought to have fewer sources of self-esteem, or valued aspects of the self, so that affirming another source would be difficult; these vulnerable individuals would have fewer resources to rely on (Roberts & Monroe, 1994; see also Steele, Spencer, & Lynch, 1993).

Resilience of Self-Esteem

It is possible that vulnerable self-esteem is generally well guarded against and becomes manifest only when individuals' defenses are down or under particularly challenging conditions. For example, Bernet et al. (1993) suggested that individuals might develop special skills, strengths, and areas of competence to compensate for an underlying negative core sense of self-esteem (cf. Adler, 1956). Consistent with this formulation, cognitive theorists have suggested that underlying negative thoughts and self-representations remain latent until activated by certain types of priming, such as stressful life events and dysphoric mood (Persons & Miranda, 1992; Riskind & Rholes, 1984; Segal & Ingram, 1994; Teasdale, 1983, 1988).

This hypothesis was supported by two studies conducted by Miranda and Persons (1988; Miranda, Persons, & Byers, 1990), who found that dysfunctional contingencies of self-worth were highly correlated with dysphoric mood in people with previous episodes of depression but were relatively uncorrelated with mood in never-depressed people. These findings suggest that negative mood states activate or make accessible dysfunctional thinking in previously depressed people but not in those who have never been depressed. Until primed by negative mood, these underlying dysfunctional contingencies of self-worth remain latent and inaccessible. Recently, Roberts and Kassel (1996) found a similar pattern of results for experienced self-esteem: Self-esteem was more highly correlated with negative affect in individuals who reported previous episodes of depressive symptoms ($r = -.45$, $p < .001$) than in never-depressed individuals ($r = -.16$, ns). It is important to note that the magnitudes of these correlations were significantly different. This differential pattern of association was not demonstrated with positive affect, suggesting that the loss of positive affect is unrelated to the deflation of self-esteem. Of related interest is the work of Brown and Mankowski (1993), who investigated the relation between mood and self-evaluation in persons with high and low self-esteem. In two studies, these authors found that both groups evaluated themselves favorably after elation mood inductions but that only low-self-esteem participants evaluated themselves negatively following depressive mood inductions. In a third study, they found the same relationship under conditions of naturally occurring fluctuations in daily mood. Together, these results suggest that both individuals with previous episodes of depression and individuals with low self-esteem experience a tighter linkage between dysphoric mood and negative thoughts about themselves than do individuals with relatively positive self-esteem who have never been clinically depressed. It may be that negative mood states act as a prime that activates negative self-conceptions. Furthermore, these studies suggest that the self-representations of depression-prone individuals are less resilient to the effects of dysphoric mood than are those of individuals who are less depression prone. Can stressful life events also act as a prime?

Miranda (1992) tested the hypothesis that stressful life events activate or make accessible dysfunctional beliefs in depression-prone individuals. She found that stressful life events were more highly correlated with negative thoughts concerning the self in previously depressed individuals than in never-depressed individuals. Subsequently, Butler et al. (1994) examined the resilience of self-esteem to daily environmental events. The authors collected 30 daily ratings of self-esteem and life hassles from college students. A measure of the reactivity of self-esteem to the environment was derived using autoregression. It is interesting that previously depressed individuals were found to have more highly reactive self-esteem than never-depressed people. Furthermore, stressful life events predicted changes in depressive symptoms over a 5-month prospective interval more strongly in individuals with relatively reactive self-esteem (with baseline symptoms controlled). These results suggest that depression-prone individuals' self-esteem is less resilient to the effects of daily life stressors than that of people who are less vulnerable to depression. Unfortunately, daily affective states were not measured in this study, leaving it unclear whether depression-prone individuals experience difficulties specifically in regulating self-esteem or have more general deficits in affect regulation (cf. Gross & Munoz, 1995; Westen, 1994).

Together, these studies suggest that the self-esteem of depression-prone individuals (even when nonepisodic) is relatively reactive to dysphoric moods and stressful life events compared with the self-esteem of less vulnerable individuals. As a result of this poor resilience, difficult interpersonal relationships are likely to have a major negative impact on depression-prone individuals' self-evaluations. For example, a conflictual marriage is likely to contribute to frequent self-esteem depletions as a result of both the daily stress endured in such a relationship and the negative affective states that would be generated from ongoing fights. As we have discussed, depression-prone people are particularly likely to have these types of conflictual relationships. Unfortunately, these individuals also might be more vulnerable to suffering from such relationships as well: Both daily stressors and negative emotions are more likely to deplete self-esteem of depression-prone people than of less vulnerable individuals.

Stability of Self-Esteem

Consistent with the foregoing discussion, theorists and researchers have suggested that temporal instability in self-esteem might characterize people at risk for depression. Barnett and Gotlib (1988) were among the first to state this hypothesis explicitly. They suggested that because of excessive interpersonal dependency and reliance on others to provide self-esteem, people at risk for depression would experience labile or temporally unstable self-esteem. These individuals' sense of self-worth would be held hostage to the external world and would rise and fall with the vicissitudes of their social environments. Likewise, Swallow and Kuiper (1988) posited that the self-evaluations of people vulnerable to depression would be temporally unstable and would fluctuate in relation to positive and negative feedback received from the social environment. According to these theorists, instability in depression-prone individuals' self-evaluations would be a consequence of their acceptance of both downward and upward social comparisons (Swallow & Kuiper, 1988).

In four recent studies with college student samples, investigators directly tested the hypothesis that vulnerability to depressive symptoms is in part characterized by temporally unstable self-esteem. In the first, Roberts and Monroe (1992) measured self-esteem on nine occasions over a 3-week period in 192 individuals. Temporal instability in self-esteem was operationalized as within-person variance scores in self-esteem. A measure of academic disappointment was developed on the basis of the discrepancy between the grade that participants "expected/hoped for" (measured 3 weeks before an examination) and actual performance, weighted by how important academic achievement was for the student (see Metalsky, Halberstadt, & Abramson, 1987). Results indicated that the combination of labile self-esteem and academic disappointment prospectively predicted increases in depressive symptoms (with baseline symptoms controlled). The fact that this effect held only for individuals who were initially nondepressed, however, suggests that labile self-esteem primarily contributes to the onset of depressive symptoms rather than to their maintenance.

Roberts and Kassel (1997) conducted a follow-up study to replicate and extend these initial findings concerning instability in self-esteem. In this investigation, a more comprehensive assessment of stressful life events and a longer prospective interval (8 weeks) were used. Instability in self-esteem was operationalized as within-person standard deviation scores in seven daily ratings of self-esteem in a sample of 213 college students. Results were consistent with previous findings: Stressful life events had a more depressogenic impact on people with unstable self-esteem than on those with stable self-esteem, and this effect held only for people who were initially low in symptoms. These findings again suggest that instability in self-esteem primarily contributes to the onset of depressive symptoms rather than to their maintenance. In addition, results indicated that the interaction between unstable self-esteem and life stress for initially low-symptom individuals was confined to people with relatively severe worst lifetime episodes of depressive symptoms. The latter finding suggests that unstable self-esteem is particularly relevant to people who appear to be prone to developing more severe depression. Consequently, temporal instability in self-esteem has *potential* relevance to the relapse of depressive episodes. However, this hypothesis needs to be directly tested in a sample of individuals who have been diagnosed on the basis of structured interviews as having episodes of major depressive disorder but who are in remission.

In a sample of 94 female college students who were initially low in depressive symptoms, Roberts and Gotlib (1996) obtained further support for the hypothesis that temporal instability in self-esteem is associated with risk for developing depressive symptoms. Unstable self-esteem was again operationalized as within-person standard deviation scores in self-esteem measured daily over the course of 1 week. Consistent with earlier findings, the interaction between temporally unstable self-esteem and stressful life events predicted the onset of depressive symptoms over a 6-week prospective interval, and this effect was confined to individuals who reported relatively severe worst lifetime episodes of depressive symptoms. It is interesting that instability in affective states failed to predict onset of depressive symptoms, suggesting that vulnerability effects are specific to dysregulation in self-esteem rather than related to more general affective dysregulation. Furthermore, results indicated that the interaction between instability in self-esteem and stressful life events failed to predict changes in anxiety. This finding suggests that effects of unstable self-esteem are specific to symptoms of depression and are not predictive of general psychological distress. In contrast to these specificity results, another investigator found that relatively high but temporally unstable self-esteem is associated with negative affective reactions involving anger and hostility following academic disappointment (Kernis et al., 1989).

Finally, the vulnerability findings discussed previously were recently replicated by independent investigators with a sample of 98 college students (Kernis et al., 1998). Increases in depressive symptoms over time were predicted by the interaction of self-esteem instability and daily hassles. Individuals with both unstable self-esteem and high levels of hassles reported the greatest increases in depressive symptoms. Of importance, these results remained significant after other presumed cognitive vulnerabilities, such as negative attributional style, were controlled statistically. Together, these four studies suggest that temporally unstable self-esteem is associated with increased risk for the development of depressive symptoms subsequent to life stress.

INTERPERSONAL BASIS OF SELF-ESTEEM

As we have mentioned, a number of theorists and investigators have suggested that self-esteem is rooted in one's social relationships. This hypothesis dates back to early psychoanalytic formulations, which suggested that negative self-esteem results from internalized anger toward an important person, or "object" (Freud, 1917/1986), and that positive self-esteem develops during infancy from an internalization of parental affection and attention (Fenichel, 1945; Kohut, 1984). From a different theoretical perspective, Cooley (1902), who wrote of the "looking-glass self," also emphasized the role of other people's reactions in determining self-esteem, and Mead (1934) posited that self-esteem is shaped by the reflected appraisals of others. In other words, Cooley and Mead both suggested that individuals' self-images, including self-esteem, are formed from the views that other people who are important in their lives have of them. Rosenberg (1979) stated that the research has generally borne out Cooley's and Mead's ideas and that "we are more or less unconsciously seeing ourselves as we think others who are important to us and whose opinion we trust see us"

(p. 97). More recently, Bowlby (1980) hypothesized that positive self-esteem arises through the development of secure attachment relationships in childhood, suggesting that interpersonal relationships in early development might be particularly important. In this section, we selectively review studies addressing the interpersonal basis of self-esteem.

Childhood Interpersonal Relationships and Traumas

Does the quality of one's interpersonal relationships in childhood contribute to the development of self-esteem? Early work by Coopersmith (1967) suggested that the answer was clearly yes and that parenting style was an important antecedent of self-esteem. In particular, Coopersmith found that children with higher self-esteem had parents who were more actively involved, emotionally warm and accepting, and respectful. Likewise, Whisman and Kwon (1992) found that college students who reported that their parents were more caring and warm endorsed fewer dysfunctional contingencies of self-esteem, whereas Brewin, Firth-Cozens, Furnham, and McManus (1992) found that medical students with stable high levels of self-criticism reported low levels of maternal care and high levels of maternal overprotection during childhood. In another study that included women with bipolar disorder, with nonbipolar depression, and with no psychiatric disorder (controls), investigators found that higher levels of dependency were associated with reports of having a distant relationship with one's father during childhood, whereas self-criticism was associated with difficulties in the quality of affective bonds with both one's father and one's peer group (Rosenfarb, Becker, Khan, & Mintz, 1994). Finally, in a large survey sample of adolescents, Rosenberg (1965) found that extreme parental indifference was associated with low self-esteem and suggested that such indifference might be even more deleterious to self-esteem than either parental punitiveness or parental criticism.

What is the role of childhood experiences involving parental loss, such as parental death and divorce? Although the evidence is mixed, some researchers have suggested that these experiences adversely affect self-esteem in children (Rosenberg, 1965) and increase risk for depression later in life (Kessler & Magee, 1993; McLeod, 1991; Roberts & Gotlib, 1997b). However, it is becoming apparent that these types of childhood loss events largely contribute to inadequate self-esteem and vulnerability to depression indirectly through their impact on parental care and family conflict. For example, Harris, Brown, and Bifulco (1990) found that early loss of a parent through death or divorce frequently led to deficient care during childhood, which in turn contributed to the development of a sense of helplessness and inadequate self-esteem throughout life. Poor self-esteem, in turn, increased risk for developing depression in adulthood, particularly after major stressful life events. Parental loss that did not lead to deficient care was not associated with later negative outcomes. Parental conflict also has a major negative impact on children's adjustment (Grych & Fincham, 1990), and it appears to mediate the effects of divorce on the child's psychological well-being (Emery, 1982). For example, Franklin, Janoff-Bulman, and Roberts (1990, Study 2) reported that high levels of unresolved parental conflict subsequent to divorce, rather than divorce per se, contributed to negative psychological outcomes. In fact, in a recent epidemiological study it was found that parental violence was more highly associated with adult depression than was parental death or divorce (Kessler & Magee, 1993).

There also is evidence that severely threatening childhood experiences, such as physical and sexual abuse, contribute to adult depression, at least in part, through the mediating role of negative thoughts and feelings about the self. It is becoming increasingly clear that physical and sexual abuse are associated with lower self-esteem (Egeland, Sroufe, & Erickson, 1983; Kaufman & Cicchetti, 1989) and with symptoms of depression (Kazdin, Moser, Colbus, & Bell, 1985; Toth, Manly, & Cicchetti, 1992) during childhood, as well as with the development of persistent forms of depression, such as early-onset dysthymia (Lizardi et al., 1995) and chronic and recurrent forms of major depression (Andrews, 1995; Andrews, Valentine, & Valentine, 1995), during adulthood. Single episodes of depression lasting less than 12 months are more directly related to adult abuse than to earlier adversities (Andrews, 1995). It is interesting that a recent study revealed that the impact of childhood abuse on adult depression was largely due to its association with an important aspect of self-evaluation: feelings of bodily shame (Andrews, 1995).

Studies consistently have documented associations between retrospective reports of the quality of early interpersonal relationships or early traumatic experiences and current levels of self-esteem (or related constructs such as self-criticism and dysfunctional contingencies of self-worth); longitudinal studies would clearly be an important complement to this cross-sectional work. In addition, given that level of self-esteem might not be a particularly good indicator of vulnerability to depression, future studies should examine the early interpersonal antecedents of aspects of self-esteem regulation and maintenance, such as the reactivity of self-esteem to stressors and negative moods and the stability of self-esteem over time. Furthermore, it would be important to investigate interpersonal relationships other than those with parents. One might expect that relationships with siblings and peers become increasingly important contributors to children's developing sense of self-esteem as they grow older. Finally, it is likely that negative experiences limited to the very early stages of development before a self-concept has begun to form would have little impact (Rutter & Rutter, 1993).

Attachment Security Across the Life Span

From the preceding discussion, it is apparent that interpersonal experiences throughout the life span contribute to the ability to maintain a positive view of oneself. We suggest that attachment theory offers one promising perspective for understanding these associations. Attachment is thought to be an evolution-based biobehavioral system that provides safety and security to infants and young children (Ainsworth, Blehar, Waters, & Wall, 1978; Bowlby, 1980); that is, the attachment system has provided a survival advantage to the species by maintaining proximity between infants and their caregivers. It is abundantly clear—and important to note—that there are individual differences in the form that particular attachment relationships take, which, in part, are determined by parenting styles and behaviors (Ainsworth et al., 1978). These individual differences in attachment style are thought to play a crucial role in interpersonal and psychological functioning throughout the life span. It is generally assumed that there is continuity in attachment across development. In fact, empirical evidence suggests that the notion of continuity is tenable, particularly if the social environment remains relatively stable (Hazan & Shaver, 1994; for conflicting findings, see Belsky, Campbell, Cohn, & Moore, 1996).

Of most relevance is the empirical evidence suggesting that in addition to a variety of interpersonal difficulties, insecure attachment styles are associated with psychological distress and clinical disorders, such as anxiety disorders and major depression, both in childhood (Armsden, McCauley, Greenberg, Burke, & Mitchell, 1990; Toth & Cicchetti, 1996) and in adulthood (Carnelley et al., 1994; Kobak & Sceery, 1988; Markley & Simons, 1995; West, Rose, & Sheldon, 1993). Hammen et al. (1995) documented that adult attachment insecurity is associated with exacerbated subclinical depressive reactions to stressful life events. In contrast, secure attachment appears to buffer against the impact of stressors. Likewise, Mikulincer, Florian, and Weller (1993) found that attachment security buffered the negative psychological effects of war stress in the Middle East, whereas attachment insecurity was associated with heightened depressive and posttraumatic stress symptoms. Nonetheless, it is unclear how attachment insecurity operates in increasing risk for psychological difficulties, such as symptoms of depression. What are the underlying mechanisms?

We propose that difficulties in self-esteem regulation and maintenance might be an important underlying mechanism. We suggest that one of the reasons individuals with insecure attachment styles are prone to depressive symptoms is that they have difficulties in regulating and maintaining self-esteem. Attachment theory suggests that early relationships with caregivers give rise to internal working models, or cognitive representations, concerning the self and others (Main, Kaplan, & Cassidy, 1985). These are essentially operating rules and expectations concerning the availability of support from caregivers as well as the implications of the caregiver's responsiveness in terms of the self, including self-esteem and lovableness (Bretherton, 1987). Unresponsive caregivers would give rise to working models of others as unreliable and models of the self as unworthy of support or worthy only if particular conditions are met. The child is likely to develop "if, then" rules concerning self-worth, or what Kuiper and Olinger (1986) have referred to as *dysfunctional contingencies of self-worth*. Because these working models involve fragile and difficult-to-maintain contingencies of self-worth, they are thought to increase risk for depletions in self-esteem.

In an initial test of this model (Roberts, Gotlib, & Kassel, 1996), our group posited that attachment insecurity would predict higher levels of dysfunctional contingencies of self-worth. Higher levels of these fragile contingencies of self-worth would prospectively predict depleted levels of self-esteem, which would directly contribute to depressive symptoms. The model was examined in two nonclinical college samples that were prospectively followed for 8 and 6 weeks (which allowed for statistical control of initial depressive symptoms). Data from the first study suggested that attachment security does not directly contribute to depressive symptoms but operates indirectly through its effects on self-worth contingencies and self-esteem (Roberts et al., 1996, Study 2). These relations were replicated in a second, 6-week prospective study in which both neuroticism and initial depressive symptoms were statistically controlled (Roberts et al., 1996, Study 3). Consistent with the results of these two studies are findings of Whisman and McGarvey (1995) that dysfunctional attitudes partly mediated the association between attachment to one's primary caregiver and symptoms of depression in a cross-sectional sample of college students (see also Randolph & Dykman, in press).

In another study (Roberts & Gotlib, 1995), our group was interested in investigating other processes involved in mood and self-esteem regulation that potentially are associated with attachment security. A number of studies have suggested that clinical depression is associated with difficulties in retrieving specific positive autobiographical memories (e.g., Goddard, Dritschel, & Burton, 1996; Williams & Broadbent, 1986; Williams & Scott, 1988), possibly because of a failure in adequately attending to the details and nuances of positive life events during encoding. It is thought that these details can serve as tags that allow memory search to move from a general category to the specific event within that category. It is relevant that difficulties in retrieving specific positive memories could interfere with self-esteem and mood regulation: Depression-prone people would have particular trouble in recruiting specific positive memories of themselves when their self-esteem is threatened and when they are in dysphoric moods. In contrast, nonvulnerable people would be able to buffer and protect their self-esteem and to repair negative moods by readily generating such memories (see Hartlage et al., 1993).

We speculated that insecurely attached individuals would be more likely to show such problems. To assess the self-esteem-regulating effects of autobiographical memories, participants were instructed to describe three self-defining memories on separate pages of paper (see Singer & Salovey, 1993). After describing these memories, participants were instructed to rate each memory in terms of its positive and negative impact on self-esteem as well as how much sadness, happiness, and fear were associated with each memory. Participants were selected on the basis of Bartholomew and Horowitz's (1991) attachment typology, which delineates four major adult attachment styles. *Secure* individuals are comfortable with both intimacy and autonomy. *Dismissing* individuals discount the importance of intimacy and appear to be counterdependent. *Fearful* individuals are afraid of intimacy and tend to be socially avoidant. Finally, *preoccupied* individuals are overinvolved with relationships and intimacy.

It is interesting that Bartholomew and Horowitz's (1991) typology is based on the concept of working models of self and others. Secure individuals are thought to have positive models of both the self and others. Dismissing individuals are thought to have positive models of the self but negative models of others. Preoccupied individuals have negative models of the self but positive models of others, whereas fearful individuals have negative models of both the self and others. Bartholomew and Horowitz's typology leads to interesting predictions regarding emotional distress and self-esteem regulation, and it suggests that only certain forms of attachment insecurity contribute to these problems. In particular, this model predicts that only preoccupied and fearful individuals are prone to depressive symptoms. Dismissing individuals would be protected by their relatively positive working models of the self.

Consistent with our predictions, compared with securely attached participants, individuals with fearful and preoccupied attachment styles reported higher levels of depressive symptoms and lower self-esteem, whereas dismissing individuals did not. Also consistent with our model, self-esteem mediated the association between attachment styles and depressive symptoms: Depression effects were rendered nonsignificant when self-esteem was statistically controlled. Furthermore, fearful and preoccupied individuals reported that their self-defining memories were associated with relatively high levels of sadness and negative impact on their self-esteem. It is interesting to note that we found an unanticipated gender difference across attachment styles. In particular, dismissing individuals were far more likely to be men (84%), whereas fearful individuals were far more likely to be women (81%). These results might have important implications in terms of women's heightened vulnerability to depression: When men develop an insecure attachment style, it tends to take a form that does not render them vulnerable to depression and loss of self-esteem.

Together, these findings suggest that attachment security across the life span protects against vulnerability to depressive symptoms and, perhaps, to clinical episodes. In contrast, attachment insecurity is associated with depression both concurrently and prospectively. Of most relevance to the current chapter are the results of several studies suggesting that attachment security contributes to the regulation of self-esteem and that deficits in self-esteem mediate the association between attachment security and symptoms of depression. However, there is a need to test this hypothesis with clinical samples of patients diagnosed by means of structured interviews. Furthermore, the concept of working models of self and others remains somewhat vague and needs further development, in terms of both its conceptualization and its measurement. Finally, attention needs to be paid to the question of specificity: It is likely that attachment insecurity also contributes to vulnerability to anxiety disorders and symptoms.

CLINICAL IMPLICATIONS

The conceptualization of self-esteem and interpersonal functioning outlined in the present chapter has a number of implications in terms of the psychological treatment of depressive disorders. Most generally, this approach suggests the need for therapeutic approaches that integrate both cognitive and interpersonal methods. Depression clearly involves deficits in both of these domains. Of perhaps greater importance is the possibility that deficits in these two domains might be self-reinforcing and reciprocally related. For example, poor social functioning likely makes it difficult to maintain a positive sense of self-worth. However, an insecure sense of self-esteem can lead to overly clingy and needy interpersonal behaviors that could contribute to social rejection (Coyne, 1976). Consequently, psychological interventions are needed to bridge these two areas of functioning.

Psychologists conducting traditional cognitive therapy for depression (Beck, Rush, Shaw, & Emery, 1979) tend to focus somewhat more on the role of cognitions or thoughts that lead to inadequate self-esteem than on interpersonal dysfunctions. More recent trends, however, are toward cognitive–interpersonal integrations. For example, Safran and Segal (1990) suggested practitioners' using the therapeutic relationship as a laboratory for exploring not only maladaptive interpersonal patterns but also dysfunctional cognitions related to interpersonal issues. We suggest that greater attention be given to how particular interpersonal relationships affect the patient's self-esteem. To what extent and in what ways might unfavorable social comparisons and insecure attachments contribute to the patient's vulnerable self-esteem?

It also is apparent that greater cognizance needs to be given to the limitations and difficulties involved in self-monitoring negative cognitions and self-representations (which tend to be related to self-esteem). Self-monitoring might be an arduous task if these cognitions are typically latent, as theory suggests. As suggested in the current chapter, these negative self-cognitions might become accessible only when primed by stressors and negative affect. Consequently, within-session moments of intense affect likely are ripe times for inquiring about stream-of-consciousness automatic thoughts and images. These thoughts and images might then be traced back to underlying dysfunctional beliefs through Socratic questioning, a process that is consistent with traditional cognitive therapy. Important negative self-representations are far more likely to be accessible during these within-session moments of hot affect than during more intellectualized moments.

Psychologists conducting interpersonal therapy (Klerman, Weissman, Rounsaville, & Chevron, 1984) have focused primarily on improving problematic interpersonal relationships in the depressed patient's social world. To some extent, this approach has deemphasized the other side of the coin: the role played by an insecure sense of self-worth as both a contributor to and a consequence of maladaptive interpersonal relationships. We believe that it would be useful for therapists taking interpersonal approaches to help depressed patients explore the ways in which their interpersonal behaviors are driven by self-esteem needs, as well as how dysfunctional relationships interfere with self-esteem regulation. Although individual-based interpersonal therapy potentially can address the interplay between social dysfunctions and vulnerable self-esteem in depression, we suggest that group therapy might be particularly effective. Dysfunctional interpersonal patterns often become readily apparent in group settings (Yalom, 1995).

The perspective we have been developing also suggests that individuals who are successfully treated for depression but who continue to show deficits in self-esteem regulation, such as temporally unstable and highly reactive self-esteem, will be at heightened risk for relapse. Such people might be in need of more prolonged treatment subsequent to their remission. Although their symptoms of depression might have abated, they have not developed healthy strategies for maintaining their self-esteem under conditions of threat, such as failures and losses. Consequently, they might be at increased risk for relapse subsequent to stressful life events. Future research is needed to test this hypothesis with clinical samples.

CONCLUSION AND FUTURE DIRECTIONS

Problems with both self-esteem and interpersonal relationships have been implicated in vulnerability to depressive symptoms and episodes. The general approach that we have been advancing in the current chapter is that to a certain extent self-esteem is rooted in and regulated by important close interpersonal relationships beginning in early childhood. The notion of self-esteem regulation (in contrast to level of self-esteem) seems to be potentially fruitful and productive for understanding the role of self-esteem in depression. As we have discussed, it has been difficult to demonstrate that chronic low self-esteem persists beyond episodes of depression or predicts the onset of future episodes or symptoms of depression. It seems likely that low self-esteem is not a trait vulnerability characteristic but acts as a symptom or correlate of depression. It is also possible that cross-sectional associations between self-report measures of level of self-esteem and depression are simply the result of item overlap between measures (Coyne & Gotlib, 1983). In contrast to chronic low levels of self-esteem, difficulties in regulating and maintaining stable positive self-esteem might prove to be indicative of risk for the development of depressive symptoms and perhaps depressive episodes. These difficulties in self-esteem regulation include deficits in the strategies and processes used in protecting self-esteem during threat (e.g., social comparison, self-affirmation), heightened reactivity of self-esteem to negative affect and daily stressors, and, finally, temporal instability of self-esteem. However, these are somewhat novel ideas that have been empirically examined only in a limited manner. Further research is required to establish the degree to which these aspects of self-esteem confer vulnerability to depression; prospective and remission designs are required.

We should note that it is still quite possible that major depletions in self-esteem act as a proximal cause of the onset of depression. It would be difficult to test this hypothesis in prospective studies in which self-esteem is measured well in advance of the onset of depression (see Brown, Andrews, et al., 1986). The self-esteem of individuals who eventually develop depression might be in normal ranges at the time it is evaluated in such designs but might fall sometime during the prospective interval. This acute drop in self-worth could be critically involved in the genesis of depression, but only studies based on daily assessments of self-esteem and depression would be able to detect this type of effect. We also should note that some research suggests that particularly low levels of self-worth and dysfunctional contingencies of self-worth during an episode of depression might contribute to the maintenance of the disorder, such that clinically depressed individuals with lower self-esteem and more dysfunctional contingencies take longer to recover (Brown et al., 1990b; Simons, Gordon, Monroe, & Thase, 1995). Likewise, low self-esteem appears to be associated with more prolonged periods of subclinical depressive symptoms (Dykman, 1996; Roberts & Monroe, 1992). Nonetheless, there is little empirical support for the hypothesis that low level of self-esteem is a trait vulnerability that is characteristic of the *onset* of depressive episodes or symptoms.

Unfortunately, most researchers investigating the interpersonal nature of self-esteem have focused on global trait levels of self-esteem, which do not appear to be associated with vulnerability to the onset of depression. Clearly, it is important for future investigators to concentrate on revealing whether and how interpersonal processes contribute to aspects of self-esteem *regulation*, as opposed to simply focusing on *level* of experienced self-esteem. In particular, are social and interpersonal factors associated with the mechanisms and processes an individual uses in maintaining self-esteem in the face of threat? Are they related to the degree of one's reactivity of self-esteem to such threats? Finally, do they contribute to the stability or instability of an individual's daily self-esteem over time?

As we have discussed, it seems likely that interpersonal relationships and experiences have a major impact on self-esteem through the development of working models of attachment security. Within attachment theory, *working models* refer to the cognitive representations of the self and others that are formed by young children through their interactions with caregivers. Although the concept of working models remains somewhat vague and elusive, our group has suggested that an important feature of working models involves rules and expectations concerning obtaining support from caregivers (see Roberts et al., 1996). Within this perspective, working models would involve procedural knowledge concerning what it takes to obtain love, affection, and attention from caregivers. As children mature, working models would include procedural knowledge concerning what it takes for the children themselves to feel worthy and lovable. Future work needs to be done to develop more refined measures of these constructs. Previous research has relied too heavily on self-report measures of attachment security and contingencies of self-worth.

Although interpersonal experiences likely play a role in self-esteem and depression throughout the lifetime, there is some evidence that childhood is a critical period in terms of vulnerability to certain severe forms of depression. Early traumatic interpersonal experiences appear to be associated with the development of chronic forms of depression, whereas such experiences in adulthood (as well as less traumatic interpersonal experiences throughout the life span) are more closely associated with acute episodic depression. Likewise, Brown and Harris (1978) found that parental death in childhood was associated with psychotic episodes of depression in adulthood, whereas parental loss through other causes was associated with nonpsychotic episodes. It may be that early childhood experiences of abuse and traumatic loss create particularly pathogenic working models and perhaps alter the biological structure of the developing brain (Kolk, 1987). It is also possible that childhood abuse and loss are associated with acute episodes of depressive disorder and that such early experiences with depression sensitize the individual and create vulnerability to recurrent and persistent episodes (Post, 1992). In this regard, there is evidence that having an episode of depression is associated with an increased risk for having subsequent episodes (Belsher & Costello, 1988). It is possible that childhood depression greatly increases risk for repeated, and perhaps chronic, depression over the life span.

Because much of the research discussed here is based on subclinical levels of depressive symptoms in relatively healthy samples (typically college students), it is unclear to what degree the ideas developed in the current chapter apply to clinical depression. Future research is needed to test these hypotheses with more severely depressed, clinical samples. Furthermore, most research conducted with adult samples has relied on self-report measures of interpersonal processes, such as parenting styles and attachment security. It would be important to complement this work with observational ratings, reports by others who know the subject well, and, when possible, experimental manipulations. Finally, longitudinal work investigating the long-term impact of interpersonal experiences in childhood, such as attachment relationships, on later self-esteem regulation and vulnerability to emotional disorders would be a major advance.

If further empirical support is obtained for this type of integration between interpersonal relationships and self-esteem regulation in clinical depression, future theoretical and empirical work will be needed to address the issue of *how* these processes contribute to depression. How do deficits in self-esteem regulation lead to depressive episodes? How do these processes cause particular symptoms of depression, such as sleep disturbance, changes in appetite, and concentration difficulties? What are the underlying mechanisms that link self-esteem to the other symptoms of depression and to the syndrome of depression? It remains for future work to address these important challenges.

REFERENCES

Adler, A. (1956). *The individual psychology of Alfred Adler* (H. L. Ansbacher & R. R. Ansbacher, Eds.). New York: Harper & Row.

Ainsworth, M. D. S., Blehar, M. C., Waters, E., & Wall, S. (1978). *Patterns of attachment: A psychological study of the strange situation.* Hillsdale, NJ: Erlbaum.

Alloy, L. B., & Abramson, L. Y. (1988). Depressive realism: Four theoretical perspectives. In L. B. Alloy (Ed.), *Cognitive processes in depression* (pp. 223–265). New York: Guilford Press.

Alloy, L. B., & Clements, C. M. (1992). Illusion of control: Invulnerability to negative affect and depressive symptoms after laboratory and natural stressors. *Journal of Abnormal Psychology, 101,* 234–245.

Alloy, L. B., Hartlage, S., & Abramson, L. Y. (1988). Testing the cognitive diathesis–stress theories of depression: Issues of research design, conceptualization, and assessment. In L. B. Alloy (Ed.), *Cognitive processes in depression* (pp. 31–73). New York: Guilford Press.

Altman, J. H., & Wittenborn, J. R. (1980). Depression-prone personality in women. *Journal of Abnormal Psychology, 89,* 303–308.

Andrews, B. (1995). Bodily shame as a mediator between abusive experiences and depression. *Journal of Abnormal Psychology, 104,* 277–285.

Andrews, B., Valentine, E. R., & Valentine, J. D. (1995). Depression and eating disorders following abuse in childhood in two generations of women. *British Journal of Clinical Psychology 34,* 37–52.

Armsden, G. C., McCauley, E., Greenberg, M. T., Burke, P. M., & Mitchell, J. R. (1990). Parent and peer attachment in early adolescent depression. *Journal of Abnormal Child Psychology, 18,* 683–697.

Aspinwall, L. G., & Taylor, S. E. (1993). Effects of social comparison direction, threat, and self-esteem on affect, self-evaluation, and expected success. *Journal of Personality and Social Psychology, 64,* 708–722.

Axford, S., & Jerrom, D. W. A. (1986). Self-esteem in depression: A controlled repertory grid investigation. *British Journal of Medical Psychology, 59,* 61–68.

Barnett, P. A., & Gotlib, I. H. (1988). Psychosocial functioning and depression: Distinguishing among antecedents, concomitants, and consequences. *Psychological Bulletin, 104,* 97–126.

Bartholomew, K., & Horowitz, L. M. (1991). Attachment styles among young adults: A test of a four-category model. *Journal of Personality and Social Psychology, 61,* 226–244.

Baumeister, R. F., Tice, D. M., & Hutton, D. G. (1989). Self-presentational motivations and personality differences in self-esteem. *Journal of Personality, 57,* 547–579.

Beach, S. R. H., Sandeen, E. E., & O'Leary, K. D. (1990). *Depression in marriage: A model for etiology and treatment.* New York: Guilford Press.

Beck, A. T. (1967). *Depression: Clinical, experimental, and theoretical aspects.* New York: Hoeber.

Beck, A. T., Rush, A. J., Shaw, B. F., & Emery, G. (1979). *Cognitive therapy of depression.* New York: Guilford Press.

Becker, J. (1979). Vulnerable self-esteem as a predisposing factor in depressive disorders. In R. A. Depue (Ed.), *The psychobiology of the depressive disorders: Implications for the effects of stress* (pp. 317–333). New York: Academic Press.

Belsher, G., & Costello, C. G. (1988). Relapse after recovery from unipolar depression: A critical review. *Psychological Bulletin, 104,* 84–96.

Belsky, J., Campbell, S. B., Cohn, J. F., & Moore, G. (1996). Instability of infant–parent attachment security. *Developmental Psychology, 32,* 921–924.

Bernet, C. Z., Ingram, R. E., & Johnson, B. R. (1993). Self-esteem. In C. G. Costello (Ed.), *Symptoms of depression* (pp. 141–159). New York: Wiley.

Bibring, E. (1953). The mechanism of depression. In P. Greenacre (Ed.), *Affective disorders* (pp. 13–48). New York: International Universities Press.

Blatt, S. J., & Zuroff, D. C. (1992). Interpersonal relatedness and self-definition: Two prototypes for depression. *Clinical Psychology Review, 12,* 527–562.

Bowlby, J. (1980). *Attachment and loss: Vol. 3. Loss, sadness, and depression.* New York: Basic Books.

Bretherton, I. (1987). New perspectives on attachment relations: Security, communication and internal working models. In J. D. Osofsky (Ed.), *Handbook of infant development* (2nd ed., pp. 1061–1100). New York: Wiley.

Brewin, C. R. (1989). Cognitive change processes in psychotherapy. *Psychological Review, 96,* 379–394.

Brewin, C. R., Firth-Cozens, J., Furnham, A., & McManus, C. (1992). Self-criticism in adulthood and recalled childhood experience. *Journal of Abnormal Psychology, 101,* 561–566.

Brown, G. W., Andrews, B., Bifulco, A., & Veil, H. (1990). Self-esteem and depression. *Social Psychiatry and Psychiatric Epidemiology, 25,* 200–209.

Brown, G. W., Andrews, B., Harris, T., Adler, Z., & Bridge, L. (1986). Social support, self-esteem and depression. *Psychological Medicine, 16,* 813–831.

Brown, G. W., Bifulco, A., & Andrews, B. (1990a). Self-esteem and depression: III. Aetiological issues. *Social Psychiatry and Psychiatric Epidemiology, 25,* 235–243.

Brown, G. W., Bifulco, A., & Andrews, B. (1990b). Self-esteem and depression: IV. Effect on course and recovery. *Social Psychiatry and Psychiatric Epidemiology, 25,* 244–249.

Brown, G. W., Bifulco, A., Harris, T., & Bridge, L. (1986). Life stress, chronic subclinical symptoms and vulnerability to clinical depression. *Journal of Affective Disorders, 11,* 1–19.

Brown, G. W., & Harris, T. O. (1978). *Social origins of depression.* New York: Free Press.

Brown, J. D., & Mankowski, T. A. (1993). Self-esteem, mood, and self-evaluation: Changes in mood and the way you see you. *Journal of Personality and Social Psychology, 64,* 421–430.

Butler, A. C., Hokanson, J. E., & Flynn, H. A. (1994). A comparison of self-esteem lability and low trait self-esteem as vulnerability factors for depression. *Journal of Personality and Social Psychology, 66,* 166–177.

Carnelley, K. B., Pietromonaco, P. R., & Jaffe, K. (1994). Depression, working models of others, and relationship functioning. *Journal of Personality and Social Psychology, 66,* 127–140.

Cofer, D. H., & Wittenborn, J. R. (1980). Personality characteristics of formerly depressed women. *Journal of Abnormal Psychology, 89,* 309–314.

Cohen, S., & Wills, T. A. (1985). Stress, social support, and the buffering hypothesis. *Psychological Bulletin, 98,* 310–357.

Cooley, C. F. (1902). *Human nature and the social order.* New York: Scribner.

Coopersmith, S. (1967). *The antecedents of self-esteem.* New York: Freeman.

Coyne, J. C. (1976). Toward an interactional description of depression. *Psychiatry, 39,* 14–27.

Coyne, J. C., Burchill, S. A. L., & Stiles, W. B. (1991). An interactional perspective on depression. In C. R. Snyder & D. R. Forsyth (Eds.), *Handbook of social and clinical psychology: The health perspective* (pp. 327–349). New York: Pergamon Press.

Coyne, J. C., & Gotlib, I. H. (1983). The role of cognition in depression: A critical appraisal. *Psychological Bulletin, 94,* 472–505.

Coyne, J. C., & Gotlib, I. H. (1986). Studying the role of cognition in depression: Well-trodden paths and cul-de-sacs. *Cognitive Therapy and Research, 10,* 695–705.

Coyne, J. C., Kessler, R. C., Tal, M., Turnbull, J., Wortman, C. B., & Greden, J. F. (1987). Living with a depressed person. *Journal of Consulting and Clinical Psychology, 55,* 347–352.

Crocker, J., & Major, B. (1989). Social stigma and self-esteem: The self-protective properties of stigma. *Psychological Review, 96,* 608–630.

Depue, R. A., & Monroe, S. M. (1986). Conceptualization and measurement of human disorder in life stress research: The problem of chronic disturbance. *Psychological Bulletin, 99,* 36–51.

Dykman, B. M. (1996). Negative self-evaluations among dysphoric college students: A difference in degree or kind? *Cognitive Therapy and Research, 20,* 445–464.

Dykman, B. M., Horowitz, L. M., Abramson, L. Y., & Usher, M. (1991). Schematic and situational determinants of depressed and nondepressed students' interpretation of feedback. *Journal of Abnormal Psychology, 100,* 45–55.

Egeland, B., Sroufe, L. A., & Erickson, M. F. (1983). Developmental consequence of different patterns of maltreatment. *Child Abuse and Neglect, 7,* 459–469.

Emery, R. E. (1982). Interparental conflict and the children of discord and divorce. *Psychological Bulletin, 92,* 310–330.

Epstein, S. (1980). The self-concept: A review and the proposal of an integrated theory of personality. In E. Staub (Ed.), *Personality: Basic aspects and current research* (pp. 82–132). Englewood Cliffs, NJ: Prentice Hall.

Feather, N. T., & Barber, J. G. (1983). Depressive reactions and unemployment. *Journal of Abnormal Psychology, 92,* 185–195.

Fenichel, O. (1945). *Psychoanalytic theory of neurosis.* New York: Norton.

Festinger, L. (1954). A theory of social comparison processes. *Human Relations, 7,* 117–140.

Franklin, K. M., Janoff-Bulman, R., & Roberts, J. E. (1990). Long-term impact of parental divorce on optimism and trust: Changes in general assumptions or narrow beliefs? *Journal of Personality and Social Psychology, 59,* 743–755.

Freud, S. (1986). Mourning and melancholia. In J. Coyne (Ed.), *Essential papers on depression* (pp. 48–63). New York: New York University Press. (Original work published 1917)

Gara, M. A., Woolfolk, R. L., Cohen, B. D., Goldston, R. B., Allen, L. A., & Novalany, J. (1993). Perception of self and others in major depression. *Journal of Abnormal Psychology, 102,* 93–100.

Giesler, R. B., Josephs, R. A., & Swann, W. B. (1996). Self-verification in clinical depression: The desire for negative evaluation. *Journal of Abnormal Psychology, 105*, 358–368.

Gilbert, P. (1992). *Depression: The evolution of powerlessness.* New York: Guilford Press.

Gilbert, P., Price, J., & Allan, S. (1995). Social comparison, social attractiveness and evolution: How might they be related? *New Ideas in Psychology, 13*, 149–165.

Gilboa, E., Roberts, J. E., & Gotlib, I. H. (1997). The effects of induced and naturally occurring dysphoric mood on biases in self-evaluation and memory. *Cognition and Emotion, 11*, 65–82.

Goddard, L., Dritschel, B., & Burton, A. (1996). Role of autobiographical memory in social problem solving and depression. *Journal of Abnormal Psychology, 105*, 609–616.

Gotlib, I. H. (1982). Self-reinforcement and depression in interpersonal interaction: The role of performance level. *Journal of Abnormal Psychology, 91*, 3–13.

Gotlib, I. H., & Beach, S. R. H. (1995). A marital/family discord model of depression: Implications for therapeutic intervention. In N. S. Jacobson & A. S. Gurman (Eds.), *Clinical handbook of couple therapy* (pp. 411–436). New York: Guilford Press.

Gotlib, I. H., & Hammen, C. L. (1992). *Psychological aspects of depression: Toward a cognitive interpersonal integration.* Chichester, England: Wiley.

Gross, J. J., & Munoz, R. F. (1995). Emotion regulation and mental health. *Clinical Psychology and Scientific Practice, 2*, 151–164.

Grych, J. H., & Fincham, F. D. (1990). Marital conflict and children's adjustment: A cognitive-contextual framework. *Psychological Bulletin, 108*, 267–290.

Gurtman, M. B. (1987). Depressive affect and disclosures as factors in interpersonal rejection. *Cognitive Therapy and Research, 11*, 87–100.

Hamilton, E. W., & Abramson, L. Y. (1983). Cognitive patterns and major depressive disorder: A longitudinal study in a hospital setting. *Journal of Abnormal Psychology, 92*, 173–184.

Hammen, C. L., Burge, D., Daley, S. E., Davila, J., Paley, B., & Rudolph, K. D. (1995). Interpersonal attachment cognitions and prediction of symptomatic responses to interpersonal stress. *Journal of Abnormal Psychology, 104*, 436–443.

Harris, T., Brown, G. W., & Bifulco, A. (1990). Loss of parent in childhood and adult psychiatric disorder: A tentative overall model. *Development and Psychopathology, 2*, 311–328.

Hartlage, S., Alloy, L. B., Vazquez, C., & Dykman, B. (1993). Automatic and effortful processing in depression. *Psychological Bulletin, 113*, 247–278.

Hartlage, S., Ardvino, K., & Alloy, L. B. (1998). Depressive personality characteristics: State dependent concomitants of depressive disorder and traits independent of current depression. *Journal of Abnormal Psychology, 107,* 349–354.

Hazan, C., & Shaver, P. R. (1994). Attachment as an organizational framework for research on close relationships. *Psychological Inquiry, 5,* 1–22.

Hewstone, M., Hooper, D., & Miller, K. (1981). Psychological change in neurotic depression: A repertory grid and personal construct theory approach. *British Journal of Psychiatry, 139,* 47–51.

Hickie, I., Parker, G., Wilhelm, K., & Tennant, C. (1991). Perceived interpersonal risk factors of nonendogenous depression. *Psychological Medicine, 21,* 399–412.

Hobfoll, S. E., & Leiberman, J. R. (1987). Personality and social resources in immediate and continued stress resistance among women. *Journal of Personality and Social Psychology, 52,* 18–26.

Hobfoll, S. E., & London, P. (1986). The relationship of self-concept and social support to emotional distress among women during war. *Journal of Social and Clinical Psychology, 4,* 189–203.

Hokanson, J. E., Rubert, M. P., Welker, R. A., Hollander, G. R., & Hedeen, C. (1989). Interpersonal concomitants and antecedents of depression among college students. *Journal of Abnormal Psychology, 98,* 209–217.

Hyland, M. E. (1987). Control theory interpretation of psychological mechanisms of depression: Comparison and integration of several theories. *Psychological Bulletin, 102,* 109–121.

Ingham, J. G., Kreitman, N. B., Miller, P. M., Sashidharan, S. P., & Surtees, P. G. (1987). Self-appraisal, anxiety and depression in women: A prospective enquiry. *British Journal of Psychiatry, 151,* 643–651.

Jacobson, E. (1975). The regulation of self-esteem. In E. J. Anthoney & T. Benedek (Eds.), *Depression and human existence* (pp. 169–181). Boston: Little, Brown.

James, W. (1890). *Principles of psychology* (Vol. 1). New York: Holt.

John, O. P., & Robins, R. W. (1994). Accuracy and bias in self-perception: Individual differences in self-enhancement and the role of narcissism. *Journal of Personality and Social Psychology, 66,* 206–219.

Joiner, T. E. (1994). Contagious depression: Existence, specificity to depressed symptoms, and the role of reassurance seeking. *Journal of Personality and Social Psychology, 67,* 287–296.

Joiner, T. E. (1995). The price of soliciting and receiving negative feedback: Self-verification theory as a vulnerability to depression theory. *Journal of Abnormal Psychology, 104,* 364–372.

Joiner, T. E., Alfano, M. S., & Metalsky, G. I. (1992). When depression breeds contempt: Reassurance seeking, self-esteem, and rejection of depressed college students by their roommates. *Journal of Abnormal Psychology, 101,* 165–173.

Joiner, T. E., Alfano, M. S., & Metalsky, G. I. (1993). Caught in the crossfire: Depression, self-consistency, self-enhancement, and the response of others. *Journal of Social and Clinical Psychology, 12,* 114–135.

Joiner, T. E., & Metalsky, G. I. (1995). A prospective test of an integrative inter-personal theory of depression: A naturalistic study of college roommates. *Journal of Personality and Social Psychology, 69*, 778–788.

Josephs, R. A., Larrick, R. P., Steele, C. M., & Nisbett, R. E. (1992). Protecting the self from the negative consequences of risky decisions. *Journal of Personality and Social Psychology, 62*, 26–37.

Kaufman, J., & Cicchetti, D. (1989). The effects of maltreatment on school-aged children's socioemotional development: Assessments in a day camp setting. *Developmental Psychology, 25*, 516–524.

Kazdin, A. E., Moser, J., Colbus, D., & Bell, R. (1985). Depressive symptoms among physically abused and psychiatrically disturbed children. *Journal of Abnormal Psychology, 94*, 298–307.

Kernis, M. H., Cornell, D. P., Sun, C., Berry, A., & Harlow, T. (1993). There's more to self-esteem than whether it is high or low: The importance of the stability of self-esteem. *Journal of Personality and Social Psychology, 65*, 1190–1204.

Kernis, M. H., Grannemann, B. D., & Barclay, L. C. (1989). Stability and level of self-esteem as predictors of anger arousal and hostility. *Journal of Personality and Social Psychology, 56*, 1013–1022.

Kernis, M. H., Whisenhunt, C. R., Waschull, S. B., Greenier, K. D., Berry, A. J., Herlocker, C. E., & Anderson, C. A. (1998). Multiple facets of self-esteem and their relations to depressive symptoms. *Personality and Social Psychology Bulletin, 24*, 657–668.

Kessler, R. C., & Magee, W. J. (1993). Childhood adversities and adult depression: Basic patterns of association in a U.S. national survey. *Psychological Medicine, 23*, 679–690.

Klerman, G. L., Weissman, M. M., Rounsaville, B. J., & Chevron, E. S. (1984). *Interpersonal psychotherapy for depression*. New York: Basic Books.

Kobak, R. R., & Sceery, A. (1988). Attachment in late adolescence: Working models, affect regulation, and representations of self and others. *Child Development, 59*, 135–146.

Kohut, H. (1984). *How does analysis cure?* (A. Goldberg, Ed.). Chicago: University of Chicago Press.

Kohut, H. (1987). *The Kohut seminars on self psychology and psychotherapy with adolescents and young adults* (M. Elson, Ed.). New York: Norton.

Kolk, B. A. (1987). The drug treatment of post-traumatic stress disorder. *Journal of Affective Disorders, 13*, 203–213.

Kuiper, N. A., & McCabe, S. B. (1985). The appropriateness of social topics: Effects of depression and cognitive vulnerability on self and other judgments. *Cognitive Therapy and Research, 9*, 371–379.

Kuiper, N. A., & Olinger, L. J. (1986). Dysfunctional attitudes and a self-worth contingency model of depression. *Advances in Cognitive-Behavioral Research and Therapy, 5*, 115–142.

Lakey, B. (1988). Self-esteem, control beliefs, and cognitive problem-solving skill as risk factors in the development of subsequent dysphoria. *Cognitive Therapy and Research, 12,* 409–420.

Laxer, R. M. (1964). Relations of real self-rating to mood and blame and their interaction in depression. *Journal of Consulting Psychology, 28,* 538–546.

Leary, M. R., Tambor, E. S., Terdal, S. K., & Downs, D. L. (1995). Self-esteem as an interpersonal monitor: The sociometer hypothesis. *Journal of Personality and Social Psychology, 68,* 518–530.

Lewinsohn, P. M., Hoberman, H. M., & Rosenbaum, M. (1988). A prospective study of risk factors for unipolar depression. *Journal of Abnormal Psychology, 97,* 251–264.

Lewinsohn, P. M., Roberts, R. E., Seeley, J. R., Rohde, P., Gotlib, I. H., & Hops, H. (1994). Adolescent psychopathology: II. Psychosocial risk factors for depression. *Journal of Abnormal Psychology, 103,* 302–315.

Lewinsohn, P. M., Steinmetz, J. L., Larson, D. W., & Franklin, J. (1981). Depression-related cognitions: Antecedent or consequence? *Journal of Abnormal Psychology, 90,* 213–219.

Linville, P. W. (1987). Self-complexity as a cognitive buffer against stress-related illness and depression. *Journal of Personality and Social Psychology, 52,* 663–676.

Lizardi, H., Klein, D. N., Ouimette, P. C., Riso, L. P., Anderson, R. L., & Donaldson, S. K. (1995). Reports of the childhood home environment in early-onset dysthymia and episodic major depression. *Journal of Abnormal Psychology, 104,* 132–139.

MacKinnon, A., Henderson, A. S., & Andrews, G. (1993). Parental "affectionless control" as an antecedent to adult depression: A risk factor refined. *Psychological Medicine, 23,* 135–141.

Main, M., Kaplan, N., & Cassidy, J. (1985). Security in infancy, childhood, and adulthood: A move to the level of representation. *Monographs of the Society for Research in Child Development, 50*(1–2), 66–104.

Markley, D. K., & Simons, A. D. (1995). *"Me" men versus "we" women: Sex-specific attachment styles associated with depressive symptomatology.* Manuscript submitted for publication.

Markus, H., & Nurius, P. (1986). Possible selves. *American Psychologist, 41,* 954–969.

Marsh, H. W. (1986). Global self-esteem: Its relation to specific facets of self-concept and their importance. *Journal of Personality and Social Psychology, 51,* 1224–1236.

Marsh, H. W. (1993). Relations between global and specific domains of self: The importance of individual importance, certainty, and ideals. *Journal of Personality and Social Psychology, 65,* 975–992.

McLeod, J. D. (1991). Childhood parental loss and adult depression. *Journal of Health and Social Behavior, 32,* 205–220.

Mead, G. H. (1934). *Mind, self, and society.* Chicago: University of Chicago Press.

Metalsky, G. I., Halberstadt, L. J., & Abramson, L. Y. (1987). Vulnerability to depressive mood reactions: Toward a more powerful test of the diathesis–stress causal mediation components of the reformulated theory of depression. *Journal of Personality and Social Psychology, 52,* 386–393.

Metalsky, G. I., Joiner, T. E., Hardin, T. S., & Abramson, L. Y. (1993). Depressive reactions to failure in a naturalistic setting: A test of the hopelessness and self-esteem theories of depression. *Journal of Abnormal Psychology, 102,* 101–109.

Mikulincer, M., Florian, V., & Weller, A. (1993). Attachment styles, coping strategies, and posttraumatic psychological distress: The impact of the Gulf War in Israel. *Journal of Personality and Social Psychology, 64,* 817–826.

Miller, P. M., Kreitman, N. B., Ingham, J. G., & Sashidharan, S. P. (1989). Self-esteem, life stress and psychiatric disorder. *Journal of Affective Disorders, 17,* 65–75.

Miranda, J. (1992). Dysfunctional thinking is activated by stressful life events. *Cognitive Therapy and Research, 16,* 473–483.

Miranda, J., & Persons, J. B. (1988). Dysfunctional attitudes are mood-state dependent. *Journal of Abnormal Psychology, 97,* 76–79.

Miranda, J., Persons, J. B., & Byers, C. N. (1990). Endorsement of dysfunctional beliefs depends on current mood state. *Journal of Abnormal Psychology, 99,* 237–241.

Monroe, S. M., & Roberts, J. E. (1990). Conceptualizing and measuring life stress: Problems, principles, procedures, progress. *Stress Medicine, 6,* 209–216.

Monroe, S. M., & Simons, A. D. (1991). Diathesis–stress theories in the context of life stress research: Implications for the depressive disorders. *Psychological Bulletin, 110,* 406–425.

Monroe, S. M., & Steiner, S. C. (1986). Social support and psychopathology: Interrelations with preexisting disorder, stress, and personality. *Journal of Abnormal Psychology, 95,* 29–39.

Mruk, C. (1995). *Self-esteem: Research, theory, and practice.* New York: Springer.

Oatley, K., & Bolton, W. (1985). A social-cognitive theory of depression in reaction to life events. *Psychological Review, 92,* 372–388.

Pelham, B. W., & Swann, W. B. (1989). From self-conceptions to self-worth: On the sources and structure of global self-esteem. *Journal of Personality and Social Psychology, 57,* 672–680.

Persons, J. B., & Miranda, J. (1992). Cognitive theories of vulnerability to depression: Reconciling negative evidence. *Cognitive Therapy and Research, 16,* 485–502.

Post, R. M. (1992). Transduction of psychosocial stress into the neurobiology of recurrent affective disorder. *American Journal of Psychiatry, 149,* 999–1010.

Potthoff, J. G., Holahan, C. J., & Joiner, T. E. (1995). Reassurance seeking, stress generation, and depressive symptoms: An integrative model. *Journal of Personality and Social Psychology, 68,* 664–670.

Power, M., & Brewin, C. R. (1991). From Freud to cognitive science: A contemporary account of the unconscious. *British Journal of Clinical Psychology, 30,* 289–310.

Pretzer, J. L., & Beck, A. T. (1996). A cognitive theory of personality disorders. In J. F. Clarkin & M. F. Lenzenweger (Eds.), *Major theories of personality disorder* (pp. 36–105). New York: Guilford Press.

Price, J., Sloman, L., Gardner, R., Gilbert, P., & Rohde, P. (1994). The social competition hypothesis of depression. *British Journal of Psychiatry, 164,* 309–315.

Pyszczynski, T., & Greenberg, J. (1987). Self-regulatory perseveration and the depressive self-focusing style: A self-awareness theory of reactive depression. *Psychological Bulletin, 102,* 122–138.

Rado, S. (1928). The problem of melancholia. *International Journal of Psychoanalysis, 9,* 420–438.

Rado, S. (1951). Psychodynamics of depression from an etiologic point of view. *Psychosomatic Medicine, 13,* 51–55.

Randolph, J. J., & Dykman, B. M. (in press). Perceptions of parenting and depression-proneness in the offspring: Dysfunctional attitudes as a mediating mechanism. *Cognitive Therapy and Research.*

Rhodewalt, F., Morf, C., Hazlett, S., & Fairfield, M. (1991). Self-handicapping: The role of discounting and augmentation in the preservation of self-esteem. *Journal of Personality and Social Psychology, 61,* 122–131.

Riskind, J. H., & Rholes, W. S. (1984). Cognitive accessibility and capacity of cognition to predict future depression: A theoretical note. *Cognitive Therapy and Research, 8,* 1–12.

Roberts, J. E., & Gotlib, I. H. (1995, November). *Attachment insecurity and symptoms of depression: Breakdowns in self-esteem regulation?* Paper presented at the meeting of the Association for the Advancement of Behavior Therapy, Washington, DC.

Roberts, J. E., & Gotlib, I. H. (1997a). Temporal variability in global self-esteem and specific self-evaluation as prospective predictors of emotional distress: Specificity in predictors and outcome. *Journal of Abnormal Psychology, 106,* 521–529.

Roberts, J. E., & Gotlib, I. H. (1997b). Lifetime episodes of dysphoria: Gender, early childhood loss, and personality. *British Journal of Clinical Psychology, 36,* 195–208.

Roberts, J. E., Gotlib, I. H., & Kassel, J. D. (1996). Adult attachment security and symptoms of depression: The mediating roles of dysfunctional attitudes and low self-esteem. *Journal of Personality and Social Psychology, 70,* 310–320.

Roberts, J. E., & Kassel, J. D. (1996). Mood-state dependence in cognitive vulnerability to depression: The roles of positive and negative affect. *Cognitive Therapy and Research, 20,* 1–12.

Roberts, J. E., & Kassel, J. D. (1997). Labile self-esteem, stressful life events, and depressive symptoms: Prospective data testing a model of vulnerability. *Cognitive Therapy and Research, 21,* 569–589.

Roberts, J. E., & Monroe, S. M. (1992). Vulnerable self-esteem and depressive symptoms: Prospective findings comparing three alternative conceptualizations. *Journal of Personality and Social Psychology, 62,* 804–812.

Roberts, J. E., & Monroe, S. M. (1994). A multidimensional model of self-esteem in depression. *Clinical Psychology Review, 14,* 161–181.

Robinson, N. S., Garber, J., & Hilsman, R. (1995). Cognitions and stress: Direct and moderating effects on depressive versus externalizing symptoms during the junior high school transition. *Journal of Abnormal Psychology, 104,* 453–463.

Robson, P. J. (1988). Self-esteem—A psychiatric view. *British Journal of Psychiatry, 153,* 6–15.

Rosenberg, M. (1965). *Society and the adolescent self-image.* Princeton, NJ: Princeton University Press.

Rosenberg, M. (1979). *Conceiving the self.* New York: Basic Books.

Rosenfarb, I. S., Becker, J., Khan, A., & Mintz, J. (1994). Dependency, self-criticism, and perceptions of socialization experiences. *Journal of Abnormal Psychology, 103,* 669–675.

Rutter, M., & Rutter, M. (1993). *Developing minds: Challenge and continuity across the life span.* New York: Basic Books.

Safran, J. D., & Segal, Z. V. (1990). *Interpersonal process in cognitive therapy.* Northvale, NJ: Jason Aronson.

Sedikides, C. (1993). Assessment, enhancement, and verification determinants of the self-evaluation process. *Journal of Personality and Social Psychology, 65,* 317–338.

Segal, Z. V., & Ingram, R. E. (1994). Mood priming and construct activation tests of cognitive vulnerability to unipolar depression. *Clinical Psychology Review, 14,* 663–695.

Segrin, C., & Abramson, L. Y. (1994). Negative reactions to depressive behaviors: A communication theories analysis. *Journal of Abnormal Psychology, 103,* 655–668.

Showers, C. (1992). Compartmentalization of positive and negative self-knowledge: Keeping bad apples out of the bunch. *Journal of Personality and Social Psychology, 62,* 1036–1049.

Silverman, J. S., Silverman, J. A., & Eardley, D. A. (1984). Do maladaptive attitudes cause depression? *Archives of General Psychiatry, 41,* 28–30.

Simons, A. D., Gordon, J. S., Monroe, S. M., & Thase, M. E. (1995). Toward an integration of psychologic, social, and biologic factors in depression: Effects on outcome and course of cognitive therapy. *Journal of Consulting and Clinical Psychology, 63,* 369–377.

Singer, J. A., & Salovey, P. (1993). *The remembered self: Emotion and memory in personality.* New York: Free Press.

Steele, C. M. (1988). The psychology of self-affirmation: Sustaining the integrity of the self. *Advances in Experimental Social Psychology, 21,* 261–302.

Steele, C. M., Spencer, S. J., & Lynch, M. (1993). Self-image resilience and dissonance: The role of affirmation resources. *Journal of Personality and Social Psychology, 64,* 885–896.

Stein, K. F., & Markus, H. R. (1994). The organization of the self: An alternative focus for psychopathology and behavior change. *Journal of Psychotherapy Integration, 4,* 317–353.

Suls, J., & Wills, T. A. (Eds.). (1991). *Social comparison: Contemporary theory and research.* Hillsdale, NJ: Erlbaum.

Swallow, S. R., & Kuiper, N. A. (1988). Social comparison and negative self-evaluations: An application to depression. *Clinical Psychology Review, 8,* 55–76.

Swallow, S. R., & Kuiper, N. A. (1992). Mild depression and frequency of social comparison behavior. *Journal of Social and Clinical Psychology, 11,* 167–180.

Swallow, S. R., & Kuiper, N. A. (1993). Social comparison in dysphoria and nondysphoria: Differences in target similarity and specificity. *Cognitive Therapy and Research, 17,* 103–122.

Swann, W. B. (1983). Self-verification: Bringing social reality into harmony with the self. In J. Suls & A. G. Greenwald (Eds.), *Social psychological perspectives on the self* (Vol. 2, pp. 33–66). Hillsdale, NJ: Erlbaum.

Swann, W. B., Wenzlaff, R. M., Krull, D. S., & Pelham, B. W. (1992). Allure of negative feedback: Self-verification strivings among depressed persons. *Journal of Abnormal Psychology, 101,* 293–306.

Tarlow, E. M., & Haaga, D. A. F. (1996). Negative self-concept: Specificity to depressive symptoms and relation to positive and negative affectivity. *Journal of Research in Personality, 30,* 120–127.

Taylor, S. E., & Brown, J. D. (1988). Illusion and well-being: A social psychological perspective on mental health. *Psychological Bulletin, 103,* 193–210.

Teasdale, J. D. (1983). Negative thinking in depression: Cause, effect, or reciprocal relationship? *Advances in Behaviour Research and Therapy, 5,* 3–25.

Teasdale, J. D. (1988). Cognitive vulnerability to persistent depression. *Cognition and Emotion, 2,* 247–274.

Tesser, A. (1988). Toward a self-evaluation maintenance model of social behavior. *Advances in Experimental Social Psychology, 21,* 181–227.

Toth, S. L., & Cicchetti, D. (1996). Patterns of relatedness, depressive symptomatology, and perceived competence in maltreated children. *Journal of Consulting and Clinical Psychology, 64,* 32–41.

Toth, S. L., Manly, J. T., & Cicchetti, D. (1992). Child maltreatment and vulnerability to depression. *Development and Psychopathology, 3,* 445–460.

Wayment, H. A., & Taylor, S. E. (1995). Self-evaluation processes: Motives, information use, and self-esteem. *Journal of Personality, 63,* 729–757.

West, M. L., Rose, M. S., & Sheldon, A. (1993). Anxious attachment as a determinant of adult psychopathology. *Journal of Nervous and Mental Disease, 181,* 422–427.

Westen, D. (1994). Toward an integrative model of affect regulation: Applications to social-psychological research. *Journal of Personality, 62*, 641–667.

Whisman, M. A., & Kwon, P. (1992). Parental representations, cognitive distortions, and mild depression. *Cognitive Therapy and Research, 16*, 557–568.

Whisman, M. A., & Kwon, P. (1993). Life stress and dysphoria: The role of self-esteem and hopelessness. *Journal of Personality and Social Psychology, 65*, 1054–1060.

Whisman, M. A., & McGarvey, A. L. (1995). Attachment, depressotypic cognitions, and dysphoria. *Cognitive Therapy and Research, 19*, 633–650.

Williams, J. M. G., & Broadbent, K. (1986). Autobiographical memory in suicide attempters. *Journal of Abnormal Psychology, 95*, 144–149.

Williams, J. M. G., & Scott, J. (1988). Autobiographical memory and depression. *Psychological Medicine, 18*, 689–695.

Wills, T. A. (1981). Downward comparison principles. *Psychological Bulletin, 90*, 245–271.

Wood, J. V. (1989). Theory and research concerning social comparisons of personal attributes. *Psychological Bulletin, 106*, 231–248.

Yalom, I. D. (1995). *The theory and practice of group psychotherapy* (4th ed.). New York: Basic Books.

8

STRIVING FOR CONFIRMATION: THE ROLE OF SELF-VERIFICATION IN DEPRESSION

R. BRIAN GIESLER AND WILLIAM B. SWANN, JR.

Depression may someday be understood in terms of its paradoxes.
(Aaron T. Beck, 1967)

Perhaps the most baffling paradox associated with depression is that depressed people persistently behave and think in ways that undermine their well-being. In fact, using maladaptive modes of action and thought is so pervasive in depression that scholars across the ages have felt compelled to comment on or to empirically document this tendency (e.g., A. T. Beck, 1967, 1976; Coates & Wortman, 1980; Coyne, 1976a, 1976b; Freud, 1955/1985; Galen, trans. 1976; Kraepelin, 1899/1990; Pinel, 1801/1962; Segrin & Abramson, 1995).

Consider the following, well-replicated findings. First, depressed people enact a wide assortment of inappropriate verbal and nonverbal social behaviors that tend to elicit hostility and rejection from others (Coyne, 1976a; Gotlib & Beatty, 1985; Gurtman, 1987; Joiner, Alfano, & Metalsky, 1992; Segrin & Abramson, 1995; Strack & Coyne, 1983; Swann, Wenzlaff, Krull, & Pelham, 1992, Study 3). Through their behavior, depressed individuals create around themselves social worlds that virtually guarantee a steady supply of negative evaluations. Second, on those occasions when depressed people do receive feedback indicating that they possess positive

189

characteristics and are individuals of worth, they seem particularly loathe to accept such reassurances (e.g., Coyne, 1976b; Joiner, Alfano, & Metalsky, 1992; Swann, Wenzlaff, & Tafarodi, 1992, Study 2). Moreover, explicitly conveying positive evaluations to depressed people often has the opposite effect of the one intended: Instead of fostering positive feelings of well-being, favorable feedback often appears to intensify the expression of depressive symptom's (Grinker, 1964; D. A. Schwartz, 1964; Watzlawick, Weakland, & Fisch, 1974). Finally, numerous studies have demonstrated that depressed individuals are especially likely to process information about themselves in a way that casts an unfavorable light on their abilities and attributes (e.g., Derry & Kuiper, 1981; Gotlib, 1983; Kovacs & Beck, 1978; Kuiper & MacDonald, 1982; Roth & Rehm, 1980).

In short, depressed people appear to behave and think in ways that suggest that they desire unfavorable evaluations from others. At first blush, such a statement may seem unnecessarily provocative. But consider again the picture that emerges from the studies cited earlier: It is not just that depressed people enact behaviors that evoke negative reactions from their interaction partners; when they do receive positive (or ambiguous) feedback, they either reject it outright, behave in ways that explicitly countermand the feedback, or construe it in a way that supports their negative self-views. Why? We propose that a functional relation binds together and accounts for these features of depression, a relation that has largely been overlooked in the past (cf. Andrews, 1989; Shustack & West, 1985). Specifically, we suggest that the three aspects of depression we have described—behaving in ways that elicit negative feedback, avoiding or denying favorable feedback, and selectively processing evaluative information about the self—act to confirm and thereby preserve depressed individuals' self-views. Whereas the desire for self-confirmation is adaptive among people with positive self-views, among depressed people, striving for confirming feedback typically means striving for unfavorable feedback. Self-verification theory articulates the psychological mechanisms that give rise to such paradoxical activities.

In the following sections, we first describe self-verification theory and its theoretical underpinnings, then review empirical research documenting self-verification effects in nondepressed and depressed populations. Next, we address misconceptions that often arise concerning self-verification's role in depression. Finally, we present a theoretical account of how self-verification processes contribute to the onset, maintenance, remission, and treatment of depressive episodes.

SELF-VERIFICATION THEORY

The central tenet of self-verification theory is that people are motivated to confirm their firmly held self-views out of a desire to bolster perceptions of prediction and control. More than a decade of research conducted by Swann and his colleagues has supported and elaborated self-verification theory (see Swann, 1990, 1996, 1997, for reviews). In summary, both laboratory and field studies have shown that people are motivated to preferentially solicit self-confirming feedback (Swann & Read, 1981a, 1981b; Swann, Wenzlaff, Krull, & Pelham, 1992, Swann, Wenzlaff, & Tafarodi, 1992), as well as to attend to (Swann & Read, 1981a), to recall (Crary, 1966; Suinn, Osborne, & Page, 1962; Swann & Read, 1981a), and to impute more credibility to feedback that fits with their self-views (Crary, 1966; Swann, Griffin, Predmore, & Gaines, 1987). Moreover, not only do people prefer verifying evaluations but they also choose interaction partners who view them as they view themselves (Swann, Hixon, & de La Ronde, 1992; Swann, Wenzlaff, Krull, & Pelham, 1992; Swann, Wenzlaff, & Tafarodi, 1992). Finally, people actively behave in ways that serve to bring interaction partners' perceptions of them in line with their own self-views (McNulty & Swann, 1994; Swann & Ely, 1984; Swann & Hill, 1982; Swann & Read, 1981b).

Of particular importance is the fact that these conclusions hold whether one is discussing positive or negative self-views. People with high self-esteem, who typically possess relatively positive self-views, prefer favorable feedback and interaction partners who provide positive appraisals. Depressed individuals and people with low self-esteem, who tend to possess relatively negative self-views, tend to solicit unfavorable appraisals and are drawn to others who provide such feedback. For example, in a study of married couples, Swann, Hixon, and de La Ronde (1992) found that spouses who conceived of themselves in unfavorable terms reported greater commitment to their relationship partners if their partners also viewed them negatively. Spouses with positive self-views, however, reported greater commitment to partners who conceived of them in favorable terms. This general pattern of results has been replicated in other studies of married people (Katz, Beach, & Anderson, 1996; Ritts & Stein, 1995; Schafer, Wickrama, & Keith, 1996) as well as college roommates (Broxton, 1963; Swann & Pelham, 1998).

What motivates people, especially people with negative self-views, to seek feedback and interaction partners who confirm those self-views? According to self-verification theory, people self-verify out of the desire to bolster their perceptions of prediction and control. From an epistemic perspective, confirming feedback tells people that their perceptions in general, and self-perceptions in particular, are veridical and reliable. Disconfirming feedback, however, explicitly threatens perceptions of prediction and control by calling into question one's most basic form of insight, apprehension of one's self. Pragmatic concerns also compel people to seek confirming feedback and interaction partners who deliver such feedback. That is, social transactions are more likely to proceed smoothly if both parties establish perceptions of each other that are neither overly negative nor overly positive. To this end, people take steps to ensure that their partners see them as they see themselves.

Critics of self-verification theory have been reluctant to accept it as an adequate explanation of the feedback-seeking activities of people with negative self-views. Some have suggested that people with low self-esteem seek negative feedback to reduce uncertainty about problematic characteristics, thereby permitting the possibility of self-improvement (e.g., Steele, 1988; Trope, 1986). This interpretation, however, is undermined by evidence that people are most likely to seek and receive confirming feedback on self-views about which they are most rather than least certain (Maracek & Mettee, 1972; Pelham & Swann, 1994; Swann & Ely, 1984; Swann & Pelham, 1998; Swann, Pelham, & Chidester, 1988). In their study, Swann, Stein-Seroussi, and Giesler (1992) also cast doubt on the self-improvement explanation; high- and low-self-esteem participants were told to "think aloud" as they chose between interacting with an unfavorable or a favorable evaluator. An independent panel of judges who rated the "think aloud" protocols found that the low-self-esteem participants who chose the unfavorable evaluator, about 78% of the sample, tended to voice epistemic and pragmatic concerns over other possible reasons; a desire for self-improvement was scarcely mentioned (see also Swann, de La Ronde, & Hixon, 1994).

This is not to imply that self-verification strivings are the sole impetus behind people's quest for feedback or that such strivings inevitably determine all their reactions to feedback. For example, as Swann and others have noted, people with negative self-views often find themselves caught in a "cognitive–affective crossfire." On the one hand, a considered desire to bolster their perceptions of prediction and control leads them to embrace confirming (i.e., negative) feedback. On the other hand, receiving unfavorable feedback makes them feel unhappy, depressed, and anxious (Shrauger, 1975; Swann et al., 1987; Swann, Wenzlaff, Krull, & Pelham, 1992, Study 4). In fact, initial research suggested that people with low self-esteem and those with high self-esteem tended to feel equally badly after receiving unfavorable feedback and equally well after receiving favorable feedback, regardless of how well the feedback matched their self-views. These studies seemed to indicate that people's positivity strivings (i.e., the desire to feel good about oneself) control affective reactions to feedback, whereas their self-verification strivings control choice of feedback and perceptions of its accuracy.

Recently, Swann and his colleagues (e.g., Hixon & Swann, 1993; Swann, Pinel, & Tafarodi, 1996; Swann & Schroeder, 1995) have revised and extended their initial conceptualization of the cognitive–affective crossfire. Whereas the valence of feedback does indeed channel a person's initial affective reaction to feedback, an entirely different affective reaction may ensue if sufficient cognitive resources and motivation are available to examine the implications of the feedback. For example, Swann, Pinel, and Tafarodi (1996) found that an initial piece of favorable but nonverifying feedback evoked pleasant feelings in people with low self-esteem. However, when those same people received an additional piece of favorable feedback, their positive affect gave way to anxiety. Swann et al. suggested that the accumulation of positive feedback forced participants to recognize the mismatch between their self-views and the feedback, which consequently threatened their perceptions of prediction and control and led to feelings of angst and anxiety. The foregoing analysis suggests that people with low-self-esteem may be in a no-win situation: For such people, just as unfavorable feedback produces sadness, too much favorable feedback engenders anxiety.

How do people with negative self-views reconcile their conflicting desires for positive and self-verifying feedback? Swann and Schroeder (1995) recently identified several factors that determine the interplay of these two motives. As noted earlier, part of the answer to this question may come from a consideration of what response one examines. Positivity strivings tend to control initial affective reactions, whereas self-verification strivings tend to influence the cognitive reactions that unfold more slowly (Shrauger, 1975).

Also important is the nature of the social context in which feedback is sought and conveyed. People are more likely to seek self-verification within relatively enduring relationships in which there is a premium placed on authenticity and accurate self-disclosure (e.g., Swann, de La Ronde, & Hixon, 1994). Whereas married people seem to prefer confirming feedback, people who are dating seem to care only about how positively they are appraised by their partner.

Perhaps the most critical moderator of self-verification strivings is the certainty of self-views: Because firmly held self-views are apt to be more important in people's efforts to predict and control their worlds than are weakly held ones, people are especially likely to work to verify them. Researchers have discovered that people are indeed more likely to seek unfavorable feedback if they are highly certain of a negative self-view. In contrast, disconfirmation of self-views that are held with little conviction offers minimal threat to perceptions of prediction and control. Thus, people tend to seek positive feedback regarding self-views of which they are uncertain (Maracek & Mettee, 1972; Swann & Pelham, 1998; see also Swann & Ely, 1984; Swann et al., 1988).

In summary, a large body of research demonstrates that people are motivated to seek and confirm their negative as well as positive self-views by seeking feedback and partners who are apt to verify their conceptions of themselves. Nevertheless, under specifiable conditions other desires, such as positivity strivings, may guide the solicitation of feedback. When these two motives conflict, moderating factors such as the certainty of self-views dictate which motive prevails. This is bad news for depressed people because they typically hold their negative self-views with great conviction (A. T. Beck, Rush, Shaw, & Emery, 1979). As a result, when depressed people seek feedback, it often is negative.

SELF-VERIFICATION AND DEPRESSION: EMPIRICAL EVIDENCE

Self-verification theory suggests that the desire for confirming feedback explains why depressed people seek negative feedback, eschew positive feedback, and interpret evaluative information in ways that confirm their relatively negative self-views. Until now, however, we have focused on people who have negative self-views (i.e., people with low self-esteem) but are not necessarily depressed. Because depressed people differ from nondepressed people in a variety of ways (e.g., depressed individuals typically possess heightened self-awareness, impaired cognitive processing, persistent negative mood, and comorbid disorders), previous findings on self-verification may not generalize to them.

To investigate self-verification processes in people who are likely to be depressed, Swann, Wenzlaff, Krull, and Pelham (1992) conducted three studies, using college students whose depressive status was assessed by the short-form of the Beck Depression Inventory (BDI–SF; A. T. Beck & R. Beck, 1972). In Study 1, under the guise of a "getting acquainted" investigation, Swann et al. found that when given a choice of partners to become acquainted with, mildly depressed participants preferred to interact with an evaluator who had appraised them negatively (i.e., had assigned them an average rating of 3 on a series of 10-point bipolar trait scales) over a favorable evaluator, who had assigned them an average rating of 9 on the same scales. Nondepressed participants reported the opposite preference. It is also consistent with self-verification theory that participants expressed more desire to interact with their chosen partner to the extent that they perceived their partner's appraisal to be accurate.

In Study 2, mildly depressed participants and nondepressed participants were asked directly how they wished to be appraised by friends and dating partners on various attributes. In general, depressed people wished to be perceived more negatively by their friends and dating partners than did nondepressed people. In line with self-verification theory, regression analyses indicated that the preferred appraisals of both nondepressed and depressed participants correlated with their respective self-views.

Finally, in a prospective study of college roommates (Study 3), Swann, Wenzlaff, Krull, and Pelham (1992) found that mildly depressed students reported a greater desire for negative feedback and a lesser desire for positive feedback from their roommates, compared with nondepressed students. Furthermore, their desire for negative feedback at midsemester was associated with more unfavorable appraisal and rejection by their roommate at semester's end.

Taken together, the results of these three studies suggest that people exhibiting mild levels of depression prefer to interact with others who see them as they see themselves and gravitate toward partners who provide confirming appraisals. Moreover, findings suggest that the feedback-seeking activities of depressed people allowed them to modify their relationship partners' evaluations of them such that partners came to view depressed people as negatively as they viewed themselves. Although this process should make these partners more attractive to depressed people, as the partners' evaluations become more negative, the partners themselves may sour on the relationship. Indeed, as demonstrated by Swann, Wenzlaff, Krull, and Pelham (1992, Study 3), the more negative partners' appraisals became, the more inclined the partners were to abandon the relationship. Unfortunately, self-verification strivings seem to compel depressed people to transform their interaction partners into people who are most apt to reject them.

Several critics challenged the conclusions of Swann, Wenzlaff, Krull, and Pelham (1992; see Hooley & Richters, 1992; Alloy & Lipman, 1992). To address these criticisms, Swann, Wenzlaff, and Tafarodi (1992) conducted two additional studies using the long form of the BDI (A. T. Beck, 1967) to identify depressed people. In Study 1, mildly depressed participants and nondepressed participants were led to believe they had been evaluated by a potential interaction partner. Some learned that they had been evaluated favorably (i.e., as well adjusted, self-confident, happy, and untroubled), whereas others learned they had been evaluated unfavorably (i.e., as chronically unhappy, unconfident, and uncomfortable around others). Participants chose between staying and interacting with the evaluator or leaving and taking part in another experiment on an unrelated topic. Sixty percent of the depressed people who had been evaluated unfavorably chose to stay and interact with the evaluator, whereas only 20% of the depressed individuals who had been evaluated favorably chose to stay and interact. Nondepressed individuals displayed the opposite pattern of preference. As in previous studies, the more accurately participants believed they were evaluated, the more they wanted to interact with the evaluator. This study demonstrates that depressed people may enact self-verification strivings both by seeking negative evaluations (i.e., gravitating toward others who appraise them unfavorably) and by eschewing positive evaluations (i.e., avoiding those who appraise them favorably).

Results of a follow-up study by Swann, Wenzlaff, and Tafarodi (1992) supported the assumption that the preference for unfavorable feedback exhibited by depressed individuals in previous studies was motivated by their desire for confirming evaluations. Mildly depressed and nondepressed participants were initially exposed to feedback that disconfirmed or verified their global self-appraisal. All participants were then given the opportunity to solicit feedback regarding their strengths or limitations. Swann, Wenzlaff, and Tafarodi reasoned that participants in the group whose global self-appraisal had been contradicted by feedback should be particularly motivated to bolster their perceptions of prediction and control by choosing verifying feedback. This is exactly what happened: Depressed participants were more likely to solicit information about their weaknesses following exposure to positive (i.e., disconfirming) as compared with negative (i.e., confirming) feedback, whereas nondepressed participants were more likely to solicit information about their strengths following exposure to negative (i.e., disconfirming) as opposed to positive (i.e., confirming) feedback.

The findings of Swann, Wenzlaff, Krull, and Pelham (1992) and Swann, Wenzlaff, and Tafarodi (1992) thus demonstrate that people whose BDI scores indicate mild depression are motivated to seek feedback and interaction partners that confirm their self-views (see also Joiner, 1995; Joiner, Alfano, & Metalsky, 1993, for related work). Nevertheless, people who exceed specified cutoff points on self-report inventories do not necessarily meet diagnostic criteria for major depression (e.g., Coyne, 1994; Hooley & Richter, 1992; Tennen, Hall, & Affleck, 1995). This may be problematic because at least some research has indicated that clinically depressed individuals differ qualitatively from those who do not meet full criteria for the disorder (see Coyne, 1994). In light of such concerns, Hooley and Richters suggested that the work by Swann and his colleagues may not generalize to people suffering from clinical depression. For example, the aversive affective state associated with clinical depression may motivate "true" depressives to avoid feedback that would make them feel even worse about themselves.

Giesler, Josephs, and Swann (1996) addressed this possibility by investigating the types of feedback desired by people who were clinically depressed, nondepressed with low self-esteem, or nondepressed with high self-esteem. Initial classification in the three groups was made on the basis of self-report inventories, and depression was confirmed by means of the Structured Clinical Interview for the *Diagnostic and Statistical Manual of Mental Disorders*, American Psychiatric Association, 1987; Spitzer, Williams, Gibbon, & First, 1990). During an interview session, participants were told that two clinical psychologists-in-training were preparing in-depth personality profiles of them on the basis of their earlier responses to a battery of "personality inventories." All participants were given the opportunity to examine the profiles. Because of supposed time constraints, participants were asked to choose the one profile they most wanted to see on the basis of summarized versions of each profile. One summary was favorable (e.g., this person seems well adjusted, self-confident); one was negative (e.g., this person seems unconfident, uncomfortable around others). After selecting a profile, participants rated how much they wished to examine each profile.

The results supported self-verification theory. Of the depressed people, 82% chose to examine the negative profile, compared with 64% of the low-self-esteem participants and only 25% of the high-self-esteem participants (see Figure 1). Moreover, participants' continuous ratings of their desire to examine each profile tended to reflect their choice of feedback. Depressed people preferred the unfavorable over the favorable profile; low-self-esteem participants displayed no preference; and high-self-esteem participants preferred the favorable over the unfavorable profile. Also as predicted by self-verification theory, several different analyses indicated that the perceived accuracy of the feedback drove feedback choice and prefer-

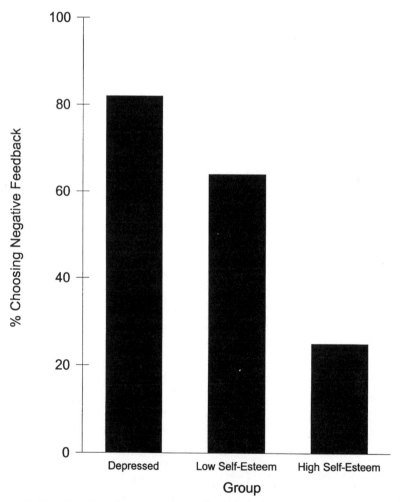

Figure 1. Feedback choice across groups.

ence. Participants in all three groups chose the summary that they perceived to be self-descriptive.

The foregoing evidence that people prefer and seek confirming feedback suggests that depressed people might seek favorable feedback if they also perceived it as verifying. Indirect support for this proposition comes from a study by Swann, Pelham, and Krull (1989). These authors discovered that even people whose global self-appraisal was negative (i.e., individuals with low-self-esteem) preferred verifying feedback about their best attributes over verifying feedback about their worst attributes, presumably because soliciting favorable information that is also confirming simultaneously satisfies self-verification and positivity strivings.

To determine whether depressed people might seek positive feedback that was also verifying, Giesler et al. (1996) told participants at the beginning of the interview session that the clinicians-in-training would provide them with feedback on some specific attributes (e.g., intellectual ability, social ability) and then asked them to indicate about which attributes they most desired feedback. Linear trend analyses indicated that depressed people, like high- and low-self-esteem participants, tended to rank their best attributes (i.e., attributes on which they rated themselves highly) ahead of their worst attributes (i.e., attributes on which they rated themselves poorly). Nevertheless, follow-up analyses of participants' rankings of their best attribute showed a decreasing linear trend across the three groups: High-self-esteem participants were most likely to desire feedback about their best attribute, followed by low-self-esteem participants, followed by depressed participants, who were least likely to want feedback about their best attribute. These findings suggest that depressed people do not fully exploit opportunities to acquire feedback that is both confirming and positive.[1]

The overall pattern of data reported by Giesler et al. (1996) suggests that the feedback-seeking activities of depressed people may be detrimental for two reasons. First, when given a choice between an unfavorable but confirming evaluation and a favorable but disconfirming evaluation, depressed individuals select the former. Second, when presented with the opportunity to acquire evaluations that are confirming and favorable, depressed individuals fail to take full advantage of the situation.

In summary, recent investigations, including several that are described elsewhere (e.g., Joiner, 1995; Joiner et al., 1993), have provided strong support for the presence of self-verification processes in mildly and clinically depressed samples. These studies demonstrate that depressed people

---

[1]This finding is probably due to the positive valence of the expected feedback. Although specific, positive feedback would be consistent with and thus confirm a specific, favorable self-view, its positivity would still be inconsistent with a depressed person's global, negative self-appraisal. This may be sufficiently threatening to mute a depressed participant's desire for this sort of feedback.

desire negative appraisals that confirm their self-views and eschew positive appraisals that do not. Moreover, several of these investigations provide evidence that depressed people's preference for negative feedback depends on the perceived accuracy of the feedback.

SELF-VERIFICATION AND DEPRESSION:
CORRECTING MISCONCEPTIONS

Aspects of self-verification theory and its role in depression have sometimes been misconstrued in the past. In the following section, we attempt to clarify several key issues by focusing on the role of perceived accuracy, the importance of the desire for prediction and control, and the specificity of self-verification effects in depression.

The Role of Perceived Accuracy

First, we wish to stress that when depressed people seek unfavorable feedback, they are seeking appraisals that provide verification of their self-views, not negative appraisals per se. From the perspective of self-verification theory, feedback is regarded as desirable to the extent that it seems accurate and self-descriptive. This means that depressed individuals are embarked on a "rational" search for self-confirmation rather than on a masochistic quest for disapproval.

The reader should bear in mind, however, that feedback perceived by depressed people as accurate varies in its degree of unfavorableness, depending on a variety of methodological factors that have nothing to do with the depressed people's psychological predispositions. For example, in the study by Giesler et al. (1996), depressed individuals preferred the negative evaluation over the positive one because it seemed more accurate to them. However, had we made the negative evaluation extremely unfavorable (e.g., this person has no redeeming value whatsoever, is totally bereft of social skills), we would have expected depressed participants to prefer the positive appraisal, because they would have perceived it as more accurate than the extremely negative one. Had we obtained these results, however, we would have been in error if we had concluded on the basis of such evidence that depressed people prefer positive feedback. Similarly, a researcher could systematically alter the positivity of preferred feedback by changing the domains for which feedback is sought. For example, the desire for confirming feedback would drive most people to solicit unfavorable feedback concerning the ability to compete in the Olympics, because most people are not world-class athletes. However, the same desire would cause most people to seek positive feedback concerning their ability to drive a car, prepare a sandwich, or perform other tasks they successfully engage in every day. Thus, focusing only on the positivity of sought-after feedback can lead to faulty conclusions. By carefully selecting and framing the type of feedback that is presented to participants, one could find evidence of a positivity bias, a negativity bias, or an evenhandedness without saying anything about the underlying psychological propensities of participants.

We make this point precisely because results of previous investigations (e.g., Swann, Wenzlaff, Krull, & Pelham, 1992; Study 3) in which depressed individuals expressed only a relative preference for negative evaluations sometimes were interpreted as evidence of a desire for balanced feedback on the part of depressed people (e.g., Hooley & Richters, 1992; Alloy & Lipman, 1992). As past research has demonstrated, this interpretation is more apparent than real, with perceived accuracy accounting for the ostensible preference for balanced feedback. Moreover, Swann, Wenzlaff, and Tafarodi (1992) and Giesler et al. (1996) definitively showed that depressed people, whether they are identified by self-report inventories or standardized clinical interviews, do not solicit feedback evenhandedly.

The Role of Prediction and Control Strivings

According to self-verification theory, the search for confirming feedback is driven by the need to bolster perceptions of prediction and control. Some readers may question whether this motive can account for self-verification effects in depression because the interpretation may seem to contradict several assumptions about the nature of depression (see A. T. Beck, 1976; Abramson, Metalsky, & Alloy, 1989; Abramson, Seligman, & Teasdale, 1978). For example, helplessness–hopelessness research suggests that depression is associated with a failure to engage in behaviors that typically signify the presence of prediction and control strivings.

Bolstering perceptions of prediction and control can be accomplished through numerous means, however. Although results of research suggest that depressed people have abandoned "proactive and dynamic" attempts to exert control over their environment, depressed individuals may seek to bolster their perceptions of prediction and control by using alternative methods, such as self-verifying. This interpretation is supported by research showing that when initial attempts to exert control fail, people switch to alternative strategies that will enable them to maintain their perception that they can at least understand, if not control, the events they experience (Pittman & Pittman, 1980; Swann, Stephenson, and Pittman, 1981; Taylor, 1983). For example, investigators have shown that mildly depressed people compared with nondepressed individuals seek more information when confronted with stressful events (Coyne, Aldwin, & Lazarus, 1981), engage in more effortful information processing in interpersonal situations (Edwards & Weary, 1993; Flett, Pliner, & Blankstein, 1989; Gleicher & Weary,

1991), and are highly interested in obtaining feedback about the self (Gasparikova-Krasnec & Post, 1984). Furthermore, Giesler et al. (1996) found that prior to the interview session, clinically depressed individuals reported that they were very interested in obtaining evaluative information about themselves, more interested even than people with low self-esteem. Moreover, during the interview session, they reported a greater desire to examine the feedback they had chosen compared with nondepressed participants overall.

Apparently, then, depressed people retain prediction and control strivings but abandon the relatively dynamic, instrumental behaviors through which nondepressed people express these strivings (see Weary & Edwards, 1994). The absence of these relatively active strategies not only is consistent with the helplessness–hopelessness perspective but also suggests that depressed people, compared with nondepressed people, may be more likely to employ alternative means to express their prediction and control strivings, such as engaging in self-verification.[2]

The Specificity Issue

Because researchers in the past did not attempt to control for potential confounds between depression and its natural covariates (e.g., anxiety), it has been suggested that self-verification effects may be due to one of these covariates and thus are not specific to depression. Two issues here require comment.

First, the motivation for confirming feedback is not (and has never been claimed to be) a desire specific to depression. Rather, as long as people possess self-views they are certain about and possess the requisite cognitive resources (see Swann, Hixon, Stein-Seroussi, & Gilbert, 1990), they should seek feedback that confirms their self-views. This should be the case regardless of what those self-views are and whether that person is depressed, anxious, or suffering from other psychological disorders. It therefore is incorrect to state that self-verification processes are specific to or are a specific cause of depression (although as we propose in a later section, self-verification processes sometimes play a critical role in the onset and maintenance of depressive episodes).

Second, because findings from numerous studies have firmly established that both depressed and nondepressed individuals seek confirming feedback, factors unique to one group (e.g., conditions comorbid with de-

---

[2]Before closing this section, we note that allowing strivings for prediction and control to guide behavior probably holds some short-term adaptive value for depressed people. For example, by avoiding interaction partners who hold overly positive expectations, depressed individuals evade social interactions that would overtax their abilities. Eventually, however, the long-term consequences of continually seeking confirming (i.e., negative) feedback are likely to outweigh the short-term benefits.

pression) cannot be driving effects common to both groups. Therefore, it is not parsimonious to assume that anxiety can account for the self-verification effects found in past research focusing on depressed people. However, if anxiety were present as a comorbid condition, it could conceivably affect the type of feedback depressed persons regard as confirming (e.g., someone who is anxious will perceive feedback indicating he or she is fearful and nervous as self-descriptive).[3]

SELF-VERIFICATION PROCESSES IN THE ONSET, MAINTENANCE, AND REMISSION OF DEPRESSIVE EPISODES: A THEORETICAL ACCOUNT

The nature and function of self-verification activities are likely to vary over the course of the depressive episode. In what follows, we consider some of the key contributions of self-verification strivings during each successive phase of depression.

Onset

Joiner (1995) reported findings suggesting that college students who solicit and receive negative feedback from their roommates exhibit increased levels of depressive symptoms over time. As predicted by self-verification theory, feedback seeking in this sample was correlated with self-esteem; persons who viewed themselves unfavorably reported a greater preference for negative feedback. Such findings suggest that self-verification processes may play an etiological role in the onset of a depressive episode.

How might self-verification processes lead to depression? Consider a person who, although not depressed, has begun to experience feelings that are intensely negative. (It is not necessary to identify the proximal cause of these feelings in the account that follows.) Whatever their origin, intense feelings of negativity are likely to have two effects: (a) They will prime similarly valenced constructs in memory such as negative self-views (Blaney, 1986; Bower, 1981; Sedikides, 1992), especially for people with low self-esteem (J. D. Brown & Mankowski, 1993), and (b) they will increase levels of self-awareness (Salovey, 1992; Wood, Saltzberg, & Goldsamt, 1990). Together, these two processes compel people to focus attention on negative aspects of themselves (see Ingram, 1990). As suggested by several major stress–diathesis theories of depression (e.g., A. T. Beck's cognitive theory), the initial experience of negative affect may also trigger

---

[3]It is interesting to note that because some anxiety disorders arise out of people's concern that they cannot predict and control important events, people suffering from anxiety disorders ought to be more likely than nonanxious people to engage in behaviors, like self-verification, that bolster their sense of prediction and control.

the emergence of previously latent depression-specific schemas or dysfunctional beliefs (Haaga, Dyck, & Ernst, 1991; Hedlund & Rude, 1995). Once activated, these information-processing structures will further increase the salience of the person's negative self-views, especially self-views specific to depression. Such heightened salience of negative self-views may cause people to "see" negativity everywhere, both in the world in general and in themselves in particular.[4]

As negative self-views become increasingly accessible, they are more likely to guide the solicitation of feedback and to be used as a standard against which to judge the perceived accuracy of incoming feedback. Over time, this process should result in an increased receipt of and receptiveness to unfavorable feedback, which in turn should foster negative affect (Shrauger, 1975; Swann, Wenzlaff, Krull, & Pelham, 1992, Study 4; Swann et al., 1987) and heighten levels of depressive symptoms (Joiner, 1995). Eventually, a depressogenic cycle may develop: The receipt of negative feedback will induce increased levels of depressive affect and related symptoms, which in turn will increase self-focus and the salience of negative self-views, thereby perpetuating the cycle. Because this cycle feeds on itself, it may escalate fairly quickly and could help trigger the onset of an episode of clinical depression.[5]

To be sure, the experience of intense negative affect does not always lead to depression. One factor that may moderate the link between negative affect and depression is the interpersonal environment inhabited by the person experiencing the negative affect. Joiner (1995), for example, indicated that it is the receipt of negative feedback that induces depressive symptoms. Therefore, whether interaction partners honor attempts to evoke negative feedback ought to play a key role in determining whether an episode of clinical depression develops.

Unfortunately for people with negative self-views, their partners are especially likely to honor such requests. Because people with low self-esteem tend to gravitate toward interaction partners who confirm their negative attributes (e.g., Buckner & Swann, 1995; Swann, Hixon, & de La Ronde, 1992), their partners are usually accustomed to providing unfavorable appraisals. The intimates of high-self-esteem persons, however, may refuse to "play ball" if negative appraisals are solicited, because they will not want to deviate from patterns of behavior (e.g., providing positive feedback) that have maintained the relationship in the past.

It is interesting that low-self-esteem persons who lack long-term in-

---

[4]It is worth noting that theories concerning depressive attributional style (Abramson, Metalsky, & Alloy, 1989) also fit well within this framework. Attributing negative events to internal causes, for example, has been linked to lowered self-esteem, which functionally would be similar to increasing the salience and accessibility of one's negative self-views.

[5]In keeping with this formulation, Bargh and Tota (1988) showed that mildly depressed people, who are characterized by high levels of negative affect but cannot be considered clinically depressed, possess automatized access to their depressotypic self-views.

teraction partners are likely to be more vulnerable to depression than their more attached counterparts. Once the depressogenic cycle described previously has begun, these people do not have anyone to insulate them against their own attempts to acquire unfavorable feedback (see Swann & Predmore, 1985). Instead, they gravitate toward any available interaction partner who seems likely to accede to requests for negative appraisal. However, compared with people with low-self-esteem, those with high self-esteem are likely to possess a greater preponderance of positive self-views. Thus, even when some unhappy event makes their negative self-views more salient and accessible, its impact on feedback seeking will be muted by the relatively high number of positive self-views they possess (see also J. D. Brown & Mankowski, 1993).

Some support for the preceding formulation exists. For example, low self-esteem has been linked prospectively to depression (e.g., Roberts, Kassel, & Gotlib, 1995), although not always (e.g., Ingham, Kreitman, Miller, Sashidharan, & Surtees, 1987; Lewinsohn, Steinmetz, Larson, & Franklin, 1981). The self-verification formulation accounts for these inconsistent findings by suggesting that low self-esteem leads to depression only under certain conditions, most notably when intimates are willing to provide negative feedback. For example, Brown and his colleagues (e.g., G. W. Brown & Andrews, 1986; G. W. Brown, Andrews, Bifulco, & Veiel, 1990) have reported prospective data indicating that low self-esteem coupled with the occurrence of a stress-inducing event predicted future episodes of clinical depression in British women; however, the presence of a supportive partner tended to mitigate this effect. From a self-verification perspective, the positive support may have acted to counter attempts to garner negative feedback, thereby decreasing the chances of a depressive episode occurring.

In summary, a cyclical mechanism is proposed to account for the possible etiological role of self-verification processes in the development of clinical depression, in which the experience of negative affect promotes the accessibility of negative self-views, which in turn leads to the elicitation of increasingly negative feedback and induces a depressogenic response (see Wachtel, 1994, for a general discussion of cyclical processes in psychopathology). Whereas this cycle is disrupted among people with high self-esteem because they tend to enter relationships with partners who provide them with positive feedback, among people with low self-esteem the cycle is augmented because they surround themselves with partners who provide them with a steady supply of negative feedback.

Maintenance

In the foregoing section, we described how the unfavorable self-views of people could be made more accessible by the experience of intense, negative affect, thereby beginning a depressogenic cycle that operates as a risk factor for depression. In this section, we describe in more concrete detail how self-verification processes affect individuals who are currently depressed.

Regardless of the origins of their depression, depressed individuals tend to have lower self-esteem and more negative self-views than nondepressed individuals (Battle, 1978; A. T. Beck, 1967; Giesler et al., 1996). According to self-verification theory, therefore, depressed people should be especially inclined to solicit negative feedback from interaction partners because such feedback is particularly likely to confirm their own self-perceptions, thereby bolstering their perceptions of prediction and control.[6] As suggested earlier, this process should reinforce and entrench depressed people's negative self-views, especially if such feedback comes from a close relationship partner (e.g., Swann & Predmore, 1985). Evaluations that verify depressed people's unfavorable self-beliefs, when coupled with the negative affect that accompanies such evaluations, should serve to maintain or to exacerbate a depressive episode.

Depressed people can verify their negative self-views in several ways. First, they may gravitate toward partners who see them negatively and may avoid ones who see them positively. Second, if they happen to encounter someone who thinks well of them, they can evoke hostility and rejection from that person by acting in a belligerent, irresponsible, or irritating manner. Third, if their efforts to evoke confirming reactions fail, they may still manage to "see" their world as more confirming than it is by selectively attending to feedback, selectively retrieving it, or interpreting it in ways that are compatible with their negative self-views.

Swann (1990) described several strategies that people with negative self-views use to ensure that they receive verifying reactions from others. Swann and Read (1981b, Study 2) found that if people with negative self-views thought that their interaction partner viewed them favorably, they intensified their efforts to appear unworthy of their interaction partner's positive regard. In a similar manner, when depressed people feel they are being misconstrued, they may act to correct these misconceptions by behaving in a hostile manner (Coyne, 1976a; Gotlib & Robinson, 1982), by becoming argumentative and demanding (e.g., Linden, Hautzinger, & Hoffman, 1983; Ruscher & Gotlib, 1988), or by enacting other behaviors commonly observed in depression to correct the misperceptions of their interaction partners (see Segrin & Abramson, 1995, for an in-depth review of work on depressive communication style).

It is interesting that one of the most frequently documented behaviors associated with depressed people's communication style is inappropriate self-disclosure (Segrin & Abramson, 1995). For example, Jacobson and

---

[6]See E. S. Becker (1964) for an intriguing alternative explanation of how strivings for prediction and control can cause and maintain depression.

Anderson (1982) reported that depressed people were more likely to make spontaneous unsolicited and negative statements about the self than were nondepressed persons. From the standpoint of a depressed individual, this is an extremely potent strategy to use: Directly informing an interaction partner of one's negative qualities practically guarantees that one will be viewed in a negative (i.e., confirming) manner, at least regarding specific characteristics. Simultaneously, because inappropriate self-disclosure by definition entails breaking social norms, it tends to evoke dislike and rejection in interaction partners (Gurtman, 1987), which provides further confirmation of one's negative attributes. From the self-verification standpoint, then, it is not surprising that inappropriate self-disclosure occurs so frequently in depression.

As depression deepens, depressed people may discover that relatively active modes of self-verification are not needed to elicit confirming feedback and instead may come to rely on relatively passive modes to do the trick. For example, they may (nonconsciously) come to rely on the natural correlates of depression to evoke unfavorable reactions, such as negative facial expressions (G. E. Schwartz, Fair, Salt, Mandel, & Klerman, 1976; Waxer, 1974) and monotonic speech (Teasdale, Fogarty, & Williams, 1980). At the same time, other relatively passive means of eliciting confirming feedback, described earlier, may begin to play an increasingly important role in the self-verification process. For example, instead of attempting to correct the perceptions of those who provide overly positive feedback, depressed people near the trough of a depressive episode may simply fail to respond or may withdraw from those whose appraisals they perceive to be disconfirming (e.g., Swann, Wenzlaff, Krull, & Pelham, 1992, Study 1). Such behaviors also offer a naturally occurring instance of the failure to seek positive appraisals displayed by the depressed participants studied by Giesler et al. (1996). In situations in which a depressed person cannot easily withdraw from a partner who provides favorable feedback (e.g., a spouse), selective information processing may offer the sole means of obtaining evaluative information that matches the depressed person's self-views.

It is worth noting that the existence of self-verification strivings provides one explanation for the fact that depression is often so difficult to shake: At some level, depressed people are motivated to cling to the negative self-conceptions that fuel their depressive states (see McNulty & Swann, 1994, for a further discussion). Indeed, if depressed people abandon active attempts to predict and control their environments, as past research suggests they do, one of the few remaining ways to satisfy prediction and control strivings is through self-verifying. Bewildered by events that seem to have spun out of control, depressed people should be especially loathe to relinquish the one thing that seems stable: their firmly held self-views.

Remission

A feature common to many theories of depression is the cyclical nature of the processes that are thought to contribute to the maintenance of depressive episodes. Although these approaches have contributed significantly to the understanding of the persistence of depression over time, relatively little is known about how and why recovery from depression occurs (Needles & Abramson, 1990). Indeed, given that the majority of processes hypothesized to maintain depression (e.g., depressive schemas, attributional style, self-focusing styles) are self-perpetuating, it is difficult to explain why depressive episodes often appear to remit spontaneously (A. T. Beck, 1967).

Although recovery is undoubtedly a complex, multiple determined process, one factor that may play a key role is the disruption of depressed individuals' self-verification processes. If self-verification strivings do indeed maintain depressive episodes, then nullifying them should allow other motives, like positivity strivings, to play a greater role in determining the valence of solicited feedback. It follows that factors that have been linked to recovery (e.g., social support, cognitive therapy) may be successful in part because of their ability to discourage people from allowing self-verification strivings to drive preferences for feedback.

For example, recall that Giesler et al. (1996) found that clinically depressed people preferred to receive verifying feedback about their strengths over verifying feedback about their weaknesses, although this preference was somewhat attenuated when compared with that of nondepressed participants. These data suggest that even clinically depressed people may seek positive information about the self if such information will not disconfirm their self-views (see also Dunning & Story, 1991; Pelham, 1991). Given that positivity strivings persist in depressed people, one potential mechanism for alleviating depression is to identify a strategy that encourages such strivings to gain control of behavior. One such mechanism may be to undermine the certainty with which depressed individuals cling to their unfavorable self-views—a strategy that some cognitive therapists have championed (A. T. Beck et al., 1979). This makes sense because people tend to seek verifying feedback for self-views of which they are certain but solicit positive feedback for self-views that are not firmly held (Maracek & Mettee, 1972; Pelham, 1991; Swann & Ely, 1984). Thus, the more uncertain depressed people become of their negative self-views, the less likely it is that they will desire to verify those self-views. Instead, other motives, such as positivity strivings, should begin to control the types of appraisals they seek regarding those attributes.

A caveat is worth mentioning here. If one attempts to undermine certainty by issuing direct challenges to specific self-views, the threat to a depressed person's global self-view could be substantial enough to cause him or her to repudiate the threat by seeking verification of some other negative aspect of the self (Swann, Pinel, & Tafarodi, 1996; Swann, Wenzlaff, & Tafarodi, 1992). This means that therapists must be cautious to avoid triggering such compensatory reactions.[7]

Perhaps the most effective means of avoiding such compensatory reactions is first to provide depressed people with small amounts of confirming (i.e., negative) feedback. Once the therapist has satisfied the depressed person's desire for negative feedback (and bolstered his or her credibility in the process), the therapist may be in a better position to "defuse" the effects of self-verification processes safely by challenging the depressed person's negative self-views. Finn and Tonsager (1992), for example, established a warm and supportive relationship with depressed patients and then gave them feedback that confirmed their self-views. Two weeks later, those who had received congruent feedback displayed improved psychological functioning and higher self-esteem than did members of a no-feedback control group, despite the fact that the congruent feedback was sometimes decidedly negative (e.g., "You are depressed, thought disordered, angry, obsessional"). Patients seemed to benefit enormously from the perception that "You seem to know all my shortcomings but still like me."

Why are confirming, negative evaluations beneficial? One reason is that congruent feedback delivered in a supportive context may increase people's perceptions that they are competent in at least one sphere: knowing themselves. This realization may foster a feeling of psychoepistemological competence, a sense of mastery, and heightened perceptions of predictability and control—perceptions that may reduce anxiety. In addition, being understood by a therapist may reduce feelings of alienation, for it tells patients that someone thought enough of them to learn who they are. For these and related reasons, when provided in a supportive context, self-verifying feedback may have beneficial effects, even when it is negative.

There are, of course, additional strategies that may be exploited in attempting to change the self-views of depressed people. The more general point here, however, is that those who are interested in changing self-views should recognize that people's desire for positive evaluations may be overriden by a general psychological desire for self-verification (Swann, 1997). The desire for self-verification may compel people to work to maintain their positive—and negative—self-views by embracing confirming feedback; eschewing disconfirming feedback; and surrounding themselves with friends, intimates, and associates who act as accomplices in maintaining their self-views.

---

[7]Therapists might use such compensatory reactions to facilitate the changes they desire. For example, therapists could impute qualities to patients that are more extreme than patients' actual qualities (e.g., characterizing an unassertive person as a complete doormat) in the hope that they will behaviorally resist the innuendo (e.g., become more assertive) and adopt corresponding self-views (e.g., Watzlawick, Weakland, & Fisch, 1974; for a discussion of a laboratory analogue of this technique, see Swann, Pelham, & Chidester, 1988).

CONCLUSION

Several decades ago, A. T. Beck (1967) noted with some puzzlement that the attitudes and behaviors of patients diagnosed with depression "seem to contradict some of the most strongly established axioms of human nature. According to the 'pleasure principle,' the patient should be seeking to maximize ... satisfactions and minimize ... pain" (p. 3). Instead, as Beck noted, depressed patients "often perform acts that seem to enhance their suffering" (p. 3). Since that time, the results of numerous empirical investigations have confirmed Beck's observations: Depressed people frequently seem compelled to engage in actions and modes of thinking that perpetuate their unhappiness.

Self-verification theory provides one explanation for the seemingly paradoxical patterns of behavior and thought enacted by depressed people. As we have discussed, depressed people, like nondepressed people, are motivated by strivings for prediction and control to seek feedback and to build social worlds that confirm their self-views. However, unlike nondepressed people, depressed people tend to possess negative self-views. Thus, for these individuals, striving for confirmation typically means soliciting negative appraisals and avoiding positive appraisals. Unfortunately, whereas seeking confirming feedback is normally adaptive, in depressed people this activity produces the added and unwanted effect of entrenching negative self-views and increasing levels of negative affectivity, which in turn exacerbate and maintain a depressive episode.

Despite the foregoing, it is also true that the depressed person retains positivity strivings, albeit in diminished form (i.e., depression does not appear to extinguish the "pleasure principle" in all but the most severe of cases). Indeed, we have suggested that disabling self-verification processes and allowing positivity strivings to guide interpersonal behavior should prove effective therapy for depression. However, as we also took pains to note, such attempts must be performed with care. The depressed person will cling to his or her self-views, as negative as they may be, because they provide a solid anchor in an environment that may otherwise appear to be uncontrollable and unpredictable. Attempts to deprive the depressed person of that anchor may be viewed as particularly threatening and may be met with great resistance.

The foregoing suggests that strivings for prediction and control and the desire for positivity operate in complex ways to determine the onset, maintenance, and remission of depressive episodes. Increasing the understanding of how these motives contribute to depression requires integration with other approaches (e.g., see Swann, Wenzlaff, Krull, & Pelham, 1992). For example, positivity strivings appear to lie at the root of the well-documented tendency of mildly depressed people to demand reassurance signifying they are valued by their interaction partners (Coyne, 1976a;

Joiner et al., 1992). However, self-verification theory explains why such reassurances (i.e., positive appraisals) leave the depressed person feeling anxious and dissatisfied, thereby provoking further requests for feedback, resulting in a cycle that frequently culminates in rejection of the depressed person.[8] In a similar vein, exploring how self-verification processes can be integrated with other risk factors for depression, such as labile self-esteem or sociotropic and autonomous personality styles, may permit greater insight into factors that cause and maintain depression.

In conclusion, self-verification theory provides one explanation for depressed individuals' paradoxical tendency to seek negative appraisals from their interaction partners. By seeking feedback and interaction partners that verify self-views, avoiding appraisals and interaction partners that provide disconfirming feedback, and selectively processing evaluative information about the self, depressed individuals create around themselves social environments that, although hostile and rejecting, provide a sense of inter- and intrapersonal coherence.

REFERENCES

Abramson, L. Y., Metalsky, G. I., & Alloy, L. B. (1989). Hopelessness depression: A theory-based subtype of depression. *Psychological Review, 96*, 358–372.

Abramson, L. Y., Seligman, M. E. P., & Teasdale, J. (1978). Learned helplessness in humans: Critique and reformulation. *Journal of Abnormal Psychology, 87*, 49–74.

Alloy, L., & Lipman, A. (1992). Depression and selection of positive and negative social feedback: Motivated preference or cognitive balance? *Journal of Abnormal Psychology, 101*, 310–313.

American Psychiatric Association. (1987). *Diagnostic and statistical manual of mental disorders* (3rd ed., rev.). Washington, DC: Author.

Andrews, J. D. (1989). Psychotherapy of depression: A self-confirmation model. *Psychological Review, 96*, 576–607.

Bargh, J. A., & Tota, M. E. (1988). Context-dependent automatic processing in depression: Accessibility of negative constructs with regard to self but not others. *Journal of Personality and Social Psychology, 54*, 925–939.

Battle, J. (1978). Relationship between self-esteem and depression. *Psychological Reports, 42*, 745–746.

Beck, A. T. (1967). *Depression: Clinical, experimental and theoretical aspects.* New York: Hoeber.

Beck, A. T. (1976). *Cognitive therapy and the emotional disorders.* New York: International Universities Press.

---

[8]Note that rejection is exactly the sort of interpersonal event that self-verification processes should drive a depressed individual toward (i.e., rejection offers compelling proof of one's worthlessness and social ineptitude).

Beck, A. T., & Beck, R. (1972). Screening depressed patients in family practice: A rapid technique. *Postgraduate Medicine, 52*, 81–85.

Beck, A. T., Rush, A. J., Shaw, B. F., & Emery, G. (1979). *Cognitive therapy of depression*. New York: Guilford Press.

Becker, E. S. (1964). *The revolution in psychiatry*. New York: Free Press.

Blaney, P. H. (1986). Affect and memory: A review. *Psychological Bulletin, 99*, 229–246.

Bower, G. H. (1981). Mood and memory. *American Psychologist, 36*, 129–148.

Brown, G. W., & Andrews, B. (1986). Social support and depression. In M. H. Appley & R. Trumbull (Eds.), *Dynamics of stress: Physiological, psychological and social perspectives* (pp. 257–282). New York: Plenum Press.

Brown, G. W., Andrews, B., Bifulco, A. T., & Veiel, H. O. (1990). Self-esteem and depression: I. Measurement issues and prediction of onset. *Social Psychiatry and Psychiatric Epidemiology, 25*, 200–209.

Brown, J. D., & Mankowski, T. A. (1993). Self-esteem, mood, and self-evaluation: Changes in mood and the way you see you. *Journal of Personality and Social Psychology, 64*, 421–430.

Broxton, J. A. (1963). A test of interpersonal attraction predictions derived from balance theory. *Journal of Abnormal and Social Psychology, 66*, 394–397.

Buckner, C. E., & Swann, W. B., Jr. (1995, August). *Physical abuse in close relationships: The dynamic interplay of couple characteristics*. Paper presented at the annual meeting of the American Psychological Society, New York.

Coates, D., & Wortman, C. B. (1980). Depression maintenance and interpersonal control. In A. Baum & J. E. Singer (Eds.), *Advances in environmental psychology* (Vol. 2, pp. 149–182). Hillsdale, NJ: Erlbaum.

Coyne, J. C. (1976a). Depression and the response of others. *Journal of Abnormal Psychology, 85*, 186–193.

Coyne, J. C. (1976b). Toward an interactional description of depression. *Psychiatry, 39*, 28–40.

Coyne, J. C. (1994). Self-reported distress: Analog or ersatz depression? *Psychological Bulletin, 116*, 29–45.

Coyne, J. C., Aldwin, C. A., & Lazarus, R. S. (1981). Depression and coping in stressful events. *Journal of Abnormal Psychology, 90*, 439–447.

Crary, W. G. (1966). Reactions to incongruent self-experiences. *Journal of Consulting Psychology, 30*, 246–252.

Derry P. A., & Kuiper, N. A. (1981). Schematic processing and self-reference in clinical depression. *Journal of Abnormal Psychology, 90*, 286–297.

Dunning, D., & Story, A. L. (1991). Depression, realism, and the over-confidence effect: Are the sadder wiser when predicting future actions and events? *Journal of Personality and Social Psychology, 61*, 521–532.

Edwards, J. A., & Weary, G. (1993). Depression and the impression-formation continuum: Piecemeal processing despite the availability of category information. *Journal of Personality and Social Psychology, 64*, 636–645.

Finn, S. E., & Tonsager, M. E. (1992). Therapeutic impact of providing MMPI-2 feedback to college students awaiting therapy. *Journal of Psychological Assessment, 4*, 278–287.

Flett, G. L., Pliner P., & Blankstein, K. R. (1989). Depression and components of attributional complexity. *Journal of Personality and Social Psychology, 56*, 757–764.

Freud, S. (1985). Mourning and melancholia (J. Strachey, Trans.). In J. Coyne (Ed.), *Essential papers on depression* (pp. 48–63). New York: New York University Press. (Reprinted from *The standard edition of the complete psychological works of Sigmund Freud*, Vol. 17, by J. Strachey, Ed., 1955, London: Hogarth Press)

Galen. (1976). *Galen on the affected parts: Translation from the Greek text with explanatory notes* (R. E. Siegel, Trans.). New York: Karger.

Gasparikova-Krasnec, M., & Post, R. D. (1984). Motivation to obtain self-relevant feedback in depressed college students. *Journal of Clinical Psychology, 40*, 1190–1193.

Giesler, R. B., Josephs, R. A., & Swann, W. B., Jr. (1996). Self-verification in clinical depression: The desire for negative evaluation. *Journal of Abnormal Psychology, 105*, 358–368.

Gleicher, F., & Weary, G. (1991). Effect of depression on quantity and quality of social inferences. *Journal of Personality and Social Psychology, 61*, 105–114.

Gotlib, I. H. (1983). Perception and recall of interpersonal feedback: Negative bias in depression. *Cognitive Therapy and Research, 7*, 399–412.

Gotlib, I. H., & Beatty, M. E. (1985). Negative responses to depression: The role of attributional style. *Cognitive Therapy and Research, 9*, 91–103.

Gotlib, I. H., & Robinson, L. A. (1982). Responses to depressed individuals: Discrepancies between self-report and observer-rated behavior. *Journal of Abnormal Psychology, 91*, 231–240.

Grinker, R. R. (1964). Communications by patients in depressive states. *Archives of General Psychiatry, 10*, 576–580.

Gurtman, M. B. (1987). Depressive affect and disclosures as factors in interpersonal rejection. *Cognitive Therapy and Research, 11*, 87–100.

Haaga, D. A., Dyck, M. J., & Ernst, D. (1991). Empirical status of cognitive theory of depression. *Psychological Bulletin, 110*, 215–236.

Hedlund, S., & Rude, S. S. (1995). Evidence of latent depressive schemas in formerly depressed individuals. *Journal of Abnormal Psychology, 104*, 517–525.

Hixon, J. G., & Swann, W. B., Jr. (1993). When does introspection bear fruit? Self-reflection, self-insight, and interpersonal choices. *Journal of Personality and Social Psychology, 64*, 35–43.

Hooley, J., & Richters, J. (1992). Allure of self-confirmation: A comment on Swann, Wenzlaff, Krull, and Pelham. *Journal of Abnormal Psychology, 101*, 307–309.

Ingham, J. G., Kreitman, N. B., Miller, P. M., Sashidharan, S., & Surtees, P. G.

(1987). Self-appraisal, anxiety and depression in women: A prospective enquiry. *British Journal of Psychiatry, 151,* 643–651.

Ingram, R. E. (1990). Self-focused attention in clinical disorders: Review and conceptual model. *Psychological Bulletin, 107,* 156–176.

Jacobson, N. S., & Anderson, E. A. (1982). Interpersonal skill and depression in college students: An analysis of the timing of self-disclosures. *Behavior Therapy, 13,* 271–282.

Joiner, T. E. (1995). The price of soliciting and receiving negative feedback: Self-verification theory as a vulnerability to depression theory. *Journal of Abnormal Psychology, 104,* 364–372.

Joiner, T. E., Alfano, M. S., & Metalsky, G. I. (1992). When depression breeds contempt: Reassurance seeking, self-esteem, and rejection of depressed college students by their roommates. *Journal of Abnormal Psychology, 101,* 165–173.

Joiner, T. E., Alfano, M. S., & Metalsky, G. I. (1993). Caught in the crossfire: Depression, self-consistency, self-enhancement, and the response of others. *Journal of Social and Clinical Psychology, 12,* 113–134.

Katz, J., Beach, S. R. H., & Anderson, P. (1996). Self-enhancement versus self-verification: Does spousal support always help? *Cognitive Therapy and Research, 20,* 345–360.

Kovacs, M., & Beck, A. T. (1978). Maladaptive cognitive structures in depression. *American Journal of Psychiatry, 135,* 525–533.

Kraepelin, E. (1990). *Clinical psychiatry: A text-book for students and physicians* (H. Metoui & S. Ayed, Trans.). Canton, MA: Science History Publications. (Original work published 1899)

Kuiper, N. A., & MacDonald, M. R. (1982). Self and other perception in mild depressives. *Social Cognition, 1,* 223–239.

Lewinsohn, P. M., Steinmetz, J. L., Larson, D. W., & Franklin, J. (1981). Depression-related cognitions: Antecedent or consequence? *Journal of Abnormal Psychology, 90,* 213–219.

Linden, M., Hautzinger, M., & Hoffman, N. (1983). Discriminant analysis of depressive interactions. *Behavior Modification, 7,* 403–422.

Maracek, J., & Mettee, D. R. (1972). Avoidance of continued success as a function of self-esteem, level of esteem certainty, and responsibility for success. *Journal of Personality and Social Psychology, 22,* 90–107.

McNulty, S. E., & Swann, W. B., Jr. (1994). Identity negotiation in roommate relationships: The self as architect and consequence of social reality. *Journal of Personality and Social Psychology, 67,* 1012–1023.

Needles, D. J., & Abramson, L. Y. (1990). Positive life events, attributional style, and hopefulness: Testing a model of recovery from depression. *Journal of Abnormal Psychology, 99,* 156–165.

Pelham, B. W. (1991). On the benefits of misery: Self-serving biases in the depressive self-concept. *Journal of Personality and Social Psychology, 61,* 670–681.

Pelham, B. W., & Swann, W. B., Jr. (1994). The juncture of intrapersonal and interpersonal knowledge: Self-certainty and interpersonal congruence. *Personality and Social Psychology Bulletin, 20,* 349–357.

Pinel, P. (1962). *A treatise on insanity* (D. D. Davis, Trans.). New York: Hafner. (Original work published 1801)

Pittman, T. S., & Pittman, N. L. (1980). Deprivation of control and the attribution process. *Journal of Personality and Social Psychology, 39,* 377–389.

Ritts, V., & Stein, J. R. (1995). Verification and commitment in marital relationships: An exploration of self-verification theory in community college students. *Psychological Reports, 76,* 383–386.

Roberts, J. E., Kassel, J. D., & Gotlib, I. H. (1995). Level and stability of self-esteem as predictors of depressive symptoms. *Personality and Individual Differences, 19,* 217–224.

Roth, D., & Rehm, L. P. (1980). Relationships among self-monitoring processes, memory, and depression. *Cognitive Therapy and Research, 4,* 149–157.

Ruscher, S. M., & Gotlib, I. H. (1988). Marital interaction patterns of couples with and without a depressed partner. *Behavior Therapy, 19,* 455–470.

Salovey, P. (1992). Mood-induced self-focused attention. *Journal of Personality and Social Psychology, 62,* 699–707.

Schafer, R. B., Wickrama, K. A. S., & Keith, P. M. (1996). Self-concept disconfirmation, psychological distress, and marital happiness. *Journal of Marriage and the Family, 58,* 167–177.

Schwartz, D. A. (1964). The paranoid-depressive existential continuum. *Psychiatric Quarterly, 38,* 690–706.

Schwartz, G. E., Fair, P. L., Salt, P., Mandel, M. R., & Klerman, G. L. (1976, April 30). Facial muscle patterning to affective imagery in depressed and nondepressed subjects. *Science, 192,* 489–491.

Sedikides, C. (1992). Changes in the valence of the self as a function of mood. *Review of Personality and Social Psychology, 14,* 271–311.

Segrin, C., & Abramson, L. Y. (1995). Negative reactions to depressive behaviors: A communication theories analysis. *Journal of Abnormal Psychology, 103,* 655–668.

Shrauger, J. S. (1975). Response to evaluation as a function of self-perceptions. *Psychological Bulletin, 82,* 581–596.

Shustack, B., & West, M. (1985). Chronic depression reconsidered: Maladaptive competence as an explanatory concept. *Clinical Psychology Review, 5,* 569–579.

Spitzer, R. L., Williams, J. B., Gibbon, M., & First, M. B. (1990). *Structured clinical interview for DSM–III–R.* Washington, DC: American Psychiatric Press.

Steele, C. M. (1988). The psychology of self-affirmation: Sustaining the integrity of the self. In L. Berkowitz (Ed.), *Advances in experimental social psychology* (Vol. 21, pp. 261–302). San Diego, CA: Academic Press.

Strack, S., & Coyne, J. C. (1983). Social confirmation of dysphoria: Shared and private reactions to depression. *Journal of Personality and Social Psychology, 44,* 798–805.

Suinn, R. M., Osborne, D., & Page, W. (1962). The self-concept and accuracy of recall of inconsistent self-related information. *Journal of Clinical Psychology, 18,* 473–474.

Swann, W. B., Jr. (1990). To be adored or to be known: The interplay of self-enhancement and self-verification. In R. M. Sorrentino & E. T. Higgins (Eds.), *Handbook of motivation and cognition* (Vol. 2, pp. 408–480). New York: Guilford Press.

Swann, W. B., Jr. (1996). *Self traps: The elusive quest for higher self-esteem.* New York: Freeman.

Swann, W. B., Jr. (1997). The trouble with raising self-esteem. *Psychological Science, 8,* 177–180.

Swann, W. B., Jr., de la Ronde, C., & Hixon, J. G. (1994). Authenticity and positivity strivings in marriage and courtship. *Journal of Personality and Social Psychology, 66,* 857–869.

Swann, W. B., Jr., & Ely, R. J. (1984). A battle of wills: Self-verification versus behavioral confirmation. *Journal of Personality and Social Psychology, 46,* 1287–1302.

Swann, W. B., Jr., Griffin, J. J., Predmore, S., & Gaines, B. (1987). The cognitive-affective crossfire: When self-consistency confronts self-enhancement. *Journal of Personality and Social Psychology, 52,* 881–889.

Swann, W. B., Jr., & Hill, C. A. (1982). When our identities are mistaken: Re-affirming self-conceptions through social interaction. *Journal of Personality and Social Psychology, 43,* 59–66.

Swann, W. B., Jr., Hixon, J. G., & de La Ronde, C. (1992). Embracing the bitter "truth": Negative self-concepts and marital commitment. *Psychological Science, 3,* 118–121.

Swann, W. B., Jr., Hixon, J. G., Stein-Seroussi, A., & Gilbert, D. T. (1990). The fleeting gleam of praise: Cognitive processes underlying behavioral reactions to self-relevant feedback. *Journal of Personality and Social Psychology, 58,* 17–26.

Swann, W. B., Jr., & Pelham, B. W. (1998). *Self-certainty and self-verification.* Manuscript in preparation, University of Texas at Austin.

Swann, W. B., Jr., Pelham, B. W., & Chidester, T. (1988). Change through paradox: Using self-verification to alter beliefs. *Journal of Personality and Social Psychology, 54,* 268–273.

Swann, W. B., Jr., Pelham, B. W., & Krull, D. S. (1989). Agreeable fancy or disagreeable truth? How people reconcile their self-enhancement and self-verification needs. *Journal of Personality and Social Psychology, 57,* 672–680.

Swann, W. B., Jr., Pinel, E. C., & Tafarodi, R. W. (1996). *The cognitive-affective crossfire revisited: Is self-verification an anxiety avoidance mechanism?* Unpublished manuscript, University of Texas at Austin.

Swann, W. B., Jr., & Predmore, S. C. (1985). Intimates as agents of social support:

Sources of consolation or despair? *Journal of Personality and Social Psychology,* *49,* 1609–1617.

Swann, W. B., Jr., & Read, S. J. (1981a). Acquiring self-knowledge: The search for feedback that fits. *Journal of Personality and Social Psychology, 41,* 1119–1128.

Swann, W. B., Jr., & Read, S. J. (1981b). Self-verification processes: How we sustain our self-conceptions. *Journal of Experimental Social Psychology, 17,* 351–372.

Swann, W. B., Jr., & Schroeder, D. G. (1995). The search for beauty and truth: A framework for understanding reactions to evaluations. *Personality and Social Psychology Bulletin, 21,* 1307–1318.

Swann, W. B., Jr., Stein-Seroussi, A., & Giesler, R. B. (1992). Why people self-verify. *Journal of Personality and Social Psychology, 62,* 392–401.

Swann, W. B., Jr., Stephenson, B., & Pittman, T. S. (1981). Curiosity and control: On the determinants of the search for social knowledge. *Journal of Personality and Social Psychology, 40,* 635–642.

Swann, W. B., Jr., Wenzlaff, R. A., Krull, D. S., & Pelham, B. W. (1992). Allure of negative feedback: Self-verification strivings among depressed persons. *Journal of Abnormal Psychology, 101,* 293–306.

Swann, W. B., Jr., Wenzlaff, R. A., & Tafarodi, R. W. (1992). Depression and the search for negative evaluations: More evidence of the role of self-verification strivings. *Journal of Abnormal Psychology, 101,* 314–317.

Taylor, S. E. (1983). Adjustment to threatening events: A theory of cognitive adaptation. *American Psychologist, 38,* 1161–1173.

Teasdale, J. D., Fogarty, S. J., & Williams, M. G. (1980). Speech rate as a measure of short-term variation in depression. *British Journal of Social and Clinical Psychology, 19,* 271–278.

Tennen, H., Hall, J. A., & Affleck, G. (1995). Rigor, rigor mortis, and conspiratorial views of depression research. *Journal of Personality and Social Psychology, 68,* 895–900.

Trope, Y. (1986). Self-enhancement and self-assessment in achievement behavior. In R. M. Sorrentino & E. T. Higgins (Eds.), *Handbook of motivation and cognition: Foundations of social behavior* (Vol. 1, pp. 350–378). New York: Guilford Press.

Wachtel, P. L. (1994). Cyclical processes in personality and psychopathology. *Journal of Abnormal Psychology, 103,* 51–54.

Watzlawick, P., Weakland, J., & Fisch, R. (1974). *Change: Principles of problem formation and problem resolution.* New York: Norton.

Waxer, P. (1974). Nonverbal cues for depression. *Journal of Abnormal Psychology, 83,* 319–322.

Weary G., & Edwards, J. A. (1994). Social cognition and clinical psychology: Anxiety, depression, and the processing of social information. In R. S. Wyer & T. K. Srull (Eds.), *Handbook of social cognition* (Vol. 1, pp. 289–338). Hillsdale, NJ: Erlbaum.

Wood, J. V., Saltzberg, J. A., & Goldsamt, L. A. (1990). Does affect induce self-focused attention? *Journal of Personality and Social Psychology, 58,* 899–908.

III

EMERGING INTERPERSONAL MODELS OF DEPRESSION

9

SILENCING THE SELF: INNER DIALOGUES AND OUTER REALITIES

DANA CROWLEY JACK

And I think on my inside, private things I say to myself, I still really feel that I'm not—I wrote it down—that I'm not patient enough, I'm too selfish. I mean I haven't gotten that self-acceptance, I just haven't. With my husband, I would say we, I have to be able to say my feelings of anger or resentment, or wanting things different when they happen. And he has to be able to hear them without being too defensive, and say his feelings back so that we can have a mutual understanding of each other.

(Carol, age 41, physician in practice 13 years, married with two children, ages 9 and 11. Diagnosed with unipolar major depression.)

How does one listen to themes that recur in depressed women's talk— of negative self-judgment, low self-esteem, and moral failure? Are they merely symptomatic distortions of depression? Or do these themes offer a new path to understanding the complexities of women's vulnerability to depression?

Women's rates of depression are two times higher than those of men in most Western industrialized countries (Nolen-Hoeksema, 1990). Among women in three major ethnic groups within the United States—Blacks, Whites, and Hispanics—the 2:1 sex ratio holds, even though the lifetime prevalence of depression is lower among Blacks than among Whites and Hispanics (Blazer, Kessler, McGonagle, & Swartz, 1994). Researchers have not found a satisfactory explanation for this gender difference (Coyne & Downey, 1991; McGrath, Keita, Strickland, & Russo, 1990; Nolen-Hoeksema, 1990), although they have identified social factors that make women vulnerable to depression. Circumstances associated with increased depression in women include the dual impact of poverty and young children; the psychological disadvantage of women's negative social status; the lack of a close, confiding relationship; and the difficulty of communicating with a partner who is hostile and critical and cannot be relied on in times of crisis (Coyne & Downey, 1991). Furthermore, exposure to stress is socially organized in gender-specific ways; women are more often victims of partner violence and poverty than are men, for example (Stoppard, 1989).

Not only women in poverty are vulnerable to depression; professional women have a higher incidence of depression and suicide than do women in the general population (McGrath et al., 1990). Known stressors that affect this privileged group of women come from discriminatory institutional structures (Whitley, Gallery, Allison, & Revicki, 1989), including sexual harassment, and from family responsibilities historically arranged to accommodate men's careers (Gross, 1992; Myers, 1988; Sells & Sells, 1989).

To understand women's higher rates of depression, it is not enough to detail the social stressors that affect women more often than men. Individuals moderate stress differently. Not all women become depressed in a given environment, yet little is known about how social factors translate into the meaning women make of themselves in their world or about how these factors work interpersonally and psychodynamically to affect women's vulnerability to depression.

To learn more about how social factors become internalized and affect depression, researchers need to listen carefully to women's inner dialogues and negative self-assessments. In what follows, I offer a phenomenology of clinically depressed women's subjectivity, particularly focused on what their negative self-assessment reveals about underlying images of relatedness. Such images, and the dynamic of silencing the self, have been found to be reliably associated with depressive symptoms, as I describe later.

SILENCING THE SELF

My work on silencing the self theory began by listening to 12 clinically depressed women participating in a longitudinal study in an attempt to understand their experience in their own terms (Jack, 1987, 1991). In addition to the frameworks provided by relational theorists such as Bowlby (1980, 1988) and Mitchell (1988), who have documented the fundamentally social nature of the self, new theoretical frameworks for the psychology of women provided a standpoint from which I heard and interpreted women's inner worlds within specific social contexts. Feminist theorists point to specific female ego strengths, weaknesses, and fears that grow out of women's ego identity development (Chodorow, 1978; Gilligan, 1982; Miller, 1986). Relational feminists stress that as part of gender-identity processes and socialization, women's sense of self is organized around connection, mutuality, and relationships. Self-esteem is tied to the quality of attachments; feelings of guilt, shame, and depression are associated with the failure of intimate ties (Gilligan, 1982; Miller, 1986). The challenge of development is not to separate (or to loosen emotional bonds) from core relationships but to stay connected to one's own feelings, goals, and voice while developing and changing within relationships (Brown & Gilligan, 1992; Gilligan, 1982; Jack, 1991).

According to the relational viewpoint, depression is interpersonal for both genders; despair arises when the person feels hopeless about the possibility of intimate connection with others (Bowlby, 1980). However, beliefs about how to relate interpersonally are powerfully influenced by gender as well as by power differentials. To learn how a person's gendered beliefs about relatedness affected depression, I listened closely to the moral themes in depressed women's narratives.

Not surprisingly, depressed women constantly use moral language—words such as *selfish*, *bad*, and *worthless*—as they assess themselves and their role in causing problems in their relationships. Because both the fall in self-esteem and negative self-evaluation are considered basic symptoms of depression according to the *Diagnostic and Statistical Manual of Mental Disorders* (4th ed.; American Psychiatric Association, 1994), researchers often overlook the vital information they contain. Developmental and psychoanalytic theorists have consistently portrayed differences in the formation and functioning of women's and men's moral concerns. Regardless of theoretical perspective, observers find a female morality attuned to relationships and affection, and a male morality based on abstract principles expressed in laws and rules (Freud, 1925/1961; Gilligan, 1982; Kohlberg, 1981; Piaget, 1932).

I have found that standards used for self-evaluation are key in understanding gender differences in the prevalence and dynamics of depression. In a person's self-reproach, standards for the ideal self are used to judge the actual self. These standards alert researchers and clinicians about what a person believes she or he should be like and how she or he should interact in order to be loved, socially valued, and safe. They come from three major sources: the individual's family, the current social context, and the wider culture. Thus, self-evaluation provides a window through which to view the social standards a person accepts and uses to judge the self, how competing standards may come into conflict within the self, and how such standards are embedded in images of relatedness that direct interpersonal behaviors. Because standards of "goodness," including measures of social worth, vary by gender, ethnicity, and social context, inquiry into moral language allows a way to honor each person's individuality, in its fully contextualized richness, by observing what values she or he strives to attain.

Gender inequality also affects the standards women and men use to evaluate the self. Inequality affects the lives of all women through the culturally explicit or implicit message of women's inferiority to men (Fredrickson & Roberts, 1997; Westkott, 1986). However, the degree to which any woman internalizes this message varies by social class, ethnicity, and personal history, and it is powerfully influenced by the gender relations she sees modeled as she grows up. Particularly when the mother displays sub-missiveness in relation to dominating men, a girl can incorporate gender inequality into her images of relatedness. Inequality then becomes part of an understanding of how to interact with others, particularly in intimate relationships, and also becomes part of the standards used to direct behavior and evaluate the self.

Searching for the standards depressed women use to judge themselves negatively, I found a model of goodness that, although varying from woman to woman in specifics, contains norms of the "good wife" and "good mother." At the core of these roles lies the belief that selflessness is good, a standard that is unattainable and self-defeating in relationships. Such women believe that in order to be loved, they have to put the needs of others first. If a girl learns that others' needs always come first, the unspoken corollary is "my needs are less important than those of others and they will never be met, or they will be met reciprocally only if I care for others first." This childhood learning, passed on through the daughter's identification with her mother (and her mother's relational position), in tandem with a social structure in which women hold a lesser position, lays the basis for pervasively low self-esteem as well as for repressed anger over unmet needs. An internalized hierarchy of needs, with hers lower than those of the people she cares for, can then become part of a girl's feminine identity and understanding of feminine goodness.

When being "selfless" in relationship is linked in a woman's mind with "goodness" (morality), with femininity (out of identification with a mother who was "selfless" and subordinate in relationship), and with in-timacy (providing safety from abandonment), she must deny whole parts of herself, including negative feelings and direct self-assertion. Yet for many such women, the measure of goodness and social worth also includes the image of "superwoman." Being a superwoman requires behaviors premised on self-reliance, aggressiveness, integrity, and self-esteem. Thus, "goodness" can include measuring up to two sets of norms that oppose each other. One requires selfless behavior; the other, "self-full" behavior. Later in this chapter, I provide examples of how these factors are reflected in depressed physicians' inner dialogues.

How are images of relatedness, including moral standards about how one should interact as a "good" woman or man, associated with depression? If one accepts the idea of relational theorists that making and maintaining relationships is the primary motivation throughout life (Bowlby, 1980; Mitchell, 1988), then analysis of images and beliefs about the self-in-relation becomes vital to research and treatment of depression. Silencing the self theory proposes that early experiences of growing up female (or male) provide a basis for forming certain images about relatedness: how to make and keep attachments and how to remain safe within them. These images are experienced as moral beliefs about how to be a good woman or man, or as what one must be like to be loved or socially valued. Depressed women's narratives are filled with examples of how such images led them to subordinate their own needs and voices to those of others and to believe that acting on their own behalf is selfish or will lead to isolation or retaliation.

Depressed women describe how certain images of relatedness—"oneness," "goodness," "self-sacrificing," "pleasing"—direct them to silence vital aspects of self out of fear that voicing them would threaten their relationships or their safety. Self-silencing contributes to a fall in self-esteem and feelings of a "loss of self." As depressed women use the metaphor *loss of self*, it serves as a verbal shorthand for a complex process that includes, most centrally, a loss of voice. *Voice* does not mean the literal act of speaking but refers to the ability to manifest and affirm in relationships aspects of self that feel central to one's identity. Speaking one's feelings and thoughts in relationship is part of creating, maintaining, and recreating one's relational identity. Thus, *voice* refers more to the *substance* of what is communicated or hidden in relationship than to speech acts themselves.

Self-silencing, therefore, refers to removing critical aspects of self from dialogue for specific relational purposes. How a person uses his or her voice is profoundly affected by the anticipated response from the social context. Women and men face different cultural and relational consequences for voicing their anger, oppositional feelings, or demands; women are often more at risk for negative economic, physical, or interpersonal consequences than are men (Christensen & Heavey, 1990; Dobash & Dobash, 1979; Jacobson & Gottman, 1998). For women and men, behavior that appears outwardly similar (such as self-silencing) may come from a different origin and carry a different intent regarding its desired effect on relationship. In distressed couples, for example, men are more likely to use "stonewalling"—withdrawal through silence or passive resistance—from the partner's "demand" behaviors for change, intimacy, or engagement (Babcock, Waltz, Jacobson, & Gottman, 1993; Gottman, 1994). These researchers have hypothesized that men's withdrawal behavior (which can look like self-silencing) may be an attempt to control women's emotional, engaging style and to maintain the status quo of power relations. In other words, when men self-silence, they may intend to create distance and to control interactions in relationship. Researchers must look behind self-silencing for its gendered meanings and its relational intent, recognizing that the meanings and uses of voice and silence vary in relation to power (Hurtado, 1996) and by culture (Goldberger, 1996; Gratch, Bassett, & Attra, 1995). Self-silencing does not *always* derive from powerlessness or indicate depression.

In women, silencing the self—that is, stopping certain thoughts, words, and actions—often leads to the outer appearance of passivity and dependence. Because the actions required to silence the self are outwardly invisible, researchers have mistakenly focused on depressed women's supposed passive style of coping (McGrath et al., 1990; Nolen-Hoeksema, 1991) without observing the "cognitive activity required to appear outwardly passive and compliant" with traditional female behaviors expected by certain partners, social contexts, and personal beliefs about goodness (Jack, 1991, pp. 129–139). Whereas from the outside women look passive and compliant, on the inside it requires tremendous self-monitoring and self-inhibition to present this appearance. Depressed women's statements such as "I have learned, don't rock the boat with my partner" and "I won't cause waves, I won't say anything" show their conscious awareness of making themselves appear passive or compliant for an intended effect: to keep outer harmony, to preserve relationship. Self-silencing becomes obvious when women try to change their thoughts and when they tell themselves how they "ought" to feel. Women take the cognitive actions required to adapt themselves to existing structures for many reasons: the fear of retaliation, the desire to keep relationship, or the lack of models for alternative behaviors. Rather than outwardly challenge the forms of their relationships, they take this inward action against themselves.

Entering a person's experience through her or his moral language allows one to analyze how gender ideologies can masquerade as moral precepts about how one "should" behave in relationships. I noticed that moral language most often occurs within a person's inner dialogues. In depressed people, this dialogue most often takes the form of a divided self, with a judging, condemning voice and an answering voice that defends the self, most often on the basis of lived experience. Inner dialogues not only reflect the standards used to judge the self but also reveal a place of dynamism where new meanings and actions coalesce, where a person challenges accepted truths and formulates new perspectives. Culture not only is reproduced in inner dialogues but it is also changed. Given that a person may choose among competing ideologies that specify what a woman or man "should" be like, researchers can learn which ideologies carry the most power for women and men in particular ethnic groups and social contexts as well as which ideologies cause the most inner conflict and self-alienation (Jack, in press-b).

Listening to a person's inner dialogue, one hears how actively silencing the self leads to the inward experience of a divided self—the condition of self-alienation. Living out the images of relatedness, a woman begins to experience two opposing selves: an outwardly conforming, "nice," compliant self trying to keep relationships and to please and an inner, hidden self that is angry, resentful, and *increasingly hopeless about the possibility of genuine relationship or self-expression.* Women describe trying to keep hidden aspects of self out of relationship, with the result of overwhelming feelings of loss of connection, inauthenticity, and loss of self. This experience of inner division, in which one part turns against the other with rage, is a key aspect of depression.

In summary, the obstacles to voice that I have found to be associated with depression in women are described below.

Images of Relatedness

These images are experienced as beliefs about how one "should" behave in order to make and maintain relationships or to stay safe within them. Specific attachment behaviors—pleasing, helping, oneness, self-sacrifice, self-silencing—that are *culturally defined as feminine* have been prescribed for generations of women interacting intimately with men who had direct power over them. They contain inequality in the understanding of relatedness, how one resolves conflict, what it means to give and care for another person, and one's own worth and importance. If a woman adopts these images of relatedness based on selflessness, she envisions the most important issues in her life—how to relate to others and protect herself—as an either–or choice that presents her with loss on either side. The choice is either *isolation* (*lose relationships* if she acts on her own needs or speaks her voice) or *subordination* (*lose herself* if she silences her voice) —either loss of self or loss of other. Such dichotomous thinking leads to feelings of hopelessness about the prospects for authenticity *and* connection. Furthermore, if a woman enacts these culturally prescribed attachment behaviors, they lead to "compliant relatedness" (Jack, 1991, p. 40), a type of connection that appears to offer intimacy and safety. Characterized by restriction of initiative and freedom of expression within a relationship, compliant relatedness looks like dependence or an anxious attachment behavior.

Shame or Fear

Many depressed women appear convinced that voicing opposition, anger, or "selfishness" will be met with some type of negative consequence. Behind this fear, which often feels "inner" or uniquely personal, lie specific outer social factors that influence fear, such as violence, sexual and racial discrimination, and poverty, each of which is a known factor for women's depression vulnerability (McGrath et al., 1990). Directed by the belief that voicing authentic feelings leads to danger, and that silence offers safety, a woman will "bite her tongue" or aggress indirectly or with ineffective explosiveness, rather than state dangerous feelings or thoughts directly. Fear of consequences for voicing one's self depends partly on personal history and partly on current social context. When both conspire to reinforce fear (e.g., when personal history corresponds to current critical or abusive relationships), the images of relatedness based on inequality in relationships are reinforced. If a woman's circumstances allow few options, she may see silencing herself as the least harmful choice, far preferable to other possibilities she perceives, such as retaliation, divorce, or suicide. Because silencing does not mean literally an absence of voice, it is critical to examine what aspects of self arouse a woman's shame and are kept out of relationships, directed by what images of relatedness and fears and with what imagined consequences for the person's sense of possibility for authentic, intimate relations with others.

Prohibitions Against Women's Anger and Aggression

Women's fears about the negative consequences of self-assertion (which many equate with aggression) appear to be related to the inhibited behaviors and cognitive styles researchers find associated with female depression (Jack, in press-a). The relevance of aggression inhibition to depression vulnerability in women is underscored by meta-analyses of research on gender differences in aggression. Mediators of aggression in women include guilt and anxiety over display of their aggressive behaviors or feelings, anticipated danger to the self, and empathy (concern about harm that aggression causes to the recipients; Eagly & Steffen, 1986). Like other social behaviors, aggression can be viewed as regulated by gender-specific social role norms that traditionally have deemphasized women's aggression (particularly in middle-class White women) and have encouraged their nurturance. Likewise, depression researchers emphasize that women's social roles affect their vulnerability to depression (Klerman & Weissman, 1980; McGrath et al., 1990). Particularly when a woman's background emphasizes nurturance, goodness, and sensitivity and precludes aggressive actions, often defined broadly as "standing up for myself" and "saying what I think and feel," society's prohibitions against female aggression enter to reinforce self-silencing behaviors. I am investigating this hypothesized relationship in a qualitative study of 60 women's accounts of their own aggression, with attention to variations of ethnicity and class (Jack, in press-a).

If a woman thinks aggression is "bad"—unfeminine, pushy, selfish, destructive—she will work hard to inhibit what she perceives as aggressive behavior in herself. On the outside, this can look like a "failure of action and mastery strategies" (McGrath et al., 1990); it may also appear that the woman is ineffectively "ruminating" on her negative thoughts (rather than restricting her initiatory, assertive behavior). Interviews with women about their aggressive actions and fantasies have led me to a different conclusion: Women focus intensely on how to balance their aggressiveness (what many would call appropriate self-assertion, or standing up for themselves) against their wish to be "good," to be safe, and to keep harmony in relationships.

Furthermore, as they calculate the social costs of speaking up—the costs to their relationships, their jobs, and the physical safety and security of themselves and their children—they often silence themselves rather than incur feared consequences (Jack, in press-a).

Silencing the self theory postulates that women whose backgrounds or current contexts encourage them to meet their relational needs in self-sacrificing, inauthentic ways are more likely to adopt gender-specific schemas about how to make and maintain intimate relationships. These schemas, or images of relatedness, reflect cultural prescriptions for feminine relationship behavior that are based on inequality. Self-silencing contributes to decreased possibilities for intimacy, to a loss of self-esteem, to the experience of a divided self, and to a heightened vulnerability to depression.

SILENCING THE SELF SCALE

Given the need for multiple methodological strategies, I constructed the Silencing the Self Scale (STSS; Jack & Dill, 1992) to measure the association between self-silencing and depression. Thirty-one scale items, with Likert scores ranging from *strongly agree* to *strongly disagree* with a range of 1 to 5, represent the themes that were heard most often in the narratives of clinically depressed women.

Four rationally derived subscales represent the proposed dynamic of depression: *Externalized Self-Perception* (judging oneself by "external" standards); *Care as Self-Sacrifice* (securing attachments by putting the needs of others before the self); *Silencing the Self* (inhibiting one's self-expression and action to avoid conflict, possible loss, and retaliation); and the *Divided Self* (presenting an outer self that does not express personal, authentic thoughts and feelings; the experience of inner division). Each subscale was conceptualized to be part of a pattern that is associated with a dynamic of depression. Subscales are considered to work together in a dynamic, interactive fashion, so that as one aspect is strengthened, it heightens the other three.

Researchers using the STSS consistently find self-silencing associated with depressive symptoms in different samples of women (Brazaitis, 1995; Carr, Gilroy, & Sherman, 1996; Gratch et al., 1995; Penza, Reiss, & Scott, 1997; Thompson, 1995), with levels of self-silencing varying in predicted directions with differing social contexts (Jack & Dill, 1992). Construct validity of the scale has been affirmed through replication of subscale structures with samples of Asian American, African American, Hispanic, and non-Hispanic Caucasian women and men (Duarte & Thompson, 1998; (Gratch et al., 1995; Gratch & Jack, 1998; Stevens & Galvin, 1995). Construct validity has also been affirmed through studies of the scale's association with predicted variables, for example, with eating disorders (Cawood, 1998), "loss of self" (Drew & Heesacker, 1998), lack of mutuality (Penza et al., 1997), marital distress (Thompson, 1995; Whisman, Uebelacker, & Courtnage, 1998), and perceived power in relationship (Cowan, Bommersbach, & Curtis, 1995).

Although silencing the self theory was proposed in the context of women's depression, samples of men score consistently higher than women on the STSS (Cowan et al., 1995; Gratch et al., 1995; Hart & Thompson, 1996; Jack & Dill, 1992; Thompson, 1995; Whisman et al., 1998). Whereas initially this finding appears to create a problem for construct validity, researchers have found that the correlates of self-silencing vary by gender in predicted ways. For example, in Thompson's (1995) study of heterosexual couples, silencing the self was more closely related to depressive symptoms for women than for men, and women's silencing was negatively associated with both their own and their partners' relationship satisfaction, whereas men's was not. Also, the meanings of self-silencing appear to differ for each gender. Cowan et al. (1995) speculated that perceived power is more critical than gender as a variable that influences the level of self-silencing. The STSS appears to correlate reliably with depressive symptoms (although differently) in both women and men; thus, further investigation into patterns, meanings, and correlates of self-silencing by gender is warranted, with particular focus on genesis and relational intent.

In my view, while both genders endorse a set of social conventions about goodness in relationships, how they translate those conventions into interpersonal behaviors differs and is affected by perceived power and social context. Content analysis of standards used for self-evaluation (Scale Item 31) may further the understanding of high male STSS scores. In the Jack and Dill (1992) scale construction study, responding to Item 31 ("I never seem to measure up to the standards I set for myself"), male college students referred to, in order of frequency, grades and then stereotypical male role requirements, such as sports ability, wage-earning ability, or interpersonal issues revealing problems of socialization to the male role, such as "play it safe in relationships." Female college students also first listed grades and then specified the following gender-based standards in order of frequency: physical appearance, weight, and having good personal qualities that make them attractive to others. Content analysis may further the understanding of how social imperatives translate into self-alienating standards used to judge the self and into images of relatedness that do not foster genuine connection.

ASSUMPTIONS OF SELF-SILENCING THEORY

Silencing the self theory assumes that the images of relatedness measured by the STSS are reflexive, that is, that they interact with the individual's life history and with situational variables, particularly with how the social context and close relationships "expect" a person to behave interpersonally. This "reflexive model" of depressive vulnerability asserts that "the categories of thought that people bring to actively interpret their worlds, guide their behavior, and assess the self are socially constructed and are reflexive with social institutions and contexts. Gender-specific aspects of socialization practices and of material social power are reflected in these social categories of thought" (Jack & Dill, 1992, p. 99). Rather than being permanent and internal, called into use by events in the environment, images of intimate relatedness measured by the STSS are presumed to be reinforced, challenged, and changed by current social contexts. The degree to which women, for example, engage in self-silencing is related to their personal history (their identification with the mother's power in relation to men), their current relationship context (e.g., their partner's dominating, coercive behaviors or the setting they work in), and their personal functioning (e.g., depression, level of self-esteem) and, reflexively, will also affect their relationship functioning (e.g., interpersonal behavior, intimacy).

Silencing the self theory differs from a diathesis–stress model, including Beck's (1983) cognitive–personality model, Blatt, Quinlan, Chevron, McDonald, and Zuroff's (1982) psychodynamic personality model, and Nolen-Hoeksema's (1991) coping response model, in two respects: (a) stability of trait and (b) location of problem. Regarding stability of trait, diathesis–stress models assume that the trait in question is an enduring, stable aspect of personality that interacts with factors in the environment to create a vulnerability to depression. Highest risk for depression is assumed to occur with a congruency between negative life events and the personality domain of value. Although these theories attempt to take account of the social context more fully than did earlier cognitive–behavioral models, they still inadequately account for the impact of social context on the person (Coyne & Whiffen, 1995). Furthermore, the personality domains of value seem artificially divided into achievement and interpersonal realms, and they do not take into account how people often construe the achievement realm as an interpersonal field, and vice versa. They also do not consider how norms directing gendered social behavior affect women's and men's interactions both in the achievement realm and in their intimate relationships. In contrast, self-silencing relational images and behaviors are not considered permanent features of personality but rather are susceptible to the affects of changing social contexts and specific relationships.

Regarding location of the problem, diathesis–stress models clearly include consideration of the social environment as it interacts with aspects of personality, but the vulnerability factor is considered to reside within the individual (Coyne, 1992). In silencing the self theory, the focus and conceptualization of the problem differ. The focus is on images of relatedness and their *reflexivity* with social factors. These images of relatedness, open to influence from social contexts, are hypothesized to relate to depressive symptoms through the specific dynamic previously described: self-silencing, loss of self, inner division, anger, and self-condemnation. The problem is not considered to lie in a deficit (such as ruminative coping style) or in a favored personality orientation (dependency–autonomy) that interacts with environmental events to create depression. Rather, the problem is considered to lie in specific forms of unequal, negative intimate relationships as well as larger social structures that demean an individual's sense of social worth. Such specific conditions are assumed to be internalized differentially (depending on personal history and social contexts) and to manifest in images of relatedness that contain moral standards, which then affect the individual's behaviors, self-evaluation, and self-esteem. Endorsement of self-silencing schemas is linked to depression through the mechanisms described earlier (see also Jack, 1991).

Although findings regarding the association of the STSS with depressive symptoms are promising, they do not address which of many causal pathways might account for the correlations. The theoretical assumptions regarding variations of self-silencing with particular social, relational contexts throughout the life span need to be investigated through prospective, longitudinal studies with clinically diagnosed samples of women and men.

CASE EXAMPLES

To demonstrate the phenomenology of depression associated with silencing the self, I present three case examples of depressed physicians. I chose these examples to explore how social contexts are manifest in standards used to judge the self and to offer a beginning illustration of the gender-specific nature of such standards. Women and men from other social contexts will sound very different (Jack, 1991, in press-b); the critical factor is to examine the interaction of social context with experience of self through the images of relatedness that guide interpersonal behavior and that supply standards used to judge the self.

Known factors that put professional women at higher risk for depression are found in medical training and practice (McGrath et al., 1990). Male doctors were assumed to have a "wife" who would take care of family and home; historically, two people supported one career. Currently, even when a partner supports her career, a woman still does more of the household chores and parenting than her partner, if a man (Myers, 1988; Sells & Sells, 1989). Not surprisingly, career–family conflict was cited as a stressor by many more female (46.3%) than male (6.1%) physicians in a study of perceived stressors in medical practice (Gross, 1992). Studies of medical students have shown that women experience more work-related stress and negative emotional reactions than do men (Coombs & Hovanessian, 1988; Janus, Janus, & Price, 1983) and that women in residency training report significantly greater levels of stress and depression than do men (Whitley et al., 1989); the suicide rate in women doctors is four times that of the general population (Craig & Pitts, 1968; Rucinski & Cybulska, 1985).

Women in professions struggle against a social backdrop that sexualizes and trivializes their work and aspirations. An early study of depression in 111 women physicians and 103 women PhDs (Welner et al., 1979) was undertaken at a time when women began entering medical schools in large numbers; the authors documented the relationship of social stresses, particularly sex discrimination, with depressive onset. Fifty-one percent of the physicians and 32% of the PhDs were diagnosed as having primary affective disorder; depression among psychiatrists was significantly higher (73%) than among other physicians (46%). More than 50% of the women reported prejudice in training or employment, and depressed women reported more prejudice. Onset of depression occurred during training or residency (33%) or during practice (39%) rather than prior to medical school (28%), leading to the easy conclusion that the structures of this profession did not support women. These issues of gender discrimination in medicine continue. For example, in the January 20, 1992, issue of *The Nation*, Dr. Adriane Fugh-Berman highlighted issues of harassment, hostility, and threats throughout her training at Georgetown Medical School in the late 1980s.

How are these social factors manifest through processes described in silencing the self theory? Images of relatedness, inner division, and standards used to judge the self negatively, apparent in the following examples, can help guide clinicians in listening to, interpreting, and intervening with depressed clients.

The following excerpt comes from a taped interview with a physician, Carol (age 41, White, diagnosed with major depression), who is currently taking the antidepressant trazodone (Desyrel). She has been in practice for 13 years. Married to another physician for 15 years, her children are 9 and 11. In this passage, Carol explains her strong agreement with Item 7 (Externalized Self-Perception subscale) of the Silencing the Self Scale, which reads "I feel dissatisfied with myself because I should be able to do all the things people are supposed to be able to do these days." Her words reveal what, in her mind, she's "supposed" to be doing and how she imagines she falls short:

> You can't be Supermom and can't do it all, and yet we all have this image that we can, and we measure ourselves by the standards of our mothers in terms of raising kids. You know, I feel guilty when I'm not there with the warm milk and cookies and when I'm not putting every Band-Aid on. And then I'm guilty because I'm not enough of a spouse for my husband, and I'm guilty because I'm not doing an adequate job professionally and never quite getting it all right. And there's not a

role model of a successful woman doing all this except this illusion of a superwoman someplace. On the outside, people, residents, tell me, "You're such a wonderful role model." And I think, "You don't know the half of it." So there is an illusion of role models, but there's not a real role model of what a good mother is who's working. (*Q: When the residents say that to you, what do you say back?*) Actually, to be honest, I usually don't tell them the truth. I say, "Thank you," or something.

Carol presents a persona that lives up to role demands—both feminine and professional—while her silenced, observing self thinks that observers "You don't know the half of it." She does not alert newcomers to medicine to her private struggles in managing to be mother, wife, and doctor. Her silence does not indicate an inability to speak; it reveals a choice to hide certain aspects of self. Looking at what aspects of self a professional woman chooses to silence and why she does so alerts the clinician to a number of issues: what she thinks self-revelation might cost her, what images of relatedness guide her behavior and self-evaluation, and how she begins to feel a "loss of self" as she removes key aspects of self from dialogue with others.

The achievement and interpersonal spheres (autonomy and sociotropy) do not stay neatly divided in people's lives but spill over to affect each other profoundly. Carol, the president of a national organization, successful as a physician, is undermined by negative self-judgments that carry from home into work, even though her rational self has plenty of ammunition to oppose such judgments. The phenomenology of the divided self emerges in her self-commentary:

> I feel like there are two me's. There's the successful me that I could never incorporate. I guess that I always felt deep underneath that I wasn't very skilled and so when I would see myself as reflected as being successful it didn't match my image of myself. I don't have a history of failures and so that's so bizarre, and yet somewhere underneath that all, I don't measure up, and I'm kind of just beginning to come to grips with that. *I feel like I'm too selfish, too self-centered, all those, on a personal level all those kinds of issues that somehow then translate into feeling incompetent on a professional level as well.* . . . I do more than the average woman doctor by a mile. By 2 miles. And it's kind of an overcompensation proving to myself that I can do this and that I am capable.

Carol's attempts to integrate opposing social expectations translate into an experience of inner division, of "two me's," with the harshly judged self that is "too selfish, too self-centered" covered over by a professional self that tries to overcome these feelings by proving she is capable. Yet her considerable achievements pale next to her sense that she is failing to be a "good" wife and mother; interpersonal issues "translate" into her experience of the achievement realm. The terms *successful professional* and *woman* each carry specific expectations and images for interpersonal behaviors. How a woman physician "should" fulfill the norms of her profession carries one set of expectations; how a woman "should" interact in intimate relationship carries a different set. The requirements for success in each sphere—the romantic and the professional—are opposed: How can a woman be both lovable and a successful professional if norms for feminine behavior require being deferential to others whereas professional success demands competition and self-assertion? (See also R. Jack & D. C. Jack, 1989, and Westkott, 1986.) For Carol, the beliefs that direct her behavior and self-evaluation appear to be most strongly based on an ideal of selflessness that undermines her in both spheres.

As one might predict, in response to Item 4 (Subscale 2: Care as Self-Sacrifice) "Considering my needs to be as important as those of the people I love is selfish," Carol circled "agree." The standard of selflessness, derived from the feminine role requirement to care for others by putting their needs first, directs her vision of the hierarchy of needs within relationship. Selflessness directs behavior by dictating how she should choose when her needs conflict with those of others she loves; it provides a standard for harsh self-judgment if she veers from its command. Furthermore, the standard of selflessness arouses anger as, following its dictates, she places her needs second to those of others; yet it also commands the repression of anger by purporting a moral basis for the suppression of her own needs. Disguised as moral demands, such role requirements are difficult to challenge. Selflessness reinforces a woman's low self-esteem by affirming that she is not as worthy or important as others, and finally, it legitimizes the historical and still prevalent view of woman's nature as essentially self-sacrificing and maternal (Jack, 1991).

Another depressed physician reveals how this same image of how she "should" relate to others affects her self-silencing and feelings of anger, inner division, and lowered self-esteem. In practice 6 years, Sue (age 36, White) has been married 9 years and has two daughters, ages 2 and 5. Her husband, also a physician, is fully aware of the demands of the profession. At the time of this interview, Sue had been diagnosed with unipolar major depression by a psychiatrist and had been taking fluoxetine (Prozac) for 3 months. Like Carol, Sue agreed with Item 4 in the STSS, "Considering my needs to be as important as those of the people I love is selfish." She said:

> Right now, I'm struggling with the fact that—I keep telling myself, there's this voice in my head that tells me that I'm a bad mother and the reason why I'm a bad mother is because when I come home after working for a day, my husband is lying on the floor playing games with my kids and all I want to do is sit on the couch and read a newspaper. And I feel like then I'm deficient, you know, because I enjoy or I need time to do something—that I would prefer doing something other than being with my kids. I mean I struggle with that. And then my husband

wants me to join them, and I do but I don't feel good and I can't tell him. When I'm by myself I don't have to struggle with that—whose needs are more important and whether my needs are valid and okay and whether someone's going to think that I'm silly or stupid or unreasonable or irrational. I can just be who I am.

Like Carol, Sue describes a "voice in [her] head" that tells her she's a bad mother; this voice is directed by the standard of feminine goodness as self-sacrificing nurturance. The voice pronounces self-condemnation ("I'm deficient in my lack of selflessness"), which arouses her anger as she accedes to its demands. Then the voice demands anger's repression. Sue struggles with the dilemma of how to act, how to judge herself, and how to relate within her family. Yet the cognitive activity, the "struggle," required to curb her own needs or voice is not visible to others. What they see is her outward compliance with her husband's wish that she join the family, a demand that coincides with her own images of what a "good woman" does. Sue joins them but does not feel good about doing so. This important issue of how to balance her own needs with those of her family is silenced by the belief that she "can't tell" her husband about her feelings. Sue imagines how her husband would respond to her voice ("think I'm silly or stupid"), blames him for her compliance, and feels resentful.

Of course, silencing one's needs in order to give to others does not always lead to self-alienation and depression. The context within which the giving occurs and the giver's ability to choose when, how, and in what form to care are critical. If a woman experiences selflessness as a requirement because of inner images or outer coercion, she enacts subservience to others' needs and becomes increasingly angry, resentful, and confused.

Both Carol and Sue value being physicians and attempt to live up to ideals about how to be a "good doctor," which contradict behaviors demanded of them as wives and mothers. The voice of harsh self-judgment can align with both sets of norms to critique the self for not "measuring up" to either of them. Sue goes on to talk about how she feels as a physician:

> I think I've always been perceived as very competent and, you know, bright and responsible, but have never taken that in, and all my life I wondered, you know, when somebody was really going to find me out. (Q: And what would they find out?) That I wasn't—that I was not competent and—not bright and a lousy physician. I don't think I think the way I imagine physicians should think. You know, the kind of analytical, rational, sort of step-by-step thinking that I imagine physicians do. For me, medicine is very intuitive, it's very creative, there are certain kind of leaps that I make.... I think the whole process of medical education ... is very, very brutal, very dehumanizing, very damaging, especially for a woman. All the attributes that are traditionally womanly are discouraged and belittled. I was even once told

by one of my residents to "be a man." You know, be a man. Be decisive. Be, you know, be aggressive. Be a man. And that's essentially what they want you to be. They don't want you to have any womanly virtues. They don't want you to be compassionate or caring, or loving, or humble, or emotional. They don't want you to be any of those things. . . . And I think part of what I'm really angry about is the fact that I buy into it.

Social factors, specifically Sue's personal experiences of being objectified, devalued, and punished as a woman in a profession designed by men for men, contribute to her inner division. Her narrative reveals how these social factors are structured in thought and work to affect her self-alienation and vulnerability to depression. Sue uses the language of the culture to devalue and deny what, on another level, she values and desires. Listening, one hears how she has judged her abilities against a dominant standard that says one must leave "womanly virtues" aside to be a physician. Sue reflects on her capabilities and strengths not on the basis of who she is and what she needs but in terms of how colleagues in her profession and others see her. Her capacity for creative, intuitive thinking and for listening to people, advocating for people, and seeing herself as a hand-holder go unacknowledged as strengths. Rather than reflecting a shortcoming of the profession, the problem is identified as her feminine style. Listening to Sue's feelings about self-worth, her confusion about what she values and what the culture says she *should* value, one hears that the self-alienation and separation from feelings are reflexive with her social context.

In Sue's inner dialogue, her harsh, critical voice condemns her as "a lousy physician." This voice reflects male values and ordains what a woman "should" be like from a male perspective. I call this voice of the inner dialogue the Over-Eye because it judges the self from the perspective of the culture's Eye, reflecting women through the male gaze (Jack, 1991). She is the "outsider" to medicine, and she is expected to adapt to a stereotyped version of the physician role: "Be a man. Be decisive. Be . . . aggressive." Sue adopts a male standard, "how physicians should think," and sees her style as different and *deficient*. These exclusionary practices arouse Sue's anger and contribute to her feeling "like a fake." To succeed, she believes she must present the *appearance* that her values accord with those of the profession, particularly those of commitment, objectivity, impersonal professionalism, and rationality. Doing so requires separating from valued aspects of self.

The other voice in Sue's inner dialogue, the perspective that emerges when she is "by herself," is that of the authentic self. As Sue describes it, when experiencing her authentic self "I can just be who I am" and not struggle over whose needs are more important or "whether my needs are valid and okay." It is a self that does not worry about "whether someone's going to think that I'm silly or stupid or unreasonable or irrational" if she acts on the basis of her own needs. When Sue enacts the perspective of her authentic self, she does not silence herself (take cognitive actions against herself to create compliance with the perceived expectations of others) nor does she feel self-alienated or self-condemning.

As Sue uses competing personal ("be selfless") and professional ("be aggressive") norms to judge herself, she undergoes a profound silencing of valued aspects of self in both realms. Afraid that honest self-expression may lead to retaliation, loss, or both (as well as violate images of relatedness), she turns her anger against herself rather than against the structures that devalue her: "And I think part of what I'm really angry about is the fact that I buy into it." This anger, arising from her self-enforced compliance to standards she knows are self-alienating, reveals both her acquiescence and her resistance to dominant stereotypes. Such anger and self-awareness offer a point for therapeutic intervention. What is paralyzing and leads to the sense of hopelessness is Sue's belief that if she let the oppositional, authentic self speak, she would not be accepted but would be harshly judged by others—her husband, her colleagues—with negative consequences. Thus, the authentic self remains in hiding and feels increasingly resentful, angry, and hopeless. The Over-Eye takes this angry, nonconformist self as its object and evaluates it as "deficient," "a bad mother," "not competent," and "a lousy physician."

The phenomenology of depression—self-silencing, inner division, and negative self-judgment—appears to be similar in men. However, men often internalize images of "goodness" from the culture that cluster around different attributes of self. As a group, they enjoy different levels of material and social power than women, and they appear to silence different aspects of self. As a result, their images of relatedness—how to make and maintain relationships—appear to differ from women's in terms of some of the "shoulds" that direct behavior and self-judgment. Given more permission from the culture to be aggressive in their own behalf and living in a social world in which their dominance is still most often assumed, their dilemmas appear to have less to do with fears of asserting their voices in relationship and more to do with feeling inadequate in gender-specific roles, such as breadwinner, successful professional, or father, or with revealing vulnerability to others. The following example of Dan, age 48, in a medical practice similar to Sue's and Carol's, illustrates a similar phenomenology of depression, but there is variation in the standards used to judge the self, directed by different images of relatedness.

Married for 25 years and the father of two children now in college, Dan has been in practice for approximately 20 years. At age 48, his episode of major depression remitted after a 2-month vacation from medical practice, but it returned gradually after he resumed work. At the time of his interview, he was in combined drug and cognitive therapy.

On the STSS, Dan received the highest possible score on the Externalized Self-Perception subscale. In discussing his agreement with Item 7, "I feel dissatisfied with myself because I should be able to do all the things people are supposed to be able to do these days," he explained:

> A lot comes up about work. I should be able to see more patients more efficiently and have a life, and should be able to adapt to the changes [in medical practice], and should be able to keep up in medicine, do the reading I need to do, and somehow it's a defect in me or a deficiency that I can't do it.

Dan's litany of "shoulds" contains not only an implied perfectionism but also an image of selflessness focused on professional role: He should be "selflessly" married to medicine. His "shoulds" require his adaptation to what he perceives as unlimited claims of medical practice. Rather than question the demands of his profession, he turns against himself, requiring acquiescence to unrealistic standards and condemning himself for an inability to keep up. He explains that increasing overhead costs and his role as sole financial provider for his family exacerbate the pressure to continue in his untenable professional position. Professional demands, then, gain coercive power as they mesh with capitalistic competition and the valued roles of husband, father, and economic provider. Whereas Sue and Carol locate the sources of their depression in the conflicting demands of wife–mother and physician, Dan focuses solely on the impossible demands of his professional role.

Dan also explores his agreement with Item 16 ("Often I look happy enough on the outside, but inwardly I feel angry and rebellious") from the Divided Self subscale:

> I think of the office a lot. I really feel stressed or angry about something, but I don't let the patients see that because they aren't coming to me to see that. I feel like I need to put on my professional face and my caring face and something like it, because if I'm feeling like that, it's not their fault. I rationalize it as my issue.

Dan's inner division occurs primarily within the context of the profession. When he thinks of presenting a false face, of hiding his anger, he locates these actions within his work setting.

Dan does not mention feeling silenced by "shoulds" from his role of husband and father, only from his role as physician. Speaking of his relationship with his wife, he said, "I think she obviously looks out for me, and I think other people do." Selflessness does not guide his images of how he should interact within his family, only of how he should behave as a physician. In contrast to Carol and Sue, whose concerns revolve around whether they are focused enough on family members, Dan assumes that others in his family look out for him.

Elaborating on why he disagreed with the statement "I feel that my partner does not know my real self" (Item 25), with which both Sue and Carol agreed, Dan said:

> I think that my wife probably sees me better than most people do, knowing how I act. Even though my mouth may say something, she knows from my actions in the past [the words] may mean something else.

Dan does not feel he has to hide his authentic self in his primary relationship; even if he tries to hide, his wife sees his real feelings because of her extensive knowledge of him.

Although intimate relationships carry emotional importance to Dan, different "shoulds" and images of relatedness, as well as different power dynamics, guide his participation in them. Likewise, although profession is central to all three physicians, fitting into the norms of the profession requires that men and women silence different aspects of the self or judge the self as "deficient" for differing reasons. Both women and men engage in self-silencing; how it differentially affects their lives and their vulnerability to depression remains open to further investigation.

IMPLICATIONS FOR THERAPY

Depression is profoundly existential and social, affecting all aspects of a person's felt experience. Moral themes provide a direct, vital entry into the heart of experiential aspects of depression. Encouraging a client to be more self-affirming, or "arguing" about the accuracy of a person's self-perception, often does not touch the core of negative self-judgments. To challenge these core issues, clients need to explore the origins of their images of relatedness; how they are tied to gender, inequality, and culture; and how they became moralized. Sue, one of the physicians quoted earlier, explained that when a therapist tries to convince her that she's "not dumb,"

> I can carry on this very involved argument in my head: "Well, you are dumb because of this, this, this, and this." You know, any sort of argument that someone can throw at me, I can think of five things, five examples to counter it.

Sue has been advised to counter "you're dumb" with accurate self-statements and to challenge global thoughts with instances that demonstrate that she is not dumb. Sue finds the advice unhelpful because it misses the point. The issue is not accuracy of self-regard; her struggle is developmental, existential, and moral. It is a struggle about identity: Through whose eyes does she see and evaluate herself? How does she position herself in relation to inner and outer voices that say her perspective is wrong? Feeling "dumb" represents a long-term theme in Sue's life that preceded her depression. This negative self-judgment becomes a critical point of entry into understanding how the social context interacts with her images of relatedness to contribute to vulnerability to depression.

How can therapy help move Sue from spinning her wheels in this rut of self-perception? First, sorting out the different strands of interpersonal history that form the standards used for negative self-evaluation allows a person to gain a perspective on the power of such standards. Such an exploration leads to Sue's awareness of her physician father's assessment of family medicine as a profession in which one has to "know everything. He couldn't hear that you didn't have to know everything . . . so he couldn't understand my wanting to go into family medicine." This awareness, then, links back to her feelings of being "dumb," of not being "good enough," in her father's or in her male colleagues' eyes, and an awareness that the vision of her inner authority (Over-Eye) parallels that of her father and the predominately male profession she works within. She sees and judges herself from the perspective of a devaluing male gaze.

Second, helping Sue voice inner arguments about her "dumbness" to an attempt to decide which voice "in her head" she wants to align with can give her a sense of choice regarding self-judgment. According to whose standards is she dumb? How does that judgment render her voiceless and powerless in situations that matter to her? How does that judgment reinforce the authority of those she may wish to challenge—both inner and outer authorities? Her refusal to see herself through her father's or her colleagues' eyes can become part of her ongoing quest to invent herself as distinct from family and professional dictates, and it can support her healthy resistance to damaging self-images. Where can she get support and help from others who are in her position so that she does not pathologize aspects of experience that have more to do with discriminatory practices in medicine than with "deficits" in an individual personality? This exploration leads Sue to a discussion of the realities of the external difficulties she faces and how she can strengthen her own perspectives on her profession through participation in a support group with other female physicians.

To facilitate a client's movement out of the trap of negativity, therapists may want to direct close attention to that person's inner dialogues. Once aware of the voices of their different selves, individuals can hear and decide which voice (or potential self) they want to align with. Many people have not acknowledged silenced aspects of self or attended to their whisperings; this is a task of therapy. If the therapist is intrusive and suggests, for example, that a woman's behavior is too compliant, that she needs to become more assertive, without engaging with the relational images and prohibitions against aggression, the risks of her outer compliance and inner self-alienation, anger, and despair are heightened. For example, Carol said, "It's kind of like how do you disagree with somebody? Being assertive has felt bad all along and I would intuitively do it, but then what I would feel really was 'was that OK? was I wrong? was I . . . ?' " Again, Carol questions not the "correctness" of her behavior but its moral meaning and its conformity with her images of relatedness.

Third, a therapist can foster a change in self-perception by helping a woman see that her compliance or "passivity" requires a tremendous amount of cognitive activity. As a woman explores how and why she silences herself, she can watch the specific cognitive actions she takes against herself and what her expectations are regarding the interpersonal consequences. Her self-silencing can be understood as a self-defensive strategy instead of as "self-defeating thoughts." She can work with the fears that underlie bringing her voice into dialogue. What would happen if she did not silence herself? What does she consider her own aggressive behaviors to be, and how does she feel about them? What does she expect as a social response to her self-assertion, disagreement, or anger (which she may see as aggressive)? Do these issues figure into her "inhibited mastery and action styles"? For men, explorations can similarly focus on what aspects of self are being silenced, on the activity required to live up to self-alienating role demands, and on what fears accompany change.

The Silencing the Self Scale can be a useful adjunct in therapy with groups, individuals, and couples to explore issues of moral meaning, self-silencing, inner division, and depression. Using the STSS in treatment groups with depressed clients provides a structure for short-term therapy that quickly deepens discussion. In couples therapy, responses to the STSS provide a useful entry into discussion of issues of power and silence. After each person separately responds to the scale, each also writes how he or she thinks the partner would answer. The couple can explore together their responses, and each person can gain a greater awareness of the uses of silence, as well as standards the partner uses to judge the self and find it lacking. Such exploration often leads to greater empathy and understanding for each other concerning issues of gender, "passivity," voice, and aggression. It also makes clear underlying issues of inequality within relationship.

CONCLUSION

Depression affects a person's sense of self and identity at the deepest levels; its roots lie in the complex interactions between person and social context. Silencing the self theory offers one possible understanding of how images of relatedness and standards for self-evaluation are reflexive with social contexts. Studies using the Silencing the Self Scale have not yet confirmed whether the phenomenology sketched here is a cause or effect of depression. In the meantime, attending to moral themes and images of relatedness offers new possibilities for listening to and engaging with the harsh inner dialogues of depression. Such a dialogue can become a vehicle for change rather than self-blame as a person shifts the focus from the shortcomings of the self to explore how outer social conditions interact with inner beliefs to create alienation and anger. Because silence itself carries complex, multiple meanings, researchers and therapists must acknowledge the complex thicket of power, choice, and intent that surrounds acts of self-silencing while also exploring the contribution of self-silencing to depression.

REFERENCES

American Psychiatric Association. (1994). *Diagnostic and statistical manual of mental disorders* (4th ed.). Washington, DC: Author.

Babcock, J. C., Waltz, J., Jacobson, N. S., & Gottman, J. M. (1993). Power and violence: The relation between communication patterns, power discrepancies, and domestic violence. *Journal of Consulting and Clinical Psychology, 61,* 40–50.

Beck, A. T. (1983). Cognitive therapy of depression: New perspectives. In P. J. Clayton & J. E. Barrett (Eds.), *Treatment of depression: Old controversies and new approaches* (pp. 265–290). New York: Raven Press.

Blatt, S. J., Quinlan, D. M., Chevron, E. S., McDonald, C., & Zuroff, D. (1982). Dependency and self-criticism: Psychological dimensions of depression. *Journal of Consulting and Clinical Psychology, 50,* 113–124.

Blazer, D. B., Kessler, R. C., McGonagle, K. A., & Swartz, M. S. (1994). The prevalence and distribution of major depression in a national community sample: The National Comorbidity Survey. *American Journal of Psychiatry, 151,* 979–986.

Bowlby, J. (1980). *Attachment and loss: Vol. 3. Loss, sadness and depression.* New York: Basic Books.

Bowlby, J. (1988). *A secure base: Parent-child attachment and healthy human development.* New York: Basic Books.

Brazaitis, S. (1995, August). *The psychological constructs of voice and silence across racial identities.* Paper presented at the 103rd annual meeting of the American Psychological Association, New York.

Brown, L., & Gilligan, C. (1992). *Meeting at the crossroads: Women's psychology and girls' development.* Cambridge, MA: Harvard University Press.

Carr, J. G., Gilroy, F. D., & Sherman, M. F. (1996). Silencing the self and depression among women: The moderating effects of race. *Psychology of Women Quarterly, 20,* 375–392.

Cawood, R. M. (1998). *Self in relationship in women who engage in disordered eating.* Unpublished doctoral dissertation, University of Florida, Gainesville.

Chodorow, N. (1978). *The reproduction of mothering: Psychoanalysis and the sociology of gender.* Berkeley: University of California Press.

Christensen, A., & Heavey, C. L. (1990). Gender and social structure in the demand/withdraw pattern of marital conflict. *Journal of Personality and Social Psychology, 59*, 73–81.

Coombs, R. H., & Hovanessian, H. C. (1988). Stress in the role constellation of female resident physicians. *Journal of the American Medical Women's Association, 43*, 21–27.

Cowan, G., Bommersbach, M., & Curtis, S. R. (1995). Codependency, loss of self, and power. *Psychology of Women Quarterly, 19*, 221–236.

Coyne, J. C. (1992). Cognition in depression: A paradigm in crisis. *Psychological Inquiry, 3*, 232–235.

Coyne, J. C., & Downey, G. (1991). Social factors in psychopathology. *Annual Review of Psychology, 42*, 401–425.

Coyne, J. C., & Whiffen, V. E. (1995). Issues in personality as diathesis for depression? The case of Sociotropy/Dependency and Autonomy/Self-Criticism. *Psychological Bulletin, 118*, 358–378.

Craig, A. G., & Pitts, F. N. (1968). Suicide by physicians. *Diseases of the Nervous System, 29*, 763–772.

Dobash, R. E., & Dobash, R. P. (1979). *Violence against wives*. New York: Free Press.

Drew, S. S., & Heesacker, M. (1998). *The role of relationship loss and self loss in depression: Understanding differences between women and men*. Manuscript submitted for publication.

Duarte, L. M., & Thompson, L. M. (1998). *Gender differences in self-silencing*. Manuscript submitted for publication.

Eagly, A. H., & Steffen, V. J. (1986). Gender and aggressive behavior: A meta-analytic review of the social psychological literature. *Psychological Bulletin, 100*, 309–330.

Fredrickson, B., & Roberts, T. A. (1997). Objectification theory: Toward understanding women's lived experience and mental health risks. *Psychology of Women Quarterly, 21*, 173–206.

Freud, S. (1961). Some psychical consequences of the anatomical distinction between the sexes. In J. Strachey (Ed. and Trans.), *The standard edition of the complete psychological works of Sigmund Freud* (Vol. 19, pp. 248–258). London: Hogarth Press. (Original work published 1925)

Fugh-Berman, A. (1992, January 20). Man to man at Georgetown: Tales out of medical school. *The Nation, 37*, 54–56.

Gilligan, C. (1982). *In a different voice: Psychological theory and women's development*. Cambridge, MA: Harvard University Press.

Goldberger, N. (1996). Cultural imperatives and diversity in ways of knowing. In N. R. Goldberger, J. M. Tarule, B. M. Clinchy, & M. F. Belenky (Eds.), *Knowledge, difference and power* (pp. 335–371). New York: Basic Books.

Gottman, J. M. (1994). *Why marriages succeed or fail*. New York: Simon & Schuster.

Gratch, L. V., Bassett, M. E., & Attra, S. L. (1995). The relationship of gender and ethnicity to self-silencing and depression among college students. *Psychology of Women Quarterly, 19*, 509–515.

Gratch, L. V., & Jack, D. C. (1998). *Gender issues and factor structure on the Silencing the Self Scale*. Manuscript submitted for publication.

Gross, E. B. (1992). Gender differences in physician stress. *Journal of the American Medical Women's Association, 47*, 107–114.

Hart, B. I., & Thompson, J. M. (1996). Gender role characteristics and depressive symptomatology among adolescents. *Journal of Early Adolescence, 16*, 407–426.

Hurtado, A. (1996). Strategic suspensions: Feminists of color theorize the production of knowledge. In N. R. Goldberger, J. M. Tarule, B. M. Clinchy, & M. F. Belenky (Eds.), *Knowledge, difference and power* (pp. 372–392). New York: Basic Books.

Jack, D. C. (1987). Silencing the self: The power of social imperatives in female depression. In R. Formanek & A. Gurian (Eds.), *Women and depression: A lifespan perspective* (pp. 161–181). New York: Springer.

Jack, D. C. (1991). *Silencing the self: Women and depression*. Cambridge, MA: Harvard University Press.

Jack, D. C. (in press-a). *Facing aggression: Hidden aspects of women's psychology*. Cambridge, MA: Harvard University Press.

Jack, D. C. (in press-b). Ways of listening to depressed women in qualitative research: Interview techniques and analysis. *Canadian Psychology*.

Jack, D. C., & Dill, D. (1992). The Silencing the Self Scale: Schemas of intimacy associated with depression in women. *Psychology of Women Quarterly, 16*, 97–106.

Jack, R., & Jack, D. C. (1989). *Moral vision and professional decisions: The changing values of women and men lawyers*. New York: Cambridge University Press.

Jacobson, N., & Gottman, J. (1998). *When men batter women*. New York: Simon & Schuster.

Janus, C. L., Janus, S. S., & Price, S. (1983). Residents: The pressure's on the women. *Journal of the American Medical Women's Association, 38*, 18–21.

Klerman, G., & Weissman, M. M. (1980). Depressions among women: Their nature and causes. In M. Guttentag, S. Salasin, & D. Belle (Eds.), *The mental health of women* (pp. 57–92). San Diego, CA: Academic Press.

Kohlberg, L. (1981). *The philosophy of moral development: Moral stages and the idea of justice*. New York: Harper & Row.

McGrath, E., Keita, G. P., Strickland, B. R., & Russo, N. F. (1990). *Women and depression: Risk factors and treatment issues*. Washington, DC: American Psychological Association.

Miller, J. B. (1986). *Toward a new psychology of women* (2nd ed.). Boston: Beacon Press.

Mitchell, S. A. (1988). *Relational concepts in psychoanalysis: An integration*. Cambridge, MA: Harvard University Press.

Myers, M. F. (1988). *Doctors' marriages: A look at the problems and their solutions*. New York: Plenum Medical Books.

Nolen-Hoeksema, S. (1990). *Sex differences in depression*. Stanford, CA: Stanford University Press.

Nolen-Hoeksema, S. (1991). Responses to depression and their effects on the duration of depressive episodes. *Journal of Abnormal Psychology, 100,* 569–582.

Penza, K., Reiss, A., & Scott, H. (1997, May). *Sexual orientation and communication in relationships: Self-silencing, mutuality and power in heterosexual and lesbian relationships*. Paper presented at the American Psychological Society, Washington, DC.

Piaget, J. (1932). *The rules of the game*. London: Routledge & Kegan Paul.

Rucinski, J., & Cybulska, E. (1985). Mentally ill doctors. *British Journal of Hospital Medicine, 33,* 90–94.

Sells, J. M., & Sells, C. J. (1989). Pediatrician and parent: A challenge for female physicians. *Pediatrics, 84,* 355–361.

Stevens, H. B., & Galvin, S. L. (1995). Structural findings regarding the Silencing the Self Scale. *Psychological Reports, 77,* 11–17.

Stoppard, M. M. (1989). An evaluation of the adequacy of cognitive/behavioural theories for understanding depression in women. *Canadian Psychology, 30,* 39–47.

Thompson, M. M. (1995). Silencing the self: Depressive symptomatology and close relationships. *Psychology of Women Quarterly, 19,* 337–353.

Welner, A., Marten, S., Wochnick, E., Davis, M. A., Fishman, R., & Clayton, P. J. (1979). Psychiatric disorders among professional women. *Archives of General Psychiatry, 36,* 169–173.

Westkott, M. (1986). *The feminist legacy of Karen Horney*. New Haven, CT: Yale University Press.

Whisman, M. A., Uebelacker, L. A., & Courtnage, E. S. (1998). *Depression and marital dissatisfaction: The role of marital processes*. Manuscript submitted for publication.

Whitley, T. W., Gallery, M. E., Allison, E. J., & Revicki, D. A. (1989). Factors associated with stress among emergency medicine residents. *Annals of Emergency Medicine, 18,* 1157–1161.

10

SOCIOPHYSIOLOGY AND DEPRESSION

RUSSELL GARDNER, JR. AND JOHN S. PRICE

SOCIOPHYSIOLOGY

Psychiatry and related clinical sciences lack a basic science of the type that underlies other medical specialties (Gardner, 1997). Such a framework would allow an understanding of the conditions treated by clinicians as variations of normal physiological and biochemical operations just as congestive heart failure is understood in terms of a pathogenetic story concerning the cardiovascular system (heart muscle falters causing blood flow backup). Knowledge of the normal cardiovascular system and its operations informs treatment of this mechanism pharmacologically (digitalis preparations) and by counsel (bed rest and low-salt diet). In parallel, we propose that knowledge of normal systems and their operations would inform the treatment and counseling of depression. In this chapter, we hope to formulate this framework with respect to the normal communicative processes basic to depression and to describe how the condition is a variant of normal sociophysiological operations. We suggest that this framework will provide guidance for the best counsel and pharmacological treatment of this serious malady, which is diagnosed more than any other psychiatric condition.

Sociophysiological theory assumes that psychiatric disorders are pathological variants of the motivation, emotions, and conflict involved in normal communicational processes. Interpersonal processes thereby are functions of the brain's normal operation; when they transpire aberrantly, pathology may result (Gardner, 1996). Correction may result after amelioration from interpersonal means. People who panic frequently become calm when someone else is around. Reaction patterns seem to have evolved to serve adaptive purposes, but they may be wrongly deployed by threshold effects, environmental circumstances, timing, and other factors. Dunbar (1996) noted that people are highly social and that this tendency correlates with the enlarged size of the human brain. Therefore, fear responses—an ancient form of reaction pattern—may persist, but more recently evolved features unique to humans modulate them. The point is that across-species comparisons in behavioral, genomic, and neural mechanisms are part of a sociophysiological approach, but contrasts are an equally integral component. Another human means of reducing fear stems from the use of medication. The role of medical doctor, with the availability of scientifically based drugs, is unique to the human species.

The eventual complete description of the pathological sociophysiology of depression will entail detailed expositions of how neurotransmitters and cell and brain systems operate in the normal states and aberrantly when pathological; we are concerned in this chapter with postulated brain modules that mediate individual motives and group effects, only touching on other levels of analysis. A basic tenet of sociophysiology holds psychopathological states to be exaggerations or inappropriate deployments of behavioral modules encoded in the nervous system as normal adaptive features. We propose that a normal module underlying depression and dysthymic disorder is one of *subordination*. One of us has labeled the correlated organismic state *in-group omega psalic*, wherein *psalic* is an acronym for *propensity state antedating language in communication* (Gardner, 1988). This term refers to the communicational state associated with being the lowest ranking animal in a grouping.

INVOLUNTARY SUBORDINATE STRATEGY

The Strategy

At the right time and place, and under the right circumstances, subordination represents a highly adaptive approach to solving problems of survival for oneself and one's offspring. One survives now to compete at a later time under better circumstances. Game theorists label as *strategy* behavioral sequences that imply the possibility of particular outcomes (Maynard Smith, 1982). In the presently described work, the intent to seem defeated represents a strategy. Deployment of such strategies results in behavioral evidence of particular states, such as depression and mania. With respect to the strategy interpretation of depressed states, we suggest that they represent states of *involuntary* subordination. We return to the involuntary–voluntary distinction in a later section.

Alternative Theory of Attachment Disruption

Depression theorists have traditionally considered depression to represent an organismic state resulting from separation or loss (Bowlby, 1980). Here, we instead consider it to be fundamentally a side effect of the biology of competition of the same kind that determines territoriality and social rank (Gardner, 1982; Price, 1967). It would still be sociophysiological, of course, if further data and hypothesis testing eventually showed the neuronal programs and behavioral modules that mediate separation responses to be more critical than those that subserve subordination.

Separation and social rank hypotheses seem at this time to be opposing hypotheses, but this may represent a false dichotomy similar to that labeled *nature–nurture*. We expect that more information from research will reconcile the two positions. We propose that some biological components evolved before others and may have formed a platform or basic plan on which subsequent developments were erected. That is, attachment behaviors are likely the result of less conserved molecular and cellular processes than are behaviors involving competition and rank; indeed, the permutations of social rank and in-group bonding may show a high degree of interdependence. Whatever the future of these research endeavors holds, the social rank hypothesis has received less scientific attention, and in this chapter we redress that neglect.

Handling Ranking Stress

We have labeled as the *involuntary subordinate strategy* (ISS) the behavioral component of a proposed normal module that underlies depression (Price, Sloman, Gardner, Gilbert, & Rohde, 1994). We invoke the term *involuntary* because the ISS is one of at least two levels of decision-making processes used by the brain to deal with ranking stress (the environmental circumstances that elicit the ISS reaction). The voluntary strategy is a higher order, more recently evolved reaction (on a level similar to that deployed by a patient with a height phobia who has his son drive over a very high bridge).

Ranking stress refers to the organism's need to cope with a conspecific challenge (a member of the same species vying for resources such as territory, status, or mating opportunity). This formulation originally involved fighting capacity as measured by the concept of resource-holding potential (RHP). Such competition exists in nearly all arthropods and vertebrates.

Primates including humans exhibit its workings behaviorally, and so do dung beetles, the species on whose behavior game theory was originally based (Parker, 1974). We hypothesize that like fight-or-flight reactions, ISS represents an ancient strategy, but one remaining functional in intervening species that therefore has not been abandoned.

Is ISS Homologous Among Varied Species?

Does the similarity of beetle and primate aggression represent homology (the attribute is traceable to a common ancestor) or convergent evolution (the attribute evolved to a functional similarity but from different sources)? Molecular correlates of arthropod subordination mechanisms may vary from those of vertebrates similar to the way that mechanisms of flight vary in birds and bats (convergent evolution). It is possible that in vertebrate ancestral species such as cephalochordata, competition among conspecifics dwindled so much that the mechanisms for competition needed to be newly formed from natural selection subsequently. This is uncertain of course; many conserved molecules held in common by arthropods and vertebrates have been discovered (Carroll, 1995), and how these relate to conspecific behavior mechanisms is not yet known. For all vertebrates, however, we conjecture that core mechanisms probably hold, because there has been no discernible lapse in conspecific competition, just as all land vertebrates possess similar locomotory devices (spinal reflexes and arrangements of musculature of the extremities). Spinal mechanisms ancestral to these indeed were pioneered by fish before the lobe-finned ancestors of both land-based vertebrates and present-day fish made their transition to land. MacLean (1990) usefully noted that in vertebrates there have evolved overlapping and emergent neuroanatomical and behavioral stages, which he labeled *reptilian*, *paleomammalian*, and *neomammalian*. The extent to which his conception is true awaits more definitive analysis in the form of the eventual deciphering of neuronal programs or genomic codings for such programs, including extensive use of across-species contrast–comparisons.

Involuntary Decision Making Contrasts With Voluntary Thought and Planning

Subordination at a voluntary level may have evolved in mammalians. A general rule seems to hold that when responses to the same stress can be actuated at two brain levels, the higher, more recently evolved response preempts or terminates the lower level, primitive response. For instance, in response to cold, switching on the central heating may preempt or terminate shivering. In response to bright light, putting on sunglasses may preempt or terminate blinking. Similarly, voluntary subordination may preempt or terminate the involuntary subordinate strategy (ISS), which otherwise might manifest as depression. For this reason, depressed patients may not manifest voluntary subordination (if they did, the ISS would have been terminated). Indeed, depressed patients whose brains are engaged in a subordination behavioral module may appear insubordinate—rebellious, aggressive, and stubborn—which is the reverse of the commonly understood meaning of the term *subordinate*. This distinction between voluntary and involuntary levels of subordination may clarify the complex relations between depression and environmental events.

Comparison to Hibernation

The ISS is hard to recognize because it is composed largely of an *absence* of behavior. The ISS consists of an absence of aggression, place seeking, lobbying for influence, and entry into social arenas "where the action is" (Goffmann, 1969). Like the dog that barked in the night, it is easier to recognize the presence of something than the absence of something. More active, positive elements of subordinate behavior, such as flattery and ingratiation, belong to the category of voluntary subordination, and even these may be inhibited in the ISS (e.g., flattery is more likely to occur in mania than in depression).

ISS may be compared with hibernation, a behavior that occurs in a number of animal species, in an attempt to conceptualize what ISS represents. The ISS is analogous to hibernation in the following respects:

- Both states are characterized by a reduction in active behavior.
- Both occur in response to stress (social adversity and climatic adversity).
- Most of the population has the capacity to perform the behavior given the right circumstances (e.g., the arctic ground squirrel, of which a proportion of the population hibernates every winter).
- In the absence of "the right circumstances," a few individuals manifest the behavior anyway (depression may occur without manifest, environmental cause; squirrels kept in constant climatic conditions may nevertheless hibernate).
- The trigger may be a predictor of the stress rather than the stress itself (shortening day length predicts the onset of winter; loss of an ally or patron predicts ranking stress).
- In both states there seems to be a "hypothalamic functional shift" (Pollitt, 1960).
- Exit from the state happens after a fixed lapse of time (the hibernating animal is not in a state to assess the weather; the

depressed patient is not in a state to make an accurate assessment of the social environment).

If one were to study the pathologies of hibernation, one might expect to identify states in which the body temperature dropped too low, hibernation occurred in the absence of the usual precipitating events, or arousal from hibernation failed to occur in the spring. In parallel, the pathology of depression may represent an intensification, prolongation, or inappropriate occurrence of a normal behavioral module encoded in the nervous system.

Strategy Set

Although the ISS may be simply a reaction or single strategy, another useful hypothesis holds it to be a member of a strategy set. An obvious fellow member of the set is the involuntary dominant strategy (IDS); when the strategy set is accessed, a decision is made between the ISS and the IDS. Patients with bipolar disorder exhibit, of course, both depression and mania. We conjecture that if the IDS is chosen, mania results. One of us has elsewhere discussed a related formulation for mania using a concept similar to the IDS—that the patient assumes an alpha status (psalic) similar to that of leaders (Gardner, 1982). Whether individuals exhibit IDS or ISS may stem in part from appraisal of the environment, including appraisal of a perceived opponent, and in part from the operation of random processes.

When the genomic coding for these strategies evolved, probably before the reptilian stage of 300 million years ago, the strategy set was probably accessed in the context of agonistic behavior, referring to competition among conspecifics. The eliciting stimulus was probably an evenly matched opponent. Pairwise contests of agonistic behavior are easily settled if two adversaries are unevenly matched. Then, the smaller or weaker gives way to the other, and a damaging contest is avoided. In his initial work, for instance, Parker (1974) noted that the larger of two competing dung beetles invariably won.

In the case of equal matching, however, something more is needed, such as an agonistic strategy set. When an individual engaged in a contest perceives itself as being evenly matched, with neither victory nor defeat as likely immediate outcomes, that individual may deploy either the IDS winning strategy or the ISS losing strategy. By pumping more energy and confidence into the system, the IDS may swing an evenly matched encounter into one wherein the IDS-using contestant wins. On the other hand, by draining energy and confidence, deployment of ISS ensures that the user will rapidly lose.

Of course, there is least conflict and damage if both competitors access the agonistic strategy set at the same time and choose opposite strategies. They then develop complementary roles and are likely to establish a stable but asymmetrical relationship. If they both deploy the IDS at the same time, a serious fight may ensue in which one is likely to be damaged or killed. What if they both deploy the ISS at the same time? Schjelderup-Ebbe (1935) described this situation in barnyard fowl. What usually happens is that one bird recovers from its submissive posture and switches to the IDS.

The choice between IDS and ISS may occur on a randomized basis (compare with the unpredictability of whether a manic or depressive episode will next occur for most bipolar patients; Goodwin & Jamison, 1990). If competitors do not want their rivals to be able to predict their future strategy, unpredictability from randomization may be the surest route of ensuring this. Each individual then has a phenotypic character of p(IDS), which is the probability of deploying the IDS rather than the ISS when the agonistic strategy set is accessed. It does not matter for this purpose whether p(IDS) is genetically, environmentally, or randomly determined. To the extent that it is genetically determined, it is likely to be influenced by the occurrence of negative frequency-dependent selection, as Maynard Smith (1982) showed with his hawk and dove model. Thus, rarer occurrences of the genotype are more likely to enhance fitness. Perhaps the familial inheritance of manic-depressive illness (bipolar disorder) fits such a paradigm and may echo the deployment of an agonistic strategy set. We suspect, however, that the access to the agonistic strategy set is likely a property of any human, not limited to those who inherit a tendency to have mania and depression as inappropriate exacerbations of the deployment of IDS and ISS.

Modern Ranking Stress

Of course, humans are now 300 million years down the evolutionary slope beyond the reptilian stage, and the agonistic strategy set is unlikely to be accessed simply when two contestants are evenly matched. Ranking stress now happens when uncertainty prevails about ranking relationships. This may be uncertainty about rank, some form of bullying by superiors, or threats of insurrection by subordinates. It may occur when there is loss of an ally on whose support one's rank depended. Using different terminology, one can say that ranking stress occurs when people are not able to impose their own definition on a relationship or situation, particularly when someone else imposes a definition that is difficult or unacceptable. Then the two are in a contest about whose definition prevails. This is formally similar to the situation of two reptiles contesting dominance.

In summary, we suggest that an agonistic strategy set is accessed when a person suffers ranking stress. This in turn occurs when one is unable to be confident about controlling the definition of an important relationship. When such a definition is unclear, one "chooses," perhaps partly by a process of randomization, between the IDS and the ISS. Because the simultaneous choice of the IDS by both contestants leads to damaging fights, the ISS may be the most common strategy for most people. In the rest of this discussion we concentrate on the ISS.

Perception of ISS

Proximate triggers of the agonistic strategy set (and hence simulation of the ISS) entail how the individual becomes aware of ranking stress. Probably there are a number of such proximal triggers. There may be cognitive appreciation of a conflict of wills. There may be a sensation of being put down by the other, either from the receipt of interpersonal signals or from the feeling that one is being manipulated into a one-down position. There may be pain, either mental pain from insults or physical pain from blows. Or there may be the sensation that one is unable to reciprocate the blows of the rival, with the well-known uncomfortable feeling that one's blows are not "getting home" on the rival.

The reciprocation of blows and insults is important for the maintenance of symmetry. We suggest that the receipt of nonreciprocated blows or insults causes loss of personal resources (R), which may be experienced as loss of self-esteem. The person who does not reciprocate adequately may then be more likely to access the agonistic strategy set, either by presaging an incipient asymmetry or by monitoring his own and the other person's R. Subjectively, this may take the form of impotent anger, a realization that the action tendency of one's anger (attack) is blocked.

The Function of the ISS

The ISS functions to stop the fighting by allowing the contestant to lose as quickly as possible. This involves signaling to the rival that one has lost and is no longer a threat to him, so that the other individual exercises "the mercy of the victor" (Weisfeld, 1977) and stops inflicting punishment; this could be called a *damage limitation function*. In addition, if one has allies, one must signal to them that they should stop giving agonistic support because their warlike signals may jeopardize one's own submission.

In humans, these signals to both rival and allies may be expressed in the form of metaphor, such as the metaphor of physical illness. The competitor signals to the rival, "I am too sick to be a threat to you," and to his supporters, "I am too sick to enter the arena on your behalf, so stop giving me agonistic support and give me nurturant support instead" (Price & Gardner, 1995).

The ISS deployer must, of course, switch off his own aggressive behavior and carry out whatever flight—escape—submit routines are appropriate in the circumstances. In fact, one could say that the person accesses a losing strategy set, which contains the alternatives of flight and submission.

A further function of the ISS may be to alter the cognitive activity of the individual in such a way that the ISS may be supplemented, or preferably replaced, by voluntary behavior appropriate to the reduced situation. In a cognitive stage of "acceptance," the new situation is reframed in such a way that it does not give rise to anger or resentment. For example, the former rival is no longer seen as a presumptuous challenger but rather as someone who is to be respected, obeyed, and looked to for support and patronage. This change of cognition makes possible the prosocial behaviors that lead to reconciliation. Because reconciliation removes the social conditions that gave rise to the ISS in the first place, after using up any momentum or inertia it might have, the ISS is likely to be switched off. The end result is for the ISS to remove the conditions that led to the agonistic strategy set being accessed. This process could be described as "functional agonism," and its various stages are summarized in the following list:

1. Unacceptable situation (e.g., one's definition of a relationship is not accepted by a rival)
2. Conflict of interest recognized by both, leading to confrontation.
3. Fighting, with no clear outcome discernible
4. Losing becomes likely
5. Receipt of unreciprocated blows or insults
6. Mental or physical pain
7. Fall in R (R is an evaluative assessment of oneself and others that we assume was originally indexed in ancestral species by fighting capacity or resource-holding potential [RHP])
8. Agonistic strategy set accessed and ISS selected
9. ISS consists of a further fall in R (and other components of self-esteem); also, a fall in resource value and ownership (see later explanation)
10. Acceptance of previously unacceptable situation; anger toward rival changes to respect
11. Decision to yield voluntarily
12. Act of submission
13. Submission accepted by other
14. Reconciliation

If any of the last five stages fails to occur, reconciliation is blocked; the ISS continues to operate and may be recognized behaviorally and experientially as a depressive state. Depression facilitates Stages 10, 11, and 12 because it lowers R, resource value, and ownership. This alters cognition in such a way that the person feels unworthy (of anything better than the unacceptable situation), loses interest in whatever was being fought about, and feels no right to possess it anyway. The person is more likely then to yield voluntarily.

When Does the ISS Present as Depression?

If the ISS fails to remove the circumstances that caused the agonistic strategy set to be accessed in the first place, it is liable to be intensified and prolonged. When this occurs, there is a state of either dysthymic disorder or major depression.

Probably the most common block to reconciliation is that the cognitive state of "giving in—giving up" is not sufficiently intense to persuade the individual to alter the goals or attitudes in which blockage led to accessing the agonistic strategy set. Some goals are held very strongly and are resistant to change. Clinging to such goals may be described as pride or stubbornness or, more approvingly, as determination or courage. However, it is sometimes regarded as courageous to back down and admit one was in the wrong. A fictional example in which a severe degree of depression did not succeed in getting the protagonist to back down is found in the figure of Mr. Trevelyan in Anthony Trollope's novel *He Knew He Was Right*. An earlier example is Satan in *Paradise Lost*. The first book of Milton's poem is like a textbook of dysfunctional agonism. Satan has been thoroughly defeated, and he knows that he has been defeated and that he will never win, but he still refuses to yield; as in a dysfunctional human family, he forms what might be called a cross-generational coalition with Eve. Moreover, the coalition is not talked about but is symbolized by an apple.

Sometimes third parties block voluntary submission. One patient had a dominating husband who objected to her going to visit her even more dominating mother. Her mother would not allow her to submit to her husband. Consequently, her ISS became extended and intensified, and she needed treatment for depression. She only recovered fully when her mother died, whereupon she could become a satisfactory wife.

Sometimes the dominant partner demands something that the willing subordinate cannot supply. A husband may demand an enthusiastic sexual response, and his bullying because this is not forthcoming makes the wife depressed and even less sexy. A woman may demand that her husband stop fidgeting when he is unable to exert voluntary control over a tic. One spouse may insist that the other give up smoking.

Sometimes patients do not know what to do to please their partner. Sometimes there is nothing that they can do. If an older sister is bullying her younger brother because he is a boy, there is not much he can do about it. A wife who is bullied because her husband is bullied at work experiences a similar bind. The same may happen if a dominant spouse gets depressed for any reason; the depression means such a person becomes more irritable with the subordinate spouse. Sometimes, as in the victim–victimizer interactions mentioned by Sloman (1995), it may be difficult to know who is responsible for the block; in that case, one should take a systemic view. One marital therapist, treating a woman with depression, successfully gave the antidepressant to the husband to take himself, rather than to the wife!

The Components of the ISS

There are three hypothetical constructs that behavioral ecologists have found to be essential for making mathematical models of fighting behavior:

1. *Resource-holding potential* is an estimate of an individual's fighting capacity and is therefore a component of R (sum of the individual's total resources).
2. *Resource value* is an estimate of the value of whatever is being fought over.
3. *Ownership* is a widespread convention in the animal world; an owner or resident of a territory wins a contest and an intruder loses it.

The higher these values are, the more the individual is likely to attack rather than back off. Therefore, we can expect all the components to be reduced in the ISS. It is an interesting exercise to see how many of the features of depressive illness can be accounted for by reduction in these three variables.

R is an evaluative assessment of oneself and others that we assume was originally indexed in ancestral species by fighting capacity, or RHP, only. Evolution of social complexity, however, requires modification of the concept to include the capacity to control adversarial social situations. There are many resources that people have in addition to RHP, including allies, wealth and territorial holdings, and group-conferred attributes such as membership and leadership. Recognition of one's R is probably an important component of human self-esteem. That self-esteem may have evolved from R accounts for some otherwise puzzling features of self-regard, such as its global nature and the wide interindividual variation. Lowered R accounts for the reduced self-esteem that is a common feature of depression; it also bears on related features such as guilt, shame, self-blame, inferiority, and other forms of negative self-perception.

Resource value expresses the investment of the individual in goals and incentives that have to be given up. These may be particular goals such as getting one's own way over some issue; they may be more general such as ambition and desire for social enhancement; or they may be symbolic such as the achievement of a meaningful philosophy or religion. To the extent that rewards are dependent on social status, resource value represents ambition and all forms of status seeking. Reduction in resource value in the depressed patient accounts for the global loss of interest, apathy, and loss of reinforcer effectiveness.

Whereas R represents the "can" of motivation, resource value represents the "will." When both "can" and "will" are high, motivation is high, which is represented by a liberal provision of energy. Conversely, when "can" and "will" are low, one can expect the individual to feel tired and lacking in energy.

Sense of ownership is impaired in depression, and in the extreme case the patient feels no right to exist, in contrast to the patient with elevated mood, for whom "the world is his oyster." One depressed golfer expressed this impairment in the statement "I have no standing on the course of life." In summary, we suggest that reduction in these basic variables accounts for a considerable proportion of depressive states.

The preceding conceptualizations concern analysis of normal sociophysiological processes that have eventuated in depressed states. There are many treatment implications, and we now turn to a few that we have found useful.

NEW METAPHORS FOR THE CLINIC

Explaining Depression to Patients as Pathological ISS

Explaining depression as a "biochemical imbalance" is less useful for rationalizing the use of medication and other treatments than explaining it as an ISS. Depression may be viewed as a normal and biologically ancient method of fending off danger from another person, loss of resources, or something signaling one of these. Although it is clearly a disorder and potentially a dangerous state, depression as a brain reaction and bodily state takes center stage. As reviewed earlier, however, responses to the same stressor may occur at two brain levels, and there seems to be a general rule that the more recently evolved response abolishes the more primitive one. The question then becomes how to invoke higher level response sets.

In our experience, patients find the model rational, simple, and understandable. Depending on circumstances, one may mention that the strategy is typically out of awareness. If there is no obvious deception, possible antagonists find the communication more convincing. In other words, this state in which patients find themselves is not something planned, not a question of choice, not something bad (depressed people are prone to think they are "bad"). Rather, it is something they find themselves saddled with, a fact of life, not under personal control.

The story of Thorlief Schjelderup-Ebbe may be useful. This lonely Norwegian boy discovered pecking order as a child, when he had often been left to his own devices in a country place, and chickens were almost his only companions. Nearly all patients already have at least some awareness of pecking order (as well as some acquaintance with loneliness). The discovery by one of us (Price, 1967) of these descriptions a half-century after Schjelderup-Ebbe made them may become part of the story. Particularly important was the resemblance of the behavior of low-ranking chickens to the behavior of depressed people, implying the possible ancientness of the response pattern.

One can also mention Martin Seligman (1975) and the behavior of "learned helplessness" he discovered in dogs that were treated inconsistently with electric shocks. The dogs became nonunreactive, apparently enduring only to live another day. Later, other researchers found that rats behave similarly when so treated. This research currently represents the most usable animal model for major depression and its recovery. For example, Petty and Sherman (1979) found that the antidepressant imipramine, when injected into the forebrains of rats, reversed their "helpless" behavior with a time course similar to that of human depression.

Patients may recognize in themselves a physiological reaction pattern in common with that of these animals. Both the animals and the depressed patients may be behaving according to a basic biological plan that resembles the response of fear in situations of imminent danger. It should be emphasized that this is probably a normal phenomenon that for the afflicted person has become abnormal. Today, the pattern has become a psychiatric problem—abnormal because its expression is stimulated too much, with wrong timing, or without present-day necessity; an ISS turned to depression is like inadvertently suggesting that a servant should weed the garden only to find the plot trampled by a monster.

As in other medical interventions, the clinician should be careful to check patient understanding. Monitoring nonverbal and verbal expressions helps one to learn whether the story makes sense in the situation at hand. The clinician should avoid imposing undue authority beyond the patient's understanding and sense of well-being, and he or she should be alert to the possibility that the treater may easily become the feared antagonist. One should take pains not to condescend to the patient and not to imply that the person is merely a lower animal.

Basic Plans

Other metaphors may be deployed to explain the idea of biological basic plan; one may note, for example, that not only people but chickens and lizards—even clams and earthworms!—have blood cells, a basic plan structure common to invertebrates, birds, and humans. Many other body devices seem to have been modified to fit what has become the human body, but despite modifications, structures such as blood cells, limbs, and the ISS all exemplify a common device multiply appearing through the vertebrate lineage. Basic plan or platform ideas take on meaning when compared with the steering wheel in automobiles. Invented early in the history of self-propelled locomotion without racks, this ordinary device has been such a useful tool that it has not needed reinvention. It may vary from car model to car model in details of appearance and dimensions, but design functions remain much the same. Of course, basic plans in biology are transmitted down the generations not by a culturally transmitted blueprint but by the genomic coding for key molecules in the brain that in turn direct certain behaviors. The behaviors of interest in the consultation session are communicative in nature, patterns of messages to other people.

Surviving with the ISS in a competitive world may have been a useful innovation for people in the past and for people in terrible environments, but it generally is not helpful for the depressed patient. Pathological ISS may resemble the pain-producing blood cells in people with homozygous sickle cell anemia. These cells lengthen and then, knifelike, stab vessel sidewalls when relative hypoxia occurs in the bloodstream. Like suicidal major depression, this disorder can be fatal at times, but we know that the less severe heterozygous version may significantly help survival from malaria in some parts of Africa. When depressed, the patient may not be aware of deploying ISS. Like the dog whose trainer stopped shocking it but did not behave differently, the patient seems no longer capable of reacting to improved circumstances; the patient does not easily undertake a plan of action involving an assessment of changed circumstances. An ISS is an involuntary bodily state that resembles shivering, such as when one enters a stand-up freezer and stays longer than anticipated.

ISS Is Like a Shiver: Foundation for a Treatment Strategy

The most important metaphor we develop for patients—leading to an explanation of how treatment works—elaborates the shiver model. This is easily illustrated on a chalkboard, one component at a time, starting with the shiver experience itself. Everyone has shivered and seen others, even dogs, shiver, so that the metaphor becomes palpable and understandable. That one shivers because of the cold is equally palpable, and what one does to remedy the shiver response by getting warmer in various ways requires little imagination. The beginning stages of this model are shown in Table 1.

TABLE 1
Brain–Body Response Shared With Other Animals

Stimulus	Response
Cold	Shiver
Bright light	Blinking
Height	Fear of falling
Ranking stress	ISS

Note. ISS = involuntary subordinate strategy.

Advantages of a Big Brain

The differences between humans and other animals are critical to this stage of discussion with patients, after one has developed the similarities and achieved agreement that breathing, blood, shivers, and other body structures and functions are held in common and that other animals also have social rank hierarchies. The differences of language, laughter, and the extensiveness of human relationships, although obvious, now need to come to the forefront. One can point out to patients that humans have a large brain, three times greater in size than that of the nearest primate relatives and of human ancestors of 3 million years ago. What happened to bring about that change? What additional, potentially helpful functions does the larger mass entail?

Three points of the human–nonhuman difference are relevant to the meaningful metaphor for therapy:

A = *allies:* People are gregarious; they attach or bond intensively to many other people. They have an extensive ability to elicit allies. They use language and nonverbal cues to exchange information.

T = *thought:* Humans extensively deploy cognition to solve problems.

P = *plan:* People can analyze their circumstances to gain new perspectives on shiverlike involuntary responses and then act to forestall or prevent unfortunate and maladaptive reflexive or automatic reactions.

Therefore, to handle ISS and other automatic responses, people benefit from the help of others who are friendly and have their best interests at heart; they can better think through the problem using language-based conversation, reassured by indications of involvement, investment, and friendliness (the hedonic mode of Chance, 1988). With such people, one can better plan for what *should* happen the next time the analyzed circumstance appears in one's life. Instead of responding with the equivalent of shivering—automatically and involuntarily—one can respond more specifically and adaptively to present surroundings, which are better analyzed if done soberly, carefully, and while supported. One's conscious thinking goes better with the help of other people.

TABLE 2
Treatment Strategy Using Allies, Thought, and Planning

Stimulus	Response
Cold	Switch on central heating
Bright light	Sunglasses
Height	Avoid cliffs
Ranking stress	Talk to doctor or other friendly person (ally)
	Sort out problem (thought)
	Design method of handling the stressor (plan)

As noted in Table 2, the human features are not completely unique. Many animals, for instance, huddle together for warmth. Moreover, ethologist Franz de Waal (1989) detailed how chimpanzee alpha males (dominants) need to enlist the aid of allies to achieve the status. Humans as animals display unusual amounts and duration of attachment behaviors.

The point can be made when talking to patients that the major helpful factor in the larger human brain mass may be that humans are storytelling animals (Deacon, 1997). With the help of the bigger brain, humans somehow became capable of constructing whole worlds and sequences of actions that other people have done, or might do, or that we ourselves did (with varying degrees of certainty) in the past. We all are avid for such stories as evidenced by the popularity of television and novels or, for that matter, the daily newspaper, radio talk shows, and stockmarket reports. We have preferred and less preferred story lines; how they work often depends on various groups to which we belong and their values, ethnic and religious allegiances, personal experiences, and education. We seem to be able to escape the iron boot by retreat into fantasy. Anne Frank had her diary as her audience in terrible times. We use metaphors like we drink fluids; they are everyday and essential features of our existence.

Other animals drink fluids as humans do, of course, and they may have some humanlike features, as pets do. They may relate to humans and our signals, but construing signals in the first place is a human idea. Their relating through story lines and metaphors is rudimentary compared with that of humans.

Serotonin Speaks

When people recover from feeling depressed, they newly or even uniquely feel in charge. This phenomenon was nicely depicted by Peter Kramer in *Listening to Prozac*, the best-selling book on antidepressant drugs, particularly those enhancing serotonin concentration in neuronal synapses (Kramer, 1993). Kramer described a woman whose low-key depression was relieved with the selective serotonin reuptake inhibitor (SSRI) fluoxetine (Prozac) and who was no longer subject to a kind of addiction to a man who treated her inconsistently and badly. Somehow, as she felt better, she no longer fussed about him. He left her life dismissed, no longer worth her time.

Patient A.O. (seen by Russell Gardner) presented a similar scenario. She had avoided medication for some months, but she was also unable to let go of a philandering man who would indicate interest in living with her but then show up with another woman in a pattern that enraged her repeatedly. She continued to hope that he would match her idealized version of him, despite repeated evidence to the contrary. With medication indicated by her major depression, she was finally able to say good-bye and then to feel pride in her decision (rather than grief at her loss). Perhaps a placebo unknown as such to the patient and the doctor would have had the same result, but in either event, her synaptic serotonin might have become elevated.

The recently developed SSRI drugs have achieved widespread notoriety because of their position on the covers of national magazines and best-selling books; however, Michael Raleigh and colleagues discovered well before these drugs came into vogue that serontonin in the blood of dominant vervet monkeys is twice as high as in subordinates (Raleigh, McGuire, Brammer, & Yuwiler, 1984). In work with humans, this research group found higher levels of whole blood serotonin in fraternity leaders and in men with higher ratings on Type A personality measures (people who are more driven, active, and energetic).

When it became clear that fluoxetine and its relatives, the other serotonergic drugs, made people feel better—not only those with major but also those with lesser depressions as well—these investigators asked what these drugs would do to the ranks of subordinates who received them. They gave them selectively to lower ranking monkeys, and the answer was definitive. Male vervet subordinates newly and clearly took dominant positions (Raleigh, McGuire, Brammer, Pollack, & Yuwiler, 1991).

We know that this is not the case with humans. Someone who is less depressed from a drug that raises serotonin in the body is not thereby a dominant bully. Indeed, less—not more—aggression correlates with rising serotonin in the human body. Conversely, people dying from violent suicides, arsonists, and people more willing to give electric shocks to other people (bullies?) have lower—not greater—amounts of serotonin in their bodies (Linnoila & Virkkunen, 1992). Humans seem to be less hurtfully aggressive and more comfortably in charge when the level of serotonin is increased.

People have the capacity to belong to many groups and to have many allegiances (each with its own story line). John Birtchnell observed that humans extend relationship story lines to nonhumans, even nonanimate objects (Birtchnell, 1993). We stop or go at a stoplight, a commander for the moment. We relate readily not only to other people but also to parts of ourselves or to ourselves of the past or future. We may say, "My hurting back is letting me down." The now-abstinent but sick alcoholic or cigarette smoker says that she or he treated the self badly in the past or expresses anger at the things lost by the substance-abusing person of the past. This metaphoric capacity enables people to have a sensible goal in the ISS column of Table 2. Parallel to warmth in the shiver column is the idea that one can be in charge of oneself or one's parts, particularly those parts of one's self that behave involuntarily and maladaptively.

Being "In Charge" by "Giving Way" Rather Than "Giving In"

To illustrate how "taking charge" may involve an attitude that a person takes toward the self and others with respect to ISS, one can relate to patients the story of a woman who told Dr. Leon Sloman (1995) of being fired from a position in city government. An election had swept in the opponent of the person appointing her, but she felt that "they can't do that!" Humiliated and furious, she was readying herself to sue. With careful questioning, Dr. Sloman ascertained the reality of the "spoils" system in that city at that time, and he suggested that she not eventually "give in," that is, resentfully battle toward a certain loss in a fight-or-flight reaction —in this case "fight like a cornered rat" does out of desperation and with little hope of winning. Rather than deploy an aggression-laden, face-saving sure-loss strategy, she was advised to "give way" instead. He suggested that she collect maximum severance pay and put her energies into taking charge of a new job search. She took his advice and soon thereafter reapplied her energies happily toward a new job.

The story points out that a person can take charge of the unruly parts of his or her own life, including issues with other people after an assessment of circumstances. This departs from the image of the authority who causes others to defer or do his or her bidding. Instead, one's own unruly wishes, impulses, inhibitions, and other inner forces must be shepherded, constrained, or encouraged. "Taking charge" as a metaphor says that a person has the capacity to look at his or her parts and consider them to be individuals who will respond to the person's taking a commanding position with respect to them. The way to combat an ISS is to realize fundamentally the involuntary nature of the response, to recognize intellectually and with the aid of allies that reality is not tested by the perceptions that stimulated the state, and to plan one's strategy for personally taking charge.

Sometimes there is great advantage to detecting and revealing hidden ways that the patient persists in battling hopeless battles and to realize thereby that a cleverer method of coping is indicated. One may suggest to a patient, in line with the insight of Beck's cognitive therapy, that the fundamental premises on which the patient is operating may have flaws.

Automatic responses (i.e., automatic negative thoughts) may operate, well apart from conscious decision making.

Our model involves allies, thought, and planning (ATP). The shiver–ATP–take charge model entails some elements of therapy; however, it should not be called psychotherapy (involving the disembodied psyche) but sociophysiological therapy, which fully enfranchises the body. It differs from cognitive therapy because it focuses on the normal physiology of behaviors that we propose are basic to the pathophysiology of the patient's troubles. Biochemical defects may in fact exist, such as different thresholds for illness onset in vulnerable people, and the ways that they operate must be subject to future investigation. But surely there must also be long-standing physiological systems that involve preparatory sets for interactions with other people. This idea is in line with the science of medical specialties other than psychiatry, each of which has a well-understood normal anatomy and physiology.

Case Examples

The Sculptor's Anger

O.C., a 40-year-old metal-working artist in financial difficulty, loves his wife, called here Cynthia, although he finds her uncompromising manner disconcerting. When first seen (by Russell Gardner), O.C. met criteria for major depression (dysphoria, guilt, problems with concentration, sleep disturbance, and lowered energy). An SSRI antidepressant caused him to feel better, but when he was furious at his wife, he continued episodically to damage his shop equipment. He reported a longer fuse on his temper after taking the medication, but the temper remained. At one point, he yelled at a secretary for the doctor's relative lack of availability, but he was calm and polite when, a few minutes later, he spoke to the doctor himself. Partly, he had cooled off, but as is typical in depression, he expressed anger down-hierarchy but not up-hierarchy. He damages his tools (symbolic subordinates) and yells at human subordinates, but to his wife and doctor, he displays politeness and even submissiveness.

His wife attacks him if she has any perception of a tie to another woman, particularly one, Jan, with whom O.C. lived prior to knowing Cynthia. He feels that Jan is well in his past; she is married and far away. However, Cynthia angrily confronted him with an implication of interest when she discovered that he had produced a commissioned work for Jan's brother, who lives nearby. O.C. had held off telling Cynthia because she was in the midst of grief for the sudden death of her own brother and he wished to protect her (as well as to avoid the predictable hassle). When she discovered the sale because the brother wanted to buy something else, she was furious. The ensuing argument caused O.C. to feel beaten down and helpless.

During O.C.'s individual therapy session, the shiver–ATP–take charge model was outlined on a chalkboard; it was suggested that both O.C. and Cynthia were in "shiver mode" for much of their argument. She would not give up and maintained the argument; he felt that selling a commission to anyone was important given their financial straits. He needed to take charge and win, although he wanted to do this as much as possible "without rubbing it in" to her. He later reported feeling better when he implemented methods to augment his marketing without sacrificing his artistry. To celebrate, he gave a party in her honor, which surprised and pleased her.

The No-Longer Helpless Daughter

Patient A.I. is 48 years old and approached treatment because she had depressive symptoms meeting criteria for major depression and because she wished "to get over my mother." Her mother, dead for 3 years, had been alcoholic and subtly controlling throughout the patient's life. A.I. felt that her depression was related to her relationship with her mother. An SSRI drug caused her to feel better but did not affect recurrences of sharp painful episodes of angry depression that had no apparent cause. In each episode, the patient wondered whether she should cause her own death— for example, leaving the car running in her enclosed garage. These episodes were very disturbing; A.I. was powerfully tempted by the idea during the relatively short periods the idea held sway.

A.I. was interested in the shiver–ATP–take charge model, and after practicing using it in sessions, she systematically deployed it outside the sessions. As a consequence, she reduced the session frequency to the level of occasional visits. When a powerful depressed feeling would take over, she "knew exactly what do do"—she sought out a variety of allies, ranging from her husband to her daughter to a good friend. At times, she recalled what had been discussed in the session and enlisted me in imagination as her ally of the moment, again illustrating the power of the human imagination in solving problems.

CONCLUSION

Use of the shiver–ATP–take charge model in combination with antidepressant medication exemplifies sociophysiological therapy, a conceptual integration of the otherwise disembodied *psycho*therapy with pharmacotherapy. New metaphors relate present woes to propensity states antedating language—to basic plans and ancient strategies that have stemmed from reaction patterns to conspecifics that were well established long before humans existed. Therapeutically, deliberate use of allies, thought, and planning (ATP) helps people plagued by automatic reactions, especially the ISS, to overcome the deleterious effects of maladaptive basic plans. Human-specific cognitive attributes that are correlated with the enlarged human brain include storytelling and the metaphoric representation of one's components as subordinates over which one can be in charge.

REFERENCES

Birtchnell, J. (1993). *How humans relate: A new interpersonal theory*. Westport, CT: Praeger.

Bowlby, J. (1980). *Attachment and loss: Vol. 3. Loss: Sadness and depression*. London: Hogarth Press.

Carroll, S. B. (1995). Homeotic genes and the evolution of arthropods and chordates. *Nature, 376*, 479–485.

Chance, M. R. A. (Ed.). (1988). *Social fabrics of the mind*. Hillsdale, NJ: Erlbaum.

Chance, M. R. A., & Jolly, C. (1970). *Social groups of monkeys, apes and men*. New York: Jonathan Cape/Dutton.

de Waal, F. (1989). *Chimpanzee politics: Power and sex among apes* (2nd ed.). Baltimore: Johns Hopkins University Press.

Deacon, T. W. (1997). *The symbolic species: The co-evolution of language and the brain*. New York: Norton.

Dunbar, R. (1996). *Grooming, gossip, and the evolution of language*. Cambridge, MA: Harvard University Press.

Gardner, R., Jr. (1982). Mechanisms in manic-depressive disorder: An evolutionary model. *Archives of General Psychiatry, 39*, 1436–1441.

Gardner, R., Jr. (1988). Psychiatric syndromes as infrastructure for intraspecific communication. In M. R. A. Chance (Ed.), *Social fabrics of the mind* (pp. 197–226). Hillsdale, NJ: Erlbaum.

Gardner, R., Jr. (1996). Psychiatry needs a basic science titled sociophysiology. *Biological Psychiatry, 39*, 833–834.

Gardner, R., Jr. (1997). Sociophysiology as the basic science of psychiatry. *Theoretical Medicine, 18*, 335–356.

Goffmann, E. (1969). *Where the action is*. London: Penguin Books.

Goodwin, F. K., & Jamison, K. R. (1990). *Manic-depressive illness*. New York: Oxford University Press.

Kramer, P. D. (1993). *Listening to Prozac: A psychiatrist explores antidepressant drugs and the remaking of the self*. New York: Penguin Books.

Linnoila, M., & Virkkunen, M. (1992). Biological correlates of suicidal risk and aggressive behavioral traits. *Journal of Clinical Psychopharmacology, 12*, 19S–20S.

MacLean, P. D. (1990). *The triune brain in evolution: Role in paleocerebral functions*. New York: Plenum Press.

Maynard Smith, J. (1982). *Evolution and the theory of games*. Cambridge, England: Cambridge University Press.

Parker, G. A. (1974). Assessment strategy and the evolution of fighting behaviour. *Journal of Theoretical Biology, 47*, 223–243.

Petty, F., & Sherman, A. D. (1979). Reversal of learned helplessness by imipramine. *Communications in Psychopharmacology, 3*, 371–373.

Price, J. S. (1967). Hypothesis: The dominance hierarchy and the evolution of mental illness. *Lancet, 2*, 243–246.

Price, J. S., & Gardner, R. (1995). The paradoxical power of the depressed patient: A problem for the ranking theory of depression. *British Journal of Medical Psychology, 68*, 193–206.

Pollitt, J. D. (1960). Depression and the functional shift. *Comprehensive Psychiatry, 1*, 381–390.

Price, J. S., & Sloman, L. (1987). Depression as yielding behavior: An animal model based on Schjelderup-Ebbe's pecking order. *Ethology and Sociobiology, 8*(Suppl. 3), 85–98.

Price, J. S., Sloman, L., Gardner, R., Jr., Gilbert, P., & Rohde, P. (1994). The social competition hypothesis of depression. *British Journal of Psychiatry, 164*, 309–315.

Raleigh, M. J., McGuire, M. T., Brammer, G. L., Pollack, D. B., & Yuwiler, A. (1991). Serotonergic mechanisms promote dominance acquisition in adult male vervet monkeys. *Brain Research, 55*, 181–190.

Raleigh, M. J., McGuire, M. T., Brammer, G. L., & Yuwiler, A. (1984). Social and environmental influences on blood serotonin concentrations in monkeys. *Archives of General Psychiatry, 41*, 405–410.

Schjelderup-Ebbe, T. (1935). Social behavior in birds. In C. Murchison (Ed.), *Handbook of social psychology* (pp. 947–972). Worcester, MA: Clark University Press.

Seligman, M. E. P. (1975). *Helplessness: On depression, development, and death*. New York: Freeman.

Sloman, L. (1995, December). *The ASCAP Newsletter, 8*(12), 3–4.

Weisfeld, G. E. (1977). A sociobiological basis for psychotherapy. In M. T. McGuire & L. A. Fairbanks (Eds.), *Ethological psychiatry* (pp. 111–126). New York: Grune & Stratton.

IV

DEPRESSION AND THE RESPONSE OF SIGNIFICANT OTHERS

11

MARITAL DISCORD AND DEPRESSION: THE POTENTIAL OF ATTACHMENT THEORY TO GUIDE INTEGRATIVE CLINICAL INTERVENTION

PAGE ANDERSON, STEVEN R. H. BEACH, AND NADINE J. KASLOW

Clinicians, marital researchers, and family members have long noted that poor relationships often appear to lead to feelings of depression. Beach, Sandeen, and O'Leary (1990) developed a marital discord model of depression to explain links between troubled relationships and depression. This model focuses on the roles of stress and social support in marital discord. About the same time that the marital discord model was being articulated, the concept of adult attachment was also being described (Hazan & Shaver, 1987). Since that time, the adult attachment literature has burgeoned, to the extent that it now provides a powerful foundation from which to explore close relationships (Shaver, Collins, & Clark, 1996) and to develop clinical implications (Kobak, Ruckdeschel, & Hazan, 1994).

We gratefully acknowledge support from National Science Foundation Grant SBR-9511385, which facilitated the preparation of this chapter.

One exciting aspect of this development is that the adult attachment literature might provide a complementary framework to the marital discord model for conceptualizing depression in marriage. Similar to the marital discord model, the attachment perspective focuses on stress and social support, but in addition, the attachment perspective emphasizes other functions of the attachment system: maintaining closeness and serving as a "secure base" for exploring the environment (Bowlby, 1969/1982). Furthermore, the marital discord model is grounded in cognitive–behavioral approaches to therapy for couples, whereas the attachment perspective is grounded in an object–relations understanding of relationships. The similarities and differences between the marital discord model and the attachment perspective suggest the potential for attachment theory to inspire a range of new interventions for use with depressed and discordant couples and to act as a bridge for integrating ideas about close relationships from different theoretical perspectives.

In this chapter, we begin with a description of the evidence linking marital discord to depression and a report of the data from recent clinical trials regarding the effectiveness of marital therapy for depression. Next, we review attachment theory and recent research on attachment and depression. We then consider the usefulness of conceptualizing attachment processes and attachment styles in clinical work with depressed individuals in troubled relationships. Finally, we discuss the potential of an attachment framework to facilitate integrative approaches to couples therapy for depression (Murray, 1983; Norcross & Freedheim, 1992).

EVIDENCE LINKING MARITAL DISCORD AND DEPRESSION

Are Marital Discord and Depression Clinically Intertwined?

Several bodies of literature provide empirical support for the marital discord model of depression and show that marital discord and depression are related. For example, on the basis of analyses of Epidemiologic Catchment Area research data collected from more than 3,000 interviews (Regier et al., 1984), Weissman (1987) reported a 25-fold increase in the relative risk of major depression for people in unhappy marriages. Likewise, using standard self-report questionnaires with a sample of 328 newly married couples, O'Leary, Christian, and Mendell (1993) found that maritally discordant spouses had a 10-fold increase in risk for depression compared with nondiscordant spouses. There seems little room for doubt that depression and marital discord are associated cross-sectionally (cf. Beach, Fincham, & Katz, in press).

Do Poor Marriages Predict Increased Vulnerability to Depression?

In a longitudinal study of 400 women, Brown and Harris (1986) examined the effect of marital support on depression. They found that at the time of the initial interview, negative marital interactions, such as arguing, strain, violence, and coldness, predicted greater vulnerability to depression. Indeed, women confronted with a severe difficulty or negative life event were more than three times as likely to become depressed if their marriage had been characterized by negative marital interactions. In a second study (Coryell, Endicott, & Keller, 1992), with less detailed measures but a larger sample (N = 3,119), researchers examined risk factors for onset of first episodes of depression. Over a 6-year interval, 12% of the participants experienced first episodes of major depression according to semistructured interviews and Research Diagnostic Criteria. Marital discord was found to be one of the primary predictors of onset of a first episode.

Does Marital Discord Predict Later Depression?

In the first longitudinal test with a national random probability sample of women working full time (N = 577), Beach and coworkers (Beach, Harwood, Horan, Katz, Blum, & Roman, 1996) found a significant effect of marital satisfaction on depressive symptoms 1 year later. Specifically, women who endorsed low levels of marital satisfaction showed greater depressive symptoms, even after investigators controlled for the relationship between marital satisfaction and depression at the initial assessment. These findings may represent a conservative estimate of the prospective effect of marital satisfaction on depressive symptoms among women, because prior research has suggested that employment mitigates the effects of marital stress on women's depression (Kandel, Davies, & Raveis, 1985), and all women in the Beach et al. sample were working full time. Because the sample was selected as a random probability sample of the United States, the findings can be generalized further than is the case when samples of convenience are used to estimate effects. Thus, the study by Beach et al. has helped to establish the presence of a reliable prospective effect of marital satisfaction on depressive symptoms.

In a more recent test of the hypothesized relationship between marital problems and depressive symptoms, Fincham and colleagues (Fincham, Beach, Harold, & Osborne, 1997) examined a series of complementary causal models in a sample of 150 newlywed couples. Couples were assessed at two time points separated by an 18-month interval. In a replication of earlier work, marital satisfaction and depressive symptoms were found to be related to each other cross-sectionally. For husbands, causal modeling suggested a greater causal effect going from earlier depressive symptoms to later marital satisfaction. For wives, marital satisfaction affected later depressive symptoms, but depressive symptoms did not exert a significant effect on later marital satisfaction. Accordingly, the Fincham et al. results suggest that the flow of causality from marital dissatisfaction to depression may be more pronounced when it is the wife rather than the husband who is depressed.

Does Marital Discord "Cause" Depression?

In a quasi-experimental study designed to examine the potential causal role of marital events in the formation of depressive symptoms, Christian, O'Leary, and Avery (1993) recruited 50 women who recently had experienced a significant negative marital event, such as abuse or discovery of a trust violation. Women were excluded from the sample if they had ever had a major depressive episode, because these researchers were interested in whether negative marital events would create an increased risk for a major depressive episode. Thirty-six percent of the women experiencing recent negative marital events were clinically depressed as assessed by the Structured Clinical Interview for the *Diagnostic and Statistical Manual of Mental Disorders* (3rd ed., rev.; American Psychiatric Association, 1987). This level of depression far exceeds both the point prevalence rate of depression for women generally (5%–9%; American Psychiatric Association, 1994) and the incidence of depression for women in the general population (2% per year; Kaelber, Moul, & Farmer, 1995). Accordingly, these data provide considerable support for the hypothesis that much of the excess risk for depression among maritally discordant couples may be attributable to the occurrence of negative marital events.
ol6

Can Depression "Cause" Marital Discord?

It is important to note that theory and data supporting prospective effects of marital discord on depression do not preclude instances of depression leading to marital discord. There is evidence that spouses of depressed people sometimes view their depressed partner as a burden (Barling, MacEwen, & Kelloway, 1991; Coyne et al., 1987). They also often see their partner's depressive behavior as putting them in an unpleasant bind (Biglan, Rothlind, Hops, & Sherman, 1989), and certain patterns of behavior, such as seeking reassurance from others, have more profound interpersonal consequences when combined with depression (Joiner, 1994; Joiner & Metalsky, 1995). In addition, recent longitudinal research on newlyweds implicates premarital dysphoria in husbands as a precursor of later marital discord for both partners, although much of the effect is attributable to lower premarital relationship adjustment (Beach & O'Leary, 1993). As these results make clear, the effect of marital discord or negative marital events on depression does not preclude an influence of depression on marital discord. It is important to note that the effect of marital discord on depression is not restricted to the general population or to those not seeking treatment. In a clinical sample, 70% of depressed and maritally discordant women believed their marital discord preceded their depression; 60% of these women believed that their marital discord was the primary cause of their depression (O'Leary, Risso, & Beach, 1990). It appears that marital discord can exert considerable influence over individual well-being and may precipitate episodes of depression.

CAN MARITAL THERAPY RELIEVE DEPRESSION?

There is evidence from well-controlled outcome research that supports the efficacy of marital therapy for treatment of depression in the context of marital discord. In three recent outcome studies, researchers examined reasonably well-specified marital therapies for depression and compared their effectiveness with that of widely used individual therapies (for a more detailed review of the treatment literature, see Beach, Whisman, & O'Leary, 1994). First, Beach and O'Leary (1992; O'Leary & Beach, 1990) randomly assigned 45 heterosexual couples with a depressed member to individual cognitive therapy (CT), conjoint behavioral marital therapy (BMT), or a 15-week waiting list condition. Both CT and BMT reduced depressive symptoms and were clearly superior to the wait-list control group in reducing those symptoms. However, only BMT improved the marital relationship, and there were large differences among the three conditions in marital outcome.

In a similar study, Jacobson, Dobson, Fruzzetti, Schmaling, and Salusky (1991) provided a broad brush replication and extension of the O'Leary and Beach (1990) results. Jacobson et al. randomly assigned 60 married women who had been diagnosed with depression to individual CT, BMT, or a treatment combining BMT and CT. Couples were not selected for the presence of marital discord. Accordingly, it was possible to examine directly whether BMT was helpful for maritally nondiscordant–depressed people. Contrary to the authors' prediction, Jacobson et al. found that the marital intervention was not helpful for alleviating depression in the absence of marital discord. However, in the half of the sample who reported some marital discord, BMT was as effective as CT in reducing depression. Furthermore, only BMT resulted in significant improvement in marital adjustment among discordant–depressed couples. Finally, CT also was effective in ameliorating depressive symptoms among the maritally discordant–depressed.

Both of the preceding studies involved BMT. Another research group randomly assigned 18 couples to either individual interpersonal psychotherapy (IPT; Klerman, Weissman, Rounsaville, & Chevron, 1984) or a newly developed version of IPT for couples (Foley, Rounsaville, Weissman, Sholomaskas, & Chevron, 1989). Foley et al. found that participants in both treatment groups exhibited a significant reduction in symptoms of depression, but they found no differential improvement on measures of depressive symptoms between the two groups. The interventions also produced equal enhancement of general social functioning. However, higher scores of marital adjustment were found for couple IPT than individual IPT at Session 16. Finally, Foley et al. reported that couple IPT was well received by participants when there was ongoing marital discord. Although based on a small sample, the results are consistent with those of the other two studies in this area.

This brief review suggests that marital therapy is an effective treatment of depression that occurs in the context of marital discord. In such cases, it is capable of reducing both marital difficulties and depressive symptoms, and it is well accepted by couples in which one partner is depressed. It is important to note that marital therapy for depression appears to be most appropriate for couples whose marital problems preceded the current depressive episode and who are experiencing problems in areas most likely to be addressed effectively by marital therapy. When marital problems are relatively mild or are viewed by clients as unrelated to their depression, individual approaches may be more appropriate (cf. O'Leary et al., 1990). For spouses who see their depression as directly related to their marital problems and who want to work on their marriage, clinicians should seriously consider marital therapy as either an adjunctive or a primary treatment. Although marital therapy appears promising as a treatment for depression, there is also considerable room for improvement in outcome and marked variability in response to marital therapy. To the extent that attachment theory can suggest new avenues of intervention that are complementary to those already tested, it is important to explore the implications of an attachment framework for intervention with co-occurring marital discord and depression.

ATTACHMENT THEORY

Infant Attachment Theory

Bowlby (1969/1980, 1982) proposed that infants develop a behavioral attachment system in order to keep caregivers nearby. The attachment system is activated under conditions of stress or discomfort, particularly during periods of separation from the caregiver. He observed that infants' responses to separation were characterized by a predictable sequence of emotions: protest, despair, and detachment. Protest includes such responses as crying, active searching for the caregiver, and resistance to others' attempts to soothe. Despair includes such responses as passivity and sadness. The final phase is emotional detachment.

In adulthood, individuals may exhibit similar types of responses to separations from the primary attachment figure, presumably the romantic partner. Protest behaviors may include nagging, pleading, and attempting to control the partner. It is interesting that these types of behaviors have been documented in depressed individuals' interactions with their spouses (Biglan, Lewin, & Hops, 1990; Coyne, 1976). Despair behaviors might include sadness and anhedonia. Finally, depressed individuals' defensive withdrawal and separation from their partners may be conceptualized as detachment. Of course, adult attachment behavior is not presumed to be an exact reenactment of infant attachment behavior. Instead, one might expect to find adult "versions" of infant responses. Attachment theorists typically look for "heterotypic continuity" (Sroufe, Carlson, & Schulman, 1993) or conceptual rather than literal continuity over time (Caspi & Herbener, 1990).

Bowlby (1969/1980, 1982) also described three defining functions of the attachment system. First, the attachment system serves a proximity-maintenance function, which keeps infants near their caregivers. A second function of the attachment system is to increase the availability of caregivers as a safe haven during times of distress. Bowlby noted that when infants are distressed or fearful, they are especially likely to turn to caregivers for support and comfort. This safe haven aspect of the attachment system is consistent with the focus on stress and social support of the marital discord model. Finally, infants use caregivers as a secure base from which they may explore the environment and engage in nonattachment, growth-oriented behavior (see also Hazan & Shaver, 1994).

In adulthood, individuals may exhibit behaviors that serve proximity-maintenance, safe haven, and secure base functions. These responses are most likely to be exhibited when the attachment system is activated. In particular, it is likely that marital discord activates the attachment system (Greenberg & Johnson, 1988; Kobak et al., 1994), which suggests that depressive behavior may serve some or all of these functions.

Infant Attachment Styles

In addition to articulating a sequence of attachment behaviors and describing the function of those behaviors, researchers on attachment also have focused on the identification of "attachment styles." Ainsworth and her colleagues (Ainsworth, Blehar, Walters, & Wall, 1978) described three styles of attachment in children on the basis of their responses to a "strange situation": secure, anxious–ambivalent, and avoidant. Children with secure attachment use the caregiver as a source of support during stress;

children with avoidant attachment do not use the caregiver as a source of support during stress; and children with anxious–ambivalent attachment make inconsistent attempts to use the caregiver as a source of support. Subsequent research has found that approximately 60% of infants are classified as secure, 25% are classified as avoidant, and 15% are classified as anxious–ambivalent (Campos, Barrett, Lamb, Goldsmith, & Sternberg, 1983). Empirical evidence suggests that the secure style is associated with better adjustment in childhood (Sroufe, 1983; Sroufe & Fleeson, 1988). The insecure styles are associated with a variety of adjustment difficulties, including increased dependence, less social competence, and less ego resilience (Elicker, Englund, & Sroufe, 1992; Urban, Carlson, Egeland, & Sroufe, 1991).

Adult Attachment Theory

Almost a decade after Ainsworth's (Ainsworth, 1978) initial research, Hazan and Shaver (1987) used their descriptions of attachment patterns to examine the way adults experience romantic relationships; they found proportions of adults classified as secure, avoidant, and anxious–ambivalent similar to those in infants. Although there is considerable debate as to whether there is a continuity between infant and adult attachment (Baldwin & Fehr, 1995), there is accumulating evidence that attachment processes operate in adulthood and are consequential in romantic relationships. However, the particular aspects of the attachment system that are most pertinent to relationship satisfaction may change as the relationship develops (Hazan & Shaver, 1994). When a person initially is attracted to a partner, his or her behavior is characterized by proximity maintenance, such as wanting to spend as much time as possible with the potential partner. Once the relationship is more established, safe haven types of behaviors increasingly become important. For example, at this stage, it is important not only to be physically close to the partner but also for the partner to be psychologically available during times of distress.

Adult Attachment Styles

Bartholomew and Horowitz (1991) developed an influential typology of attachment styles based on internal working models of self and others. Internal working models of self reflect the extent to which people view themselves as lovable. Internal working models of others reflect the extent to which people view others as dependable and capable of providing valuable resources. These researchers described four styles of attachment based on the combination of the positivity or negativity of the model of self with the positivity or negativity of the model of others: secure (positive self, positive others), dismissive (positive self, negative others), preoccupied (anxious–ambivalent; negative self, positive others), and fearful (negative self, negative others). Subsequent research has supported the construct validity of the four-category model (Griffin & Bartholomew, 1994), and the model has been extended to the study of dysphoria and marital discord.

Attachment Processes and Styles in Depression and Marriage

Over the past decade, attachment theory increasingly has been found to be a useful framework for explaining and understanding adult interactions and socioemotional reactions. In addition to predicting the quality of close relationships in adulthood, attachment style appears to have important implications for individual well-being and coping with interpersonal or major life stressors (Mikulincer, Florian, & Weller, 1993). It currently is believed that attachment styles reflect highly organized individual differences in cognition and affect that may play a central role in the way individuals deal with stressful or challenging life events and regulate emotion (Shaver et al., 1996). Because attachment styles have been associated with processes that are important in depression and marital interactions (Feeney & Noller, 1990), a consideration of attachment styles may contribute to an understanding of the relationship between marital discord and depression.

At a minimum, people with a "negative internal model of self" may be more vulnerable to the depressogenic effects of marital discord and perhaps less able to use social resources effectively in response to stress and dysphoria. In addition, "negative internal models of others" may be related to the propensity to engage in destructive, defensive, or self-protective relationship behavior. In turn, such reactions are predictive of relationship deterioration and marital dissatisfaction (Fincham & Beach, in press). Also, because relationship distress is likely to activate the attachment system, one might expect to observe behaviors that serve proximity-maintenance, save haven, or secure base functions. Next, we consider the ways in which depressive behavior may serve these functions in troubled relationships, as well as the impact of attachment styles on the expression of such behaviors.

PROXIMITY SEEKING IN THE CONTEXT OF DEPRESSION

Implications of Attachment Theory

Feelings of dysphoria and the perceived unavailability of the partner may energize and engage the attachment system, leading the individual to engage in protest behavior. As discussed earlier, dysphoria often occurs in the context of relationship dissatisfaction, and either relationship distress or dysphoria may act as a "threat" to the relationship. Thus, relationship distress may orient people toward protest behavior. There has been considerable empirical work examining interactions between depressed people and their spouses. Interactions with depressed partners have been found to include such behaviors as nagging, reassurance seeking, pleading, and attempting to control the partner's behavior (Biglan et al., 1990; Coyne, 1976; Joiner & Metalsky, 1995). Many of these interactions may be viewed as protest behaviors on the part of the depressed person in response to relationship distress.

Empirical work examining depressed individuals' interactions with their partners has come from differing orientations, such as behavioral and systemic perspectives. Both of these perspectives highlight the function of depressive behaviors in marital interactions. Biglan et al. (1990) proposed that depressive behavior, such as complaining, may be functional, although coercive, behaviors that are most likely to be reinforced in a home environment that is characterized by high levels of negative verbal behavior. This model is similar to a model developed from a family systems perspective by Coyne (1976), who proposed that depressive behavior is maintained or increased by the social environment. Coyne suggested that depressed people demand attention through complaints about the depression. Initially, these complaints serve to elicit caretaking behavior or ward off aggressive behavior on the part of the partner. However, over time, the depressed behavior that once elicited care and concern, and reduced the likelihood of aggressive behavior, begins to act as a "turnoff" to important others. Research has supported the role of depressive behavior in the context of potentially conflictual discussions with the partner (Schmaling & Jacobson, 1990). Depressive behavior is less likely than aggressive behavior to elicit hostile behavior from the partner, and it is therefore maintained (Biglan et al., 1985; Nelson & Beach, 1990; Schmaling & Jacobson, 1990). In summary, research from differing perspectives suggests that depressed people behave in a way that elicits attention and wards off hostility from their spouses, which may be conceptualized as protest under conditions of duress.

The way that depressed people go about eliciting responses from partners seems to have consequences for the marital relationship, which in turn may exacerbate depressive symptoms. Sexual behavior may also be conceptualized as a type of proximity-seeking behavior. Hazan and Zeifman (1994) suggested that sexual contact is likely to facilitate the development and maintenance of adult attachments. Given that lack of interest in sex is a common symptom of depression, it is interesting to conceptualize lack of sexual desire as a disruption in attachment. Lack of sexual desire could then be viewed as an adult manifestation of detachment and despair.

Implications of Attachment Styles

Attachment styles may help identify individual differences in both the quantity and the type of proximity-seeking behaviors that occur in response to dysphoria or relationship distress. People with a secure attachment (positive self, positive other) are likely to believe that important others will be consistently available to meet their needs. Thus, individuals with secure attachments may engage in proximity-seeking behaviors with a sense of efficacy that their needs will be met by the partner. Individuals with a dismissive attachment (positive self, negative other) are likely to believe that others do not have valuable resources to offer them in times of need. Thus, people who are dismissively attached might be less likely to engage in proximity-seeking behavior or to attempt to elicit proximity through protest or despair behaviors. People with a preoccupied attachment style (negative self, positive other) may believe that others do have valuable resources to offer them but that they are not the kind of person to whom others would spontaneously respond. People who have a preoccupied style may feel that they must "work overtime" to get attention from others. They may engage in excessive proximity-seeking behaviors, such as clinging, pleading, and seeking reassurance. For example, Sinclair and McCluskey (1996) found that couples who were having difficulties after the birth of a baby displayed more invasive behaviors, such as anxious following, than couples who were not having difficulties. The invasive behaviors were also related to gender, to attachment styles of each partner, and to communication patterns. Persons with a fearful attachment style (negative self, negative other) may feel conflicted in their attempts to seek others in time of distress. They may believe that important others are unlikely to meet needs but that there is nowhere else to turn (e.g., they cannot turn to the self).

MARRIAGE AS A SAFE HAVEN: THE ROLE OF SOCIAL SUPPORT IN DEPRESSION

Implications of Attachment Theory

Another primary function of the attachment system is to orient individuals to the attachment figure for comfort and support during times of need or distress. That is, the attachment figure serves as a "safe haven" for the individual. For example, an infant might search for her mother when she has been frightened by a loud noise. The notion of a safe haven seems relevant for adults, as well. The concept of "social support" seems to constitute an adult version of a safe haven because social support is presumed to reflect comfort and support offered by others.

Lack of social support or of a save haven may act as a vulnerability factor for developing depression. Brown and his colleagues have addressed this issue in their research. These authors found that the lack of a confiding relationship is a vulnerability factor in the development of depression in women (Brown & Harris, 1978). Furthermore, Brown and his colleagues (Brown, Andrews, Harris, Adler, & Bridge, 1986; Brown & Harris, 1986) found that women confronted with a severe difficulty or negative life event were more than three times as likely to become depressed if their marriage also had been characterized by negative interactions. Retrospective reports of these women suggested that the depression may have been attributable to the lack of support from the partner in times of need, especially if the women had expected support from the partner. Kobak and Hazan (1991) also described links between attachment, marital distress, emotional communication, and support. These researchers found that distressed couples were more likely than nondistressed couples to display negative affect during discussions about solving problems. Distressed couples also showed less support for each other than did nondistressed couples. Finally, lower attachment security scores were related to marital adjustment and behavior during problem-solving tasks.

These studies suggest that lack of social support in the face of negative life events may put an individual at risk for the development of a depressive episode. The stress of the acute negative life event activates the attachment behavioral system; therefore, the person encountering stress is likely to seek the attachment figure for comfort and support. If the person perceives that the attachment figure is not available, he or she may respond with "despair" and may be at a greater risk for the development of depressive symptoms.

In keeping with this view, recent empirical work suggests that attachment and negative life events are related to depression. Hammen et al. (1995) found that attachment style, interpersonal stresses, and their interaction predicted depression and other adjustment problems in women. For example, they found that women who reported that they could not depend on others and who were experiencing a greater number of stressful life events were more likely to be depressed than other women. In addition, they found that women who reported that they feared being abandoned in relationships and that they were experiencing a greater number of stressful life events were more likely to be depressed than other women. These findings suggest that attachment can act as a vulnerability factor in the face of negative life events.

In another series of studies involving college students, researchers, found that insecure attachment styles were associated with increases in depression over time (Roberts, Gotlib, & Kassel, 1996). It is interesting that these authors also found that the relationship between attachment and depression was mediated by dysfunctional attitudes and low self-esteem. These researchers suggested that attachment influences depressive symptoms through its impact on negative cognitions and self-esteem. This finding has been partially replicated by Whisman and McGarvey (1995), who found that the effect of perceived attachment to caretakers on dysphoria was partially mediated by dysfunctional attitudes in a college sample. Finally, Burge, Hammen, Davila, and Daley (1997) found that attachment-related cognitions interacted with initial symptoms to predict future depression (and other psychiatric symptoms) in a longitudinal study of female high school seniors. There is evidence from several studies, therefore, that attachment is related to cognition, which in turn affects depressive symptoms. It is possible that a positive relationship protects individuals with insecure attachment from developing depressive symptoms to the extent that the partner can challenge negative self-views. Alternatively, an insecurely attached individual in a poor relationship may be at greater risk for developing and confirming self-deprecating thoughts.

Implications of Attachment Styles

Whether individuals conceptualize marriage as a potential safe haven may be related to attachment styles. Individuals who are securely attached (positive self, positive others) may believe that they are "worth" the attention of others and that important others are available to meet their needs. During stressful times, these individuals may be prone to seek support and comfort from the attachment figure. Individuals who are dismissively attached (positive self, negative others) may be less likely to seek support from their spouse because they believe that the spouse does not have anything to offer. Individuals characterized by a preoccupied style (negative self, positive others) may be likely to engage in excessive support seeking during times of stress and may place unreasonable demands on the partner. This may be especially problematic; some research suggests that excessive reassurance seeking combined with negative affect and negative feedback seeking is likely to elicit negative responses from others (Joiner, Alfano, & Metalsky, 1992, 1993). This dynamic is likely to confirm preoccupied individuals' beliefs that they are not the kind of person to whom others will readily provide positive responses. Finally, fearfully attached (negative self, negative others) individuals' attempts at seeking support may be conflicted and are not likely to be effective.

Empirical work has shown that persons with different attachment styles respond differentially to social support, in terms of both support giving and support seeking. As discussed earlier, securely attached women were found to engage in more support-seeking behavior in the face of an anxiety-provoking situation (Simpson, Rholes, & Nelligan, 1992). Another group of researchers replicated these findings in a real-world situation. Mikulincer et al. (1993) examined responses to the threat of Iraqi scud missile attacks in Israel during the Gulf War. They found that securely attached individuals made greater use of social support as a way of coping with the anxiety associated with the threat of bombardment than did insecurely attached individuals. Avoidantly attached people showed increased use of distancing strategies relative to the other individuals. The results of these two studies suggest that individuals who are insecurely attached are less likely to use social support in times of need. Their reluctance to use social support may increase their vulnerability to depression in the face of negative life events. Priel and Shamai (1995) found that college students' subjective satisfaction with social support contributed to felt distress beyond the impact of attachment styles and that securely attached students perceived more social support than did insecurely attached students. The lack of use of social support among insecurely attached individuals may confirm prior expectations that the partner is unavailable to meet needs, which may perpetuate the cycle of failing to elicit social support as well as contribute to relationship distress. If social support can serve as a proxy for safe haven processes in attachment relationships, then attachment style acts as a moderator of the use of marriage as a safe haven.

MARRIAGE AS A SECURE BASE

Implications of Attachment Theory

The idea of marriage as a secure base points to the potential of the attachment system in adulthood to facilitate exploration and interaction with the world. Cummings and Davies (1996) suggested that as children develop, emotional "felt-security" becomes a goal in itself, rather than simply serving as a thermometer for the availability of caretakers in childhood. When emotional security is low, a child (or an adult) may be prompted to respond cognitively, emotionally, or behaviorally to increase felt-security. Adults may become more focused on the relationship and therefore have fewer resources to explore the environment to meet nonattachment needs. Such individuals may restrict employment opportunities or curb other interpersonal relationships in their efforts to increase felt-security in the romantic relationship. Restriction of outside activities in response to lowered felt-security (i.e., relationship distress) may place individuals at risk for developing depressive symptoms (Lewinsohn, 1974).

The ways that adults go about trying to restore felt-security with the primary attachment figure may be influenced by attachment styles. For example, the level of felt-security necessary to engage the attachment system may differ for individuals with different models of self. Those with preoccupied and fearful attachment styles may respond to smaller decreases in felt-security by engaging the attachment behavioral system.

Implications of Attachment Styles

In adulthood, a secure base allows individuals to explore the environment to meet other, nonattachment related needs and perhaps other attachment-related needs as well, such as relationships with peers. The extent and the quality of this exploratory behavior is likely to vary according to individuals' attachment style. People with secure attachment styles may feel more comfortable having some needs met outside the relationship through friendships, hobbies, or work satisfaction. Insecurely attached individuals who also are depressed may have great difficulty looking for such outside sources of satisfaction.

ATTACHMENT AND AN INTEGRATIVE MARITAL THERAPY FOR DEPRESSION

As discussed earlier, knowledge of attachment processes and attachment styles may increase the understanding of depression in the context of marriage. Next, we discuss how knowledge of attachment processes and attachment styles may suggest new approaches and help integrate existing approaches for the treatment of couples who are discordant and depressed.

Attachment Theory

Attachment theory helps integrate insights from behavioral, cognitive, emotion-focused, and object-relations orientations for therapy. For example, in traditional behavioral marital therapy with a depressed partner, couples are taught how to communicate effectively so that they can work toward compromise and change constructively (Jacobson & Margolin, 1979). Interventions are aimed at decreasing the mind reading and other inferences of one partner about the motivations of another partner. Emotion-focused therapy often tries to get at the softer, more basic emotions behind superficial conflict. For example, a wife's anger at a husband for being late is conceptualized as a reaction to a fear of abandonment on the part of the wife when the husband is not on time. An attachment framework might be presented to a couple as a way of highlighting the power of early experiences with parents and how those experiences may lead people to develop certain beliefs about the world. The couple's "hot spots" can be talked about in the context of this framework. This serves the dual advantage of externalizing the problem and taking the sting out of conflict (see Notarius, Lashley, & Sullivan, 1997).

Safe Haven

As previously discussed, the perceived availability of social support during times of stress maps on to the safe haven function in attachment relationships. Because an elevated level of depressive symptoms is associated with a problematic pattern of simultaneously seeking reassurance and negative feedback (Coyne, 1976; Joiner et al., 1993; Swann, Wenzlaff, Krull, & Pelham, 1992), it seems appropriate to help couples recognize and change the dysfunctional patterns of interaction that are likely to elicit rejection, even if the changes do not result in immediate reductions in symptoms of depression.

Secure Base

Attachment theory proposes the importance of marriage as a secure base from which spouses explore the environment to meet nonattachment needs. Increasingly, marital therapists are encouraging partners to take seriously the needs left unmet in the relationship and to explore alternative means of need satisfaction other than the partner (Christensen, Jacobson, & Babcock, 1996). Recognizing that the relationship will not be able to meet all needs, obtaining permission to explore the environment to meet these needs, and developing self-care strategies outside the relationship may increase relationship satisfaction (Beach et al., 1990). Increased relationship satisfaction may serve as a protective factor against the development of a depressive episode.

Attachment Styles

Recent work on attachment and marriage has suggested the potential value of expanding the cognitive–behavioral model of therapy for couples to include elements aimed at increasing understanding of, and changing, basic attachment style. Object-relations marital therapy has attended to these processes for quite some time, and it may be appropriate to borrow strategies for dealing with problematic attachment relationships from this perspective (e.g., Scharff & Scharff, 1991; Siegel, 1992), from interpersonal therapy approaches in the Sullivanian tradition (Benjamin, 1993; Klerman et al., 1984), and from emotion-focused therapy (Greenberg & Johnson, 1988). Particularly in cases in which early learning and attachment problems appear to have given rise to problematic internal representations of relationships (i.e., object representations), it may be that better understanding of depressed patients' working models of relationships will be critical in designing interventions (Blatt, 1974; Blatt, Quinlan, Chevron, McDonald, & Zuroff, 1982; Blatt & Zuroff, 1992). Furthermore, a consideration of attachment-related variables may be helpful in designing gender-sensitive object-relational therapy with depressed women (Kaslow & Carter, 1991). Indeed, in such cases, interventions more commonly associated with insight-oriented traditions may be critical in resolving long-standing problematic interaction patterns.

In addition, knowledge of attachment styles may help identify those at risk for developing depressive symptoms. Using a large, nationally representative sample, Mickelson and her colleagues found that individuals with an insecure attachment were more likely to experience a major depression episode and dysthymia (Mickelson, Kessler, & Shaver, 1997). Furthermore, Kobak and Hazan (1991) found that the percentage of securely attached individuals is higher in married couples than in unmarried individuals. This finding, which has been replicated in a sample of Dutch couples (Gerlsma, Brunk, & Mutsaers, 1996), suggests that marital status may confer some advantage on securely attached individuals and perhaps partially explain their decreased likelihood of depression. In addition, couples with two securely attached partners report significantly more intimacy than couples containing one or two insecure spouses (Senchak & Leonard, 1992). Thus, couples in marriages in which both spouses have a secure attachment style may be less likely to experience marital discord, and the individuals subsequently may be less likely to develop depressive symptoms in the context of marital discord.

Knowledge of attachment style may help the clinician generate hypotheses about the ways in which a particular client goes about soliciting social support, its likely effectiveness, and its likely impact on the partner. For example, an individual who is dismissively attached may not solicit social support during times of stress. This knowledge may guide clinicians in constructing interventions to facilitate support seeking. Another aspect of this issue is a consideration of the partner's attachment style. There is some evidence that there is complementary mating with regard to attachment style (Carnelley, Pietromonaco, & Jaffe, 1994) such that partners confirm self-views. This finding is consistent with other work examining the basic motive of affirmation of one's self-views, even if those self-views are negative (Swann, 1983; Swann, Hixon, & de La Ronde, 1992). For example, securely attached people are likely to be coupled with other securely attached people (Caspi & Herbener, 1990). Individuals who have a preoccupied attachment style are likely to be coupled with individuals with a dismissive attachment style. In this scenario, the preoccupied individual might seek the other during times of stress, only to find the other is not responsive to needs, which serves to confirm the preoccupied individual's belief that he or she is not worthy of true regard from others but instead must work all the time to obtain affection.

Knowledge of attachment styles may help clinicians, therefore, as they fine-tune general interventions for specific couples. The use of social support has been a mainstay in the treatment of depression in the context of marriage. A consideration of individuals' attachment styles may be helpful in implementing strategies aimed at increasing social support. For example, if an individual is dismissively attached, the clinician may spend a considerable amount of time explaining the importance and potential usefulness of social support and help the dismissively attached individual recognize when support is being offered by the partner. Finally, an assessment of the individual's attachment style may give the therapist ideas about how the client is likely to attach to the therapist and how to make appropriate interventions. This knowledge may help the therapist in structuring interactions for building rapport.

CASE ILLUSTRATION

Quite often, women presenting with depression in the context of marital discord report problems in the relationship having to do with lack of opportunity to express their feelings and to feel understood and accepted by their partner. Husbands of depressed wives often show a minimal response to their wives' complaints. From an attachment perspective, this problem might be viewed as a symbolic failure of the safe haven function of the marriage. Empathic listening may be one way to break through repetitive cycles of defensive interaction and to allow the couple to reestablish a well-functioning secure base. Alternatively stated, such skills may help create a "holding environment" that reduces defensive processes and allows for growth. From an attachment perspective, it is not so much that new skills that are being learned as it is that anxieties are being overcome. Accordingly, the therapist informed by an attachment perspective might listen for evidence of unspoken anxiety regarding abandonment or dismissive rejection of "intrusive control." Whereas such issues might not be addressed in the initial attempt at empathic listening, being aware of their presence may enhance the therapist's ability to follow the unspoken subtext of the interaction. The following transcript illustrates these attachment-related problems in a couple with a depressed wife.

> Husband: Wednesday night ... somebody called up, one of our clients, and asked if I wanted to go out to dinner with him ... and usually in that kind of situation, I come home and Ellie is asleep ... that night you were sitting up. It was just puzzling for me why you were ... knowing that Thursday was a workday.

> Wife: Is this the paraphrasing you're talking about? You're puzzled as to why I was waiting. When you had called, you said that you would be home at 10 or 11 ... 10 or 11 came and went and you weren't home, so I was getting worried. It was 20 after 1 when you came home. The later it got, the more awake I got. I was worried, that's all.

Husband:	I wouldn't have expected you to be awake because normally by that time you would have been tired and you would have gone to sleep.
Wife:	Yeah, but before that you said ...
Therapist:	Why don't you try paraphrasing that before you do anything else?
Wife:	You didn't expect me to be awake because usually I'm too tired to stay up that late. Normally, maybe, I couldn't have stayed up that late but the later ... it got so late and I thought something was wrong. I couldn't imagine a restaurant that would be open that late where people were allowed to stay and talk over business. The other thing that was keeping me awake was that when you had called to say you were going out to dinner, you said that he called on your night number, and I didn't even have a night number for you and this client has a night number? The more I thought about it, the more upset I got.
Husband:	OK, so you didn't ... you became upset because of not knowing about this night number. . . . So, you were thinking about the night number and that's what kept you awake.
Wife:	Yes, I wanted to discuss that with you.
Husband:	Why?
Wife:	Why? ... there are a million things running around in my mind right now ... umm ...
Therapist:	Why were you hurt?
Wife:	Because I thought that you didn't want me to be able to reach you ... that if you left the building ... I think it was a lack of trust and the more I thought ... about ... what if you wanted to leave the building, I would have no way of knowing. If I called, I am not able to call you. You could leave the building at 4:30 and not come home until 8 and say you were there, but I can't reach you, I don't know ... I have no way of checking on you.
Husband:	So, you were hurt really from not knowing about the number.
Wife:	Right ... first of all. But also, you have had this new night number in for a week or two, and you're telling me that the occasion hasn't come up for you to tell me about it. This is what I'm talking about.

Therapist: [Interrupting] Can you rephrase that more positively?

Wife: More positively .... It would have been nice if you had come home from work the day that they did that and said, "Guess what, you can reach me.' ... It would make me feel very good for you to offer me a way of communicating with you that I haven't been able to do.

Therapist: That was good.

Wife: It would make me feel very ... you know, like I'm part of your life. That you want me to be able to reach you when I need to.

Husband: So you're more comfortable with the situation when you can contact me.

Wife: Yeah.

Therapist: Did he get all of what you wanted to say? If not, maybe you can say it again in a different way and give him another chance to paraphrase.

Wife: Yeah. [To husband] There are little things that are going on in your life day to day, there has to be and they don't seem very important to you or very earth shattering.... You don't have to wait for major things in your life to let me know that is happening. If you could come home and share little things along the way then that lets me into what's going on with you. I try to do that with you, talk about very insignificant things, and I don't even know whether you're listening to me or not but I communicate to you.

Husband: So, what you're looking for is really the little communication, the little things that are going on in my life, just like your conversation to me as to what's going on in your class.

Wife: The difference I can see in ... I feel very ... I feel like a very unimportant part of your life when you don't share with me. I feel ... that I'm not worth your time ... it makes me get down on myself if you can't talk to me.

Husband: So, you feel basically down. You don't feel important if I don't talk to you about these little things. It affects your confidence ... because I'm not telling you the little things that are going on.

Therapist: That was pretty good as far as accepting responsibility for your feelings instead of attacking or criticizing George.

And George that was a pretty good job of paraphrasing and staying with Ellie instead of just nodding or giving a very short response.

Ellie's concern about her husband's possible infidelity maps on to the basic attachment concern of abandonment and availability of the partner. Such concerns are likely to activate the attachment system, and the couple might understand Ellie's desire to stay up and discuss relationship issues as a "protest" behavior. Also, as the couple makes progress in developing a secure base of their marriage, other relationship and personal issues can be addressed.

CONCLUSION

The preceding discussion highlights the usefulness of attachment theory in considering interpersonal processes in romantic relationships and how those processes might increase the understanding of the development of depression in the context of relationship dissatisfaction. Consideration of attachment processes (proximity maintenance, safe haven, secure base) and attachment styles serves as a potential bridge in the arena of treatment of depression in the context of couple distress. An attachment perspective reinforces and expands the important role of social support and stress, as described in the marital discord model of depression. A continuing focus on attachment processes in romantic relationships may help ground observations regarding attachment styles and clinical problems more firmly in attachment theory. In turn, this should facilitate the use of research in clinical practice and ease the translation of techniques between clinical orientations.

REFERENCES

Ainsworth, M., Blehar, M., Waters, E., & Wall, S. (1978). *Patterns of attachment: A psychological study of the strange situation.* Hillsdale, NJ: Erlbaum.

American Psychiatric Association. (1987). *Diagnostic and statistical manual of mental disorders* (3rd ed., rev.). Washington, DC: Author.

American Psychiatric Association. (1994). *Diagnostic and statistical manual of mental disorders* (4th ed.). Washington, DC: Author.

Baldwin, M. W., & Fehr, B. (1995). On the instability of attachment style ratings. *Personal Relationships, 2,* 247–261.

Barling, J., MacEwen, K. E., & Kelloway, E. K. (1991, November). *Effects of short term role overload on marital interactions.* Paper presented at the 25th annual convention of the Association for the Advancement of Behavior Therapy, New York.

Bartholomew, K., & Horowitz, L. (1991). Attachment styles among young adults: A test of a four-category model. *Journal of Personality and Social Psychology, 61*, 226–244.

Beach, S. R. H., Fincham, F. D., & Katz, J. (in press). Marital therapy in the treatment of depression: Toward a third generation of therapy and research. *Clinical Psychology Review.*

Beach, S. R. H., Harwood, E. M., Horan, P. M., Katz, J., Blum, J. C., & Roman, P. M. (1996, June). *Marriage and depression: Longitudinal effects.* Paper presented at the annual meeting of the International Network on Personal Relationships, Seattle, WA.

Beach, S. R. H., & O'Leary, K. D. (1992). Treating depression in the context of marital discord: Outcome and predictors of response to marital therapy vs. cognitive therapy. *Behavior Therapy, 23*, 507–528.

Beach, S. R. H., & O'Leary, K. D. (1993). Dysphoria and marital discord: Are dysphoric individuals at risk for marital maladjustment? *Journal of Marital and Family Therapy, 19*, 355–368.

Beach, S. R. H., Sandeen, E. E., & O'Leary, K. D. (1990). *Depression in marriage: A model for etiology and treatment.* New York: Guilford Press.

Beach, S. R. H., Whisman, M., & O'Leary, K. D. (1994). Marital therapy for depression: Theoretical foundations, current status, and future directions. *Behavior Therapy, 25*, 345–371.

Benjamin, L. S. (1993). *Interpersonal diagnosis and treatment of personality disorders.* New York: Guilford Press.

Biglan, A., Hops, H., Sherman, L., Friedman, L. S., Arthur, J., & Osten, V. (1985). Problem solving interactions of depressed women and their spouses. *Behavior Therapy, 16*, 431–451.

Biglan, A., Lewin, L., & Hops, H. (1990). A contextual approach to the problem of aversive practices in families. In G. R. Patterson (Ed.), *Depression and aggression in family interaction* (pp. 103–129). Hillsdale, NJ: Erlbaum.

Biglan, A., Rothlind, J., Hops, H., & Sherman, L. (1989). Impact of distressed and aggressive behavior. *Journal of Abnormal Psychology, 98*, 218–228.

Blatt, S. J. (1974). Levels of object representation in anaclitic and introjective depression. *Psychoanalytic Study of the Child, 29*, 107–157.

Blatt, S. J., Quinlan, D. M., Chevron, E. S., McDonald, C., & Zuroff, D. (1982). Dependency and self-criticism: Psychological dimensions of depression. *Journal of Consulting and Clinical Psychology, 50*, 113–124.

Blatt, S. J., & Zuroff, D. C. (1992). Interpersonal relatedness and self-definition: Two prototypes for depression. *Clinical Psychology Review, 12*, 527–562.

Bowlby, J. (1980). *Attachment and loss: Vol. 3. Loss.* New York: Basic Books.

Bowlby, J. (1982). *Attachment and loss: Vol. 1. Attachment.* New York: Basic Books. (Original work published 1969)

Brown, G. W., Andrews, B., Harris, T., Adler, Z., & Bridge, L. (1986). Social support, self-esteem and depression. *Psychological Medicine, 16*, 813–831.

Brown, G. W., & Harris, T. (1978). *Social origins of depression: A study of psychiatric disorders in women.* New York: Free Press.

Brown, G. W., & Harris, T. (1986). Establishing causal links: The Bedford College studies of depression. In H. Katschnig (Ed.), *Life events and psychiatric disorders: Controversial issues* (pp. 107–187). Cambridge, England: Cambridge University Press.

Burge, D., Hammen, C., Davila, J., & Daley, S. E. (1997). The relationship between attachment cognitions and psychological adjustment in late adolescent women. *Development and Psychopathology, 9,* 151–167.

Campos, J. J., Barrett, K., Lamb, M. E., Goldsmith, H. H., & Sternberg, C. (1983). Socioemotional development. In P. H. Mussen (Ed.), *Handbook of child psychology: Vol. 2. Infancy and developmental psychopathology* (pp. 783–915). New York: Wiley.

Carnelley, K. B., Pietromonaco, P. R., & Jaffe, K. (1994). Depression, working models of others, and relationship functioning. *Journal of Personality and Social Psychology, 96,* 127–140.

Caspi, A., & Herbener, E. S. (1990). Continuity and change: Assortive marriage and the consistency of personality in adulthood. *Journal of Personality and Social Psychology, 58,* 250–258.

Christensen, A., Jacobson, N. S., & Babcock, J. (1996). Integrative behavioral couples therapy. In N. S. Jacobson & A. S. Gurman (Eds.), *Clinical handbook of marital therapy* (2nd ed., pp. 31–64). New York: Guilford Press.

Christian, J. L., O'Leary, K. D., & Avery, S. (1993). *The impact of negative events in marriage and depression.* Unpublished manuscript, State University of New York at Stony Brook.

Coryell, W., Endicott, J., & Keller, M. (1992). Major depression in a nonclinical sample: Demographic and clinical risk factors for first onset. *Archives of General Psychiatry, 49,* 117–125.

Coyne, J. C. (1976). Depression and the response of others. *Journal of Abnormal Psychology, 85,* 186–193.

Coyne, J. C., Kessler, R. C., Tal, M., Turnbull, J., Wortman, C. B., & Greden, J. F. (1987). Living with a depressed person. *Journal of Consulting and Clinical Psychology, 55,* 347–352.

Cummings, E. M., & Davies, P. (1996). Emotional security as a regulatory process in normal development and the development of psychopathology. *Development and Psychopathology, 8,* 123–139.

Elicker, J., Englund, M., & Sroufe, L. A. (1992). Prediction of peer competence and peer relationships in childhood from early parent–child relationships. In R. D. Parke & G. Ladd (Eds.), *Family–peer relationships: Models of linkage* (pp. 77–106). Hillsdale, NJ: Erlbaum.

Feeney, J. A., & Noller, P. (1990). Attachment style as a predictor of adult romantic relationships. *Journal of Personality and Social Psychology, 58,* 281–291.

Fincham, F. D., & Beach, S. R. H. (in press). Marital conflict. *Annual Review of Psychology.*

Fincham, F. D., Beach, S. R. H., Harold, G. T., & Osborne, L. N. (1997). Marital satisfaction and depression: Different causal relationships for men and women? *Psychological Science, 8*, 351–357.

Foley, S. H., Rounsaville, B. J., Weissman, M. M., Sholomaskas, D., & Chevron, E. (1989). Individual versus conjoint interpersonal therapy for depressed patients with marital disputes. *International Journal of Family Psychiatry, 10*, 29–42.

Gerlsma, C., Brunk, B. P., & Mutsaers, W. C. M. (1996). Correlates of self-reported adult attachment styles in a Dutch sample of married men and women. *Journal of Social and Personal Relationships, 13*, 331–320.

Greenberg, L. S., & Johnson, S. M. (1988). *Emotionally focused therapy for couples.* New York: Guilford Press.

Griffin, D. W., & Bartholomew, K. (1994). The metaphysics of measurement: The case of adult attachment. In K. Bartholomew & D. Perlman (Eds.), *Attachment processes in adulthood: Advances in personal relationships* (Vol. 5, pp. 17–52). London: Jessica Kingsley.

Hammen, C. L., Burge, D., Daley, S. E., Davila, J., Paley, B., & Rudolph, K. D. (1995). Interpersonal attachment cognitions and prediction of symptomatic responses to interpersonal stress. *Journal of Personality and Social Psychology, 104*, 436–443.

Hazan, C., & Shaver, P. (1987). Romantic love conceptualized as an attachment process. *Journal of Personality and Social Psychology, 52*, 511–524.

Hazan, C., & Shaver, P. R. (1994). Attachment as an organizational framework for research on close relationships. *Psychological Inquiry, 5*, 1–22.

Hazan, C., & Zeifman, D. (1994). Sex and the psychological tether. In K. Bartholomew & D. Perlman (Eds.), *Attachment processes in adulthood: Advances in personal relationships* (Vol. 5, pp. 151–178). London: Jessica Kingsley.

Jacobson, N. S., Dobson, K., Fruzzetti, A. E., Schmaling, D. B., & Salusky, S. (1991). Marital therapy as a treatment for depression. *Journal of Consulting and Clinical Psychology, 59*, 547–557.

Jacobson, N. S., & Margolin, G. (1979). *Marital therapy: Strategies based on social learning and behavior exchange principles.* New York: Brunner/Mazel.

Joiner, T. E., Jr. (1994). Contagious depression: Existence, specificity to depressed symptoms, and the role of reassurance-seeking. *Journal of Personality and Social Psychology, 67*, 287–296.

Joiner, T. E., Alfano, M. S., & Metalsky, G. I. (1992). When depression breeds contempt: Reassurance-seeking, self-esteem, and rejection of depressed college students by their roommates. *Journal of Abnormal Psychology, 101*, 165–173.

Joiner, T. E., Alfano, M. S., & Metalsky, G. I. (1993). Caught in the crossfire: Depression, self-consistency, self-enhancement, and the response of others. *Journal of Social and Clinical Psychology, 12*, 113–134.

Joiner, T. E., Jr., & Metalsky, G. I. (1995). A prospective test of an integrative interpersonal theory of depression: A naturalistic study of college roommates. *Journal of Personality and Social Psychology, 69*, 778–788.

Kaelber, C. T., Moul, D. E., & Farmer, M. E. (1995). Epidemiology of depression. In E. E. Beckham & W. R. Leber (Eds.), *Handbook of depression* (pp. 1–35). New York: Guilford Press.

Kandel, D., Davies, M., & Raveis, V. H. (1985). The stressfulness of daily social roles for women: Marital, occupational and household duties. *Journal of Health and Social Behavior, 26,* 64–78.

Kaslow, N. J., & Carter, A. S. (1991). Gender-sensitive object-relational family therapy with depressed women. *Journal of Family Psychology, 5,* 116–135.

Klerman, G. L., Weissman, M. M., Rounsaville, B. J., & Chevron, E. S. (1984). *Interpersonal psychotherapy of depression.* New York: Basic Books.

Kobak, R. R., & Hazan, C. (1991). Attachment in marriage: Effects of security and accuracy of working models. *Journal of Personality and Social Psychology, 58,* 273–280.

Kobak, R., Ruckdeschel, K., & Hazan, C. (1994). From symptom to signal: An attachment view of emotion in marital therapy. In S. M. Johnson & L. S. Greenberg (Eds.), *The heart of the matter* (pp. 46–71). New York: Brunner/Mazel.

Lewinsohn, P. M. (1974). A behavioral approach to depression. In R. M. Friedman & M. M. Katz (Eds.), *The psychology of depression: Contemporary theory and research* (pp. 157–185). New York: Wiley.

Mickelson, K. D., Kessler, R. C., & Shaver, P. R. (1997). Adult attachment in a nationally representative sample. *Journal of Personality and Social Psychology, 73,* 1092–1106.

Mikulincer, M., Florian, V., & Weller, A. (1993). Attachment styles, coping strategies, and posttraumatic psychological distress: The impact of the Gulf War in Israel. *Journal of Personality and Social Psychology, 64,* 817–826.

Murray, E. J. (1983). Beyond behavioral and dynamic therapy. *British Journal of Clinical Psychology, 22,* 127–128.

Nelson, G. M., & Beach, S. R. H. (1990). Sequential interaction in depression: Effects of depressive behavior on spousal aggression. *Behavior Therapy, 21,* 167–182.

Norcross, J. C., & Freedheim, D. K. (1992). Into the future: Retrospect and prospect in psychotherapy. In D. K. Freedheim (Ed.), *History of psychotherapy: A century of change* (pp. 881–900). Washington, DC: American Psychological Association.

Notarius, C. I., Lashley, S. L., & Sullivan, D. J. (1997). Angry at your partner? Think again. In R. J. Sternberg & H. Hojjat (Eds.), *Satisfaction in close relationships* (pp. 219–248). New York: Guilford Press.

O'Leary, K. D., & Beach, S. R. H. (1990). Marital therapy: A viable treatment for depression and marital discord. *American Journal of Psychiatry, 147,* 183–186.

O'Leary, K. D., Christian, J. L., & Mendell, N. R. (1993). A closer look at the link between marital discord and depressive symptomatology. *Journal of Social and Clinical Psychology, 13,* 31–41.

O'Leary, K. D., Risso, L. P., & Beach, S. R. H. (1990). Attributions about the marital discord/depression link and therapy outcome. *Behavior Therapy, 21*, 413–422.

Priel, B., & Shamai, D. (1995). Attachment style and perceived social support: Effects on affect regulation. *Personality and Individual Differences, 19*, 235–241.

Regier, D. A., Myers, J. K., Kramer, M., Robins, L. N., Blazer, D. G., Hough, R. L., Eaton, W. W., & Locke, B. Z. (1984). The NIMH Epidemiologic Catchment Area program: Historical context, major objectives, and study population characteristics. *Archives of General Psychiatry, 41*, 934–941.

Roberts, J. E., Gotlib, I. H., & Kassel, J. D. (1996). Adult attachment security and symptoms of depression: The mediating roles of dysfunctional attitudes and low self-esteem. *Journal of Personality and Social Psychology, 70*, 310–320.

Scharff, D. E., & Scharff, J. S. (1991). *Object relations couple therapy.* Northvale, NJ: Jason Aronson.

Schmaling, K. B., & Jacobson, N. S. (1990). Marital interaction and depression. *Journal of Abnormal Psychology, 99*, 229–236.

Senchak, M., & Leonard, K. E. (1992). Attachment styles and marital adjustment among newlywed couples. *Journal of Social and Personal Relationships, 9*, 51–64.

Shaver, P. R., Collins, N., & Clark, C. L. (1996). Attachment styles and internal working models of self and relationship partners. In G. J. O. Fletcher & J. Fitness (Eds.), *Knowledge structures in close relationships* (pp. 25–61). Hillsdale, NJ: Erlbaum.

Shaver, P. R., & Hazan, C. (1993). Adult romantic attachment: Theory and evidence. In W. H. Jones & D. Perlman (Eds.), *Advances in personal relationships* (Vol. 4, pp. 29–70). London: Jessica Kingsley.

Siegel, J. (1992). *Repairing intimacy.* Northvale, NJ: Jason Aronson.

Simpson, J. A., Rholes, W. S., & Nelligan, J. S. (1992). Support seeking and support giving within couples in an anxiety-provoking situation: The role of attachment styles. *Journal of Personality and Social Psychology, 62*, 434–446.

Sinclair, I., & McCluskey, U. (1996). Invasive partners: An exploration of attachment, communication and family patterns. *Journal of Family Therapy, 18*, 61–78.

Sroufe, L. A. (1983). Infant–caregiver attachment and patterns of adaptation in preschool: The roots of maladaptation and competence. In M. Perlmutter (Ed.), *Minnesota Symposium in Child Psychology* (Vol. 16, pp. 41–83). Hillsdale, NJ: Erlbaum.

Sroufe, L. A., Carlson, E., & Schulman, S. (1993). Individuals in relationships: Development from infancy through adolescence. In D. Funder, R. Parke, C. Talminson-Keasey, & K. Widaman (Eds.), *Studying lives through time* (pp. 315–342). Washington, DC: American Psychological Association.

Sroufe, L. A., & Fleeson, J. (1988). The coherence of family relationships. In

R. A. Hinde & J. Stevenson-Hinde (Eds.), *Relationships within families: Mutual influences* (pp. 27–47). Oxford, England: Oxford University Press.

Swann, W. B., Jr. (1983). Self-verification: Bringing social reality into harmony with the self. In J. Suls & A. G. Greenwald (Eds.), *Social psychological perspectives on the self* (Vol. 2, pp. 33–66). Hillsdale, NJ: Erlbaum.

Swann, W. B., Jr., Hixon, J. G., & de La Ronde, C. (1992). Embracing the bitter "truth": Negative self-concepts and marital commitment. *Psychological Science, 3*, 118–121.

Swann, W. B., Jr., Wenzlaff, R. M., Krull, D. S., & Pelham, B. W. (1992). Allure of negative feedback: Self-verification strivings among depressed persons. *Journal of Abnormal Psychology, 101*, 293–306.

Urban, J., Carlson, E., Egeland, B., & Sroufe, L. A. (1991). Patterns of individual adaptation across childhood. *Development and Psychopathology, 1*, 237–255.

Weissman, M. M. (1987). Advances in psychiatric epidemiology: Rates and risks for major depression. *American Journal of Public Health, 77*, 445–451.

Whisman, M. A., & McGarvey, A. L. (1995). Attachment, depressotypic cognitions, and dysphoria. *Cognitive Therapy and Research, 19*, 633–650.

12

DEPRESSED PARENTS AND FAMILY FUNCTIONING: INTERPERSONAL EFFECTS AND CHILDREN'S FUNCTIONING AND DEVELOPMENT

E. MARK CUMMINGS AND PATRICK T. DAVIES

In comparison to the historical focus on genetic (Kashani et al., 1981) and cognitive (Abramson, Metalsky, & Alloy, 1989) models, the role of the interpersonal experiences of depressed individuals has only recently reached ascendance. Interpersonal approaches stress how reciprocal links between individuals and their social environments contribute to the causes and consequences of depression (Coyne, 1976a, 1976b). As such, the focus on socioemotional domains complements genetic and cognitive approaches.

Broader, more inclusive models are required to account for the causes, origins, and course of depression. Although cognitive processes are integral to the symptoms of depression, the effects may be based on interpersonal experience and do not provide a complete account of the phenomenon (Coyne & Gotlib, 1983; Gotlib & Hammen, 1992). With roots in transactional models, interpersonal approaches focus on the dynamic, reciprocal interaction between depressive social contexts and individuals over time.

In contrast to a mechanistic conceptualization of causes and consequences of depression as simple, additive, linear chains of factors (e.g., dominant gene theory) or the statistical interaction of a limited number of factors (e.g., Personal Constitution × Environment = Psychopathology), in interpersonal approaches depression is viewed as an integral part of a broad, complex matrix of interdependent social and emotional processes (Cummings & Cicchetti, 1990; Sameroff, 1995).

Interpersonal approaches stress how individuals relate to key persons in their lives. Relationships with family members form a core of the environmental and interpersonal circumstances pertinent to depression (Cummings & Cicchetti, 1990). A major category of interpersonal effects within families concerns the children, who are affected by, and also affect, depressed parents. Children of depressed parents are two to five times more likely to develop psychopathology, including depression, than children of nondepressed parents (Beardslee, Bemporad, Keller, & Klerman, 1983). The interpersonal perspective provides a useful guidepost for explicating the processes responsible for the outcomes of children with depressed parents by underscoring the significance of (a) the dynamic, interdependent nature of relations among children of depressed parents, their families, and extrafamilial contexts over time; (b) family and ecological characteristics accompanying depression that serve as mediators of children's developmental trajectories; and (c) interpersonal resources that protect children from risk by promoting psychological resilience and competence (Cicchetti & Toth, 1995).

Inspired by the accumulating evidence for the significance of close relationships in interpersonal approaches (e.g., Downey & Coyne, 1990), we previously advanced a family model for conceptualizing the link between depressed parents and child adjustment (Cummings & Davies, 1992, 1994b). Within the model, depressive family environments marked by complex, reciprocal relations among (a) impairments in child-management techniques (e.g., lax monitoring, harsh and inconsistent discipline), (b) exposure to parental characteristics and symptoms of depression (e.g., sad affect, unresponsiveness), (c) marital discord, and (d) child characteristics (e.g., temperament, sex, developmental level) were conceptualized as proximal causes and conditions responsible for the impact of parental depression on children.

In this chapter, we further develop this model by advancing a theory that builds on attachment theory to address the reasons children are affected by depressive family environments. In this theory, referred to as the *emotional security hypothesis* (Cummings & Davies, 1996; Davies & Cummings, 1994), we propose that family-wide influences extending beyond traditional notions of parent–child interaction (e.g., marital conflict, parent–child attachment, exposure to family emotional climates of sadness and dysphoria) increase children's risk for psychopathology by threatening their emotional security. Furthermore, emphases are placed on the role of emotional as well as cognitive processes in children's organization and motivation to respond in the face of family events and stressors.

We begin by providing justification for our contention that interpersonal theories emphasizing social and emotional processes are necessary for understanding the adjustment of children of depressed parents. Next, we review the primary pathways between parental depression, family process, and child adjustment in our model, including factors less often considered in models for the transmission of risk from depressed parents to their children (i.e., parent–child emotional relationships or attachments, marital conflict). Throughout, we pay particular attention to findings published since the most recent reviews (Cummings & Davies, 1994b; Downey & Coyne, 1990; Gelfand & Teti, 1990). At various points, we outline an emotional security hypothesis for understanding the effects of multiple family contexts on children of depressed parents, and we close with a systematic treatment of various points significant to the interpretation of our model.

WHY ARE SOCIAL AND EMOTIONAL MODELS OF DEPRESSION NECESSARY?

Interpersonal perspectives on depression do not exclude cognitive processes but advance a more inclusive domain of experiential and contextual influences (see Coyne & Gotlib, 1983). As we illustrate later, although evidence for cognitive models of relations between parental depression and child adjustment has been reported, complementary social and emotional models also receive considerable support and are necessary for an understanding of the impact of parental depression on children (e.g., Hammen et al., 1995).

The negative social–cognitive processes of depressed parents may shape and organize their responses to children's behavior, thereby affecting the children. Associations have been reported between maternal depression, negative cognitions about the children, and parenting impairments (Christensen, Phillips, Glasgow, & Johnson, 1983; Richard, Forehand, Wells, Griest, & McMahon, 1981). For example, in one recent study investigators found statistical evidence for a model whereby depressed mothers distorted or exaggerated their children's behavior problems (Fergusson, Lynskey, & Horwood, 1993). However, it is also possible on the basis of these analyses that (a) mothers' appraisals accurately reflected children's greater behavior problems at home in comparison to school (e.g., according to teacher reports) or (b) relations between parental depression and negative appraisals were an artifact of "third" variables such as maternal personality characteristics, marital distress, or family discord. Another group reported evidence that negative attributions of child behavior mediated relations between maternal depressed mood and child psychological problems by fueling harsh parenting practices (Geller & Johnston, 1995). However, analyses again left room for the possibility that other family processes accounted for effects. Furthermore, relations between depressed mood, attributions, and parenting impulses were moderate at best.

Lower levels of self-efficacy about parenting in depressed mothers may impair parenting (Teti, Gelfand, & Pompa, 1990). For example, researchers recently reported that depressed mothers perceived more difficulty in caring for their infants and regarded their infants as more bothersome than did nondepressed mothers, and infants of depressed mothers performed more poorly on Bayley tests (Whiffen & Gotlib, 1989). However, the infants were also rated by observers as more tense, less content, and deteriorating more quickly under stress than children of nondepressed mothers, so that preexisting emotional problems may have negatively affected their performance in testing situations.

Depressed parents may communicate with children in ways that increase the children's sense of responsibility and guilt for the adult depression (Zahn-Waxler, Kochanska, Krupnick, & McKnew, 1990). Children of depressed parents are exposed to negative emotions and despair as well as negative attributional strategies—that is, mixed expressions of personal responsibility and helplessness (Garber, Braafladt, & Zeman, 1991; Hoeksema, Wolfson, Mumme, & Guskin, 1995; Thompson & Caulkins, 1996). These parental cognitions may induce in the children excessive or inappropriate caregiving for the parents. However, relatively little is known about the impact of these exposures on children's behavior. Furthermore, elevated caregiving toward parents might also be explained by processes of emotional and behavioral sensitization that are due to repeated exposure to parental negative emotions and conflicts. Elevated exposure to parental negative emotions and conflicts has been shown both in studies of children's responding in the home and in controlled analogue studies in the laboratory to increase children's caregiving toward parents (Cummings & Davies, 1994a; also see El-Sheikh & Cummings, 1995; El-Sheikh, Cummings, & Reiter, 1996). Also, children's caregiving behaviors may reflect efforts to regulate, reduce, or terminate their parents' negative emotions or conflicts in the service of their own sense of emotional security, because these events threaten the safety and security of the family, rather than being a response to the cognitive contents of the parents' behavior per se (Davies & Cummings, 1994).

Whereas exposure to depressed parents' cognitive processes clearly affects children, the evidence suggests that cognitive factors provide no more than a partial explanation for children's adjustment outcomes. In recent studies, weak relations have been reported for teaching or puzzle-completion tasks (Goldsmith & Rogoff, 1995; Nolen-Hoeksema, Wolfson, Mumme, & Guskin, 1995), IQ (Kershner & Cohen, 1992), linguistic measures of communication deviance (Hamilton, Jones, & Hammen, 1993), and academic performance (Davies & Windle, 1997; Tannenbaum & Forehand, 1994). Also, because children have no direct access to internal processes of parental cognitions, such constructs are more precisely seen as only indirectly affecting children by affecting parental interaction within the family. Furthermore, socioemotional processes are also clearly implicated in studies that identify the operation of cognitive processes. In one recent study, it was reported that depressed and well mothers could not be distinguished in their descriptions of child behavior expressed in affectively neutral tones but that depressed mothers were more negative when affectively hostile statements were considered (Goodman, Adamson, Riniti, & Cole, 1994).

At the same time, the evidence indicates that socioemotional processes in interpersonal relations are important for understanding the links between parental depression and child development (see commentaries by Cummings, 1995a; Hops, 1992, 1995; Kershner & Cohen, 1992; Lyons-Ruth, 1995). Again, in recent studies only, one finds repeated support for the roles of emotionality, emotion regulation, and related socioemotional processes in relations between parental depression, child functioning, and child adjustment (Goodman et al., 1994; Hamilton, Hammen, Minasian, & Jones, 1993; Hamilton, Jones, & Hammen, 1993; Kershner & Cohen, 1992; Tannenbaum & Forehand, 1994; Tarullo, DeMulder, Martinez, & Radke-Yarrow, 1994; Whiffen & Gotlib, 1989; see conceptualizations and reviews by Cummings & Davies, 1994b; Downey & Coyne, 1990; Lee & Gotlib, 1991; Thompson & Caulkins, 1996).

In addition, similar themes are evident in recent research on childhood depression, which is one psychopathological outcome associated with parental depression (Cummings & Davies, 1994b; Downey & Coyne, 1990). Researchers found that whereas depression, social competence, and academic competence were intercorrelated, social relations were a proximal cause of depression but academic competence was not (D. A. Cole, Martin, Powers, & Truglio, 1996), thereby supporting a social, but not an academic, deficit model of depression (D. A. Cole, 1990, 1991).

In summary, the evidence suggests that whereas cognitive factors are significant influences (see Cummings & Davies, 1994b, for a more extensive review of the research), they do not provide a complete explanation for the greater risk for the development of psychopathology among children of depressed parents. Again, a significant, even primary, role of social and emotional processes in relations between parental depression, family functioning, and child development is indicated; these themes are more fully developed in the following sections.

FAMILY PROCESSES AND PARENTAL DEPRESSION: SOCIAL AND EMOTIONAL INFLUENCES ON CHILDREN

Numerous patterns of dysfunctional relationships linked with depression have been identified, including marital disruption and hostility, insecure attachment relationships (see chapters 7 and 11, this volume; Hammen et al., 1995), and disturbed parent–child interactions (Downey & Coyne, 1990; Gotlib & Hammen, 1992). Figure 1 presents an overview of our family process model of depression (Cummings & Davies, 1994b), which places special emphasis on parent–child relations and marital conflict as key pathways of influence on children but also recognizes the role of the child in reciprocal family relationships. Because of space limitations, the review that follows can only be illustrative, providing a selection of recent findings (see Cummings & Davies, 1994b; Downey & Coyne, 1990, for more extensive treatments). However, before proceeding with the review, we briefly consider the tenets of an emotional security hypothesis.

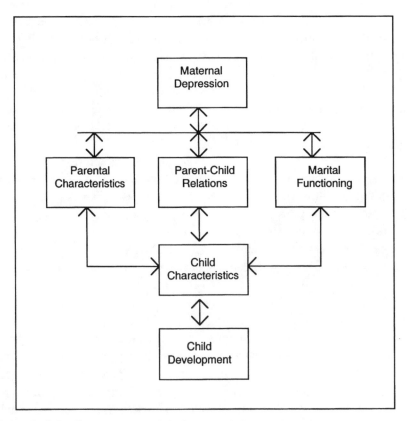

Figure 1. A family process model of parental depression.

THEORETICAL CONSIDERATIONS: EMOTIONAL SECURITY AS A MEDIATOR OF THE EFFECTS OF PARENTAL DEPRESSION ON CHILDREN

A family process perspective lays a foundation for a family-wide model for children's emotional security as a mediator or moderator of adjustment outcomes. Although family processes do not influence children solely as a function of the implications for emotional security, our hypothesis is that emotional security is one important mediator of the effects of parental depression and other family processes on children.

As we demonstrate later, multiple family systems are influenced by parental depression. Our hypothesis is that children's emotional security derives from various family systems that may be influenced by parental depression and that these relations have implications for children's adjustment. Specifically, we postulate that multiple relations within the family affect children's emotional security, which regulates, and is regulated by, interpersonal events within the family. Children's concerns about emotional security—that is, their interpretation of the meaning of family relations, for their own well-being and the well-being of the family—play a role in their regulation of emotional arousal and in their organization and motivation to respond in the face of interpersonal stressors (Cummings & Davies, 1995, 1996; Davies & Cummings, 1994). Over time, the impact of these response processes and of changing internalized representations of parental, intrafamilial, and personal relations accumulates and comes to have significant implications for children's short- and long-term adjustment.

Emotional regulation and emotional security are central constructs in many accounts of both normal development and the development of psychopathology (P. M. Cole, Michel, & Teti, 1994). Similar to current approaches to emotions as regulatory processes (Thompson, 1994; Thompson & Caulkins, 1996), and to a functionalist perspective on human emotion, emotional security is seen as central to the regulation of action, as constructive and organizing, and not just as a by-product of experience to be controlled and modulated—that is, essentially disorganizing. Felt-security as a goal is defined from an organizational perspective, reflecting the entire pattern of the individual's reactions to events in relation to emotional security as a goal (emotions, behaviors, thoughts, and physiological responses) as opposed to simply those reactions that are "conscious" and reported as "feelings." Emotional security is a response not only to the immediate person–environment context but also to the historical context of the person's experience with familial situations (e.g., past exposures to interparental hostility). Finally, consistent with a commitment to testable theory, component regulatory systems are specified, including processes of emotional regulation, regulation of exposure to family affect, and internal representation of family events (Davies & Cummings, 1994; Cummings & Davies, 1995, 1996). Following is a definition of emotional security from Cummings and Davies (1996), which provides a framework to relate while reviewing the evidence for our model; later, we return to themes concerning an emotional security hypothesis for relations between parental depression and child adjustment.

> Emotional security is a latent construct that can be inferred from the overall organization and meaning of children's emotions, behaviors, thoughts, and physiological responses, and serves as a set goal by which children regulate their own functioning in social contexts, thereby directing social, emotional, cognitive, and physiological reactions. (p. 126)

PARENTAL CHARACTERISTICS: BEHAVIORAL AND EMOTIONAL PATTERNS OF DEPRESSION

Depressed parents are more negative, unsupportive, and intrusive with their children than nondepressed parents (Cox, Puckering, Pound, & Mills, 1987). In comparison to nondepressed parents, depressed parents evidence more negative affective styles (fewer supportive statements, guilt induction, criticism, intrusive statements; Hamilton, Jones, & Hammen, 1993) and more depressed affect (sadness, anxiety, downcast eyes; Radke-Yarrow, Nottleman, Belmont, & Welsh, 1993) in interactions with their children. These behaviors are linked with critical coping styles in children, which are, in turn, associated with later symptoms of affective disorders (Hamilton, Hammen, et al., 1993; Tarullo, DeMulder, Martinez, & Radke-Yarrow, 1994). Analogue studies have shown that exposure to parental dysphoria and withdrawal in infants and toddlers induce responses of distress, disorganization, aggression, withdrawal, and lack of focused activity (e.g., Cohn, Campbell, Matias, & Hopkins, 1990; Cohn & Tronick, 1983; Seiner & Gelfand, 1995).

Although an "internalizing" profile is characteristic of depression, high levels of irritability and aggression are also manifested during depressive episodes (Weissman & Paykel, 1974). Patterns of parental emotional insensitivity, withdrawal, and hostility are linked with children's adjustment problems (Cummings & Davies, 1994b). One group recently reported strong evidence that poor mother–child interactional quality was a partial mediator of the link between maternal depressive symptoms and child externalizing problems (Harnish, Dodge, Valente, & the Conduct Problems Prevention Research Group, 1995).

Symptoms of depression repeatedly have been related to children's socioemotional functioning and adjustment, therefore, including their emotional regulation and quality of interpersonal relations within the family. Because parental unavailability, withdrawal, unsupportiveness, and hostility are linked with children's emotional security within the family (Cummings & Davies, 1995), these data are consistent with an emotional security hypothesis.

DEPRESSION AND PARENT–CHILD RELATIONS

Besides effects of exposure to depressive symptoms, or carryover of depressive symptoms into parent–child interaction, there also are effects of changes in parent–child relations, that is, child-management practices and parent–child attachment (see Figure 1).

Depression and Child-Management Practices

On the one hand, in comparison to nondepressed parents, depressed parents are more inconsistent, lax, and generally ineffective in child management and discipline. On the other hand, when they are not yielding to the child's demands, they are more likely to engage in direct, forceful control strategies and are less likely to end disagreements in compromise (Fendrich, Warner, & Weissman, 1990; Forehand, Lautenschlager, Faust, & Graziano, 1986; Kochanska, Kuczynski, Radke-Yarrow, & Welsh, 1987; Zahn-Waxler, Iannotti, Cummings, & Denham, 1990). Recently, investigators found particularly strong support (i.e, replicated across different regions, parental gender, and different measures for the same constructs) for a conceptual model whereby parental depressive symptoms, induced by stressful events, compromised child-management practices, leading to adolescent deviance (antisocial behavior, low academic achievement, poor peer relations; Conger, Patterson, & Ge, 1995; see also Ge, Conger, Lorenz, Shanahan, & Elder, 1995).

The processes traditionally proposed to account for the effects of ineffective child management are not as obviously related to emotionality or emotional security as those in other interpersonal contexts within the family (e.g., parent–child attachment). The explanatory constructs involve behavioral contingencies or social–cognitive mechanisms, but they may provide only a limited explanation of the impact of depression in these contexts. The complexity and richness of communication and expression between parents and children may be lost in such explanations. For example, emotionality is salient in discipline situations. Fear and anxiety may disrupt children's internalization of parental disciplinary messages (Grusec & Goodnow, 1994). When negative emotional arousal is induced, social interpretations and judgments of others may become distorted, especially when children are already susceptible to emotional dysregulation (Dodge & Somberg, 1987). There is also evidence that children's sense of emotional security provides an "emotional context" for their behavior in disciplinary situations, affecting the likelihood of disobedience or noncompliance with parents' wishes (Lay, Waters, & Park, 1989; Londerville & Main, 1981). In short, there is increasing recognition of the role of emotion in child management and of the need for more satisfactory accounts of emotional processes (Cummings & Davies, 1995; Davies & Cummings, 1994).

Depression and Attachment

There has been interest, both historically and in recent years, in the contribution of disturbances in parent–child attachment to the transmission of depression within families (Cummings & Cicchetti, 1990). Although the case has not yet been made in long-term longitudinal research, there are empirical and conceptual bases for postulating that parental depression contributes to the development of insecure parent–child attachment that might, in turn, increase children's risk for adjustment problems, including depression. For example, parental emotional unavailability and psychological insensitivity are highly associated with parental depression and insecure parent–child attachment. Furthermore, the cognitive and emotional contents of models of the self and others thought to characterize insecurely attached children bear similarities to patterns characteristic of depression (Cummings & Cicchetti, 1990).

Parental depression increases the probability of insecure parent–child attachments (Lyons-Ruth, Connell, Zoll, & Stahl, 1987; Radke-Yarrow, Cummings, Kuczynski, & Chapman, 1985; Radke-Yarrow, McCann, DeMulder, Belmont, Martinez, & Richardson, 1995; van Ijzendoorn, Goldberg, Kroonenberg, & Frenkel, 1992; see reviews by Cicchetti & Toth, 1995; Cummings & Davies, 1994b). In one recent study, maternal depression during infancy predicted insecure attachment 13 months later for infants and preschoolers; in particular, disorganized–disoriented attachments were three to four times more likely in children of depressed mothers than in children of well mothers (Teti, Gelfand, Messinger, & Isabella, 1995). It is notable that a substantial literature indicates that insecure attachments are associated with a wide range of adjustment problems in children (Cummings & Davies, 1994a).

A case study serves to illustrate the extent of children's emotional insecurity within the parent–child relationship that can be associated with parental depression. For infants and young children, attachment security is assessed in a laboratory procedure called the Strange Situation, in which children are briefly separated from their parents, and assessments focus on the parent–child reciprocity, the emotional quality of interactions, and, in particular, the effectiveness of parents in fostering children's emotional regulation following stressors, especially reunions. Securely attached children evidence positive emotionality and reciprocity with parents during the reunions, are seldom distressed before separations, and effectively use the parents as a source of security following reunion and other stressors. In contrast, the following case study, adapted from Cummings (1990), illustrates the emotional insecurity of a 34-month-old child of a parent with bipolar depression:

> Before the first separation, the child was already whiny toward the mother and hyperactive. The approach of another adult upset the child, and the child had difficulty being comforted. The child cried loudly when the mother left the first time and could not be comforted by another adult. The child was extremely difficult for the mother to comfort in reunion, and her cries had an odd quality. The child assumed a huddled, depressed posture and showed sad affect, not looking at the mother in response to her overtures. The child was affectless and disconnected in appearance during the second separation and didn't greet the mother, averted her gaze, and was unresponsive to the mother's overtures.

This example illustrates the extreme disturbances in the functioning of the interpersonal relationship of attachment in the provision of security that have been reported in children of depressed parents. The documented effects of parental depression on children's attachment security are evidence for an emotional security hypothesis. However, there is a need for further articulation of these relations. Traditional attachment classifications, for example, may not adequately characterize attachment patterns in the special case of children of depressed parents. Children of depressed parents may be exposed to emotional communications that are especially ambiguous, changeable, unreliable with regard to meaning, and negative, which may contribute in unknown ways to emotional insecurity in the children. In addition, standard approaches of characterizing parent–child interactions in terms of emotional sensitivity, responsivity, and warmth, which may be adequate for normal samples, may only partially capture critical dimensions of emotionality in families with parental depression, leaving important questions about the possible extremity of disturbances in security provision in the context of parent–child relations in these family environments.

DEPRESSION AND MARITAL FUNCTIONING

A traditional view is that children are affected by family functioning only as a result of parent–child interaction. However, recent work makes clear the need for a broader systems view of family influences on children. In particular, there is now substantial evidence for the impact of marital conflict on children's adjustment (Emery, 1982; Grych & Fincham, 1990; also see Figure 1). Furthermore, children are affected by their observations as bystanders. A case study adapted from work by Cummings, Zahn-Waxler, and Radke-Yarrow (1981) shows the sensitivity of even very young children, in this instance 20-month-old Clara, to marital conflict. The mother is the narrator.

> I was very upset and I wasn't feeling well. The house was a shambles, where the children had been pulling out toys, and the dishes had not been done, and there were clothes on the floor. I put Clara to bed and ran down to the kitchen to put away some things. Dick was in the kitchen, and I yelled at him, "I don't care if this house stays a mess forever, I am not picking up another damn thing." I screamed at the top of my lungs. And in a squeaky voice I heard Clara say, "Mommy, shut up" about three times.

The following case study, adapted from Cummings and Davies (1994a), of a 5-year-old girl's responses to anger directed at the mother by another adult woman (confederate) in an experiment illustrates further the impact on children's emotional security of even mild expressions of unresolved conflict involving the parents:

> The woman expressed anger at the mother for her negligence in filling out forms. The child showed distress and sadness while looking down at the floor, and her active play stopped. She was preoccupied with the angry scene. She looked to her mother and smiled, but the smile quickly faded. After the woman left, she said to her mother, "Doesn't she know that it takes awhile to fill out forms?" and she moved to stand near her mother. After a few seconds, she sat on the side of the mother's chair and put her arm around the mother. She paid special attention to how the mother was filling out forms and made comments, "Is your name on the forms now? Are you putting circles on them?" She pointed to specific areas on the forms as she spoke. Finally, she said, nervously, "Are you done with the forms yet?"

Adult depression has been found to covary with marital hostility, distress, and anger, and marital discord may mediate the effects of maternal depression on children; marital discord may be a more proximate predictor of certain child outcomes than is maternal depression per se (Wierson & Forehand, 1992; see reviews by Downey & Coyne, 1990; Cummings & Davies, 1994b). In one recent study, researchers found that maternal depressive symptoms were no longer a significant predictor of female adolescent depressive symptoms after family factors were controlled but that marital conflict, adverse family events, and low family socioeconomic status remained significant predictors (Fergusson, Horwood, & Lynskey, 1995). Another group found strong support for a mediational model whereby girls' greater vulnerability to family discord (e.g., marital discord, low family warmth, parenting problems) accounted for the impact of maternal depressive symptoms on their psychological adjustment (Davies & Windle, 1997).

Children's emotional security also derives from the quality of the marital relationship (Davies & Cummings, 1994). Children have excellent bases for concern about the quality of marital relations. Marital conflict can threaten children's emotional or even physical well-being, cause family life to be emotionally unpleasant, and forecast family dissolution, which causes economic and interpersonal hardships and many difficult life changes. High marital conflict may undermine children's emotional security, with implications for children's functioning in stressful situations as well as their psychological adjustment over the long term (Cummings & Davies, 1995; Davies & Cummings, 1994). Recently it was demonstrated that children's emotional security (regulation of emotions, attempts to regulate parental emotions, and representations of marital relations) mediated adjustment outcomes of marital conflict, particularly adjustment in terms of internalizing problems (Davies & Cummings, 1998). Mediators are the "generative mechanism" by which an independent variable (e.g., parental depression) influences outcomes (e.g., child adjustment; Baron & Kenny, 1986); emotional security that is based on the quality of marital relations emerges as a factor that may mediate outcomes in children of depressed parents.

Because there has been little adaptation of assessments to family environments with parental depression, is is not known whether there are peculiar forms of conflict in these families and, if so, their impact. The prevalence and impact of nonverbal communication, anger mixed with dysphoria, unresolved conflict, and lack of explanation in families with depressed parents merit investigation (Cummings & Davies, 1994b). A goal for future research should be to differentiate styles of marital conflict associated with parental depression and to study their impact (Zahn-Waxler, Cummings, McKnew, & Radke-Yarrow, 1984).

Furthermore, what are the interrelations between emotional security related to marital conflict and emotional security related to parent–child attachment? Are the models additive or multiplicative, and how do the effects sum? A central tenet of the emotional security hypothesis is that one must consider the multiple aspects of family environments (e.g., various parent–child systems, marital system) and the action of multiple systems on common processes and outcomes (e.g., emotional security) to account for effects (Cummings & Davies, 1995; Davies & Cummings, 1994). Answers to these questions must await future research.

CHILD CHARACTERISTICS

Children are important in shaping interpersonal relations in families, and their characteristics are a factor in their own risk for adjustment problems (Coyne, Burchill, & Stiles, 1991).

Temperament

Difficult temperament may moderate children's responses to depressive familial environments (Crockenberg, 1986; Wachs & Gandour, 1983). Moderators specify the strength or direction of relations between an independent variable (e.g., depression) and an outcome (e.g., child adjustment; Baron & Kenny, 1986; Holmbeck, 1997). In one study, investigators reported associations between mothers' ratings of difficult temperament and their depression, low competence, marital problems, and restricted parental role (Sheeber & Johnson, 1992). Another group found that during the first days of life, children of depressed parents were more unresponsive and lethargic, and displayed poorer orienting skills, than children of nondepressed parents (Abrams, Field, Scafidi, & Prodromidis, 1995). Other researchers have found a pattern of right frontal asymmetry in depressed mothers and their infants that may be an indicator of biological vulnerability (Field, Fox, Pickens, & Nawrocki, 1995; Field, Pickens, Fox, Nawrocki, & Gonzalez, 1995). Although relatively few studies have been done to examine this issue, there is evidence that constitutional vulnerabilities factor into children's relational problems within the family and proneness for difficulties with emotional regulation and emotional security (Cummings & Davies, 1994b, 1996).

Gender and Age

In contrast to earlier conceptualizations, recent work has suggested that boys are not necessarily at greater risk than girls. Gender differences are complexly intertwined with developmental level. In particular, it appears that whereas boys may exhibit greater susceptibility than girls to depressive family environments in childhood (Fergusson et al., 1993; Kershner & Cohen, 1992), this trend reverses in adolescence (Davies & Windle, 1997; Radke-Yarrow, Nottleman, Belmont, & Welsh, 1993; Tarullo et al., 1994; Thomas & Forehand, 1991). Hypotheses to explain this shift center around the notion that adolescent girls are socialized to value interpersonal and familial relationships more than are boys (Hops, 1995; Hops, Sherman, & Biglan, 1990) and are more likely to feel caught in the middle (Buchanan, Maccoby, & Dornbusch, 1991). From the perspective of an emotional security hypothesis, these results indicate that the implications of family events for an individual's sense of emotional security may depend on age and gender as well as on the status of interfamilial relations (e.g., parent–child, marital).

ADDITIONAL THEMES

Relations among parental depression, family processes, and child adjustment are not simple; one-to-one correspondences between depression and family processes (e.g., insecure attachment), and between family processes and child outcomes, should not be expected and, in fact, are not found. As is common in interpersonal approaches (Coyne, 1976a, 1976b), interrelations between environmental and interpersonal circumstances surrounding parental depression are complex (see Cummings, 1995a).

Adjustment Problems Are a Probability, Not a Certainty

Parental depression increases the probability, or risk, of adjustment problems in children, but adjustment problems at the level of diagnosis of psychopathology are far from inevitable. Many children of depressed parents develop adaptively and competently, and some develop into well- or even high-functioning individuals. These facts highlight the importance of protective and resilience factors in the individual and in the family (e.g., positive life events; Hamilton, Jones, & Hammen, 1993).

Degree of Depression Influences Degree of Children's Risk

The degree of risk is a direct function of the severity and chronicity of parental depression (Campbell, Cohn, & Meyers, 1995; Fergusson & Lynskey, 1993; Radke-Yarrow et al., 1993; Seifer, 1995). When parental depression is mild, transient, or short term, there may be little or no impact on the children (Campbell et al., 1995; Radke-Yarrow et al., 1985). However, percentages of children with adjustment problems may be high when the extent of parental psychopathology in the child's lifetime is high (Radke-Yarrow et al., 1985).

Relations Between Depression and Family Processes Are Reciprocal and Bidirectional

Although family processes mediate the impact of parental depression on children, these processes may not be unique to depression; they may be generally robust predictors in their own right of children's adjustment. Furthermore, family processes (e.g., levels of chronic stress, single parenthood) may be better predictors than maternal depression of parental behavior (e.g., Hamilton, Jones, & Hammen, 1993), and maternal behavior may be a better predictor of children's outcomes than maternal diagnosis per se (Hamilton, Hammen, Minasian, & Jones, 1993). Thus, relations between parental depression and family functioning are complex, with family processes influencing depression and depression influencing family processes (e.g., Beach, Arias, & O'Leary, 1987; Beach & Nelson, 1990); parental depression is complexly intertwined in the broader operation of family systems.

Risk and Protection Depend on the Broader Family Context

The effects of specific family processes may also depend on the broader family context, which highlights the importance of studying both high-risk and normal groups for a fuller understanding of causal relations in family environments (Cicchetti & Toth, 1995). For example, different relations between variables may be obtained when broader family environments are benign (i.e., normal) versus deviant (i.e., at risk). One group found that negative maternal attitudes predicted child psychopathology in depressive family environments but not in nondepressive environments (Goodman, Adamson, Riniti, & Cole, 1994). In another study, it was found that a good father–child relationship was a protective factor against the effects of high (but not low) maternal depressive symptoms on children's adjustment problems (Tannenbaum & Forehand, 1994). However, behaviors that are positive in other contexts might be precursors of later maladaptation in these family environments, which indicates the significance of interpersonal context. For example, caring behavior by children or tenderness by depressed mothers—particularly when the former is motivated by threat to self—extreme levels of concern for others, and emotional dysregulation (Radke-Yarrow, Zahn-Waxler, Richardson, Susman, & Martinez, 1994)—and when the latter is reflective of parental enmeshment, indulgence, and overprotection (Radke-Yarrow et al., 1993)—have been linked with greater adjustment problems later in development. As another example, for boys from backgrounds associated with high risk for problems of aggressiveness, maternal depression may simultaneously serve as a risk factor (i.e., increased depressive symptoms) and a protective factor (i.e., decreased aggressiveness; Wall & Holden, 1994).

These considerations underscore the importance of identifying mediating processes and process relations in terms of well-defined and specific pathways among maternal depression, family process, and child psychopathology; they indicate the diminishing returns that result from continuing simply to document correlations between diagnostic categories of parental and child adjustment. In particular, experiments, which have been neglected in clinical and family research, may be essential to establish more firmly the directions of effect and process relations (e.g., Goldsmith & Rogoff, 1995; Seiner & Gelfand, 1995; see Cummings, 1995b). It is important to "unpack" the multidimensional nature of parental depression, including the role of buffers and protective factors, and to appreciate the transactional, reciprocal nature of parent–child interaction (see the section on this subject that follows).

EMOTIONAL SECURITY AS A MEDIATOR:
COMPARISONS WITH OTHER MODELS

The literature illustrates the importance of social and emotional processes in the family for understanding the effects of parental depression on children. The problem now is to make more order out of complexity, not to advocate further for the complexity of the issues. One aim should be to differentiate between family processes and child outcomes in families at high and low risk because of parental depression. All aspects of family and child functioning are unlikely to be equally and highly negatively affected by parental depression. Furthermore, some problems may be evident in high-stress contexts but not in low-stress contexts (Tarullo et al., 1994).

The interpersonal perspective has involved a broadening of the range of factors considered to explain depression but relatively tentative suggestions concerning theory, rather than a set of formal, well-delineated theoretical propositions (Coyne, Downey, & Boergers, 1992). This area is maturing, and theory is needed to guide research to the next step, that is, the development of advanced models for processes and pathways of relations among parental depression, family dysfunction, and child development.

How and why do depressive family contexts shape children's developmental trajectories, particularly in the development of maladaptation? Disturbances in attachment have long been implicated theoretically and empirically in the development, maintenance, and intergenerational transmission of depression in families (Cummings & Cicchetti, 1990). Given the higher incidence of marital conflict and insecure attachments in homes with parental depression and the familial patterns of emotional communication and psychological unavailability linked in other research to emotional insecurity in children, it makes sense conceptually that the issue of emotional security plays a mediating role in risk for adjustment problems in children of depressed parents. Furthermore, we build on attachment theory but shift the emphasis from the evolutionary–ethological origins of attachment theory to the regulation of emotional well-being and security as a goal in itself (see our definition of emotional security, given earlier). Emotional security in our model derives from general family functioning, including marital relations, not simply the parent–child relationship. Although we certainly do not contend that emotional security is the only operational mediating process, we do argue that it is a key domain or element of process functioning. We posit a family-wide conceptualization of emotional security as a theoretically guided model for future study of the development of children of depressed parents.

Rooting Emotional Security Within a Broader Relational Systems Perspective

Our purpose here is to advance an emotional security theory for the sets of interpersonal processes in the family that are particularly affected by parental depression (e.g., attachment, marital functioning). Our theory is a specific application or subclass of the relational systems approach, with similarities to other models in its concern with contexts that focus on family subsystems and goals of interpersonal relations (i.e., emotional security).

Lee and Gotlib (1991) advanced notions to explain why different forms of family disturbance (e.g., marital discord, divorce, parental depression) predicted common child outcomes, hypothesizing that different family stressors may affect child development through common emotional processes in the family system. Presenting ideas that are similar to an emotional security hypothesis, they called for family systems perspectives in which the comorbidity of family stressors is considered. The most promising mediators were identified as those involving emotional processes of parental availability and children's sense of security or confidence in their parents. In essence, these are arguments for the construction of a family-wide emotional security model to account for the impact of depressed parents on their children. The importance of the emotional security hypothesis is the conceptualization of the *specific* processes and functions of emotional security within a family-systems framework (for other, related conceptualizations, see Feldman & Downey, 1994; Thompson & Caulkins, 1996; Wierson & Forehand, 1992).

Lyons-Ruth (1995) argued for the development of theoretical frameworks that center on relational systems, which were seen as important for understanding the intergenerational transmission of maladjustment within depressive family contexts. Consistent with the functionalist perspective on human emotion, relational systems models maintain that an individual's well-being and functioning are most usefully considered within the interpersonal context. Patterns of behavior and psychopathology are conceptualized as components and mechanisms of control systems that regulate interpersonal relations. Of fundamental importance for understanding the development of psychopathology is the specification of critical contexts of interpersonal relations, the goals within these contexts, and the success in achieving these goals. According to Lyons-Ruth, relational *contexts* that are particularly promising include (a) attachment relationships, (b) coercive parent–child interactions, and (c) hostile marital relations. The *goals* of interpersonal relations outlined as providing a significant step toward understanding maladaptation include (a) security in attachment relationships, (b) global self-worth and positive self-appraisals, and (c) extent of control in interpersonal relations. Finally, Lyons-Ruth also highlighted the importance of internal working models or implicit representational systems underlying relational and psychological disturbances.

The emotional security hypothesis also emphasizes the role of contexts of (a) parent–child emotional relationships, (b) parental control and management techniques, and (c) quality of marital relations. Furthermore, as a central issue, emotional security is viewed as a goal relevant to understanding contexts of family discord and child psychopathology. Within our conceptual framework, emotional security also has implicit theoretical ties with two other goals of relational systems. First, global self-worth and positive self-appraisals can be seen as developing from internal representations of family life. Second, whereas the lack of control or predictability in parental discipline situations may compromise children's sense of security, children's feelings of having too much control (e.g., parent–child enmeshment) may lead to psychological problems that are funneled through the issue of emotional security (Cummings & Davies, 1995).

Differences Between an Emotional Security Hypothesis and Other Relational Systems Perspectives

The emotional security hypothesis differs from other recent propositions advocating for relational perspectives primarily in its specificity. The emotional security hypothesis is a specific, well-defined application of the relational systems perspective. Rather than highlighting the potential roles of multiple, diverse goals of interpersonal relations in understanding developmental psychopathology, we focus on understanding a single goal within precisely defined family contexts. The aim is a coherent, parsimonious theory amenable to programmatic, empirical testing. The model takes full advantage of the mutual interplay between theory and research, with the theory serving as a heuristic for research and the research serving as an empirical foundation for the subsequent refinement of theory.

Our perspective also differs in its specification of the role of relational strategies and goals in the development of adaptation and maladaptation. We theorize that negative family processes (e.g., high marital conflict, insecure parent–child attachment) are vulnerability factors that increase the risk of psychopathology (outcomes) by compromising children's emotional security (i.e., they are mediators). Within our perspective, negative family factors compromise children's emotional security, which in turn is a precursor to later psychopathology. In addition to having an important role in some forms of psychopathology, therefore, emotional security may be a precursor and etiological mechanism for the development of the disorder.

CONTRIBUTIONS TOWARD A TRANSACTIONAL MODEL OF RELATIONS BETWEEN ATTACHMENT AND DEPRESSION

The emotional security hypothesis is consistent with themes of a transactional perspective on relations between attachment and depression. Cummings and Cicchetti (1990) outlined the evidence for a transactional model for relations between attachment and depression, placing attachment in the context of a broad array of experiential and biological influences that, in complex interplay during children's development, affect risk for depression. Within a model in which a multiplicity of child and environmental factors was assumed to operate in interaction during development to account for risk for depression, attachment was conceptualized as an important contributor to protection or risk because it is related to the individual's sense of security. In this chapter, we expand on this transactional model of the origins of an individual's sense of emotional security to include a consideration of family-wide events and occurrences as contributing to vulnerability.

COMPONENTS OF EMOTIONAL SECURITY AS A REGULATORY SYSTEM

Emotion-based theories are sometimes limited in terms of their operationalization of constructs (Thompson, 1994). Accordingly, a direction in the development of this model is to advance precise criteria for the operationalization of emotional security. Emotional security, therefore, is defined as a latent construct describing the set goal of regulatory functioning, with various well-defined regulatory systems that are testable subsumed within emotional security as an operating process. These components are separate but also interdependent in the organization of emotional regulation in the service of emotional security. In the following sections, we address this important theme with the aim of greater elaboration and more precise definition of emotional security as a psychological variable and regulatory system.

Emotional Regulation

This component refers to children's emotional arousal and their capacity for emotional regulation to the extent that they can be inferred from subjective feelings, physiological arousal, and overt expression of emotion; it includes consideration of intensity, latency between exposure to a stressor and response, and difficulty in reducing negative affect (Thompson, 1994). For example, insecure attachments and marital and family hostility each energize multiple emotion systems in the face of stress, reducing the capacity to regulate emotionality. One finding is that children who experience physical abuse or who witness repeated hostility between parents have greater difficulty than other children regulating their emotions (Cummings et al., 1981; Lyons-Ruth et al., 1987).

Regulation of Exposure to Family Affect

Controlling their exposure to family affect is another way for children to regulate their emotional security. Whereas these responses may appear to be signs of desirable functioning, there is evidence that high amplitudes of caregiving for parents signals underlying insecurity. For example, histories of high marital conflict are linked with children's greater disposition to mediate or by other means regulate their exposure to marital conflict (J. S. Cummings, Pellegrini, Notarius, & Cummings, 1989; O'Brien, Margolin, John, & Krueger, 1991) as well as with greater risk for adjustment problems (Emery, 1982; Grych & Fincham, 1990).

These responses make sense from the point of view of children from discordant homes. A common problem in high-conflict homes is parental mismanagement of negative affect, with the result being spiraling levels of hostility and spillover of negativity into other family subsystems (e.g., the parent–child subsystem). Consequently, children in these homes may feel more threatened by conflict and more motivated to intervene as a means of preventing increased family stress; these interventions may, in fact, effectively function to achieve this goal in the short-term, thereby restoring children's security.

Internal Representations of Family Relations

Internal representations may be both accurate representations of reality and alterations of reality in the service of emotional security (e.g., deactivation, dismissing strategies). Children's internal representations based on past experiences play an important role in their adjustment to stress, including their primary assessment of the negativity, threat, and self-relevance of events, and their secondary appraisal of why the event is occurring, who is responsible, and whether they have adequate coping skills (Grych & Fincham, 1990). As in cognitive and information-processing theories (Crick & Dodge, 1994), in emotion-based theories, children's appraisals of family events are seen as both reflecting and affecting their emotional security. A fundamental proposition is that children actively process the meaning that events have for their own well-being throughout a stressful event, with continuing implications for their responding.

CONCLUSION

We have presented evidence for relations among parental depression, family relationships, and child adjustment and have described emotional security as one of the processes that may mediate relations among these three variables. This theoretical model is intended as a stimulus for future research aimed at understanding the bases for relations among parental depression, family process, and child adjustment. In addition, we hope that this model will provide insights valuable to clinical practice in this area.

Many questions and issues remain. For example, there is the possibility of a confounding influence of genetic factors in the family processes that are emphasized. The role of biological and genetic factors in contributing to interpersonal family processes that influence child outcomes associated with parental depression merits investigation. An even more urgent need is for direct, prospective tests of this model, including samples of children of depressed parents. As we have shown, multiple familial and interpersonal contexts of children's functioning with regard to the goal of emotional security are pertinent to developmental models of emotional security as a factor in normal development and the development of psychopathology in children of depressed parents. Studies are needed that allow simultaneous examination of parental depression, family process, children's emotional security, and psychological adjustment so that researchers may begin to test this complex causal chain systematically. Such work holds promise both for theoretical models of depression and for the application of these findings to clinical practice.

REFERENCES

Abrams, S. M., Field, T., Scafidi, F., & Prodromidis, M. (1995). Newborns of depressed mothers. *Infant Mental Health Journal, 16,* 233–239.

Abramson, L. Y., Metalsky, G. I., & Alloy, L. B. (1989). Hopelessness depression: A theory-based subtype of depression. *Psychological Review, 96,* 358–372.

Baron, R., & Kenny, D. (1986). The mediator–moderator variable distinction in social psychological research: Conceptual, strategic, and statistical considerations. *Journal of Personality and Social Psychology, 51,* 1173–1182.

Beach, S. R. H., Arias, I., & O'Leary, K. D. (1987). The relationship of marital satisfaction and social support to depressive symptomatology. *Journal of Psychopathology and Behavioral Assessment, 8,* 305–316.

Beach, S. R. H., & Nelson, G. M. (1990). Pursuing research on major psychopathology from a contextual perspective: The example of depression and marital discord. In G. Brody & I. Sigel (Eds.), *Methods of family research: Biographies of research projects: Vol. II. Clinical populations* (pp. 227–259). Hillsdale, NJ: Erlbaum.

Beardslee, W., Bemporad, J., Keller, M. B., & Klerman, G. L. (1983). Children of parents with a major affective disorder: A review. *American Journal of Psychiatry, 140,* 825–832.

Buchanan, C. M., Maccoby, E. E., & Dornbusch, S. M. (1991). Caught between parents: Adolescents' experience in divorced homes. *Child Development, 62,* 1008–1029.

Campbell, S. B., Cohn, J. F., & Meyers, T. (1995). Depression in first-time mothers: Mother–infant interaction and depression chronicity. *Developmental Psychology, 31,* 349–357.

Christensen, A., Phillips, S., Glasgow, R. E., & Johnson, S. M. (1983). Parental characteristics and interactional dysfunction in families with child behavior problems: A preliminary investigation. *Journal of Abnormal Child Psychology, 11,* 153–166.

Cicchetti, D., & Toth, S. (1995). Developmental psychopathology and disorders of affect. In D. Cicchetti & D. J. Cohen (Eds.), *Developmental psychopathology: Vol. 2. Risk, disorder, and adaptation* (pp. 369–420). New York: Wiley.

Cohn, J. F., Campbell, S. B., Matias, R., & Hopkins, J. (1990). Face-to-face interactions of postpartum depressed and nondepressed mother–infant pairs at 2 months. *Developmental Psychology, 26,* 15–23.

Cohn, J. F., & Tronick, E. (1983). Three-month-old infants' reaction to simulated maternal depression. *Child Development, 54,* 185–190.

Cole, D. A. (1990). Relation of social and academic competence to depressive symptoms in childhood. *Journal of Abnormal Psychology, 99,* 422–429.

Cole, D. A. (1991). Preliminary support for a competency-based model of depression in childhood. *Journal of Abnormal Psychology, 100,* 181–190.

Cole, D. A., Martin, J. M., Powers, B., & Truglio, R. (1996). Modeling causal relations between academic and social competence and depression: A multitrait–multimethod longitudinal study of children. *Journal of Abnormal Psychology, 105,* 258–270.

Cole, P. M., Michel, M., & Teti, L. (1994). The development of emotion regulation and dysregulation: A clinical perspective. In N. Fox (Ed.), The development of emotion regulation: Biological and behavioral considerations. *Monographs of the Society for Research in Child Development, 59*(2–3, Serial No. 240), 73–102.

Conger, R. D., Patterson, G. R., & Ge, X. (1995). It takes two to replicate: A mediational model for the impact of parents' stress on adolescent adjustment. *Child Development, 66,* 80–97.

Cox, A. D., Puckering, C., Pound, A., & Mills, M. (1987). The impact of maternal depression in young people. *Journal of Child Psychology and Psychiatry, 28,* 917–928.

Coyne, J. C. (1976a). Depression and the response of others. *Journal of Abnormal Psychology, 85,* 186–193.

Coyne, J. C. (1976b). Toward an interactional description of depression. *Psychiatry, 39,* 28–40.

Coyne, J. C., Burchill, S. A. L., & Stiles, W. B. (1991). An interactional perspective on depression. In C. R. Snyder & D. O. Forsyth (Eds.), *Handbook of social and clinical psychology: The health perspective* (pp. 327–348). New York: Pergamon Press.

Coyne, J. C., Downey, G., & Boergers, J. (1992). Depression in families: A systems perspective. In D. Cicchetti & S. Toth (Eds.), *Rochester Symposium on Developmental Psychopathology: Vol. 4. A developmental approach to affective disorders* (pp. 211–249). Rochester, NY: University of Rochester Press.

Coyne, J. C., & Gotlib, I. H. (1983). The role of cognition in depression: A critical appraisal. *Psychological Bulletin, 94,* 472–505.

Crick, N., & Dodge, K. A. (1994). A review and reformulation of social information-processing mechanisms in children's social adjustment. *Psychological Bulletin, 115,* 74–101.

Crockenberg, S. B. (1986). Are temperamental differences in babies associated with predictable differences in caregiving? In J. V. Lerner & R. M. Lerner (Eds.), *Temperament and social interaction in infants and children* (pp. 53–73). San Francisco: Jossey-Bass.

Cummings, E. M. (1990). Classification of attachment on a continuum of felt-security: Illustrations from the study of children of depressed parents. In M. Greenberg, D. Cicchetti, & E. M. Cummings (Eds.), *Attachment in the preschool years: Theory, research, and intervention* (pp. 311–338). Chicago: University of Chicago Press.

Cummings, E. M. (1995a). Security, emotionality, and parental depression. *Developmental Psychology, 31,* 425–427.

Cummings, E. M. (1995b). The usefulness of experiments for the study of the family. *Journal of Family Psychology, 9,* 175–185.

Cummings, E. M., & Cicchetti, D. (1990). Towards a transactional model of relations between attachment and depression. In M. Greenberg, D. Cicchetti, & E. M. Cummings (Eds.), *Attachment in the preschool years: Theory, research, and intervention* (pp. 339–372). Chicago: University of Chicago Press.

Cummings, E. M., & Davies, P. T. (1992). Parental depression, family functioning, and child adjustment: Risk factors, processes, and pathways. In D. Cicchetti & S. Toth (Eds.), *Rochester Symposium on Developmental Psychopathology: Vol. 4. A developmental approach to the affective disorders* (pp. 283–322). Rochester, NY: University of Rochester Press.

Cummings, E. M., & Davies, P. (1994a). *Children and marital conflict: The impact of family dispute and resolution.* New York: Guilford Press.

Cummings, E. M., & Davies, P. T. (1994b). Maternal depression and child development. *Journal of Child Psychology and Psychiatry, 35,* 73–112.

Cummings, E. M., & Davies, P. T. (1995). The impact of parents on their children: An emotional security hypothesis. *Annals of Child Development, 10,* 167–208.

Cummings, E. M., & Davies, P. T. (1996). Emotional security as a regulatory process in normal development and the development of psychopathology. *Development and Psychopathology, 8,* 123–139.

Cummings, E. M., Zahn-Waxler, C., & Radke-Yarrow, M. (1981). Young children's responses to expressions of anger and affection by others in the family. *Child Development, 52,* 1274–1282.

Cummings, J. S., Pellegrini, D., Notarius, C., & Cummings, E. M. (1989). Children's responses to angry adult behavior as a function of marital distress and history of interparent hostility. *Child Development, 60,* 1035–1043.

Davies, P. T., & Cummings, E. M. (1994). Marital conflict and child adjustment: An emotional security hypothesis. *Psychological Bulletin, 116,* 387–411.

Davies, P. T., & Cummings, E. M. (1998). Exploring children's emotional security as a mediator of the link between marital relations and child adjustment. *Child Development, 69,* 124–139.

Davies, P. T., & Windle, M. (1997). Gender-specific pathways between maternal depressive symptoms, family discord, and adolescent adjustment. *Developmental Psychology, 33,* 657–668.

Dodge, K. A., & Somberg, D. R. (1987). Hostile attributional biases among aggressive boys are exacerbated under conditions of threats to the self. *Child Development, 58,* 213–224.

Downey, G., & Coyne, J. C. (1990). Children of depressed parents: An integrative review. *Psychological Bulletin, 108,* 50–76.

El-Sheikh, M., & Cummings, E. M. (1995). Children's responses to angry adult behavior as a function of experimentally manipulated exposure to resolved and unresolved conflict. *Social Development, 4,* 75–91.

El-Sheikh, M., Cummings, E. M., & Reiter, S. (1996). Preschoolers' responses to interadult conflict: The role of experimentally manipulated exposure to resolved and unresolved arguments. *Journal of Abnormal Child Psychology, 24,* 665–679.

Emery, R. E. (1982). Interparental conflict and the children of discord and divorce. *Psychological Bulletin, 92,* 310–330.

Feldman, S., & Downey, G. (1994). Rejection sensitivity as a mediator of the impact of childhood exposure to family violence on adult attachment behavior. *Development and Psychopathology, 6,* 231–247.

Fendrich, M., Warner, V., & Weissman, M. M. (1990). Family risk factors, parental depression, and psychopathology in offspring. *Developmental Psychology, 26,* 40–50.

Fergusson, D. M., Horwood, L. J., & Lynskey, M. T. (1995). Maternal depressive symptoms and depressive symptoms in adolescents. *Journal of Child Psychology and Psychiatry, 36,* 1161–1178.

Fergusson, D. M., & Lynskey, M. T. (1993). The effect of maternal depression on child conduct disorder and attention deficit behaviours. *Social Psychiatry and Psychiatric Epidemiology, 28,* 116–123.

Fergusson, D. M., Lynskey, M. T., & Horwood, L. J. (1993). The effect of maternal depression on maternal ratings of child behavior. *Journal of Abnormal Child Psychology, 21,* 245–269.

Field, T., Fox, N. A., Pickens, J., & Nawrocki, B. (1995). Relative right frontal

EEG activation on 3- to 6-month-old infants of "depressed" mothers. *Developmental Psychology, 31*, 358–363.

Field, T., Pickens, J., Fox, N. A., Nawrocki, T., & Gonzalez, J. (1995). Vagal tone in infants of depressed mothers. *Development and Psychopathology, 7,* 227–232.

Forehand, R., Lautenschlager, G. J., Faust, J., & Graziano, W. G. (1986). Parent perceptions and parent–child interactions in clinic-referred children: A preliminary investigation of the effects of maternal depressive moods. *Behaviour Research and Therapy, 24,* 73–75.

Garber, J., Braafladt, N., & Zeman, J. (1991). The regulation of sad affect: An information processing perspective. In J. Garber & K. A. Dodge (Eds.), *The development of emotion regulation and dysregulation* (pp. 208–240). New York: Cambridge University Press.

Ge, X., Conger, R. D., Lorenz, F. O., Shanahan, M., & Elder, G. H. (1995). Mutual influences in parent and adolescent distress. *Developmental Psychology, 31,* 406–419.

Gelfand, D. M., & Teti, D. M. (1990). The effects of maternal depression on children. *Clinical Psychology Review, 10,* 329–353.

Geller, J., & Johnston, C. (1995). Depressed mood and child conduct problems: Relationships to mothers' attributions for their own and their children's experiences. *Child and Family Behavior Therapy, 17,* 19–34.

Goldsmith, D. F., & Rogoff, B. (1995). Sensitivity and teaching by dysphoric and nondysphoric women in structured versus unstructured situations. *Developmental Psychology, 31,* 354–388.

Goodman, S. H., Adamson, L. B., Riniti, J., & Cole, S. (1994). Mothers' expressed attitudes: Associations with maternal depression and children's self-esteem and psychopathology. *Journal of the American Academy of Child and Adolescent Psychiatry, 33,* 1265–1274.

Gotlib, I., & Hammen, C. (1992). *Psychological aspects of depression: Towards a cognitive–interpersonal integration.* Chichester, England: Wiley.

Grusec, J. E., & Goodnow, J. J. (1994). Impact of parental discipline methods on the child's internalization of values: A reconceptualization of current points of view. *Developmental Psychology, 30,* 4–19.

Grych, J. H., & Fincham, F. D. (1990). Marital conflict and children's adjustment: A cognitive–contextual framework. *Psychological Bulletin, 108,* 267–290.

Hamilton, E. B., Hammen, C., Minasian, G., & Jones, M. (1993). Communication styles of children of mothers with affective disorders, chronic medical illness, and normal controls: A contextual perspective. *Journal of Abnormal Child Psychology, 21,* 51–63.

Hamilton, E. B., Jones, M., & Hammen, C. (1993). Maternal interaction style in affective disordered, physically ill, and normal women. *Family Process, 32,* 329–340.

Hammen, C. L., Burge, D., Daley, S. E., Davila, J., Paley, B., & Rudolph, K. (1995). Interpersonal attachment cognitions and prediction of symptomatic responses to interpersonal stress. *Journal of Abnormal Psychology, 104,* 436–443.

Harnish, J. D., Dodge, K. A., Valente, E., & the Conduct Problems Prevention Research Group. (1995). Mother–child interaction quality as a partial mediator of the roles of maternal depressive symptomatology and socioeconomic status in the development of child behavior problems. *Child Development, 66,* 739–753.

Hoeksema, S., Wolfson, A., Mumme, D., & Guskin, K. (1995). Helplessness in children of depressed and nondepressed mothers. *Developmental Psychology, 31,* 377–387.

Holmbeck, G. (1997). Towards terminological, conceptual, and statistical clarity in the study of mediators and moderators: Examples from the child clinical and pediatric psychology literatures. *Journal of Consulting and Clinical Psychology, 65,* 599–610.

Hops, H. (1992). Parental depression and child behaviour problems: Implications for behavioural family intervention. *Behaviour Change, 9,* 126–138.

Hops, H. (1995). Age- and gender-specific effects of parental depression: A commentary. *Developmental Psychology, 31,* 428–431.

Hops, H., Sherman, L., & Biglan, A. (1990). Maternal depression, marital discord, and children's behavior: A developmental perspective. In G. R. Patterson (Ed.), *Depression and aggression in family interaction* (pp. 185–208). Hillsdale, NJ: Erlbaum.

Kashani, J., Husain, A., Shekim, W., Hodges, K., Cytryn, L., & McKnew, D. H. (1981). Current perspectives on childhood depression: An overview. *American Journal of Psychiatry, 38,* 143–153.

Kershner, J. G., & Cohen, N. J. (1992). Maternal depressive symptoms and child functioning. *Journal of Applied Developmental Psychology, 13,* 51–63.

Kochanska, G., Kuczynski, L., Radke-Yarrow, M., & Welsh, J. D. (1987). Resolution of control episodes between well and affectively ill mothers and their young child. *Journal of Abnormal Child Psychology, 15,* 441–456.

Lay, K., Waters, E., & Park, K. A. (1989). Maternal responsiveness and child compliance: The role of mood as a mediator. *Child Development, 60,* 1405–1411.

Lee, C. M., & Gotlib, I. H. (1991). Family disruption, parental availability, and child adjustment. *Advances in Behavioral Assessment of Children and Families, 5,* 171–199.

Londerville, S., & Main, M. (1981). Security of attachment, compliance, and maternal training methods in the second year of life. *Developmental Psychology, 17,* 289–299.

Lyons-Ruth, K. (1995). Broadening our conceptual frameworks: Can we introduce relational strategies and implicit representational systems to the study of psychopathology? *Developmental Psychology, 31,* 432–436.

Lyons-Ruth, K., Connell, D. B., Zoll, D., & Stahl, J. (1987). Infants at social risk:

Relations among infant maltreatment, maternal behavior, and infant attachment behavior. *Developmental Psychology, 23*, 223–232.

Nolen-Hoeksema, S., Wolfson, A., Mumme, D., & Guskin, K. (1995). Helplessness in children of depressed and nondepressed mothers. *Developmental Psychology, 31*, 377–387.

O'Brien, M., Margolin, G., John, R. S., & Krueger, L. (1991). Mothers' and sons' cognitive and emotional reactions to simulated marital and family conflict. *Journal of Consulting and Clinical Psychology, 59*, 692–703.

Radke-Yarrow, M., Cummings, E. M., Kuczynski, L., & Chapman, M. (1985). Patterns of attachment in two- and three-year-olds in normal families and families with parental depression. *Child Development, 56*, 884–893.

Radke-Yarrow, M., McCann, K., DeMulder, E., Belmont, B., Martinez, P., & Richardson, D. (1995). Attachment in the context of high-risk conditions. *Development and Psychopathology, 7*, 247–266.

Radke-Yarrow, M., Nottleman, E., Belmont, B., & Welsh, J. D. (1993). Affective interactions of depressed and nondepressed mothers and their children. *Journal of Abnormal Child Psychology, 21*, 683–695.

Radke-Yarrow, M., Zahn-Waxler, C., Richardson, D. T., Susman, A., & Martinez, P. (1994). Caring behavior in children of clinically depressed and well mothers. *Child Development, 65*, 1405–1414.

Richard, K. M., Forehand, R., Wells, K. C., Griest, D. L., & McMahon, R. J. (1981). Factors in the referral of children for behavioral treatment: A comparison of mothers of clinic-referred deviant, clinic-referred nondeviant, and non-clinic children. *Behaviour Research and Therapy, 19*, 201–205.

Sameroff, A. (1995). General systems theories and developmental psychopathology. In D. Cicchetti & D. Cohen (Eds.), *Developmental psychopathology* (pp. 659–695). New York: Wiley.

Seifer, R. (1995). Perils and pitfalls of high-risk research. *Developmental Psychology, 31*, 420–424.

Seiner, S. H., & Gelfand, D. M. (1995). Effects of mothers' simulated withdrawal and depressed affect on mother–toddler interactions. *Child Development, 66*, 1519–1528.

Sheeber, L. B., & Johnson, J. H. (1992). Child temperament, maternal adjustment, and changes in family life style. *American Journal of Orthopsychiatry, 62*, 178–185.

Tannenbaum, L., & Forehand, R. (1994). Maternal depressive mood: The role of the father in preventing adolescent problem behaviors. *Behavioral Research and Therapy, 32*, 321–325.

Tarullo, L. B., DeMulder, E. K., Martinez, P. E., & Radke-Yarrow, M. (1994). Dialogues with preadolescents and adolescents: Mother–child interaction patterns in affectively ill and well dyads. *Journal of Abnormal Child Psychology, 22*, 33–51.

Teti, D., Gelfand, D. M., Messinger, D. S., & Isabella, R. (1995). Maternal depression and the quality of early attachment: An examination of infants, preschoolers, and their mothers. *Developmental Psychology, 31,* 364–376.

Teti, D. M., Gelfand, D. M., & Pompa, J. (1990). Depressed mothers' behavioral competence with their infants: Demographic and psychosocial correlates. *Development and Psychopathology, 2,* 259–270.

Thomas, A. M., & Forehand, R. (1991). The relationship between paternal depressive mood and early adolescent functioning. *Journal of Family Psychology, 4,* 260–271.

Thompson, R. A. (1994). Emotion regulation: A theme in search of definition. In N. Fox (Ed.), The development of emotion regulation: Biological and behavioral considerations. *Monographs of the Society for Research in Child Development, 59*(2–3, Serial No. 240), 25–52.

Thompson, R. A., & Caulkins, S. (1996). The double-edged sword: Emotional regulation for children at risk. *Development and Psychopathology, 8,* 163–182.

van Ijzendoorn, M. H., Goldberg, S., Kroonenberg, P., & Frankel, O. (1992). The relative effects of maternal and child problems on the quality of attachment: A meta-analysis of attachment in clinical samples. *Child Development, 63,* 840–858.

Wachs, T. D., & Gandour, M. J. (1983). Temperament, environment, and six-month cognitive–intellectual development: A test of the organismic specificity hypothesis. *International Journal of Behavioral Development, 6,* 135–152.

Wall, J. E., & Holden, E. W. (1994). Aggressive, assertive, and submissive behaviors in disadvantaged, inner-city preschool children. *Journal of Clinical Child Psychology, 23,* 382–390.

Weissman, M. M., & Paykel, E. S. (1974). *The depressed woman: A study of social relationships.* Chicago: University of Chicago Press.

Whiffen, V. E., & Gotlib, I. H. (1989). Infants of postpartum depressed mothers: Temperament and cognitive status. *Journal of Abnormal Psychology, 98,* 274–279.

Wierson, M., & Forehand, R. (1992). Family stressors and adolescent functioning: A consideration of models for early and middle adolescents. *Behavior Therapy, 23,* 671–688.

Zahn-Waxler, C., Cummings, E. M., McKnew, D. H., & Radke-Yarrow, M. (1984). Altruism, aggression, and social interactions in young children with a manic-depressive parent. *Child Development, 55,* 112–122.

Zahn-Waxler, C., Iannotti, R. J., Cummings, E. M., & Denham, S. (1990). Antecedents of problem behaviors in children of depressed mothers. *Development and Psychopathology, 2,* 271–291.

Zahn-Waxler, C., Kochanska, G., Krupnick, J., & McKnew, D. (1990). Patterns of guilt in children of depressed and well mothers. *Developmental Psychology, 26,* 51–59.

13

A SOCIAL–COGNITIVE MODEL OF INTERPERSONAL PROCESSES IN DEPRESSION

WILLIAM P. SACCO

A depressed client is seen in therapy with his wife. He has stopped working since becoming depressed. Each time the therapist raises the issue of his returning to work, his wife objects, claiming that he is "not ready." The client readily agrees. After several sessions, the wife admits that she fears her husband will embarrass himself in front of his coworkers.

In their book on cognitive therapy for depression, Beck and his colleagues (Beck, Rush, Shaw, & Emery, 1979) warned therapists against beginning to "believe the patient's persistent negative view of himself and his life situation." The therapist, they say, should not "buy into" the "patient's distorted construction of reality" (p. 59).

In a recent review of interpersonal aspects of depression, the authors (Segrin & Abramson, 1994) concluded that "depressed people reliably experience rejection from those in their social environment" (p. 655).

The divorce rate for couples with a formerly depressed spouse is 9 times greater than the rate for the general population at a 1- to 3-year follow-up (Merikangas, 1984).

The best single predictor of depression relapse was found in one study

329

to be the patient's response to a single item: "How critical is your spouse of you?" Perceived criticism surpassed marital distress and expressed emotion in predicting relapse (Hooley & Teasdale, 1989).

Parental rejection has been found to predict higher levels of depression in children 10 years later (Lefkowitz & Tesiny, 1984).

The preceding observations raise the following important questions about the interpersonal environment of depressed people:

- How do others perceive the depressed person?
- How do others explain the depressed person's successes, failures, and personal problems?
- To what extent are others' perceptions and attributions about the depressed person biased?
- How are these social–cognitive phenomena related to affective and behavioral reactions to a depressed person?
- Do perceptions and attributions regarding the depressed person change after symptoms remit?
- To what extent do depressed individuals accurately perceive how others view and respond to them?
- Do these social–cognitive processes play a role in the development, maintenance, or exacerbation of depression?

Despite considerable evidence that the way others respond to depressed people may play an important role in the development and course of depression, there has been little theory or research concerning the preceding questions. This lack of attention has occurred despite substantial advances in the study of social cognition (Wyer & Srull, 1994) and, in particular, cognition in close relationships (Berscheid, 1994; M. S. Clark, Hegleson, Mickelson, & Pataki, 1994; Fletcher & Fincham, 1991). A vast body of theory and research describing affective influences on social judgment (e.g., Forgas, 1995) has also been largely ignored. Therefore, this chapter is intended to show how this literature may enhance the understanding of interpersonal aspects of depression. A model is presented that conceptualizes depressogenic interpersonal processes in terms of social–cognitive processes that may underlie interactions involving depressed persons. This working model is intended to be integrative and heuristic. Relevant theory and research from the following areas are incorporated into the model: social cognition (e.g., attributions and trait representations), marital–relationship satisfaction, cognition and affect, and perceptions of others' appraisals. The model is most applicable to the role that interpersonal processes may play in the maintenance or worsening of depression; however, it also suggests ways that similar interpersonal processes may be involved in the development of depression.

OVERVIEW OF THE PROPOSED MODEL

The proposed model (Figure 1) assumes a bidirectional interactional process whereby both the depressed (or depression-prone) target and others in the social environment influence interpersonal outcomes.[1] Social–cognitive responses to the depressed target, caused partly by the depressed person's less socially skillful behavior (Segrin & Abramson, 1994) and partly by autonomous cognitive and affective processes that serve to perpetuate the other's negative mental construction of the depressed person (e.g., Carlston & Skowronski, 1994; Forgas, 1995), are expected to influence interpersonal interactions in a way that adversely affects the depressed person. The depressed person's reactions are then expected to reinforce the tendency of others to think negatively about him or her.

The model focuses on two social–cognitive constructs: attributions and person schemas. *Attributions* refer here primarily to causal explanations of the depressed person's behaviors (Sacco & Dunn, 1990). However, recent findings in the marital satisfaction literature suggest that responsibility attributions—the extent to which someone is held accountable for an event (e.g., blameworthiness)—may also be a useful operationalization of this construct (Bradbury & Fincham, 1990). The *person schema* refers to a mental representation of the target in memory as an individual with a unique constellation of attributes, behavioral tendencies, interests, and values (Andersen & Cole, 1990). This cognitive structure includes information such as abstract inferences (e.g., trait perceptions, their certainty and importance), concrete memories (e.g., past failures), and evaluative inferences. As a memory structure, the person schema organizes abstract and concrete information about the target, which then influences how information about the target is processed (Fiske, 1995; S. L. Murray, Holmes, & Griffin, 1996). This conceptualization of a person schema is analogous to that proposed for the self-concept as a knowledge structure or cognitive self-schema (Kihlstrom & Klein, 1994; Markus, 1980). In addition, comparable to theory and research on self-esteem, the person schema is expected to include an evaluative component (Campbell, 1990), for example, the valence of the appraisal of the depressed person's behaviors. In support of the melding of these two elements of the person schema (i.e., knowledge and evaluation), there is evidence that knowledge about a person rarely exists without evaluative connotations (S. L. Murray et al., 1996; Scott, Fuhrman, & Wyer, 1991), that self-knowledge (i.e., the self-concept) and self-esteem are inextricably linked (Greenwald, Bellezza, & Banaji, 1988), and that evaluative judgments may be largely unconditional automatic responses (Bargh, Chaiken, Raymond, & Hymes, 1996; Jarvis & Petty, 1996).

---

[1]In general, this model is expected to apply to both depressed and depression-prone individuals.

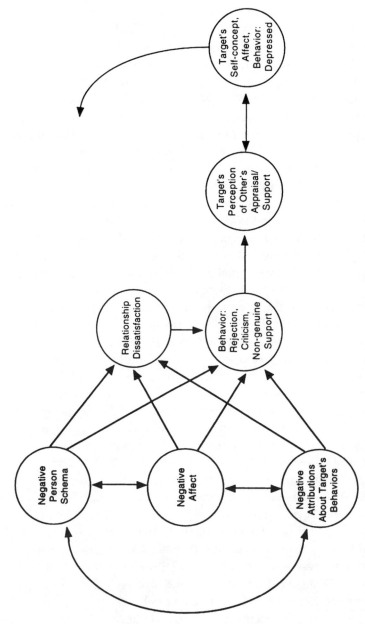

Figure 1. A social–cognitive model of interpersonal processes in depression.

Social cognition is expected to influence and be influenced by affect, as suggested by a large literature demonstrating reciprocal causation between affect and social judgment (Forgas, 1995). Affective reactions, therefore, should exaggerate the valence of social cognitions about the depressed person. The valence of affective reactions to the depressed person is expected to be largely negative (e.g., anger, shame), although researchers have less consistently shown that others may feel mixed affective reactions (e.g., both anger and concern; Sacco & Dunn, 1990; Sacco & Macleod, 1990).

Each of these factors (attributions, schema, and affect) is expected to contribute independently to other people's relationship satisfaction and behavioral reactions to depressed people. Negative behavioral reactions may take various forms such as greater criticism, argumentativeness, withdrawal, nongenuine support, and rejection. These behaviors, when accurately perceived by the depressed person, are expected to influence adversely the depressed person's self-esteem, mood, and behavior as well as to contribute to feelings of loss and alienation. Therefore, the depressed target's perceptions of others' appraisal and support are posited as the most proximal influence on depressive reactions (cf. Hooley & Teasdale, 1989).

Negatively biased information processing, commonly found among depressed individuals, is expected to alter their perception of how others appraise them and of the amount and quality of support others provide. In this way, a basic tenet of cognitive models of depression is incorporated into the model (Beck et al., 1979). However, cognitive models emphasize the depressed person's tendency to experience distorted social perceptions, whereas the present model posits a reciprocal causal relationship. That is, the depressed person's interpersonal perceptions are expected to be due partly to other persons' actual behaviors and partly to autonomous cognitive processes that serve to perpetuate the depressed person's negative mental model of the self in relation to others (Kenny & DePaulo, 1993). Perceived negative reactions from others, real or illusory, are expected to influence mood adversely and, concurrently, to activate the depressed person's self-relevant negative cognitive network, which should influence interpretations of and responses to subsequent interpersonal stimuli (Segal & Ingram, 1994).

HYPOTHESES OF THE MODEL

The proposed model is intended to be integrative and heuristic. It represents an attempt to organize diverse findings that are directly and indirectly relevant to interpersonal aspects of depression into a single conceptual framework. In a further elaboration of the model, several central hypotheses are presented, along with relevant theory and data from social and clinical psychology.

Hypothesis: *Others develop a negative schema of the depressed person that influences attention, encoding, and retrieval of information about the depressed person. As such, these negative schemas will result in faster but often biased perceptions, interpretations, and judgments about the depressed person.*

It has been reliably found that others rate depressed individuals, compared with controls, more negatively on a variety of trait descriptors. More negative ratings have been found with various trait rating forms and across various levels of acquaintanceship. For example, when asked to study and form an impression of a fellow student on the basis of responses to a self-report depression inventory, participants rated mildly depressed, relative to nondepressed, respondents more negatively on 22 of 23 trait descriptors (Hall & Sacco, 1983). In addition, therapists rated role-players enacting a depressed, compared with a nondepressed, "client" more negatively on 19 of the same 23 trait descriptors (Jenkins-Hall & Sacco, 1991). This evidence suggests that people have a negative stereotype of depressed people (cf. Cane & Gotlib, 1985).

Evidence suggests that those in close relationships with depressed individuals also hold a negative view. Children with more symptoms of depression were rated more negatively on personality traits by their mothers (Sacco, Johnson, & Tenzer, 1993), and depressed wives were rated more negatively by their husbands than were nondepressed wives (Hautzinger, Linden, & Hoffman, 1982; Sacco, Dumont, & Dow, 1993). Similarly, roommates rated relatively depressed targets more negatively on a revised Rosenberg Self-Esteem Questionnaire, which assessed overall regard for the depressed person (Joiner & Metalsky, 1995).

Other researchers have reported indirect evidence of a negative view of depressed people. For example, relatively depressed children, college students, and adults have been rated more negatively by their peers on a variety of social behaviors and on overall social competence (e.g., Bell-Dolan, Reaven, & Peterson, 1993; Cole, 1991; Dykman, Horowitz, Abramson, & Usher, 1991; Segrin & Abramson, 1994). To the extent that the literature on self-esteem is relevant to depression, it is apropos that people with low self-esteem have been shown to be viewed more negatively than people with higher self-esteem. For example, mothers' perceptions of their children's social, sports, and mathematical ability predicted the children's self-perceived ability in these areas, suggesting that children with lower self-esteem in these areas are also viewed more negatively by their mothers on relevant traits (Jacobs & Eccles, 1992).

Is the negative view of the depressed person biased? Negative trait ratings of depressed people could be due to actual behavioral differences —that is, an unbiased translation of their behavior into trait descriptors. Bias is difficult to detect (Funder, 1987; Richters, 1992); however, the study of therapist ratings mentioned earlier provided some relevant information (Jenkins-Hall & Sacco, 1991). Depressed "clients" were rated more negatively on the traits "bad-good" and "dirty-clean." The rating of depressed clients as less "good" than nondepressed clients is pejorative and suggests negative generalization, possibly negative bias. In addition, the depressed "clients" were rated as dirtier, although the same actors played both roles; therefore, rating the depressed client as dirtier appears to reflect a negatively biased perception.

A subsequent study was designed to address the question of bias (Sacco, Dumont, & Dow, 1993). Husbands of wives with or without a history of depression were asked to rate their spouses on a set of positive and negative traits. The traits were chosen according to whether they reflected behaviors that are likely to be associated with depressive symptoms (e.g., enthusiastic, unpleasant) or unlikely to be related to depressive symptoms (e.g., well read, shallow). On the one hand, it was expected that depressed spouses would be rated more negatively on depression-related traits. On the other hand, there was no reason to expect that depressed people would behave more negatively with regard to depression-unrelated traits; therefore, more negative ratings on these traits would provide further evidence of negatively biased perceptions of depressed people. In support of the negative bias hypothesis, wives with a history of depression were rated more negatively on both sets of traits, depression related and depression unrelated. A somewhat higher depression level in the husbands of depressed wives did not account for this effect. Finally, in a more recent study (Nicholson, 1997), undergraduate participants were led to believe they were evaluating a depressed or a nondepressed target on the basis of the target's performance on a memory task. Despite equal levels of success, depressed targets were rated more negatively on task-relevant traits that were unrelated to depression (e.g., unintelligent, talented, clever). These findings also lend support to the hypothesis that others have a negatively biased view of depressed people.

Do these negative ratings of depressed people reflect the operation of a negative schema (i.e., a knowledge structure that influences information processing)? In the studies cited, a "negative view" was operationally defined as the overall valence of trait ratings of the depressed person. These self-report measures are typically criticized as too explicit to tap into the covert cognitive processes suggested by the notion of a cognitive schema. However, some evidence suggests that explicit measures of trait perceptions (i.e., trait ratings) do correspond to measures indicative of schematic information processing. Fuhrman and Funder (1995) provided evidence that the extremity of trait ratings by peers predicts faster response latencies to trait descriptors, which is accepted as an indicator of schematic information processing. They also found that schemas of a target manifested the same properties of enhanced accessibility for trait-relevant information as did the individual's self-schema. That is, peers who had previously rated a friend higher on a given trait (e.g., responsibility) displayed faster reaction times when later judging whether other attributes relevant to the trait were true of the target. In addition, research on the automatic evaluation effect (e.g., Bargh et al., 1996) suggests that once a negative view of a depressed person is established, it may bias processing of subsequent "nondepressed" behaviors. This research indicates that frequently and recently activated evaluations of just about any stimulus object become automatic, interfering with the processing of information that is of the opposite valence.

Other studies have provided indirect evidence of schematic processing of individuals with psychological disorders. Signal detection analyses have indicated that parents of problem children are less able to "see" positive or praiseworthy behaviors in their children (Holleran, Littman, Freund, & Schmaling, 1982). In another study, trained raters who had reliably counted the number of positive and negative behaviors exhibited by normal and "disturbed" children were asked 8 weeks later to report the frequencies of these behaviors. Although they were accurate in their estimates of positive behaviors for both groups of children, the raters significantly overestimated the frequencies of negative behaviors by the behaviorally disturbed children (Yates, Klein, & Haven, 1978). In summary, although some evidence hints of support for the model's hypothesis concerning schematic processing of information about depressed people, more research directly addressing this question is needed. A host of methodologically sophisticated procedures are now available for the study of implicit (Greenwald & Banaji, 1995) or automatic (Bargh, 1994) cognitive processes in relation to depressed people, depression-prone people, and depressed people in remission.

How does the proposed social–cognitive model conceptualize the findings presented thus far, and what are their implications for the study of interpersonal processes in depression? A host of evidence has shown that behavioral observations lead to trait inferences stored in memory (Carlston & Skowronski, 1994; Park, 1986). The nature of encoded traits is determined partly by an actor's behavior, but selective attention, expectations, prior concepts, and knowledge influence how behavior is cognitively represented (Fiske, 1993; Wyer & Carlston, 1994). There is evidence that this inferential process occurs spontaneously and unconsciously (Carlston & Skowronski, 1994; Lewicki, Hill, & Czyzewska, 1992). Srull and Wyer (1989) argued that personality inferences involve both trait encodings and general valuative impressions, and they provided evidence that behavioral perceptions are organized around a valuative concept rather than a descriptive one. Applying their analysis here, one can speculate that people interacting with a depressed person form relatively negative trait representations and a relatively negative overall evaluation, both of which are reflected in their trait ratings. Once formed and used, these abstract trait and valuative impressions are likely to influence perceptions of subsequent behaviors (Smith & Zarate, 1992; Wyer & Carlston, 1994).

In addition, the influence of encoded abstract concepts on judgments and decisions increases over time relative to the effect of the information on which those abstractions were initially based. That is, after information is interpreted in terms of accessible concepts, reinterpretations using subsequently activated concepts are less likely (Scott et al., 1991). For example, Sherman and Klein (1994) provided evidence that initial personality impressions consist of stored behavioral exemplars but that after repeated observations, abstract impressions are constructed that alter subsequent information processing (also see Park, 1986). They noted that "ironically, the more behavioral information one has about a person, the less likely it is to play a direct role in judgments about the person" (Sherman & Klein, 1994, p. 980). Various authors also have suggested that, in contrast to positive behaviors, negative behaviors are more likely to be noticed (Pratto & John, 1991) and, when dispositionally attributed, better remembered (Ybarra & Stephan, 1996). Negative behaviors are more likely to alter perceptions of another (i.e., are more "diagnostic"; Fiedler, Asbeck, & Nickel, 1991; Reeder & Coovert, 1986), and once formed, negative trait inferences are more difficult to disconfirm than are positive ones (Rothbart & Park, 1986). In short, a large literature on social–cognitive processes suggests that those in close relationships with depressed individuals may be prone to derive negative trait and global valuative impressions that could adversely bias their processing of the depressed person's behaviors.[2]

This conceptualization yields several implications for the study and treatment of depression. First, longer or recurrent depressive episodes should result in a larger, more elaborate, and more accessible negative schema of the depressed person. By virtue of its influence on information processing, this well-developed negative person schema should lead to even more negative interpersonal reactions to the depressed person. Consistent with this hypothesis is evidence suggesting that the duration of a depressive episode is related to reductions in social support, greater rejection, and greater anger toward the depressed person (Hokanson, Hummer, & Butler, 1991; Sacco, Milana, & Dunn, 1985). Second, even after the disordered individual's symptoms remit or otherwise change, the negative person schema may remain or be easily reactivated by the appearance of any depressive symptom or other schematic cues (Higgins & Bargh, 1987), making it difficult to process nondisordered behavior accurately (Sherman & Klein, 1994; Zuroff, 1989). These cognitive processes may help explain why remitted depressed patients view themselves as showing considerable improvement on many personality traits, yet informants are more likely to see no or considerably less improvement (Peselow, SanFilipo, & Fieve, 1994).

Enduring negative perceptions may also result in negative reactions

---

[2]These social–cognitive processes may also occur in interpersonal systems in which individuals with other types of psychological disorders interact (Sacco & Murray, 1997).

to the previously depressed person. Formerly depressed individuals continue to report restricted social networks (Gotlib & Hammen, 1992) and greater marital discord (Barnett & Gotlib, 1988). Thus, negatively biased perceptions may make it difficult to revitalize formerly positive relationships and may result in overt responses that undermine recovery (Hooley & Teasdale, 1989). It is ironic that when symptoms remit, the depressed person's negative self-referential thinking (e.g., Barnett & Gotlib, 1988) and social competence (Lewinsohn, Mischel, Chaplin, & Barton, 1980) may improve to a level indistinguishable from that of nondepressed individuals. Consequently, those in close relationships with depressed people may require an extended symptom-free period to deactivate their negative schema of the person.

Hypothesis: *Others explain the behaviors of the depressed person in relatively negative ways.*

Causal attributions, another important social–cognitive construct, may also help explain interpersonal reactions to depressed people. A great deal of evidence shows that causal explanations of a target's behaviors are likely to influence cognitive, affective, and behavioral reactions to the target (Kelley & Michela, 1980; Weary, Edwards, & Riley, 1994). Despite the robustness of this social–cognitive phenomenon, little research has been done to examine how others explain the causes of a depressed person's behaviors and how these attributions may influence interpersonal reactions to the depressed person. Early evidence of the relevance of attributions was provided by Yarkin, Harvey, and Bloxom (1981). These researchers led participants to believe that a person with whom they were going to interact was (a) happy, well adjusted, and fulfilled; (b) lonely, depressed, worried about his or her mental health, and unfulfilled; or (c) unknown in this respect (no initial information given). The confederates were trained to act in an ambiguous manner in all conditions. Participants made more negative attributions and less positive attributions about the "depressed" target, and they reported less liking of the depressed target. During a subsequent interaction, the depressed target elicited more negative social responses from others (e.g., others sat further away, made less eye contact, engaged in more negatively valenced conversations, and spent less time speaking), and the valence of attributions was related to the valence of social behavior. In another experiment, it was found that the failures and personal problems of a hypothetical depressed, versus nondepressed, person were attributed more to dispositional factors (i.e., factors that are more internal, stable, global, and controllable). In contrast, the depressed person's *successes* were attributed more to situational factors (Sacco & Dunn, 1990). In an extension of these findings to naturally occurring relationships, several investigators found that spouses of partners who are more depressed or higher in negative affectivity make more negative attributions about the target's failures and negative marital behaviors (Karney, Bradbury, Fincham, & Sullivan, 1994; Sacco, Dumont, & Dow, 1993; Senchak & Leonard, 1993).

The proposed model distinguishes between others' causal attributions about the depressed person's behaviors and their schema of the depressed person. Although the valence of schematic representations is expected to be correlated with the valence of causal attributions, there are several reasons for differentiating between these two social–cognitive constructs. First, the influence of causal explanations on interpersonal relationships has received a great deal of attention (Bradbury & Fincham, 1990; Dix, 1991). In contrast, much less is known about the influence of schematic processing on relationships (e.g., effects on attention, efficiency of processing, memory, and bias). Also, attributional bias is difficult to determine, whereas measuring the extent to which perceptions about another are biased is possible. Third, a precedent for distinguishing between knowledge structures (e.g., trait representations) and attributional judgments can be found in the literature (Cantor & Kihlstrom, 1987; Hilton, Smith, & Kim, 1995; Schneider, 1991; Scott et al., 1991; Surra & Bohman, 1991). This literature suggests that these two constructs may explain independent variance in interpersonal reactions to depressed persons. For example, in arguing that nonsocial cognitive constructs may be fruitfully applied to the study of social knowledge, Cantor and Kihlstrom proposed that attributions reflect procedural social knowledge (i.e., *rules* involved in social inference, judgment, and causal attribution), whereas *concepts* about people reflect declarative social knowledge. Although rules are likely to influence the development of social concepts, these two forms of social knowledge are considered separable (Cantor & Kihlstrom, 1987). In applying Srull and Wyer's (1989) person memory model to close relationships, Scott et al. argued that responses to another's behavior are cognitively mediated by trait–event representations, which lead to inferences about consequences of the target's behavior for the observer. Such inferences do not require previous causal judgments. Causal judgments may, however, reflect the nature of the trait–event representations that are typically activated in construing the behavior (Scott et al., 1991). There is evidence that trait inferences occur automatically, whereas causal judgments require additional cognitive resources to account for situational constraints, making their occurrence less likely (Gilbert, Pelham, & Krull, 1988; Gilbert & Malone, 1995).[3] Both Bassili (1989) and Hilton et al. (1995) provided evidence

---

[3]However, attributional judgments may also become schematic and, therefore, exert automatic influences on the processing of causal inferences about another (Bugental, 1992; Weary et al., 1994). After repeated observations, others may acquire working models or schemas of the usual causes of the target's behaviors (i.e., an attributional style). These frequently activated causal inferences are likely to influence subsequent causal attributions about specific behaviors (e.g., Higgins & King, 1981).

that trait inferences and causal attributions reflect the outcome of different cognitive processes and thus are not isomorphic. Finally, evidence of the independent contributions of attributions and trait conceptions to relationship satisfaction has been reported in two studies (Sacco, Dumont, & Dow, 1993; Sacco & Weems, 1997). In summary, causal attributions and information contained in a person schema (e.g., trait representations), although likely to be correlated, appear to reflect distinguishable social–cognitive processes and thus may play separate roles with respect to interpersonal reactions to depressed people.

Hypothesis: *Social cognition about the depressed person influences affect and affect influences social cognition.*

A good deal of evidence suggests that interpersonal interactions with depressed people are often, although not always, aversive to others (Gotlib & Hammen, 1992; McNeil, Arkowitz, & Pritchard, 1987). One manifestation of this aversiveness is that others often feel more negative affect when interacting with depressed individuals (Segrin & Dillard, 1992). The proposed model posits that affective reactions to depressed people are partly mediated by social cognitions about them. In addition, regardless of its cause, affect is also expected to influence social–cognitive responses to depressed individuals (Clore, Schwarz, & Conway, 1994; Forgas, 1995).

There is much evidence that attributions mediate affective reactions to interpersonal stimuli. In general, dispositional causal attributions (e.g., internal, stable, global, controllable attributions) about another's negative behaviors lead to more negative affective reactions to the target (Kelley & Michela, 1980; Weiner, 1993). For example, causal attributions are correlated with affective reactions to a marital partner's behavior (Fincham, Beach, & Nelson, 1987; Fincham & O'Leary, 1983) and with a parent's affective reactions to children's behavior (see Dix, 1991; S. A. Miller, 1995, for reviews). Path analyses also have supported the hypothesis that attributions mediate the effect of depression (Sacco & Dunn, 1990) on others' affective reactions.

Much less is known about the influence of nonattributional cognition on affective reactions. Although researchers have amply shown that self-relevant valenced cognitions induce a corresponding change in affect (D. M. Clark, 1983), few data bear directly on the hypothesis that a significant other's cognitions about a target are causally related to affective reactions to the target. The proposed model suggests that the person schema creates a distal cognitive context that influences situation-specific cognitions about the depressed person, which, in turn, should influence affective reactions. Two studies have provided indirect evidence of this relationship by showing an association between trait perceptions of family members and affective responses. Husbands of depressed wives, compared with husbands of non-depressed wives, rated their wives more negatively on a broad list of personality traits and reported more negative affective reactions to their wives' real and hypothetical failures. Valence of trait ratings was correlated with valence of affective reactions (Sacco, Dumont, & Dow, 1993). In a second study, the valence of mothers' trait ratings of their child was associated with more negative and less positive affective reactions to hypothetical events occurring to the child (Sacco, Johnson, & Tenzer, 1993). Finally, in the Nicholson (1997) study mentioned earlier, we found that participants evaluating a depressed, as opposed to nondepressed, target gave more negative trait ratings and reported more negative affect and that trait ratings were correlated with the rater's affect. Moreover, when trait ratings were statistically controlled, the correlation between target depression level and affect dropped to a nonsignificant level. The latter finding supports the hypothesis that trait perceptions mediate affective reactions to depressed people.

However, the correlational nature of these studies allows for the possibility that negative perceptions are not causally related to emotions. In addition, trait ratings may not reflect the occurrence of situation-specific cognitions about the target. Therefore, in a subsequent study, my student–colleague and I examined whether activating valenced cognitions about a target child would influence the mother's affect. Mothers were randomly assigned to list and write about positive or negative characteristics of their child. Regardless of preexisting trait conceptions of the child, activating positive information elevated mothers' mood. In contrast, activating negative information lowered mood only in mothers with relatively negative trait conceptions of their child (D. W. Murray & Sacco, 1998). These results provide initial support for the notion that preexisting trait representations of a target provide a cognitive context that influences the nature of negative affective reactions to the target.

A sizable body of data demonstrating the powerful influence of affect on social judgment (Clore et al., 1994; Forgas, 1995) is also pertinent to the study of interpersonal processes in depression. People in good moods tend to view (and act) toward others positively; those in negative moods tend to show the opposite pattern. Several theoretical explanations for this finding have been posited (M. S. Clark et. al, 1994). Affect may increase the accessibility of mood-congruent cognitions (Bower, 1991; M. S. Clark & Isen, 1982) or simply may cue broad, general response tendencies without activating mood-congruent bits of information (Cunningham, 1988). Affect may, correctly or incorrectly, serve as information that is taken into account when social judgments are made (Schwarz, 1990). For example, negative affect incorrectly attributed to the target (rather than to a bad day at work) is likely to influence social judgments about the target. Consistent with this view is evidence showing that affective influences on evaluative judgments occur independently of the specific content by which the mood was induced (Clore et al., 1994). Motivation to maintain positive affect or to repair negative affect may also influence social judgments through cognitive-processing strategies (Sinclair & Mark, 1992). People in happy moods are said to use impressionistic processing strategies, primarily to avoid a negative mood. In response to a depressed person, they may be more likely to make global, prejudiced judgments to avoid processing negative information. Finally, Forgas (1995) proposed an affect infusion model, which posits that affect will most likely alter social judgments when constructive, generative processing strategies are adopted.

In summary, the literature on affect and social cognition may add to the understanding of interpersonal processes in depression. Affective reactions caused by cognitions about the depressed target or by factors entirely unrelated to the depressed person may shift the view of the target in the direction of the valence of the affective state. This reciprocal relationship between social cognition and affect may, therefore, create a self-perpetuating feedback loop that could serve either to deteriorate or to enhance the view of the target (M. S. Clark et al., 1994; Clore et al., 1994; Scott et al., 1991). Finally, although it is not included in Figure 1, on the basis of this literature, the proposed model would also posit that interpersonal reactions to the depressed target are influenced by extrarelationship factors that alter affect, such as when the other is depression prone (Brody & Forehand, 1986; Dumas & Serketich, 1994; Jouriles, Murphy, & O'Leary, 1988; Lewin, Hops, Aubuschon, & Budinger, 1988; Richters, 1992), experiences significant life stressors (Burge & Hammen, 1991; Dumas & Serketich, 1994), or is maritally distressed (Erel & Burman, 1995).

Hypothesis: *Relationship dissatisfaction in those involved with the depressed target is mediated by negative schematic representations and attributions about the depressed target as well as affective state.*

People tend to be less satisfied with relationships involving depressed targets (Gotlib & Hammen, 1992). For example, marital satisfaction is generally lower in both partners when one member of the dyad is depressed (e.g., Gotlib & Whiffen, 1989; Sacco, Dumont, & Dow, 1993). The divorce rate for couples with a formerly depressed spouse was nine times greater than the rate for the general population at a 1- to 3-year follow-up (Merikangas, 1984). A similar phenomenon can be found among nonmarital relationships. Roommates of depressed college students were less satisfied (e.g., Hokanson, Rubert, Welker, Hollander, & Hedeen, 1989) and children's ratings of depressed peers as less socially competent suggest the same (e.g., Blechman, McEnroe, Carella, & Audette, 1986). Evidence supports a reciprocal relationship between depression and marital satisfaction. That is, marital distress can cause depression, and depression can lead to marital dissatisfaction (Barnett & Gotlib, 1988; Gotlib & Hammen, 1992; Ulrich-Jakubowski, Russell, & O'Hara, 1988). Because the disruption of attachments and loss of social support are likely to contribute to the onset, maintenance, and worsening of depression, a better understanding of the processes underlying relationship dissatisfaction is desirable.

Although it is largely ignored by researchers studying depression (cf. Baucom, Epstein, Sayers, & Sher, 1989; Sacco, Dumont, & Dow, 1993), a great deal of evidence suggests that social cognition mediates satisfaction in close relationships (Baucom et al., 1989; Berscheid, 1994; Fletcher & Fincham, 1991). Numerous investigators have shown that marital satisfaction is linked to attributions about the marital partner's behaviors (see Bradbury & Fincham, 1990). Dissatisfied spouses tend to make more dispositional (i.e., internal, stable, global) causal attributions and to view their partner as more responsible for negative marital behaviors. This attributional style has been associated with more negative marital behaviors (Bradbury & Fincham, 1992), and longitudinal data suggest that a negative attributional style antecedes lower marital satisfaction (Fincham & Bradbury, 1987). Research on parent–child dyads, although seldom directed at the construct of relationship satisfaction, has consistently revealed that dispositional attributions about the causes of a child's negative behaviors are related to increased negative affective and behavioral reactions to the child (Dix, 1991; S. A. Miller, 1995), suggesting lower relationship satisfaction. Supporting this inference are findings of a recent study that mothers' dispositional causal attributions about negative child behaviors were associated with lower mother–child relationship satisfaction (Sacco & Murray, 1997).

Relationship satisfaction may also be mediated by other cognitive representations of the target. One such social–cognitive variable, which my group has focused on, is trait representations. Although few investigators have specifically examined the role that trait representations play in determining relationship satisfaction, there is indirect evidence to support this hypothesis (Berscheid, 1994; Park, 1986; Scott, Fuhrman, & Wyer, 1991; Surra & Bohman, 1991). As noted earlier, many studies show that behavioral observations automatically and unconsciously lead to trait inferences that are stored in memory (Carlston & Skowronski, 1994; Park, 1986). Stored trait representations influence subsequent processing of information about the other, resulting in faster but often biased perceptions, interpretations, judgments, and recall (Berscheid, 1994; Carlston & Skowronski, 1994; Scott et al., 1991; Wyer & Carlston, 1994). Given their apparent influence on interpretations of and responses to others' behaviors, trait conceptions, and in particular their overall valence, are likely to function as one determinant of relationship satisfaction. In support of this hypothesis are two recent studies in which it was found that husbands' trait conceptions of marital partners and parents' trait conceptions of their children accounted for a large amount of variance in relationship satisfaction (Sacco, Dumont, & Dow, 1993; Sacco & Murray, 1997). In both cases, this finding occurred after investigators controlled for the effects of both attributions and affect.

Do attributions about and trait conceptions of a target mediate others' relationship dissatisfaction with depressed individuals? This question has been addressed in only one study. Presence or absence of a history of depression in wives no longer contributed significantly to husbands' marital satisfaction after attributions and trait ratings were statistically controlled, whereas both social–cognitive variables made significant independent contributions when target depression was controlled (Sacco, Dumont, & Dow, 1993). In addition, my group recently extended this finding to mother–child dyads, but for nonspecific psychological problems in the child. The association between child disorder and mother's relationship satisfaction was fully mediated by trait conceptions of the child and partially mediated by attributions about the child's negative behaviors (Sacco & Murray, 1997). These findings provide early support for the hypothesis that trait conceptions and attributional judgments mediate dissatisfaction with depressed targets. The similarity of findings for depressed and nonspecified child disorder suggests that social–cognitive processes in depression may also model the dynamics of interpersonal systems in which individuals with other forms of psychological disorders interact (Sacco & Murray, 1997).

Finally, does affect contribute independently to relationship satisfaction, along with attributions and trait conceptions? Researchers found that mood made a significant contribution to marital satisfaction after controlling for attributions (Fincham, Beach, & Bradbury, 1989, Study 2; Senchak & Leonard, 1993; cf. Karney et al., 1994). Consistent with the results of these studies of marital dyads are the results of our study (Sacco & Murray, 1997) of mother–child relationship satisfaction: Mothers' state-mood was significantly correlated with relationship satisfaction but did not account for the association between social cognition and relationship satisfaction; in addition, mood significantly contributed to relationship satisfaction over and beyond the contributions of attributions and trait conceptions. D. W. Murray (1997), who in a subsequent study examined mothers of children with an attention deficit disorder, also found that trait ratings, attributions, and affect contributed significant independent variance to mothers' relationship satisfaction. Partially replicating the Sacco and Murray (1997) study, Murray also found that the relationship between child hyperactivity and relationship satisfaction was fully mediated by trait ratings and affective reactions to the child. These findings are consistent with evidence documenting the independent influence of mood on evaluative judgments (Clore et al., 1994).

Hypothesis: *Behavioral responses to a depressed person are mediated by negative schematic representations and attributions about the depressed target as well as affective state.*

Evidence indicates that others behave in more negative ways toward depressed than nondepressed people. Depressed people are more likely to be rejected than are nondepressed people (Marcus & Nardone, 1992; Segrin & Abramson, 1994). Interpersonal interactions with depressed individuals, including those involving family members, tend to be more negatively toned (Hautzinger et al., 1982; Hokanson, Sacco, Blumberg, & Landrum, 1980; Messer & Gross, 1995). Divorce rates are substantially higher for couples with a partner who has suffered from depression (Merikangas, 1984). Depressed individuals have smaller and less supportive social networks (Gotlib & Hammen, 1992). These negative interpersonal responses, viewed from the interpersonal perspective as reflecting the withdrawal of support and disruption of social attachments, are believed to play a major role in the development, maintenance, and worsening of depression.

Is there evidence that social cognition and affect mediate behavioral reactions to depressed people? In one study described earlier, confederates who were described as depressed (vs. happy), but who acted in an ambiguous manner, received more negative attributions and less positive attributions, were liked less, and during a subsequent interaction elicited more negative social responses (e.g., others sat farther away, made less eye contact, had more negatively valenced conversations, and spoke less). Valence of attributions was related to valence of social behavior (Yarkin et al., 1981). In a more recent study from our lab, Nicholson (1997) found that when depressed and nondepressed targets performed equally poorly on a memory task, raters were less likely to want the depressed target on their work team in the future. Most relevant to the present hypothesis, however, is the finding that rejection of the depressed target was fully accounted for by trait perceptions of the target. No other study could be found in which this hypothesis was directly tested with measurement of one or more of the variables specified by the model along with behavioral reactions to depressed people.

Other studies have provided indirect evidence that social–cognitive responses to depressed individuals mediate negative behavioral reactions. When primed, a negative person schema should direct attention, influence the encoding and retrieval of schema-relevant information, and thereby alter perceptions and evaluations of the target's social responses (Fiske, 1995). This cognitive process should result in more negative cognitions about the target, which should influence interpersonal behavior. College students were found to view depressed, compared with nondepressed, roommates with less esteem. This global negative view also highly correlated with their willingness to interact with their roommates (Joiner & Metalsky, 1995). During relaxed discussions and, to a greater extent, problem-solving discussions, maritally distressed couples evidenced more negative cognitions about their spouse, which predicted more negative conversational behaviors (Halford & Sanders, 1990). The valence of cognitions during conversations between married couples concerning important relationship problems, which was correlated with dyadic relationship satisfaction and depression level, explained significant amounts of independent variance in the observed verbal content and voice tone (Fletcher & Kininmonth, 1991).

Several other researchers have found an association between attributions and interactional behaviors. Maritally dissatisfied spouses exhibited higher rates of negative behaviors when told their partner was responsible, as opposed to not responsible, for writing a negative description of them (Fincham & Bradbury, 1988). Other investigators found that more negative attributions for a partner's behaviors predicted more negative and less positive interactional behaviors and less effective problem-solving behavior (Bradbury & Fincham, 1992; Sillars, 1985). Numerous authors have reported an association between attributions and self-reported interpersonal behaviors such as parenting behaviors (Dix, 1991; S. A. Miller, 1995) and helping behavior (Weiner, 1993). In one study, self-reported affective and behavioral reactions to a hypothetical depressed person were examined. Path analyses suggested that target depression influenced attributions, which influenced others' affective reactions, which in turn influenced both psychological helping and social rejection (Sacco & Dunn, 1990); these findings were consistent with the proposed model.

Negative schematic information (e.g., trait conceptions) about a depressed person should bias expectations about the depressed person's behaviors. A large literature on interpersonal expectancies suggests that expectations may alter behavior toward the target, which can ultimately influence the target's behavior, affect, attitudes, and self-concept (Darley & Fazio, 1980; D. T. Miller & Turnbull, 1986; Rosenthal, 1994). This literature indirectly suggests that a negative schema of the depressed person will influence behavior toward him or her. One study provided some support for this extrapolation. Others were found to expect the depressed person to make more requests of them to discuss personal problems. A path analysis suggested that this expectation leads to a desire to avoid the depressed person through its impact on angry feelings toward the depressed person (Sacco et al., 1985). Although these results are suggestive, much more research is needed that directly measures how mental representations of depressed people contribute to interactional behavior (Wyer & Carlston, 1994).

Interpersonal perspectives on depression suggest that negative affective reactions to depressed persons influence social behaviors toward these individuals (Coyne, 1976). Numerous investigators have found that positive affect increases positive social behaviors, such as increased helping and cooperativeness (Isen, 1987). To the extent that depressed people fail to induce positive affect in others, therefore, they are less likely to be the recipients of positive social behaviors. In contrast, the influence of negative affect on social behaviors such as helping and rejection is less clear. Negative affect such as guilt can increase helping, but feelings of anger and disgust have been found to reduce helping behavior (Schroeder, Penner, Dovidio, & Piliavin, 1995). These observations from the literature on helping have been extended to studies of psychological helping for depressed people. In response to a request for psychological help (i.e., to talk about a problem) from a hypothetical depressed or nondepressed acquaintance, others consistently report that they would feel greater anger toward the depressed target, a willingness to provide equal amounts of help to the depressed and nondepressed targets, but substantially less interest in future social interactions with the depressed target (Sacco & Dunn, 1990; Sacco et al., 1985). Similarly, distressed behaviors in social interactions were found to evoke both angry and concerned emotions in others, as well as more supportive behaviors and behavioral avoidance (Lovejoy & Busch, 1993). These observations of incongruence between others' affective state and overt behavior appear to reflect what Coyne (1976) termed *nongenuine support* for the depressed.

Findings from the study of affective influences on parenting behavior also suggest a negative outcome for depressed children, to the extent that they are prone to induce negative affect, especially anger, in parents (Messer & Gross, 1995). Dix (1991), for example, presented evidence that negative affect is more likely to result in negative parenting behaviors (e.g., punitiveness).

Hypothesis: *The depressed individual perceives others as less supportive and as appraising him or her more negatively. However, the depressed person's negative self-schema also affects the perception of appraisal and support.*

Interpersonal perspectives on depression assume that others' negative responses will influence the depressed person's affect, cognitions, and behavior. This outcome assumes that the depressed person detects, to some extent accurately, the negative reactions of others. What is known about the depressed person's perceptions of others' support and appraisals? To what extent are these perceptions accurate? To what extent are these perceptions simply mirroring the depressed person's negative self-schema?

Numerous investigators have shown that depressed people perceive their interpersonal environments more negatively than do nondepressed controls. Depressed individuals reported having smaller social networks of friends and close relationships, and they perceived their relationships as less supportive and poorer in quality (Gotlib & Hammen, 1992). Laboratory studies of perceptions of rejection also have shown that depressed people perceive greater rejection by their partners (e.g., Dobson, 1989; Segrin, 1993; Strack & Coyne, 1983). Retrospective descriptions by depressed, versus nondepressed, adults indicated that depressed people perceived their family environments as having been more negative (Gerlsma, Emmelkamp, & Arrindell, 1990).

To what extent are these perceptions accurate? The issue of accuracy of social perception is complex (Kenny & DePaulo, 1993), and an adequate review of the relevant literature on this question would require substantially more attention than is possible here. In short, the data on this question are mixed, with evidence supporting the conclusion that depressed people are likely to be most accurate in perceiving appraisals within close relationships. For example, Gotlib and Hammen's (1992) review of perceived social support and quality of close relationships suggested that depressed people's perceptions are not distorted. Richters (1992) reached a similar conclusion after reviewing studies of depressed mothers' perceptions of behavior problems in their children. In a large-scale longitudinal study of determinants of perceived support among married couples, researchers concluded that perceived support is determined strongly by actual interpersonal transactions, moderately by the perceiver's biased negative outlook, and only weakly by his or her anxiety and depression (Vinokur, Schul, & Caplan, 1987).

Some data suggest that retrospective reports of parental negativity are influenced by symptoms of depression at the time of recall (Lewinsohn & Rosenbaum, 1987). However, in a longitudinal study, Lefkowitz and Tesiny (1984) found that parental rejection during childhood predicted level of depression in young adulthood, lending some support for the accuracy of retrospective reports by depressed adults. Independent sources of information about depressed people's parents (e.g., siblings, relatives, and longtime friends) corroborated depressed patients' perceptions that their parents were more rejecting than were parents of nondepressed people (Crook, Raskin, & Eliot, 1981). Furthermore, in a review of the accuracy of retrospective assessments, Brewin, Andrews, and Gotlib (1993) concluded that concerns over the unreliability of retrospective reports are exaggerated. Research on interactions with strangers is less clear; results have suggested that depressed or low-self-esteem individuals may fail either to detect the negativity of others (Swann, Stein-Seroussi, & McNulty, 1992) or to perceive negativity that does not exist (Dobson, 1989).

Kenny and DePaulo (1993) reviewed the literature concerning the accuracy with which people can discern how much others like them and others' trait perceptions of them. Accuracy of perceptions can be evaluated in terms of generalized meta-accuracy, which is the ability of the target to know how others in general view him or her (e.g., a group of others), and dyadic meta-accuracy, which is the target's ability to know how the target is differentially regarded by others. The data suggest that generalized accuracy for liking and for trait perceptions is relatively high, in some cases substantial. Support for dyadic accuracy of perceived liking is mixed; in four studies, small-to-moderate correlations (mean $r = .34$) were found, and in three studies, small or no correlations (mean $r = -.04$) were reported. In contrast, dyadic accuracy for trait perceptions was low in seven of eight studies. Thus, targets appear to have a reasonably good idea of whether others, in general, like them and how others, in general, view their traits. To a lesser extent, targets can discern accurately the extent to which specific individuals like them.

Because self-perceptions and beliefs about others' appraisals tend to be highly correlated (Kenny & DePaulo, 1993), depressed people's self-concepts most likely account for a significant amount of variance in social perceptions. A review of the evidence suggests that the self-concept affects social perceptions because targets observe their own behavior during social interactions as they attempt to discern what impression others are forming of them (Kenny & DePaulo, 1993). Kenny and DePaulo also acknowledged that, within long-term relationships, others' appraisals are likely to have a greater impact on self-perception than is suggested by the studies they reviewed, in which participants were exclusively undergraduates.

Hypothesis: *The perception of negative appraisals and reduced support adversely influences the target's depression level.*

According to the proposed model, the perception of negative appraisals and reduced support activates existing (or leads to the development of) highly accessible and well-developed negative self-referential information stored in memory. This activation is then expected to influence mood, cognition, and behavior. Therefore, these interpersonal perceptions should function as one proximal cause of the development, maintenance, and worsening of depression.

Several investigators have shown that perceiving the interpersonal environment as unsupportive or critical predicts a slower recovery from depression, greater relapse, or an increase in symptoms of depression. For example, Billings and Moos (1985) found that perceived quality of significant relationships and perceptions of family and work correlated with the rate of recovery from depression. In several longitudinal studies of recovery from depression, similar findings have been reported (McLeod, Kessler, & Landis, 1992; I. W. Miller et al., 1992; Swindle, Cronkite, & Moos, 1989). An examination of interpersonal predictors of 9-month relapse rates among depressed women found that the single best predictor was the patient's answer to the question "How critical is your spouse of you?" (Hooley & Teasdale, 1989). The perception of criticism accounted for more variance in relapse than did the spouses' marital distress and expressed emotion (e.g., critical remarks), although each of these variables was correlated with relapse, as would be expected by the present model. In addition, hierarchical regression analyses showed that after perceived criticism was entered into the equation, expressed emotion no longer significantly contributed to relapse rate. This result is consistent with the model's hypothesis that perceived criticism mediates the effect of spouses' critical behaviors on relapse. Finally, in a prospective study of college roommates, it was found that students with a roommate who viewed them negatively experienced an increase in depressive symptoms, but only when the target also reported an interest in the roommate's negative feedback (Joiner, 1995).

Hypothesis: *The social–cognitive processes described in the proposed model contribute to the development of depression (i.e., negative self-concept and depressed mood and behavior).*

The proposed model appears to be most relevant for explaining the maintenance, worsening, or relapse of depressive symptoms. That is, others' social–cognitive responses to the depressed target, partly a function of the depressed person's behaviors and partly a function of cognitive and affective processes that serve to perpetuate mental models of the target, influence interpersonal interactions in ways that adversely affect a depressed or depression-prone target. The same social–cognitive and affective processes might also explain interpersonal processes involved in the development of depression. Social interactions culminating in depression would presumably occur over the course of a sustained relationship with a significant other.

Theory and research from a variety of sources are consistent with this hypothesis. Symbolic interactionists have long maintained that the self-concept results from the target's introjection of the significant other's view of the target (Cooley, 1902; Mead, 1934). The proposed model does not assert that the target necessarily internalizes the specific trait conceptions of the significant other (cf. Kenny & DePaulo, 1993; Shrauger & Schoeneman, 1979) but that the target's perception of the overall valence of the other's appraisals and attributions influences the valence of the target's self-concept, affect, and behavior. This effect is expected to occur as a by-product of the perception of loss and the disruption in attachments instilled by the negative responses of the other. As noted earlier, a large body of research on interpersonal expectancies suggests that how others perceive a target can ultimately influence the target's behavior, affect, attitudes, and self-concept (Darley & Fazio, 1980; D. T. Miller & Turnbull, 1986; Rosenthal, 1994). A good deal of evidence suggests that parents' perceptions and attributions about children are internalized by children (Dix, 1993). In a series of studies, Sarason and colleagues (e.g., Sarason, Pierce, Bannerman, & Sarason, 1993) showed that the valence of parents' views of their child predicted both the child's perception of parental support and the valence of the child's self-concept. Using path analyses on a large sample of randomly selected married couples, Schafer and Keith (1985) found evidence that a spouse's appraisals influence the target spouse's self-concept through the target's perception of the spouse's appraisal. Also, results of a longitudinal study by Felson (1989) indicated that parents' actual appraisals of children affected both the children's perceptions of parents' appraisals and the children's self-appraisals. There is ample evidence, therefore, to support the hypothesis that the way significant others view a target can ultimately influence the target's self-concept.

In a host of studies, it has been found that depressed adults report a history of parental rejection and criticism (e.g., Gerlsma et al., 1990; Lizardi et al., 1995), suggesting that such criticism may play a causal role in the development of depression. Although the accuracy of retrospective assessments such as these has been questioned, Brewin et al. (1993) concluded in their review that "claims concerning the general unreliability of retrospective reports are exaggerated" (p. 82) and that "recall of significant past events does not appear to be affected by mood state" (p. 94). In a 10-year longitudinal study, Lefkowitz and Tesiny (1984) assessed whether parental rejection during childhood predicted depression in young adulthood. Rejection was measured by asking parents to evaluate the child (in third grade) on such factors as responsibility, forgetfulness, compliance, manners, and schoolwork. These ratings represent a reasonable operationalization of the person schema construct in the proposed model. For items on which the child was rated negatively, parents were also asked to indicate whether they felt annoyed by the behavior. Thus, both the person schema and affective reactions to the child were incorporated into the rejection score. The results revealed that parental rejection predicted depression 10 years later, in young adulthood. Unfortunately, however, a failure to measure and to control for depression in childhood allows for the possibility that depression in the child preceded the occurrence of parental rejection. The same limitation applies to studies of retrospective reports of negative parental behaviors. Therefore, these findings provide only equivocal support for the model's hypothesis.

Finally, the results of several studies have suggested that the perception of an unsupportive or critical spouse can lead to depression. In their review of antecedents of depression, Barnett and Gotlib (1988) found evidence that marital discord antecedes depression. Likewise, in a longitudinal study, Schaefer and Burnett (1987) found that women's perceptions of their husband's behavior toward them predicted psychological well-being and future levels of psychological adjustment, after initial levels of distress were statistically controlled. Clearly, additional well-controlled, prospective studies are needed to assess whether the social–cognitive processes described in the proposed model are involved in the development of depression.

CONCLUSION AND TREATMENT IMPLICATIONS

The goal of the present chapter has been to provide a model that integrates findings from research in clinical and social psychology that are relevant to the study of interpersonal processes in depression. The model focuses on the role that social cognition plays in determining interpersonal reactions to depressed persons. These reactions are expected to play an important role in the development, maintenance, and worsening of depressive symptoms. In addition, although it is more speculative, the same model could help explain the development of depression.

To the extent that this model is valid, it has implications for the treatment of depression. First, to state the obvious, it suggests that clinical interventions must account for the potentially adverse impact of the depressed person's interpersonal environment. The therapist's attention should be directed to significant others' perceptions, attributions, and affective reactions to the depressed person during the depressive episode. Although more evidence is needed, the model suggests that others may retain a negative social–cognitive "set" that may bias interpretations of the formerly depressed person's responses for some time after symptoms remit. These biased interpretations could result in social interactions that undermine recovery. Biased perceptions would be expected to persist to a greater extent after longer durations and repeated episodes of depression, and they may also depend on the valence of the premorbid schema of the depressed client held by significant others. Successful interventions, therefore, may require extensive efforts to modify the effects of long-standing negative biases held by those who interact with individuals who have a history of depression. Negatively biased automatic information processing may be corrected by making observers aware of their prejudice or motivating them to obtain accurate information (Neuberg, 1989). The effect correction of biased information processing appears to be mediated, at least partly, by extensive and more objective information gathering, a process that is likely to be facilitated during marital therapy for depression (e.g., Beach, Whisman, & O'Leary, 1994).

REFERENCES

Andersen, S. M., & Cole, S. W. (1990). "Do I know you?": The role of significant others in general social perception. *Journal of Personality and Social Psychology, 59*, 384–399.

Bargh, J. A. (1994). The four horsemen of automaticity: Awareness, intention, efficiency, and control in social cognition. In R. S. Wyer & T. K. Srull (Eds.), *Handbook of social cognition* (Vol. 1, pp. 1–40). Hillsdale, NJ: Erlbaum.

Bargh, J. A., Chaiken, S., Raymond, P., & Hymes, C. (1996). The automatic evaluation effect: Unconditional automatic attitude activation with a pronunciation task. *Journal of Experimental Social Psychology, 32*, 104–128.

Barnett, P. A., & Gotlib, I. H. (1988). Psychosocial functioning and depression:

Distinguishing among antecedents, concomitants, and consequences. *Psychological Bulletin, 104,* 97–126.

Bassili, J. N. (1989). Trait encoding in behavior identification and dispositional inference. *Personality and Social Psychology Bulletin, 15,* 285–296.

Baucom, D. H., Epstein, N., Sayers, S., & Sher, T. G. (1989). The role of cognitions in marital relationships: Definitional, methodological, and conceptual issues. *Journal of Consulting and Clinical Psychology, 57,* 31–38.

Beach, S. R. H., Whisman, M. A., & O'Leary, K. D. (1994). Marital therapy for depression: Theoretical foundation, current status, and future directions. *Behavior Therapy, 25,* 345–371.

Beck, A. T., Rush, A. J., Shaw, B. F., & Emery, G. (1979). *Cognitive therapy of depression.* New York: Guilford Press.

Bell-Dolan, D. J., Reaven, N. M., & Peterson, L. (1993). Depression and social functioning: A multidimensional study of the linkages. *Journal of Clinical Child Psychology, 22,* 306–315.

Berscheid, E. (1994). Interpersonal relationships. *Annual Review of Psychology, 45,* 79–129.

Billings, A. G., & Moos, R. H. (1985). Life stressors and social resources affect posttreatment outcomes among depressed patients. *Journal of Abnormal Psychology, 94,* 140–153.

Blechman, E. A., McEnroe, M. J., Carella, E. T., & Audette, D. P. (1986). Childhood competence and depression. *Journal of Abnormal Psychology, 95,* 223–227.

Bower, G. H. (1991). Interpersonal relationships. *Annual Review of Psychology, 45,* 79–129.

Bradbury, T. N., & Fincham, F. D. (1990). Attributions in marriage: Review and critique. *Psychological Bulletin, 107,* 3–33.

Bradbury, T. N., & Fincham, F. D. (1992). Attributions and behavior in marital interaction. *Journal of Personality and Social Psychology, 63,* 613–628.

Brewin, C. R., Andrews, B., & Gotlib, I. H. (1993). Psychopathology and early experience: A reappraisal of retrospective reports. *Psychological Bulletin, 113,* 82–98.

Brody, G. H., & Forehand, R. (1986). Maternal perceptions of child maladjustment as a function of the combined influence of child behavior and maternal depression. *Journal of Consulting and Clinical Psychology, 54,* 237–240.

Bugental, D. D. (1992). Affective and cognitive processes within threat-oriented family systems. In I. E. Sigel, A. B. McGillicuddy-DeLisi, & J. J. Goodnow, (Eds.), *Parental belief systems* (2nd ed., pp. 219–248). Hillsdale, NJ: Erlbaum.

Burge, D., & Hammen, C. (1991). Maternal communication: Predictors of outcome at follow-up in a sample of children at high and low risk for depression. *Journal of Abnormal Psychology, 100,* 174–180.

Campbell, J. D. (1990). Self-esteem and clarity of the self-concept. *Journal of Personality and Social Psychology, 59,* 538–549.

Cane, D. B., & Gotlib, I. H. (1985). Implicit conceptualizations of depression: Implications for an interpersonal perspective. *Social Cognition, 3*, 341–368.

Cantor, N., & Kihlstrom, J. F. (1987). *Personality and social intelligence.* Englewood Cliffs, NJ: Prentice Hall.

Carlston, D. E., & Skowronski, J. J. (1994). Savings in the relearning of trait information as evidence for spontaneous inference generation. *Journal of Personality and Social Psychology, 66*, 840–856.

Clark, D. M. (1983). On the induction of depressed mood in the laboratory: Evaluation and comparison of the Velten and musical procedures. *Advances in Behavior Research and Therapy, 5*, 27–49.

Clark, M. S., Helgeson, V. S., Mickelson, K., & Pataki, S. P. (1994). Some cognitive structures and processes relevant to relationship functioning. In R. S. Wyer & T. K. Srull (Eds.), *Handbook of social cognition* (Vol. 2, pp. 189–238). Hillsdale, NJ: Erlbaum.

Clark, M. S., & Isen, A. M. (1982). Toward understanding the relationship between feeling states and social behavior. In A. H. Hastorf & A. M. Isen (Eds.), *Cognitive social behavior* (pp. 73–108). New York: Elsevier/North-Holland.

Clore, G. L., Schwarz, N., & Conway, M. (1994). Affective causes and consequences of social information processing. In R. S. Wyer & T. K. Srull (Eds.), *Handbook of social cognition* (Vol. 1, pp. 323–417). Hillsdale, NJ: Erlbaum.

Cole, D. A. (1991). Preliminary support for a competency-based model of depression in children. *Journal of Abnormal Psychology, 100*, 181–190.

Cooley, C. H. (1902). *Human nature and the social order.* New York: Scribner.

Coyne, J. C. (1976). Toward an interactional description of depression. *Psychiatry, 39*, 28–40.

Crook, T., Raskin, A., & Eliot, J. (1981). Parent–child relationships and adult depression. *Child Development, 52*, 950–957.

Cunningham, M. (1988). What do you do when you're happy or blue: Mood, expectancies, and behavioral interests. *Motivation and Emotion, 12*, 309–330.

Darley, J. M., & Fazio, R. H. (1980). Expectancy confirmation processes arising in the social interaction sequence. *American Psychologist, 35*, 867–881.

Dix, T. (1991). The affective organization of parenting: Adaptive and maladaptive processes. *Psychological Bulletin, 110*, 3–25.

Dix, T. (1993). Attributing dispositions to children: An interactional analysis of attribution in socialization. *Personality and Social Psychology Bulletin, 19*, 633–643.

Dobson, K. S. (1989). Real and perceived interpersonal responses to subclinically anxious and depressed targets. *Cognitive Therapy and Research, 13*, 37–47.

Dumas, J. E., & Serketich, W. J. (1994). Maternal depressive symptomatology and child maladjustment: A comparison of three process models. *Behavior Therapy, 25*, 161–181.

Dykman, B. M., Horowitz, L. M., Abramson, L. Y., & Usher, M. (1991). Schematic and situational determinants of depressed and nondepressed students' interpretation of feedback. *Journal of Abnormal Psychology, 100,* 45–55.

Erel, O., & Burman, B. (1995). Interrelatedness of marital relations and parent–child relations: A meta-analytic review. *Psychological Bulletin, 118,* 108–132.

Felson, R. B. (1989). Parents and reflected appraisal process: A longitudinal anlaysis. *Journal of Personality and Social Psychology, 56,* 965–971.

Fiedler, L., Asbeck, J., & Nickel, S. (1991). Mood and constructive memory effects on social judgement. *Cognition and Emotion, 5,* 363–378.

Fincham, F. D., Beach, S. R., & Bradbury, T. N. (1989). Marital distress, depression, and attributions: Is the marital distress-attribution association an artifact of depression? *Journal of Consulting and Clinical Psychology, 57,* 768–771.

Fincham, F. D., Beach, S. R., & Nelson, G. (1987). Attribution processes in distressed and non-distressed couples: 3. Causal and responsibility attributions for spouse behavior. *Cognitive Therapy and Research, 11,* 71–86.

Fincham, F. D., & Bradbury, T. N. (1987). The impact of attributions in marriage: A longitudinal analysis. *Journal of Personality and Social Psychology, 52,* 739–748.

Fincham, F. D., & Bradbury, T. N. (1988). The impact of attributions in marriage: An experimental analysis. *Journal of Social and Clinical Psychology, 7,* 122–130.

Fincham, F. D., & O'Leary, K. D. (1983). Causal inferences for spouse behavior in maritally distressed and non-distressed couples. *Journal of Social and Clinical Psychology, 1,* 42–57.

Fiske, S. T. (1993). Social cognition and social perception. *Annual Review of Psychology, 44,* 155–194.

Fiske, S. T. (1995). Social cognition. In A. Tesser (Ed.), *Advanced social psychology* (pp. 149–193). New York: McGraw-Hill.

Fletcher, G. J. O., & Fincham, F. D. (1991). *Cognition in close relationships.* Hillsdale, NJ: Erbaum.

Fletcher, G. J. O., & Kininmonth, L. (1991). Interaction in close relationships and social cognition. In G. J. O. Fletcher & F. D. Fincham (Eds.), *Cognition in close relationships* (pp. 235–255). Hillsdale, NJ: Erlbaum.

Forgas, J. P. (1995). Mood and judgment: The affect influsion model (AIM). *Psychological Bulletin, 117,* 39–66.

Fuhrman, R. W., & Funder, D. C. (1995). Convergence between self and peer in the response-time processing of trait-relevant information. *Journal of Personality and Social Psychology, 69,* 961–974.

Funder, D. C. (1987). Errors and mistakes: Evaluating the accuracy of social judgment. *Psychological Bulletin, 101,* 75–90.

Gerlsma, C., Emmelkamp, P. M. G., & Arrindell, W. A. (1990). Anxiety, depression, and perception of early parenting: A meta-analysis. *Clinical Psychology Review, 10,* 251–277.

Gilbert, D. T., & Malone, P. S. (1995). The correspondence bias. *Psychological Bulletin, 117*, 21–38.

Gilbert, D. T., Pelham, B. W., & Krull, D. S. (1988). On cognitive dizziness: When person perceivers meet persons perceived. *Journal of Personality and Social Psychology, 54*, 733–740.

Gotlib, I. H., & Hammen, C. L. (1992). *Psychological aspects of depression*. New York: Wiley.

Gotlib, I. H., & Whiffen, V. E. (1989). Depression and marital functioning: An examination of specificity and gender differences. *Journal of Abnormal Psychology, 98*, 23–30.

Greenwald, A. G., & Banaji, M. B. (1995). Implicit social cognition: Attitudes, self-esteem, and stereotypes. *Psychological Bulletin, 102*, 4–27.

Greenwald, A. G., Bellezza, F. S., & Banaji, M. R. (1988). Is self-esteem a central ingredient of the self-concept? *Personality and Social Psychology Bulletin, 14*, 34–45.

Halford, W. K., & Sanders, M. R. (1990). The relationship of cognition and behavior during marital interaction. *Journal of Social and Clinical Psychology, 9*, 489–510.

Hall, R. L., & Sacco, W. P. (1983, March). *The depression stereotype and its interpersonal impact*. Paper presented at the 29th annual meeting of the Southeastern Psychological Association, Atlanta, GA.

Hautzinger, M., Linden, M., & Hoffman, N. (1982). Distressed couples with and without a depressed partner: An analysis of their verbal interaction. *Journal of Behavior Therapy and Experimental Psychiatry, 13*, 307–314.

Higgins, E. T., & Bargh, J. A. (1987). Social cognition and social perception. *Annual Review of Psychology, 38*, 369–425.

Higgins, E. T., & King, G. (1981). Accessibility of social constructs: Information-processing consequences of individual and contextual variability. In N. Cantor & J. F. Kihlstrom (Eds.), *Personality, cognition, and social interaction* (pp. 69–121). Hillsdale, NJ: Erlbaum.

Hilton, D. J., Smith, R. H., & Kim, S. H. (1995). Processes of causal explanation and dispositional attribution. *Journal of Personality and Social Psychology, 68*, 377–387.

Hokanson, J. E., Hummer, J. T., & Butler, A. C. (1991). Interpersonal perceptions by depressed college students. *Cognitive Therapy and Research, 15*, 443–457.

Hokanson, J. E., Rubert, M. P., Welker, R. A., Hollander, G. R., & Hedeen, C. (1989). Interpersonal concomitants and antecedents of depression among college students. *Journal of Abnormal Psychology, 98*, 209–218.

Hokanson, J. E., Sacco, W. P., Blumberg, S. R., & Landrum G. C. (1980). Interpersonal behavior of depressive individuals in a mixed-motive game. *Journal of Abnormal Psychology, 89*, 320–332.

Holleran, P. A., Littman, D. C., Freund, R. D., & Schmaling, K. B. (1982). A signal detection approach to social perception: Identification of negative and positive behaviors by parents of normal and problem children. *Journal of Abnormal Child Psychology, 10,* 547–558.

Hooley, J. M., & Teasdale, J. D. (1989). Predictors of relapse in unipolar depressives: Expressed emotion, marital distress, and perceived criticism. *Journal of Abnormal Psychology, 98,* 229–235.

Isen, A. M. (1987). Positive affect, cognitive processes, and social behavior. In L. Berkowitz (Ed.), *Advances in experimental social psychology* (Vol. 20, pp. 203–253). San Diego, CA: Academic Press.

Jacobs, J. E., & Eccles, J. S. (1992). The impact of mothers' gender-role stereotypic beliefs on mothers' and children's ability perceptions. *Journal of Personality and Social Psychology, 63,* 932–944.

Jarvis, W. B. G., & Petty, R. E. (1996). The need to evaluate. *Journal of Personality and Social Psychology, 70,* 172–194.

Jenkins-Hall, K., & Sacco, W. P. (1991). Effect of client race and depression on the perceptions of white therapists. *Journal of Social and Clinical Psychology, 10,* 5–10.

Joiner, T. E. (1995). The price of soliciting and receiving negative feedback: Self-verification theory as a vulnerability to depression theory. *Journal of Abnormal Psychology, 104,* 364–372.

Joiner, T. E., & Metalsky, G. I. (1995). A prospective test of an integrative interpersonal theory of depression: A naturalistic study of college roommates. *Journal of Personality and Social Psychology, 69,* 778–788.

Jouriles, E. N., Murphy, C. M., & O'Leary, K. D. (1988). Effects of maternal mood on mother–son interaction patterns. *Journal of Abnormal Child Psychology, 17,* 513–525.

Karney, B. R., Bradbury, T. N., Fincham, F. D., & Sullivan, K. T. (1994). The role of negative affectivity in the association between attributions and marital satisfaction. *Journal of Personality and Social Psychology, 66,* 413–424.

Kelley, H. H., & Michela, J. L. (1980). Attribution theory and research. *Annual Review of Psychology, 31,* 457–501.

Kenny, D. A., & DePaulo, B. M. (1993). Do people know how others view them? An empirical and theoretical account. *Psychological Bulletin, 114,* 145–161.

Kihlstrom, J. F., & Klein, S. B. (1994). The self as a knowledge structure. In R. S. Wyer & T. K. Srull (Eds.), *Handbook of social cognition* (Vol. 1, pp. 153–208). Hillsdale, NJ: Erlbaum.

Lefkowitz, M. M., & Tesiny, E. P. (1984). Rejection and depression: Prospective and contemporaneous analysis. *Developmental Psychology, 20,* 776–785.

Lewicki, T., Hill, T., & Czyzewska, M. (1992). Nonconscious acquisition of information. *American Psychologist, 47,* 796–801.

Lewin, L., Hops, H., Aubuschon, A., & Budinger, T. (1988). Predictors of maternal satisfaction regarding clinic-referred children: Methodological considerations. *Journal of Clinical Child Psychology, 17,* 159–163.

Lewinsohn, P. M., Mischel, W., Chaplin, W., & Barton, R. (1980). Social competence and depression: The role of illusory self-perceptions. *Journal of Abnormal Psychology, 89*, 203–212.

Lewinsohn, P. M., & Rosenbaum, M. (1987). Recall of parental behavior by acute depressives, remitted depressives, and nondepressives. *Journal of Personality and Social Psychology, 52*, 611–619.

Lizardi, H., Klein, D. N., Ouimette, P. C., Riso, L. P., Anderson, R. L., & Donaldson, S. K. (1995). Reports of the childhood home environment and early-onset dysthymia and episodic major depression. *Journal of Abnormal Psychology, 104*, 132–139.

Lovejoy, M. C., & Busch, L. M. (1993). Emotional and behavioral responses to aversive interpersonal behaviors. *Journal of Abnormal Psychology, 102*, 494–497.

Marcus, D. K., & Nardone, M. E. (1992). Depression and interpersonal rejection. *Clinical Psychology Review, 12*, 433–449.

Markus, H. (1980). The self in thought and memory. In D. M. Wegner & R. R. Vallacher (Eds.), *The self in social psychology* (pp. 102–130). New York: Oxford University Press.

McLeod, J. D., Kessler, R. C., & Landis, K. R. (1992). Speed of recovery from major depressive episodes in a community sample of married men and women. *Journal of Abnormal Psychology, 102*, 277–286.

McNeil, D. E., Arkowitz, H. S., & Pritchard, B. E. (1987). The response of others to face-to-face interaction with depressed patients. *Journal of Abnormal Psychology, 96*, 341–344.

Mead, G. H. (1934). *Mind, self and society.* Chicago: University of Chicago Press.

Merikangas, K. R. (1984). Divorce and assortative mating among depressed patients. *American Journal of Psychiatry, 141*, 74–76.

Messer, S. C., & Gross, A. M. (1995). Childhood depression and family interaction: A naturalistic observation study. *Journal of Clinical Child Psychology, 24*, 77–88.

Miller, D. T., & Turnbull, W. (1986). Expectancies and interpersonal processes. *Annual Review of Psychology, 37*, 233–256.

Miller, I. W., Keitner, G. I., Whisman, M. A., Ryan, C. E., Epstein, N. B., & Bishop, D. S. (1992). Depressed patients with dysfunctional families: Description and course of illness. *Journal of Abnormal Psychology, 101*, 637–646.

Miller, S. A. (1995). Parents' attributions for their children's behavior. *Child Development, 66*, 1557–1584.

Murray, D. W. (1997). *The role of social-cognition and affect in parent–child relationship satisfaction.* Unpublished doctoral dissertation, University of South Florida, Tampa.

Murray, D. W., & Sacco, W. P. (1998). Effect of child-relevant cognitions on mother's mood: The moderating effect of child-trait conceptions. *Cognitive Therapy and Research, 22*, 47–61.

Murray, S. L., Holmes, J. G., & Griffin, D. W. (1996). The benefits of positive illusions: Idealization and the construction of satisfaction in close relationships. *Journal of Personality and Social Psychology, 70*, 79–98.

Neuberg, S. L. (1989). The goal of forming accurate impressions during social interactions: Attenuating the impact of negative expectancies. *Journal of Personality and Social Psychology, 56*, 374–386.

Nicholson, K. J. (1997). *Cognitive, affective, and behavioral reactions to depressed vs. nondepressed targets during an interactive task.* Unpublished master's thesis, University of South Florida, Tampa.

Park, B. (1986). A method for studying the development of impressions of real people. *Journal of Personality and Social Psychology, 51*, 907–917.

Peselow, E. D., SanFilipo, M. P., & Fieve, R. R. (1994). Patients' and informants' reports of personality traits during and after major depression. *Journal of Abnormal Psychology, 103*, 819–824.

Pratto, R., & John, O. P. (1991). Automatic vigilance: The attention-grabbing power of negative social information. *Journal of Personality and Social Psychology, 61*, 380–391.

Reeder, G. D., & Coovert, M. D. (1986). Revising an impression of morality. *Social Cognition, 4*, 1–17.

Richters, J. E. (1992). Depressed mothers as informants about their children: A critical review of the evidence for distortion. *Psychological Bulletin, 112*, 485–499.

Rosenthal, R. (1994). Interpersonal expectancy effects: A 30-year perspective. *Current Directions in Psychological Science, 6*, 176–179.

Rothbart, M., & Park, B. (1986). On the confirmability and disconfirmability of trait concepts. *Journal of Personality and Social Psychology, 50*, 131–142.

Sacco, W. P., Dumont, C. P., & Dow, M. G. (1993). Attributional, perceptual, and affective responses to depressed and nondepressed marital partners. *Journal of Consulting and Clinical Psychology, 61*, 1076–1082.

Sacco, W. P., & Dunn, V. K. (1990). Effect of actor depression on observer attributions: Existence and impact of negative attributions toward the depressed. *Journal of Personality and Social Psychology, 59*, 517–524.

Sacco, W. P., Johnson, S. A., & Tenzer, S. A. (1993, August). *Parent perceptions, affective reactions, and depression in children.* Paper presented at the 101st annual convention of the American Psychological Association, Toronto, Ontario, Canada.

Sacco, W. P., & MacLeod, V. A. (1990). Interpersonal responses of primary caregivers to pregnant adolescents differing on depression level. *Journal of Clinical Child Psychology, 19*, 265–270.

Sacco, W. P., Milana, S., & Dunn, V. K. (1985). Effect of depression level and length of acquaintance on reactions of others to a request for help. *Journal of Personality and Social Psychology, 49*, 1728–1737.

Sacco, W. P., & Murray, D. (1997). Mother–child relationship satisfaction: The role of attributions and trait conceptions. *Journal of Social and Clinical Psychology, 16*, 24–42.

Sarason, B. R., Pierce, G. R., Bannerman, A., & Sarason, I. G. (1993). Investigating the antecedents of perceived social support: Parents' views of and behavior toward their children. *Journal of Personality and Social Psychology, 66,* 1071–1085.

Schaefer, E. S., & Burnett, C. K. (1987). Stability and predictability of quality of women's marital relationships and demoralization. *Journal of Personality and Social Psychology, 53,* 1129–1136.

Schafer, R. B., & Keith, P. M. (1985). A causal model approach to the symbolic interactionist view of the self-concept. *Journal of Personality and Social Psychology, 48,* 963–969.

Schneider, D. J. (1991). Social cognition. *Annual Review of Psychology, 42,* 527–561.

Schroeder, D. A., Penner, L. A., Dovidio, J. F., & Piliavin, J. A. (1995). *The psychology of helping in altruism,* New York: McGraw-Hill.

Schwarz, N. (1990). Feelings as information: Informational and motivational functions of affective states. In E. T. Higgins & R. M. Sorrentino (Eds.), *Handbook of motivation and cognition: Foundations of social behavior* (Vol. 2, pp. 527–561). New York: Guilford Press.

Scott, C. K., Fuhrman, R. W., & Wyer, R. S. (1991). Information processing in close relationships. In G. J. O. Fletcher & R. D. Fincham (Eds.), *Cognition in close relationships* (pp. 37–68). Hillsdale, NJ: Erlbaum.

Segal, Z. V., & Ingram, R. E. (1994). Mood priming and construct activation in tests of cognitive vulnerability to unipolar depression. *Clinical Psychology Review, 14,* 663–695.

Segrin, C. (1993). Interpersonal reactions to dysphoria: The role of relationship with partner and perceptions of rejection. *Journal of Social and Personal Relationships, 10,* 83–97.

Segrin, C., & Abramson, L. Y. (1994). Negative reactions to depressive behaviors: A communication theories analysis. *Journal of Abnormal Psychology, 103,* 655–668.

Segrin, C., & Dillard, J. P. (1992). The interactional theory of depression: A meta-analysis of research literature. *Journal of Social and Clinical Psychology, 11,* 43–70.

Senchak, M., & Leonard, K. E. (1993). The role of spouses' depression and anger in the attribution-marital satisfaction relation. *Cognitive Therapy and Research, 17,* 397–409.

Sherman, J. W., & Klein, S. B. (1994). Development and representation of personality impressions. *Journal of Personality and Social Psychology, 67,* 972–983.

Shrauger, J. S., & Schoeneman, T. J. (1979). Symbolic interactionist view of self-concept: Through the looking glass darkly. *Psychological Bulletin, 86,* 549–573.

Sillars, A. L. (1985). Interpersonal perception in relationships. In W. Ickes (Ed.), *Compatible and incompatible relationships* (pp. 277–305). New York: Springer-Verlag.

Sinclair, R. C., & Mark, M. M. (1992). The influence of mood state on judgment and action: Effects on persuasion, categorization, social justice, person perception, and judgmental accuracy. In L. L. Martin and A. Tesser (Eds.), *The construction of social judgments* (pp. 165–193). Hillsdale, NJ: Erlbaum.

Smith, E. R., & Zarate, M. A. (1992). Exemplar-based model of social judgment. *Psychological Review, 99,* 3–21.

Srull, T. K., & Wyer, R. A. (1989). Person, memory and judgment. *Psychological Review, 96,* 58–83.

Strack, S., & Coyne, J. C. (1983). Social confirmation of dysphoria: Shared and private reactions to depression. *Journal of Personality and Social Psychology, 44,* 798–806.

Surra, C. A., & Bohman, T. (1991). The development of close relationships: A cognitive perspective. In G. J. O. Fletcher & F. D. Fincham (Eds.), *Cognition in close relationships* (pp. 281–306). Hillsdale, NJ: Erlbaum.

Swann, W. B., Jr., Stein-Seroussi, A., & McNulty, S. E. (1992). Outcasts in a white-lie society: The enigmatic worlds of people with negative self-conceptions. *Journal of Personality and Social Psychology, 62,* 618–624.

Swindle, R. W., Jr., Cronkite, R. C., & Moos, R. H. (1989). Life stressors, social resources, coping, and the 4-year course of unipolar depression. *Journal of Abnormal Psychology, 98,* 468–477.

Ulrich-Jakubowski, D., Russell, D. W., & O'Hara, M. W. (1988). Marital adjustment difficulties: Cause or consequence of depressive symptomatology? *Journal of Social and Clinical Psychology, 7,* 312–318.

Vinokur, A., Schul, Y., & Caplan, R. D. (1987). Determinants of perceived social support: Interpersonal transactions, personal outlook, and transient affective states. *Journal of Personality and Social Psychology, 53,* 1137–1145.

Weary, G., Edwards, J. A., & Riley, S. (1994). Attribution. *Encyclopedia of human behavior, 1,* 291–299.

Weiner, B. (1993). On sin versus sickness: A theory of perceived responsibility and social motivation. *American Psychologist, 48,* 957–965.

Wyer, R. S., & Carlston, D. E. (1994). The cognitive representation of persons and events. In R. S. Wyer & T. K. Srull (Eds.), *Handbook of social cognition* (Vol. 1, pp. 41–98). Hillsdale, NJ: Erlbaum.

Wyer, R. S., & Srull, T. K. (1994). *Handbook of social cognition.* Hillsdale, NJ: Erlbaum.

Yarkin, K. L., Harvey, J. H., & Bloxom, B. M. (1981). Cognitive sets, attribution, and social interaction. *Journal of Personality and Social Psychology, 41,* 243–252.

Yates, B. T., Klein, S. B., & Haven, W. G. (1978). Psychological nosology and mnemonic reconstruction: Effects of diagnostic labels on observers' recall of positive and negative behavior frequencies. *Cognitive Therapy and Research, 2,* 377–387.

Ybarra, O., & Stephan W. G. (1996). Misanthropic person memory. *Journal of Personality and Social Psychology, 70,* 691–700.

Zuroff, D. C. (1989). Judgments of frequency of social stimuli: How schematic is person memory? *Journal of Personality and Social Psychology, 56,* 890–898.

V

POSTSCRIPT

14

THINKING INTERACTIONALLY ABOUT DEPRESSION: A RADICAL RESTATEMENT

I have mixed feelings about the attention that the first publication of my career (Coyne, 1976b) continues to get in the current literature on depression. I was a graduate student when I wrote it, and I was quite lacking in clinical and research experience. A reviewer had queried, "What basis does this author have for making these claims about depression?" Fortunately, the editor missed the inadequacy of my response in the revision that was accepted for publication. The article was hardly the presentation of a formal model of depression that it was later made out to be. It was, at best, an incompletely theorized description of a set of processes linking depression to its interpersonal context. The conceptualization of depression that I offered was vague and lacking in crucial details, in part because I was attempting to set out a theoretical and research agenda for further development, but also because I was simply not very familiar with the phenomena I was trying to explain. Whereas it is gratifying that the article has not settled into obscurity, it has been disappointing that it is taking so long for subsequent work to move beyond my conceptualization. Even in my most expansive moment, I always conceived of this work as being only a rung on the ladder of theoretical development. If the article continues to deserve attention, it is in recognition of its being a first step, not a place to rest.

My dissertation study (Coyne, 1976a) was an extension of the work in my first article, but it was not a crucial test of that formulation. It involved having naive undergraduate women conversing on the telephone with either depressed or nondepressed female psychiatric outpatients or normal controls. Audiotapes of the conversations were scored for content, and the students and their conversational partners filled out questionnaires at the end of the conversation. In the earlier article, I mentioned in passing that people in the immediate interpersonal environment of depressed people become "irritated, yet inhibited, and increasingly guilt-ridden" (p. 34), but I did not state that depressed people were distressing. Even if that were the case for people who interact with depressed individuals on a prolonged or regular basis, it was a bit much to expect to be able to demonstrate this in 20-minute telephone conversations between depressed people and strangers. The hypothesis that depressed people would have a measurable impact on strangers' mood in such a brief encounter seemed a bit far-fetched, even if depressed persons actually had such effects on others' moods in more extended interactions.

In response to critics (Doerfler & Chaplin, 1985), I later defended the relevance of the study of fleeting contacts between strangers for the development of an interactional model of depression (Coyne, 1985a). I argued that such studies allow the examination of an emergent pattern of depressive interactions in the absence of a confounding history of negative experiences between participants. In retrospect, I still believe that there is some merit to this position, yet a preexisting relationship, including whatever negative experiences people have had with each other, is more than a confound in terms of its effects on current interactions. The question of the relevance of studies of contacts between strangers for the understanding of what transpires in enduring close relationships is far more complex than it first looks. Specifically, Benazon (1997) cogently argued that it is not always easy to identify direct parallels in close relationships to what has been observed in these fleeting contacts between strangers. For instance, in the Coyne (1976a) study, rejection was measured with items such as not wanting to sit next to the depressed person on a long bus trip. Not wanting to sit next to a spouse would undoubtedly point to a very different phenomenon from avoiding a stranger and would negativity be expressed differently in all but the most deteriorated of long-term relationships.

Benazon (1997) further pointed out that the original Coyne (1976b) formulation was silent on the temporal parameters of the interpersonal processes that were being described. To the extent that some sort of progression may be assumed, one should expect that many of the interpersonal processes have already taken their toll on relationships by the time depressed people enter treatment and become available for study. The paradox, therefore, is that if the processes I originally postulated actually occurred, there is reason to believe that one would not be able to observe them in current interactions between depressed patients and their spouses. One should be able to observe the sequelae of these processes, but these could be quite different from the original interactions. The accumulative effects of these processes might be reflected in resignation, tension, and emotional distance, not necessarily continued reassurance seeking. Indeed, the methodological requirement of observational studies that couples with a depressed person sit down and talk about a specific problem for 15 minutes without any distraction or either partner leaving the room might represent a profound shift in the routines the partners have tacitly negotiated. My point is that it may be much more difficult to develop, refine, and test interactional models of depression in enduring relationships than was first assumed. The Oregon Research Institute group (Biglan, Hops, & Sherman, 1988) provided a provocative demonstration of how displays of depressive behavior in the family may in the short run inhibit hostile behavior and elicit compliance from others but also serve to suppress caring behavior and to increase the likelihood of hostility subsequently being directed at the depressed family member. This finding can be taken as strong evidence that interactional processes of the kind I originally postulated can be identified in enduring relationships. However, there should be no illusions about the difficulties involved in trying to reconstruct what has been going on in a couple or family with a depressed person from the observations that can be made years into a set of relationships and months or longer into a current episode of depression.

Many interactional studies of depression suffer from a lack of original and critical thinking in their conception and execution. There have been far too many cookie-cutter variations and replications of the Coyne (1976a) study. Additional studies are unlikely to unseat the robust finding that distressed and clinically depressed people reliably get rejected after a brief conversation (Segrin & Abramson, 1994). Findings of negative mood induction are more than a "will-o'-the-wisp" phenomenon but not as robust as what is found for rejection. However, the generalizability of both positive and null findings concerning mood induction in brief encounters is uncertain. It is a lot to ask of participants that they be able to report on what are undoubtedly subtle shifts in mood occurring in such a brief period. Mood changes that are evident in nonverbal behavior may not be reflected in self-reports (Gotlib & Robinson, 1982). People living with depressed individuals may be distressed themselves (Benazon, 1997; Coyne et al., 1987; Coyne, Pepper, & Cohen, in press), but it is doubtful that the processes involved are the same as those often observed in studies of brief encounters between depressed people and strangers. If the term *mood induction* is to be applied to both fleeting encounters and enduring relationships, it should be viewed as a descriptive term referring to a heterogeneous set of processes and circumstances, not as a singular process or an explanatory term.

I intend in the present chapter to put my 1976 articles in perspective, building on them but acknowledging their limitations and renewing a call for the development of an interactional view of depression. Interest in interpersonal factors in depression appears to be alive and well. The other chapters in this volume can be taken as evidence of fresh theoretical, empirical, and clinical work. These chapters go far beyond my early work, and there is considerable original thinking here. Most of the authors take an integrative perspective, in particular linking interpersonal and cognitive conceptions of depression. This integrative turn and the emphasis on cognition reflect dominant trends in the larger field and will undoubtedly be adopted in a large body of future research. Yet I remain skeptical. If the proposed benefits of adopting an integrative approach are to be realized, it will be a result of sufficient critical scrutiny of this movement that it is saved from its excesses. Adherents of so-called integrative approaches to depression tend to make sweeping inferences from exceedingly weak data. They also discourage a struggle with the many difficulties inherent in doing meaningful research concerning the interpersonal context of depression by offering easily done but less revealing alternatives.

The crucial problem with much work on depression that is intended to be integrative is that it ends up reductionistic. Too often what is involved in such research is that depressed individuals' statements about themselves and their relationships automatically get interpreted as evidence of enduring cognitive structures, a sociotropic trait, or working models of relationships, and these reified entities are then given causal priority over any interpersonal processes. Interest in what goes on between depressed people and others and how involvement in contemporary relationships affects the functioning of depressed individuals is dulled or lost altogether.

In one of the many recent examples of this tendency, J. E. Roberts, Gotlib, and Kassel (1996) administered a set of questionnaires including a measure of attachment style to a sample of college students. This measure (Levy & Davis, 1988) involves classifying respondents as secure, ambivalent, or avoidant on the basis of which of three single-item prototypical self-descriptions they endorse most strongly. For instance, a respondent who most agreed with the following description would be classified as an "anxious–ambivalent type": "I find that others are reluctant to get as close as I would like. I often worry that my partner really doesn't love me or won't want to stay with me. I want to get very close to my partner, and this sometimes scares people away" (Hazan & Shaver, 1990, p. 272). No attempt was made to assess what recent experiences or characteristics of the partner in question or others in the respondent's life might give rise to such a set of concerns.

Instead, this classification was interpreted by J. E. Roberts et al. as a lifelong trait that developed in early childhood and that conferred vulnerability to depression throughout the life span. In two more studies reported in the same article, college students received another measure of attachment and self-report measures of distress, self-esteem, and neuroticism. The students then completed the measures of self-esteem and distress 6 or 8 weeks later, and the first battery of self-report measures was used to predict changes in distress. One might ask why the effects of this allegedly lifelong attachment style were not being expressed in the initial distress score rather than in the changes in distress observed over a short period of time. These data probably reflected students' intervening experiences in relationships that were affecting their levels of distress, but no data on such experiences were collected. Instead, the authors concluded that they had demonstrated that attachment style is associated with depressive symptoms but mediated by dysfunctional attitudes and depleted self-esteem.

The sheer repetitiousness of such claims has seemingly given them an unwarranted credibility; in each successive study, prior papers are cited in which such claims were also made without empirical evidence. One is asked to believe that the past is everything and inexorably shapes current perceptions and even the circumstances in which persons find themselves. Yet the reasonableness of these perceptions and the details of these circumstances remain unexplored. What is touted as an integration of interpersonal and cognitive factors is ultimately a head-first, cognitive reductionism with a resolutely neocryptopsychoanalytic bias. Such work is an alternative to attempting to understand the interpersonal context of depression—a barrier even—not a contribution to it.

As I indicate in the remainder of the chapter, constructing an interactional perspective is difficult, and progress is likely to be slow in disentangling the complex and reciprocal processes linking depressed persons and their contexts. Yet the payoff is likely to be great in terms of the richness of the understanding that is achieved and the radical new possibilities for intervention that can be derived from such a perspective. Furthermore, a key contribution of an interactional perspective is that it can be the source of a sustained critique of what might be termed the "fundamental attributional error in depression theory and research." That is, an interactional perspective can be used to identify how conventional models of depression ascribe intrinsic characteristics to depressed people, which are more properly seen as emerging from their exchanges with the environment, contingent on their being in particular environments, or simply features of the environment in which depression occurs, not of depressed people themselves.

For the remainder of the chapter, I outline some of the broader issues both in developing an interactional perspective and in using it as a basis for critiquing the limitations of conventional views of the disorder. These issues include how one explores and understands the importance of the past, the role of significant others in lives of depressed individuals, and the relationship of depressed people's statements about themselves to their interpersonal context. I then point to some of the unrealized potential of an interactional perspective for the development of innovative interventions aimed not only at depressed people but also at key members of their environments. Depression occurs in troubled interpersonal circumstances. The individuals who are significant in the lives of depressed patients can often profitably be enlisted directly in understanding and renegotiating their roles and relationships. These people have something to contribute to the recovery of depressed patients, but they are also likely to have unmet needs themselves that can be addressed in therapy and other forms of intervention. Before proceeding with this agenda, however, I argue for the need for theorists and researchers to come to terms with the recurrent, episodic nature of clinical depression and how it differs from self-reported distress. Once researchers recognize the nature of depression, there will be profound shift in the kinds of questions asked about the role of interpersonal factors and the kinds of answers sought. It will be seen that the attempt to justify studies of ersatz clinical depression with college students completing batteries of self-report measures poses serious problems for the development and credibility of all psychological approaches to depression, not just the interactional perspective.

THE NEED TO COME TO TERMS WITH THE NATURE OF CLINICAL DEPRESSION

The accumulation of compelling data showing that depression is a recurrent, episodic disorder with onset typically in the third decade of life has important implications for the form that models of the disorder should take (Coyne & Whiffen, 1995). The best predictor that someone will get depressed in the near future is by far a personal history of depression. Indeed, reanalyses of the Epidemiologic Catchment Area data have indicated that people who are depressed in the course of a year are 40 times more likely to have been depressed in the past than people who do not become depressed in that year (Kessler & Magee, 1994a). In my group's study of primary medical care patients, we obtained a more modest, but nonetheless impressive, relative risk of 8 for predicting current depression from past depression (Coyne, Pepper, & Flynn, in press). Long-term follow-up of depressed psychiatric patients has revealed that few if any depressed patients experience only a single episode of depression (Keller, Lavori, Lewis, & Klerman, 1983) and that once depressed people enter outpatient treatment, they are likely to spend 20% of their lives depressed (Angst, 1986).

Many psychosocial predictors of depression lose their significance or are substantially reduced in importance once a history of depression is taken into account (Kessler & Magee, 1994b). Although it is possible that some lifetime vulnerability for recurrence of depression is explained by the crystallization of stable psychological and social factors, the size of the relationship between past and current depression dwarfs the relationship between any psychosocial factors and lifetime or current depression. A more plausible explanation is that psychosocial factors, particularly features of the interpersonal context, interact with constitutional factors in producing an episode of depression. Akiskal (1991) suggested that childhood adversity moderates the expression of a constitutional vulnerability to depression, in part by being associated with an excess of stressful interpersonal experiences in adulthood. Disrupted family relationships in early life may be tied to immaturity, hostile dependency, manipulativeness, impulsiveness, and a low threshold for alcohol and drug abuse in adulthood rather than directly associated with depression. These characteristics may precipitate life events that trigger depression in vulnerable persons, and the result may be more frequent episodes without a direct effect on the lifetime risk for depression. However, an interactional perspective would suggest even more complexity. Some of the apparent effects of such a background and stormy interpersonal style on the risk for depression in adulthood may be tied to intervening events such as pregnancy before marriage (Andrews & Brown, 1988; Quinton, Rutter, & Liddle, 1984), continuities in interpersonal circumstances, and the kinds of people who are attracted to or tolerate such an interpersonal style. As I argue later, an interactional perspective calls attention to the need to consider such contingent relationships before assuming the effects of the past are fixed, like a frozen woolly mammoth in the Arctic (Wachtel, 1977). However, for present purposes, it needs to be noted that (a) the recurrent, episodic nature of depression needs to be accommodated in any model of depression, including an interactional model; (b) even in the face of constitutional vulnerabilities to depression, interpersonal variables may affect how these vulnerabilities are expressed; and (c) models of depression that assume the disorder regularly occurs in single episodes are empirically invalid. Given the overwhelming importance of history of depression, one cannot assume that most onsets of an episode of depression can be explained by a set of interpersonal circumstances in which anyone would get depressed.

The prognostication that depressed patients will average 20% of their lives depressed could be taken as pessimistic and discouraging, but it leaves open the question of how interpersonal factors might explain the other 80% of the lives of people vulnerable to depression or how such factors may explain deviations from this prognosis. Indeed, theorists need to be careful lest their efforts to explain the 20% of the time vulnerable people are depressed leave them ill equipped to accommodate the obverse fact that 80% of the time these individuals are not depressed. The risk of relapse or recurrence is particularly high immediately after recovery, but interpersonal factors may still prove decisive in whether a recovered patient remains out of episode (Coyne & Whiffen, 1995). A monthly opportunity for remitted depressed patients to review their interpersonal circumstances has been shown to extend their time until relapse substantially (Frank, Kupfer, Perel, & Cornes, 1990). Again, recognition of the recurrent, episodic nature of depression shifts only the kinds of questions asked about interpersonal factors; it does not resolve them. Furthermore, the attention that has been given to psychosocial variables as vulnerability factors in depression needs to be balanced by consideration of how psychosocial factors confer resiliency and thereby moderate lifetime risk for depression. For instance, achievement of a close, confiding relationship with a dependable spouse may substantially reduce risk of depression in otherwise vulnerable persons (Quinton & Rutter, 1988; Quinton et al. 1984).

Psychologists need to accommodate the recurrent nature of depression including the timing of first episodes in theorizing about the role of interpersonal factors such as marriage and marital problems in the disorder. Many vulnerable people experience their first episode of depression prior to getting married or at least before their current marriage, given their greater likelihood of divorce (Coyne, Pepper, & Cohen, in press). Therefore, the quality of their current marriage cannot assume all of the explanatory burden for their being at risk for depression. Here, too, what has been learned about the nature of depression alters the form of questions asked about the importance of such factors; it does not settle them.

A recurrence of depression may have different implications than a first or single episode for how depressed individuals cope and how others react. Repeated experiences with depression may generate fears about the ability to meet role demands and the likely reactions of others when depression recurs (Coyne & Calarco, 1995; Coyne, Gallo, Klinkman, & Calarco, 1998), and these effects may persist well beyond the acute episode. Similarly, the burden on family members (Coyne et al., 1987) and how they cope may be different with a recurrent disorder. Recurrence would represent both a continued cost for persons who have suffered depression and a diminution of the resources needed to avoid depression in the future (Coyne & Calarco, 1995).

Finally, the nature of depression has implications for the relevance of studies of self-reported distress in the understanding of the disorder, particularly studies conducted with college student samples. Current distress does not by itself represent a strong indicator for the disorder (Fechner-Bates, Coyne, & Schwenk, 1994; R. E. Roberts et al., 1991), and the common assumption of a continuum from everyday distress to clinical disorder may not be warranted (Coyne, 1994). The sophomore year of college, when students are typically recruited for research, may predate the time when most vulnerable persons have their first episode of depression. The high rates of distress but low rates of clinical disorder that are sometimes found in adolescent samples (almost 50% distressed, but only 2.5% depressed according to R. E. Roberts et al., 1991) suggest that distress in college students is probably even less related to clinical disorder than are the same levels of distress when reported by older, community-residing adults (Coyne & Santor, 1997). It is unfortunate that despite the strong claims that have been made for the contribution of studies of distressed college students to the understanding of depression (Vredenburg, Flett, & Krames, 1993), so little is known about the nature and character of students' distress beyond the correlations of self-reported distress with semantically similar measures (Gotlib, Lewinsohn, & Seeley, 1995). Despite the plethora of studies in which various redundant measures of subjective self-evaluation were used, there has been almost no attention to the circumstances in which this distress arises and gets resolved or to the temporal parameters of such distress. Undoubtedly, the finding of high rates of distress among college students represents in part trait neuroticism, acute distress, and error in measurement (Kenny & Zautra, 1995). This heterogeneity should be reflected in differences in social interaction. Regardless, demonstration that distressed college students share significant features with clinically depressed people is long overdue for those who make claims of equivalence.

CONSTRUCTING AN INTERACTIONAL PERSPECTIVE ON DEPRESSION: BROADER ISSUES

An interactional perspective on depression represents much more than the hypothesis that depressed people are distressing and get rejected. Fundamentally, it is a call for a different way of thinking about psychopathology, one that involves an appreciation of the rich and reciprocal links between people and their environments and of the significance of close relationships. An important first step in constructing such a perspective is to move from a consideration of the subjective experience and behavioral manifestations of depression taken in isolation to an exploration of how they might make greater sense when the interpersonal environment and depressed persons' exchanges with it are taken into account. For instance, this conceptual move can be seen in Leff and Vaughn's (1985) contextualization of depressed women's concerns about loss and rejection and their desire for continual comfort and support. The authors found that "few depressed patients described as chronically insecure or lacking in self-confidence were living with supportive or sympathetic spouses ... when this was the case, the patients were well at follow-up" (p. 95).

Observations that have led to conclusions that depressed individuals lack social skills and that this lack of skills contributes to their becoming depressed are opened to new interpretations within an interactional perspective. A study by Libet and Lewinsohn (1973) established a tendency in the literature for differences between depressed and nondepressed people in social behavior to be automatically attributed to depressed people's skills deficits. In that study, depressed individuals in group therapy scored lower on a number of measures of social activity, which the authors interpreted as a skills deficit. However, the data also revealed that the level of social behavior that was emitted by individuals in these groups was highly correlated with the level received, so that depressed people were facing a different social environment than were other members of the groups. This is an exceedingly primitive conceptualization of the notion of social skill, but after more than 25 years the study of social skills in depression has not moved far beyond it. A more sophisticated view of social skills problems in depression takes into account a number of considerations. First, as a result of their effects on others, depressed people may face environments that require more effort and special skills for them to maintain social relationships and the quality of their social behavior. Second, some of the changes in their environment that contributed to their becoming depressed—loss events in particular—also deplete social resources and contribute directly to interpersonal difficulties. Third, the anergia, anhedonia, difficulty concentrating, and other symptoms of depression may make normal social behavior more effortful and less satisfying. In these ways, depression is more impairing than many chronic physical illnesses (Wells et al., 1989). Whereas depressed people's behavior may appear as a deficit in performance, it should not be interpreted as a skills deficit.

An interactional perspective invites the balancing of historical questions about why problems are occurring with an inquiry about why they are manifested now. The identification of deficits in the functioning of depressed people needs to be followed up with exploration of the conditions in which problems were absent in the past and of contemporary conditions that might be maintaining these problems. Although residual problems persist beyond an episode of depression (Mintz, Mintz, Arruda, & Hwang, 1992; Paykel et al., 1995; Weissman & Paykel, 1974), many individuals who are vulnerable to depression function well throughout their lives or for long periods between episodes. The task is to discover how the competencies that have been demonstrated in the past can be reinstated. For instance, the fact that depression interferes with effective parenting has been used to explain the high prevalence of psychological difficulties and diagnosable disturbance found in the children of depressed parents. However, consideration of the family context of depression leads to rival interpretations, as reviewed by Downey and Coyne (1990). First, some of the difficulties of the children may be traceable to problems in this context, such as marital discord that preceded and contributed to parental depression. Second, an available nondepressed parent and the absence of overt family conflict largely eliminate the risk of disturbance among the children of depressed parents.

From an interactional perspective, the notion of interpersonal skills ought not be reduced to a fixed repertoire of behaviors. Enactment of interpersonal behavior is of course affected by context, and one must ask how the interpersonal context, including the characteristic response from others, differs for depressed people. Also, problems in important contexts can influence behavior in other contexts, as when work problems affect interactions in the home (Repetti, 1989; Repetti & Wood, 1997) or conflict with the spouse reduces the quality of a parent's interactions with children. One must also ask what might be added to an interpersonal context to elicit seemingly missing social skills. The presence of a supportive other may expand the range of positive social behaviors, and the mere anticipation of being able to report to a supportive other may increase such behavior, even when such a person is not physically present. Finally, even if depressed people have never exhibited particular behaviors that would be effective in resolving their predicament, one must ask why they have not benefited from the successful models available in their larger environment. This question can often be profitably rephrased as "What keeps depressed people feeling ineligible to make use of culturally available resources?" This question broadens the inquiry to larger social issues, including gender roles (see chapter 9, this volume).

The Role of the Past: A Woolly Mammoth or Escapable Cycles and Tracks?

Much of the current writing on depression assumes that childhood experiences have a direct, inevitable effect on adult relationships and risk for depression. This assumption is theory driven—another instance of the persistence of neocryptopsychoanalytic thinking—rather than based on data. The actual risk for adult depression conferred by childhood adversity is modest; some reviewers express doubt about an effect for parental death or separation from a parent of any substantial significance (Crook & Eliot, 1980; Richards & Dyson, 1982). Other researchers have suggested it is not loss per se that is important but a "lack of care": the antipathy and neglect by caretakers that may follow the loss of a parent (Harris, Brown, & Bifulco, 1986). Work by Kessler and his colleagues (Kessler, 1997; Kessler & Magee 1994a, 1994b) suggests that the risk for depression conferred by childhood adversity is limited to early-onset depression (onset prior to age 20). This conclusion is consistent with the results of other research suggesting that the effects of childhood adversity are conveyed through late adolescent and early adulthood experiences such as premarital pregnancy and violent and unsupportive intimate relationships (Andrews & Brown, 1988; Quinton et al., 1984). For instance, in one study, late adolescent girls whose mothers had psychiatric disorders were themselves more likely to have experienced a severe life event involving a boyfriend in the past year (Andrews, Brown, & Creasey, 1990).

An interactional perspective on depression discourages the assumption of a strong or immutable link between early childhood experience and adult depression; the appearance of such a link requires confirmation and explanation. Whatever link exists is likely to be less robust and more indirect than commonly assumed. Such a perspective also encourages attention to the dynamic interplay of people with accumulating individual histories in interaction with environments that are not entirely of their own making and not entirely yielding to their efforts (Rutter, 1989). Some of the apparent continuities in psychosocial risk for depression may reflect continuities in interpersonal circumstances in addition to individual behavior. In effect, an interactional perspective on depression is a contextual, life-span, developmental perspective (Coyne, Downey, & Boergers, 1992; Elder, George, & Shanahan, 1996) with emphases on "the fact that humans make choices but are socially constrained in the choices they make, the influence of individual choice and social constraints on the age grading of events and social roles, and the relational interdependence among human lives" (Elder et al., 1996, p. 246). Attention is directed to how individuals negotiate potential "turning points" (Strauss, 1959) or "transforming incidents" (Clausen, 1995) in their life circumstances, which either strengthen existing trajectories or present the opportunity for large-scale change. An unwed teenage mother's decision to move in with the father of her child not only may commit her to an unsupportive relationship and increase her risk of negative life events related to financial difficulties but also may decrease the likelihood she will have a relationship with a more appropriate man in the future (Pickles & Rutter, 1991). The resolution of such turning points may depend on how individuals make choices within the constraints of the options that their circumstances provide as well as on an interlinked chain of effects from both before and after such turning points. In addition, as Bandura (1982) argued, one needs to allow that "chance encounters play a prominent role in shaping the course of human lives" (p. 747).

The recurrent, episodic nature of depression necessitates acknowledgment of the reciprocal, accumulative effects of repeated episodes on deficiencies in psychosocial resources. Drawing on Caspi, Bem, and Elder's (1989) distinction between cumulative and interactional continuity, one can postulate two broad sets of processes by which individuals' lifetime risk for recurrent episodes of depression and limitations in psychosocial resources perpetuate each other. *Cumulative continuity* refers to a situation in which an individual's experience with depression channels him or her into an environment that reinforces the likelihood of future depression, thereby sustaining risk across the life course through the progressive accumulation of the consequences of depression. In addition to marital difficulties increasing risk for depression, therefore, recurrent episodes of depression may precipitate divorce and entrance into single parenthood without adequate financial resources. *Interactional continuity* refers to a situation in which recurrent depression strengthens reciprocal, sustaining responses from others in subsequent social interaction, thereby reinstating the behavior pattern across the life course whenever the relevant interactive situation is replicated. Significant others' past experiences with an individual's depression may increase their sensitivity to moodiness and their intolerance of reassurance seeking.

Taking into account the events intervening between conditions in the distal past and current risk for depression allows for a better understanding of how psychosocial vulnerabilities get expressed or modified over time and how they can be moderated by positive experiences and the development of resiliency factors. Similarly, looking beyond the skin of the individual to the larger interpersonal context and its continuities and discontinuities increases explanatory power. Yet an interactional perspective ultimately confronts the limits of prediction: "We need not be fixed by our pasts" (Lewis, 1997, p. 70).

An Interpersonal Environment Populated by Real People

Writings on depression, even those ostensibly representing an interpersonal perspective, give scant attention to the characteristics of the people who are significant in the adult lives of depressed individuals. There is little reference to their resources, their limitations, or their own pasts, which they in part have brought to the relationship with the depressed people in their lives and in part have shared with them. Drawing on a tradition established by Harry Stack Sullivan, George Herbert Mead, and others, Kiesler (1996) referred to such a person as a "significant other," defined as someone who "presently is important and influential in an adult person's life—whose presence, actions, and speech are central in sustaining that person's self-view and worldview" (p. 74). As Thomas Joiner and I indicated in the opening chapter of this volume, significant others are often reduced to the state of hapless victim in accounts of their involvement in the interactions associated with the perpetuation of depression. Other literature disembodies significant others, limiting their importance to depressed individuals' *perceptions* of the availability of social support. The social support literature has granted increasing recognition that close relationships are sources of stress, conflict, and disappointment, as well as of support (Coyne & DeLongis, 1986), but even with these negative elements acknowledged, there is still considerable reductionism involved in treating these relationships only in terms of depressed people's perceptions of support or negativity.

A look at the characteristics of significant others displaces some of the explanatory burden that would otherwise be put on the characteristics of depressed individuals. For instance, Brown, Bifulco, Harris, and Bridge (1996) attempted to determine whether the difficulties in the marital relationships of depressed women could be construed as contingent on the women's affective state; they found that only one third of the marital difficulties were rated as contingent. Two thirds of these marital difficulties involved husbands judged to be "grossly undependable." Characteristics of current partners may mediate the contribution of depressed individuals' past to their current vulnerability to depression. Background factors such as childhood adversity and adolescent deviance as well as the destructiveness of current tactics for resolving conflict are remarkably highly correlated for depressed women and their husbands (Coyne, Pepper, & Cohen, in press). Quinton et al. (1984) found that the adjustment of women who had been raised in an institution was predicted by husbands' reports of their own adolescent deviance. Furthermore, the women's current problems were associated with their spouses' current alcohol or drug problems or difficulties with the law. Birtchnell (1980) found that among women whose mothers had died in childhood and who had a poor relationship with subsequent maternal figures, those who had a good relationship with their spouse were less likely to become depressed. If they did become depressed, it occurred almost a decade later than in those with a bad relationship. Parker and Hadzi-Pavlovic (1984) found not only that an affectionate relationship with the spouse largely eliminated the influence of this negative childhood experience but also that an unaffectionate relationship with the spouse undid the influence of a positive relationship with the father and stepmother.

Significant others may be viewed as the accomplices of people who are vulnerable to depression and as key players in the vulnerable people's current circumstances, with its attendant risk and resiliency factors. Yet one also needs to understand the sources of significant others' own risk for distress (Benazon, 1997; Coyne, Pepper, & Cohen, in press; Coyne, Wortman, & Lehman, 1988). Their lives are susceptible to disruption by depression in those with whom they live (Coyne et al., 1988). Living with a person who is vulnerable to recurrent depression may require patience and understanding, and there may be emergent problems that could not be predicted from the background of either the depressed person or the significant other. The quality of others' involvement and the support they provide may deteriorate over time (Coyne et al., 1988), particularly when the persistence or return of depressive symptoms is not clearly tied to interpersonal circumstances. For those who are not themselves vulnerable to the disorder, the occurrence of depression in someone they know and the failure of this person to master the problem by shear willpower or positive thinking is puzzling enough; repeated recurrences may prove truly mysterious. It is important from both a theoretical and a practical perspective that the potentially troubled close relationships of depressed individuals not be reduced to the pure victimization of spouses and family members by depressed individuals, or vice versa. Instead, an appreciation must be developed for how all involved may have gotten caught up in difficult circumstances and how their ways of coping may perpetuate these circumstances despite intentions to the contrary.

Depressed People's Complaints About Themselves and Their Circumstances

On close inspection, a rather large literature is reducible to the observation that distressed and clinically depressed people complain. Semantically similar questionnaire items that elicit such complaints are sorted into scales whose labeling indicates researchers' intention that they represent distinct constructs (e.g., neuroticism, dysfunctional attitudes, distress). Yet examination of the content of these items often reveals that their placement on one scale rather than on another was arbitrary, and this is borne out by item–scale correlations. Sophisticated statistical analyses of a battery of these scales yield a causal ordering that is dictated by minor differences in semantic content and the breadth of the time period covered by the instructions for a particular scale. For example, a scale on which respondents are asked to indicate whether negative self-statements generally apply to them (neuroticism) is given causal priority over a scale on which similar items are to be evaluated for the "past 2 weeks" (self-reported distress or depression).

Such exercises are virtually guaranteed to yield to statistically significant associations among the scales, but an interactional perspective provides a basis for a sustained critique of the standard interpretation that these associations reflect causal relations among cognitive variables. The perspective first suggests some criteria that need to be met before a scale score is interpreted as evidence of a cognitive structure and, in particular, as evidence of an enduring cognitive bias or distortion. It is necessary to look at the circumstances in which respondents endorse negative self-statements and ask (a) what information they cite as the basis of their endorsement of these self-statements, (b) what information is available to them that is seemingly inconsistent with such statements and how they reconcile this with their responses to the scale, and (c) what would bring about a change in their responses. Presumably, one would postulate a different sort of cognitive construct if respondents were making their "depressive" self-statements in life circumstances that were rich and stable in their support of such interpretations than if these complaints persisted when there was no such environmental support. Also, the nature of this cognitive construct would be quite different if respondents readily shifted their answers to questionnaires with changes in the demands placed on them by their life circumstances or with changes in the views of their significant others. From an interactional perspective, correlations among measures of distress and measures of purported cognitive constructs are not very informative without this additional work. In evaluating this critique, it is important to keep in mind that much of the literature to which it is applied consists of cross-sectional and short-term longitudinal studies in which a set of self-report measures are simply related to each other. Evidence that respondents strongly endorse negative self-statements when they are not distressed is sorely lacking, but the discussions of the results of such studies reflect the assumption that enduring cognitive constructs are being assessed.

The interactional perspective has typically been seen as countering cognitive theorists' claim that depression is a product of biased and distorted thinking with the notion that depressed people have a basis in their experience for their self-complaints (Coyne, 1982; Coyne & Gotlib, 1983). Yet it is in no way a challenge to an interactional perspective if depressed individuals misjudge either the particular messages to them or the overall quality of their environment (Coyne, 1989b). As pointed out in Coyne (1976b), communication between depressed people and others may be inhibited, attenuated, and distorted so that discrepancies in perceptions and expectations are not clarified. Indeed, interpersonal psychotherapy for depression frequently focuses on resolving such communication difficulties without the assumption that they represent cognitive distortions on the part of depressed individuals. Furthermore, Coyne (1976b) raised the possibility that the threatening aspects of the interpersonal environment of depressed people—including the tendency of key individuals to offer false reassurance while in fact feeling critical and rejecting—may be such that negative interpretative biases make sense or even prove adaptive.

Beyond questions of bias or verticality of depressed people's complaints, the interactional perspective raises issues about their function or instrumentality (Coyne, 1989b). It is not always clear, for instance, that depressed people believe their negative self-statements in the same way that they hold to core beliefs about themselves or the world. To varying degrees, depressed individuals are able to maintain some distance from their thoughts. Many even concede they are *kvetching* (Held, in press). An adequate explanation of depressed people's complaints must also address their function as illocutionary speech acts (Austin, 1962) with the purpose of reducing demands, eliciting support from others, inhibiting others, or leaving them feeling guilty. Depressed people's complaints about themselves may also be a self-manipulative or self-handicapping strategy (Snyder & Smith, 1982) in that they allow depressed people to reduce their expectations of themselves, avoid the implications of potential failures, and otherwise guard against disappointment. For example, complaints of being incompetent may represent a strategy of self-indoctrination in a threatening situation.

In my most recent work (Coyne, 1997), I have begun to explore how the negative self-talk of depressed people may sometimes represent efforts to resist indoctrination by others. I note that depressed individuals frequently struggle with negative self-views that, on the one hand, they do not entirely accept, yet, on the other hand, they do not feel free to dismiss. Drawing on the work of Bakhtin and Vygotsky, as well as feminist theorists such as Dana Jack (1991; also see chapter 9, this volume), I have come to view some of depressed people's self-criticism as an ongoing dialogue with authoritative voices, often drawn from socializing agents and sources of criticism and disapproval in their current environment. Resolution of these complaints comes when depressed individuals are either effectively supported in resisting these judgments or able to make changes in their circumstances.

Regardless of where this work takes me, it is consistent with the notion that there is no one essential psychological process or mechanism inherent in depressive self-complaints and statements of pessimism. Before settling on the distorted cognitive processes as the core or causal disturbance in depression, researchers need to examine the readily observable features of the context in which such complaints occur and the function they serve, including the degree to which depressed people accept them as valid. As a prelude to considering what depressed individuals think, one needs to know something about their ecological niches, what judgments these circumstances support, and how depressed people and those around them are responding.

INTERVENTIONS IN THE INTERPERSONAL CONTEXT OF DEPRESSION

Interpersonal psychotherapy for depression (IPT; Klerman, Weissman, Rounsaville, & Chevron, 1984) has been validated as a treatment for acute depression as well as a maintenance therapy (Frank et al., 1990). In the National Collaborative Study, it compared well with both cognitive therapy and tricyclic medication (Elkin, Shea, Watkins, & Imber, 1989). The goals of IPT are to decrease the depressive symptoms and to improve the interpersonal problems associated with the onset and maintenance of the depressive episode. Therapy is typically focused on one or two problem areas, each broadly characterized as a role dispute, role transition, unresolved grief, or interpersonal deficit such as social isolation. In addition, recognition is given to the effects of depression on personal functioning and relationships in the explicit granting to patients of a limited sick role. It is acknowledged that some of the difficulties of depressed persons reflect genuine impairment; a burden falls on them to manage these difficulties, but it also must be accepted that they are not at their best and they need to lower expectations and renegotiate responsibilities.

It is assumed in IPT that change comes about through understanding and renegotiating the roles and relationships on which depressed patients depend. An effort is made to elicit patients' feelings about these aspects of their lives, giving particular attention to how unacknowledged feelings may be linked to unmet expectations. In turn, these expectations are examined, and discussion focuses on how they can be more effectively communicated and used as a basis for renegotiating patients' involvement in significant life contexts. Efforts to help patients develop new activities typically take the form of discussions of their options during which therapists implicitly encourage patients to consider new behaviors, rather than give them explicit directives or homework assignments. The patients' significant others are sometimes invited to take part in these discussions in conjoint sessions. The interpersonal therapist is also open to engaging patients in frank discussions of whether a particular close relationship has deteriorated to the point that dissolution needs to be considered and what options this leaves for patients. More than psychodynamic therapists, interpersonal therapists assume an active role in directing discussion, and they may adopt the role of advocate for depressed patients in discussions when patients' own sense of their rights and entitlement falters. However, IPT is marked by considerable constraint on therapists' activities in its eschewing of direct advice, strategizing, and active involvement in the planning and executing of changes in patients' lives. Even if IPT is an empirically validated, effective therapy, it is an approach that falls far short of realizing the full potential of an interactional approach to psychotherapy for depression.

Although it comes out of the behavioral, rather than the interpersonal, tradition, couples therapy is also a viable approach to treating some married depressed people. Outcome data suggest efficacy comparable to other empirically validated therapies for depression (Beach, Fincham, & Katz, in press; Jacobson, Dobson, Fruzzetti, & Schmaling, 1991). As developed by Beach, Sandeen, and O'Leary (1990), couples therapy for depression is a clinically flexible approach in which the therapist begins by facilitating closeness and shared positive experiences between the partners prior to adopting a focus on change in the relationship. Considerable effort is made to tailor interventions to meet the particular needs of the couple, and there is a "troubleshooting" component at the end of therapy to empower couples to maintain the gains they have made. In contrast, traditional behavioral marital therapy (BMT; Jacobson & Margolin, 1979) is focused on the identification of areas in which each member of the couple desires change. This emphasis may exacerbate the withdrawal of some disengaged partners of depressed people and may prove demoralizing for some depressed spouses. In particular, traditional BMT may introduce a focus on change earlier than is optimal for some depressed spouses and their emotionally disengaged partners (Cordova & Jacobson, 1993). Despite the fact that depressed married people tend to have marital problems and that marital therapy has been shown to be effective for depression, it does not necessarily follow that most married depressed individuals are candidates for conjoint couples therapy. After demonstrating the efficacy of marital therapy for depression in a clinical trial (McLean & Hakstian, 1979), one investigator group had to abandon efforts to recruit depressed women and their husbands directly from primary medical settings (McLean & Miles, 1975). Inability of the women to enlist their husbands in therapy was cited as a key reason for the failure of this program. Apparently, the husbands were either satisfied with their marriage or inclined to blame their marital problems on their wife's depression, which they saw as an individual problem.

The notion that depression can be treated by intervening directly in its interpersonal context has not been developed to its full potential. Interpersonal psychotherapy for depression is derived from the work of Harry Stack Sullivan, who probably coined the term *interpersonal,* and of the Swiss American psychiatrist Adolf Meyer, who was probably the first to use the term *interpersonal relations* (Perry, 1982). In many respects, these two men offered a radical departure from orthodox psychodynamic thinking about psychopathology and psychotherapy, but they retained many of the prohibitions from psychodynamic therapy against direct advice or collaborations with patients in strategizing about how they might implement changes in their lives (Wachtel, 1977). Ironically, this is probably due to Sullivan and Meyer's observations of the destructiveness of Freud's intrusions in to the personal lives of his American followers (Kramer, 1997). Regardless, IPT is unnecessarily limited in its vision of the range of ways in which therapists might appropriately intervene in the lives of depressed patients. Unless patients live a Robinson Crusoe existence, therapy inevitably entails intervention in the lives of more than one person. Once it is recognized that therapy and recovery from depression of necessity involve renegotiation of interpersonal relationships, the task becomes finding the most efficient and ethical ways of bringing about these changes and figuring out who should be involved (Watzlawick & Coyne, 1980).

The work of the Palo Alto Mental Research Institute group (Coyne & Segal, 1982; Fisch, Weakland, & Segal, 1982; Watzlawick, Weakland, & Fisch, 1974; Weakland, Fisch, Watzlawick, & Bodin, 1974) shares with IPT a set of roots in the work of Sullivan and Meyer, but under the influence of hypnotherapist Milton Erickson, this group shed any Sullivanian inhibitions about direct intervention and the assignment of explicit homework to patients. The group adopted the term *strategic* for this approach because of its emphasis on therapists' accepting responsibility for their role in the change process by making deliberate choices about which strategies and tactics to adopt in assisting patients (Haley, 1973; Weakland, 1992). Strategic therapy emphasizes direct intervention in patients' lives to modify the interpersonal contexts, complex feedback processes, and characteristic responses of others that maintain them in their predicaments.

Strategic therapy provides a pragmatic, goal-oriented, short-term approach to the treatment of depression. It focuses on how miscarried coping by depressed persons and those who are significant in their lives perpetuates patients' depression and their predicament and how these efforts can be redirected (Coyne, 1989a; Coyne & Pepper, 1998). Extensive use is made of extratherapy task assignments, often of a paradoxical nature and often using *reframing* (Coyne, 1985b; Watzlawick et al., 1974). In reframing, the therapist works to grasp the language with which the depressed patient and significant others describe a problem, actively acknowledges an acceptance of this perspective, and then extends or turns it in a way that allows the patient and others to initiate new behavior.

Even when depressed patients initially present as individuals, family members and friends may be invited to attend therapy sessions. When this occurs, a nonblaming stance is assumed by the therapist: Others do not have to be the cause of patients' problems to be enlisted in their solutions. Another distinctive feature of the strategic approach is its emphasis on splitting sessions and working individually with spouses and family members. In a kind of shuttle diplomacy, the therapist meets with family members separately and follows this up with a briefer conjoint meeting in which an extratherapy task assignment is suggested. The notion is that both depressed individuals and significant others will be more forthcoming, less defensive, and more compromising if they are given the opportunity to talk with the therapist alone. Many couples in which the depressed patient or spouse would not be engaged in conventional couples therapy have been amenable to this approach.

An interactional perspective calls attention to how others may contribute to the perpetuation of depressive interactions and how they can be usefully enlisted in the process of change. However, an interactional perspective is a way of viewing clinical problems, not a prescription for who must be involved in therapy. There is a preference for having as few family members in a session at one time as possible. If the depressed person's relationships are characterized by conflict and a lack of support, it may be too much to expect that members of this interpersonal system will work together collaboratively. Watzlawick and Coyne (1980) illustrated the flexibility of this approach in describing a case in which the patient, a middle-aged man who was suffering from depression secondary to two strokes, attended none of the five sessions. Rather, the therapist met with his family in an effort to modify sincere efforts that they agreed only had increased the man's demoralization and functional impairment. Therapeutic interventions focused on blocking family members' ineffectual efforts to cheer up the man and on getting him mobilized by assigning therapeutic tasks that challenged the man to take responsibility for himself.

Much of the strategic therapy literature consists of provocative case examples and transcripts; there are limited outcome data available for the approach (Shoham, Rohrbaugh, & Patterson, 1995). Ultimately, such outcome data must be generated if credible claims for the approach are to be made. However, in the interim, strong circumstantial evidence suggests the usefulness of exploring alternative formats, techniques, and foci for intervention in working with the interactional context of depression. First, IPT is effective in renegotiating the relationships of depressed individuals, even within its narrow definition of appropriate techniques and its almost exclusive focus on working with the depressed patient. However, there may be greater potential in expanding the range of acceptable therapeutic strategies and creatively engaging significant others in treatment. Second, depression is a marker for a full range of marital and family problems and identifies a context in which others may be suffering and at risk for psychiatric disorder (Coyne et al., 1992; Downey & Coyne, 1990). The unmet needs of significant others could be addressed, their own risk of disorder could be reduced, and their underused resources could be activated in interventions that focused directly on the whole interpersonal system associated with depression, capitalizing on the motives and initiative of whoever was willing to make a commitment to the process of change.

CONCLUSION: RESTORING CURIOSITY ABOUT THE INTERPERSONAL CONTEXT OF DEPRESSION

This chapter might be an exercise in paradox, if not simple self-contradiction. At the outset, I criticized my first article (Coyne, 1976b) as the naive statement of an inexperienced graduate student, and I lamented that the interactional perspective has advanced little beyond that statement. I further suggested that the strongly recurrent nature of depression might not be entirely understandable in terms of psychosocial variables, and I cautioned against expecting psychological theories to explain more than they reasonably can. Against this seemingly pessimistic backdrop, I proceeded to provide a rather optimistic view of what an interactional perspective of depression can provide, both as a distinct way of explaining the disorder and as a sustained means of criticizing conventional theories. I further suggested ways in which an interactional perspective can expand the range of interventions for both depressed individuals and those who share an environment with them.

Some readers may be frustrated because after acknowledging that my 1976 articles did not provide a formal model of depression, I did not remedy this situation by providing such a model in this chapter. I made suggestions about how the phenomena of depression may be related to its interpersonal context but provided no formalization. This was deliberate because I believe that presentation of a formal model is not appropriate at this time. As demonstrated by the helplessness model, revised helplessness model, and hopelessness theory of depression, the study of depression has already been burdened by prematurely formalized models as researchers search for the elusive model that fits the evidence. I believe that at this time, the field would benefit most from empirical research and cautious innovations in intervention that are driven by some general notions about how depression is tied to its context.

Research exploring the kinds of issues raised in this chapter is inevitably costly and labor intensive. For a start, a focus on clinical depression rather than on self-reported distress requires diagnostic assessment by trained and supervised interviewers. Some authors are already clamoring that this requirement unfairly restricts who can do research on depression (Weary, Edwards, & Jacobson, 1995). Some issues can be examined only in costly behavioral observation studies, but as I noted at the outset, many important phenomena cannot be adequately captured without a better understanding of their temporal parameters. Although the work of the Oregon Research Institute group is an outstanding exception, much of the work that has been done studying marital interaction in depression has revealed little except that these interactions are negative. Coding schemes oriented toward the specific phenomena of depression are sorely needed. Much past work even fails to distinguish between sadness and hostility in the coding of negative affect.

In my own work, I have relied on focus groups with depressed people and their family members to ensure the content validity of the measures that were subsequently developed and to check on the interpretations that were made in the resulting quantitative studies (Coyne & Calarco, 1995; Coyne et al., 1987). At the present time and given the limitations of current knowledge, semistructured interviews and contextual assessments of the kind pioneered by Brown and Harris (1978) should become the mainstay of research from an interactional perspective. The superiority of such a method over traditional self-report has clearly been demonstrated for the study of life events, and I believe that a similar case can be made for the assessment of other aspects of the interpersonal context (Coyne & Gottlieb, 1996).

Lack of resources including lack of access to individuals diagnosed as depressed will preserve the temptation to continue with studies in which college students complete a battery of measures over the course of a semester. With all due respect to contributors to this volume, I remain convinced that efforts to justify such studies are going to retard further progress in the understanding of clinical depression. The necessity of moving into the community and clinics and of adopting more expensive methods in place of self-report questionnaires is not going to be widely accepted until the bankruptcy of mass studies of captive college students is appreciated. One important contribution of the interactional perspective is the discomfort it has created with the current research on depression by repeatedly and persistently showing how little it yields.

REFERENCES

Akiskal, H. S. (1991). An integrative perspective on recurrent mood disorders: The mediating role of personality. In J. Becker & A. Kleinman (Eds.), *Psychosocial aspects of depression* (pp. 215–236). Hillsdale, NJ: Erlbaum.

Andrews, B., & Brown, G. W. (1988). Marital violence in the community: A biographical approach. *British Journal of Psychiatry, 153,* 305–312.

Andrews, B., Brown, G. W., & Creasey, L. (1990). Intergenerational links between psychiatric disorder in mothers and daughters: The role of parenting experiences. *Journal of Child Psychology and Psychiatry and Allied Disciplines, 31,* 1115–1129.

Angst, J. (1986). The course of affective disorders. *Psychopathology, 19,* 47–52.

Austin, J. L. (1962). *How to do things with words.* Oxford, England: Oxford University Press.

Bandura, A. (1982). The psychology of chance encounters and life paths. *American Psychologist, 37,* 747–755.

Beach, S. R. H., Fincham, F. D., & Katz, J. (in press). Marital therapy in the treatment of depression: Toward a third generation of treatment and research. *Clinical Psychology Review.*

Beach, S. R. H., Sandeen, E. E., & O'Leary, K. D. (1990). *Depression in marriage: A model for etiology and treatment.* New York: Guilford Press.

Benazon, N. (1997). *Predicting negative partner attitudes toward depressed persons: An empirical evaluation of two theories.* Manuscript submitted for publication.

Biglan, A., Hops, H., & Sherman, L. (1988). Coercive family processes and maternal depression. In R. J. McMahon & R. DeV. Peter (Eds.), *Marriages and families: Behavioral treatments and processes* (pp. 72–103). New York: Brunner/ Mazel.

Birtchnell, J. (1980). Women whose mothers died in childhood: An outcome study. *Psychological Medicine, 10,* 699–713.

Brown, G. W., Bifulco, A., Harris, T., & Bridge, L. (1996). Life stress, chronic subclinical symptoms and vulnerability to clinical depression. *Journal of Affective Disorders, 11,* 1–19.

Brown, G. W., & Harris, T. (1978). *Social origins of depression: A study of psychiatric disorder in women.* New York: Free Press.

Caspi, A., Bem, D. J., & Elder, G. H. (1989). Continuities and consequences of interactional styles across the life course. *Journal of Personality, 57,* 375–406.

Clausen, J. (1995). Gender, contexts, and turning points. In P. Moen, G. H. Elder, Jr., & K. Luscher (Eds.), *Examining lives in context* (pp. 365–389). Washington, DC: American Psychological Association.

Cordova, J. V., & Jacobson, N. S. (1993). Couple distress. In D. H. Barlow (Ed.), *Clinical handbook of psychological disorders* (2nd ed., pp. 481–512). New York: Guilford Press.

Coyne, J. C. (1976a). Depression and the response of others. *Journal of Abnormal Psychology, 85,* 186–193.

Coyne, J. C. (1976b). Toward an interactional description of depression. *Psychiatry, 39,* 28–40.

Coyne, J. C. (1982). A critique of cognitions as causal entities with particular reference to depression. *Cognitive Therapy and Research, 6,* 3–13.

Coyne, J. C. (1985a). Studying depressed persons' interactions with strangers and spouses. *Journal of Abnormal Psychology, 94,* 231–232.

Coyne, J. C. (1985b). Toward a theory of frames and reframing: The social nature of frames. *Journal of Marital and Family Therapy, 11,* 337–344.

Coyne, J. C. (1989a). Employing therapeutic paradoxes in the treatment of depression. In M. L. Ascher (Ed.), *Paradoxical procedures in psychotherapy* (pp. 163–183). New York: Guilford Press.

Coyne, J. C. (1989b). Thinking post-cognitively about depression. In A. Freeman, K. Simon, L. Beutler, & H. Arkowitz (Eds.), *Comprehensive handbook of cognitive therapy* (pp. 227–244). New York: Plenum Press.

Coyne, J. C. (1994). Self-reported distress: Analog or ersatz depression? *Psychological Bulletin, 116,* 29–45.

Coyne, J. C. (1997, March). *Self-talk in depression.* Invited colloquium, University of North Dakota, Grand Forks.

Coyne, J. C., & Calarco, M. M. (1995). Effects of the experience of depression: Application of focus group and survey methodologies. *Psychiatry, 58,* 149–163.

Coyne, J. C., & DeLongis, A. M. (1986). Going beyond social support: The role of social relationships in adaptation. *Journal of Consulting and Clinical Psychology, 54,* 454–460.

Coyne, J. C., Downey, G., & Boergers, J. (1992). *Rochester Symposium on Developmental Psychopathology: Vol. 4. Developmental approaches to the affective disorders* (pp. 211–249). Rochester, NY: University of Rochester Press.

Coyne, J. C., Gallo, S. M., Klinkman, M. S., & Calarco, M. (1998). Effects of recent and past major depression and distress on self-concept and coping. *Journal of Abnormal Psychology, 107,* 86–96.

Coyne, J. C., & Gotlib, I. (1983). The role of cognition in depression: A critical appraisal. *Psychological Bulletin, 94,* 472–505.

Coyne, J. C., & Gottlieb, B. (1996). The mismeasure of coping by checklist. *Journal of Personality, 64,* 959–991.

Coyne, J. C., Kessler, R. C., Tal, M., Turnbull, J., Wortman, C., & Greden, J.

(1987). Living with a depressed person. *Journal of Consulting and Clinical Psychology, 55*, 347–352.

Coyne, J. C., & Pepper, C. M. (1998). The therapeutic alliance in strategic therapy. In J. Safran & J. C. Muran (Eds.), *The therapeutic alliance in brief psychotherapy* (pp. 147–169). Washington, DC: American Psychological Association.

Coyne, J. C., Pepper, C. M., & Cohen, N. (in press). Marital distress, ways of coping with conflict, and the backgrounds of depressed patients and husbands. *Journal of Family Psychology.*

Coyne, J. C., Pepper, C. M., & Flynn, H. (in press). Significance of prior episodes of depression in two populations. *Journal of Consulting and Clinical Psychology.*

Coyne, J. C., & Santor, D. C. (1997, August). *Categories and continua: Social filters, distress, and depression.* Paper presented at the 106th Annual Convention of the American Psychological Association, Chicago.

Coyne, J. C., & Segal, L. (1982). A brief, strategic interactional approach to psychotherapy. In J. Anchin & D. Kiesler (Eds.), *Handbook of interactional psychotherapy* (pp. 248–261). New York: Pergamon Press.

Coyne, J. C., & Whiffen, V. E. (1995). Issues in personality as diathesis for depression: The case of sociotropy–dependency and autonomy–self-criticism. *Psychological Bulletin 118*, 358–378.

Coyne, J. C., Wortman, C., & Lehman, D. (1988). The other side of support: Emotional overinvolvement and miscarried helping. In B. Gottlieb (Ed.), *Marshaling social support: Formats, processes, and effects* (pp. 305–330). Newbury Park, CA: Sage.

Crook, T., & Eliot, J. (1980). Parental death during childhood and adult depression: A critical review of the literature. *Psychological Bulletin, 87*, 252–259.

Doerfler, L. A., & Chaplin, W. F. (1985). Type III error in research on interactional models of depression. *Journal of Abnormal Psychology, 94*, 227–230.

Downey, G., & Coyne, J. C. (1990). Children of depressed parents: An integrative review. *Psychological Bulletin, 108*, 50–76.

Elder, G. H., George, L. K., & Shanahan, M. J. (1996). Psychosocial stress over the life course. In H. B. (Ed.), *Psychosocial stress: Perspectives on structure, theory, life-course, and methods* (pp. 247–292). San Diego, CA: Academic Press.

Elkin, I., Shea, M. T., Watkins, J. T., & Imber, S. D. (1989). National Institute of Mental Health Treatment of Depression Collaborative Research Program: General effectiveness of treatments. *Archives of General Psychiatry, 46*, 971–982.

Fechner-Bates, S., Coyne, J. C., & Schwenk, T. L. (1994). The relationship of self-reported distress to psychopathology. *Journal of Consulting and Clinical Psychology, 62*, 550–559.

Fisch, R., Weakland, J. H., & Segal, L. (1982). *The tactics of change: Doing therapy briefly.* San Francisco: Jossey-Bass.

Frank, E., Kupfer, D. J., Perel, J. M., & Cornes, C. (1990). Three-year outcomes for maintenance therapies in recurrent depression. *Archives of General Psychiatry, 47,* 1093–1099.

Gotlib, I. H., Lewinsohn, P. M., & Seeley, J. R. (1995). Symptoms versus a diagnosis of depression: Differences in psychosocial functioning. *Journal of Consulting and Clinical Psychology, 63,* 90–100.

Gotlib, I. H., & Robinson, A. (1982). Responses to depressed individuals: Discrepancies between self-report and observer-rated behavior. *Journal of Abnormal Psychology, 91,* 231–240.

Haley, J. (1973). *Strategies of psychotherapy.* New York: Grune & Stratton.

Harris, T., Brown, G., & Bifulco, A. (1986). Loss of parent in childhood and adult psychiatric disorder: The role of lack of adequate parental care. *Psychological Medicine, 16,* 641–659.

Hazan, C., & Shaver, P. R. (1990). Love and work: An attachment-theoretical perspective. *Journal of Personality and Social Psychology, 59,* 270–280.

Held, B. (in press). The importance of kvetching in theory, research and practice. *Psychotherapy in Private Practice.*

Jack D. C. (1991). *Silencing the self: Women and depression.* Cambridge, MA: Harvard University Press.

Jacobson, N. S., Dobson, K., Fruzzetti, A. E., & Schmaling, K. B. (1991). Marital therapy as a treatment for depression. *Journal of Consulting and Clinical Psychology, 59,* 547–557.

Jacobson, N. S., & Margolin, G. (1979). *Marital therapy: Strategies based on social learning and behavior exchange principles.* New York: Brunner/Mazel.

Keller, M. B., Lavori, P. W., Lewis, C. E., & Klerman, G. (1983). Predictors of relapse in major depressive disorder. *Journal of the American Medical Association, 250,* 3299–3304.

Kenny, D. A., & Zautra, A. (1995). The trait-state-error model for multiwave data. *Journal of Consulting and Clinical Psychology, 63,* 52–59.

Kessler, R. C. (1997). The effects of stressful life events on depression. *Annual Review of Psychology, 48,* 191–214.

Kessler, R. C., & Magee, W. J. (1994a). Childhood family violence and adult recurrent depression. *Journal of Health and Social Behavior, 35,* 13–27.

Kessler, R. C., & Magee, W. J. (1994b). The disaggregation of vulnerability to depression as a function of the determinants of onset and recurrence. In W. R. Avison, & I. H. Gotlib (Eds.), *Stress and mental health: Contemporary issues and prospects for the future* (pp. 239–258). New York: Plenum Press.

Kiesler, D. J. (1996). *Contemporary interpersonal theory and research.* New York: Wiley.

Klerman, G. L., Weissman, M. M., Rounsaville, B. J., & Chevron, E. (1984). *Interpersonal psychotherapy of depression.* New York: Basic Books.

Kramer, P. D. (1997). *Should you leave?* New York: Scribner.

Leff, J., & Vaughn, C. E. (1985). *Expressed emotion in families: Its significance for mental illness.* New York: Guilford Press.

Levy, M. B., & Davis, K. E. (1988). Love styles and attachment styles compared: Their relations to each other and to various relationship characteristics. *Journal of Social and Personal Relationships, 5*, 439–471.

Lewis, M. (1997). *Altering fate: Why the past does not predict the future*. New York: Guilford Press.

Libet, J., & Lewinsohn, P. M. (1973). The concept of social skill with special reference to the behavior of depressed persons. *Journal of Consulting and Clinical Psychology, 40*, 304–312.

McLean, P. D., & Hakstian, A. R. (1979). Clinical depression: Comparative efficacy of outpatient treatments. *Journal of Consulting and Clinical Psychology, 47*, 818–836.

McLean, P. D., & Miles, J. E. (1975). Training family physicians in psychosocial care: An analysis of a program failure. *Journal of Medical Education, 50*, 900–902.

Mintz, J., Mintz, L. I., Arruda, M. J., & Hwang, S. S. (1992). Treatments of depression and the functional capacity to work. *Archives of General Psychiatry, 49*, 761–768.

Parker, G., & Hadzi-Pavlovic, D. (1984). Modification of levels of depression in mother-bereaved women by prenatal and marital relationships. *Psychological Medicine, 14*, 125–135.

Paykel, E. S., Ramana, R., Cooper, Z., Hayhurst, H., Kerr, J., & Barocka, A. (1995). Residual symptoms after partial remission—An important outcome in depression. *Psychological Medicine, 25*, 1171–1180.

Perry, H. S. (1982). *Psychiatrist of America: The life of Harry Stack Sullivan*. Cambridge, MA: Harvard University Press.

Pickles, A., & Rutter, M. (1991). Statistical and conceptual models of 'turning points' in developmental processes. In D. Magnusson, D. L. R. Bergman, G. Rudinger, & B. Torestad (Eds.), *Problems and methods in longitudinal research: Stability and change* (pp. 133–165). Cambridge, England: Cambridge University Press.

Quinton, D., & Rutter, M. (1988). *Parenting breakdown*. Brookfield, VT: Avebury.

Quinton, D., Rutter, M., & Liddle, C. (1984). Institutional rearing, parenting difficulties and marital support. *Psychological Medicine, 14*, 107–124.

Repetti, R. L. (1989). Effects of daily workload on subsequent behavior during marital interaction: The roles of social withdrawal and spouse support. *Journal of Personality and Social Psychology, 57*, 651–659.

Repetti, R. L., & Wood, J. (1997). Effects of daily stress at work on mothers' interactions with preschoolers. *Journal of Family Psychology, 11*, 90–108.

Richards, M. P. M., & Dyson, M. (1982). *Separation, divorce and the development of children: A review*. London: Department of Health and Social Security.

Roberts, J. E., Gotlib, I. H., & Kassel, J. D. (1996). Adult attachment security and symptoms of depression: The mediating roles of dysfunctional attitudes and low self-esteem. *Journal of Personality and Social Psychology, 70*, 310–320.

Roberts, R. E., Lewinsohn, P. M., & Seeley, J. R. (1991). Screening for adolescent depression: A comparison of scales. *Journal of the American Academy of Child and Adolescent Psychiatry, 30*, 58–66.

Rutter, M. (1989). Pathways from childhood to adult life. *Journal of Child Psychology and Psychiatry, 30*, 23–51.

Segrin, C., & Abramson, L. Y. (1994). Negative reactions to depressive behaviors: A communication theories analysis. *Journal of Abnormal Psychology, 103*, 655–668.

Shoham, V., Rohrbaugh, M., & Patterson, J. (1995). Problem- and solution-focused couple therapies: The MRI and Milwaukee models in A. S. Gurman & N. S. Jacobson (Eds.), *Clinical handbook of couple therapy* (pp. 142–163). New York: Guilford Press.

Snyder, C. L., & Smith, T. W. (1982). Symptoms as self-handicapping strategies: The virtue of old wine in a new bottle. In G. Weary & H. Mirels (Eds.), *Integration of clinical and social psychology* (pp. 104–127). New York: Oxford University Press.

Strauss, A. (1959). *Mirrors and masks: The search for identity.* New York: Free Press of Glencoe.

Vredenburg, K., Flett, G. L., & Krames, L. (1993). Analog versus clinical depression: A clinical reappraisal. *Psychological Bulletin, 113*, 327–344.

Wachtel, P. (1977). *Psychoanalysis and behavior therapy.* New York: Basic Books.

Watzlawick, P. W., & Coyne, J. C. (1980). Depression following stroke: Brief problem-focused family treatment. *Family Process, 19*, 13–18.

Watzlawick, P., Weakland, J. H., & Fisch, R. (1974). *Change: Principles of problem formation and problem resolution.* New York: Norton.

Weakland, J. H. (1992). Conversation—But what kind? In S. Gilligan & R. Price (Eds.), *Therapeutic conversations* (pp. 136–145). New York: Norton.

Weakland, J. H., Fisch, R., Watzlawick, P. H., & Bodin, A. (1974). Brief therapy: Focused problem resolution. *Family Process, 13*, 141–166.

Weary, G., Edwards, J. A., & Jacobson, J. A. (1995). Depression research methodologies in the *Journal of Personality and Social Psychology:* A reply. *Journal of Personality and Social Psychology, 68*, 885–891.

Weissman, M. M., & Paykel, E. S. (1974). *The depressed woman.* Chicago: University of Chicago Press.

Wells, K. B., Stewart, A., Hays, R. D., Burnam, M. A., Rogers, W., Daniels, M., Berry, S., Greenfield, S., & Ware, J. (1989). The functioning and well-being of depressed patients: Results from the medical outcomes study. *Journal of the American Medical Association, 262*, 914–919.

AUTHOR INDEX

Abbey, A., 54, *57*
Abramovitch, R., 77, *87*
Abrams, S. M., 312, *320*
Abramson, L. Y., 65, 66, 73, 81, 86, 87, 90, *91*, 116, *117*, 128, 129, 130, *143*, *146*, *147*, 155, 157, 160, 161, *175*, *179*, *183*, *185*, 189, 200, 203, 205, 207, *210*, *213*, *214*, 299, *320*, 329, 331, 334, 345, *360*, *367*, *392*
Adamson, L. B., 303, 314, *324*
Adler, A., 161, *175*
Adler, Z., 157, *177*, 282, *292*
Adrian, C., 28, 29, 30, 32, 33, 34, 67, 89, *145*
Ahrens, A. H., 65, 67, 68, 77, 88, *91*
Ainsworth, M., 277, *291*
Ainsworth, M. D. S., 74, *87*, 168, *175*
Akiskal, H. S., 371, *387*
Aldwin, C. A., 200, *211*
Alfano, M. S., 10, *18*, 47, *61*, 86, 89, 111, *117*, 136, *145*, 150, 160, *180*, 189, 190, 196, *213*, 283, *294*
Allen, D. M., 77, *87*
Allen, J. K., 53, *57*
Allen, L. A., *178*
Alloy, L., 195, 200, *210*
Alloy, L. B., 65, 81, 87, *91*, 147, 156, 161, *175*, *179*
Altman, E. O., 133, *144*
Altman, J. H., 155, *176*
Anda, R., 55, *57*
Anderson, B. L., 53, *57*
Andersen, S. M., 331, *352*
Anderson, C. A., 93, 94, 100–101, 101, 102, 104, 106, 108, 110, 111, 116, *117*, *118*, *121*, *181*
Anderson, E. A., 206, *213*
Anderson, K., 128, *147*
Anderson, K. B., 94, *117*
Anderson, R. L., *182*, *358*
Andersson, L., 106, 111, *118*
Andrews, B., 156, 157, 167, 173, *176*, *177*, 204, *211*, 282, *292*, 348, *353*, 371, 375, 376, *388*

Andrews, F. M., 54, *57*
Andrews, J. D., 190, *210*
Andrzejewski, P. L., *59*
Angst, J., 370, *388*
Appelman, A. J., 102, *118*
Arcus, D., 104, *121*
Arduino, K., 155, *179*
Arias, I., 313, *320*
Arieti, S., 27, *33*
Arkin, R. M., 102, *118*
Arkowitz, H. S., 340, *358*
Armsden, G. C., 168, *176*
Arnoult, L. H., 93, 101, 102, 111, 116, *117*, *118*
Aronson, E., 100, *118*
Arthur, J., *292*
Asarnow, J. R., 129, *144*
Asbeck, J., 337, *355*
Aseltine, R. H., 54, *63*
Aspinwall, L. G., 44, *57*, 159, *176*
Atherton, S. C., 102, *122*
Audette, D. P., 342, *353*
Austin, J. L., 380, *388*
Avison, W. R., 39, 40, *57*
Axford, S., 154, *176*

Babcock, J. C., 225, *243*
Back, K., 100, *120*
Badura, B., 53, *63*
Baird, D., 53, *61*
Baldwin, M., 103, *124*
Baldwin, M. W., 278, *291*
Banaji, M. B., 336, *356*
Bandura, A., 116, *118*, 376, *388*
Banks, S. M., 53, *57*
Barahal, R. M., 76, *87*
Barber, J. G., 154, *178*
Bardbury, T. N., 339, *357*
Bargh, J. A., 203, *210*, 331, 336, 337, *352*, *356*
Barling, J., 274, *291*
Barlow, D. H., 113, *118*
Barnes, D. R., 129, *147*

Barnett, P. A., 113, *118*, 149, 152, 153, 154, 160, 163, *176*, 338, 342, 351, *352*
Barocka, A., *392*
Baron, R., 311, 312, *320*
Baron, R. M., 67, 87
Barrett, K., 278, *293*
Barron, C. R., 109, *121*
Bartholomew, K., 170, *176*, 278, 279, 292, *294*
Bartlett, F., 73, 87
Barton, R., 133, *146*, 338, 357
Bassett, M. E., 225, *244*
Bassili, J. N., 339, *353*
Battle, J., 205, *210*
Baucom, D. H., 343, *353*
Baum, A., 116, *118*
Baum, C. G., 133, *144*
Baumeister, R. F., 153, *176*
Beach, S. R., 340, 344, *355*
Beach, S. R. H., 149, *176*, *179*, 191, 213, 271, 272, 273, 274, 275, 279, 280, 286, 292, 293, 294, 295, 313, 320, 353, 383, 388
Beardslee, W., 300, *321*
Beatty, M. E., 189, *212*
Bebbington, P., 112, *118*
Beck, A. T., 23, 27, 33, 81, 87, 110, 113, 115, 116, *118*, *124*, 127, 128, 129, 130, *144*, 152, 154, 171, *176*, *184*, 189, 190, 194, 195, 200, 202, 205, 207, 209, 210, 211, 213, 231, 243, 329, 333, *353*
Beck, R., 194, *211*
Becker, D. M., 53, *57*
Becker, E. S., 5, *17*, *211*
Becker, J., 54, 62, 152, 158, 166, *176*, *185*
Bell, I. R., 104, 105, *118*
Bell, R., 167, *181*
Bellack, A. S., 116, *118*
Bell–Dolan, D. J., 334, *353*
Bellezza, F. S., 331, *356*
Belmont, B., 140, *146*, 308, *326*
Belsher, G., *176*
Belsky, J., 168, *176*
Belyea-Caldwell, S., *122*
Bem, D. J., 376, *388*
Bemporad, J., 27, *33*, 300, *321*
Benazon, N., 366, 367, 378, *388*
Benfield, C. Y., 129, 130, *144*
Benjamin, L. S., 114, *120*, 286, *292*

Berg, 109
Berkowitz, L., 94, *119*
Bernet, C. Z., 149, 151, 154, 161, *176*
Berry, A., 150, *181*
Berry, A. J., *181*
Berry, S., *393*
Berscheid, E., 330, 343, *353*
Bertholf, M., 94, *122*
Bibring, E., 4, *17*, 151, *176*
Bifulco, A., 156, *177*, 378, *388*
Biglan, A., 274, 277, 280, 292, 367, *388*
Billings, A., 46, 47, 50, 52, 57, 62
Billings, A. G., 57, 349, *353*
Binet, A., 73, 87
Birtchnell, J., 263, 267, 378, *388*
Bishop, D. S., *358*
Blackwell, J., 68, *91*
Blai, B., 107, 109, 110, 115, *119*
Blaney, N., 100, *118*
Blaney, P. H., 202, *211*
Blankenstein, K. R., 111, *120*
Blatt, S. J., 152, *176*, 231, 243, 286, *292*
Blazer, D. B., 221, *243*
Blazer, D. G., *296*
Blechman, E. A., 342, *353*
Blehar, M., 277, *291*
Blehar, M. C., 168, *175*
Blum, J. C., 273, *292*
Blumenthal, J. A., *57*
Blumenthal, S. J., 53, *58*
Bodin, A., 384, *393*
Bohman, T., 339, 343, *361*
Bolger, N., 40, 42, 47, 55, *58*
Bolton, W., 152, *183*
Bommersbach, M., 230, *244*
Bonin, L. A., 39, 41, *60*
Bonner, R. L., 111, 113, 115, 116, *119*, *124*
Botein, S., 74, *90*
Bottomly, L., 140, *146*
Bower, G. H., 202, *211*, 341, *353*
Bowlby, J., 25, 27, *33*, 166, 168, *177*, 222, 223, 224, 243, 249, 267, 272, 276, *292*
Braafladt, N., 302, *324*
Bradburn, N., 93, 107, *119*
Bradbury, T. N., 331, 339, 343, 346, *353*, *355*
Brage, D., 107, 115, *119*
Bragg, M. E., 110, *125*
Braith, J. A., *122*
Brazaitis, S., 229, *243*

Brennan, P., 41, 60
Brennan, P. L., 43, 47, 58, 62
Brennon-Quattrock, J., 146
Bretherton, I., 74, 87, 169, 177
Brewin, C. R., 116, 120, 153, 166, 177,
 183, 348, 351, 353
Breznitz, S., 39, 40, 59
Bridge, L., 157, 177, 282, 292, 378, 388
Broadbent, K., 169, 187
Brodt, S. E., 101, 119
Brody, G. H., 342, 353
Brown, B., 93, 119
Brown, G., 30, 34, 375, 390
Brown, G. W., 6, 17, 24, 33, 110, 111,
 112, 119, 132, 144, 152, 153,
 156, 157, 158, 162, 166, 173,
 174, 177, 179, 204, 211, 273,
 282, 292, 293, 371, 375, 376,
 378, 387, 388
Brown, J. D., 159, 160, 186, 202, 204,
 211
Brown, L., 223, 243
Brown, P. J., 101, 108, 109, 124
Brownell, K. D., 45, 58
Broxton, J. A., 191, 211
Bruch, M. A., 108, 109, 119
Brunk, B. P., 287, 294
Buchanan, C. M., 312, 321
Buckner, C. E., 203, 211
Budinger, T., 342, 357
Bugental, D. D., 339, 353
Burchill, S. A. L., 160, 177, 311, 322
Burge, D., 28, 29, 30, 33, 34, 35, 78, 89,
 141, 144, 145, 179, 283, 293,
 294, 324, 342, 353
Burger, J. M., 102, 118
Burhans, K. K., 75, 85, 87
Burke, M., 133, 144
Burke, P., 66, 90
Burke, P. M., 168, 176
Burman, B., 342, 355
Burnam, M. A., 393
Burnett, C. K., 351, 360
Burney, E., 28, 34
Busch, C. M., 106, 108, 119
Busch, L. M., 347, 358
Buss, A., 101, 102, 119
Butler, A. C., 153, 155, 157, 162, 177
Butler, L. J., 81, 89

Cain, K. M., 73, 75, 82, 88, 89

Calarco, M., 372, 389
Calarco, M. M., 372, 387, 389
Campbell, J. D., 331, 352
Campbell, S. B., 168, 176, 306, 313, 321
Campos, J. J., 278, 293
Cane, D. B., 334, 354
Cantor, N., 52, 63, 339, 354
Capone, R. J., 59
Carlson, C. L., 104, 122
Carlson, E., 277, 278, 296, 297
Carlson, G. A., 129, 144
Carlston, D. E., 331, 336, 343, 346, 354,
 361
Carnelley, K. B., 56, 150, 168, 177, 287,
 293
Carnelly, K. B., 58
Carpentieri, A. M., 101, 119
Carr, J. G., 229, 243
Carroll, S. B., 250, 267
Carter, A. S., 286–287, 295
Carver, C. S., 44, 58
Caspi, A., 12, 17, 277, 287, 293, 376,
 388
Caulkins, S., 302, 305, 316, 327
Cawood, R. M., 230, 243
Cerezo, M. A., 77, 87
Chaiken, S., 331, 352
Champion, L., 52, 61
Chance, M. R. A., 261, 267
Chaplin, W. F., 366, 390
Chapman, M., 308, 326
Cheek, J. M., 101, 102, 106, 108, 114,
 119
Chelune, G., 115, 119
Chester, N. L., 56, 63
Chevron, E., 276, 294, 381, 391
Chevron, E. S., 6, 18, 172, 181, 276,
 295
Chodorow, N., 222, 243
Christensen, A., 225, 244, 286, 293,
 301, 321
Christenson, A. J., 103, 124
Christian, J. L., 272, 274, 293, 295
Cicchetti, D., 167, 168, 181, 186, 300,
 308, 314, 315, 318, 321, 322
Clark, D. M., 340, 354
Clark, K. C., 58
Clark, M. L., 108, 121
Clark, M. S., 330, 341, 342, 354
Clausen, J., 376, 388
Clayton, P. J., 246
Clements, C. M., 161, 175

Clore, G. L., 340, 341, 342, 344, *354*
Clum, G. A., 111, *125*
Coates, D., 189, *211*
Cochran, S., 25, *34*
Cochran, S. D., 111, *121*
Cofer, D. H., 155, *177*
Cohen, D., 113, *119*
Cohen, N., 12, *17*
Cohen, N. J., 303, 312, *325*
Cohen, S., 40, *58*, 149, *177*
Cohn, D. A., 74, *87*
Cohn, J. F., 306, 313, *321*
Colbus, D., 133, *145*
Cole, D. A., 67, 69, 79, 81, 83, 86, 87,
    92, 303, *321*, 334, *354*
Cole, P. M., 305, *321*
Cole, S., 303, 314, *324*
Cole, S. W., 331, *352*
Collins, N., 28, *33*, 271, *296*
Compas, B. E., 53, *62*
Conger, R. D., 307, *321*, *324*
Connell, D. B., 74, 90, 308, *325*
Conrad, M., 29, *33*
Cooley, C. F., 165, *177*
Cooley, C. H., 350, *354*
Coombs, R. H., 233, *244*
Coopersmith, S., 166, *177*
Coovert, M. D., 337, *359*
Copeland, J. R. M., *120*
Cordova, J. V., 383, *388*
Cornell, D. P., 150, *181*
Cornes, C., 372, *390*
Coryell, W., 273, *293*
Costello, C. G., *176*
Covell, K., 77, *87*
Cowan, G., 230, *244*
Cox, A. D., 306, *321*
Coyne, J., 78, *88*
Coyne, J. C., 5, 6, 7, 12, 16, *17*, *18*, *19*,
    23, 24, 28, *33*, 39, 40, 41, 47,
    48, 50, 51, 54, *58*, *59*, 77, 86,
    88, 127, 132, 138, *144*, 150,
    151, 152, 154, 160, 171, 173,
    177, *178*, 189, 190, 196, 200,
    205, 209, *211*, *214*, 221, 222,
    231, *244*, 274, 277, 280, 286,
    293, 299, 300, 301, 303, 304,
    310, 311, 313, 315, *321*, *322*,
    323, 346, 347, *354*, *361*, 365,
    366, 367, 370, 372, 373, 374,
    376, 377, 378, 380, 381, 384,

    385, 386, 387, 388, 389, 390,
    393
Craig, A. G., 233, *244*
Crary, W. G., *211*
Crick, N., 319, *322*
Crick, N. R., 72, 79, 80, 84, 86, *88*
Crockenberg, S. B., 312, *322*
Crocker, J., 158, *178*
Cronkite, R. C., 43, 46, 50, 51, 52, *59*,
    61, *62*, *63*, 349, *361*
Crook, T., 348, *354*, 375, *390*
Crook, T. II., 112, *119*
Cruet, D., 112, *121*
Cummings, E. M., 12, *17*, 76, *88*, 284,
    293, 300, 301, 302, 303, 304,
    305, 306, 307, 308, 309, 310,
    311, 312, 313, 314, 315, 317,
    318, 319, *322*, *323*, 326, *327*
Cummings, J. S., 319, *323*
Cunningham, M., 341, *354*
Cutrona, C. E., 40, 44, *59*, *62*
Cybulska, E., 233, *246*
Cytryn, L., *325*

Daley, S., 30, *33*, *34*
Daley, S. E., 30, 31, *33*, 283, *293*
Daniels, D., 52, *59*, 104, 105, 110, *123*
Daniels, M., *393*
Darley, J. M., 346, 350, *354*
Davidson, I. A., *120*
Davidson, R. J., 11, *17*
Davidson, W., 13, *18*, 82, *88*
Davies, M., 273, *295*
Davies, P., 76, *88*, 284, *293*, 302, 308,
    310, *322*
Davies, P. T., 12, *17*, 300, 301, 302, 303,
    304, 305, 306, 307, 310, 311,
    312, 317, *322*, *323*
Davila, J., 30, *33*, *34*, 179, 294, *324*
Davis, G. E., 116, *118*
Davis, K. E., 368, *391*
Davis, M. A., *246*
Deacon, T. W., 262, *267*
Dean, A. L., 77, *88*
Dean, J., 104, *122*
Deering, C. G., 12, *18*
Deiner, E., 104, *122*
De La Ronde, C., 193, *215*
de la Ronde, C., 192
DeLongis, A., 40, 54, *58*
DeLongis, A. M., 377, *389*

deMayo, R., 25, 35, 140, *144*
DeMulder, E. K., 303, 306, *326*
Denham, S., 307, *327*
DePaulo, B. M., 333, 348, 349, 350, *357*
DePaulo, J. R., *59*
Depue, R. A., 155, *178*
Derry, P. A., 190, *211*
Derryberry, D., 104, *124*
Deuser, W. E., 94, *117*
Devila, J., *30*
de Waal, F., 262, *267*
Dewey, M. E., *120*
Dill, D., 229, 230, 231, *245*
Dill, J. C., 101, *118*
Dillard, J. P., 340, *360*
Dix, T., 339, 340, 343, 346, 347, 350, *354*
Dixon, J. F., 65, 67, 68, *88*
Dobash, R. E., 225, *244*
Dobash, R. P., 225, *244*
Dobson, K., 275, 294, 383, *391*
Dobson, K. S., 347, 348, *354*
Dodge, K. A., 72, 79, 80, 84, 88, *91*, 110, *123*, 306, 307, 319, *322*, *323*, *325*
Doerfler, L. A., 366, *390*
Dolan, A. B., 104, 105, *122*
Donaldson, S. K., *182*, *358*
Dotzenroth, S. E., 114, *120*
Downey, G., 12, *18*, 24, 28, *33*, 40, 47, *58*, 77, *88*, 221, 222, *244*, 300, 301, 303, 304, 310, 316, *323*, 374, 376, 386, 389, *390*
Downey, G., 315, *322*
Downs, D. L., 14, *18*, 158, *182*
Drew, S. S., 230, *244*
Dritschel, B., 169, *179*
Duarte, L. M., 229, *244*
Dugan, E., 111, 115, *123*
Dumas, J. E., 342, *354*
Dumont, C. P., 334, 335, 339, 340, 341, 342, 343, 344, *359*
Dunbar, R., 248, *267*
Dunn, V. K., 331, 333, 338, 340, 346, 347, *359*
Dunning, D., 207, *211*
Durand, V. M., 113, *118*
Dweck, C. S., 13, *18*, 75, 82, 83, 85, 87, *88*, 89, 90, *92*
Dyck, M. J., 23, *33*, 203, *212*
Dyer, C. S., *122*

Dykman, B., *179*
Dykman, B. M., 140, *144*, 149, 169, 173, *178*, *184*, 334, *354*
Dyson, M., 375, *392*

Eagly, A. H., 228, *244*
Eaker, E., *57*
Eaton, W. W., *296*
Eaves, L. J., 40, 46, *61*
Ebata, A. T., 43, 55, *59*
Eccles, J. S., 334, *357*
Edwards, J. A., 96, *125*, 200, 201, *211*, 216, 338, 361, 387, *393*
Edwards, J. R., 40, *58*
Egeland, B., 167, *178*
Eisdorfer, C., 113, *119*
Eisemann, M., 112, 113, *119*
Eisenberg, N., 103, *120*
Eisner, J. P., 74, *88*
Ekkehard, S., 106, 109, *120*
Elder, G., 12, *17*
Elder, G. H., 307, *324*, 376, *390*
Elicker, J., 278, *293*
Eliot, J., 375, *390*
Elkin, I., 381, *390*
Ellard, J. H., 51, *58*
Ellicott, A., 27, 30, *34*
Elliot, E. S., 75, *88*
El-Sheikh, M., 302, *323*
Ely, R. J., 191, 192, 193, 207, *215*
Emery, C. F., *57*
Emery, G., 113, *118*, 127, *144*, 171, *176*, *194*, *211*, 329, *353*
Emery, R. E., 167, *178*, 309, 319, *323*
Emmelkamp, P. M. G., 348, *355*
Emslie, G., 66, *92*
Endicott, J., 273, *293*
Englund, M., 278, *293*
Enna, B., 13, *18*, 82, *88*
Epstein, N., 343, *353*
Epstein, N. B., *358*
Epstein, S., 158, *178*
Erdly, W. W., 54, *62*
Erel, O., 342, *355*
Erikson, E., 74, *88*
Ernst, D., 23, *33*
Essex, M. J., 114, *120*
Esveldt-Dawson, K., 129, 133, *145*
Evans, G. W., 116, *120*
Ewart, C. K., 55, *59*

Fabes, R. A., 103, *120*
Fair, P. L., 206, *214*
Fairfield, M., 153, *184*
Fäth, M., 106, 108, *120, 124*
Fatis, M., *120*
Fauber, R., 133, *144*
Faucher, I., *19*
Faust, J., 133, *144*
Fazio, R. H., 346, 350, *354*
Feather, N. T., 154, *178*
Fechner-Bates, S., 372, *390*
Feeney, J. A., 279, *293*
Fehr, B., 278, *291*
Feldman, S., 316, *323*
Felson, R. B., 350, *355*
Fendrich, M., 307, *323*
Fenichel, O., *18*, 151, 165, *178*
Fenn, C., 47, *62*
Fergusson, D. M., 301, 310, 312, 313, *323*
Festinger, L., 100, *120*, 158, *178*
Fiedler, L., 337, *355*
Field, T., 312, *320, 323, 324*
Fielding, R., 55, *59*
Fincham, F. D., 72, 73, 74, 76, 77, 82, 84, 88, 89, 167, *179*, 272, 273, 274, 279, *292, 293, 294*, 309, 319, *324*, 330, 331, 339, 340, 343, 344, 346, *353, 355*, 383, 388
Finchman, F. D., 53, *59*
Fine, S. L., 129, *144*
Finn, S. E., 208, *212*
Finney, J. W., 51, 52, 59, *62*
First, M. B., *214*
Firth-Cozens, J., 116, *120*, 166, *177*
Fisch, R., 384, *390, 393*
Fishman, R., *246*
Fiske, S. T., 331, 336, *355*
Fitzgerald, S. T., 53, *57*
Fleeson, J., 278, *296*
Fletcher, G. J. O., 330, 343, 346, *355*
Flett, G. L., 111, *120*, 200, *212*, 373, *393*
Florian, V., 168, *183*, 279, *295*
Foersterling, F., 116, *120*
Fogarty, S. J., 206, *216*
Foley, S. H., 276, *294*
Folkman, S., 42, 43, 44, 59, *61*
Follick, M. J., 53, *59*
Fondacaro, M., 43, 55, 59, *62*
Ford, M. E., 74, 85, *88*

Forehand, R., 133, *144*, 301, 303, 307, 310, 312, 314, 316, *324, 326, 327, 342, 353*
Forgas, J. P., 330, 331, 333, 340, 341, 342, *355*
Forrester, A. W., 53, *59*
Foster, M., 47, *58*
Fox, N. A., 11, *17*, 312, *323*
Foxall, M. J., 109, *121*
Frank, E., 372, 381, *390*
Frank, J., 142, *147*
Frankel, O., 308, *327*
Franklin, J., 154, *182*, 204, *213*
Franklin, K. M., 167, *178*
Fredrickson, B., 223–224, *244*
Freedheim, D. K., 272, *295*
Freeman, R. J., 129, *144*
French, N. H., 129, *145*
French, R., 106, *121*
Freud, S., 3, *18*, 151, 165, *178*, 189, *212*, 223, *244*
Frias, D., 77, *87*
Friedman, L. S., *292*
Friend, R., *122*
Fugh-Berman, A., *244*
Fuhrman, R. W., 331, 335, 343, *355, 360*
Fulcher, G., 53, *61*
Funder, D. C., 334, 335, *355*

Gaines, B., 191, *215*
Galen, 189, *212*
Gallery, M. E., 222, *246*
Gallo, S. M., 372, *389*
Galvin, S. L., 229, *246*
Gammon, G. D., 133, *145*
Gandour, M. J., 312, *327*
Gara, M. A., 154, *178*
Garber, J., 65, 66, 67, 68, 79, 86, 89, *91*, 110, *123*, 157, *185*, 302, *324*
Gardner, R., 254, *268*
Gardner, R., Jr., 247, 248, 249, 252, *267*
Gasparikova-Krasnec, M., 201, *212*
Ge, X., 307, *324*
Geen, R. G., 94, 103, *120*
Gelfand, D. M., 301, 302, 306, 314, *324, 326, 327*
Geller, J., 302, *324*
George, 113
George, L. K., 376, *390*
Gerlsma, C., 287, *294*, 348, 351, *355*

Giesler, R. B., 152, *179*, 196, 198, 199, 200, 201, 205, 206, 207, *212*
Gilbert, D. T., 201, *215*, 339, *356*
Gilbert, P., 158, *179*, *184*, 249, 268
Gilboa, E., 161, *179*
Gilligan, C., 222, 223, *243*, *244*
Gilroy, F. D., 229, *243*
Girgus, J. S., 66, 67, *90*
Girodo, M., 114, *120*
Gitlin, M., 27, 30, *34*
Glaser, R., *122*
Glassman, A., *57*
Gleicher, F., 96, *125*, 200, *212*
Glueckauf, R. L., 51, *62*
Goddard, L., 169, *179*
Goetz, D., *146*
Goffmann, E., 251, *267*
Goldberg, S., 308, *327*
Goldberger, L., 39, 40, *59*
Goldberger, N., 225, *244*
Goldsmith, H. H., 278, *293*
Goldsmith D. F., 303, 314, *324*
Goldston, R. B., *178*
Goldston, S. E., 110, *123*
Gong-Guy, E., 25, *33*
Gonzalez, J., 312, *324*
Goodman, S. H., 303, 314, *324*
Goodman-Brown, T., 27, *34*
Goodnow, J. J., 307, *324*
Goodwin, F. K., 253, *267*
Gordon, D., 28, *33*, *34*, *89*, *145*
Gordon, J. S., 173, *185*
Gorkin, L., *59*
Gotlib, 7, *17*
Gotlib, I., 23, *33*, 78, 88, 299, 304, *324*, 380, *389*
Gotlib, I. H., 39, 40, *57*, 83, 88, 113, *118*, 132, 133, *144*, 149, 150, 151, 152, 153, 154, 157, 160, 163, 164, 166, 169, 173, *176*, *178*, *179*, *184*, 189, 190, 205, *212*, 214, 282, 296, 299, 301, 302, 303, 316, *322*, *325*, *327*, 334, 338, 340, 342, 345, 347, 348, 351, 352, 354, *356*, 367, 368, 373, *390*, *392*
Gottlieb, B., 387, *389*
Gottman, J., 225, *245*
Gottman, J. M., 225, *243*, *244*
Granger, D. A., 104, *120*
Grannemann, B. D., 153, *181*
Gratch, L. V., 225, 229, 230, *244*, *245*

Graves, D. J., 133, *146*
Graziano, W. G., 307, *324*
Greden, J., *389*
Greden, J. F., 58, *178*, *293*
Green, B. H., 111, *120*
Greenberg, J., 112, *123*, 152, *184*
Greenberg, L. S., 277, 286, *294*
Greenfield, S., *393*
Greenier, K. D., *181*
Greenwald, A. G., 331, 336, *356*
Griest, D. L., 301, *326*
Griffin, D. W., 279, *294*
Griffin, J. J., 191, *215*
Grinker, R. R., 190, *212*
Gross, A. M., 345, 347, *358*
Gross, E. B., 222, 232, *245*
Gross, J. J., 163, *179*
Grunebaum, H. U., 74, *90*
Grusec, J. E., 307, *324*
Grych, J. H., 53, 59, 167, *179*, 309, 319, *324*
Grych, L. H., 72, 76, 77, 84, *89*
Gurtman, M. B., 160, *179*, 189, 206, *212*
Guskin, D., 78, *91*
Guskin, K., 302, 303, *325*, *326*
Gwyther, *113*

Haaga, D. A., 23, *33*, 203, *212*
Haaga, D. A. F., 154, *186*
Hadzi-Pavlovic, D., 378, *392*
Hailey, B. J., 107, *121*
Haines, B. A., 77, *89*
Hakstian, A. R., 383, *391*
Halberstadt, L. J., 66, *90*, 164, *182*
Haley, B. M. T., 129, *144*
Haley, J., 384, *390*
Halford, W. K., 346, *356*
Hall, J. A., 196, *216*
Hall, R. L., 334, *356*
Halman, J., 54, *57*
Hamilton, E. B., 303, 306, 313, *324*
Hamilton, E. W., 155, *179*
Hammen, C., 23, 25, 26, 27, 28, 29, 30, 32, *33*, *34*, 35, 48, 60, 67, 78, *89*, 112, *120*, 129, 130, 140, 141, *144*, *145*, 147, 283, *293*, 299, 303, 304, 306, 313, *324*, 342, *353*
Hammen, C. L., 24, 25, *34*, 35, 150, 168, *179*, 282, *294*, *324*, 338, 340, 342, 345, 347, 348, *356*

Hampton, C., *122*
Hanna, H. H., *147*
Hardin, T. S., 66, *90*
Haris, S. D., *58*
Harlow, T., 150, *181*
Harnish, J. D., 306, *325*
Harris, T., 6, *17*, *24*, *33*, 110, 111, 112,
    119, 132, *144*, 166, *179*, 273,
    282, 293, 375, 387, 388, *390*
Harris, T. O., 152, 156, 174, *177*
Hart, B. I., 230, *245*
Hartlage, S., 155, 156, 170, *175*, *179*
Hartmann, E., 104, *120*
Harvey, J. H., 338, *361*
Harvey, R. J., 104, 108, 110, 111, *117*
Harwood, E. M., 273, *292*
Hautzinger, M., 205, *213*, 334, 345, *356*
Havik, O. E., 53, *60*
Hayes, S. C., 56, *60*
Hayhurst, H., *392*
Hays, R. D., 42, *63*
Hazan, C., 168, *180*, 271, 277, 278, 280,
    282, *287*, 294, 295, 296, 368,
    391
Healy, J. M., 56, *63*
Heath, A. C., 40, 46, *61*
Heavey, C. L., 225, *244*
Hedeen, C., 156, *180*, 342, *356*
Hedlund, S., 203, *212*
Heesacker, M., 230, *244*
Held, B., 380, *391*
Helgeson, V. S., 54, 55, *60*, 330, *354*
Helm, S. B., 116, *121*
Henderson, A. S., 149, *182*
Henderson, V. L., 83, *89*
Henri, V., 73, *87*
Herbener, E. S., 277, 287, *293*
Herlocker, C. E., *181*
Hersen, M., 116, *118*
Herzberg, D., *33*
Hewstone, M., 154, *180*
Heyman, G. D., 75, 85, *89*
Hickie, I., 149, *180*
Higgins, E. T., 337, 339, *356*
Higley, J. D., *19*
Hill, C. A., 191, *215*
Hill, S., 102, *122*
Hill, T., 336, *357*
Hilsman, R., 65, 66, 67, 68, *89*
Hilton, D. J., 339, *356*
Himmelhoch, J., 116, *118*
Hiroto, D., *33*, 34, 67, *89*, *145*

Hixon, J. B., 201, *215*
Hixon, J. G., 191, 192, 203, *212*, *215*,
    287, 297
Hoberman, H. M., 155, *182*
Hobfoll, S. E., 157, *180*
Hock, C., 113, *123*
Hodges, K., 111, *123*, *325*
Hoeksema, S., 302, *325*
Hoffman, M. A., 101, 102, *125*
Hokanson, J. E., 133–134, *147*, 153,
    156, *177*, *180*, 337, 342, 345,
    356
Hokoda, A., 74, *89*
Holahan, C. J., 10, *19*, 39, 41, 42, 43,
    44, 45, 48, 51, 53, 54, 56, 60,
    61, 62, 63, 152, *183*
Holahan, C. K., 41, *60*
Holden, E. W., 314, *327*
Hollander, G. R., 156, *180*, 342, *356*
Holleran, P. A., 336, *356*
Hollon, S., 116, *124*
Holmbeck, G., 312, *325*
Holmes, J. G., 331, *358*
Hooley, J., 9, *18*, 195, 196, 200, *212*
Hooley, J. M., 330, 333, 338, 349, *357*
Hooper, D., 154, *180*
Hopkins, J., 306, *321*
Hops, H., 292, 303, 312, *325*, 342, *357*,
    367, 388
Horowitz, L., 278, *292*
Horowitz, L. M., 106, 107, 108, *121*,
    140, *144*, 149, 170, *176*, *178*,
    334, *354*
Horwood, L. J., 310, *323*
Hough, R. L., *296*
Hovanessian, H. C., 233, *244*
Hsu, L. R., 107, *121*
Hughes, C., 53, *61*
Hughes, C. W., 66, *92*
Hummer, J. T., 337, *356*
Hur, C., 102, *122*
Hurry, J., 112, *118*
Hurtado, A., 225, *245*
Husain, A., *325*
Hwang, S. S., 374, *392*
Hyland, M. E., 152, *180*
Hymel, S., 81, *89*
Hymes, C., 331, *352*

Iannotti, R. J., 307, *327*
Imber, S. D., 381, *390*

Inderbitzen-Pisuruk, H., 108, *121*
Ingham, J. G., 156, *180*, 204, *212, 213*
Ingram, R. E., 81, 89, 112, *121*, 149, 161, *176, 185*, 202, *213*, 333, 360
Isabella, R., *326*
Isen, A. M., 341, 346, *354, 357*
Jack, D. C., 222, 223, 226, 227, 228, 229, 230, 231, 232, 235, 237, *245*, 381, *391*
Jack, R., 235, *245*
Jackson, D. N., 51, *62*
Jackson, J., 111, *121*
Jacobs, J. E., 334, *357*
Jacobson, E., 151, *180*
Jacobson, N., 225, *245*
Jacobson, N. S., 205, *213*, 275, 280, 285, 286, *293, 294, 296*, 383, 388, *391*
Jaenicke, C., 33, 34, 78, 89, 140, *145*
Jaffe, K., 56, *58*
Jaimez, L., 142, *147*
Jaimez, T. L., *147*
James, W., 152, 158, *180*
Jamison, K., 27, *34*
Jamison, K. R., 253, *267*
Janoff-Bulman, R., 167, *178*
Janus, C. L., 233, *245*
Janus, S. S., 233, *245*
Jarrett, R. B., 56, *60*
Jarvis, W. B. G., 331, *357*
Jasnoski, M. L., 104, *118*
Jenkins, C. D., 53, *61*
Jenkins-Hall, K., 334, *357*
Jennings, D. L., 101, *118*
Jerrom, D. W. A., 154, *176*
John, K., 133, *145*
John, O. P., 161, *180*, 337, *359*
Johnson, B. R., 112, *121*
Johnson, J. E., 101, *121*
Johnson, J. H., 312, *326*
Johnson, J. L., 77, *91*
Johnson, J. M., 101, *121*
Johnson, S. A., 334, 341, *359*
Johnson, S. M., 277, 286, *294*, 301, *321*
Johnston, C., 302, *324*
Joiner, T. E., 47, 48, *61, 62*, 110, 111, *117, 121*, 136, *145*, 150, 151, 152, 157, 160, *180, 181, 183*, 189, 190, 196, 198, 202, 203, *213*, 334, 345, 350, *357*
Joiner, T. E., Jr., 8, 10, 11, 14, *18, 19*,

66, 86, 89, 90, 129, 131, 132, *146, 147*, 274, 280, 283, 286, *294*
Jolly, C., *267*
Jome, M. A., 77, *89*
Jones, D., *57*
Jones, M., 303, 306, 313, *324*
Jones, W. H., 108, *121*
Jono, R. T., 53, *61*
Jordon, C., 68, *91*
Josephs, R. A., 152, 153, 161, *179, 181*, 196, *212*
Jouriles, E. N., 342, *357*

Kaelber, C. T., 274, *295*
Kaflowitz, N. G., 108, *119*
Kagan, J., 11, *18*, 104, 105, *118, 121*
Kahn, J., 78, *88*
Kalliopuska, M., 106, 108, *121*
Kammer, D., 111, *121*
Kandel, D., 273, *295*
Kaniasty, K., 47, *61*
Kaplan, N., 168, *182*
Kaplan, R. M., 53, *61*
Karney, B. R., 339, 344, *357*
Kashani, J., 299, *325*
Kaslow, N. J., 12, *18*, 65, 66, 67, 70, 90, *91*, 112, *121*, 129, 140, *145, 147*, 286, *295*
Kassel, J. D., 153, 157, 162, 164, *184*, 204, *214*
Katz, J., 136, *145*, 191, *213*, 273, *292*
Kaufman, J., 76, *90*, 167, *181*
Kauneckis, D., 104, *120*
Kaye, A. L., *122*
Kazdin, A. E., 129, 130, 133, *145*, 167, *181*
Keaten, J., 114, *121*
Keele-Card, G., 109, *121*
Keita, G. P., 53, *61*, 221, *245*
Keith, D., 84, *91*
Keith, P. M., 350, *360*
Keitner, G. I., *358*
Keller, M. B., 370, *391*
Kelley, H. H., 86, *90*, 338, 340, *357*
Kelly, L., 114, *121*
Kendall, P. C., 129, *145*
Kendler, K. S., 40, 46, *61*
Kennedy, E., 134, *145*
Kennedy, G., 113, *119*
Kenny, D., 311, 312, *320*

Kenny, D. A., 67, 87, 333, 348, 349, 350, 357, 373, 391
Kernis, M. H., 150, 153, 165, 181
Kerns, R. D., 53, 57
Kerr, J., 392
Kershner, J. G., 303, 312, 325
Kessler, R. C., 40, 46, 54, 58, 61, 63, 166, 167, 178, 181, 221, 243, 287, 293, 295, 349, 358, 370, 371, 375, 389, 391
Ketcham, A.Sl., 58
Kiecolt-Glaser, J. K., 113, 122
Kiesler, D. J., 377, 391
Kihlstrom, J. F., 331, 339, 354, 357
King, D. S., 104, 118
King, G., 339, 356
Kininmonth, L., 346, 355
Kivett, V. R., 109, 110, 122
Kleban, M. H., 104, 122
Klein, D. N., 182, 358
Klein, M. H., 114, 120
Klein, S. B., 331, 336, 337, 357, 360, 361
Klerman, G., 23, 35, 228, 245, 370, 391
Klerman, G. L., 6, 18, 172, 181, 206, 214, 276, 286, 295, 300, 321, 381, 391
Knutson, J. F., 105, 122
Kobak, R., 271, 277, 295
Kobak, R. R., 168, 181, 282, 287, 295
Kochanska, G., 302, 307, 325, 327
Kohlberg, L., 223, 245
Kohut, H., 151, 154, 165, 181
Kolk, B. A., 174, 181
Kovacs, M., 116, 124, 190, 213
Kraepelin, E., 189, 213
Kramer, P. D., 262, 267, 384, 391
Krantz, S., 25, 34
Kreitman, N. B., 156, 180, 183, 204, 212
Krietman, N., 110, 111, 122
Krueger, L., 319, 326
Kuczynski, L., 307, 325
Kuiper, N. A., 75, 91, 129, 146, 153, 155, 159, 160, 163, 169, 181, 186, 190, 211, 213
Kupfer, D. J., 372, 390
Kusel, S. J., 80, 91
Kwon, P., 154, 157, 166, 187

Ladd, G. W., 79, 80, 86, 88
Lahey, B. B., 104, 122

Laitinen, M., 106, 108, 121
Lakey, B., 157, 181
Lamm, H., 106, 108, 120, 124
Landrum, G. C., 345, 356
Langeluddecke, P., 53, 61
Lansing, C. R., 105, 122
Larrick, R. P., 153, 181
Larsen, R. J., 104, 122
Larson, J., 44, 62
Lashley, S. L., 285, 295
Lautenschlager, G. J., 307, 324
Lavori, P. W., 370, 391
Lawton, M. P., 104, 122
Laxer, R. M., 154, 182
Lay, K., 308, 325
Lazarus, R. S., 42, 43, 61
Leary, M., 101, 102, 113, 122
Leary, M. R., 14, 18, 158, 160, 182
Lee, C. M., 316, 325
Lee, M., 94, 122
Leff, J., 373, 391
Leff, J. P., 9, 18
Lefkowitz, M. M., 75, 79, 90, 330, 348, 351, 357
Leggett, E. L., 82, 83, 88
Leiberman, J. R., 157, 180
Leitenberg, H., 106, 122, 129, 145
LeMare, L. J., 108, 124
Lenhart, L., 81, 91
Leonard, K. E., 287, 296, 339, 344, 360
Lepore, S. J., 116, 120
Levin, I., 109, 122
Levy, M. B., 368, 391
Lewicki, T., 336, 357
Lewin, L., 277, 292, 342, 357
Lewinsohn, P. M., 4, 19, 42, 62, 83, 88, 132, 133, 146, 154, 155, 156, 157, 182, 204, 213, 284, 295, 338, 348, 357, 358, 373, 374, 390, 391, 392
Lewis, M., 377, 391
Libet, J., 374, 391
Licht, B. G., 82, 90
Lichtenstein, E., 45, 58
Lilly, A. A., 19
Lindberg, N., 33
Linden, M., 205, 213, 334, 356
Linn, J. D., 140, 147
Linnoila, M., 19, 263, 267
Linville, P. W., 86, 90, 151, 153, 182
Lipman, A., 195, 200, 210
Lipsey, J. R., 59

Littman, D. C., 336, *356*
Livingston, R., 129, *145*
Lizardi, H., 149, 167, *182, 358*
Lochman, L. E., 81, *91*
Locke, B. Z., 296
Lohr, M. J., 114, *120*
Lollis, S., 108, *124*
Londerville, S., 308, *325*
London, P., 157, *180*
Lovejoy, M. C., 347, *358*
Lucas, J. A., *147*
Lucas, R., *147*
Lukens, E., *146*
Lynskey, M. T., 301, 313, *323*
Lyons-Ruth, K., 29, *35,* 74, *90,* 303, 308, 316, 319, *325*

Maccoby, E. E., 312, *321*
MacDonald, M. R., 190, *213*
Macera, C., *57*
MacEwen, K. E., 274, *291*
MacKinnon, A., 149, *182*
MacLean, P. D., 250, *267*
Maelands, J. G., 53, *60*
Magee, W. J., 166, 167, *181,* 370, 371, *375, 391*
Main, M., 168, *182,* 308, *325*
Major, B., 158, *178*
Malik, M. M., 77, *88*
Malone, P. S., 339, *356*
Mandel, M. R., 206, *214*
Mankowski, T. A., 153, 162, *177,* 202, 204, *211*
Manly, J. T., 167, *186*
Maracek, J., 192, 193, 207, *213*
Marcus, D. K., 345, *358*
Margolin, G., 285, *294,* 319, *326,* 383, *391*
Mark, M. M., 342, *361*
Markley, D. K., 168, *182*
Marks, J., *57*
Marks, T., 25, *35,* 140, *144*
Markus, H., 128, *146,* 153, *182,* 331, *358*
Markus, H. R., 153, *186*
Marlatt, G. A., 45, *58*
Marsh, H. W., 153, *182*
Marsh, K. L., 96, *125*
Marten, S., *246*
Martin, H. P., 76, *87*
Martin, J. M., 303, *321*

Martinez, P., 308, 314, *326*
Matheny, A. P., Jr., 104, 105, *122*
Matthews, K. A., 53, *58*
Maughan, B., 52, *61*
Maynard Smith, J., 248, 253, *268*
Mayol, A., 23, 25, *35*
McCabe, M., 133, *147*
McCabe, S. B., 160, *181*
McCann, K., 308, *326*
McCaul, K. D., 111, *122*
McCauley, E., 66, 67, *90,* 168, *176*
McCluskey, U., 281, *296*
McCullough, J. P., 105, 112, *122*
McCune, K. J., *122*
McDonald, C., 231, *243,* 286, *292*
McEnroe, M. J., 342, *353*
McGarvey, A. L., 169, *187,* 283, *297*
McGrath, E., 53, *61,* 221, 222, 226, 227, 228, 232, *245*
McGuire, M. T., 263, *268*
McKnew, D., 302, *327*
McKnew, D. H., *325*
McLean, P. D., 383, *391*
McLeod, J. D., 166, *182,* 349, *358*
McLeod, V. A., 333, *359*
McMahon, R. J., 301, *326*
McManus, C., 166, *177*
McNiel, D. E., 340, *358*
McNulty, S. E., 191, 206, *213*
McWilliam, C., *120*
Mead, G. H., 165, *182,* 350, *358*
Mehlman, P. T., 8, *19*
Melchior, L. A., 101, 102, 114, *119*
Mellstrom, 109
Melville, H., 4, *19*
Meredith, W., 107, *119*
Merikangas, K. R., 329, 342, 345, *358*
Messer, S. C., 345, 347, *358*
Metalsky, G. I., 10, 14, *18,* 47, *61,* 65, 66, 69, 73, 81, 86, 87, 89, *90,* 111, *117,* 128, 129, 136, *143, 145, 146,* 151, 152, 157, 160, 164, *181, 182, 183,* 200, 203, 210, 274, 280, 294, 299, 320, 334, 345, *357*
Mettee, D. R., 192, 193, 207, *213*
Michel, M., 305, *321*
Michela, J. L., 110, *125,* 338, 340, *357*
Mickelson, K. D., 287, *295*
Mikulincer, M., 168, *183,* 279, 283, *295*
Milana, S., 337, *359*
Miles, J. E., 383, *391*

Miller, D. T., 346, 350, *358*
Miller, I. W., 116, *122*, 349, *358*
Miller, J. B., 222, 223, *245*
Miller, N. E., 112, *119*
Miller, P. M., 156, *183*
Miller, R. S., 101, *118*
Miller, S. A., 340, 343, 346, *358*
Mills, M., 306, *321*
Mintz, 166, *185*
Mintz, J., 374, *392*
Mintz, L. I., 374, *392*
Miranda, J., 161, 162, *183*
Mischel, W., 133, *146*, 338, *357*
Mitchell, J. R., 66, *90*, 168, *176*
Mitchell, R. E., 50, *61*
Mitchell, S. A., 222, 224, *245*
Moffat, F. L., Jr., *58*
Monroe, S. M., 39, 40, 41, *61*, 150, 151,
        153, 154, 155, 156, 157, 161,
        164, 173, *178*, *183*, *185*
Moore, D., 106, 108, 109, 115, *123*
Moore, G., 168, *176*
Moos, B. S., 43, 48, 49, *62*
Moos, R., 46, 50, 52, *57*
Moos, R. H., 39, 40, 41, 42, 43, 44, 45,
        46, 47, 48, 49, 50, 51, 52, 54,
        55, 56, *57*, *58*, *59*, *60*, *61*, *62*,
        63, 349, *353*
Moretti, M. M., 129, *144*
Morf, C., 153, *184*
Moser, J., 167, *181*
Moss, S., 66, *90*
Moul, D. E., 274, *295*
Mruk, C., 152, *183*
Müller-Spahn, F., 113, *123*
Mullins, L. C., 111, 115, *123*
Mullins, L. L., 111, *123*, 134, *146*
Mumme, D., 78, *91*
Munoz, R. F., 163, *179*
Murphy, B. C., 103, *120*
Murphy, C. M., 342, *357*
Murray, D., 343, 344, *359*
Murray, D. W., 341, *358*
Murray, E. J., 272, *295*
Murray, S. L., 331, *358*
Myers, J. K., *296*
Myers, M. F., 222, 232, *246*

Nacht, S., 4, *19*
Nardone, M. E., 345, *358*
Nawrocki, B., 312, *323*, *324*

Neale, M. C., 40, 46, *61*
Needles, D. J., 207, *213*
Neeleman, J., 113, *123*
Nelson, G. M., 280, *295*, 313, *320*
Nelson, R. O., 56, *60*
Nelson, S., 13, *18*, 82, *88*
Neto, F., 104, 108, *123*
Neuberg, S. L., *359*
Nezu, A. M., 110, *123*
Nezu, C. M., 110, *123*
Nezu, V. A., 110, *123*
Ng, R., 47, *58*
Nicholson, K. J., 335, 341, 345, *359*
Nisbett, R. E., 153, *181*
Nolen-Hoeksema, S., 44, 62, 65–66, 67,
        68, 69, 70, 78, 83, 85, *90*, *91*,
        221, 226, 231, *246*, 303, *326*
Noller, P., 279, *293*
Norcross, J. C., 272, *295*
Noriega, V., *58*
Norman, W. H., 116, *122*
Norris, F. H., 47, *61*
Norris, S. L. W., *122*
Norwood, R. M., 93, *125*
Notarius, C. I., 285, *295*
Nottleman, E., 306, 312, *326*
Nurius, P., 153, *182*

Oatley, K., 152, *183*
O'Brien, M., 319, *326*
Ogrocki, P., *122*
O'Leary, K. D., 272, 274, 275, 276, 292,
        293, *295*, *296*, 340, *355*
Olinger, L. J., 75, *91*, 129, *146*, 153,
        155, 169, *181*
Olweus, D., 80, *91*
Osborne, D., 191, *215*
Osborne, L. N., 273, *294*
Osherow, N., 100, *118*
Osten, V., *292*

Pagel, M. D., 54, *62*
Paley, B., 30, 33, 34, *179*, *294*, *324*
Palmer, D. J., 129, *144*
Panak, W. F., 79, 86, *91*, 110, *123*
Park, B., 336, 337, 343, *359*
Parker, G., 149, *180*, 378, *392*
Parker, G. A., 250, 252, *268*
Parker, L. E., 44, *62*

Pataki, S. P., 330, *354*
Patterson, G. R., 307, *321*
Patterson, J., 106, 107, 109, *124*
Paykel, E. S., 6, *19*, 23, *35*, 306, *327*, 374, *392, 393*
Pearl, L., 108, *119*
Pearlin, L. I., 47, *62*
Pelham, B. W., 138, *147*, 153, *183, 186*, 189, 191, 192, 193, 194, 195, 196, 198, 200, 203, 206, 207, 208, 209, *213*, 215, *216*, 286, 297, 339, *356*
Pellegrini, D., 319, *323*
Penner, L. A., 347, *360*
Penza, K., 229, 230, *246*
Peplau, L. A., 107, 109, 110, *123*, 125
Pepper, C. M., 12, *17*, 367, 370, 372, 378, 384, *389*
Perez-Bouchard, L., 77, 78, *91*
Perlman, D., 107, 109, 110, *123*
Perry, D. G., 80, *91*
Perry, H. S., 384, *392*
Perry, L. C., 80, *91*
Perry, M., 111, *117*
Persons, J. B., 109, 129, *146*, 161, *183*
Peselow, E. D., 337, *359*
Peters, S. D., 24, *35*
Peterson, C., 73, 74, 82, *91*, 128, *146*, *147*
Peterson, C., 78
Peterson, L., 134, *146*
Petty, F., 259, *268*
Petty, R. E., 331, *357*
Petzel, T. P., 101, *121*
Pfaff, H., 53, *63*
Phares, V., 52, *62*
Phillips, S., 301, *321*
Piaget, J., 223, *246*
Pickens, J., 312, *324*
Pickles, A., 376, *392*
Pierce, G. R., 54, *62*, 350, *360*
Pietromonaco, P. R., 56, *58*, 150, *177*, 287, *293*
Piliavin, J. A., 347, *360*
Pilkonis, P. A., 93, 102, 106, *123*, 125
Pillow, D. R., 47, *62*
Pinel, E. C., 192, 193, 208, *215*
Pinel, P., 189, *214*
Pittman, N. L., 111, *123*, 200, *214*
Pittman, T. S., 111, *123*, 200, *214*
Pitts, F. N., 233, *244*
Pliner, P., 111, *120*, 200, *212*

Plomin, R., 104, 105, 110, *123*
Pollack, S. L., 112, *121*
Pollitt, J. D., *268*
Post, R. D., 201, *212*
Post, R. M., 174, *183*
Potthoff, J. G., 10, *19*, 48, *62*, 152, *183*
Powell, M., 104, *122*
Power, M., 153, *183*
Power, M. J., 113, *123*
Pozo, C., *58*
Pratto, R., 337, *359*
Predmore, S. C., 204, 205, *215*
Pretzer, J. L., 152, *184*
Price, J., 158, *179*, 184
Price, J. S., 249, 254, 259, *268*
Priel, B., 284, *296*
Problems Prevention Research Group, 306, *325*
Prodromidis, M., 312, *320*
Puckering, C., 306, *321*
Puig-Antich, J., 133, *146*
Pyszczynski, T., 112, *123*, 152, *184*

Quiggle, N. L., 79, 86, *91*, 110, 111, 112, *123*
Quinlan, D. M., 231, *243*, 286, *292*
Quinton, D., 371, 372, 375, 378, *392*
Quittner, A. L., 51, *62*

Rabiner, D. L., 81, *91*
Racamier, P. C., 4, *19*
Racusin, G. R., 12, *18*
Radke-Yarrow, M., 140, *146*, 303, 306, 308, 311, 312, 313, 314, 326, *327*
Rado, S., 151, 152, *184*
Raleigh, M. J., 263, *268*
Ramana, R., *392*
Randolph, J. J., 169, *184*
Range, L. M., 107, *121*
Rao, P. A., 129, *146*
Rao, U., 30, *35*
Raskin, A., 348, *354*
Read, S., 28, *33*
Read, S. J., 191, 205, *216*
Reaven, N. M., 134, *146*, 334, *353*
Redner, J. E., 83, *88*
Reeder, G. D., 337, *359*
Regier, D. A., 272, *296*

Rehm, L. P., 65, 90, 112, *121*, 190, *214*
Reiss, A., 229, *246*
Renshaw, P. D., 101, 108, 109, *124*
Repetti, R. L., 375, *392*
Resnick, J. S., 11, *18*, 104, *121*
Revenson, T. A., 107, *124*
Revicki, D. A., 222, *246*
Rhodewalt, F., 153, *184*
Rholes, W. S., 68, *91*, 161, *184*, 283, *296*
Rich, A. R., 111, 113, 115, 116, *119*, *124*
Richard, K. M., 301, *326*
Richards, M. P. M., 375, *392*
Richards, W., 77, *88*
Richardson, D., 308, *326*
Richters, J., 195, 196, 200, *212*
Richters, J. E., 334, 342, 348, *359*
Riger, A. L., 101, *118*
Riskind, J. H., 161, *184*
Riso, L. P., *182, 358*
Risso, L. P., 275, *296*
Ritts, V., 191, *214*
Roberts, J. E., 153, 154, 156, 157, 161, 162, 163, 164, 166, 169, 173, 174, *179, 183, 184, 185,* 204, *214,* 282, *296,* 368, 369, *392*
Roberts, R. E., 372, 373, *392*
Roberts, T. A., 224, *244*
Roberts, W.Cl., *122*
Robins, L. N., *296*
Robins, R. W., 161, *180*
Robinson, A., 367, *390*
Robinson, D. S., *58*
Robinson, L. A., 133, *144,* 205, *212*
Robinson, N. S., 157, *185*
Robinson, R. G., *59*
Robson, P. J., 152, *185*
Rodgers, A., 129, *145*
Rogers, W., *393*
Rogoff, B., 303, 314, *324*
Rohde, P., 42, *62,* 83, *88,* 158, *184,* 249, *268*
Rohrbaugh, M., 385, *392*
Rokeach, M., 100, *124*
Roman, P. M., 273, *292*
Rook, K., 107, 115, *124*
Rose, J., 108, *121*
Rose, M. S., 168, *186*
Rosenbaum, M., 348, *358*
Rosenberg, M., 152, 165, 166, *185*
Rosenfarb, I. S., 166, *185*

Rosenthal, R., 346, 350, *359*
Roth, D., 190, *214*
Rothbart, M., 337, *359*
Rothbart, M. K., 104, *124*
Rothlind, J., 274, *292*
Rounsaville, B. J., 6, *18,* 276, *294*
Rowe, D. C., 104, 105, *123*
Rubert, M. P., 156, 180, 342, *356*
Rubin, K. H., 108, 109, *124*
Rucinski, J., 233, *246*
Ruckdeschel, K., 271, *295*
Rude, S. S., 203, *212*
Rudolph, K., 30, *34, 35, 324*
Rudolph, K. D., 179, *294*
Ruscher, S. M., 205, *214*
Rush, A. J., 113, 116, *118, 124,* 127, *144,* 171, *176,* 194, *211,* 329, *353*
Russel, D. W., *62*
Russell, D., 108, *121*
Russell, D. W., 40, 44, *59,* 342, *361*
Russo, N. F., 53, *61,* 221, *245*
Rutter, M., 167, *185,* 371, 372, 376, *392*
Ryan, C. E., *358*
Ryan, M. C., 106, 107, 109, *124*

Sacco, 340
Sacco, W. P., 133, *146,* 331, 333, 334, 335, 337, 338, 339, 340, 341, 342, 343, 344, 345, 346, 347, 356, 357, 358, *359*
Safran, J. D., 171, *185*
Salovey, P., 170, *185,* 202, *214*
Salusky, S., 275, *294*
Salzberg, J. A., 202, *216*
Sameroff, A., 300, *326*
Sandeen, E. E., 149, *176,* 271, *292,* 383, *388*
Sanders, M. R., 346, *356*
Sandler, I., 47, *62*
SanFilipo, M. P., 337, *359*
Santor, D. C., 373, *389*
Sarason, B. R., 54, *62,* 350, *360*
Sarason, I. G., 54, *62,* 350, *360*
Sashidharan, S., 204, *212*
Sashidharan, S. P., 156, *180, 183*
Saunders, P. A., *120*
Sceery, A., 168, *181*
Schachter, S., 100, *120*
Schaefer, E. S., 351, *360*
Schaefer, J., 42, *61*

Schaefer, J. A., 40, 42, 56, *62, 63*
Schafer, R. B., 191, *214*, 350, *360*
Schamaling, K. B., *296*
Scharff, D. E., 286, *296*
Scharff, J. S., 286, *296*
Scheier, M. F., *58*
Schilling, E. A., 40, *58*
Schjelderup-Ebbe, T., 253, *268*
Schmaling, D. G., 275, *294*
Schmaling, K. B., 280, 336, *356*, 383, *391*
Schmidt, K., 140, *146*
Schmidt, K. L., 141, *147*
Schmidt, N. B., 131, 132, 142, *147*
Schneider, D. J., 339, *360*
Schoeneman, T. J., 350, *360*
Schott, T., 53, *63*
Schroeder, A., 116, *120*
Schroeder, D. A., 347, *360*
Schroeder, D. G., 192, 193, *216*
Schul, Y., 348, *361*
Schulman, P., 84, *91*
Schultz, N. R., 106, 108, 109, 115, *123*
Schuster, T. L., 54, *63*
Schwartz, D. A., 190, *214*
Schwartz, G. E., 206, *214*
Schwartz, N., 340, 341, *354, 360*
Scott, C. K., 331, 337, 339, 342, 343, *360*
Scott, J., 169, *187*
Scovel, M., 111, *124*
Secunda, S. K., 93, 110, *124*
Sedikides, C., 101, *118*, 160, *185*, 202, *214*
Seeley, J. R., 42, *62*, 83, *88*
Segal, L., 384, *390*
Segal, Z., 128, 139, *147*
Segal, Z. V., 161, 171, *185*, 333, *360*
Segrin, C., 160, *185*, 189, 205, *214*, 329, 331, 334, 340, 345, 347, *360*, 367, *392*
Seifer, R., *326*
Seigel, L. J., 111, *123*
Seiner, S. H., 306, 314, *326*
Seligman, M. E. P., 8, *19*, 65, 66, 67, 68, 69, 73, 74, 78, 82, 84, 87, *90, 91*, 116, *117, 124*, 128, 129, *143, 146, 147*, 200, 210, 259, *268*
Seligson, A. G., 110, 115, *124*
Sells, C. J., 222, 232, *246*
Sells, J. M., 222, 232, *246*

Senchak, M., 287, 296, 339, 344, *360*
Serketich, W. J., 342, *354*
Shamai, D., 284, *296*
Shanahan, M., 307, *324*
Sharma, V., *120*
Shaughnessy, M. S., 84, *91*
Shaver, P., 271, 277, 278, *294*
Shaver, P. R., 168, *180*, 271, 279, *296*, 368, *391*
Shaw, B., 113, *118*
Shaw, B. F., 75, *91*
Shaw, D. A., 4, *19*
Shea, M. T., 381, *390*
Sheeber, L. B., 312, *326*
Shelton, M. R., 67, *91*
Sher, T. G., 343, *353*
Sherbourne, C. D., 42, 45, *63*
Sherick, R. B., 129, *145*
Sherman, A. D., 259, *268*
Sherman, J. W., 337, *360*
Sherman, L., 274, *292*, 312, *325*
Shoham, V., 385, *392*
Sholomaskas, D., 276, *294*
Showers, C., 153, *185*
Shrauger, J. S., 192, 193, 203, *214*, 350, *360*
Shustack, B., 190, *214*
Shuttleworth, E. C., *122*
Siegel, A. W., 65, *90*, 112, *121*
Siegel, J., 286, *296*
Siegler, R. S., 67, *92*
Sikes, J., 100, *118*
Sillars, A. L., 346, *360*
Silverman, J. A., 155, *185*
Silverman, J. S., 155, *185*
Simons, A. D., 39, 40, 41, *61*, 156, 168, 173, *182, 183, 185*
Simpson, J. A., 283, *296*
Sinclair, I., 281, *296*
Sinclair, R. C., 342, *361*
Singer, J. A., 170, *185*
Skinner, J. R., Jr., 66, *92*
Skowronski, J. J., 331, 336, 343, *354*
Sloman, L., 158, *184*, 249, 257, 264, *268*
Smiley, P., 75, *92*
Smith, D. A. F., 50, 51, *58*
Smith, E. R., 336, *361*
Smith, R. H., 339, *356*
Smith, T. W., 59, 103, *124*, 380, *392*
Snapp, M., 100, *118*
Snider, P. R., 44, *63*
Snidman, N., 11, *18*, 104, *121*

Snyder, C. L., 380, 392
Sokol, M., 56, 63
Solano, C. H., 108, 121
Somberg, D. R., 307, 323
Speers, M. A., 128, 147
Speicher, C. E., 122
Spence, S. H., 134, 145
Spencer, S. J., 161, 186
Spitzer, R. L., 214
Sroufe, A., 80, 92
Sroufe, L. A., 25, 35, 74, 92, 167, 178,
    277, 278, 296, 297
Srull, T. K., 330, 336, 339, 361
Stablein, D., 59
Stack, S., 189, 214
Stahl, J., 308, 325
Stansbury, K., 29, 34, 78, 89
Stanton, A. L., 44, 63
Stanton, B. A., 53, 61
Stark, K. D., 129, 140, 141, 145, 147
Steele, C. M., 158, 161, 185, 186, 192,
    214
Steffen, V. J., 228, 244
Stein, J. R., 191, 214
Stein, K. F., 153, 186
Stein, S. J., 114, 120
Steiner, S. C., 150, 151, 183
Steinmetz, J. L., 154, 182, 204, 213
Stein-Seroussi, A., 192, 216, 348, 361
Stephan, C., 100, 118
Stephan, E., 108, 124
Stephan, W. G., 337, 362
Stephens, R. S., 133, 147
Stephenson, B., 200, 216
Sternberg, C., 278, 293
Stevens, H. B., 229, 246
Stewart, A., 393
Stewart, A. J., 56, 63
Stewart, S. M., 66, 92
Stickland, B. R., 53, 61
Stocker, C., 104, 123
Stokes, J. P., 109, 122
Stoppard, M. M., 222, 246
Story, A. L., 207, 211
Stowe, M. L., 129, 144
Strack, S., 347, 361
Strauss, A., 376, 393
Stringer, S. A., 77, 88
Stroup-Benham, C. A., 53, 61
Sturt, E., 112, 118
Suinn, R. M., 191, 215
Sullivan, C., 120

Sullivan, H. S., 5, 19
Sullivan, K. T., 339, 357
Suls, J., 158, 186
Sultan, F., 115, 119
Suomi, S. J., 19
Surra, C. A., 339, 343, 361
Surtees, P. G., 156, 180, 204, 212
Susman, A., 314, 326
Swallow, S. R., 153, 159, 163, 186
Swank, R. T., 53, 57
Swann, W. B., 153, 160, 183, 186
Swann, W. B., Jr., 130, 138, 140, 147,
    189, 190, 191, 192, 193, 194,
    195, 196, 198, 200, 201, 203,
    204, 205, 206, 207, 208, 209,
    211, 212, 213, 215, 216, 286,
    287, 297, 348, 361
Swartz, M. S., 221, 243
Sweeney, P. D., 128, 147
Swindle, R. W., 46, 63
Swindle, R. W., Jr., 349, 361
Szasz, T. S., 5, 19

Tal, M., 58
Tambor, E. S., 14, 18, 158, 182
Tanenbaum, R. L., 67, 90, 91, 147
Tannenbaum, L., 303, 314, 326
Tarlow, E. M., 154, 186
Tarnowski, K. J., 77, 87
Tarullo, L. B., 303, 306, 312, 315, 326
Taub, D. M., 19
Taylor, H., 124
Taylor, S. E., 44, 57, 153, 159, 160, 176,
    186, 200, 216
Teasdale, J., 9, 18, 65, 87
Teasdale, J. D., 116, 117, 152, 158, 161,
    186, 206, 216, 330, 333, 338,
    349, 357
Teglasi, H., 84, 91, 101, 102, 125
Teitelbaum, M. L., 59
Telch, M. J., 131, 142, 147
Tems, C. L., 66, 83, 92
Tennant, C., 53, 61, 112, 118, 149, 180
Tennen, H., 196, 216
Terdal, S. K., 14, 18
Tesiny, E. P., 75, 79, 90, 330, 348, 351,
    357
Tesser, A., 158, 186
Teti, D., 302, 326, 327
Teti, D. M., 301, 324
Thase, M. E., 173, 185

Thoits, P. A., 40, 42, *63*
Thomas, A. J., 106, *125*
Thomas, A. M., 312, *327*
Thompson, J. M., 230, *245*
Thompson, L. M., 229, *244*
Thompson, M. M., 229, 230, *246*
Thompson, R. A., 74, 85, 88, 302, 305, 316, 318, *327*
Tice, D. M., 153, *176*
Tilson, M., 42, *62*
Todak, G., *146*
Tomkins, S. S., 101, *125*
Tonsager, M. E., 208, *212*
Tota, M. E., 203, *210*
Toth, S., 300, 308, 314, *321*
Toth, S. L., 167, 168, *186*
Townshend, P., 109, 110, *125*
Traub, G. S., 111, *125*
Triesch, S. K., 77, *89*
Tronick, E., 306, *321*
Trope, Y., 192, *216*
Troy, M., 80, *92*
Truglio, R., 303, *321*
Tsai, S. L., 129, *145*
Turk, D. C., 128, *147*
Turnbull, J., 58, *178*, 293, *389*
Turnbull, W., 346, 350, *358*
Turner, J. E., Jr., 67, 69, 83, 87, *92*

Uebelacker, L. A., 230, *246*
Ulrich-Jakubowski, D., 342, *361*
Urban, J., 278, *297*
Usher, M., 140, *144*, 149, *178*, 334, *354*

Valentine, E. R., 167, *176*
Valentiner, D. P., 45, *63*
van der Molen, H. T., 101, *125*
van Ijzendoorn, M. H., 308, *327*
Vaugh, C. E., 9, *18*
Vaughn, C. E., 373, *391*
Veiel, H., 156, *177*
Veiel, H. O., 204, *211*
Vella, D. D., *147*
Vickers, J., *19*
Vinokur, A., 348, *361*
Vinokur, A. D., 47, *58*
Virkkunen, M., 263, *267*
Visco, J., *59*
Vredenburg, K., 373, *393*

Wachs, T. D., 312, *327*
Wachtel, P., 371, 384, *393*
Wachtel, P. L., 204, *216*
Wagner, E., 81, *89*
Wall, J. E., 314, *327*
Wall, S., 168, *175*, 277, *291*
Walters, C., 68, *91*
Waltz, J., 225, *243*
Waltz, M., 53, 54, *63*
Ware, J., *393*
Warner, V., 133, *145*, 307, *323*
Waterman, J., 76, *87*
Waters, E., 308, *325*
Watson, A. K., 102, *119*
Watzlawick, P., 190, 208, *216*, 384, *393*
Watzlawick, P. W., 16, *19*, 384, 385, *393*
Waxer, P., 206, *216*
Wayment, H. A., 153, 159, *186*
Weakland, J., 190, 208, *216*
Weakland, J. H., 384, 390, *393*
Weary, G., 96, 111, *125*, 200, 201, *211*, *212*, 216, 338, 339, *361*, 387, *393*
Weeks, D. J., 110, 111, 115, *125*
Weems, 340
Weiner, B., 111, *125*, 340, 346, *361*
Weinstein, M. S., 4, *19*
Weisfeld, G. E., 254, *268*
Weiss, J. R., 104, *120*
Weiss, R. S., 110, *125*
Weissman, M. M., 6, *18*, *19*, 23, 35, 172, *181*, 228, *245*, 272, 276, 295, 297, 306, *327*, 374, 381, 391, *393*
Weisz, J., 30, *35*
Welker, R., 134
Wells, K. B., 42, *63*, 374, *393*
Welner, A., 233, *246*
Welsh, J. D., 306, 307, 312, *325*, *326*
Wenzlaff, R. A., 189, 190, 191, 192, 194, 195, 196, 200, 203, 206, 208, 209, *216*
Wenzlaff, R. M., 138, 140, *147*, *186*, 286, *297*
West, M., 190, *214*
West, M. L., 168, *186*
Westen, D., 163, *187*
Westkott, M., 224, 235, *246*
Wheaton, B., *63*
Whiffen, V. E., 7, *17*, 39, 40, 41, *59*, 231, *244*, 302, 303, *327*, 342, 356, 370, 372, *390*

Whisenhunt, C. R., *181*
Whisman, M., 275, *292*
Whisman, M. A., 154, 157, 166, 169,
    187, 230, 246, 283, 297, *353*
Whitley, T. W., 222, 233, *246*
Wickrama, K. A. S., 191, *214*
Wierson, M., 310, 316, *327*
Wierzbicki, M., 133, *147*
Williams, C., 115, *119*
Williams, J. B., *214*
Williams, J. M. G., 169, *187*
Williamson, D., *57*
Williard, L. C., 80, *91*
Wills, T. A., 149, 158, 159, *177*, 186,
    187
Wilson, G. T., 45, *58*
Windle, M., 303, 310, 312, *323*
Wise, E. H., 129, *147*
Wisnicki, K. S., 112, *121*
Wisnieski, W., 113, *119*
Wittenborn, J. R., 155, *176*, 177
Wolfson, A., 78, *91*, 302, 303, *325*, 326
Wood, J., 375, *392*
Wood, J. V., 158, *187*, 202, *216*
Woodward, J., 107, *119*
Woolfolk, R. L., *178*
Wortman, C., 378, 389, *390*
Wortman, C. B., 58, *178*, 189, *211*, 293
Wyer, R. A., 336, 339, *361*

Wyer, R. S., 330, 336, 343, 346, *361*

Yalom, I. D., 172, *187*
Yang, B., 111, *125*
Yarkin, K. L., 338, 345, *361*
Yates, B. T., 336, *361*
Ybarra, O., 337, *362*
Yost, L. W., 129, *145*
Young, J., 130, *147*
Young, J. E., 114, *125*
Young, L. D., 53, *63*
Yuwiler, A., 263, *268*

Zahn-Waxler, C., 302, 307, 310, 311,
    314, *323*, 326, *327*
Zajonc, R. B., 103, *125*
Zarate, M. A., 336, *361*
Zautra, A., 373, *391*
Zautra, A. J., 47, *62*
Zeifman, D., 280, *294*
Zimbardo, P. G., 93, 94, 101, 106, 108,
    119, 122, *125*
Zirkel, S., 52, *63*
Zupan, B., *89*
Zupan, B. A., 112, *120*, 129, 130, *145*,
    147
Zuroff, D., 231, *243*, 286, *292*
Zuroff, D. C., 152, *176*, 292, 337, *362*

SUBJECT INDEX

Abramovitch, R., 77
Abramson, L. Y., 128
Ause. *See* child abuse; substance abuse
Adaptation, 40
Adaptive interpersonal functioning, 11, 42
ADHD. *See* attention deficit hyperactivity disorder
Adolescents
  parental depression and, 310, 312, 375–376
  stress and coping processes and, 52–53
Affect
  negative social behaviors and, 346–347
  relationship satisfaction and, 344
  social cognitions and, 333, 340–342
Affect infusion model (AIM), 342
"Affective style," 11
Aggression in women, 228–229
Ahrens, A. H., 68
AIM. *See* affect infusion model
Ainsworth, M., 277–278
Akiskal, H. S., 371
Allen, D. M., 77
Allies, thought, and planning (ATP), 261, 265
Anderson, C. A., 10–11, 12, 13, 14, 15, 93–125
Anderson, P., 11–12, 15–16, 271–297
Anger inhibition in women, 228–229
Anxiety, and self-esteem, 165. *See also* social anxiety
Approach coping strategies, 11, 42–43
ATP. *See* allies, thought, and planning
Attachment styles
  in adults, 278–279
  Coyne's interactional theory and, 7
  in infants, 277–278
  in marriage, 279, 281, 283–284, 285
  proximity seeking and, 281
  self-esteem regulation and, 170–171, 368–369
Attachment theory
  adult attachment theory and, 278–279

depression vulnerability and, 31
emotional security hypothesis and, 315
functions of attachment system and, 277
infant attachment theory and, 276–278
integrative marital therapy and, 15–16, 285–291
maintenance of self-esteem and, 14, 168–171
marital discord model and, 271–272
marital factors in depression and, 11–12, 277
marriage as safe haven and, 281–284
marriage as secure base and, 284–285
origins of interpersonal perspective and, 25–26, 27–28
proximity seeking in marital discord and, 279–281
Attention deficit hyperactivity disorder (ADHD), 140–141
Attributional style. *See also* negative attributional style
  cognitive therapy and, 116
  Coyne's interactional theory and, 7
  heuristic model for origins of, 70–84
  hopelessness theory and, 128–129
  link between depression and, 69–70, 111–112
  maladaptive, and everyday problems of living, 100–101, 116
  stability of, 69–70
Attributions, in social-cognitive model, 331, 338–340
  affective reactions and, 340
  negative, by others, 338–340
  vs. person schemas, 339–340
  responses to depressed people and, 344–347
Avoidant coping strategies, 11, 15, 42

Barahal, R. M., 76
Barnett, P. A., 163
Bartholomew, K., 170, 278
Beach, S. H., 271–297

Beck, A., 23, 81, 329
Beck, A. T., 129–130, 209
Behavioral inhibition, 11
  genetic factors and, 104–105
  intervention and, 15
Behavioral interpersonal model, 132–133
Behavioral marital therapy (BMT), 275–
  276, 383–384
Behavioral modification, 114
Bell, I. R., 105
Benazon, N., 366–367
Bernet, C. Z., 161
Biased perceptions by others, 334–338,
  346, 352
Bibring, E., 4
Biglan, A., 280
Birtchnell, J., 263–264, 378
Blai, B., 109
Blalock, J., 3–19
Bloxom, B. M., 338
BMT. See behavioral marital therapy
Bonin, L. A., 11, 39–63. See also adap-
  tive interpersonal functioning
Bonner, R. L., 116
Bowlby, J., 25–26, 27, 166, 276–277
Brown, G. W., 6, 24–25, 152, 174
Brown, J. D., 162
Burhams, K. K., 75–76, 85–86
Busch, C. M., 108
Butler, A. C., 162–163

Cain, K. M., 73–74
Cardamone, A. I., 65–92
Cardiac patients, 53–56
Causal attributions. See attributional
  style; attributions, in social-
  cognitive model
Causal unity, 32
Causes of depression, 9–13, 32. See also
  onset of depression
Cerezo, M. A., 77
Cheek, J. M., 101, 102, 108
Child abuse
  attributional style and, 76–77
  self-esteem and, 167
Child-management practices, 307–308
Children. See also parental depression;
  parent-child relationships; peer
  relationships
  caregiving for parents and, 302

characteristics of, and family processes,
  311–312
depression in, and negative attributional style, 66–70
development of attributional style and,
  70–85
development of self-esteem and, 166–
  167
early episode of depression and, 83–84
integrative framework and, 140–141
link between depression and early experiences and, 74–75, 375–377
methodological issues and, 85
parental rejection and, 330
parental stress and coping processes
  and, 51–52
transmission of depression and, 28–29
vulnerability factors and, 9
Clinical depression. See also silencing the
  self theory
recurrent nature of, and theory construction, 370–373, 374, 375–
  377, 378–379
self-esteem and, 175
self-verification and, 196–198
Cognitive characteristics of shyness, 102
Cognitive models, 127–132
  Beck's model and, 129–130, 152
  children of depressed parents and,
    301–304
  Coyne's interactional theory and, 6–7
  development of attributional style and,
    70–73, 81, 85, 86
  origins of interpersonal perspective
    and, 23
  self-esteem and, 152
Cognitive phenomena associated with depression, 111–112, 116
Cognitive therapy (CT)
  loneliness and, 115
  maritally depressed people and, 275–
    276
Cole, D. A., 61–62, 67–68
Complaints, 379–381
Compliant relatedness, 227
Control. See prediction and control strivings
Cooley, C. F., 165
Coping strategies. See also stress and coping framework
  approach vs. avoidant strategies, 11,
    42–43

mediation of depression and, 14, 43–45

predictors of, 43

Couples therapy

attachment perspective and, 15–16, 285–291

behavioral marital therapy and, 275–276, 383–384

efficacy of, 275–276, 383–384

integrative approach to, 15–16, 285–291

Covell, K., 77

Coyne, J. C., 3–19, 154, 365–393

integrative frameworks and, 7, 368–369

interpersonal theory of, 5, 6–7, 24, 133–134, 160, 365–368

intervention and, 16, 381–386

Crick, N. R., 79–80, 84

Cummings, E. M., 12, 16, 284, 299–327

Cumulative vs. interactional continuity, 376–377

Damage limitation function, 253

Davies, P. T., 12, 16, 299–327

Dean, A. L., 77

DePaulo, B. M., 348–349

Depression

antecedents of, 111–113

clinician impressions of impacts of, 3–4

consequences of, 113–114

vs. dysphoria, 95–96

importance of social and emotional models of, 301–303

maintenance of, 204–206

onset of, 202–204, 350–351, 370, 372

periods of healthy functioning and, 374, 375–377

prevalence of, 93

prevalence of maladaptive behavior in, 189–190

as problem of living, 95–96, 110–111

recurrent nature of, 370–373, 374, 375–377, 378–379

remission of, 207–208

risk for relapse of, 9, 330, 349–350

self-verification and, 194–199

single-episode models of, 371

societal costs of, 94

studies on self-esteem and, 154–165

types of, 95–96

Developmental psychopathology, and origins of interpersonal approach, 25–26

Development of depression. *See* onset of depression

de Waal, Franz, 262

Diathesis-stress models

attachment cognitions and, 27–28

hopelessness theory and, 65–66, 67–69, 128–129

integrative stress and coping framework and, 41

level of self-esteem and, 156–157

maladaptive self-schemas and, 130–131

negative attributional style and, 67–69

silencing the self model and, 231–232

stress generation and, 29–30

Dill, J. C., 10–11, 12, 13, 14, 15, 93–125

Disconnection schema cluster, 131

Dispositional optimism, 43–44

Dixon, J. F., 68

Dodge, K. A., 80, 84

Dotzentroth, S. E., 114

Dweek, C. S., 75–76, 82–83, 85–86

Dysphoria

vs. depression, 95–96

reactivity of self-esteem and, 162–163

Early maladaptive schema (EMS) theory

adult interpersonal behavior and, 9–10

interpretation of social feedback and, 137–140

predictive power of EMSs, 130–132

schema-based resiliency and, 141–142

ECA data. *See* epidemiologic catchment area data

Eisenberg, N., 103

Elder, G. H., 376

Elderly persons, 109–110, 115. *See also* loss

Emotional security. *See also* emotional security hypothesis

defined, 12, 306

family process model and, 305–306

as mediator, 305–306, 311, 315–318

Emotional security hypothesis, 300–301, 306

attachment theory and, 315, 318

Emotional security hypothesis
    (*continued*)
  child characteristics and, 311–312
  emotional regulation and, 318–319
  emotional security as mediator and,
      305–306, 311, 315–318
  exposure to family affect and, 318–319
  family process model and, 304
  importance of social and emotional
      models and, 301–303
  internal representations of family rela-
      tions and, 319
  marital functioning and, 309–311
  parental characteristics and, 306–307
  parent-child relations and, 307–309
Empirical investigations. *See also* method-
      ological issues
  integrative interpersonal and schematic
      framework and, 140–141
  of self-esteem and depression, 154–165
  on self-verification and depression,
      194–199
  underpinning interpersonal perspective,
      26–30
EMS theory. *See* early maladaptive
      schema theory
Environmental stressors, 67, 78
Epidemiologic catchment area (ECA)
      data, 370
Epstein, S., 158
Erickson, Milton, 384
Everyday problems of living approach.
      See also loneliness; shyness
  attributional style and, 100–101
  definitions of, 95–96
  interrelationships among, 96–99
  prevention and, 99–100
  treatment implications and, 99
Exaggerated Standards schema cluster,
      131–132
Expressed emotion, and relapse, 9

Fabes, R. A., 103
Family environment. *See also* family pro-
      cess model; parental depression;
      parent-child relationships
  adolescent adjustment and, 52–53
  approach coping strategies and, 11, 43
  development of attributional style and,
      73–78
  emotional security hypothesis and,
      300–301

interdependencies between spouses
      and, 50–51
  negative evaluation and, 9
  parent-child relationships and, 12, 51–
      52, 300
  prevention and, 50–53
  recurrent nature of depression and,
      372, 378–379
  short- vs. long-term effects in, 367
Family interventions, 50–53, 384–385
Family process model, 304. *See also* emo-
      tional security hypothesis
  broader family context and, 314
  emotional security and, 305–306
  parental depression and, 300
  reciprocity and, 313–314
Feedback. *See also* negative feedback
      seeking
  affective reactions to, 192–193
  perception of, and integrative ap-
      proach, 137–140
  positive, and self-verification processes,
      190, 195, 198, 206, 207–208
"Felt-security," 284–285
Feminist theory, 222–223. *See also* silenc-
      ing the self theory
Fincham, F. D., 73–74, 76, 84, 273–274
Foley, S. H., 276
Ford, M. E., 85
Forgas, J. P., 342
Freud, S., 3
Frias, D., 77
Fugh-Berman, Adriane, 233
Fuhrman, R. W., 355–356
"Functional agonism," 255–256
"Fundamental attributional error in de-
      pression theory and research,"
      369
Funder, D. C., 355–356

Garber, J., 68, 79
Gardner, R., Jr., 8, 10, 247–268
Gender differences. *See also* women
  in aggression, 228
  attachment security and, 170–171
  correlates of self-silencing and, 230
  emotional security hypothesis and, 312
  origins of interpersonal perspective
      and, 23–24

standards for self-evaluation and, 223–224
Gender inequality, 223–224, 227
Genetic factors, 84, 104–105
Giesler, R. B., 10, 12, 14, 15, 189–217
Gilbert, P., 158
Girodo, M., 114
"Goodness," 224–225
Gotlib, I. H., 154, 163, 164–165, 316, 368–369
Grief, 15. See also loss
Grych, L. H., 76, 77, 84

Hadzi-Pavlovic, D., 378
Haines, B. A., 12–13, 15, 16, 65–92, 77
Hammen, C., 10, 21–35, 282
Harris, T., 6, 24–25, 152, 174
Hartmann, E., 104
Harvey, J. H., 338
Hazan, C., 278, 280
Hearing loss, and social skills, 105–106
He Knew He Was Right (Trollope), 256
Henderson, V. L., 83
Heterogeneity of depression, 32
Hibernation, 251–252
Hilsman, R., 68
Hokoda, A., 74
Holahan, C. J., 11, 14, 15, 39–63. See also adaptive interpersonal functioning
Hopelessness theory, 65–66, 67–69, 128–129. See also diathesis stress models
Horowitz, L., 278
Horowitz, L. M., 170
Hostile attributional bias, 79, 112

IDS. See involuntary dominant strategy
Images of relatedness, 227
Inappropriate self-disclosure, 205–206
Individual interventions, 45–50. See also interventions
Ingram, R. E., 81
Inner dialogues, 226–227, 241–242
Inner division. See self-alienation
Integrative frameworks, 134–140. See also social-cognitive model; stress and coping framework
Coyne's critique of, 7, 368–369

empirical investigations based on, 140–141
general conceptual framework, 142–143
interventions and, 142, 171–172
perception of interpersonal feedback and, 137–140
perception of stressors and, 135–136
reassurance seeking and, 137
self-esteem and, 150, 171–172
Interactional perspective
challenges to construction of, 369–370
childhood experiences and, 12
Coyne's formulation of, 5, 6–7, 366–367
integration with cognitive approach and, 7
issues in development of, 370–381
link between early experience and depression and, 375–377
problems with conception of studies, 367–368
study of enduring relationships and, 366–367
theoretical precedents to, 5–7
Interactional vs. cumulative continuity, 376–377
Interdependence, 40, 50–51
Intergenerational transmission of depression, 12, 28–29, 308–309. See also parental depression
Internalizing behavior problems, 104
Internal representations of family relations, 319. See also schemas
Interpersonal perspective
causes of depression and, 9–13
emergence of, 21–32
empirical investigations underpinning, 26–30
focus of, 299–300
fundamental nature of depression and, 7–9
future research directions and, 16–17, 31–32, 85–86, 172–175
historical contributions to, 22–26
integrative approach and, 134–140
key aspects of, 132–134
mediation of depression and, 13–14
remediation of depression and, 15–16
Interpersonal psychotherapy (IPT)
as approach to depression, 15–16, 381–383, 384, 385–386

Interpersonal psychotherapy (IPT)
   (*continued*)
   for couples, 276
   self-esteem and, 172
Interpersonal stressors. *See also* life stress
   attachment cognitions and vulnerabil-
      ity to, 27–28
   attributional style and, 67
   cardiac patients and, 54–55
   specific vulnerability to, 26–27
Interventions, 116–117. *See also* couples
      therapy; family interventions; in-
      terpersonal psychotherapy
   attachment theory and, 15–16, 285–
      291
   behavioral marital therapy and, 275–
      276, 383–384
   clinical metaphors and, 258–266
   integrative cognitive and interpersonal
      model and, 142, 171–172
   integrative marital therapy and, 285–
      291
   integrative stress and coping framework
      and, 45–56
   involuntary subordinate strategy and,
      258–266
   medical patients and, 53–56
   negative perceptions by others and,
      337–338
   range of, and interactional approach,
      381–386
   self-verification theory and, 207–208
   shiver–ATP–take charge model and,
      260–266
   silencing the self theory and, 240–242
   social-cognitive model and, 351–352
   treatment of loneliness and, 115–116
   treatment of shyness and, 114
Invasive behaviors, 281
Involuntary dominant strategy (IDS),
      252–253
Involuntary subordinate strategy (ISS), 8,
      10, 248–258
   attachment disruption theory and, 249
   basic biological plan and, 259–260
   case examples and, 265–266
   characterization of, 248–249
   clinical metaphors and, 258–266
   compared with hibernation, 251–252
   components of, 257–258
   function of, 253–256
   as homologous, 250
   human–non human differences and,
      261–262

involuntary dominant strategy and,
      252–253
   occurrence as depression and, 256–257
   as part of strategy set, 252–253
   pathological ISS and, 258–259
   perception of, 253
   ranking stress and, 249–250, 253–254
   serotonin levels and, 262–264
   shiver model and, 260–261
   taking charge metaphor and, 264–265
   vs. voluntary subordination, 250–251
IPT. *See* interpersonal psychotherapy
Irrational thoughts, 102
ISS. *See* involuntary subordinate strategy

Jack, D. C., 8–9, 10, 13, 16, 221–246
Jacobson, N. S., 275
James, William, 152
Joiner, T., 3–19, 65–92, 202–204
Jome, M. A., 77

Kaslow, N. J., 271–297
Kassel, J. D., 162, 164, 368–369
Kaufman, J., 76
Keaton, J., 114
Keith, D., 84
Kelly, L., 114
Kenny, D. A., 348–349
Kessler, R. C., 375
Kiesler, D. J., 376
Knutson, J. F., 105–106
Kuiper, N. A., 163

Lack of connection schema, 9
Ladd, G. W., 79–80
Lansing, J. R., 105–106
Learned helplessness model, 128, 259. *See
      also* hopelessness theory
Leary, M., 101, 160
Lee, C. M., 316
Leggett, E. L., 82–83
Lenhart, L., 81
Lewinsohn, P. M., 4, 132–133, 155, 156,
      374
Libet, J., 374
Life stressors. *See also* diathesis stress
      models; everyday problems of liv-
      ing approach; *Social Origins of*

Depression; stress and coping framework; stress generation patterns; traumatic life events
attachment security and, 168
controllability of, 44–45
interpersonal factors in vulnerability to, 6, 26–28
level of self-esteem and, 156–157
life context profiles and, 48–49
maladaptive schemas vs. hopelessness theory and, 130–132
ongoing stressors and resources and, 47
relevant to schemas, 140
resilience of self-esteem and, 162–163
stability of self-esteem and, 164–165
Life Stressors and Social Resources Inventory (LISRES), 48–49
Listening to Prozac (Kramer), 262–263
Lochman, L. E., 81
Loneliness
antecedents of, 107–110
as causal factor, 10–11
causes of, 97–98
consequences of, 110, 114
definitions of, 106–107
as mediator, 13, 99
relationships between depression and, 96–99, 111, 113–114
relationships between shyness and, 96–99, 106, 107–108, 115
Loss, 109–110, 374, 378. *See also* elderly persons; silencing the self theory
in childhood, 74–75, 166–167, 375
Lyons-Ruth, K., 316–317

McCabe, M., 133
McCullough, J. P., 105
Maintenance of depression, 204–206
Malik, M. M., 77
Mankowski, T. A., 162
Marital conflict. *See* marital discord model; marital distress; parental depression
Marital discord model, 271–272
evidence for, 272–275
marital therapy and, 275–276
Marital distress, 309–311
as cause of depression, 274
children and, 76–77, 309–311
as contingent on affective state, 378
depression as cause of, 274–275

development of attributional style and, 76–77
development of self-esteem and, 167
mediation of, 342–344
as risk factor, 11–12, 273–274
social-cognitive model and, 342–344
Marital therapy. *See* couples therapy
Martin, H. P., 76
Mate selection, 30, 31–32
Mead, G. H., 165
Mediators, 13, 14, 67
emotional security as, 305–306, 311, 315–318
of responses to depressed people, 344–347
Medical patient rehabilitation, 53–56
Melchior, L. A., 101, 102
Melville, H., 4–5
Memory retrieval, and self-esteem regulation, 169–170
Metalsky, G. I., 65–92
Methodological issues. *See also* empirical investigations
brief encounters vs. enduring relationships and, 366–367
formal models and, 386
item-scale correlations and, 379–380
self-reported distress and, 372–373
Meyer, Adolf, 384
Miranda, J., 161–162
Modeling, and development of attributional style, 73–74
Moderator variable, 67
Modern society, characteristics of, 94–95
Monroe, S. M., 13–14, 149–187, 164
Mood induction, as term, 367–368
Moore, D., 108
Moos, R. H., 11, 39–63. *See also* adaptive interpersonal functioning
Motivational model, 75, 82–83
Murphy, B. C., 103
"Myth of materialism," 95

Nacht, S., 4
Negative attributional style. *See also* attributions, in social-cognitive model; negative cognitions
hopelessness theory and, 65–66
interpersonal events and, 12–13
intervention and, 15
low self-esteem and, 157

Negative attributional style (*continued*)
origins of attributional style and, 70–84
research on depression in children and, 66–70
Negative cognitions. *See also* negative attributional style
attentiveness to negative information and, 111–112, 190
interactional approach to self-complaints and, 379–381
shyness and, 10–11
Negative evaluation by others. *See also* feedback; negative feedback seeking; negative schemas in others
development of attributional style and, 12–13, 75–76, 82
vulnerability to depression and, 9
women and, 13
Negative feedback seeking, 10, 15, 140, 190. *See also* negative schemas in others
empirical evidence on, 194–199
motivation for, 191–194, 201
Negative schemas in others
bias and, 334–338, 346
responses to depressed people and, 344–347
"Negative view," 335–336
Nicholson, K. J., 345
Nolen-Hoeksema, S., 68, 69
Nongenuine support, 347

Onset of depression. *See also* relapse of depression
contribution of social-cognitive processes to, 350–351
self-verification and, 202–204
timing of, 370, 372
Oregon Research Institute group, 367
Overconnection schema, 9–10, 131
Over-Eye, 237, 241
Ownership, 257, 258

Palo Alto Mental Research Institute Group, 16, 384
Panak, W. F., 79
Paradise Lost (Milton), 256
Parental depression
behavioral patterns and, 306–307
broader family context and, 374–375
child characteristics and, 311–312
emotional patterns of depression and, 306–307
emotional security as mediator and, 305–306, 311
family processes and, 300, 304
marital functioning and, 309–311
negative attributional style in children and, 78
risk for depression in children and, 28–29, 300, 313
self-efficacy about parenting and, 302
transmission of, 12, 28–29, 308–309
Parent-child relationships
attachment and, 308–309
child-management practices and, 307–308
development of attributional style and, 73–78
development of self-esteem and, 166–167
emotional security model and, 307–309
parental messages to children and, 141, 302, 309
social-cognitive model and, 341, 343–344, 347, 350–351
stress and coping processes and, 51–52
transmission of depression and, 12, 28–29
Parker, G., 378
Peer relationships
development of attributional style and, 78–81
development of self-esteem and, 167
Pennsylvania State University (PSU) Reticence Program, 114
Peplau, L. A., 109
Perceptions of depressed persons. *See also* attributional style; negative attributional style; negative cognitions
accuracy of, 348–349
perceived criticism and, 9, 330, 349–350, 351
of social support, 347–349
of stressors, and integrated model, 135–136
Perez-Bouchard, L., 77
Perlman, D., 109

Personal resources. *See* social support; stress and coping framework
Person memory model, 339
Persons, J. B., 161–162
Person schema, in social-cognitive model, 331, 339–340. *See also* negative schemas in others
Pessimistic worldview, development of, 12–13, 85. *See also* negative attributional style
Peterson, C., 73, 82
Physiological arousal, and shyness, 103–104
Pilkonis, P. A., 102
Pittman, N. L., 111
Pittman, T. S., 111
Posttraumatic stress syndrome, 168
Prediction and control strivings, 200–201, 209–202
Preemptive processing, 84
Price, J. S., 8, 10, 247–268
Proximity seeking, 279–281
PSU Reticence Program. *See* Pennsylvania State University Reticence Program
Psychotherapeutic treatment, 45–46. *See also* interventions

Quiggle, N. L., 86
Quinton, D., 378

Rabiner, D. L., 81
Racamier, P. C., 4
Raleigh, M. J., 263
Reassurance seeking
  intervention and, 15
  mediation of depression and, 14, 133
  perception of stressors and, 135–136
  self-perception of, 137
  stress generation and, 48
  as vulnerability factor, 10
Reciprocity
  family process model and, 313–314
  as issue for interactional approach, 373
Reflexivity, 230–232
Reframing, 384–385
Rejection. *See also* parent-child relationships; peer relationships
  parental, and depression in children, 330, 351

perceptions of, 347–348
  as response to depressed people, 345
  self-esteem and, 159–160
Relapse of depression
  perceived criticism and, 9, 330, 349–350
  periods of healthy functioning and, 374, 375–377
  recurrent nature of depression and, 370–373, 374, 375–377, 378–379
Relational pathology, 29
Relational systems models, 222–223, 316–317
Relationship satisfaction, mediation of, 342–344
Remission of depression
  research designs on self-esteem and, 154
  self-verification and, 207–208
Resource holding potential (RHP), 249–250, 257–258
Resource value, 257–258
RHP. *See* resource holding potential
Rich, A. R., 116
Richards, W., 77
Roberts, J. E., 13–14, 149–187
  attachment styles and, 282–283, 368–369
  self-esteem and, 162, 163–165
Role disputes and transitions, 15
Rook, K., 107
Rosenberg, M., 165
Rumination, 44

Sacco, W. P., 9, 329–362
Safe haven, marriage as, 281–284, 286
Sarason, B. R., 350
Schema Questionnaire, 131
Schemas. *See also* cognitive models; early maladaptive schema theory; integrative frameworks; internal representations; working models, concept of
  acquisition of, 32
  Coyne's interactional theory and, 7
  defined, 127–128
  disrupted emotional security and, 12
  mediation of depression and, 14
  models based on, 127–132

Schemas (*continued*)
  person schema in social-cognitive
      model and, 331
  process elements of, 139
  resiliency and, 141–142
  structural elements of, 139
Schjelderup-Ebbe, Thorlief, 259
Schmidt, K. L., 9–10, 127–142
Schmidt, N. B., 9–10, 12, 14, 15, 127–
      142
Schulman, P., 84
Schultz, N. R., 108
Secure base, 284–285, 286
Selective serotonin reuptake inhibitors
      (SSRIs), 262–264
Self-alienation, and self-silencing, 226–
      227
Self-complaints, interactional approach
      to, 379–381
Self-disclosure, inappropriate, 205–206
Self-enhancement strategies, 160–161
Self-esteem
  attributional style and, 81
  development of, 166–167
  empirical studies of depression and,
      154–165
  facets of, 153–154
  interpersonal basis of, 165–171
  interventions and, 171–172
  level of, 152–153, 155–158, 173–174
  mediation of depression and, 13–14,
      157–158
  nature of, 152–154
  negative feedback seeking and, 10
  regulation of, 153, 158–161, 169, 173,
      174
  resilience of, 153, 161–163
  self-silencing and, 225
  self-verification processes and, 203–
      204
  sociometer theory of, 14, 160
  stability of, 153, 1630165
  theories of depression and, 151–152
  women and, 222–223
Self-esteem theory of depression with in-
      terpersonal mediator, 14
Self-evaluation
  bodily shame and, 167
  gender differences in standards of,
      223–224, 238–240
  interactional approach to self-
      complaints and, 379–381

negative, and onset of depression,
      156–157
  process vs. product of, 152–153
  self-esteem regulation and, 160–161
  silencing the self and, 237, 238
  social perceptions and, 349
Self-focused thought, 112
Selfishness standard, and self-silencing,
      234–235, 236
Self-monitoring, 172
Self-sacrifice schema, 9, 10
Self-silencing theory. *See* silencing the
      self theory
Self-verification, 10. *See also* negative
      feedback seeking
  correction of misconceptions and,
      199–202
  empirical evidence on depression and,
      194–199
  maintenance of depression and, 204–
      206
  mediation of depression and, 14
  onset of depression and, 202–204
  perceived accuracy and, 199–200
  remission of depression and, 207–208
  self-esteem regulation and, 160
  specificity to depression, 201–202
  theory of, 190–194
Self-worth
  contingent, 75–76, 85–86, 161–162,
      163, 168–169
  experienced, 153
Seligman, M. E. P., 68, 69, 73, 77, 82,
      84, 128, 259
Shame, 227–228
Shaughnessy, M. S., 84
Shaver, P. R., 278
Shaw, D. A., 4
Shiver–ATP–take charge model, 260–
      266
Shyness, 10–11. *See also* "involuntary
      subordinate strategy"
  antecedents of, 103–106
  causal role of, 97
  consequences of, 106
  definitions of, 101–102
  public vs. private, 102
  relationship between depression and,
      96–99, 111, 113–114
  relationship between loneliness and,
      96–99, 107–108, 115
  treatment of, 114

Significant others. *See also* couples therapy; family interventions
  characteristics of, 377–379
  interventions and, 382, 386
Silencing the Self Scale (STSS), 229–230, 242
Silencing the self theory, 8–9, 10, 222–229
  association between self-silencing and depression and, 229–230
  assumptions of, 230–232
  case examples and, 232–240
  images of relatedness and, 227
  intervention and, 16
  men and, 225, 238–240
  obstacles to voice and, 227–229
  shame and, 227–228
Sloman, Leon, 264
Social anxiety
  loneliness and, 108
  shyness and, 101–102, 103–104
Social-cognitive model, 329–352
  hypotheses of, 333–351
  overview of, 331–333
Social comparison processes, 158–160
Social context, 40
Social-ecological perspective
  interventions programs and, 46–47
  principles in, 39–40
Social information-processing model, 72
Social model of depression , 6, 24–25, 152. *See also* emotional security hypothesis
Social networks
  loneliness and, 109
  perception of support and, 347–348
  self-esteem regulation and, 159–160
Social Origins of Depression (Brown & Harris), 24–25
Social skills
  conceptualization of, 373–374
  IPT and, 15
  Lewinsohn's model and, 132–133, 374
  loneliness and, 108–109
  perception of reassurance seeking and, 137
  shyness and, 102, 103, 105–106
  training in, and shyness, 114
Social support. *See also* attachment theory; family environment
  cardiac patients and, 54–55

depressed person's perception of, 347–349
  interventions and, 115
  marriage as safe haven and, 281–283
  nongenuine, 347
  persons low in, 8, 11
  vulnerability to depression and, 112–113
Sociometer theory of self-esteem, 14, 160
Sociophysiological perspective, 247–267. *See also* involuntary subordinate strategy
Specificity
  development of attributional style and, 86
  emotional security hypothesis and, 317
  of interpersonal factors to depression, 31
  of self-verification effects, 201–202
  of vulnerability to interpersonal stressors, 26–27
Srull, T. K., 339
SSRIs. *See* selective serotonin reuptake inhibitors
Steele, C. M., 161
Stein, S. J., 114
Strange Situation procedure, 308–309
Strategic therapy, 384–385
Stress and coping framework
  conceptualization of, 40–45
  family interventions, 50–53
  individual treatment, 45–50
  rehabilitation of medical patients and, 53–56
Stress generation patterns, 10, 29–30, 47–48
Stringer, S. A., 77
STSS. *See* Silencing the Self Scale
Substance abuse, 77–78
Sullivan, Harry Stack, 5, 384
Swallow, S. R., 163
Swann, W. B., 10, 12, 14, 15, 189–217
Symbolic interactionism, 350

Tarnowski, K. J., 77
Taylor, S. E., 159
Teacher relationships, 81–83
Teglasi, H., 84
Thompson, R. A., 85

Traumatic life events
    development of attributional style and,
        74–75
    maintenance of self–esteem and, 13–
        14
    negative feedback seeking and, 10
    precipitation of depression and, 6
Triesch, S. K., 77
Turner, J. E., Jr., 67–68
"Turning points," 376

van der Molen, H. T., 101–102
Voice, 225
    inner dialogues and, 226–227, 241–
        242
    obstacles to, 227–229

Waterman, J., 76
Wayment, H. A., 159
Weinstein, M. S., 4
Weissman, Myrna, 23
Wierzbicki, M., 133

Women. *See also* couples therapy; gender
        differences; parental depression;
        silencing the self theory
    active coping and, 44
    characteristics of spouses and, 373, 378
    interventions and, 16
    LISRES profiles and, 48–49
    moral themes in narratives of, 223–
        226
    negative feedback and, 13
    in professions, 232–233
    rates of depression among, 221–222
    Social Origins of Depression and, 24–25
Working models, concept of, 170–171,
        174
Wyer, R. A., 339

Yarkin, K. L., 338
Young, J. E., 9–10, 127–142
    schematic theory of, 130–131

Zeifman, D., 280

ABOUT THE EDITORS

Thomas Joiner received his PhD in clinical psychology in 1993 from the University of Texas at Austin, and is Associate Professor of Clinical Psychology at Florida State University. His recent papers on the psychology of depression, anxiety, and eating disorders have established him as a leader in the field. Author of 82 peer-reviewed publications and over 45 conference presentations, Dr. Joiner is Associate Editor of the journal *Behavior Therapy* and sits on the editorial board of the *Journal of Abnormal Psychology*. He received the Young Investigator Award from the National Alliance for Research on Schizophrenia and Depression, the Shakow Award for Early Career Achievement from the Division of Clinical Psychology of the American Psychological Association, as well as research grants from the National Institute of Mental Health and the American Suicide Foundation.

James C. Coyne is Professor of Psychology in the Department of Psychiatry and in the Department of Family Medicine and is Program Leader, Behavioral Sciences, in the Cancer Center at the University of Pennsylvania Health System. He received his PhD in clinical psychology from Indiana University. In addition to the interactional perspective on depression, his research interests include psychological aspects of genetic testing, individual and couples' adaptation to physical illness, and depression in primary care and community settings. He is the co-author of *Father Knows Best: The Use and Abuse of Power in Freud's Case of Dora* with Robin Lakoff and of *Relationships in Chronic Illness and Disability* with Renee Lyons, Michael Sullivan, and Paul Ritvo. He maintains an active clinical practice working with depressed individuals and their marriages and families.